Emerging Trends in Applications and Infrastructures for Computational Biology, Bioinformatics, and Systems Biology

Systems and Applications

Emerging Trends in Applications and Infrastructures for Computational Biology, Bioinformatics, and Systems Biology

Systems and Applications

Quoc Nam Tran

Hamid R. Arabnia

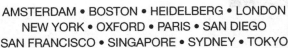

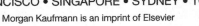

AMSTERDAM • BOSTON • HEIDELBERG • LONDON
NEW YORK • OXFORD • PARIS • SAN DIEGO
SAN FRANCISCO • SINGAPORE • SYDNEY • TOKYO
Morgan Kaufmann is an imprint of Elsevier

Morgan Kaufmann is an imprint of Elsevier
50 Hampshire Street, 5th Floor, Cambridge, MA 02139, USA

British Library Cataloguing in Publication Data
A catalogue record for this book is available from the British Library

Library of Congress Cataloging-in-Publication Data
A catalog record for this book is available from the Library of Congress

ISBN: 978-0-12-804203-8

For information on all MK publications visit our website at https://www.elsevier.com/

Publisher: Todd Green
Acquisition Editor: Brian Romer
Editorial Project Manager: Amy Invernizzi
Production Project Manager: Punithavathy Govindaradjane
Designer: Maria Inês Cruz

Typeset by SPi Global, India

Contents

List of Contributors

V. Abedi
Nutritional Immunology and Molecular Medicine Laboratory, Virginia Bioinformatics Institute, Virginia Tech, Blacksburg, VA, United States

J. Albasri
Prince Sultan Military Medical City, Riyadh, Saudi Arabia

D.J. Andrews
Cancer Research UK Cambridge Institute, University of Cambridge, Cambridge, United Kingdom

A.A. Bahrami
IT Consultation, Savannah, GA, United States

M.S. Baptista
Chemistry Institute, University of São Paulo, São Paulo, SP, Brazil

J. Bassaganya-Riera
Nutritional Immunology and Molecular Medicine Laboratory, Virginia Bioinformatics Institute, Virginia Tech, Blacksburg, VA, United States

T.B. Baturalp
Department of Mechanical Engineering, Texas Tech University, Lubbock, TX, United States

B. Ben Youssef
Department of Computer Engineering, King Saud University, Riyadh, Saudi Arabia

J. Beyerer
Vision and Fusion Laboratory IES, Karlsruhe Institute of Technology KIT, Karlsruhe, Germany; Fraunhofer Institute of Optronics, System Technologies and Image Exploitation IOSB, Karlsruhe, Germany

S.D. Bhavani
SCIS University of Hyderabad, Hyderabad, Telangana, India

E. Black
Data Analysis Australia, Perth, WA, Australia; Department of Mathematics and Statistics, Curtin University, Perth, WA, Australia

J.W. Brooks
Premier Education Group, New Haven, CT, United States

A. Carbo
BioTherapeutics Inc., Blacksburg, VA, United States

A. Chan
Department of Statistics, University of California, Los Angeles, CA, United States

Y. Chang
Department of Computer Science and Engineering Technology, University of Houston-Downtown, Houston, TX, United States

C.A. Cole
Department of Computer Science and Engineering, University of South Carolina, Columbia, SC, United States

R.M. Cordeiro
Center for Natural and Human Sciences, Federal University of ABC, Santo André, SP, Brazil

E.B. Costa
Center for Natural and Human Sciences, Federal University of ABC, Santo André, SP, Brazil

P. Costa
Department of Systems Engineering and Operations Research, George Mason University, Fairfax, VA, United States

C.A. de Luna Ortega
Universidad Politécnica de Aguascalientes, Aguascalientes, Mexico

A. Deeter
Integrated Bioscience Program, Department of Computer Science, The University of Akron, Akron, OH, United States

J.R. Deller
Michigan State University, East Lansing, MI, United States

C. Di Ruberto
Department of Mathematics and Computer Science, University of Cagliari, Cagliari, Italy

Z.-H. Duan
Integrated Bioscience Program, Department of Computer Science, The University of Akron, Akron, OH, United States

C. Early
Department of Science and Engineering Technology, University of Houston-Clear Lake, Houston, TX, United States

C.S. Ee
Multimedia University, Melaka, Malaysia

A. Ertas
Department of Mechanical Engineering, Texas Tech University, Lubbock, TX, United States

A. Fahim
Department of Computer Science and Engineering, University of South Carolina, Columbia, SC, United States

A.C. Ferraz
Physics Institute, University of São Paulo, São Paulo, SP, Brazil

Y. Fischer
Fraunhofer Institute of Optronics, System Technologies and Image Exploitation IOSB, Karlsruhe, Germany

B.D. Fleet
Michigan State University, East Lansing, MI, United States

A. Fronville
Computer Science Department, University of Western Brittany, Brest, France

J. Garza
Department of Computer Science and Engineering Technology, University of Houston-Downtown, Houston, TX, United States

P. Gong
Environmental Laboratory, U.S. Army Engineer Research and Development Center, Vicksburg, MS, United States

J. Gonya
The Research Institute at Nationwide Children's Hospital, Columbus, OH, United States

R.M. Gonzalez
Computer Science Department, Instituto Tecnologico de Aguascalientes, Aguascalientes, Mexico

E.D. Goodman
Michigan State University, East Lansing, MI, United States

V. Gupta
Borgess Medical Center, Borgess Research Institute, Kalamazoo, MI, United States

R.R. Hashemi
Department of Computer Science, Armstrong State University, Savannah, GA, United States

N. Hazzazi
Department of Computer Science, George Mason University, Fairfax, VA, United States

D. Hempel
Steinbeis-Transfer-Institut Klinische Hämatoonkologie, Donauwörth, Germany

M. Hennig
Nutrition Research Institute, University of North Carolina at Chapel Hill, Kannapolis, NC, United States

V. Hodges
Premier Education Group, New Haven, CT, United States

R. Hontecillas
Nutritional Immunology and Molecular Medicine Laboratory, Virginia Bioinformatics Institute, Virginia Tech, Blacksburg, VA, United States

S. Hoops
Nutritional Immunology and Molecular Medicine Laboratory, Virginia Bioinformatics Institute, Virginia Tech, Blacksburg, VA, United States

S. Irausquin
Department of Computer Science and Engineering, University of South Carolina, Columbia, SC, United States

D. Ishimaru
Department of Biochemistry and Molecular Biology, Medical University of South Carolina, Charleston, SC, United States

W. Ji
East China Normal University, Shanghai, China

N.T. Juni
Nutritional Immunology and Molecular Medicine Laboratory, Virginia Bioinformatics Institute, Virginia Tech, Blacksburg, VA, United States

T.K. Kho
Multimedia University, Melaka, Malaysia

W. Koh
School of Computing, University of Southern Mississippi, Hattiesburg, MS, United States

M. Kumar
Department of Computer Science and Engineering, National Institute of Technology Rourkela, Rourkela, India

A. Leber
Nutritional Immunology and Molecular Medicine Laboratory, Virginia Bioinformatics Institute, Virginia Tech, Blacksburg, VA, United States

Y. Li
Department of Mathematics, Illinois State University, Normal, IL, United States

H. Lin
Department of Computer Science and Engineering Technology, University of Houston-Downtown, Houston, TX, United States

W.W. Liou
Western Michigan University, Kalamazoo, MI, United States

P. Lu
Nutritional Immunology and Molecular Medicine Laboratory, Virginia Bioinformatics Institute, Virginia Tech, Blacksburg, VA, United States

A.G. Lynch
Cancer Research UK Cambridge Institute, University of Cambridge, Cambridge, United Kingdom

V. Manca
Department of Computer Science, University of Verona, Verona, Italy; Center for BioMedical Computing (CBMC), University of Verona, Verona, Italy

A. Manzourolajdad
National Center for Biotechnology Information, National Library of Medicine, National Institutes of Health, Bethesda, MD, United States

T. Maruo
Graduate School of Applied Informatics, University of Hyogo, Hyogo, Japan

A. Maxwell
School of Computing, University of Southern Mississippi, Hattiesburg, MS, United States

R. Miotto
Center for Natural and Human Sciences, Federal University of ABC, Santo André, SP, Brazil

E.A. Mohamed
Department of Management Information Systems, College of Business Administration, Al Ain University of Science and Technology, Al Ain, United Arab Emirates

Á. Monteagudo
Department of Computer Science, University of A Coruña, A Coruña, Spain

L.M. Montoni
Complex System and Security Laboratory, University Campus Bio-Medico of Rome, Rome, Italy

J.L. Mustard
Division of Basic Sciences, Laboratory of Bioinformatics and Computational Biology, Kansas City University of Medicine and Biosciences, Kansas City, MO, United States

A.J.P. Neto
Center for Natural and Human Sciences, Federal University of ABC, Santo André, SP, Brazil

M.E. Nia
Multimedia University, Melaka, Malaysia

H. Nishimura
Graduate School of Applied Informatics, University of Hyogo, Hyogo, Japan

S. Nobukawa
Department of Management Information Science, Fukui University of Technology, Fukui, Japan

P. Philipp
Vision and Fusion Laboratory IES, Karlsruhe Institute of Technology KIT, Karlsruhe, Germany

C.W. Philipson
BioTherapeutics Inc., Blacksburg, VA, United States

L. Putzu
Department of Mathematics and Computer Science, University of Cagliari, Cagliari, Italy

T.S. Rani
SCIS University of Hyderabad, Hyderabad, Telangana, India

S.K. Rath
Department of Computer Science and Engineering, National Institute of Technology Rourkela, Rourkela, India

W.C. Ray
The Research Institute at Nationwide Children's Hospital, Columbus, OH, United States

V. Rehbock
Department of Mathematics and Statistics, Curtin University, Perth, WA, Australia

V.L. Rivas
Computer Science Department, Instituto Tecnologico de Aguascalientes, Aguascalientes, Mexico

V. Rodin
Computer Science Department, University of Western Brittany, Brest, France

J.C.M. Romo
Computer Science Department, Instituto Tecnologico de Aguascalientes, Aguascalientes, Mexico

F.J.L. Rosas
Computer Science Department, Instituto Tecnologico de Aguascalientes, Aguascalientes, Mexico

R.W. Rumpf
The Research Institute at Nationwide Children's Hospital, Columbus, OH, United States

R. Sahoo
SCIS University of Hyderabad, Hyderabad, Telangana, India

I. Samoylo
I.M. Sechenov First Moscow State Medical University, Moscow, Russia

J. Santos
Department of Computer Science, University of A Coruña, A Coruña, Spain

A. Sarr
Computer Science Department, University of Western Brittany, Brest, France

G. Schreiber
Chevron-Phillips Chemical Company, Houston, TX, United States

A. Schrey
Department of Biology, Armstrong State University, Savannah, GA, United States

N.W. Seidler
Division of Basic Sciences, Laboratory of Bioinformatics and Computational Biology, Kansas City University of Medicine and Biosciences, Kansas City, MO, United States

R. Setola
Complex System and Security Laboratory, University Campus Bio-Medico of Rome, Rome, Italy

M. Shen
Shantou Polytechnic, Shantou, Guangdong, PR China

K.S. Sim
Multimedia University, Melaka, Malaysia

I. Ştirb
Computer and Software Engineering Department, "Politehnica" University of Timişoara, Timişoara, Romania

S. Subedi
Department of Computer Science and Engineering Technology, University of Houston-Downtown, Houston, TX, United States

D. Swain Jr.
Department of Computer Science, Armstrong State University, Savannah, GA, United States

C.S. Ta
Multimedia University, Melaka, Malaysia

Z. Tao
Suzhou Vocational University, Suzhou, China

S. Tavaré
Cancer Research UK Cambridge Institute, University of Cambridge, Cambridge, United Kingdom

Q.N. Tran
The University of South Dakota, Vermillion, SD, United States

G.G. Trellese
Center for Natural and Human Sciences, Federal University of ABC, Santo André, SP, Brazil

C.P. Tso
Multimedia University, Melaka, Malaysia

N.R. Tyler
School of Pharmacy, University of Georgia, Athens, GA, United States

H. Valafar
Department of Computer Science and Engineering, University of South Carolina, Columbia, SC, United States

G.M. Veloz
Universidad Tecnológica del Norte de Aguascalientes, Aguascalientes, Mexico

M. Verma
Nutritional Immunology and Molecular Medicine Laboratory, Virginia Bioinformatics Institute, Virginia Tech, Blacksburg, VA, United States

G.A. Vess
Nutritional Immunology and Molecular Medicine Laboratory, Virginia Bioinformatics Institute, Virginia Tech, Blacksburg, VA, United States

D. Wijesekera
Department of Computer Science, George Mason University, Fairfax, VA, United States

J.B. Worley
Division of Basic Sciences, Laboratory of Bioinformatics and Computational Biology, Kansas City University of Medicine and Biosciences, Kansas City, MO, United States

X. Wu
School of Computing, University of Southern Mississippi, Hattiesburg, MS, United States

B. Yang
School of Computing, University of Southern Mississippi, Hattiesburg, MS, United States

M. Yao
East China Normal University, Shanghai, China

Y. Yao
Central Michigan University, Mt. Pleasant, MI, United States

B. Yu
Department of Computer Science, George Mason University, Fairfax, VA, United States

N. Zaki
College of Information Technology, United Arab Emirates University, Al Ain, United Arab Emirates

C. Zhang
School of Computing, University of Southern Mississippi, Hattiesburg, MS, United States

Q. Zhang
Shantou University Medical College, Shantou, Guangdong, PR China; Shantou University, Shantou, Guangdong, PR China

Y. Zhang
North Dakota State University, Fargo, ND, United States

H. Zhao
Integrated Bioscience Program, Department of Computer Science, The University of Akron, Akron, OH, United States

B. Zheng
Shantou University, Shantou, Guangdong, PR China

D. Zhukov
Moscow State Technical University of Radio Engineering, Electronics and Automation "MIREA", Moscow, Russia

B.B. Zobel
Department of Diagnostic Imaging, University Campus Bio-Medico of Rome, Rome, Italy

Preface

It gives us great pleasure to introduce this collection of chapters to the readers of the book series "Emerging Trends in Computer Science and Applied Computing" (Morgan Kaufmann/Elsevier). This book is entitled "Emerging Trends in Computational Biology, Bioinformatics, and Systems Biology — Systems and Applications." This is the second book in the series about the topic. We are indebted to Professor Quoc-Nam Tran (Professor and Department Chair) of the University of South Dakota for accepting our invitation to be the senior editor. His leadership and strategic plan made the implementation of this book project a wonderful experience.

Computational Biology is the science of using biological data to develop algorithms and relations among various biological systems. It involves the development and application of data-analytical and algorithms, mathematical modeling, and simulation techniques to the study of biological, behavioral, and social systems. The field is multidisciplinary in that it includes topics that are traditionally covered in computer science, mathematics, imaging science, statistics, chemistry, biophysics, genetics, genomics, ecology, evolution, anatomy, neuroscience, and visualization where computer science acts as the topical bridge between all such diverse areas (for a formal definition of Computational Biology, refer to http://www.bisti.nih.gov/docs/compubiodef.pdf). Many consider the area of Bioinformatics to be a subfield of Computational Biology that includes methods for acquiring, storing, retrieving, organizing, analyzing, and visualizing biological data. The area of Systems Biology is an emerging methodology applied to biomedical and biological scientific research. It is an area that overlaps with computational biology and bioinformatics. This edited book attempts to cover the emerging trends in many important areas of Computational Biology, Bioinformatics, and Systems Biology with particular emphasis on systems and applications.

The book is composed of selected papers that were accepted for the 2014 and 2015 International Conference on Bioinformatics & Computational Biology (BIOCOMP'14 and BIOCOMP'15), July, Las Vegas, USA. Selected authors were given the opportunity to submit the extended versions of their conference papers as chapters for publication consideration in this edited book. Other authors (not affiliated with BIOCOMP) were also given the opportunity to contribute to this book by submitting their chapters for evaluation. The editorial board selected 34 chapters to comprise this book.

The BIOCOMP annual conferences are held as part of the World Congress in Computer Science, Computer Engineering, and Applied Computing, WORLDCOMP (http://www.world-academy-of-science.org/). An important mission of WORLDCOMP includes "*Providing a unique platform for a diverse community of constituents composed of scholars, researchers, developers, educators, and practitioners. The Congress makes concerted effort to reach out to participants affiliated with diverse entities (such as: universities, institutions, corporations, government agencies, and research centers/labs) from all over the world. The congress also attempts to connect participants from institutions that have **teaching** as their main mission with those who are affiliated with institutions that have **research** as their main mission. The congress uses a quota system to achieve its institution and geography diversity objectives.*" As this book is mainly composed of the extended versions of the accepted papers of BIOCOMP annual conferences, it is no surprise that the book has chapters from a highly qualified and diverse group of authors.

We are very grateful to the many colleagues who offered their services in organizing the BIOCOMP conferences (and its affiliated topical tracks). Their help was instrumental in the formation of this book. The members of the editorial committee included:

- Prof. Abbas M. Al-Bakry. University President, University of IT and Communications, Baghdad, Iraq
- Prof. Nizar Al-Holou. Professor and Chair, Electrical and Computer Engineering Department; Vice Chair, IEEE/SEM-Computer Chapter; University of Detroit Mercy, Detroit, Michigan, USA
- Dr. Hamid Ali Abed Alasadi. Head, Department of Computer Science, Basra University, Iraq; Member of Optical Society of America (OSA), USA; Member of The International Society for Optical Engineering (SPIE), Bellingham, Washington, USA
- Prof. Christine Amaldas. Ritsumeikan Asia Pacific University, Kyoto, Japan
- Prof. Hamid R. Arabnia (Coeditor). Professor of Computer Science; The University of Georgia, USA; Editor-in-Chief, *Journal of Supercomputing* (Springer); Editor-in-Chief, *Emerging Trends in Computer Science and Applied Computing* (Elsevier); Editor-in-Chief, *Transactions of Computational Science & Computational Intelligence* (Springer); Elected Fellow, Int'l Society of Intelligent Biological Medicine (ISIBM); USA
- Prof. Juan Jose Martinez Castillo. Director, The Acantelys Alan Turing Nikola Tesla Research Group and GIPEB, Universidad Nacional Abierta, Venezuela
- Dr. En Cheng. Department of Computer Science, The University of Akron, Akron, Ohio, USA
- Dr. Ravi Chityala. Elekta Inc, Sunnyvale, California, USA; and the University of California Santa Cruz Extension, San Jose, California, USA
- Prof. Kevin Daimi. Director, Computer Science and Software Engineering Programs, Department of Mathematics, Computer Science, and Software Engineering, University of Detroit Mercy, Michigan, USA
- Prof. Youping Deng. Director of Bioinformatics and Biostatistics, Rush University Medical Center, Chicago, Illinois, USA
- Dr. Lamia Atma Djoudi. Synchrone Technologies, France
- Prof. Mary Mehrnoosh Eshaghian-Wilner. Professor of Engineering Practice, University of Southern California, California, USA; Adjunct Professor, Electrical Engineering, University of California Los Angeles, Los Angeles (UCLA), California, USA
- Arjang Fahim. Department of Computer Science and Engineering; University of South Carolina, Columbia, South Carolina, USA
- Prof. George A. Gravvanis. Director, Physics Laboratory & Head of Advanced Scientific Computing, Applied Math & Applications Research Group; Professor of Applied Mathematics and Numerical Computing and Department of ECE, School of Engineering, Democritus University of Thrace, Xanthi, Greece; former President of the Technical Commission on Data Processing, Social Security for the Migrant Workers, European Commission, Hellenic Presidency, Greece
- Prof. Houcine Hassan. Universitat Politecnica de Valencia, Spain
- Prof. Mohammad Shahadat Hossain (PhD, UMIST, Manchester), MBCS. Department of Computer Science and Engineering, University of Chittagong, Bangladesh; Visiting Academic Staff, The University of Manchester, UK

- Prof. George Jandieri. Georgian Technical University, Tbilisi, Georgia; Chief Scientist, The Institute of Cybernetics, Georgian Academy of Science, Georgia; Editorial Board: *International Journal of Microwaves and Optical Technology*, *The Open Atmospheric Science Journal*, *American Journal of Remote Sensing*
- Dr. Abdeldjalil Khelassi. Associate Professor and Head of Knowledge and Information Engineering Research Team, Computer Science Department, University of Tlemcen, Algeria
- Prof. Byung-Gyu Kim. Multimedia Processing Communications Lab. (MPCL), Department of Computer Science and Engineering, College of Engineering, SunMoon University, South Korea
- Prof. Tai-hoon Kim. School of Information and Computing Science, University of Tasmania, Australia
- Assoc. Prof. Dr. Guoming Lai. Computer Science and Technology, Sun Yat-Sen University, Guangzhou, P.R. China
- Dr. Ying Liu. Division of Computer Science, Mathematics, and Science, St. John's University, Queens, New York, USA
- Dr. Yan Luo. National Institutes of Health, Bethesda, Maryland, USA
- Prof. George Markowsky. Professor & Associate Director, School of Computing and Information Science; Chair International Advisory Board of IEEE IDAACS; Director 2013 Northeast Collegiate Cyber Defense Competition; President Phi Beta Kappa Delta Chapter of Maine; Cooperating Prof. Mathematics & Statistics Department UMaine; Cooperating Prof. School of Policy & Int'l Affairs UMaine; University of Maine, Orono, Maine, USA
- Dr. Andrew Marsh. CEO, HoIP Telecom Ltd (Healthcare over Internet Protocol), UK; Secretary General of World Academy of BioMedical Sciences and Technologies (WABT) at UNESCO NGO, The United Nations
- Prof. G.N. Pandey. Vice-Chancellor, Arunachal University of Studies, Arunachal Pradesh, India; Adjunct Professor, Indian Institute of Information Technology, Allahabad, India
- Prof. James J. (Jong Hyuk) Park. Department of Computer Science and Engineering (DCSE), SeoulTech, Korea; President, FTRA, EiC, HCIS Springer, JoC, IJITCC; Head of DCSE, SeoulTech, Korea
- Prof. R. Ponalagusamy. Department of Mathematics, National Institute of Technology, Tiruchirappalli, India; and Editor-in-Chief, *International Journal of Mathematics and Engineering with Computers*
- Dr. Alvaro Rubio-Largo. University of Extremadura, Caceres, Spain
- Prof. Khemaissia Seddik. University of Tebessa, Algerie, Algeria
- Dr. Akash Singh. IBM Corporation, Sacramento, California, USA; Chartered Scientist, Science Council, UK; Fellow, British Computer Society; Member, Senior IEEE, AACR, AAAS, and AAAI; IBM Corporation, USA
- Prof. Fernando G. Tinetti. School of Computer Science, Universidad Nacional de La Plata, La Plata, Argentina; Coeditor, *Journal of Computer Science and Technology* (JCS&T)
- Prof. Quoc-Nam Tran (Coeditor). Professor and Chair, Department of Computer Science, University of South Dakota, USA
- Prof. Shiuh-Jeng Wang. Department of Information Management, Central Police University, Taiwan; Program Chair, Security & Forensics, Taiwan; Director, Information Crypto and Construction Lab (ICCL) & ICCL-FROG

- Prof. Xiang Simon Wang. Head, Laboratory of Cheminfomatics and Drug Design, Howard University College of Pharmacy, Washington, DC, USA
- Prof. Mary Q. Yang. Director, Mid-South Bioinformatics Center and Joint Bioinformatics Ph.D. Program, Medical Sciences and George W. Donaghey College of Engineering and Information Technology, University of Arkansas, USA
- Prof. Jane You. Associate Head, Department of Computing, The Hong Kong Polytechnic University, Kowloon, Hong Kong
- Peng Zhang. Biomedical Engineering Department, Stony Brook University, Stony Brook, New York, USA
- Prof. Wenbing Zhao. Department of Electrical and Computer Engineering, Cleveland State University, Cleveland, Ohio, USA

We are grateful to all authors who submitted their contributions to us for evaluation. We express our gratitude to Brian Romer and Amy Invernizzi (Elsevier) and their staff.

We hope that you enjoy reading this book as much as we enjoyed editing it.

On Behalf of Editorial Board:
Hamid R. Arabnia, PhD
Editor-in-Chief, "Emerging Trends in Computer Science and Applied Computing"
Professor, Computer Science
Department of Computer Science, The University of Georgia, Athens, GA, United States

Introduction

It gives us immense pleasure to present this edited book to the Computational Biology, Bioinformatics, and Systems Biology research community. As stated in the Preface of this book, Computational Biology is the science of using biological data to develop algorithms and relations among various biological systems. It involves the development and application of data-analytical and algorithms, mathematical modeling, and simulation techniques to the study of biological, behavioral, and social systems. The field is multidisciplinary in that it includes topics that are traditionally covered in computer science, mathematics, imaging science, statistics, chemistry, biophysics, genetics, genomics, ecology, evolution, anatomy, neuroscience, and visualization where computer science acts as the topical bridge between all such diverse areas. We consider the area of Bioinformatics to be an important subfield of Computational Biology, which includes methods for acquiring, storing, retrieving, organizing, analyzing, and visualizing biological data. The area of Systems Biology is an emerging methodology applied to biomedical and biological scientific research. It is an area that overlaps with computational biology and bioinformatics. This edited book attempts to cover the emerging trends in many important areas of Computational Biology, Bioinformatics, and Systems Biology with special emphasis on systems and applications. The book is composed of 35 chapters divided into five broad sections.

SECTION I, entitled "Computational Biology — Methodologies and Algorithms" is composed of five chapters. These chapters present various technologies, software tools, and algorithms, to solve and address important problems. More specifically, the methods include validation experiments and issues related to polymerase chain reaction, computational morphogenesis, image analysis, the use of neural networks, and distributed processing and frameworks.

The collection of 13 chapters compiled in SECTION II presents a number of important applications and describe novel uses of methodologies, including in bioinformatics, data mining and machine learning, simulation and modeling, pattern discovery, and prediction methods.

SECTION III, entitled "Systems Biology and Biological Processes" is composed of three chapters. These chapters provide an insight and understanding of how different technologies are intertwined and used in concert to solve real and practical problems. More specifically, the topics presented in this section include tissue growth models, detecting multiprotein complexes, and computational genomics.

SECTION IV is composed of two chapters that discuss data analytics and numerical modeling in computational biology.

Lastly, the 12 chapters that form SECTION V present a number of medical applications, medical systems, and devices. In particular, these chapters present various cancer studies, a novel heart simulator, clinical guidelines and methods, the novel uses of MRI and CT, treatment evaluation studies, imaging systems, signal processing (EEG analysis), and health informatics.

Many of the 35 chapters that appear in the five sections outlined above are extended versions of selected papers that were accepted for presentation at the 2014 and 2015 International Conference on Bioinformatics & Computational Biology (BIOCOMP'14 and BIOCOMP'15), July, Las Vegas, USA. Other authors (not affiliated with BIOCOMP) were also given the opportunity to contribute to this book by submitting their chapters for evaluation. We were fortunate to be coeditors of the proceedings of the above annual conferences where the preliminary versions of many of these chapters first appeared. We are grateful to all authors who submitted papers for consideration. We thank the referees and members of the editorial board of BIOCOMP and the federated congress, WORLDCOMP. Without their help this book project would not have been initiated nor finalized.

We hope that you learn from and enjoy reading the chapters of this book as much as we did.

Prof. Quoc Nam Tran, PhD
Senior Editor, Emerging Trends in Computational Biology, Bioinformatics, and Systems Biology — Systems and Applications
Professor of Computer Science and Department Chair
University of South Dakota, Vermillion, SD, United States

Prof. Hamid R. Arabnia, PhD
Co-editor, Emerging Trends in Computational Biology, Bioinformatics, and Systems Biology — Systems and Applications
Editor-in-Chief, "Emerging Trends in Computer Science and Applied Computing"
Professor, Computer Science
Department of Computer Science, The University of Georgia, Athens, GA, United States

Acknowledgments

We are very grateful to the many colleagues who offered their services in preparing and publishing this edited book. In particular, we would like to thank the members of the Program Committee of BIOCOMP'14 and BIOCOMP'15 Annual International Conferences; their names appear at: http://www.worldacademyofscience.org/worldcomp14/ws/conferences/biocomp14/committee.html, http://www.world-academy-of-science.org/worldcomp15/ws/conferences/biocomp15/committee.html. We would also like to thank the members of the Steering Committee of Federated Congress, WORLDCOMP 2015; http://www.world-academy-of-science.org/ and the referees that were designated by them. The American Council on Science and Education (ACSE: http://www.americancse.org/about) provided the use of a computer and a web server for managing the evaluation of the submitted chapters. We would like to extend our appreciation to Brian Romer (Elsevier Executive Editor) and Amy Invernizzi (Elsevier Editorial Project Manager) and their staff at Elsevier for the outstanding professional service that they provided to us. We are also very grateful to Ron Rouhani and Kaveh Arbtan for providing IT services at each phase of this project.

SECTION

I

COMPUTATIONAL BIOLOGY - METHODOLOGIES AND ALGORITHMS

CHAPTER

USING METHYLATION PATTERNS FOR RECONSTRUCTING CELL DIVISION DYNAMICS: ASSESSING VALIDATION EXPERIMENTS

1

D.J. Andrews, A.G. Lynch, S. Tavaré

Cancer Research UK Cambridge Institute, University of Cambridge, Cambridge, United Kingdom

1.1 INTRODUCTION

Understanding the lineage relationships among cells and the dynamics of cell division is of great interest in developmental biology, cancer dynamics, stem cell dynamics, immunology, neurobiology, and reproductive medicine, to name just a few. The most celebrated success story is arguably the identification of the complete cell lineage tree of the nematode *Caenorhabditis elegans* [1]. For reviews of approaches for lineage tracing up to the end of the 20th century (see [2, 3] for example). As might have been anticipated, it has proved technically difficult to produce detailed lineage trees in higher organisms such as mouse and human. As a result, evolutionary approaches for constructing and interpreting lineage trees, which exploit changes in molecular markers during cell division as a surrogate for direct observation, have become common in the last 15 years (reviewed in [4–6] for example).

Several types of molecular marker have been used for this purpose. Microsatellite variability has been exploited in [4, 7–11], mitochondrial variation in [12], and variation in methylation status in [13–17]. In this chapter we focus on the use of methylation markers, which we now describe in more detail.

1.1.1 USING METHYLATION PATTERNS

The measurement of the methylation patterns present in a cell population can inform us about the way the cells are organized and how the population is sustained. Methylation is inheritable through cell divisions but changes can occur as a result of methylation replication error. Hence, variation in methylation patterns in a cell population at a given time captures information about the history of the cell population.

An example of a cell population that has been studied in this way is the human colon crypt. The colon crypt is found in the epithelium of the colon, has a cylindrical shape, and consists of about 2000 cells. Residing at the bottom of the cylinder are stem cells from which originate the cell lineages of all the other cells found in the crypt. When a stem cell divides it will usually produce a daughter cell, which is committed to differentiation, as well as another stem cell. More rarely the stem cell will divide symmetrically to produce either two stem cells or two differentiating cells. Any cells committed to differentiation will move up toward the top of the cylinder, differentiating as they go, until they become mature epithelial cells.

The methylation data we obtain are typically composed of methylation patterns obtained from bisulfite converted DNA sequenced at a small number of CpG sites in an amplicon a few hundred base pairs in length. Such patterns can be used to infer aspects of the dynamics of cells in the colon crypt by exploiting a probabilistic model for the cell population organization and for the observation process [18]. The authors fit a full probabilistic model for the stem cell genealogy, the methylation/demethylation process, and the sampling, and perform inference using a Markov chain Monte Carlo (MCMC) algorithm. In [19] a cellular Potts model of crypt evolution is used, while the inference about stem cell structure is performed using approximate Bayesian computation (ABC). As another example, Siegmund et al. [20] infer the topological nature of the ancestral tree for tumor cells from methylation patterns and spatial data. They simulate methylation patterns and also use an ABC algorithm for the inference.

It is, of course, important that the observed methylation patterns are representative of those patterns in the cell population. However, we know that bisulfite sequencing may introduce new patterns, and degradation may eliminate rare patterns. Clearly, this is an occasion when studying the data generation process in more detail may prove beneficial. Here we investigate how bisulfite degradation may be expected to affect the data, and how inference could be made in light of this.

1.1.2 BISULFITE TREATMENT

The methylation states of CpG sites can be measured by encoding this information into the DNA sequence. This is achieved by treating the DNA with bisulfite, which causes the complete deamination of cytosine to make uracil, while leaving 5-methyl-cytosine (5mC) unchanged. Thus, from a number of CpG sites, some will be indicated as methylated and others not; we call this the methylation pattern. Bisulfite treatment is followed by polymerase chain reaction (PCR) where uracil is converted to thymine. These DNA molecules, with the methylation patterns encoded as substitutions, can be prepared and sequenced in the usual way. The sequenced reads can be compared to a reference sequence and the methylation patterns can be inferred.

Bisulfite treatment introduces errors and biases, investigated by Grunau et al. [21] and Warnecke et al. [22]. The method is based on the complete conversion of cytosine and the complete nonconversion of 5mC. If either of these does not happen, that is, if a cytosine fails to convert or a 5mC does convert, then an incorrect methylation pattern will be encoded, which may subsequently be sequenced.

DNA degradation is an undesired side effect of bisulfite treatment; degraded molecules will not be sequenced and hence the methylation patterns of these will be absent from the read data. Grunau et al. [21] conclude that complete conversion of cytosine can be achieved when the incubation of alkaline denatured DNA with a saturated bisulfite solution is performed for 4 h at 55°C. They estimate that using these conditions between 84% and 96% of DNA is degraded. With such a high fraction of molecules being degraded there is a high chance that some of the more rare methylation patterns in the population may not be observed at all. This would be particularly concerning if the diversity of methylation patterns was of interest, because degradation is likely to decrease this diversity.

We consider a theoretical experiment where a single colon crypt, with approximately 2000 cells, is bisulfite-sequenced (using 454 sequencing technology). We consider methylation patterns made up from 9 CpG sites contained in a single amplicon sequence, numbers that are typical of real data (cf. [13, 14, 18, 19]). Specifically, we investigate how the measurement process affects inference of two quantities: the number of haploid genomes (out of the total of 4000) that have the most common pattern, and how many distinct patterns are present in the entire population. While we consider a specific case for illustration, the reader can generalize to other examples.

1.2 ERRORS, BIASES, AND UNCERTAINTY IN BISULFITE SEQUENCING

To understand how the steps in the bisulfite sequencing protocol affect the analysis of methylation patterns we start by describing a naive statistical method for this type of data. Suppose we know that there are $N^{(0)}$ genomes in our sample and we observe k different patterns with counts $y_1,\ldots,y_k$. Then the naive estimator of the number of distinct patterns is k and the estimator of the number of genomes with pattern i is $N^{(0)}y_i/Y$, where $Y = y_1 + \cdots + y_k$ is the total number of reads.

There are many ways that errors, biases, and uncertainty can be introduced in the course of bisulfite sequencing, and that may consequently result in these estimators being biased or highly variable. For this study we limit the sources of error and bias that we consider. We consider only those biases that result from the loss of molecules from the experiment: for example, by bisulfite degradation, by sampling, by ligation, and by bead placement. We expect that the loss of molecules from observation will affect estimates for the methylation pattern frequencies as well as estimation of the total number of distinct methylation patterns. In summary, we are focusing on the affect of losing molecules from the experiment, and we assess how small the degradation probability can be while still achieving small bias and variance in estimation.

1.3 MODEL FOR DEGRADATION AND SAMPLING

1.3.1 MODELING

We focus on the experimental steps of bisulfite degradation and other sampling steps; the resultant protocol can be described as follows. Let b be the number of CpGs at which the methylation status will be observed. Then there are $k = 2^b$ possible patterns which *wlog* we can label 1, ..., k. A quantitative model for the protocol is as follows.

1. We start with a total of $N^{(0)}$ molecules containing the CpG sites, and with $n_i^{(0)}$ of pattern i for $i = 1,\ldots,k$; $n_1^{(0)} + \cdots + n_k^{(0)} = N^{(0)}$.
2. Bisulfite treatment causes the failure of a fraction $(1 - p)$ of the molecules leaving a total of $N^{(1)}$ molecules, which is $N^{(0)}p$ on average, and $n_i^{(1)}$ with pattern i for $i = 1,\ldots,k$.
3. PCR amplifies the number of each pattern by a constant factor M.
4. The number of reads Y will be smaller than $M \times N^{(1)}$ due to loss of molecules during ligation, bead placement, and other sampling steps that happen after PCR.

We can describe this model probabilistically as

$$n_i^{(1)} \sim \text{Binomial}(n_i^{(0)}, p) \text{ independently for } i = 1, \ldots, k$$

$$y|n^{(1)}, Y \sim \text{Multinomial}(Y, q) \text{ where } q_i = \frac{n_i^{(1)}}{\sum_j n_j^{(1)}}$$

Whether this model is accurate depends on the validity of a number of assumptions and approximations (beyond those made by ignoring the sources of bias and error as described above). These are as follows:

(i) Each molecule independently, and with probability $1 - p$, fails the bisulfite treatment.

(ii) Each molecule that survives the bisulfite treatment is independently and equally likely to be successfully read. With this assumption alone and supposing we knew the probability of a molecule being read to be r, then the second part of the model would be

$$y_i \sim \text{Binomial}(Mn_i^{(1)}, r) \text{ independently for } i = 1, \ldots, k$$

However, the probability r is the product of the probabilities of several (assumed) independent events: and that a molecule has adapters successfully ligated to it; that a molecule is successfully hybridized to a bead; that a molecule survives any other sampling steps; that a molecule is not adsorbed onto any of the containers it is held in. Hence we will treat it as unknown. The natural way to remove r from the likelihood is by conditioning on $Y := y_1 + \cdots + y_k$, which is observed, leaving

$$p(y|n^{(1)}, Y) = \binom{MN^{(1)}}{Y}^{-1} \prod_{i=1}^{k} \binom{Mn_i^{(1)}}{y_i}$$

In other words, y is distributed as taking Y objects from an urn containing $Mn_i^{(1)}$ balls of color i, *without* replacement (a multivariate hypergeometric random variable).

(iii) If the PCR is successful then M is large; for example, if PCR has 20–30 rounds with replication probability in 0.7–1.0, then M is between 4.1×10^4 and 1.1×10^9. We shall hence assume that $M \times N^{(1)}$ is many times larger than Y. Taking the limit as $M \to \infty$, y becomes distributed as above but *with* replacement (a multinomial random variable).

$$p(y|n^{(1)}, Y) = Y! \prod_{i=1}^{k} \frac{(n_i^{(1)} / \sum_j n_j^{(1)})^{y_i}}{y_i!}$$

Assuming that r is unknown weakens our ability to make inference about $N^{(0)}$. However, for application to tissues such as colon crypts this is acceptable because the range of plausible values of $N^{(0)}$ is known in advance.

1.3.2 SIMULATION STUDY: EFFECTS OF DEGRADATION

Now that we have a model for the bisulfite sequencing protocol we can investigate by simulation the consequences of degradation by bisulfite treatment.

In Fig. 1.1 we investigate the affect of the bisulfite survival probability p on the bias of the naive estimator of the starting number of distinct patterns. The more patterns that were present in the starting

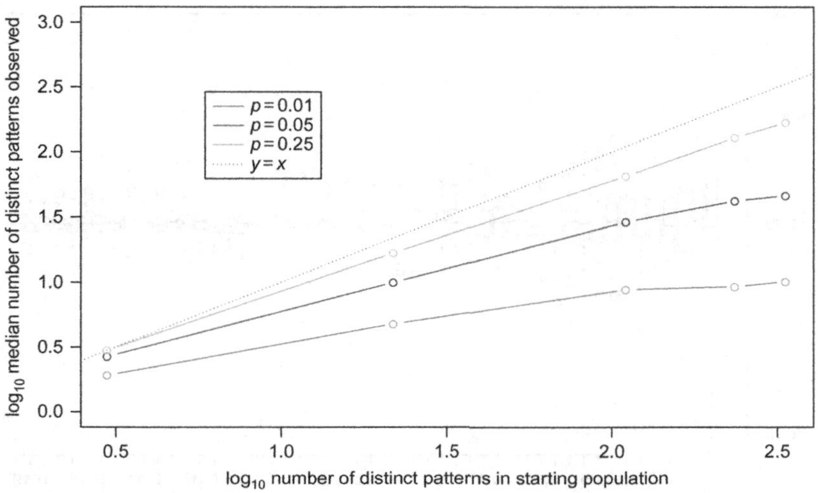

FIGURE 1.1

For five different starting pattern populations with number of distinct patterns, 3,22,111,237,337 (out of a total of $2^9 = 512$), and for different degradation probabilities $p = 0.01, 0.05, 0.25$ (bottom, middle, and top lines respectively), the data y were sampled 100 times according to the model with $Y = 10^4$. The naive estimate of the number of distinct patterns is more biased for smaller p. (The starting populations are realizations of the prior discussed later in the article, with $\alpha \in (0,1)$.)

population (and hence the more rare patterns that are present) the more bias the estimator will have. This is because the fewer molecules that have a given pattern the more likely it is that all of them will be degraded. When $p = 0.25$ (top line) the bias is quite small, but it is very large for $p = 0.05$ (middle line) and $p = 0.01$ (bottom line); the estimates being over 10 times too small in the latter case when there were more that 100 patterns present originally.

In Fig. 1.2 we investigate the affect of p on the variance of the observed pattern count for a pattern originally present in 2000 out of the 4000 haploid genomes. When $p > 0.1$ this variance changes little, but as p decreases below this level the variance increases rapidly.

The consequences for estimation are that when p is small we expect large uncertainty about the frequency of any pattern and vary large uncertainty about the number of distinct patterns, especially when more than 100 patterns are observed.

1.4 STATISTICAL INFERENCE METHOD

We have seen that the naive estimator for the starting number of distinct patterns is biased. We now present a Bayesian approach to inference, and develop an MCMC algorithm to generate samples that we will treat as being samples from the posterior.

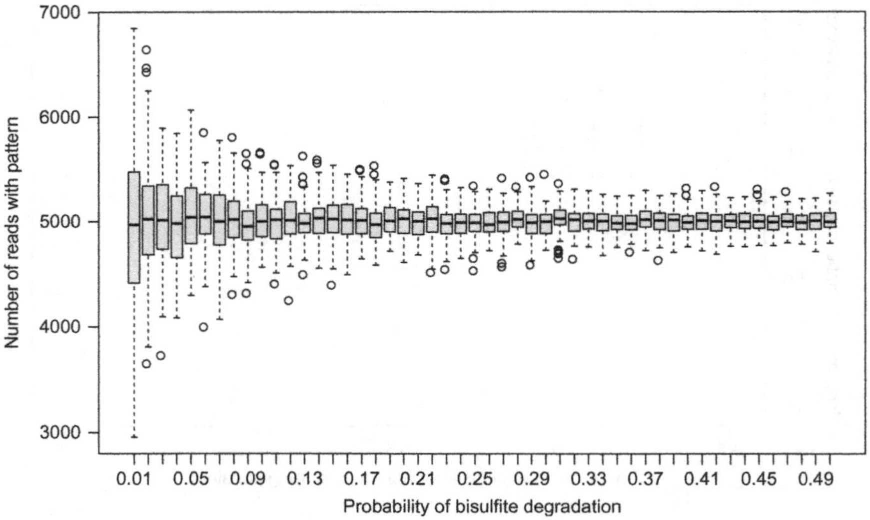

FIGURE 1.2

For an initial population $n^{(0)}$ such that the most frequent pattern was present in 50% of genomes, the data y were simulated 100 times, with $Y = 10^4$, and each for a range of p in (0,0.5). The observed number of this pattern has very large variation, but is unbiased, when p is small.

Choice of noninformative prior. We need to specify a prior for $(n_1^{(0)}, \ldots, n_k^{(0)})$. Considering this inference problem in isolation from everything known about the evolutionary process that created the population of methylation patterns, a simple three-level prior would be

$$(n_i^{(0)})_{i=1}^k \sim \text{Multinomial}(N^{(0)}, (q_i)_{i=1}^k), \quad (q_i)_{i=1}^k \sim \text{Dirichlet}(\alpha \mathbf{1}_k), \quad \text{and} \quad \alpha \sim \pi$$

where $\mathbf{1}_k$ is a k-vector of ones, and π is a density function on $(0, \infty)$ that is yet to be decided. The priors in this family satisfy the sensible property of being exchangeable in $n^{(0)}$; that is, $\mathbb{P}(n_1^{(0)} = x_1, \ldots, n_k^{(0)} = x_k) = \mathbb{P}(n_{\sigma(1)}^{(0)} = x_1, \ldots, n_{\sigma(k)}^{(0)} = x_k)$ for any permutation $\sigma \in S_k$. Equivalently, our prior knowledge is invariant to the way the patterns are labeled. Simulations from

$$\pi(\alpha) = \frac{1}{3 \times 1.4} \alpha^{-2/3} \mathbf{1}_{(0, 1.4^3)}(\alpha)$$

show that this prior is less informative for the number of distinct methylation patterns; see Chapter 2 of [23] for further details.

Algorithm development. Fig. 1.3 shows a directed acyclic graph (DAG) representation of the model, including the prior and observation model. We shall show how $n^{(0)}$ and q can be integrated out.

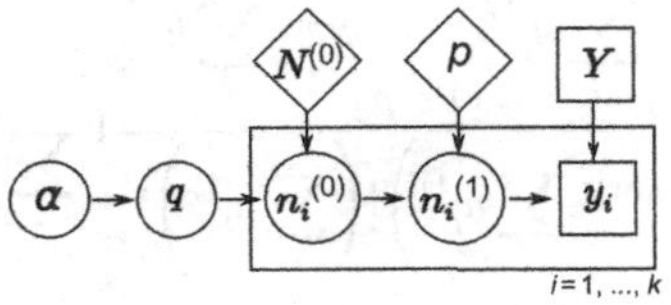

FIGURE 1.3

A directed acyclic graph (DAG) representation of the model. The circular nodes are those that are not observed; the square nodes are observed; the diamond nodes are assumed known. The arrows represent the conditional relationships: the conditional density of a node given all its ancestors is only a function of said node and its parent nodes. The nodes in the plate exist in k copies; two nodes in different plates are independent conditional on the parents of the plate nodes.

The full conditional for $(n^{(0)}, q)$ is

$$p(n^{(0)},q|n^{(1)},\alpha,y) \propto \prod_{i=1}^{k} \binom{n_i^{(0)}}{n_i^{(1)}} p^{n_i^{(1)}} (1-p)^{n_i^{(0)}-n_i^{(1)}} \mathbf{1}_{\{0 \le n_i^{(1)} \le n_i^{(0)}\}}$$

$$\times N^{(0)}! \prod_{i=1}^{k} \frac{q_i^{n_i^{(0)}}}{n_i^{(0)}!} \mathbf{1}_{\{0 \le n_i^{(0)}\}} \mathbf{1}_{\left\{\sum_j n_j^{(0)} = N^{(0)}\right\}}$$

$$\times \Gamma(\alpha k) \prod_{i=1}^{k} \frac{q_i^{\alpha-1}}{\Gamma(\alpha)} \mathbf{1}_{\{0 \le q_i \le 1\}} \mathbf{1}_{\left\{\sum_j q_j = 1\right\}}$$

which is proportional (in $n^{(0)}$ and q) to

$$p(n^{(0)},q|n^{(1)},\alpha,y) = \left(N^{(0)} - \sum_{j=1}^{k} n_j^{(1)}\right)! \prod_{i=1}^{k} \frac{q_i^{n_i^{(0)}-n_i^{(1)}}}{(n_i^{(0)}-n_i^{(1)})!} \mathbf{1}_{\left\{\sum_j n_j^{(0)} = N^{(0)}\right\}} \mathbf{1}_{\{n_i^{(1)} \le n_i^{(0)}\}}$$

$$\times \Gamma\left(\sum_{j=1}^{k} n_j^{(1)} + \alpha k\right) \prod_{i=1}^{k} \frac{q_i^{n_i^{(1)}+\alpha-1}}{\Gamma(n_i^{(1)}+\alpha)} \mathbf{1}_{\{0 \le q_i \le 1\}} \mathbf{1}_{\left\{\sum_j q_j = 1\right\}}$$

Hence

$$n^{(0)} - n^{(1)}|n^{(1)},q,y \sim \text{Multinomial}\left(N^{(0)} - \sum_{j=1}^{k} n_j^{(1)}, q\right)$$

and

$$q|n^{(1)},\alpha,y \sim \text{Dirichlet}(n^{(1)} + \alpha \mathbf{1}_k)$$

Dividing $p(n^{(0)}, n^{(1)}, q, \alpha|y)$ by $p(n^{(0)}, q|n^{(1)}, \alpha, y)$ this leaves the joint posterior for $n^{(1)}$, α

$$p(n^{(1)},\alpha|y) \propto \frac{N^{(0)}!p^{\sum_j n_j^{(1)}}(1-p)^{N^{(0)}-\sum_j n_j^{(1)}}}{\left(N^{(0)}-\sum_j n_j^{(1)}\right)!\left(\sum_j n_j^{(1)}\right)!}\mathbf{1}_{\{\sum_j n_j^{(1)} \le N^{(0)}\}}$$

$$\times \frac{\left(\sum_j n_j^{(1)}\right)!\Gamma(\alpha k)}{\Gamma\left(\sum_j n_j^{(1)}+\alpha k\right)}\prod_{i=1}^{k}\frac{\Gamma(n_i^{(1)}+\alpha)}{(n_i^{(1)})!\Gamma(\alpha)}\left(\frac{n_i^{(1)}}{\sum_j n_j^{(1)}}\right)^{y_i}\mathbf{1}_{\{0\le n_i^{(1)}\}}$$

$$\times \pi(\alpha)$$

which cannot obviously be written in terms of simpler distributions.

The fact that the posterior distribution can be decomposed in this way suggests a program for sampling using a MCMC algorithm: get a sample from $n^{(1)}, \alpha|y$, then sample directly from the exact conditional distributions of $q|n^{(1)}, \alpha, y$, and then $n^{(0)}|n^{(1)}, q, y$. This should be better than sampling all the variables in a MCMC scheme, due to decreased correlation between samples.

The full conditionals for the random variables $\alpha, n_1^{(1)}, \ldots, n_k^{(1)}$ are

$$p(\alpha|n^{(1)},y) \propto \frac{\left(\sum_j n_j^{(1)}\right)!\Gamma(\alpha k)}{\Gamma\left(\sum_j n_j^{(1)}+\alpha k\right)}\prod_{i=1}^{k}\frac{\Gamma(n_i^{(1)}+\alpha)}{(n_i^{(1)})!\Gamma(\alpha)}\pi(\alpha)$$

and

$$p(n_i^{(1)}|s_{(-i)},\alpha,y) \propto \frac{(n_i^{(1)}+s_{(-i)})!\Gamma(\alpha k)}{\Gamma(n_i^{(1)}+s_{(-i)}+\alpha k)}\frac{\Gamma(n_i^{(1)}+\alpha)}{(n_i^{(1)})!\Gamma(\alpha)}\frac{n_i^{(1)y_i}}{(n_i^{(1)}+s_{(-i)})^{Y}}$$

$$\times \frac{N^{(0)}!p^{n_i^{(1)}+s_{(-i)}}(1-p)^{N^{(0)}-n_i^{(1)}-s_{(-i)}}}{(N^{(0)}-n_i^{(1)}-s_{(-i)})!(n_i^{(1)}+s_{(-i)})!}\mathbf{1}_{0\le\{n_i^{(1)}\le N^{(0)}-s_{(-i)}\}}$$

where $s_{(-i)} = \sum_{j\ne i} n_j^{(1)}$.

One iteration of the MCMC algorithm proceeds as

1. update $n^{(1)}$ by k Metropolis-Hastings steps: for each $i = 1,\ldots,k$ update $n_i^{(1)}$ given $s_{(-i)}$ and α;
2. update α by a Metropolis-Hastings step;
3. sample q given $n^{(1)}$ and α;
4. sample $n^{(0)}$ given $n^{(1)}$, q and α.

There is one issue with this scheme that would prevent it working well in certain cases: if Y is large then the posterior for $n^{(0)}$ has local modes at vectors approximately integer multiples of the truth. If the algorithm is initialized near to a local mode then it will not converge to the true posterior.

Rather than altering the algorithm to get around this problem we set the initial $n^{(1)}$ to be sampled from

$$n^{(1)} \sim \text{Multinomial}\left(N^{(0)}p, \left\{\frac{y_i}{\sum_j y_j}\right\}_{i=1}^{k}\right)$$

to have a good chance of convergence to the true posterior around the global mode.

1.5 SIMULATION STUDY: BAYESIAN INFERENCE

We investigate how our Bayesian inference method performs under different circumstances.

Investigating frequency estimates. For a given starting population of patterns $\{n_i^{(0)}\}_{i=1}^{512}$ we simulate the observation process 100 times, with $Y = 10^4$, each time computing the maximum a posteriori (MAP) estimate of the starting number of genomes with the truly most frequent pattern; this pattern is originally present with count 779 out of 4000. This we repeat with values of $p = 0.01, 0.05, 0.1, 0.25$.

Fig. 1.4 shows that for small p the MAP estimator is biased downward and highly variable. Both the bias and variance of this estimator decrease as p increases. The naive estimator seems to be much less biased than the MAP for smaller p, and performs equally well for larger p. The bias in the MAP estimate is due to the prior. The smaller p is, the more the posterior is more influenced by the prior, and the estimator is more biased.

Investigating diversity inference. Fig. 1.5 shows the result of a simulation study investigating the performance of the Bayesian MAP estimator of the number of distinct patterns. When a $\log_{10}$ transformation is taken of the estimates it seems that the variance is stabilized; this means that the coefficient of variation of the estimate does not depend on the true number of distinct patterns. The estimator variance is larger when $p = 0.01$ than when $p = 0.05$. It seems like the estimator is more or less unbiased, unlike the naive estimator that underestimates.

1.6 DISCUSSION

We have seen in this chapter that degradation caused by bisulfite treatment has the potential to make the observed methylation patterns very unrepresentative of those present in the cell population. We developed a Bayesian MCMC method to infer the methylation patterns present in the cell population. We showed that the method allows us to accurately infer the number of distinct patterns originally present. However, when p is small, this method performs worse than the naive method at estimating the original count of a given pattern.

In this experiment it would seem that 99% degradation is too small to achieve accurate and precise estimation. This equates to an average of 40 molecules not being degraded. When degradation is this high the uncertainty about the original pattern counts is high and cannot be reduced by using methods based on models of the data generation process.

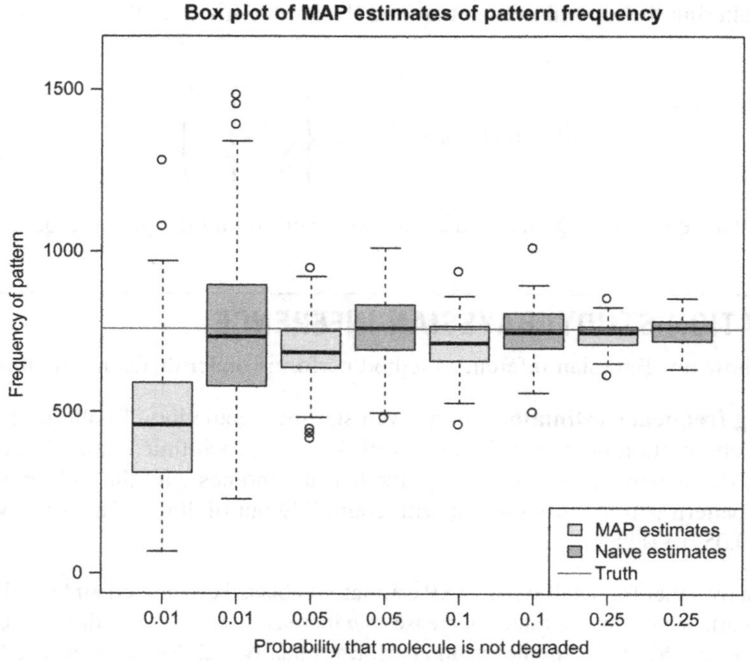

FIGURE 1.4

A starting population was simulated from the prior with $\alpha = 0.3^3$, resulting in a most frequent pattern of 779 out of 4000 and a total of 88 distinct patterns. For values of $p = 0.01, 0.05, 0.1, 0.5$, 100 sets of observed patterns were simulated from the model with $Y = 10^4$. For each of these data sets the MCMC algorithm produced MAP estimators of the frequency of the most frequent pattern (left-hand box plot in pair). Also shown are box plots of the naive estimates for the pattern count (right-hand box plot in pair). For small p the MAP estimator is biased with a median of around 450. The bias and variance of the MAP estimator decreases with increasing p.

1.6.1 DIFFERENT EXPERIMENTS

This limited study has been concerned with a particular experiment when the number of starting molecules is $N^{(0)} = 4000$, the number of CpG sites is $b = 9$, and the number of reads is $Y = 10^4$. The question remains as to how things would be different if these experimental parameters were different.

Concerning $N^{(0)}$. We expect that increasing $N^{(0)}$ and keeping the number of distinct patterns constant will have a very similar effect to increasing p; that is, more accurate inference of the pattern frequencies. If the pattern diversity also increases then there may be little improvement in the precision in estimating the starting number of distinct patterns, as the number of rare patterns may not change.

Concerning Y. The variance in the estimate of the proportion of molecules with pattern i comes from two sources: the variance in sampling $n_i^{(1)}$ and the variance in sampling y_i. Increasing Y will reduce the latter variance but not the former. Hence, there will be diminishing returns from increasing Y.

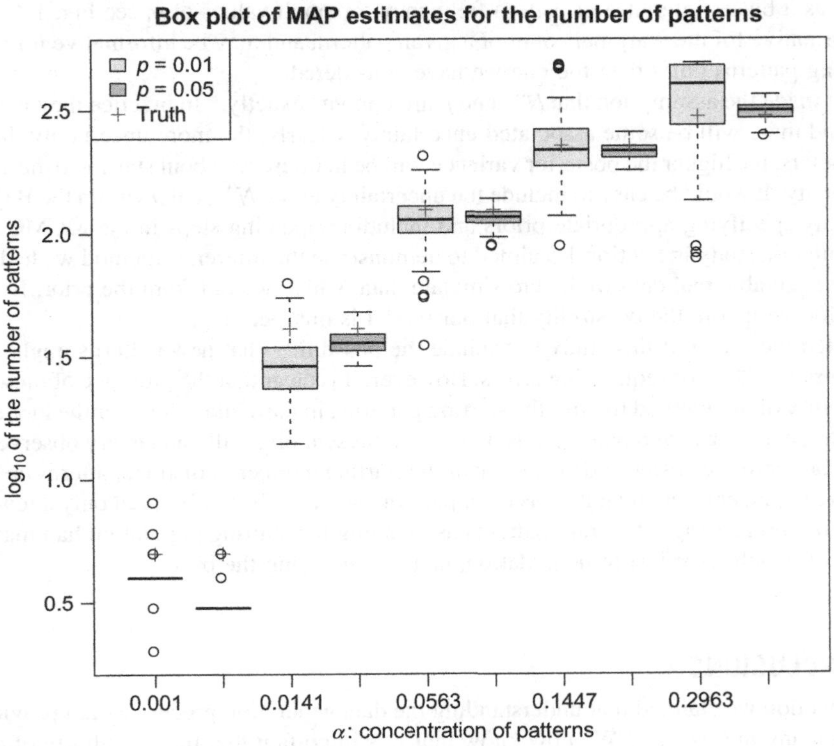

FIGURE 1.5

A range of starting populations was sampled from the prior with values of α such that $0 < \alpha < 0.3$. For each population 100 sets of observed patterns were simulated from the model with $Y = 10^4$. For each data set our MCMC algorithm was run and the MAP estimate of the starting number of distinct patterns was computed. Shown are box plots of $\log_{10}$ of these estimates when $p = 0.01$ and $p = 0.05$ (left-hand and right-hand box plot in pairs respectively).

Concerning k. In this study we considered methylation patterns made up from 9 CpG sites, equivalently 512 possible patterns. If a different number of CpGs were used then it is likely that the prior would need to change to keep it uninformative for the number of distinct patterns. The number of possible patterns is $k = 2^b$ where b is the number of CpG sites. The MCMC algorithm is $O(2^b)$ and hence will become very slow for moderate b. This method would need to be adapted in that case.

1.6.2 OPPORTUNITIES

In this study we rejected the uniform prior on the starting pattern counts as it was very informative for the number of patterns with nonzero count. We manufactured a prior that appeared uninformative for this function of the starting patterns, which we used for subsequent analysis. This prior is not entirely satisfactory as it biases inference of pattern frequency for small values of p; see Fig. 1.4. Clearly this prior is informative for the marginal count of a given pattern, and may be informative for any function of the starting patterns other than the one we have considered.

We have made the assumption that $N^{(0)}$ and p are known "exactly." In practice they will have been estimated and there will be some associated uncertainty. Clearly, the more uncertainty there is about these parameters, the higher the posterior variance will be in inference about starting pattern counts and pattern diversity. It would be easy to include the uncertainty about $N^{(0)}$ and p within the Bayesian analysis by simply specifying appropriate priors and including updating steps in the MCMC algorithm.

Our simulation study in Section 1.5 aimed to demonstrate the inference method we had developed. As we had no suitable real data we had to simulate data, which we did from the prior. By simulating from the prior we ignore the possibility that our model is misspecified.

We limited the scope of this study to exclude the possibility that new patterns might arise by bisulfite conversion, PCR, or sequencing errors. However, it is clear that the presence of these errors will affect the ability of our method to infer the starting patterns. In particular, as under the model described in this chapter, every observed pattern must have been present originally and every observed error pattern will at least shift the posterior distribution of the starting number of distinct patterns up by one. It is likely to have a greater effect than this, as error patterns will mostly be observed only a few times. The model will interpret seeing a few rare patterns as meaning the starting population had many rare patterns, some of which were lost to degradation, hence amplifying the bias.

1.6.3 CONCLUSIONS

In the introduction we claimed that understanding the data generation process would provide benefits. Have we seen any in this case? We now know that it is important that the probability of degradation $(1-p)$ is small. Given a real experiment with some $N^{(0)}$, we could simulate the data generation process and investigate when p will be too small. Having a model for the data generation process has also made it possible for us to estimate the starting number of distinct patterns in a more accurate way.

REFERENCES

[1] Sulston JE, Schierenberg E, White JG, Thomson JN. The embryonic cell lineage of the nematode *Caenorhabditis elegans*. Dev Biol 1983;100(1):64–119.
[2] Clarke JD, Tickle C. Fate maps old and new. Nat Cell Biol 1999;1(4):E103–9.
[3] Stern CD, Fraser SE. Tracing the lineage of tracing cell lineages. Nat Cell Biol 2001;3(9):E216–8.
[4] Frumkin D, Wasserstrom A, Kaplan S, Feige U, Shapiro E. Genomic variability within an organism exposes its cell lineage tree. PLoS Comput Biol 2005;1(5):e50.
[5] Shibata D, Tavaré S. Counting divisions in a human somatic cell tree: how, what and why? Cell Cycle 2006; 5(6):610–4.
[6] Shibata D, Tavaré S. Stem cell chronicles: autobiographies within genomes. Stem Cell Rev 2007; 3(1):94–103.
[7] Tsao JL, Zhang J, Salovaara R, Li ZH, Järvinen HJ, Mecklin JP, et al. Tracing cell fates in human colorectal tumors from somatic microsatellite mutations: evidence of adenomas with stem cell architecture. Am J Pathol 1998;153(4):1189–200.

[8] Tsao JL, Tavaré S, Salovaara R, Jass JR, Aaltonen LA, Shibata D. Colorectal adenoma and cancer divergence. Evidence of multilineage progression. Am J Pathol 1999;154(6):1815–24.
[9] Tsao JL, Yatabe Y, Salovaara R, Järvinen HJ, Mecklin JP, Aaltonen LA, et al. Genetic reconstruction of individual colorectal tumor histories. Proc Natl Acad Sci U S A 2000;97(3):1236–41.
[10] Salipante SJ, Horwitz MS. Phylogenetic fate mapping. Proc Natl Acad Sci U S A 2006;103(14):5448–53.
[11] Salipante SJ, Thompson JM, Horwitz MS. Phylogenetic fate mapping: theoretical and experimental studies applied to the development of mouse fibroblasts. Genetics 2008;178(2):967–77.
[12] Humphries A, Cereser B, Gay LJ, Miller DSJ, Das B, Gutteridge A, et al. Lineage tracing reveals multipotent stem cells maintain human adenomas and the pattern of clonal expansion in tumor evolution. Proc Natl Acad Sci U S A 2013;110(27):E2490–9.
[13] Yatabe Y, Tavaré S, Shibata D. Investigating stem cells in human colon by using methylation patterns. Proc Natl Acad Sci U S A 2001;98(19):10839–44.
[14] Siegmund KD, Marjoram P, Woo YJ, Tavaré S, Shibata D. Inferring clonal expansion and cancer stem cell dynamics from DNA methylation patterns in colorectal cancers. Proc Natl Acad Sci U S A 2009;106 (12):4828–33.
[15] Graham TA, Humphries A, Sanders T, Rodriguez-Justo M, Tadrous PJ, Preston SL, et al. Use of methylation patterns to determine expansion of stem cell clones in human colon tissue. Gastroenterology 2011;140(4). 1241–50.e1–9.
[16] Sottoriva A, Spiteri I, Shibata D, Curtis C, Tavaré S. Single-molecule genomic data delineate patient-specific tumor profiles and cancer stem cell organization. Cancer Res 2013;73(1):41–9.
[17] Koyanagi KO. Inferring cell differentiation processes based on phylogenetic analysis of genome-wide epigenetic information: hematopoiesis as a model case. Genome Biol Evol 2015;7(3):699–705.
[18] Nicolas P, Kim KM, Shibata D, Tavaré S. The stem cell population of the human colon crypt: analysis via methylation patterns. PLoS Comput Biol 2007;3(3):e28.
[19] Sottoriva A, Tavaré S. Integrating approximate Bayesian computation with complex agent-based models for cancer research. In: Saporta G, Lechevallier Y, editors. COMPSTAT 2010 — Proceedings in computational statistics. Berlin: Springer, Physica Verlag; 2010. p. 57–66.
[20] Siegmund KD, Marjoram P, Shibata D. Modeling DNA methylation in a population of cancer cells. Stat Appl Genet Mol Biol 2008;7(1):Article 18.
[21] Grunau C, Clark SJ, Rosenthal A. Bisulfite genomic sequencing: systematic investigation of critical experimental parameters. Nucleic Acids Res 2001;29(13):E65–5.
[22] Warnecke PM, Stirzaker C, Melki JR, Millar DS, Paul CL, Clark SJ. Detection and measurement of PCR bias in quantitative methylation analysis of bisulphite-treated DNA. Nucleic Acids Res 1997;25(21):4422–6.
[23] Andrews D. Statistical models of PCR for quantification of target DNA by sequencing. Ph.D. thesis, University of Cambridge; 2015.

CHAPTER

2

A DIRECTIONAL CELLULAR DYNAMIC UNDER THE CONTROL OF A DIFFUSING ENERGY FOR TISSUE MORPHOGENESIS: PHENOTYPE AND GENOTYPE

A. Sarr, A. Fronville, V. Rodin
Computer Science Department, University of Western Brittany, Brest, France

2.1 INTRODUCTION

Facing the complexity of in vivo experiments, understanding of the living is more and more focused on in silico models. Nowadays, the relative ease of implementation of a *virtual lab* has made possible the formulation and testing of many hypotheses in *biology*, particularly in *morphogenesis*. *Morphogenesis* is an important research field within *developmental biology*. It can be defined as the set of processes that causes an organism to develop its shape. Many models exist in the area depending on the main factors considered in biological form creation and also on the studied organisms (prokaryotes, animals, plant, etc.). *Tensegrity model* is for example interested in cells' shape changing. This model considers biomechanical forces between cells and the extracellular matrix. The stretching of cells adhering to the extracellular matrix may result from local reshuffle in this latter [1]. However, the question of cell diversity arises even before the acquisition of shape [2]. Indeed, when the embryo has only a few pairs of cells, we can already see a diversification in the biochemical content of the embryonic cells or even in their morphology. *Artificial regulatory networks* have also been used in morphogenesis modeling. They define a series of regulatory genes and structural genes. The first consists of a network of rules determining the evolution of the system and the latter are intended to each generate a simple specific pattern [3]. However, even if the detailed knowledge of genomic sequences allow us to determine where and when different genes are expressed in the embryo, it is insufficient to understand how the organism emerges [4]. The mechanisms of cell morphogenesis also include the reaction-diffusion models. A.M. Turing presented in 1952 his well-known model where it is suggested that a system of chemical substances, called morphogens, reacting together and diffusing through a tissue, is adequate to account for the main phenomena of morphogenesis [5]. In this model, patterns or structures emerge due to an instability of the homogeneous equilibrium, which is triggered by random disturbances. This model can surely produce structures, like spots and stripes, for a range of organisms but it does not give the process by which the global shape emerges. Besides, because the model relies on random disturbances to produce spotted patterns, we cannot follow in a deterministic way cell division and differentiation from the first cell of the organism and along with development of its shape. Another approach commonly used for modeling multicellular systems is to make an integration of the dynamic interactions between different spatial and/or temporal scales. This approach introduces some complexities in models that limit their understanding and effectiveness with respect to their purpose. Thus, we consider that the cell must be the focus, which determines both causalities and downgrades. In other words, as a first step to a better understanding, observations must be restricted to a single spatial and temporal scale of the biological organization.

Thanks to advances in microscopy and imaging, very detailed data on components and structures of living organisms are now available. Melani et al. achieved a tracking of cell nuclei and the identification of cell divisions in live zebra fish embryos using `3D+time` images acquired by confocal laser scanning microscopy [6]. While the zebrafish embryo contains a few pairs of cells, we noticed (see Fig. 2.1):

1. A geometrical segmentation during cellular proliferation.
2. A specific arrangement of cells at each stage guided by a deterministic process.

These observations allow us to formulate a set of principles so as to propose a model. First, the noted geometrical segmentation allows us to adopt a discrete model in time and space to study the forms

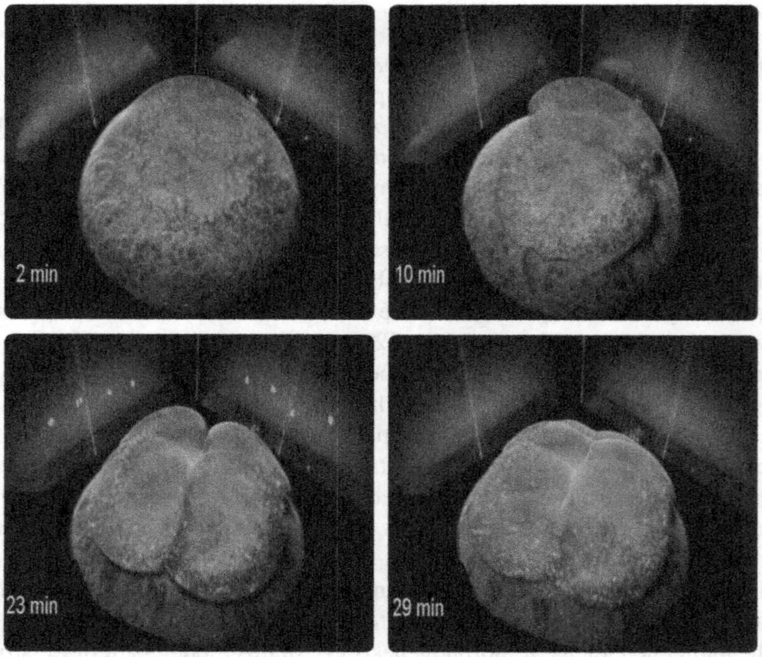

FIGURE 2.1

The four images are a collection of screenshots from the video produced with the framework designed in [7]. It was used for imaging and reconstructing the whole zebrafish embryo at its first 10 cell division cycles. These images depict the first three division cycles when the embryo includes 2, 4, and 8 cells.

appearing in the early stages of morphogenesis. For now, we restrict to a 2D model. Besides, we make the hypothesis that, based on spatial choices of cells, we can define a morphological dynamic of tissues emergence and growth at the early stage of the embryo during which the mechanical influences are insignificant. Furthermore, we assume that this dynamic is the fundamental principle of morphogenesis and is therefore able to describe all evolutions of a tissue, both those that modify it and those that maintain it.

Our main goal in this chapter is to develop, implement, and simulate a mathematical model that embodies the crucial features of our hypothesis. At the same time, we show how such a model is accurate to describe behaviors of cells and aggregation of cells. This chapter is organized as follows, Section 2.2 presents the mathematical morphological dynamic of a multicellular system. It relies on the viability theory [8], which offers an approach especially well suited for the biological systems whose complexity would render a purely analytic approach unrealistic. Using computer simulations, by mimicking the tissue growth, the dynamic model allows us to generate in Section 2.3 all possible phenotypes at the early stage of the embryo and their underlying genotype. Building on the back of the phenotypes and their associated genotype, we present in Section 2.4 a prediction tool to simulate tissue evolution at the later stages of the embryo. Because we are focusing on animal growth, cellular exchange has been taken into account through a coupling of an energy diffusion model with the morphogenesis model. Thereby, cells are endowed with the ability to consume, lose, and transfer energy from and to their environment. The main contribution of this chapter is the coupling of the two dynamic models: differential equations manage the energy of the system and morphological equations govern its growth. That coupling implies a coevolution in the system. On one hand, the global energy fed in the system depends on the size of the tissue, and on the other hand, the local morphological dynamics of cells that locally transforms the tissue depends on their available energy reserve. Finally, Section 2.5 concludes this chapter by giving some applications achieved with this work and then open some perspectives to explore in coming ones in terms of simulation.

2.2 MATHEMATICAL MORPHOLOGICAL DYNAMICS

In *mathematics*, the *viability theory* offers concepts and methods to control a dynamical system in a given fixed environment, to maintain it in a set of constraints of viability. Applied to *morphogenesis*, this means that we should have at least one coviable evolution of the cells' state and their environment among all the available pairs of state-environment of each developmental step. This formalization allows us to establish rules in terms of `cell plus action` as spatial choices of cells under logical and temporal conditions. The application of such rules causes some biological effects on the cells individually but they also impact the overall tissue. However, relying on that theory to tackle issues in morphogenesis requires first to properly define some of its concepts in the case of a multicellular system. In [9], we described mathematically the state, controls, and both local and global morphological dynamics of tissues. Some points of that formalization are highlighted in this section.

$\mathcal{K} \subset \mathcal{P}(X)$[1] denotes the *morphological environment*[2] ($X = \mathbb{R}^2$ denotes the set of containment cells contained in the complement of *vitellus*[3]). Cells $x \in X \cup \emptyset$ are either characterized by their position

[1]Supplied with the structure of max-plus algebra for the operation $\cup$ and + (where $K + \emptyset := \emptyset$ with K a cell tissue).
[2]For instance, $\mathcal{K} := \{K \subset M\}$ is the family of subsets contained in a given subset M.
[3]In biology, the vitellus is the energy reserve used by the embryo during its development.

(living cells) or by their death made of tissues L, which are subsets of cells ($L \in \mathcal{P}(X)$). The subset of eight genetic actions d of cells is

$$\mathcal{A} := \{(1,0,0), (-1,0,0), (0,1,0), (0,-1,0), (0,0,1), (0,0,-1), (0,0,0), \emptyset\}$$

$\mathcal{A}$ is made of the six geometric directions, the origin, and the empty set. Here, we restrict morphogenesis in the plan:

$$\mathcal{A} := \{(0,1), (0,-1), (1,0), (-1,0), (0,0), \emptyset\}$$

For convenience, we replace (0,1), (0,−1), (1,0), (−1,0), (0,0) and Ø, respectively, by 1, 2, 3, 4, 5, and 6.

$$\mathcal{A} := \{1,2,3,4,5,6\}$$

These genetic actions allow to describe cells' behaviors:

1. *Transitions* $x \mapsto x + d$, where $d \in \{1,2,3,4\}$ (action)
2. *Quiescence* $x \mapsto x + 5 = x$ (no action)
3. *Apoptosis* $x \mapsto x + 6 = 6$ (programmed cell death)

This injunction $(d^{\wedge}, d^{<})$ is described by the genetic inclusion

$$x \rightsquigarrow \{x + d^{\wedge}, x + d^{<}\}$$

where the *mother* cell x

- first migrates from x to $x + d^{\wedge}$ using the migration action $d^{\wedge} \in \mathcal{A}$ at a new position (including x or Ø),
- then divides, giving birth to a cell at position $x + d^{<}$ using the division action $d^{<} \in \mathcal{A} \setminus \{5\}$.

The composition of these actions produce a *mother-daughter* cell pair $\{x + d^{\wedge}, x + d^{<}\}$.

Hence, the basic behaviors of the *mother* cell are described by

1. *Sterile migration* by taking $d^{\wedge} \in \mathcal{A}$ and $d^{<} = 6$.
2. *Stationary division* by taking $d^{\wedge} = 5$ and $d^{<} \in \mathcal{A}$.
3. *Migrating division* by taking $d^{\wedge} \in \mathcal{A} \setminus \{5\}$ and $d^{<} \in \mathcal{A} \setminus \{5\}$.

In this implementation, we do not take into account *migration* and *death* and all cell transitions are all stationary divisions. Hence, the injunction $(d^{\wedge}, d^{<})$ can be likened to the `genetic action` singleton $d^{<} := d$.

2.2.1 GENE AND STATUS EXPRESSION

A *genetic process*, G, is a possible combination of genetic actions $G := \{d^1, \ldots, d^i\} \in \mathcal{A}^i$. Operating a *genetic process* under a given criterion, either for migration or for division, means that the process scans successively $x + d^1, \ldots, x + d^i$ until the first time when the criterion is satisfied. For any tissue (phenotype), there exists a set of *genetic processes* (genotype) that allows to achieve its creation. Starting with a single cell, at each step, we compute from the previous tissues all the possible configurations of tissue we can reach through cell division. In computer science, this issue is a case of polyominoes enumeration, except that we have added some biological constraints. The configurations are saved on the edges of the graph and all the events involved have also been saved in the vertices: division, quiescence, and differentiation. Thereby, from any edge in the graph, we can reconstruct the way back to the single cell. This characterization results in the determination of the lineage of any phenotype. Then, using that lineage, we construct the underlying genotype with respect to our model. A *genetic process* is identified by its color. All cells, whose last division is achieved with this *genetic process*, carry its color, and thus, define a pattern called a gene expression. The color levels during this division cycle highlights the status expression. Light colored cells are already divided, and dark cells are newly created in the cycle; they are both quiescent. The third category represents the proliferating cells, which are awaiting division, which are medium colored. Differentiations can occur while generating tissues. Indeed, if a cell has to change a *genetic process* in order to be able to divide, its color, and that of its daughter, are set to the color of the new *genetic process*. A tissue appearing with one color would mean that it is made of just one *genetic process* with no genetic differentiation occurring, ie, all cells were able to divide using the same ordered sequence of genetic actions.

The action of one cell, x, involves a local morphological dynamic which locally transforms the tissue, L, at a local process time. The global morphological dynamic transforms the morphological environment, K, at the end of every cell division cycle after the processing of all cells. The only constraints this growth can face are spatial ones that arise from the morphological environment, and from the cells themselves.

2.3 ATTAINABLE SETS OF PHENOTYPES

Giving a mathematical formalization of cells' actions and behaviors, defining the gene and status expressions, and describing the morphological dynamics, we now use this mathematical foundation to explore a case study stated as follows. From a single cell,

1. What are the all possible tissues that can be obtained after a given number of division cycles (phenotypes)?
2. For each attained tissue, what are the minimal underlying `genetic processes` that have governed cell division and differentiation (genotypes)?

2.3.1 IMPLEMENTATION

Our 2D model consists of a grid of automaton elements, which represent our biological cells. The state of each element is defined by a state vector, including three components that correspond to the features of interest in this case study: (i) occupation, ie, an element is either occupied by a cell or is an empty space; (ii) cell status, ie, the cell is either in a proliferative state (allowed to divide), quiescent (the newly created cell is prevented from dividing), or divided (the cell is already processed in the current division cycle); and (iii) cell color that identifies the *genetic process* that the cell is associated with. The program is developed in `C++`, sets are represented with the library `Boost Graph` and the algorithm operates a redundancy control in sets to ensure that either a phenotype (shape plus gene and status expressions) or its different geometrical transformations (symmetries, rotations, and translations) are stored only once (**reduced a set by** 87%). As the sets' size increase asymptomatically, we have also developed a parallel implementation with `Boost Thread` that allowed us a significant gain in execution time (**more that** `30x` **faster**). The program offers a view in details on each generated phenotype:

- at each time, which cell was created (tagging system),
- which one created it and by which `genetic action` (symbolized by arrows),
- and what is its current cell type (color) and status (color level).

Besides, while generating a phenotype, the underlying genotype is being built gradually. The output results are displayed with `Scilab` where all tissues and their `genetic processes` generated after the given number of division cycles can be visualized. Results are depicted in Figs. 2.2–2.11.

On this basis, we are able to reconstruct the early stages of zebra fish morphogenesis depicted in Fig. 2.1 and, most importantly, to shed light on the potential processes that could differentiate cells and how they could be applied to them at different states (see Fig. 2.5). The program offers the possibility to keep only tissues passing through some defined paths during their generation (see Fig. 2.6). These paths are defined in a *filter catalog* that has to be set at the beginning of the program. The number of division cycles after which to apply it also has to be defined.

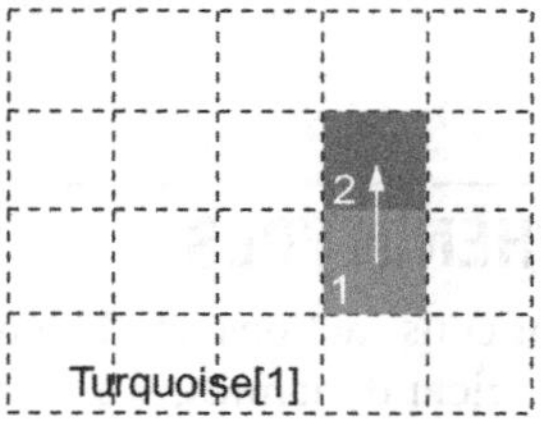

FIGURE 2.2

Attainable set of tissues after one division (size 1).

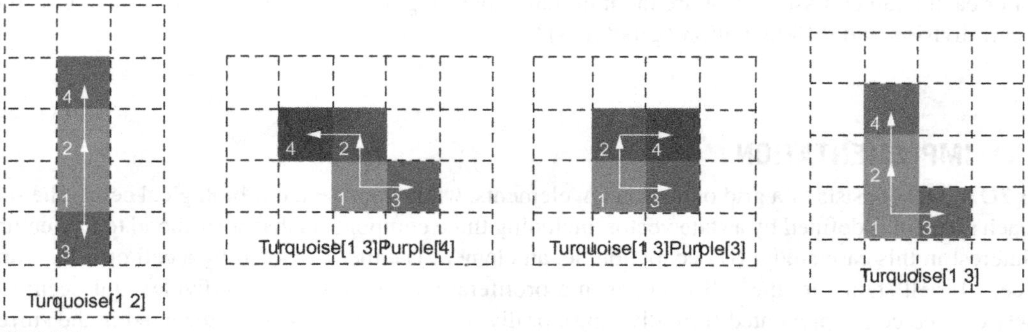

FIGURE 2.3

Attainable set of tissues after two divisions (size 4). The second tissue shows two colors representing two *genetic processes*: turquoise and purple. Each is an ordered sequence of the four genetic actions (1 is north, 2 is south, 3 is east, and 4 is west). These *genetic processes* are the minimum required to design this tissue. The arrows distinguish cell lineage as the creation of the tissue goes on.

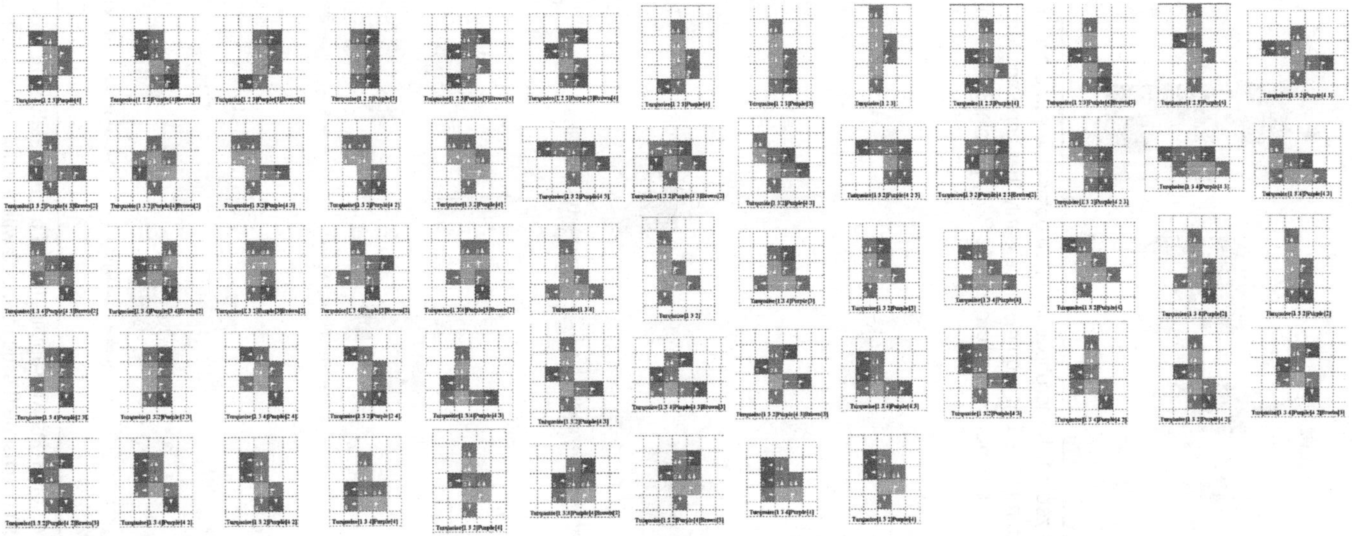

FIGURE 2.4

Attainable set of tissues after three divisions (size 61).

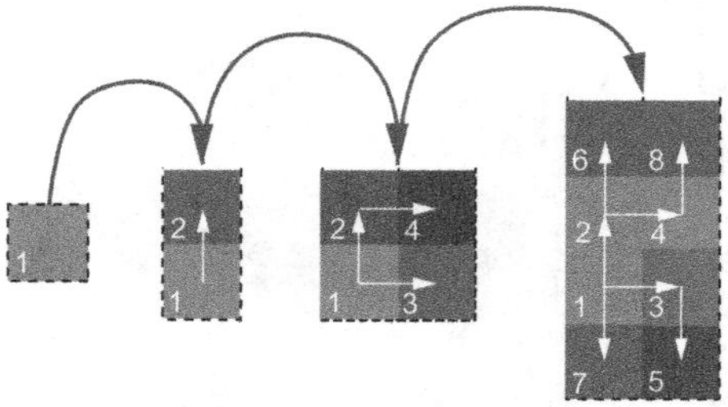

FIGURE 2.5

Simulation of the early stages of zebra fish morphogenesis. To obtain the same cell arrangement at the first three division cycles as depicted in Fig. 2.1, it requires necessarily that gene and status expressions be underlying by the following `genetic processes`: Turquoise[1 3 2], Purple[3], Brown[2].

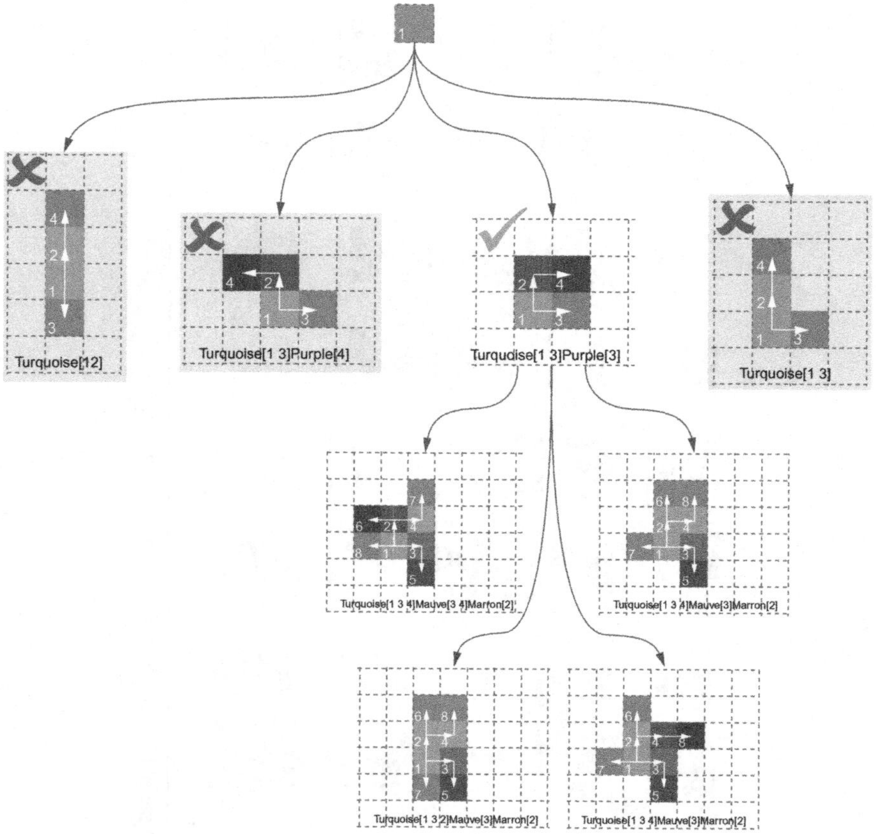

FIGURE 2.6

Attainable set of tissues after three divisions with application of a filter catalog after two divisions (size 4). Here, the filter catalog includes just one tissue (tissue stamped with a tick). The paths that go through the tissues that are not defined in the filter catalog are discarded (tissues stamped with a red cross).

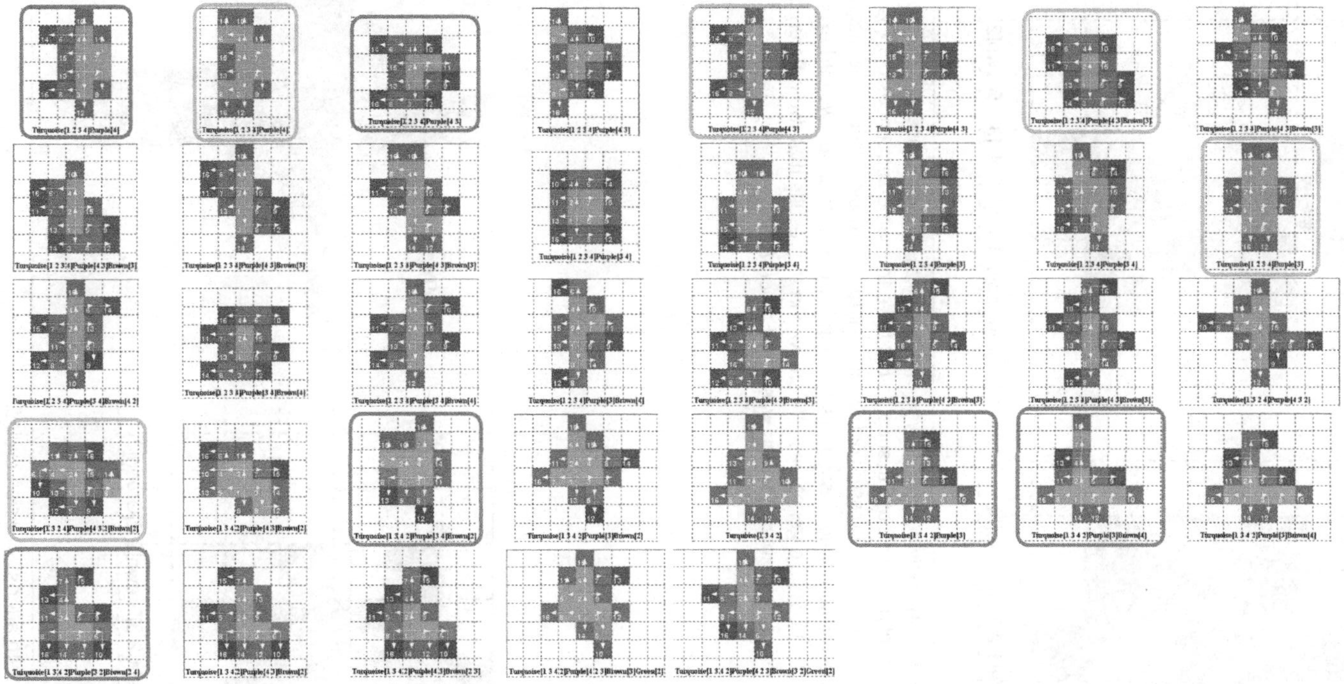

FIGURE 2.7

Attainable set of tissues after four divisions (size 1029). We show that with just 16 cells, we have some interesting patterns emerging in terms of symmetry, bioinspiration, and robustness.

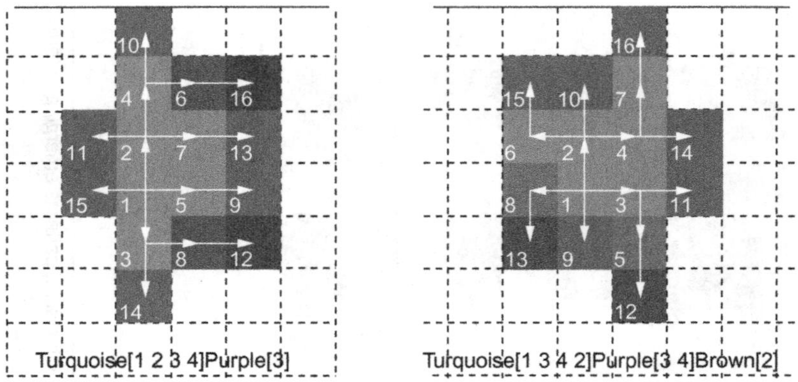

FIGURE 2.8

An example that highlights the link between phenotype and genotype. We can observe how the variations on the genotypes affect the phenotypes. The two tissues do not have the same sequences of cells division and then do not have either the same gene expression or the same status expression despite the fact that their overall shape is the same. We have previously addressed this issue in [10]. In that paper, we had explored and simulated the entire base of all possible genotypes. We showed in the results that two different genotypes in the base could achieve the same phenotype, which was *The French Flag*.

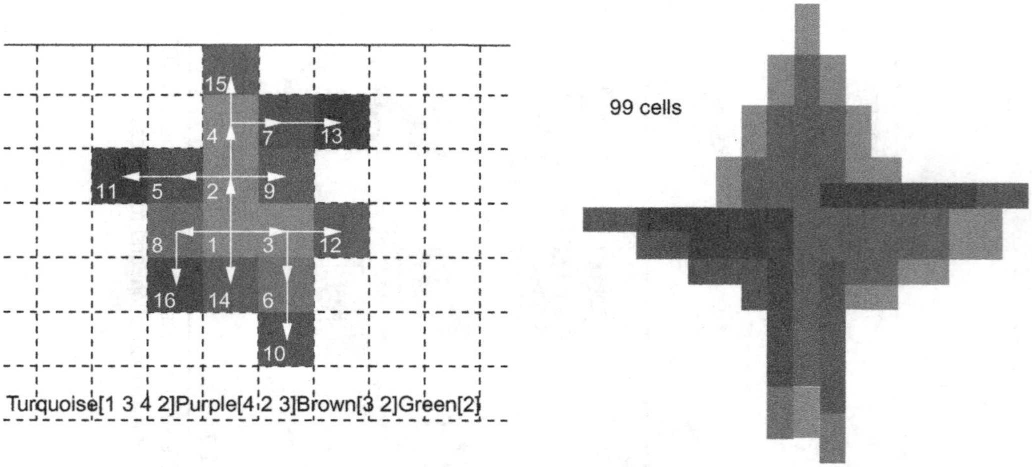

FIGURE 2.9

The result of the tissue growth after six division cycles.

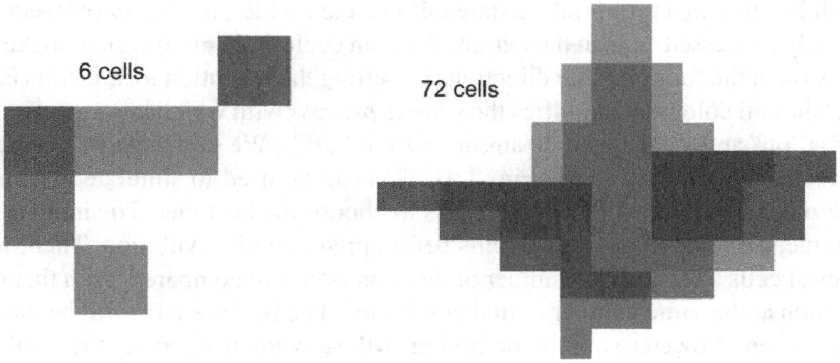

FIGURE 2.10

A scenario of irradiation, which stunts the normal growth of the tumor presented in Fig. 2.9. Indeed, after six division cycles, we have 72 cells instead of 99.

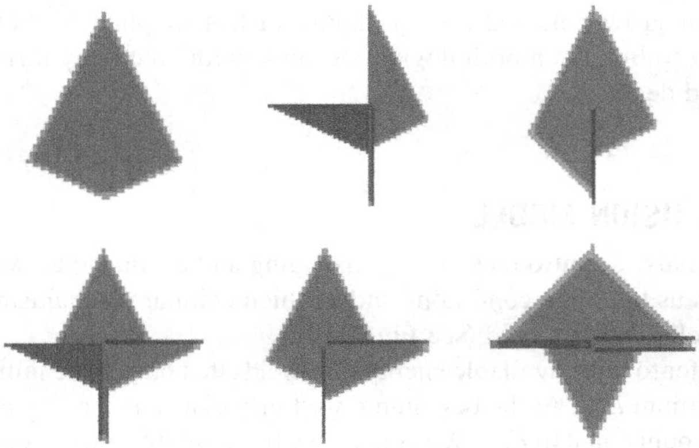

FIGURE 2.11

Tree and leaf phenotypes (made of 1000 cells at least) achieved with directional division instructions defined by the genetic processes.

2.4 PREDICTION TOOL BASED ON A COEVOLUTION OF A DYNAMIC TISSUE WITH AN ENERGY DIFFUSION

2.4.1 PREDICTION OF TISSUE GROWTH

Having generated all possible phenotypes at the early stages of the embryo and highlighted the underlying genotype for each, we can now select some of them (by bioinspiration for example) to see how they could evolve after a given number of division cycles. During the division cycles, cells are processed sequentially and their status is updated asynchronously. In the case study of prediction, the second and the third components of the state vector define each element of the automaton change defined in Section 2.3.1. Indeed, cell status and cell color of the automaton have a new meaning: (ii) cell status, ie, the cell is either in a proliferative state (allowed to divide), quiescent (preventing newly created cells or already processed cells in the current division cycle from dividing), or locked due to a lack of space for division in the four possible directions by setting the evolution lock factor (ELF) of the cell to "on"; and (iii) the cell color that identifies the *genetic process* with which it is associated (a dark level means that ELF is "on" and a light level means that ELF is "off"). We stop the growth when we meet the required number of division cycles (see Fig. 2.9). This can be used to simulate responses to several scenarios of radiotherapy in terms of effectiveness to choose the best one. To simulate an irradiation scenario on a tissue, we remove a group of cells before predicting its evolution. Then, we observe the obtained number of cells after a given number of division cycles to compare it with that obtained without any cell deletion at the same number of division cycles. The best scenario will be the one where the deleted cells have been allowed to obtain the best growth slowdown, meaning the smallest number of cells (see Fig. 2.10).

However, even though plant morphogenesis can be analyzed and understood almost entirely in terms of directional cell division and expansion, in growing animals, these mechanisms are by no means solely responsible. Cell migration, neighbor exchange, and elective cell death are critically important [11]. Up to now, tissue grows in our model by a mere reading and application of directions of division. This model of growth indeed results mainly in leaf or plant phenotypes (see Fig. 2.11). Therefore, we aim now to link the morphological dynamic with an energy diffusion model to ensure a cellular exchange and death.

2.4.2 ENERGY DIFFUSION MODEL

To model growing animals, we introduce energy managing and exchange between cells and their environment. This allows us to define conditions under which cellular mechanisms such as quiescence, mitosis, and elective cell death are held (see Fig. 2.12).

These conditions refer to three available energy thresholds that have to be initialized: minimum E_{mi}, medium E_{me}, and maximum E_{ma}. At the beginning, we fairly distribute energy to cells' location. Each cell has access to an amount equal to E_{ma}. We note $E_n(x)$, the available energy of cell x at the beginning of a given division cycle n. Prior to reading its `genetic process` G_x, x compares its current available energy $E(x)$ to these thresholds, then behaves appropriately by choosing the corresponding mechanism. The correspondences between threshold and mechanism are described in what follows.

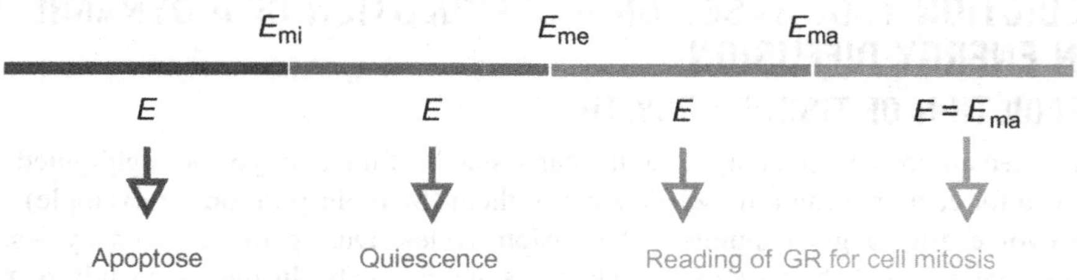

FIGURE 2.12

Cellular mechanisms execution according to the available energy.

2.4.2.1 Mitosis

$E(x)$ cannot go beyond E_{ma}. If it is the case, we set $E(x) = E_{ma}$. Otherwise, the cell tries a mitosis with its `genetic process`.

$$G = G_x \text{ and } K_n(x) := \varphi(n, K_n, x; G)$$

For $E(x)$ use at reproduction, Kooijman proposed the *k-rule* in his study of dynamic energy and mass budgets in biological systems [12]. This rule assumes that a fixed proportion $k \in]0,1[$ of energy mobilized from the reserves is spent on somatic maintenance plus growth while the remaining portion $1 - k$ on maturity maintenance plus maturation plus reproduction. Given α and $\beta \in]0,1[$, the energy use at mitosis is (as depicted in Fig. 2.13):

- αk for somatic maintenance
- $\beta(1 - k)$ for maturity maintenance
- $\dfrac{(1-\alpha)k}{1+\delta(1-\alpha)k}$ for cell growth. The parameter δ indicates that each cell type has its own energy consumption rate for growth. To have a fair consumption rate between cell types, we can set $\delta = 0$. Thus, δ has to be defined for each genetic process or not.
- As the reserve density at birth equals that of the mother at egg formation [12], the remaining $\dfrac{(1-\beta)(1-k)+2\delta(1-\beta)^2(1-k)^2}{1+\delta(1-\beta)(1-k)}$ is fairly shared after reproduction between x and its daughter.

While x is dividing, each of its neighboring cells y is in a proliferating state. They have hence used a part k' of their available energy for somatic maintenance and another part $\beta'(1 - k')$ for maturity maintenance. The parameters of energy distribution and consumption vary depending on processes that

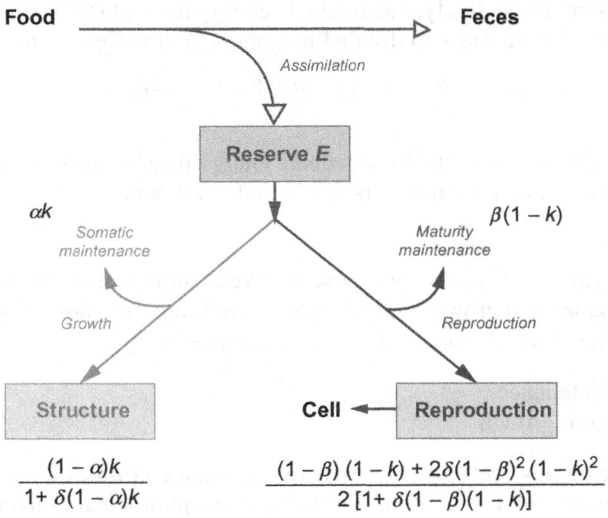

FIGURE 2.13

Energy reserve use at mitosis.

the cell achieves according to its current behavior (mitosis, proliferating or quiescent). Thereby, for each neighbor y, $(1-\beta')(1-k')$ is available and x can retrieve an amount inversely proportional to the number of neighbors of y. For instance, if y has V_y neighbors, x can receive $\frac{(1-\beta')(1-k')}{V_y}E(y)$. Which is to say, the more x is subject to spatial constraints (great number of neighbors), the more it gathers energy after reproduction. The rate change of $E(x)$ from one cycle to the other is described as follows:

$$\dot{E}_n(x) = \frac{(1-\beta)(1-k)+2\delta(1-\beta)^2(1-k)^2}{2[1+\delta(1-\beta)(1-k)]}\dot{E}_{n(i)}(x) + \sum_{j=1}^{V_x}\frac{(1-\beta')(1-k')}{V_y^j}\dot{E}_{n(i)}(y^j)$$

$\dot{E}_{n(i)}(x)$ is the rate change of $E_n(x)$ throughout the cycle n. These changes occurred during the local processing of the cells preceding x and include losses due to transfers to its divided neighbors. If V_{xd} is the number of divided neighbors prior to x and V_x its total number of neighbors:

$$\dot{E}_{n(i)}(x) = E_n(x) - (1-\beta')(1-k')\frac{V_{xd}}{V_x}E_n(x)$$

$\dot{E}_{n(i)}(y^j)$ is the energy rate change of a given neighbor y^j of x throughout the cycle n. These changes might occur by two behaviors of y^j:

1. Mitosis $\dot{E}_{n(i)}(y^j) = E_n(y^j) - \left[\alpha k + (1-k)\beta + \frac{(1-\alpha)k}{1+\delta(1-\alpha)k}\right]E_n(y^j)$

$$-(1-\beta')(1-k')\frac{V_{y^jd}}{V_y^j}E_n(y^j) + \sum_{l=1}^{V_{y^j}}\frac{(1-\beta')(1-k')}{V_z^l}E_n(z^l)$$

   The terms represent, respectively, the available energy for y^j at the beginning of the cycle n, the losses during mitosis, the transfers to divided neighbors, and the gains during mitosis.

2. Quiescence $\dot{E}_{n(i)}(y^j) = E_n(y^j) - k''E_n(y^j) - (1-\beta')(1-k')\frac{V_{y^jd}}{V_y^j}E_n(y^j)$

   The terms represent, respectively, the available energy for y^j at the beginning of the cycle n, the losses during quiescence, and the transfers to divided neighbors.

2.4.2.2 Quiescence

When $E(x)$ is below or equal to E_{me}, x stays quiescent. We assume that in this state, cells have only to ensure somatic maintenance and growth. Indeed, when conditions are poor, allocation to reproduction can be blocked [12]. Therefore, the use of $E(x)$ at quiescence is

- $\alpha' k''$ for somatic maintenance
- $(1-\alpha')k''$ for structure growth

Which is to say that during this cycle where x stays quiescent, it consumes k'' of its available energy to satisfy these two processes and $1-k''$ remains. Its local morphological dynamic is given by

$$G = \{5,\ldots\} \Rightarrow K_n(x) := K_n$$

$$\dot{E}_n(x) = (1-k'')\dot{E}_{n(i)}(x)$$

2.4.2.3 Apoptosis

When $E_n(x)$ is as low as E_{mi} or below to it, x is brought to death and its available energy is released.

$$G=\{6,\ldots\} \Rightarrow K_n(x) := K_n \backslash \{x\}$$

$$E(x)=0$$

We have shown that local transitions on the tissue K_n depend on the available local energy. Likewise, the amount of the global energy supplied to cells environment at the beginning of each cycle n, is proportional to the cardinal of $\phi(n-1, K_{n-1}) := \varphi(K_{n-1}(x_1, \ldots, x_{p_{K_{n-1}}}); G)$. Indeed, Kooijman asserts in his book that reserve and structure grow in harmony, and the specific somatic maintenance costs is some function of the structural volume. Thereby, assuming that card $\phi(n-1, K_{n-1}) = N$, the energy supply amount at the location of each cell x_i is

$$E_{ma} - 1/N \sum_{i=1}^{N} E_n(x_i)$$

It may happen to stop the growth before reaching the targeted number of division cycles. This decision is made when the global energy of the system is below or equal to $\frac{N}{2}E_{mi}$, meaning that if the global energy was fairly distributed to the cells, at least half would be brought to death. In such an energy level condition, we consider that growth is not safe for the tissue.

2.4.3 RESULTS

The tissues are displayed in a way that emphasizes the available energy for cells. A new color levels code highlights the status that the cell is ready to get (quiescence, mitosis, or death) according to the interval where its available energy is situated.

- dark: going to die
- intermediate: going to stay quiescent
- light: ready to divide

In the deb model, it is taken into account the intraspecies and interspecies variations of parameter values, which is to say that the energy devoted to the processes of feeding, digestion, maintenance, growth, and reproduction change between individuals of a specie and also from a specie to another. For the implementation of our model, we make the choice to set the parameter values in a way that allows a fair allocation between processes: $k = 1/2$; $\alpha = 1/2$; $\beta = 1/2$; $k' = 2/3$; $\alpha' = 1/2$; $\beta' = 1/2$; and $k'' = 1/2$.

In Fig. 2.14, we present the simulations results of several phenotypes among those generated in Section 2.3. We set E_{ma} too high (2000) for these cases.

Then to obtain more specific results, we set the thresholds as follows:

- $E_{mi} = 0.01$
- $E_{me} = 0.03$
- $E_{ma} = 0.08$
- We set $\delta \in \{-2, -1, 1, 2\}$ for the different energy consumption rates during growth.

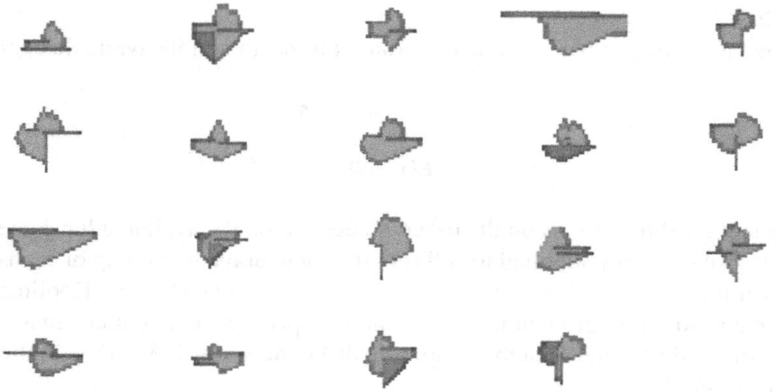

FIGURE 2.14

Simulation of 19 tissues with a high initial energy level. Cell quiescence is enabled.

Simulations of the mixed model with some phenotypes have yielded some noteworthy results. Indeed, we have observed that

1. There is no more high proliferation with regular shapes and energy uptake is well observed from the outside to the inside of the tissue (see Fig. 2.15).
2. There is a kind of cell sort by the end of the growth when the energy level becomes too low (see Fig. 2.16).
3. Every tissue has a certain number of cycles after which it no longer has enough energy and stops growing.
4. There is a symmetry acquisition during development and the tissue can stay in a homeostasis a certain number of cycles (see Fig. 2.17).

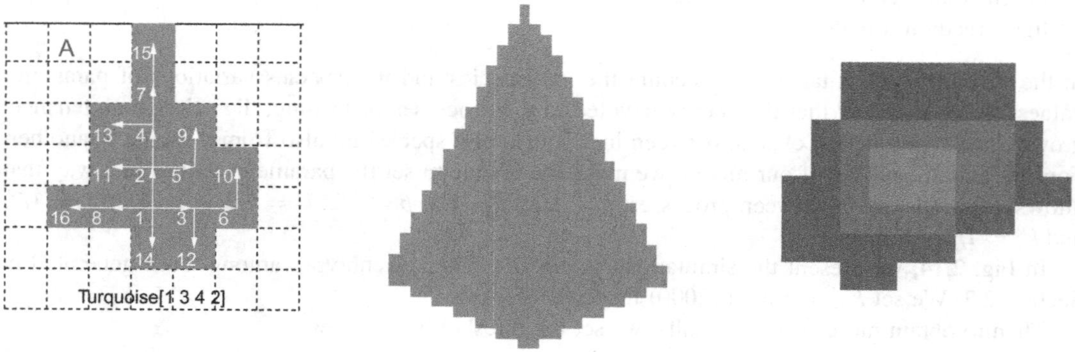

FIGURE 2.15

Phenotype A after 18 division cycles, without coupling the directional division dynamic with an energy diffusion, appears regular and reaches 448 cells (in the middle). By the coupling, apoptosis is now possible and after 18 cycles, the tissue is made of just 54 cells and looks different.

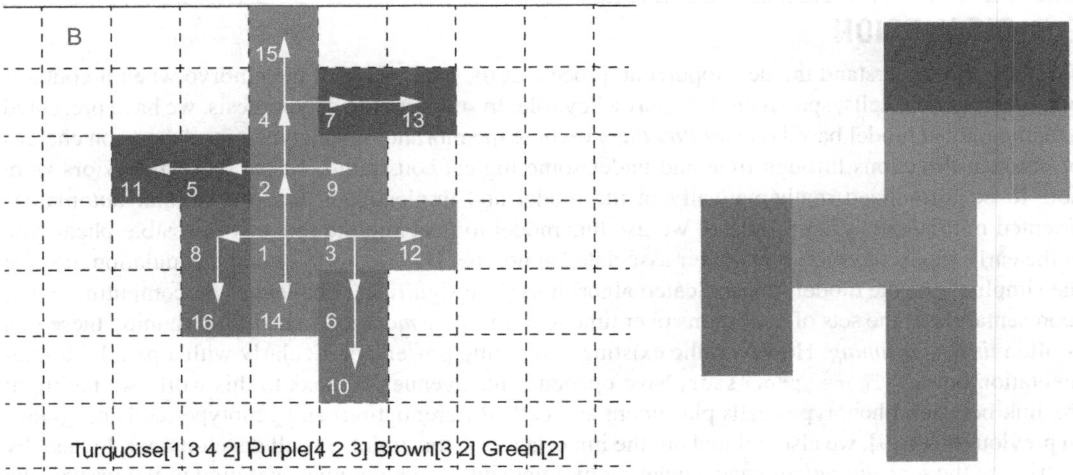

FIGURE 2.16

Phenotype B after 23 division cycles is made of 10 cells and does not have enough energy to pursue growth. We observe that the cell are separated into top, middle, and down groups (or head, body, and legs).

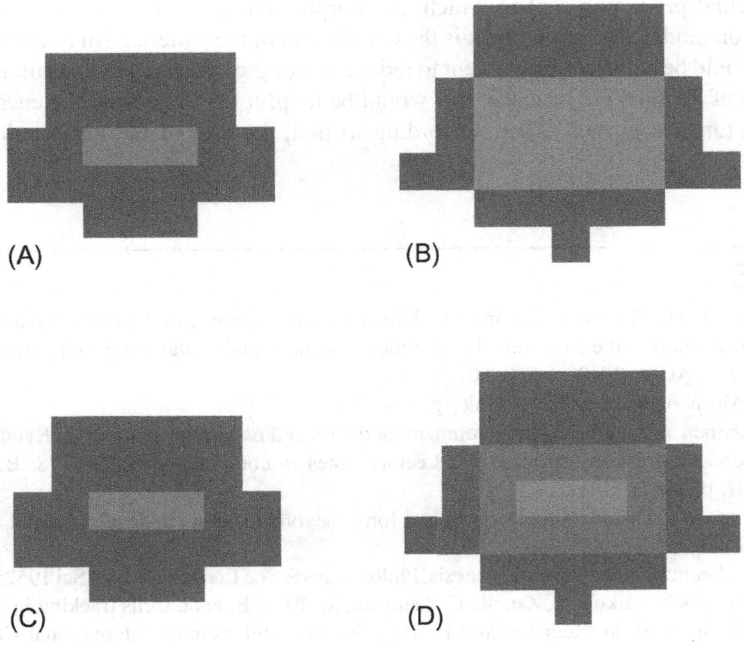

FIGURE 2.17

Phenotype A acquires a symmetry at the 20th (A) and the 21st (B) cycle with 27 and 39 cells, respectively. Then at the 26th (C) and the 27th (D) cycle, the same scenario recurs with the same number of cells. However, energy is not spread in the same way in (D) as in (B).

2.5 DISCUSSION

To study and understand the developmental process at the early stage of the embryo when it contains just a few pairs of cells, spatial choices play a key role. In support of this hypothesis, we have presented a mathematical model based on *viability theory* where the morphological dynamics depend on choices of division directions through time and under some logical constraints. Major cells' behaviors were able to be formalized mathematically in the model and implemented using a cellular automaton-oriented multiagent system. Indeed, we use this model to generate the spaces of possible phenotype at the early stages of embryo and their associated genotype. Due to this systematic simulation, despite the simplicity of the model, the dedicated algorithms pose significant challenges on computing. First, representation of the sets of evolutions over time requires *huge memory*. In addition, running these sets is often *time-consuming*. However, the existing computing powers, particularly with a parallel implementation on `multicores processor`, have opened some avenues. Thanks to this work, we highlight the link between phenotype (cells placement and cells differentiation) and genotype (cells program). In previous work [9], we also pointed out the importance of constraints in cell development. Indeed, by restricting the *morphological environment* or by imposing a *commutative evolution* to the tissues, the possibilities of growth had been significantly reduced.

We have shown that the application could be, on the one hand, to determine the genotype of any form of tissue (pathological tissue mainly), and on the other hand, the use of this genotype to predict their evolution in later times (*pattern prediction* and *growth controlling*). For this purpose, we have designed an original prediction tool in which the morphological dynamic of tissue coevolves with an energy diffusion model. The main result is the enrichment of the patterns. An interesting application of this coupling could be caloric management to reduce tumor growth. Indeed, this latter depends on the nutritional status of the host [13]. Hence, this would be helpful for evaluating the energy reserve that better stunts the tumor's growth. Then, according to that, the diet of the host could be controlled consequently.

REFERENCES

[1] Fernández JD, Vico F, Doursat R. Complex and diverse morphologies can develop from a minimal genomic model. In: Proceedings of the 14th annual conference on genetic and evolutionary computation, GECCO '12. Philadelphia, PA: ACM; 2012. p. 553–60.

[2] Peyriéras N. Morphogenèse animale; 2006; p. 179–201.

[3] Chavoya A, Duthen Y. An artificial development model for cell pattern generation. In: Randall M, Abbass H, Wiles J, editors. Progress in artificial life. Lecture notes in computer science, 4828. Berlin/Heidelberg: Springer; 2007. p. 61–71.

[4] Müller G, Newman S. Origination of organismal form: beyond the gene in developmental and evolutionary biology. Cambridge, MA: MIT Press; 2003.

[5] Turing A. The chemical basis of morphogenesis. Philos Trans R Soc Lond Ser B Biol Sci 1952;237(641):37–72.

[6] Melani C, Peyriéras N, Mikula K, Zanella C, Campana M, Rizzi B, et al. Cells tracking in the live zebrafish embryo. In: Engineering in Medicine and Biology Society, 29th Annual International Conference of the IEEE, 1; 2007. p. 1631–4.

[7] Olivier N, Luengo-Oroz MA, Duloquin L, Faure E, Savy T, Veilleux I, et al. Cell lineage reconstruction of early zebrafish embryos using label-free nonlinear microscopy. Science 2010;329(5994):967–71.

[8] Aubin JP. Viability theory. Basel: Birkhauser; 1991.

[9] Sarr A, Fronville A, Rodin V. Morphogenesis model for systematic simulation of forms co-evolution with constraints: application to mitosis. In: TPNC 2014, 3rd international conference on the theory and practice of natural computing, 8890. Berlin/Heidelberg: Springer; 2014. p. 230–41.

[10] Sarr A, Fronville A, Ballet P, Rodin V. French flag tracking by morphogenetic simulation under developmental constraints. In: Formenti E, Tagliaferri R, Wit E, editors. Computational intelligence methods for bioinformatics and biostatistics. Lecture notes in computer science, 8452. Berlin/Heidelberg: Springer International Publishing; 2014. p. 90–106.

[11] Davies JA. Chapter 22 — growth, proliferation and death: a brief overview. In: Davies JA, editor. Mechanisms of morphogenesis. 2nd. Boston: Academic Press; 2013. p. 283–305.

[12] Kooijman S. Dynamic energy and mass budgets in biological systems. Cambridge: Cambridge University Press; 2008.

[13] van Leeuwen IMM, Zonneveld C, Kooijman S. The embedded tumour: host physiology is important for the evaluation of tumour growth. Br J Cancer 2003;89(12):2254–63.

CHAPTER

A FEATURE LEARNING FRAMEWORK FOR HISTOLOGY IMAGES CLASSIFICATION

3

C. Di Ruberto, L. Putzu

Department of Mathematics and Computer Science, University of Cagliari, Cagliari, Italy

3.1 INTRODUCTION

Histology is the study of the microscopic structure of cells and tissues of organisms. Pathologists examine the tissue under a microscope slide observing it at various levels of magnification to identify the morphological characteristics that indicate the presence of diseases, such as cancer. But such a diagnosis is subjective. Then, a quantitative evaluation of these images is really essential for an objective diagnosis. In the last 10 years, many computer-assisted disease systems have been developed to help histological diagnosis and reduce subjectivity. All these systems attempt to mimic pathologists by extracting features from histological images [1]. In Ref. [2] various types of descriptors have been tested for different image classification problems. In Ref. [3] a framework based on the novel and robust collateral representative subspace projection modeling has been used for histology image classification. In Ref. [1] the authors proposed the use of Fourier shape descriptors to capture the distribution of stain-enhanced cellular and tissue structures in renal tumor image. In Ref. [4] an automatic method for detecting and segmenting glands in prostate images has been proposed. In Ref. [5] a novel image analysis methodology for automatically distinguishing low and high grades of breast cancer has been presented. In Ref. [6] the authors used an unsupervised feature learning framework for the automatic detection of basal cell carcinoma. In Ref. [7] the authors realized a new ensemble of descriptors for the classification of transmission electron microscopy images of viruses based on texture analysis. Although there are a large number of works dealing with histology images, only few of them use color information. In fact, most of the works previously appointed operate on the gray-level images obtained through a conversion from the original color ones. Other works, such as [8], use a different kind of conversion averaging the three color channels to obtain an intensity image in which cells' structures are more visible. In some works instead [1,9] the color information of histological images have been used for the extraction of statistical texture features. Finally, in Ref. [10] an exhaustive comparison of color texture features and classification methods for histological images has been made, but the authors validated their method using only one database dealing with only one medical problem, consisting of discrimination of cells categories in histological images of fish ovary. Mainly the research progress lies in developing computer-based systems targeted at specific clinical fields. In particular, the research direction focuses on extracting specific features of certain data sets to represent the characteristics of the objects better in specific clinical fields. As a consequence, they are clinical-domain dependent.

Developing general applications not dependent on specific histology data sets is still a challenging open problem. Our effort was to develop a general classification system for histology images. A color texture-based histology image classification framework is proposed and tested using very different public biological image data sets. In the proposed system color and texture features are used in combination to avoid the data set dependency. Another aspect we consider of great importance for histology images analysis is color. Indeed, the biopsy samples are usually prepared with some chemical solution that enhances the contrast and stains in very distinctive colors of specific parts of the cells or tissue. As a consequence, color-based features are important in histology applications as biologists stain tissues to highlight special structures. But there are many color spaces used to apply in the analysis of histology images. So, another challenging task consists of analyzing histology images in different color spaces to individuate a general representation able to solve the classification problem efficiently without any dependence on a specific image data set or a specific clinical field. Summarizing, our goal was to build a broad and general histology image classification system for assisting the pathologists in any clinical field for disease diagnosis by extracting significant features starting from the image representation that contains the disease-independent characteristics of the objects better and more discriminant for classification. The rest of this chapter is organized as follows. In Section 3.2 we introduce some basic background information. Section 3.3 describes the proposed approach. Section 3.4 presents the databases used to test our framework. Section 3.5 shows the experimental results. Finally, in Section 3.6 we present our conclusions and some possible future works.

3.2 METHODS

3.2.1 COLOR AND COLOR SPACES

Color is very important in histology systems because biologists stain tissues to highlight spatial structures. The color is the brain's reaction to a specific visual stimulus. The aim of color spaces is to aid the process of describing color, either between people or between machines or programs. The classical color spaces are classified into three main families: primary spaces, luminance-chrominance spaces, and perceptual spaces. The primary spaces, based on trichromatic theory, assume that is possible to match any color by mixing appropriate amounts of the three primary colors. Examples are RGB, CMY(K), and XYZ. In general, color images are acquired through the RGB color space, called the image acquisition color space. So, all the color spaces are expressed thanks to transformations of the R, G, and B channels. The luminance-chrominance spaces are used when it is useful to separate the color definition into luminance, represented by one component, and chrominance represented by the two other components. Among these there are the television transmission color spaces, sometimes known as transmission primaries, YIQ and YUV for analogical standard and YCbCr for digital standard. For this reason only the YCbCr has been taken into account. The International Commission on Illumination (CIE) has defined a system that classifies color according to the human visual system to specify any color in terms of its CIE coordinates. There are two main CIE-based color spaces, CIELUV (Luv) and CIELAB (Lab), nearly linear with visual perception with the L parameter, having a good correlation with perceived lightness, and the other two parameters expressing the chrominance. The perceptual spaces quantify the subjective human color perception by means of intensity, hue, and saturation. This family represents a wealth of similar color spaces; alternative names include

HSI, HSV, HSL, HCI, and so on. We consider only HSV, which is the most used and can be obtained from the RGB color space.

3.2.2 FEATURES EXTRACTION AND CLASSIFICATION

Feature extraction is a fundamental step for automated methods based on machine learning approaches. Its goal is to extract useful characteristics from the data, which in computer vision corresponds to calculating values from input images. A feature, or descriptor, is defined as a function of one or more measurements, specifying some quantifiable property (ie, color, texture, or shape) of the whole image or subimage or of a single object. Many different methods for managing texture have been developed that are based on the various ways texture can be characterized, including the scale-invariant feature transform [11], speeded up robust feature [12], histogram of oriented gradients [13], local binary patterns (LBPs) [14], Gabor filters [15], and others. In this work we focus on improving some of the earliest methods used for the analysis of gray-level texture-based on statistical approaches: gray-level cooccurrence matrix (GLCM), gray-level difference matrix (GLDM), gray-level run-length matrix (GLRLM). Motivated by the wide diffusion of these methods and by the increasing numbers of medical data sets presenting color images, we wished to investigate the possibility to improve their accuracy using color information. Some interesting methods have been presented to extend the original implementation of GLCM. In Ref. [16] the authors evaluate different values for the distance parameter that influence the matrices computation, in Ref. [17] the GLCM descriptors are extracted by calculating the weighted sum of GLCM elements, and in Ref. [18] the GLCM features are calculated by using the local gradient of the matrix. In Ref. [19] to calculate the features, the gray levels and the edge orientation of the image are considered. In Ref. [20] the authors propose to use a variable window size by multiple scales to extract descriptors by GLCM. The method in Ref. [21] uses the color gradient to extract from GLCM statistical features. In Ref. [2] various types of GLCM descriptors and GLRLM features are extracted. Although the color information to extract GLCM has already been used by other authors such as [22], one of the goals of this work is to evaluate the performance improvement that can arise from computing not only GLCM but also GLDM, GLRLM, and LBP, using the color information. GLCM is one of the most powerful models for texture analysis proposed by Haralick in Ref. [23]. A GLCM represents the probability of finding two pixels i and j with distance d and orientation θ. Obviously, the d and θ values can assume different values, but the most used are $d=1$ and $\theta=$[0 degree; 45 degree; 90 degree; 135 degree]. Haralick proposed 13 descriptors that can be extracted from these matrices: angular second moment, contrast, correlation, variance, inverse difference moment, sum average, sum variance, sum entropy, entropy, difference variance, difference entropy and measures of correlation 1 and 2. The GLDM [24] collects the absolute difference between pairs of pixel values. From this matrix it is possible to compute easily nine descriptors: mean, angular second moment, contrast, variance, inverse difference moment, entropy, product moment, cluster shade and cluster prominence. The GLRLM [25] is based on information of higher order statistics as it contains information on a particular number of equal gray levels (run) in a given direction. So, a run-length matrix is defined as a set of consecutive pixels having the same gray level. The element (i, j) of a run-length matrix specifies the number of times that the image contains a run of length j composed by all pixels with gray level i. The GLRLMs are calculated by considering the main 4 orientations and for each matrix 11 descriptors can be extracted: short-run emphasis, long-run emphasis, gray-level nonuniformity, run-length nonuniformity, run percentage, low gray-level run emphasis, high gray-level run emphasis, short-run low gray-level emphasis, short-run high gray-level emphasis, long-run low gray-level emphasis, and long-run high gray-level emphasis. Another useful and more recent tool for texture analysis is the LBP, originally proposed in Ref. [14] and widely used for gray-level texture classification, due to its simplicity and robustness. This operator transforms the image by thresholding the neighborhood of each pixel and by coding the result as a binary number. The resulting image histogram can be used as a feature vector for texture classification. Also, two main parameters must be defined, which are the radius r and the number of neighborhood n pixels. For example, $LBP_{8,1}$ is the operator with r and n equal to 1 and 8, respectively. The extracted features must be inserted in a process that classifies them based on hematological concepts. Thus, given a collection of records characterized by a set of features x and a label of class y the objective is to define a classification model that associates a class label to record. Recently, the classification by support vector machine (SVM) has received a growing interest in the field of pattern recognition. This technique has been designed for binary classification problems, but it can be easily extended to multiclass problems.

3.3 PROPOSED SYSTEM

To extend the classical gray-level texture features to color texture features we start by decomposing the color image into the three channels Ch_1, Ch_2, and Ch_3, obtaining three different images. The most intuitive way to take into account color information in computing texture feature is to use the classical implementation and pass to them every time a different color channel. This approach could be very useful thanks to a higher number of significant descriptors extracted and passed to the classifier. To take into account not only repeated pattern inside the same color channel, but also the correlation between the color channels, we have combined the color channels in pairs $(Ch_k, Ch_{k'})$ with $k, k' = [1, 2, 3]$. The results of this combination is a feature vector nine times longer than the classical feature vector, composed by three intrachannels feature vector (Ch_1, Ch_1), (Ch_2, Ch_2), and (Ch_3, Ch_3) and six extrachannels feature vector (Ch_1, Ch_2), (Ch_2, Ch_1), (Ch_1, Ch_3), (Ch_3, Ch_1), (Ch_2, Ch_3), and (Ch_3, Ch_2). However, not all these combinations make sense. In fact, for features extracted from GLCM or GLDM, combining the channels in pairs means that the occurrences or differences for $(Ch_k, Ch_{k'})$ are calculated by storing on each (i, j) the number of occurrences or differences of $i \in Ch_k$ and $j \in Ch_{k'}$ and the number of occurrences or differences of $i \in Ch_{k'}$ and $j \in Ch_k$. So, the vice versa produces the same result. Thus, for GLCM and GLDM we have used only three extrachannels combinations, (Ch_1, Ch_2), (Ch_1, Ch_3) and (Ch_2, Ch_3). Therefore, from these six combinations we have computed the occurrences with $d = 1$ and $\theta = [0$ degree; 45 degree; 90 degree; 135 degree$]$ producing 24 GLCMs and 312 features. Similarly we have computed 24 GLDMs and 216 features. The GLRLMs can be computed by using the three classical bands only, producing 12 GLRLMs and 132 descriptors. The only method that could benefit from all the extrachannels combination is the LBP. Thus, we have used the nine channel combination to extract the $LBP_{8,1}$, bringing to 2304 features. The overall system is shown in Fig. 3.1. Each feature subset has been used to train a multiclass SVM, considered one of the best classification models for color medical image applications [26]. The SVM classifier is trained using the one versus all approach because it is the fastest both in training and in testing phase. After a process of cross-validation we have selected the best kernels and parameters. The selected kernel function is the RBF that uses a Gaussian radial basis function, with c parameter equal to $1e3$ and γ equal to $1e2$. Given the variable size of the data sets, we have performed the validation of our system using a five time repeated stratified

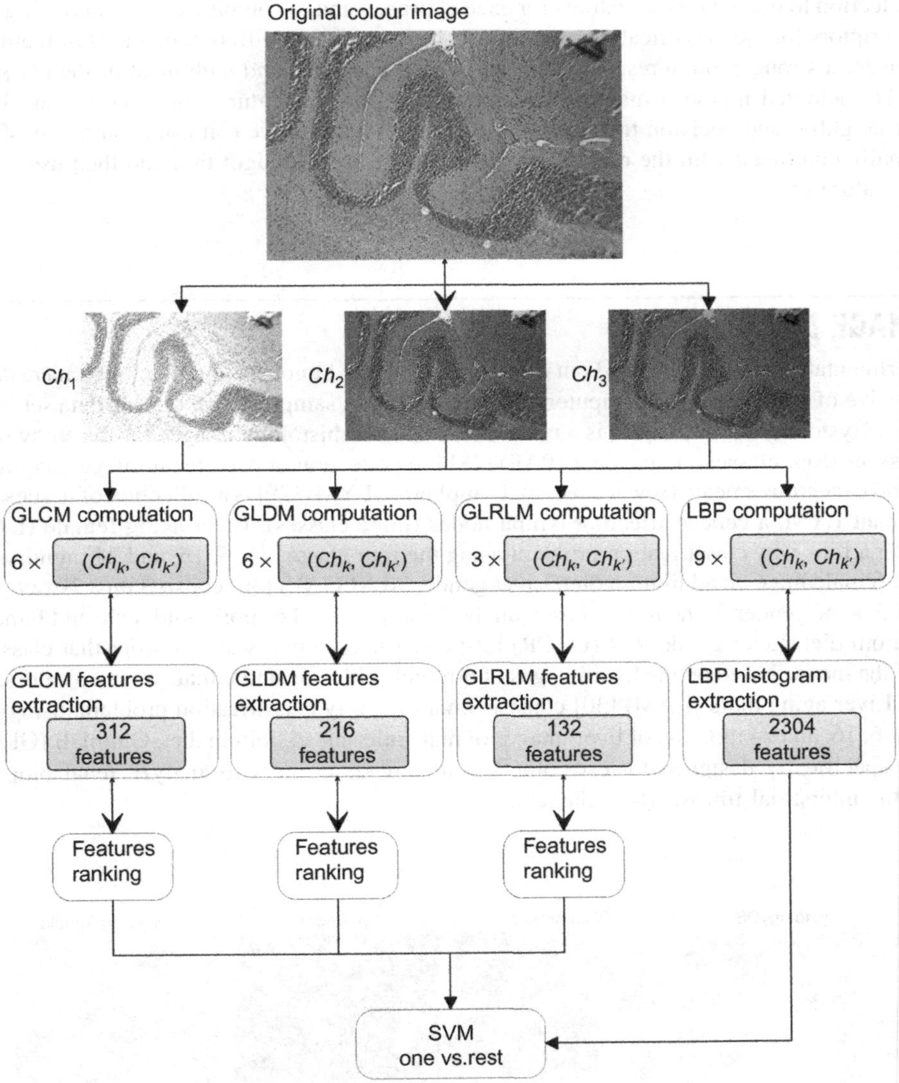

FIGURE 3.1

Diagram of the proposed system for histology image analysis.

holdout, which guarantees that each class is properly represented both in the training and in the test set and at the same time it averages the roles of each subset. In our experiments, training and test sets are represented by 80% and 20% of the samples, respectively. The performance has been evaluated by calculating the accuracy, which gives us a good indication of the efficiency because it considers each class of equal importance. After the extraction each feature subset has been subjected to a process of feature selection to trace the best features for each approach and to combine them for creating the final set of descriptors for the classification process. We have combined different methods of feature selection to ensure a strong enough result to be used in each condition and with most of the classification models. The adopted methods make use of sequential forward feature selection and are based on k-nearest neighbor and decision trees. From the selected features we can establish a sort of ranking that is finally combined with the ranking provided by the ReliefF algorithm and then used to derive the final feature set.

3.4 IMAGE DATA SETS

The experimentation has been carried out on eight of the most famous color histology image databases representative of really different computer vision problems. A sample image of each data set is showed in Fig. 3.2. HystologyDS (HIS) [27] is a collection of 20,000 histology images for the study of fundamental tissues (four classes). Pap-smear (PAP) [28] is a collection of pap-smear images acquired from healthy and cancerous smears (seven classes). Lymphoma (LYM) [29] is a collection of tissues affected by malignant LYM, a cancer affecting lymph nodes (three classes). Liver aging female (LAF) [30] consists on a four-way classification problem using the four classes (1, 6, 16, and 24 months) of liver images of female mice on ad libitum diet. Liver gender AL (LGAL) [30] consists on a 2-way classifier that classifies the gender of the mouse based on the liver images of 6-month-old male and female mice on ad libitum diet. Liver gender CR (LGCR) [30] consists on a two-way classifier that classifies the gender of the mouse based on the liver images of 6-month-old male and female mice on caloric restriction diet. Liver aging male (LAM) [30] consists on a four-way classification problem, using the four classes (1, 6, 16, and 24 months) of liver images of male mice on ad libitum diet. GlomDB (GLOM) [9] has been specifically designed to test color and texture descriptors to analyze renal biopsies and quantify the interstitial fibrosis (two classes).

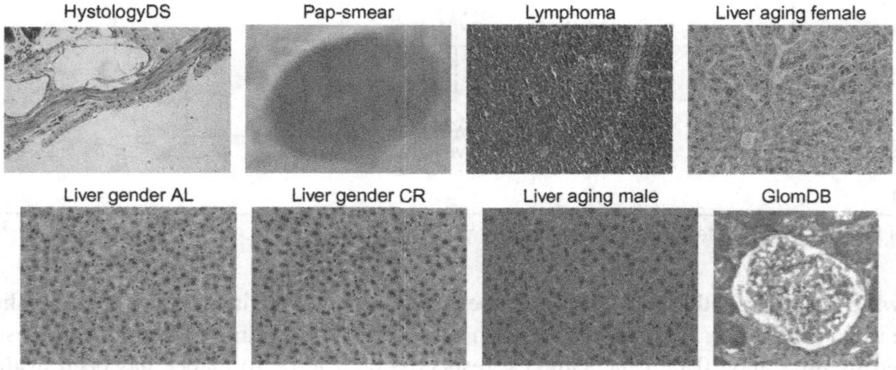

FIGURE 3.2

Illustration of database diversity with a sample image representative of each of the eight data sets.

3.5 EXPERIMENTAL RESULTS

Our first goal is to compare all the feature subsets to individuate the color space leading to better performances. We have considered five color spaces representative of the three color space families: RGB, HSV, Lab, Luv, and YCbCr. We have tested the original features subsets on each database separately. The numerical results are reported in Table 3.1: the last column shows the average result for each database. In this table and in the followings the best accuracy values have been represented in bold. In general, we can confirm that HSV is the color space that outperforms the others.

To the features extracted from the HSV color space we have applied the ranking step, which provides the features sorted by relevance, as shown in Table 3.2. To consider all the most relevant descriptors, we have performed a series of experiments by selecting each time a different number of descriptors ranging from 1 to the maximum number of descriptors. The obtained results have confirmed

Table 3.1 Usefulness of Analyzing Features in Different Color Spaces

Color Space	Database	GLCM	GLDM	GLRLM	LBP	Average Results
RGB	LYM	94.7±2.9	87.6±5.9	84.4±2.3	97.2±2.5	91.0±5.9
	PAP	92.5±1.8	87.2±1.8	88.9±1.4	85.6±2.3	88.5±2.9
	HIS	92.5±1.3	84.6±1.0	86.9±1.6	89.0±1.2	88.2±3.4
	LAF	99.8±0.3	98.6±0.6	99.2±0.8	99.6±0.5	99.3±0.5
	LAM	99.6±0.5	97.3±1.3	99.1±1.0	99.3±0.8	98.8±1.0
	LGAL	100.0±0.0	100.0±0.0	99.8±0.6	100.0±0.0	**99.9**±0.1
	LGCR	100.0±0.0	100.0±0.0	99.2±0.9	99.7±0.7	99.7±0.37
	GLOM	96.6±0.9	94.3±0.7	92.5±1.1	92.9±1.2	**94.0**±1.8
HSV	LYM	94.9±2.7	88.1±4.3	88.1±3.8	92.7±2.9	91.0±3.4
	PAP	93.6±2.0	88.3±1.9	90.4±1.2	86.9±1.9	**89.8**±2.9
	HIS	93.1±1.4	87.7±1.6	89.9±1.8	89.0±1.9	**89.9**±2.3
	LAF	100.0±0.0	99.8±0.6	99.8±0.4	99.6±0.7	**99.8**±0.2
	LAM	99.9±0.3	99.4±1.0	99.1±1.4	99.9±0.3	**99.6**±0.4
	LGAL	100.0±0.0	99.6±0.8	98.9±1.8	99.8±0.6	99.6±0.5
	LGCR	100.0±0.0	100.0±0.0	100.0±0.0	100.0±0.0	**100.0**±0.0
	GLOM	97.4±0.5	94.5±1.0	93.8±0.8	82.0±1.2	91.9±6.8
Lab	LYM	92.9±2.9	83.7±3.7	86.1±2.8	91.1±2.4	88.4±4.3
	PAP	93.9±2.0	87.3±2.0	90.1±1.4	87.0±3.1	89.6±3.2
	HIS	93.4±0.8	86.1±1.2	90.7±0.7	87.9±0.8	89.5±3.2
	LAF	100.0±0.0	99.0±1.2	99.4±0.5	99.7±0.5	99.5±0.4
	LAM	99.9±0.3	97.7±1.4	99.3±0.7	99.0±0.7	99.0±0.9
	LGAL	100.0±0.0	100.0±0.0	98.3±1.7	100.0±0.0	99.6±0.8
	LGCR	100.0±0.0	100.0±0.0	100.0±0.0	100.0±0.0	**100.0**±0.0
	GLOM	97.4±0.8	96.2±0.9	95.8±0.6	88.4±1.6	94.9±4.1

Continued

Table 3.1 Usefulness of Analyzing Features in Different Color Spaces—cont'd

Color Space	Database	GLCM	GLDM	GLRLM	LBP	Average Results
Luv	LYM	92.8±2.7	82.5±4.1	88.7±2.1	83.7±1.9	86.9±4.7
	PAP	93.6±1.7	87.2±2.5	90.4±2.1	85.0±2.0	89.0±3.7
	HIS	92.3±1.0	83.6±1.4	90.4±0.9	80.3±1.6	86.6±5.6
	LAF	99.7±0.5	99.8±0.4	99.9±0.3	98.8±1.0	99.6±0.5
	LAM	99.5±0.5	99.2±0.9	99.0±0.9	98.8±1.3	99.1±0.3
	LGAL	100.0±0.0	100.0±0.0	99.6±1.2	99.8±0.6	99.8±0.2
	LGCR	100.0±0.0	100.0±0.0	100.0±0.0	99.3±0.8	99.8±0.3
	GLOM	97.4±1.1	96.2±0.9	96.1±1.1	91.1±1.1	**95.2**±2.8
YCbCr	LYM	95.1±2.4	84.8±3.7	91.5±2.3	95.3±1.7	**91.7**±4.9
	PAP	93.2±1.4	87.8±2.2	89.9±1.3	86.2±2.4	89.2±3.0
	HIS	93.2±0.8	86.1±1.6	90.8±1.0	86.9±1.9	89.2±3.3
	LAF	100.0±0.0	99.3±0.6	98.9±2.3	99.3±0.6	99.4±0.4
	LAM	99.3±0.7	98.5±1.0	99.6±0.5	99.5±0.7	99.2±0.5
	LGAL	100.0±0.0	99.8±0.6	99.6±0.8	100.0±0.0	99.8±0.2
	LGCR	100.0±0.0	100.0±0.0	100.0±0.0	100.0±0.0	**100.0**±0.0
	GLOM	97.9±0.5	96.3±0.6	96.1±0.7	88.5±1.4	94.7±4.2

Table 3.2 Extracted Descriptors Ranked by Relevance

Ranking	GLCM	GLDM	GLRLM
1	Cor	μ	LRE
2	MC1	Ent	HGRE
3	MC2	IDM	SRE
4	Sav	ASM	RLN
5	Den	Con	SRLGE
6	Sen	Var	GLN
7	IDM	PM	RP
8	Ent	CS	LGRE
9	Con	CP	LRHGE
10	ASM		LRLGE
11	Dva		SRHGE
12	Var		
13	Sva		

that the ranking is correct for all the tested databases but, above all, that by using only the descriptors leading to better performances we can reduce significantly the dimensionality of each feature subset.

As a consequence, our final feature set will be based on the first six GLCM, the first five GLDM, and the first four GLRLM descriptors. To find the complete feature set able to classify correctly images belonging to different databases, we have performed various tests with different combination of features. In Table 3.3 we report the classification of images using different combinations of features leading to better results. As can be noted, none of the combinations presents the LBP. With this descriptor the performances are excellent only for some datasets, so it cannot be used for a general framework. On the contrary, the other descriptors provide good results for each database, up to excellent results when combined together.

Finally, in Table 3.4 we report a comparison between our results and others present in literature. As can be seen, the proposed approach outperforms all the others for all the tested databases. In particular, we would like to highlight that only a few authors have analyzed more than one database and that none used all the databases containing different histological images and therefore representative of different medical problems. Finally, we make some observations on the execution time. The final feature set is extracted on average in about 1.6 ± 0.04 s/image. The training phase is completed in 2.6 s in the worst case, with HIS presenting the highest number of images, while the test phase is performed on average in 0.018 ± 0.002 s. Thus, in a real case of application you can reach a computer-aided diagnosis in less than 2 s.

Table 3.3 Classification of Images According to Different Features Combinations

Database	Features Combination			
	GLCM GLDM	GLDM GLRLM	GLCM GLRLM	GLCM GLDM GLRLM
LYM	94.8±2.0	95.1±2.5	96.0±1.5	**97.4**±0.9
PAP	93.7±2.5	93.6±1.2	94.2±1.3	**96.6**±0.3
HIS	93.2±0.9	92.6±1.0	92.7±1.0	**96.0**±0.9
LAF	100.0±0.0	100.0±0.0	100.0±0.0	**100.0**±0.0
LAM	99.9±0.2	99.7±0.5	99.9±0.3	**100.0**±0.0
LGAL	100.0±0.0	100.0±0.0	100.0±0.0	**100.0**±0.0
LGCR	100.0±0.0	100.0±0.0	100.0±0.0	**100.0**±0.0
GLOM	97.3±0.6	96.3±0.9	97.4±0.8	**97.7**±0.7

Table 3.4 Comparison of Our Results With the State-of-the-art Approaches

Database	Nanni et al. [2]	Shamir et al. [29]	Meng et al. [3]	Arevalo et al. [6]	Herv et al. [9]	dos Santos et al. [7]	Our System
LYM	–	85.0	92.7	–	63.3	–	**97.4**
PAP	92.5	–	–	–	–	91.4	**96.5**
HIS	92.4	–	–	94.1	–	92.4	**96.0**
LAF	–	51.0	96.4	–	–	–	**100**
LAM	–	–	–	–	–	–	**100**
LGAL	–	69.0	99.4	–	97.3	–	**100**
LGCR	–	99.0	–	–	–	–	**100**
GLOM	–	–	–	–	97.4	–	**97.7**

3.6 CONCLUSION

In this chapter we have proposed a color texture-based histology image classification framework. The features have been obtained by generalizing the existent gray-scale approaches (GLCM, GLDM, GLRLM, and LBP) to color images and extracted from the HSV color space, which performs better than the other color spaces. The features have been used to train a SVM model. The experimental results have shown that the best feature subset has been obtained from the generalized GLCM, demonstrating very good performance. The feature-ranking step has permitted individuating of the best descriptors for each approach for use in combination as the final feature set. The proposed framework has been tested using very different public biological image databases, obtaining excellent results and outperforming the existing methods present in the literature. The next step for this work will include a further reduction of the feature set, by using also PCA and LDA, to decrease the training time, being able to apply our approach on bigger databases with other significant medical problems and to study different stages of pathology, if present. Further research will be devoted to improve robustness and accuracy in the rotation invariant classification task, which is an important issue especially for medical images that can occur in different and uncontrolled rotation angles.

ACKNOWLEDGMENTS

Lorenzo Putzu gratefully acknowledges the Sardinia regional government for the financial support of his PhD scholarship (P.O.R. Sardegna F.S.E. Operational Programme of the Autonomous Region of Sardinia, European Social Fund 2007-2013 — Axis IV Human Resources, Objective l.3, Line of Activity l.3.1.).

REFERENCES

[1] Kothari S, Phan JH, Young AN, Wang MD. Histological image classification using biologically interpretable shape-based features. BMC Med Imaging 2013;13(9):1–16.

[2] Nanni L, Brahnam S, Ghidoni S, Menegatti E, Barrier T. Different approaches for extracting information from the co-occurrence matrix. PLoS One 2013;8(12):e83554.

[3] Meng T, Lin L, Shyu ML, Chen SC. Histology image classification using supervised classification and multimodal fusion. In: Proceedings of IEEE international symposium on multimedia (ISM2010), Taichung, Taiwan; 2010. p. 145–52.

[4] Naik S, Doyle S, Madabhushi A, Feldman M, Tomaszewski J. Gland segmentation and computerized gleason grading of prostate histology by integrating low-, high-level and domain specific information. In: Proceedings of 2nd workshop on microsopic image analysis with applications in biology, Piscataway, NJ, USA; 2007.

[5] Doyle S, Agner S, Madabhushi A, Feldman M, Tomaszewski J. Automated grading of breast cancer histopathology using spectral clustering with textural and architectural image features. In: Proceedings of 5th IEEE international symposium on biomedical imaging, Paris, France; 2008. p. 496–9.

[6] Arevalo J, Cruz-Roa A, Arias V, Romero E, Gonzalez FA. An unsupervised feature learning framework for basal cell carcinoma image analysis. Artif Intell Med 2015;64(2):131–45.

[7] dos Santos FLC, Paci M, Nanni L, Brahnam S, Hyttinen J. Computer vision for virus image classification. Biosys Eng 2015;138:11–22.

[8] Lessmann B, Nattkemper TW, Hans VH, Degenhard A. A method for linking computed image features to histological semantics in neuropathology. J Biomed Inform 2007;40(6):631–41.

[9] Herv N, Servais A, Thervet E, Olivo-Marin J-C, Meas-Yedid V. Statistical color texture descriptors for histological images analysis. In: IEEE international symposium on biomedical, imaging; 2011. p. 724–7.

[10] Gonzlez-Rufino E, Carrin P, Cernadas E, Fernndez-Delgado M, Domnguez-Petit R. Exhaustive comparison of color texture features and classification methods to discriminate cells categories in histological images of fish ovary. Pattern Recogn 2013;46(9):2391–407.

[11] Lowe DG. Distinctive image features from scale-invariant keypoints. Int J Comput Vis 2004;60(2):91–110.

[12] Bay H, Tuytelaars T, Van Gool L. SURF: speeded up robust features. In: European conference on computer vision (ECCV). Lecture notes in computer science, vol. 3951; 2006. p. 404–17.

[13] Dalal N, Triggs B. Histograms of oriented gradients for human detection. In: IEEE computer society conference on conference on computer vision and pattern recognition (CVPR), vol. 1; 2005. p. 886–93.

[14] Ojala T, Pietikinen M, Harwood D. A comparative study of texture measures with classification based on featured distributions. Pattern Recogn 1996;29(1):51–9.

[15] Jain AK, Farrokhnia F. Unsupervised texture segmentation using Gabor filters. In: IEEE international conference on systems, man and cybernetics; 1990. p. 14–9.

[16] Gelzinis A, Verikas A, Bacauskiene M. Increasing the discrimination power of the co-occurrence matrix-based features. Pattern Recogn 2007;40(9):2367–72.

[17] Walker R, Jackway P, Longstaff D. Genetic algorithm optimization of adaptive multi-scale GLCM features. Int J Pattern Recogn Artif Intell 2003;17(1):17–39.

[18] Chen S, Chengdong W, Chen D, Tan W. Scene classification based on gray level-gradient co-occurrence matrix in the neighborhood of interest points. In: IEEE international conference on intelligent computing and intelligent systems (ICIS); 2009. p. 482–5.

[19] Mitrea D, Mitrea P, Nedevschi S, Badea R, Lupsor M. Abdominal tumor characterization and recognition using superior-order cooccurrence matrices, based on ultrasound images. Comput Math Methods Med 2012;2012. Article ID 348135, 17 pp.

[20] Hu Y. Unsupervised texture classification by combining multi-scale features and k-means classifier. In: Chinese conference on pattern recognition; 2009. p. 1–5.

[21] Gong R, Wang H. Steganalysis for GIF images based on colors-gradient co-occurrence matrix. Opt Commun 2012;285(24):4961–5.

[22] Benco M, Hudec R. Novel method for color textures features extraction based on GLCM. Radioengineering 2007;4(16):64–7.

[23] Haralick RM, Shanmugam K, Dinstein I. Textural features for image classification. IEEE Trans Syst Man Cybern 1973;3(6):610–21.

[24] Conners RW, Harlow CA. A theoretical comparison of texture algorithms. IEEE Trans Pattern Anal Mach Intell 1980;2(3):204–22.

[25] Tang X. Texture information in run-length matrices. IEEE Trans Image Process 1998;7(11):1602–9.

[26] Putzu L, Di Ruberto C. Investigation of different classification models to determine the presence of leukemia in peripheral blood image. In: International conference on image analysis and processing (ICIAP). Lecture notes in computer science, vol. 8156; 2013. p. 612–21.

[27] Cruz-Roa A, Caicedo JC, Gonzlez FA. Visual pattern mining in histology image collections using bag of features. Artif Intell Med 2011;52(2):91–106.

[28] Jantzen J, Dounias G. Analysis of pap-smear data. In: NISIS 2006, Puerto de la Cruz, Tenerife, Spain; 2006.

[29] Shamir L, Orlov N, Eckley DM, Macura T, Goldberg IG. A proposed benchmark suite for biological image analysis. Med Biol Eng Comput 2008;46(9):943–7.

[30] Zahn JM, Poosala S, Owen AB, Ingram DK, Lustig A, Carter A, et al. AGEMAP: a gene expression database for aging in mice. PLoS Gene 2007;3(11):e201.

CHAPTER

SPONTANEOUS ACTIVITY CHARACTERIZATION IN SPIKING NEURAL SYSTEMS WITH LOG-NORMAL SYNAPTIC WEIGHT DISTRIBUTION

4

S. Nobukawa*, H. Nishimura†, T. Maruo†

*Department of Management Information Science, Fukui University of Technology, Fukui, Japan**

Graduate School of Applied Informatics, University of Hyogo, Hyogo, Japan†

4.1 INTRODUCTION

Cortical networks are generally known to sustain some degree of electrical activity representing the brain's noisy internal state even in the absence of sensory stimulation. This fluctuating appearance is called spontaneous activity or ongoing activity [1,2] and is typically accompanied by irregular neuronal spiking with a low firing rate ($\approx$1 Hz) in the cerebral cortex but a high coherent spike transmission between specific neurons. Further, in this activity, the subthreshold membrane potential has two distinctively different states; that is, the depolarized state near the threshold of spiking (called the upstate) and the hyperpolarized state (called the downstate) where spikes cannot arise [3–5]. Recently, to account for the genesis of this spontaneous activity in the brain, Teramae et al. [6] proposed, based on the experimental findings, that the above-mentioned features could be caused by synaptic weights that follow a log-normal distribution [7,8]. They also used a leaky integrate-and-fire (LIF) neuron model to propose that the amplitude of the excitatory postsynaptic potentials between cortical neurons obey a non-Gaussian long-tailed, typically log-normal distribution.

The Hodgkin-Huxley model [9] is known as the most important spiking neuron model. It simulates the neurodynamics by describing the capacitance of the membrane and the characteristic of the ion channel resistance. It can reproduce almost all of the spiking activities observed in neural systems by tuning its parameters. However, because of the complexity of the physiological parameters, many simpler neuron models with a smaller number of parameters have been proposed to focus on the membrane potential behavior (spiking activity), including the LIF neuron model and FitzHugh-Nagumo neuron model [10].

Among these, the Izhikevich neuron model [11,12], which combines continuous spike-generation mechanisms and a discontinuous resetting process after spikes, can reproduce the major spike patterns observed in the cerebral cortex simply by tuning a few parameters, and it has a large variety of spiking properties in comparison with other models [12]. In particular, a comparison of the Izhikevich neuron model and the LIF neuron model, which includes the resetting process (called a hybrid spiking neuron model), shows that the former contains the dynamics of the spike generation and refractoriness after spiking, whereas the latter does not contain these dynamics. Thus, a question arises about whether the Izhikevich neuron model, as a more realistic neuron model, can reproduce the previously mentioned spontaneous activity in a cortical network. To answer this question, it is necessary to study the influence of the neurodynamics on this spontaneous activity.

In this chapter, following up on our previous work [13], we introduce new evaluation measures and indices and reanalyze the spike transmission characteristics in the LIF neural system with a log-normal synaptic weight distribution. Then, we examine the spike transmission characteristics in the Izhikevich neural system, and compare the results to those of the LIF neural system.

4.2 MODELS OF SPONTANEOUS ACTIVITY

Spontaneous activity has the following typical characteristics: (1) sustained spiking activity without external input, (2) a low firing rate ($\approx$1 Hz), (3) irregular spiking, (4) spike coherence between specific neurons, and (5) irregular transitions between up/down states [3–5]. Several studies have been conducted over the last decade on the genesis of this spontaneous activity, utilizing spiking neuron models. In the literature [14], it has been reported that the spiking activity of low-threshold spike neurons may induce the emergence of this spontaneous activity. This approach included all of the previously mentioned characteristics except the fourth. However, all of the neurons exhibited low coherence (the cross-correlation among neuron spikes was less than 0.05); that is, a highly coherent group of neurons was not confirmed. In another approach, the spontaneous activity was produced by the structures of the neural network such as the small-world property [15], sparse random connections [16], and log-normal distribution of synaptic weights [6]. In particular, the models proposed by Teramae et al. [6] and Vogels and Abbott [16] satisfy the above five conditions.

Based on the literature [6], the following sections discuss the spontaneous activity in a neural network with a log-normal distribution of synaptic weights.

4.3 MODEL AND METHODS

A neural system with a log-normal distribution of synaptic weights is described using the LIF neuron model and Izhikevich neuron model in Sections 4.3.1 and 4.3.2, respectively. Next, we introduce the evaluation indices used to check the physiological validity and measure the synchronization between the preneuron spike train and postneuron spike train in Section 4.3.3.

4.3.1 LIF NEURAL SYSTEM APPLIED SYNAPTIC INPUT

We first consider a neural system receiving spike trains from several preneurons, as shown in Fig. 4.1. The postneuron membrane potential $v(t)$ in the neural system is described by the conductance based on a LIF neuron as follows:

$$\frac{dv(t)}{dt} = -\frac{1}{\tau_m}(v(t) - V_L) - g_E(t)(v(t) - V_E) - g_I(t)(v(t) - V_I) \tag{1}$$

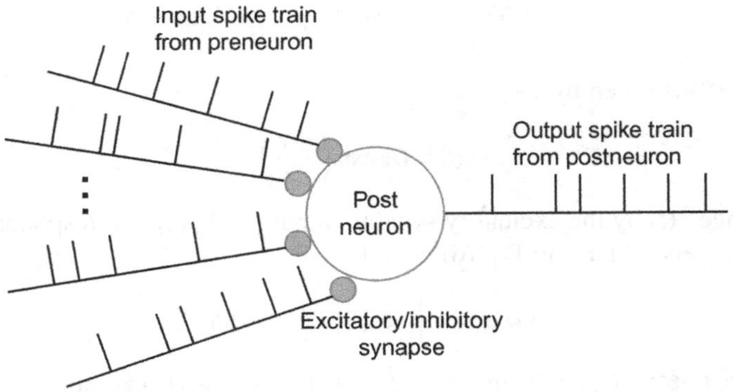

FIGURE 4.1

Neural system with postneuron receiving spike trains from several presynaptic neurons.

$$\text{If } v(t) \geq V_{\text{thr}}, \text{ then } v(t) = V_{\text{r}} \tag{2}$$

where τ_{m} is the membrane decay constant; and V_{E}, V_{I}, and V_{L} are the reversal potentials of the AMPA-receptor-mediated excitatory synaptic current, inhibitory synaptic current, and leak current, respectively. The excitatory synaptic conductance $g_{\text{E}}(t)$ and inhibitory synaptic conductance $g_{\text{I}}(t)$ are given by

$$\frac{dg_{\text{E}}(t)}{dt} = -\frac{g_{\text{E}}(t)}{\tau_{\text{s}}} + \sum_j G_{\text{E},j} \sum_{s_j} \delta(t - s_j) \tag{3}$$

$$\frac{dg_{\text{I}}(t)}{dt} = -\frac{g_{\text{I}}(t)}{\tau_{\text{s}}} + \sum_j G_{\text{I},j} \sum_{s_j} \delta(t - s_j) \tag{4}$$

Here, τ_{s} is the decay constant of the excitatory and inhibitory synaptic conductances. $G_{\text{E},j}$ and $G_{\text{I},j}$ are the synaptic weights of the excitatory and inhibitory synapses, respectively. In our simulation, we set $V_{\text{I}} = -80$ mV, $V_{\text{L}} = -70$ mV, $V_{\text{r}} = -60$ mV, $V_{\text{thr}} = -50$ mV, $V_{\text{E}} = 0$ mV, $\tau_{\text{m}} = 20$ ms, and $\tau_{\text{s}} = 2$ ms. The preneurons consist of 1000 excitatory neurons and 1000 inhibitory neurons [6]. s_j indicates the spiking time in preneuron j and is given by a Poisson process obeying $p(k) = \frac{(\lambda T)^k}{k!} e^{-\lambda T}$, where k is the sum of the spikes during the evaluation duration $[0, T]$.

The amplitudes of excitatory postsynaptic potential V_{EPSP} are generated from a log-normal distribution:

$$P(V_{\text{EPSP}}) = \frac{1}{\sqrt{2\pi}\sigma V_{\text{EPSP}}} \exp\left(-\frac{(\ln V_{\text{EPSP}} - \mu)^2}{2\sigma^2}\right) \tag{5}$$

In our simulation, we set $\sigma = 1.0$ and the mode of the distribution $\mu - \sigma^2 = \log 0.2$. Here, the V_{EPSP} observable must be translated into synaptic weight G_{E} to solve Eq. (3). Next, we consider the case where a postneuron receives spike input from a single excitatory synapse at $t = 0$ ms. In this case, the dynamics of the membrane potential $v(t)$ can be found as follows:

$$\frac{dv(t)}{dt} = -\frac{1}{\tau_{\text{m}}}(v(t) - V_{\text{L}}) - g_{\text{E}}(t)(v(t) - V_{\text{E}}) \tag{6}$$

$$\frac{dg_E(t)}{dt} = -\frac{g_E(t)}{\tau_s} + G_E\delta(t) \tag{7}$$

The solution of Eq. (7) is given by

$$g_E(t) = G_E \exp\left(-\frac{t}{\tau_s}\right) \tag{8}$$

The amount of change $v(t)$ by the excitatory synaptic input (ie, V_{EPSP}) corresponds to the integration between $[0, \tau_s]$ of the second term in Eq. (6), as follows:

$$V_{EPSP} \approx -\int_0^{\tau_s} g_E(t)(v(t) - V_E)dt \tag{9}$$

Under the condition $\tau_s \ll \tau_m$ ($\tau_m = 20$ ms, $\tau_s = 2$ ms), $v(t)$ and $g_E(t)$ can approximate $v(t) \approx V_r$ and $g_E(t) \approx G_E$, respectively. The relationship between V_{EPSP} and G_E is derived from these calculations as follows:

$$V_{EPSP} \approx -\tau_s G_E(V_r - V_E) = 120G_E \tag{10}$$

For simplicity, the excitatory-to-inhibitory synapses have a uniform value of $G_{I,j} = 0.002$. Based on the results of a previous physiological experiment [7], the excitatory-to-excitatory synaptic transmissions fail depending on an EPSP amplitude. Thus, we adopt the probability of this failure in the process of synaptic transmissions: $\frac{\alpha}{V_{EPSP+\alpha}}$, where $\alpha = 0.1$ mV.

4.3.2 IZHIKEVICH NEURAL SYSTEM USED FOR SYNAPTIC INPUT

The Izhikevich neuron model [11,12] is a two-dimensional system of ordinary differential equations with the following form:

$$C\frac{dv}{dt} = k(v - V_r)(v - V_t) - u - g_I(v - V_I) - g_E(v - V_E) \tag{11}$$

$$\frac{du}{dt} = a\{b(v - V_r) - u\} \tag{12}$$

with the auxiliary after-spike resetting

$$\text{If } v \geq 30(\text{mV}), \text{ then} \begin{cases} v \leftarrow c \\ u \leftarrow u + d \end{cases} \tag{13}$$

Here, v and u represent the membrane potential of the neuron and a membrane recovery variable, respectively. v has the millivolt scale, and the time t has the millisecond scale. C is the membrane capacitance, V_r is the resting membrane potential, V_t is the instantaneous threshold potential, and $-\ g_I(v - V_I) - g_E(v - V_E)$ is the input current term, where g_E and g_I follow Eqs. (3), (4), respectively. The parameters k and b are related to the neuron's rheobase and input resistance. The parameter a is the recovery time constant. As the threshold value V_{thr}, we adopt the saddle-node bifurcation point, $V_{thr} = \frac{kV_t + kV_r + b}{2k}$ (mV), which is derived from the condition for the multiple roots of v-nullcline ($v' = 0$) and u-nullcline ($u' = 0$). Our simulation uses the following parameter values: $C=5$, $k=0.04$, $a=0.02$, $b=0.2$, $c=-65$, $d=30$, $V_r=-70$, $V_t=-35$, $\tau_s=2$. Note that the threshold for the spiking V_{thr} corresponds to -50 mV under these parameters. This model is discretized using a difference interval $\Delta t=10^{-1}$ ms. Additionally, the relationship between V_{EPSP} and G_E ($V_{EPSP}=137G_E$) is derived by utilizing the simulation for the amount of $v(t)$ change in a case where a spike is input from a single excitatory synapse with G_E. Because an analytical estimation such as Eq. (9) is difficult to perform using the Izhikevich neural system, we used this numerical estimation. The settings for the excitatory-to-inhibitory synaptic weights and excitatory-to-excitatory synaptic transmission failures are the same as those for the LIF neuron model case.

4.3.3 EVALUATION INDICES

We introduce evaluation indices to compare the spontaneous activities observed in physiological experiments and the spiking activities produced by the models discussed in Sections 4.3.1 and 4.3.2.

As an index for the synchronization between the preneuron's spike train, $X(l)\left(l=1,2,\ldots,m\left(\frac{T}{m}=\Delta t\right)\right)$, and the postneuron's spike train, $Y(l)$, during a long interval, T is measured using the cross-correlation:

$$C=\frac{\sum_{l=1}^{m}\left(X(l)-\overline{X(l)}\right)\left(Y(l)-\overline{Y(l)}\right)}{\sqrt{\sum_{l=1}^{m}\left(X(l)-\overline{X(l)}\right)^2\sum_{l=1}^{m}\left(Y(l)-\overline{Y(l)}\right)^2}} \tag{14}$$

Here, if the preneuron fires within the l-th time bin, $X(l)=1$, otherwise $X(l)=0$. For the postneuron, $Y(l)$ is given in the same way.

To evaluate the uniformity of the neuron spikes, we adopt the following coefficient of variation for interspike intervals [17]:

$$CV=\frac{\sqrt{Var(T_k)}}{\langle T_k\rangle} \tag{15}$$

T_k is the k-th inter spike interval (ISI) ($T_k=t_{k+1}-t_k$). $Var(T_k)$ and $\langle T_k\rangle$ are the deviation and mean of T_k, respectively. Here, CV becomes zero in the periodic state and positive in the aperiodic state. In the case of a cerebral cortex neuron, CV has a value of about 1.0 [5,18].

4.4 RESULTS AND EVALUATIONS

In this section, we first investigate the effect of an input spike from the weak synapses in the LIF neural system in Section 4.1. Next, the spike transmission is evaluated in an environment with a log-normal synaptic weight distribution using the LIF neuron model and Izhikevich neuron model in Sections 4.2 and 4.3, respectively.

4.4.1 EFFECT OF INPUT SPIKE FROM WEAK SYNAPSE IN LIF NEURAL SYSTEM

Let us first demonstrate the relationship between the mean frequency of an input spike ($\Lambda=\lambda\times10^3$(Hz)) from preneurons with a weak synaptic weight ($V_{EPSP}<3$mV) and the postneuron

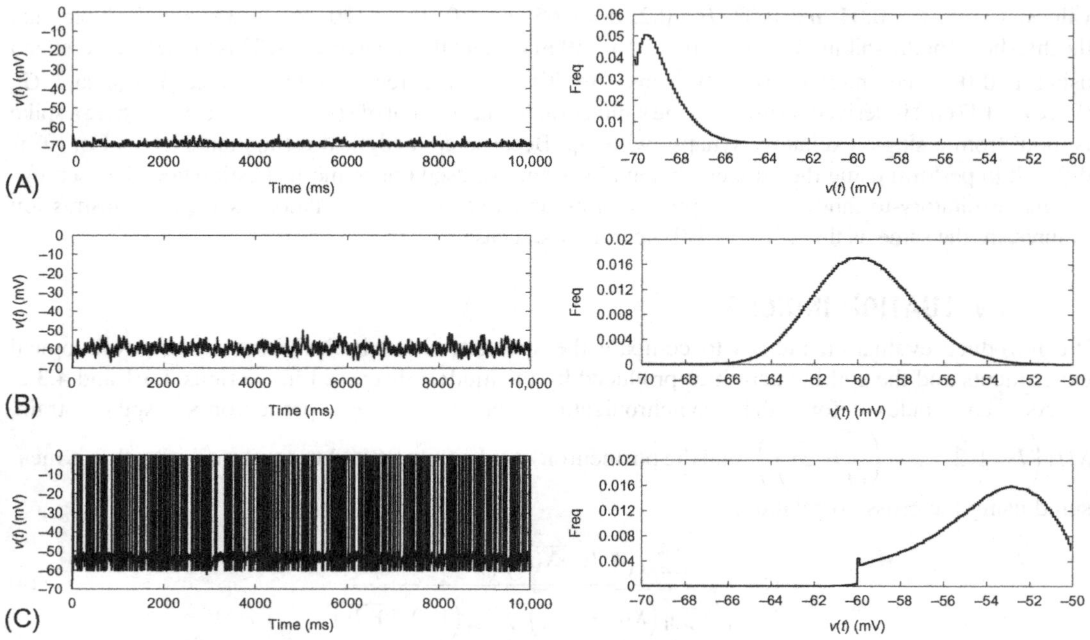

FIGURE 4.2

Time series of membrane potential $v(t)$ (left) and histogram of $v(t)$ (right) under a condition where large synaptic weights (>3 mV) are removed: (A) $\Lambda = 0.1$ Hz, (B) $\Lambda = 1.0$ Hz, and (C) $\Lambda = 2.5$ Hz ($\tau_m = 20, \tau_s = 2$, $V_L = -70$, $V_r = -60$, $V_E = 0$, $V_I = -80$, $V_{thr} = -50$).

membrane potential $v(t)$ using the LIF neuron model. Fig. 4.2 shows the time series of membrane potential $v(t)$ (left) and the appearance frequency of the $v(t)$ value during$[0, 10^6]$ (ms) (right) at $\Lambda = 0.1, 1.0, 2.5$Hz under a condition where the large synaptic weights ($V_{EPSP} > 3$mV) are removed. Note that the $v(t)$ values for the spiking and refractory states are removed from the appearance frequency. In the case of $\Lambda = 0.1$ Hz (Fig. 4.2(A)), the appearance frequency concentrates around the resting membrane potential V_L (mV) because of the small fluctuation in $v(t)$. The mean frequency of the input spike increases the mode of the appearance frequency to V_{thr}=50 mV with an increase in the base of the $v(t)$ time series, as shown in Fig. 4.2(B). In a case where a postneuron fires with high frequency at $\Lambda = 2.5$Hz (Fig. 4.2(C)), the mode of the appearance frequency is close to −50 mV.

Furthermore, Fig. 4.3 shows the mean and mode of the $v(t)$ dependence on Λ in relation to the appearance frequency given by Fig. 4.2. The mean and mode of $v(t)$ increase with an increase in Λ, and the postneuron begins firing at $\Lambda > 1.5$ Hz. The mean converges to about −54.5 mV, whereas the mode increases at $\Lambda \gtrsim 2.0$ Hz and reaches a value of about $V_{thr} = -50$ mV. The different tendency between the mean and mode at $\Lambda \gtrsim 2.0$ Hz is caused by the break in the symmetry of the mode in the appearance frequency distribution, as shown in Fig. 4.2(C).

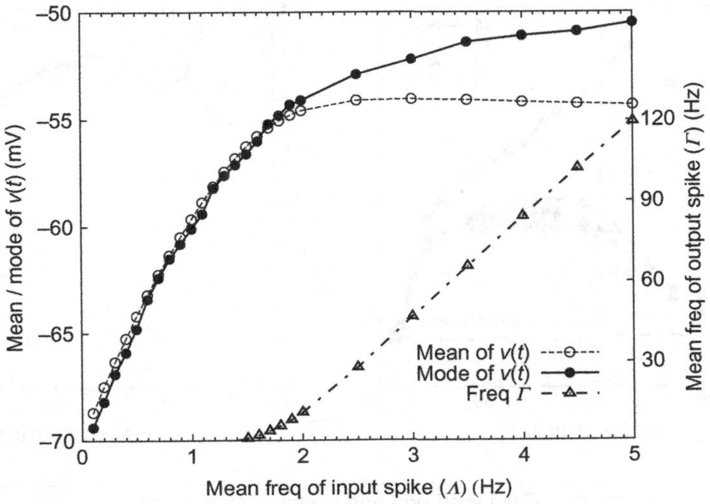

FIGURE 4.3

Dependence of mean/mode of $v(t)$ and mean frequency of output spike (Γ (Hz)) on mean frequency of input spike (Λ(Hz)) under a condition where large synaptic weights (>3 mV) are removed ($\tau_m = 20, \tau_s = 2, V_L = -70, V_r = -60, V_E = 0, V_I = -80, V_{thr} = -50$).

4.4.2 SPIKE TRANSMISSION IN LIF NEURAL SYSTEM

Under a synaptic weight distribution that includes strong synapses ($V_{EPSP} > 3$ mV), we examine the postneuron responses to input spike trains with strong synapses, which rank in the top five of all synaptic weights, and the weak synapse located in the mode of the synaptic weight distribution ($V_{EPSP} \approx 0.2$). Fig. 4.4(A) indicates the dependence of the cross-correlation C between the spike train of the postneuron and that of the preneuron on the mode of $v(t)$ given by Fig. 4.3. Here, the time window and evaluation duration T are set to 4.0 ms and 10^6 ms, respectively. When $-70 \lesssim$ mode of $v(t) \lesssim -65$ mV, the preneuron with the strongest synapse ($G_{E,380} \approx 0.1486(\#1)$) does not synchronize ($C \lesssim 0.1$). However, the C value increases with the rising mode of $v(t)$ and has a peak (≈ 0.25) at around -60 mV. In addition, as shown in Fig. 4.4(B), the ISI value of the postneuron near the peak of C exhibits a high irregularity ($CV \approx 1.0$) corresponding with the observed data in the cerebral cortex [5,18]. If it is assumed that the input spike train from the strong synapse and the weak synapses are a signal and background noise, respectively, this phenomenon can be interpreted to be the signal response enhanced by noise with an appropriate strength; that is, stochastic resonance (SR) [19]. In the cases of the other strong synapses ($G_{E,82} \approx 0.0965\,(\#2), G_{E,572} \approx 0.0899\,(\#3), G_{E,973} \approx 0.0880\,(\#4), G_{E,220} \approx 0.0861\,(\#5)$) in Fig. 4.4(A), the peak values of C decrease depending on the synaptic weight, and ultimately the value of C approaches zero in the case of $V_{EPSP} \approx 0.2$.

Furthermore, we demonstrate the spike train in the preneuron and the time series of $v(t)$ in the postneuron in the SR case. Fig. 4.5 shows the spike trains from the largest synapse (#1 in Fig. 4.4) and weak synapse (V_{EPSP}= 0.2 mV case in Fig. 4.4) at $\Lambda = 0.9$ Hz. We can find that the postneuron responds

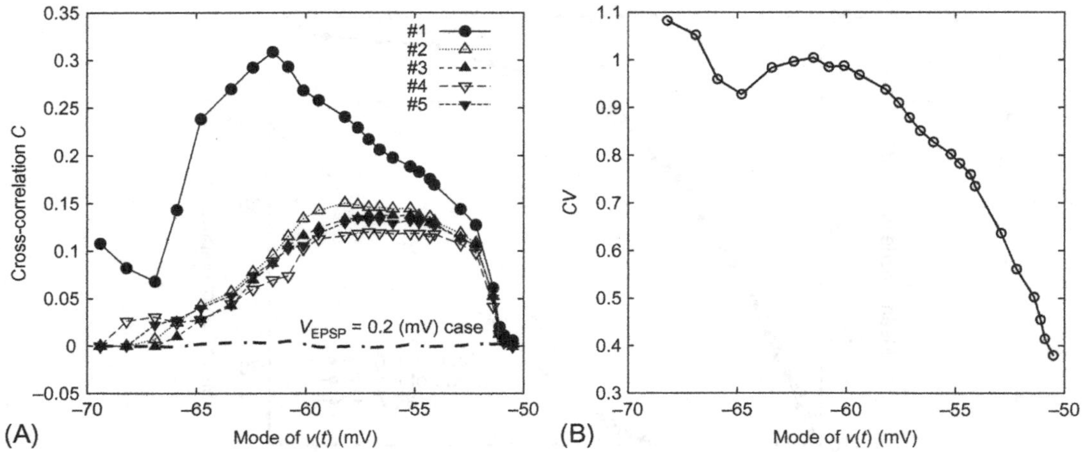

FIGURE 4.4

(A) Dependence of cross-correlation C between pre- and postneurons on mode of $v(t)$ (time window: 4 ms). (B) Dependence of coefficient of variation for interspike intervals CV in postneuron on mode of $v(t)$ ($\tau_m = 20$, $\tau_s = 2$, $V_L = -70$, $V_r = -60$, $V_E = 0$, $V_I = -80$, $V_{thr} = -50$, evaluated duration $[0, 10^6]$ (ms)).

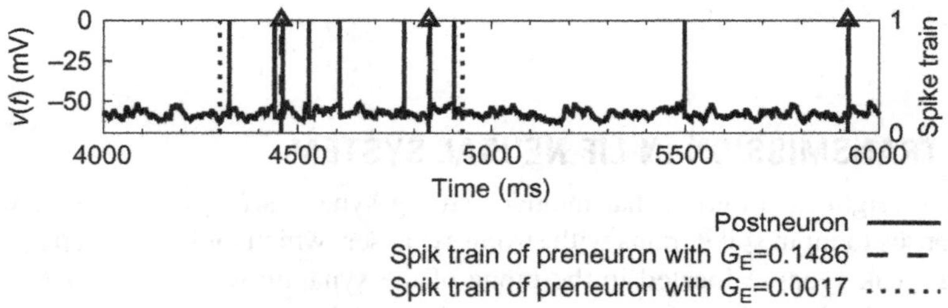

FIGURE 4.5

Spike trains of preneuron and $v(t)$ in $\left[4\times10^3, 6\times10^3\right]$ (ms) ($\tau_m = 20$, $\tau_s = 2$, $V_L = -70$, $V_r = -60$, $V_E = 0$, $V_I = -80$, $V_{thr} = -50$).

to the spike train from the strongest synapse promptly at $t = 4450, 4840, 5910$ ms (indicated by *open triangles*), where the time delay is within 4 ms. These precise spike trains between the pre- and postneuron have been observed physiologically in the brain of behaving animals [20].

4.4.3 SPIKE TRANSMISSION IN IZHIKEVICH NEURAL SYSTEM

In this section, we evaluate the signal response in a neural system with the input-output structure discussed in Section 4.1 using the Izhikevich neuron model and compare the characteristics of the LIF and Izhikevich neuron models.

Fig. 4.6 shows the mean and mode of the $v(t)$ dependence on Λ under the condition where the large synaptic weights (>3 mV) are removed. The mean and mode of $v(t)$ increase with an increasing Λ, and the postneuron begins firing at $\Lambda > 5.5$Hz. The mean converges to about -53 mV because of the break

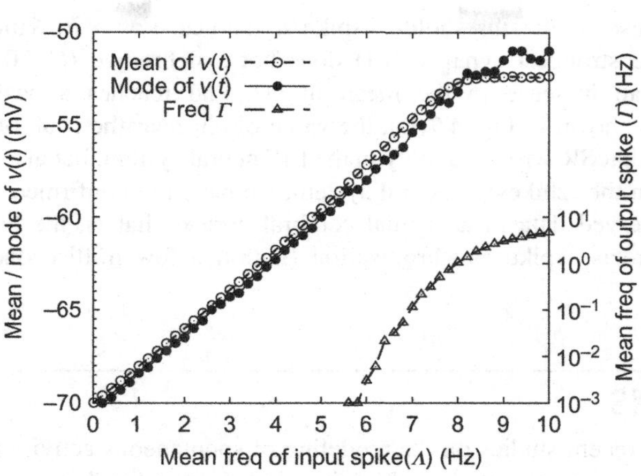

FIGURE 4.6

Dependence of mean/mode of $v(t)$ and mean frequency of output spike (Γ (Hz)) on mean frequency of input spike (Λ (Hz)) under a condition where large synaptic weights (>3 mV) are removed in an Izhikevich neuron model case ($C=5, k=0.04, a=0.02, b=0.2, c=-65, d=30, V_r=-70, V_t=-35, \tau_s=2$).

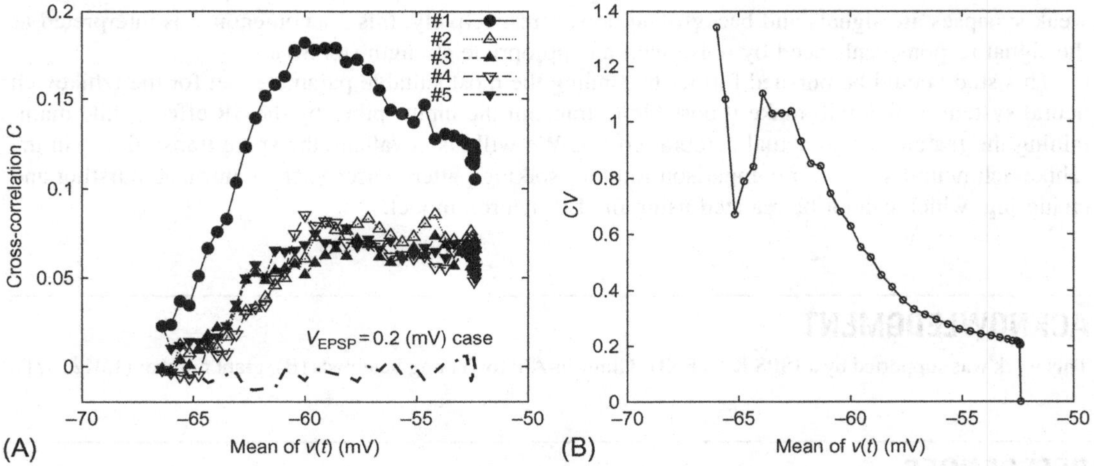

FIGURE 4.7

(A) Dependence of C between pre- and postneurons on mean of $v(t)$ (time window: 40 ms). (B) Dependence of CV in postneuron on mean of $v(t)$ in an Izhikevich neuron model case ($C=5, k=0.04, a=0.02, b=0.2, c=-65, d=30, V_r=-70, V_t=-35, \tau_s=2$, evaluated duration $[0, 10^6]$ (ms)).

in the symmetry of the appearance frequency distribution, whereas the mode increases at $\Lambda \gtrsim 8.0$ Hz and reaches a value of about $V_{thr} = -50$ mV. Fig. 4.7(A) indicates the dependence of C on the mean of $v(t)$, which is given by Fig. 4.6 under a synaptic weight distribution that includes strong synapses. Here, we set the time window and the evaluation duration T to 40 ms and 10^6 ms, respectively. Note that the Izhikevich neuron model needs a larger time window than the LIF neuron model to obtain a high value of C because of the threshold-to-spike dynamics. For $-70 \lesssim \text{mean of } v(t) \lesssim -65$ mV, the preneuron with the strongest synapse (#1) does not synchronize ($C \lesssim 0.01$). However, the C value increases with an increase in the mean of $v(t)$ and reaches a peak (≈ 0.18) at around -60 mV. Moreover, as shown in Fig. 4.7(B), the value of CV near the peak of C is about 0.6.

These results show that SR arises, not only in the LIF neural system, but also in the Izhikevich neural system. However, in the Izhikevich neural system, we have not confirmed spiking activity corresponding with the observed data in an actual cerebral cortex; that is, the high irregularity of ISI ($CV \approx 1.0$), and the precise spike synchronization (within a few milliseconds) between pre- and postneurons.

4.5 CONCLUSIONS

In this chapter, several recent studies on the modeling of spontaneous activity have been introduced. Next, a neural system that uses synaptic weights with a log-normal distribution was described using the LIF neuron model and Izhikevich neuron model, and we introduced the evaluation indices of CV and C. Furthermore, the spike transmission characteristics were evaluated in a neural system using the LIF neuron model and Izhikevich neuron model. The results revealed that the generation of internal fluctuating activity by long-tailed weight distributions produces an optimal solution for efficient spike transmission in both neuron models. By recognizing that the input spike trains from the strong and weak synapses are signals and background noises, respectively, this phenomenon was interpreted as the signal response enhanced by noise with an appropriate strength (ie, SR).

This study could be pursued further by finding the most suitable parameter set for the Izhikevich neural system, which will make it possible to transmit the input spikes by the SR effect while maintaining the features of an actual cerebral cortex. We will also evaluate the spike transmission in the Izhikevich neural system in comparison to other spiking pattern cases such as intrinsic bursting and chattering, which cannot be realized using the LIF neuron model.

ACKNOWLEDGMENT

This work was supported by a JSPS KAKENHI Grant-in-Aid for Young Scientists (B), grant number (15K21471).

REFERENCES

[1] Fiser J, Chiu C, Weliky M. Small modulation of ongoing cortical dynamics by sensory input during natural vision. Nature 2004;431:573–8.
[2] McCormick DA. Spontaneous activity: signal or noise? Science 1999;285(5427):541–3.
[3] Hromádka T, DeWeese MR, Zador AM. Sparse representation of sounds in the unanesthetized auditory cortex. PLoS Biol 2008;6(1):e16.
[4] Sakata S, Harris KD. Laminar structure of spontaneous and sensory-evoked population activity in auditory cortex. Neuron 2009;64(3):404–18.
[5] Softky W, Koch C. The highly irregular firing of cortical cells is inconsistent with temporal integration of random EPSPs. J Neurosci 1993;13:334–50.

[6] Teramae J, Tsubo Y, Fukai T. Optimal spike-based communication in excitable networks with strong-sparse and weak-dense links. Sci Rep 2012;2:485.
[7] Lefort S, Tomm C, Floyd Sarria JC, Petersen CC. The excitatory neuronal network of the C2 barrel column in mouse primary somatosensory cortex. Neuron 2009;61(2):301–16.
[8] Song S, Sjöström PJ, Reigl M, Nelson S, Chklovskii DB. Highly nonrandom features of synaptic connectivity in local cortical circuits. PLoS Biol 2005;3(3):e68.
[9] Hodgkin AL, Huxley AF. A quantitative description of membrane current and application to conduction and excitation in nerve. J Physiol 1952;117(4):500–44.
[10] Rabinovich MI, Varona P, Selverston AI, Abarbanel HDI. Dynamical principles in neuroscience. Rev Mod Phys 2006;78(4):1213–65.
[11] Izhikevich EM. Simple model of spiking neurons. IEEE Trans Neural Netw 2004;14(6):1569–72.
[12] Izhikevich EM. Which model to use for cortical spiking neurons? IEEE Trans Neural Netw 2004;15(5):1063–70.
[13] Nobukawa S, Maruo T, Nishimura H. Spontaneous activity modeling in spiking neural systems with log-normal synaptic weight distribution. In: Proceedings of the SICE annual conference (SICE2014); 2014. pp. 130–6.
[14] Destexhe A. Self-sustained asynchronous irregular states and up-down states in thalamic, cortical and thalamocortical networks of nonlinear integrate-and-fire neurons. J Comput Neurosci 2009;27(3):493–506.
[15] Guo D, Li C. Self-sustained irregular activity in 2-D small-world networks of excitatory and inhibitory neurons. IEEE Trans Neural Netw 2010;21(6):895–905.
[16] Vogels TP, Abbott LF. Signal propagation and logic gating in networks of integrate-and-fire neurons. J Neurosci 2005;25(46):10786–95.
[17] Pikovsky AS, Kurths J. Coherence resonance in a noise-driven excitable system. Phys Rev Lett 1997;78(5):775–8.
[18] Compte A, Constantinidis C, Tegnér J, Raghavachari S, Chafee MV, Goldman-Rakic PS, et al. Temporally irregular mnemonic persistent activity in prefrontal neurons of monkeys during a delayed response task. J Neurophysiol 2003;90(5):3441–54.
[19] Gammaitoni L, Hänggi P, Jung P, Marchesoni F. Stochastic resonance. Rev Mod Phys 1998;70(1):223–87.
[20] Abeles M, Bergman H, Margalit E, Vaadia E. Spatiotemporal firing patterns in the frontal cortex of behaving monkeys. J Neurophysiol 1993;70(4):1629–38.

CHAPTER

COMPARISON BETWEEN OpenMP AND MPICH OPTIMIZED PARALLEL IMPLEMENTATIONS OF A CELLULAR AUTOMATON THAT SIMULATES THE SKIN PIGMENTATION EVOLUTION

5

I. Ştirb

Computer and Software Engineering Department, "Politehnica" University of Timişoara, Timişoara, Romania

5.1 INTRODUCTION

The Game of Life cellular automaton simulates the change of state of all cells once, each time the automaton moves to a new generation. The cells are the elements of a matrix that is associated with the human skin. The live cells of the matrix are considered to be the pigmented human cells regardless of their color shade and the dead cells are associated with the rest of the human cells that are not pigmented. The continuous transition to a new generation of cells is correlated with the evolution of the human skin cells during the entire lifetime. The transitions can be automated using a parallel algorithm that speeds up the computation of the evolutionary process.

Modern architectures are designed to be multicore to be able to obtain physical parallelism that involves many processes that each can run on different cores. Physical parallelism is meant to obtain execution time improvement by minimizing the time in which processes are in idle state. This way, when the number of processes is equal to the number of cores, the processes do not enter at all in idle state, as each process is assigned to a core. On the other hand, logical parallelism is obtained when the there is more than one process assigned per core. In this case, processes become idle, waiting one after another to get into execution, which will cause a performance degradation in terms of execution time as the overhead spent on dealing with multiple processes may be bigger than the time gained by parallelizing the execution. Thus, the target is to obtain physical parallelism.

Parallel computation provides means to obtain real-time performances using different compiling directives or libraries, by making use of processes or threads to obtain parallelism [1]. Programs are manually parallelized today through such application program interfaces (APIs). One of these is open multiprocessing (OpenMP) which is based on the concept of shared memory between multiple threads. The code does not need to be written in a parallel manner because the OpenMP directives are inserted straightforward in the serial code similar to how comments are inserted. Vendors implement OpenMP in their programming language compilers, such as in the case of C++ compiler [2]. OpenMP compiler directives can be used in several programming languages (C/C++, Fortran) and represent a powerful and portable manner to obtain parallelism.

Message passing interface (MPI) is another ways to implement high-level parallelism. As opposed to OpenMP, MPI involves a communication between processes through exchange of data via messages, because the processes do not share a common memory as threads do. MPI is available in C/C++, Fortran, and Java.

If the underlying architecture is a multicore one, MPI would be a better choice rather than OpenMP because unlike threads, processes can be executed on several cores and, thus, the overall idle state time of all processes is minimized.

This paper proposes two optimized implementations in a parallel manner, one using MPI and the other using OpenMP of the Game of Life cellular automaton and, as well, a comparison between the two implementations with respect to their performances in terms of execution time.

5.1.1 THE CELLULAR AUTOMATON GAME OF LIFE

Game of Life is a mathematical model that automates the natural phenomenal of evolution in time of the skin pigmentation, described briefly by the fact that the natural color of a skin cell is inhibited (ie, the cell becomes pigmented) when a certain number of surrounding cells are pigmented as well.

Game of Life is a cellular automaton that describes the evolution in time during multiple generations of the cells in a matrix, starting from an initial state that is associated with the skin color gene of a person. No input is required for the evolution to take place. The evolution of skin cells is triggered by itself, regardless of the internal or external factors that influence the human body at that moment. A cell can be in one of the two states at a time, either alive or dead, and it goes into the next state according to the following rules:

- A live cell with less than two alive neighbors dies in the next generation because it is considered to be underpopulated.
- A live cell with two or three alive neighbors lives in the next generation.
- A live cell with more than three alive neighbors dies because it is considered to be overcrowded.
- A dead cell with exactly three alive neighbors becomes alive in the next generation, by reproduction.

A personal view is that the rules above are carefully chosen so as to reproduce the observable pigmentation phenomenon, based on the following conditions:

- The growth of the live cell should not be explosive; that is, the population of cells should not grow beyond an upper limit. In biological terms, this condition reflects the fact that, in most cases, the pigmented cells are limited to the face region of the human body.
- A chaotic and unpredictable initial state can occur and the evolution based on the Game of Life's rules must be supported starting from such initial states. Obviously, the human configuration of cells before the formation of the fetus is unpredictable.
- The rules of skin pigmentation evolution must be modeled as simple as possible because the human body configuration is already extremely complex.

5.2 MPICH OPTIMIZED APPROACH OF THE CELLULAR AUTOMATON

Messaging passing interface Chameleon (MPICH) is an implementation of the MPI that is a standardized and portable message passing system. In the following sections some MPI concepts will be detailed. Afterwards, the MPICH approach of the Game of Life will be described, followed by the code section along with the explanations that state the performances of the current implementation.

5.2.1 MPI STANDARD

MPI provides two ways of communication, one that can be done between groups of processes that are connected through a communicator object and the other simply between the processes within a group. The communicator object gives processes unique identifiers and arranges them in an ordered topology. MPI supports point-to-point communication through message exchange between two processes using MPI_Send and MPI_Recv functions and collective communication that involves the existence of a group of processes in which one of the processes may broadcast a message to all of the other processes, members of the group.

Optimization algorithms for collective communication such as all-gather, broadcast, all-to-all, reduce-scatter, reduce, and all-reduce are currently released for MPICH [3].

5.2.2 DESCRIPTION OF THE MPICH APPROACH OF THE CELLULAR AUTOMATON

The topology is established based on the direction of the message flow [4]. A ring topology is chosen for the implementation of Game of Life cellular automaton using MPICH. Precisely, the ring topology leads to an optimized implementation. The Dijkstra-Scholten algorithm assures that the processes receive confirmation signals of their sent messages [4].

The master process is chosen to be process number zero and all the other processes in the ring are slaves. The distinction between the master and the slaves is made at the code level, not at the operating system level. The master process executes a slightly different section of code than the slaves do, while the same other section of code is shared by all slaves. Because the underlying topology is a ring one and not a star topology, the master slave concept used in the implementation should not be interpreted as task farming. Task farming would imply that the master process decomposes the problem into subproblems and sends the subproblems to the slaves [5], which does not apply in this case.

Any cell in the matrix of cells has eight neighbors. The matrix is considered to be wrapped around; thus, the cells in the borders of the matrix are considered to have the same number of neighbors as the rest of the cells in the interior of the matrix. Thereby, a cell located in the position (0, 0) would have three neighbors (ie, the cells at positions (0, 1), (1, 0), and (1, 1)). Beside the three, it has five other neighbors (ie, the cells located at positions (0, MAX_LENGTH_C), (1, MAX_LENGTH_C), (MAX_LENGTH_R, 0), (MAX_LENGTH_R, 1), and (MAX_LENGTH_R, MAX_LENGTH_C), where MAX_LENGTH_C and MAX_LENGTH_R is the maximum index of a column or row in the matrix, respectively. The five are neighbors of cell (0, 0) although they are not located in the proximity of the cell, but in a symmetrical position relative to the vertical and horizontal midline and second diagonal that cross the matrix.

Al cells in the matrix, each described by its state (ie, whether alive or dead) represents a generation. Once passing into a new generation, each cell in the matrix changes its state to a new one, which may happen with a high probability to be the same as the previous state of the cell because the number of possible states is limited to only two. With respect to the implementation of the transition between generations of cells, two matrices are used to store the current and the next generation of cells. If a single matrix is used to store both the current and the next generation, the state of the cells in the current generation would have been altered. An altered current state of a cell becomes the next generation state of the cell before the entire matrix of cells passes into the next generation. This would cause next generation state of the neighboring cells to be computed erroneously because of the dependence on the cell that has already passed into the next generation. This would violate the principle of transition between generations, which asserts that the state of a cell belonging to the next generation is computed only according to the state of the neighbor cells belonging to the current generation.

For starters, let us consider that matrix no. 1 keeps the current generation and matrix no. 2 keeps the next generation. When passing to the next generation, the first matrix is assigned to the content of the second matrix, so the next generation at that time becomes the current one and the roles of the matrices are switched: now the second matrix keeps the current generation and the first matrix will keep the next generation. The switching is continuously performed.

Two vectors of pointers are used to keep the addresses of the first element of each of the rows in the two matrices. The first vector, p_1, references to the content of the current generation matrix and the second vector, namely p_2, points to the content of the next generation matrix (p_1 and p_2 are vectors of pointers to the first element in each row of the first and second matrix, respectively). The computation of the next generation is performed by reading from memory the state of cells in the current generation matrix, which is manipulated using the vector of pointers p_1 and the result is stored in the elements of the next generation matrix, which is accessed using the vector of pointers p_2. Then, the elements at the same index in the two vectors are swapped by the corresponding process that deals with those elements (elements are equal to saying rows in the matrix). This way, the next generation vector (which references to the next generation matrix) becomes the current generation vector on which the computation is exclusively done afterwards to determine the following generation.

Each slave process is in charge of a number of n/p rows in the matrix of cells, where n is the number of rows in the matrix and p is the total number of processes. Thus, for the master process it has remained a number of $n\%p$ rows in the matrix to be in charge of. From a total number of n/p rows which slave process i takes care of, the next generation for a number of $n/p-2$ rows is computed requiring no data sent via messages from the surrounding processes in the ring, namely process $i-1$ and process $i+1$, while the next generation for the first and last row of the n/p rows corresponding to process i is computed depending on the data received from process $i-1$ and $i+1$, respectively. Thereby, slave process i sends the first row of the list of rows it is in charge of to process $i-1$ and the last row to process $i+1$, via messages. Process $i-1$ uses the received row to compute the next generation of the last row which it is in charge of and process $i+1$ uses the received row to compute the first row of the list of rows that it is in charge of.

In this case, the program code gathers all the characteristics of a data parallel program, because it achieves parallelism by dividing the data (ie, the matrix of cells) among processes and having each process apply (more or less) the same operation to its portion of the data.

The messages between processes are sent through functions:

- `MPI_IRecv(buf, count, datatype, source, tag, comm, request)`
- `MPI_ISend(buf, count, datatype, dest, tag, comm, request)`,

which provide a nonblocking manner of message passing as opposed to the functions:

- `MPI_Send(buf, count, datatype, dest, tag, comm)`
- `MPI_Recv(buf, count, datatype, source, tag, comm)`,

which are the blocking version of message passing. Nonblocking message passing allows the process to continue its execution after sending a message and while waiting to receive a message. The functions are called specifying a parameter that describes the tag of the message. There are two tags when it comes to this implementation, the first one is assigned to messages that are sent from the current process to the previous one and received by the current process from the next one in the ring topology, while the second tag is matched with the messages that are sent from the current process to the next one and are received by the current process from the previous one.

To reduce the number of messages sent between processes and, thus, to ease the computation, the last row of the matrix is cloned and kept at the index zero in the current generation vector of pointers because the next generation of the first row of the matrix of cells, kept at index 1, will be computed according to index 0 row. This way, the last slave process will not need to send its last row to the process number zero anymore, that is the master. In the same manner, another row will be added at index $n+1$, where n is the number of rows in the matrix, and this row will be identical to the row at index 1, which is the first row in the matrix of cells. By adding the row at index $n+1$, the master process does not need to send anymore, via a message, to the first row of its list of rows, to the last slave, which needs it to compute the next generation of the last row in the matrix of cells. The content of the current generation vector of pointers is shown in Eq. (1).

$$\begin{aligned} &p1[0] = \&m1[n-1][0] \\ &p1[i] = \&m1[i-1][0], \quad 0 < i \le n \\ &p1[n+1] = \&m1[0][0] \end{aligned} \tag{1}$$

Thus, the row at index zero and at index $n+1$ in the matrix need to be swapped as well for the correctness of the computation, even though they are not part of the matrix of cells, being only the clones of the last and the first row of the matrix, respectively. The swap between the current and the next generation of the row at index zero is assigned to master process. In the case of the swap of row at index $n+1$, because all slaves execute the same section of code, if the swap is placed in the section of code common for all slaves, it would have been performed many times, once for each slave process. So, the swap must be guarded to be executed once per generation transition, meaning by a single process, which may be, for instance, the last slave process in the ring topology.

5.2.3 MPICH IMPLEMENTATION OF THE CELLULAR AUTOMATON

Matrices m_1 and m_2 represent the current and the next generation matrix, respectively. First, the current generation matrix is initialized with the initial state of the cells. The two vectors of pointers p_1 and p_2 store the addresses of the first element in the rows of the two matrices, m_1 and m_2, respectively. The first row in each vector references to the last row in the corresponding matrix and the last row references to the first row in the matrix. The rest of the content of the vector are addresses that point to the rows in the corresponding matrix, namely element at position i in the vector points to row $i-1$ in the matrix, where i is greater than 1 and less than or equal to the size of the matrix. After the initializations are done, the execution of the program spins into multiple processes using the MPI functions:

- `MPI_Init(argc, argv)`
- `MPI_Comm_size(comm, size)`
- `MPI_Comm_rank(comm, rank)`
- `MPI_Get_processor_name(name, resultlen)`

The algorithm is successively applied to multiple generations of cells and it is divided into two sections, one that is being executed by the master and the other that is executed by each slave. The master is in charge of a number of *er* rows and an additional row that has index 0 in the vector p_1. Each slave with *rank* identifier is in charge of a number of *rpp* rows, starting from `(rank - 1) * rpp+1+er` and ending with `(rank - 1) * rpp+er+rpp`, where *rank* is the number of the slave process in the ring as in Eq. (2).

$$(\text{rank}-1)*\text{rpp}+1+\text{er}<i<(\text{rank}-1)*\text{rpp}+\text{er}+\text{rpp} \tag{2}$$

Both the master and the slave processes compute the next generation of their own rows that are not dependent on data from other processes, and they do the processing while sending and receiving messages. Then, when the required data is received, the next generation for the first and the last row of the list of rows the process it is in charge of is computed, as well, before moving to the next generation. Each process swaps its corresponding list of rows. In addition, the master swaps the address at index zero in the vector and the last slave swaps the address at the last index in the vector. Swapping is to be understood as passing to a next generation.

CODE 1. PROGRAM CODE OF THE MPICH VERSION OF GAME OF LIFE

```
int main (int argc, char *argv[])
{
  liveness m1[SIZE][SIZE], m2[SIZE][SIZE];
  liveness *p1[SIZE + 2], *p2[SIZE + 2];
  int nr, nc, ng;
  int i, k, rpp, er, offset;
  int nt, len, rank, next, prev;
  int tag1 = 1, tag2 = 2;
  char hostname[MPI_MAX_PROCESSOR_NAME];
  MPI_Status stats[2];
  MPI_Request reqs[4];
  ...
  initP(p1, m1, p2, m2, nr);
  MPI_Init(&argc,&argv);
  MPI_Comm_size(MPI_COMM_WORLD, &nt);
  MPI_Comm_rank(MPI_COMM_WORLD, &rank);
  MPI_Get_processor_name(hostname, &len);
```

```
er = nr % nt;
if(er == 0) er = nr / nt;
rpp = nr / nt;
for(k = 0; k < ng; k++)
{
  if(rank == MASTER)
  {
   if(nt > 1)
   {
     MPI_Isend(p1[1], nc, MPI_INT, nt - 1, tag2, MPI_COMM_WORLD,
              &reqs[0]);
     MPI_Isend(p1[er], nc, MPI_INT, 1, tag1, MPI_COMM_WORLD, &reqs[1]);
     MPI_Irecv(p1[nr], nc, MPI_INT, nt - 1, tag1, MPI_COMM_WORLD,
              &reqs[2]);
     MPI_Irecv(p1[er+1], nc, MPI_INT, 1, tag2, MPI_COMM_WORLD,
              &reqs[3]);
   }
   for(i = 2; i < er; i++)
     computeRow(p1[i - 1], p1[i], p1[i+1], nc, p2[i]);
   if(nt > 1) MPI_Waitall(4, reqs, stats);
   computeRow(p1[0], p1[1], p1[2], nc, p2[1]);
   if(er > 1) computeRow(p1[er - 1], p1[er], p1[er+1], nc, p2[er]);
   swap(p1, p2, 0, er);
  }
  if(rank > MASTER)
  {
   prev = rank - 1;
   next = rank+1;
   if (rank == (nt - 1))  next = 0;
   MPI_Isend(p1[(rank - 1) * rpp + er + 1], nc, MPI_INT, prev, tag2,
            MPI_COMM_WORLD, &reqs[0]);
   MPI_Isend(p1[rank * rpp - 1 + er + 1], nc, MPI_INT, next, tag1,
            MPI_COMM_WORLD, &reqs[1]);
   MPI_Irecv(p1[(rank - 1) * rpp + er], nc, MPI_INT, prev, tag1,
            MPI_COMM_WORLD, &reqs[2]);
   MPI_Irecv(p1[rank * rpp - 1 + er + 1 + 1], nc, MPI_INT, next, tag2,
            MPI_COMM_WORLD, &reqs[3]);
   offset = (rank - 1) * rpp +1 + er + 1;
   for(i = 0; i < rpp - 2; i++)
   computeRow(p1[offset - 1 + i], p1[offset + i], p1[offset+1 + i],
             nc, p2[offset + i]);
   MPI_Waitall(4, reqs, stats);
   computeRow(p1[(rank - 1) * rpp + er], p1[offset - 1], p1[offset], nc,
             p2[offset - 1]);
```

```
      if(rpp > 1)
        computeRow(p1[offset + rpp - 2 - 1], p1[offset + rpp - 2], p1[rank *
                    rpp - 1 + er + 1 + 1], nc, p2[offset+rpp - 2]);
      swap(p1, p2, er + 1 + (rank - 1)* rpp, rpp - 1);
      if(rank == nt - 1) swap(p1, p2, nr+1, nr+1);
    }
  }
  MPI_Finalize();
}
```

5.3 OpenMP OPTIMIZED APPROACH OF THE CELLULAR AUTOMATON

OpenMP provides a series of compiler directives that are extensions to programming languages such as C/C++ and Fortran. The focus is on the C compiler directives that will be used in this OpenMP approach of this optimized implementation of the Game of Life that will be detailed in the following.

5.3.1 OPEN MULTIPROCESSING

OpenMP directives are applied to structured blocks that are statements with a single entry at the top and a single exit at the bottom. The execution of the program spins into multiple threads using the compiler directive `#pragma omp parallel shared`, which is inserted on the program code. The threads are numbered as well as the processes and a master thread is assigned to be a thread with the identifier zero.

OpenMP facilitates access to the enhanced parallel computing provided by the underlying operating system and hardware architecture [6]. Thus, it is a portable manner of parallelism that does not have to deal with message passing as MPI does. The compiler directives are inserted as comments and treated as so when the compiler is sequential.

5.3.2 DESCRIPTION OF THE OpenMP APPROACH OF THE CELLULAR AUTOMATON

The initial state of the matrix of cells is initialized in a `#pragma omp parallel shared` construct, which creates a team of threads with shared memory (the data shared is the matrix of cells, the dimensions of the matrix) and their own private variables. Next, for each generation, the same construct as mentioned before is applied to the section of code, which computes the new state of the cells. Precisely, for each generation, the computation of the next generation of cells is divided among multiple threads. The cells are grouped in chunks and the chunks are assigned dynamically to threads, so that when a thread finishes a chunk, another chunk is assigned to it.

5.3.3 OpenMP IMPLEMENTATION OF THE CELLULAR AUTOMATON

The matrices m_1 and m_2 represent the current and the next generation matrices as well, as in case of the MPICH approach. p_1 and p_2 represent pointers to the first element of the first row in matrices m_1 and m_2, respectively. When computing the next generation of the cells, a number of *chunk* iterations of the loops that iterate through the cells in the matrix is assigned to each thread and when the thread finishes the current chunk, it receives another chunk. The question that raises is: Which is the proper number of iterations per chunk depending on the matrix dimension so as to obtain the best execution time?

CODE 2. PROGRAM CODE OF THE OPENMP VERSION OF GAME OF LIFE

```
int main (int argc, char *argv[])
{
  int nthreads, i, j, k, chunk = 10;
  int noOfRows, noOfColoumns, noOfGeneration;
  liveness m1[SIZE][SIZE], m2[SIZE][SIZE], *p, *p2, *aux;
  #pragma omp parallel shared(f,m1,noOfRows,noOfColoumns,nthreads,chunk)
                      private(tid,i,j)
  {
    #pragma omp for schedule (static, chunk)
    for(i = 0; i < noOfRows; i++)
      for(j = 0; j < noOfColoumns; j++)
        fscanf(f,"%d ", &m1[i][j]);
  }
  fclose(f);
  p = &m1[0][0];
  p2 = &m2[0][0];
  for(k = 0; k < noOfGenerations; k++)
  {
     #pragma omp parallel shared(m1,m2,noOfRows,noOfColoumns,chunk)
                         private(i,j)
     {
        #pragma omp for schedule (dynamic, chunk)
        for(i = 0; i < noOfRows; i++)
          for(j = 0; j < noOfRows; j++)
            *(p2+i * noOfColoumns + j) =
                              computeCell(i,j,p,noOfRows,noOfColoumns);
     }
     aux = p;
     p = p2;
     p2 = aux;
  }
}
```

5.4 EXECUTION TIME COMPARISON OF THE TWO PARALLEL IMPLEMENTATIONS

Ring topology makes the MPICH approach optimized in terms of execution time. If all slaves would communicate directly with the master process, through message exchange, like it happens in a star topology, than the master would be overloaded. In the ring, all processes have the same amount of message overhead, which enhances the improvement in terms of execution time, as the message overhead is spread across multiple processes that run in parallel, so the time spent with the overhead is also parallelized.

When it comes to OpenMP implementation, the optimization arises from the fact that the matrix is initialized in parallel and from the number of iterations executed by each thread called chunk, which is carefully chosen. The proper number of iterations to be executed by a thread is 10 when the dimensions of the matrix are under 100 × 100.

Table 5.1 presents the execution time in seconds of both the MPICH and OpenMP program code that is executed by a certain number of processes in the case of MPICH and threads in the case of OpenMP for a matrix of dimension 10 × 10. Table 5.2 is based on the same configurations, except that the matrix dimension is 100 × 100.

An MPI application that uses thousands of processors faces many scalability issues that can drastically decrease the overall performance of any parallel application. Some of the issues are process control, resource exhaustion, latency awareness and management, fault tolerance, and optimized collective operations for a common communication pattern [7].

If Game of Life's program code runs on a number of processes bigger than 10, the execution time is much bigger than if the program runs on the same number of threads as in case of OpenMP implementation. In the second case, the matrix of cells is shared by all threads, as opposed to the case of processes that have their own memory. The lack of shared memory makes the MPICH implementation execution time less effective when the number of processes is bigger than 10.

The execution time of the serial version of Game of Life cellular automaton, in the case of the matrix dimension 10 × 10 is 0.14 s and in the case of the matrix dimensions 100 × 100 is 0.33 s.

Table 5.1 Parallel Execution Time for Small Dimension Matrix of Cells

MPI Version — No. of Generations 100		*OpenMP Version* — No. of Generations 100	
No. of Processes	**Matrix Size 10 × 10 (s)**	**No. of Threads**	**Matrix Size 10 × 10 (s)**
1	0.033	1	0.007
2	0.134	2	0.036
4	0.374	4	0.046
8	0.409	8	0.06
10	0.964	10	0.115

Table 5.2 Parallel Execution Time for Medium Dimension Matrix of Cells

MPI Version — No. of Generations 100		*OpenMP Version* — No. of Generations 100	
No. of Processes	**Matrix Size 10 × 10 (s)**	**No. of Threads**	**Matrix Size 10 × 10 (s)**
1	0.243	1	0.273
2	0.29	2	0.322
4	0.39	4	0.263
8	0.976	8	0.17
10	1.008	10	0.335
20	2.521	20	0.404
50	4.224	50	0.484

The results in Tables 5.1 and 5.2 are registered on an AMD Athlon X2 64-bit dual core hardware architecture, Windows 7 operating system. Thus, because of the reduced number of cores, the results are considered the worst case for parallel hardware architectures. Because the worst case improves the execution time compared to the serial version, the experimental results are considered to be significantly optimized for a hardware architecture with a greater number of cores.

5.5 CONCLUSIONS

The Game of Life cellular automaton simulates the evolution in time of the pigmented human cells according to certain rules clearly established, during multiple and possibly an infinite number of transitions from one generation to another. A transition describes a change of the state of all the cells in the matrix (ie, human skin) compared to the previous generation (a new state is allowed to be the same as the one in the previous generation). The pigmented cells are considered to be the live cells of the Game of Life automaton, regardless of their color shade.

An interesting discovery was made by Bill Gosper and his team from Massachusetts Institute of Technology: it states that there are different initial patterns (ie, initial states) that produce an infinite growth of the live cells. This situation corresponds to persons who have their pigmentation extended on their back and keeps extending throughout their body during their entire lifetime.

A mathematical model that gets even closer to the biological phenomenon of evolution of the skin pigmentation can be one in which the shape of the cells is a hexagon. The number of neighbors of such a cell could be 6 or 12 and the evolution process of a cell would be conducted by a slightly modified version of the rules presented in the Introduction section of this chapter. Thus, the rules would be changed, but the core of the implementation of the parallel algorithms would be kept the same; that is, the number of chunks will not be modified in the case of OpenMP implementation of the cellular automaton and the topology will be unchanged in the case of MPICH implementation).

The OpenMP version of the implementation of the Game of Life is considered to be optimized as the number of iterations per thread is chosen to be 10 for a matrix dimension less than 100×100, which produces a reasonable amount of work to do for each thread and avoids assigning chunks to threads so often, which would be time-consuming.

The MPICH approach of the implementation of the Game of Life cellular automaton has been chosen to be based on a ring topology of processes that exchange messages with the neighbor processes as this proves to be the most optimized version of the cellular automaton because the ring topology avoids the message overhead of the master process that occurs in the case of a star topology.

> The parallel implementations of the Game of Life automaton anticipate and speed up the computation of the evolutionary process of skin pigmentation during the lifetime of a human.

Regarding the actual trends with respect to parallel API's, Pthreads, and OpenMP are the most widely used in shared memory systems. Pthreads may often require reorganization of the program's structure, as opposed to OpenMP directives. OpenMP does not yet provide expression of locality and modularity that may be needed for multicore applications [8]. Besides MPICH, another implementation of MPI is MPICH-G2 (a grid-enabled implementation of the MPI), which allows a user to run MPI programs across multiple computers, at the same or different sites, using the same commands that would be used on a parallel computer. This library extends the Argonne MPICH implementation of MPI to use services as "authentication, authorization, resource allocation, executable staging, and I/O, as well as process creation, monitoring, and control" [9].

REFERENCES

[1] Wah BW. Wiley encyclopedia of computer science and engineering. Canada: Wiley and Sons; 2009. p. 305.
[2] Dagum L, Menon R. OpenMP: an industry standard API for shared memory programming. IEEE Comput Sci Eng 2002;5:46.
[3] Thakur R, Rabenseifner R, Gropp W. Optimization of collective communication operations in MPICH. Int J High Perform Comput Appl 2005;19(1):49–66.
[4] Cristea V. Algorithmi de prelucrare paralela. Romania: MatrixRom Publishing; 2002. p. 116.
[5] Niculescu V. Calcul parallel. Proiectare si dezvoltare formala a programelor paralele. Romania: Presa Universitara Clujeana Publishing; 2005. p. 52.
[6] Chandra R, Dagum L, Kohr D, Maydan D, McDonald J, Menon R. Parallel programming in OpenMP. San Francisco, CA: Morgan Kaufmann; 2001. p. 4.
[7] Nicholas TK, Toonen B, Foster I. MPICH-G2: a grid-enabled implementation of the message passing interface. J Parallel Distrib Comput 2003;63(5):551–563.
[8] Chapman B, Huang L. Parallel computing: architectures, algorithms and applications. Advances in parallel computing, vol. 15. Netherlands: Ios Press Publishing; 2008. p. 4.
[9] Gabriel E, et al. Open MPI: goals, concepts and design of the next generation MPI implementation. In: Recent advances in parallel virtual machines and message passing interface. Lecture notes in computer science, vol. 3241. Springer Berlin Heidelberg; 2004. p. 98.

SECTION

II

BIOINFORMATICS, SIMULATION, DATA MINING, PATTERN DISCOVERY, AND PREDICTION METHODS

CHAPTER

STRUCTURE CALCULATION OF α, α/β, β PROTEINS FROM RESIDUAL DIPOLAR COUPLING DATA USING REDCRAFT

6

C.A. Cole*, D. Ishimaru†, M. Hennig‡, H. Valafar*

*Department of Computer Science and Engineering, University of South Carolina, Columbia, SC, United States**
Department of Biochemistry and Molecular Biology, Medical University of South Carolina, Charleston, SC, United States† Nutrition Research Institute, University of North Carolina at Chapel Hill, Kannapolis, NC, United States‡

6.1 INTRODUCTION

Calculation of protein structures plays a critical role in establishing their biological function and the mechanism by which they accomplish their function. Therefore an understanding of protein structure serves as the first and critical step in understanding the molecular basis of nearly all diseases. Traditional means of structure determination by nuclear magnetic resonance (NMR) spectroscopy and X-ray crystallography have made significant advances in the past decades. However, despite these advances, their deployment is confined to only a limited class of proteins while imposing a substantial financial cost. Therefore development of more cost-effective and inclusive means of structure determination is the subject of pursuit in the international scientific community.

In recent years, the use of residual dipolar coupling (RDC) data acquired from NMR spectroscopy has become a potential avenue for a significant reduction in the cost of structure determination of proteins. Recent work [1–4] has demonstrated the challenges in structure calculation of proteins from RDC data alone, and some potential solutions have been introduced [2,3,5]. One such approach, named residual dipolar coupling-based residue assembly and filter tool (REDCRAFT) [1,4–6], has been demonstrated to be successful in structure calculation of proteins from a reduced set of RDC data. Although REDCRAFT's ability in structure calculation of proteins has been documented with experimental data from aqueous [7–9] and membrane [10] proteins, the limitations of its capabilities have not been explored under controlled conditions. Therefore the primary objective in this research is to perform a feasibility study for structure calculation of a representative collection of proteins using synthetic RDCs. Our feasibility study will establish the minimum required data for unambiguous structure calculation for α, β, and α/β proteins, and explore REDCRAFT's robustness to experimental noise. A better understanding of minimum data requirement will help to alleviate the cost of structure determination by avoiding acquisition of unneeded data.

6.2 BACKGROUND AND METHOD

6.2.1 RESIDUAL DIPOLAR COUPLINGS

RDCs can be acquired via NMR spectroscopy. The theoretical basis of RDC interaction had been established and experimentally observed in 1963 [11]. However, it has only become a more prevalent source of data for structure determination of biological macromolecules in recent years due to the availability of alignment media. Upon the reintroduction of order to an isotropically tumbling molecule, RDCs can be easily acquired. The RDC interaction between two atoms in space can be formulated as shown in Eq. (1).

$$D_{ij} = D_{\max}\left\langle \frac{3\cos^2(\theta_{ij}(t)) - 1}{2} \right\rangle \tag{1}$$

$$D_{\max} = \frac{-\mu_0 \gamma_i \gamma_j h}{(2\pi r)^3} \tag{2}$$

In this equation, D_{ij} denotes the RDC in units of Hz between nuclei i and j. The θ_{ij} represents the time-dependent angle of the internuclear vector between nuclei i and j with respect to the external magnetic field, and the angle brackets signify time averaging. In Eq. (2), $D_{\max}$ represents a scalar multiplier dependent on the two interacting nuclei. In this equation, γ_i and γ_j are nuclear gyromagnetic ratios, r is the internuclear distance (assumed fixed for directly bonded atoms), h is the modified Planck's constant, and μ_0 represents the permeability of free space.

6.2.2 REDCRAFT STRUCTURAL FITNESS CALCULATION

While generating a protein structure from a given set of RDCs is nontrivial, it is straightforward to determine how well a given structure fits a set of RDCs. Through algebraic manipulation of Eq. (1) RDC interaction can be represented as shown in Eq. (3),

$$D_{ij} = v_{ij} * S * v_{ij}^T \tag{3}$$

where S represents the Saupe order tensor matrix [11] and v_{ij} denotes the normalized interacting vector between the two interacting nuclei i and j. REDCRAFT takes advantage of this principle by quantifying the fitness of a protein to a given set of RDCs (in units of Hz) and calculating a root-mean-squared deviation as shown in Eq. (4). In this equation D_{ij} and D'_{ij} denote the computed and experimentally acquired RDCs, respectively, N, represents the total number of RDCs for the entire protein, and M represents the total number of alignment media in which RDC data have been acquired. In this case a smaller fitness value indicates a better structure.

$$Fitness = \sqrt{\frac{\sum_{j=1}^{M}\sum_{i=1}^{N}\left(D_{ij} - D'_{ij}\right)^2}{M * N}} \tag{4}$$

The REDCRAFT algorithm and its success in protein structure elucidation has been previously described and documented in detail [1,7,8,10,12]. Here we present a brief overview. REDCRAFT calculates structures from RDCs using two separate stages. In the first stage (*Stage-I*), a list of all possible discretized torsion angles is created for each pair of adjoining peptide planes. This list is then filtered based on allowable regions within the Ramachandran space [13]. The list of torsion angles that remain are then ranked based on fitness to the RDC data. These lists of potential angle configurations are used to reduce the search space for the second stage.

Stage-II begins by constructing the first two peptide planes of the protein. Every possible combination of angles from *Stage-I* between peptide planes i and $i+1$ are evaluated for fitness with respect to the collected data, and the best n candidate structures are selected, where n denotes the search depth. The list of dihedral angles corresponding to the top n structures are then combined with every possible set of dihedral angles connecting the next peptide plane to the current fragment. Each of these candidate structures is evaluated for fitness and the best n are again selected and carried forward for additional rounds of elongation. All combination of dihedral angles worse than the best n are eliminated, thus removing an exponential number of candidate structures from the search space. This elongation process is repeated iteratively, incrementally adding peptide planes until the entire protein is constructed.

The number of RDCs required to correctly fold a novel protein with a bundle of four nearly parallel helices with REDCRAFT has not been previously examined in a systematic manner. Here we investigate the effect of reducing the available RDCs on the quality of the resulting computational structure. Collecting fewer RDCs per peptide plane can substantially reduce data collection times. In particular, ^{15}N-^{1}H RDCs are easily collected because they avoid expensive ^{13}C labeling. Furthermore, ^{15}N-^{1}H RDC values are typically large in magnitude, reducing the effect of measurement error. C_α-H_α RDCs are large in magnitude but require ^{13}C labeling, complicating sample preparation. RDCs for additional vectors can be collected, but with a decreasing utility and at a greater expense.

6.2.3 THE ENSEMBLE OF TEST PROTEINS

To better investigate the limits of our structure calculation strategy across different classes of protein structures, we have selected a sample protein from each of the three main protein structure classification database (CATH) [14] classes: (I) all α helical proteins, (II) all β strand proteins, and (III) α/β proteins.

Our representative protein from CATH I (α helical proteins) is a novel, 71 residue protein PF2048.1 (seen in Fig. 6.1A). This protein has less than 17% sequence identity to any structurally characterized protein in PDB (as of October, 2015). PF2048.1 was expressed in *Escherichia coli* as an N-terminal His_6-GB1 fusion that can be efficiently cleaved by tobacco etch virus (TEV) protease introducing a single (nonnative) Gly residue at position −1. Nearly complete assignments for backbone and side-chain

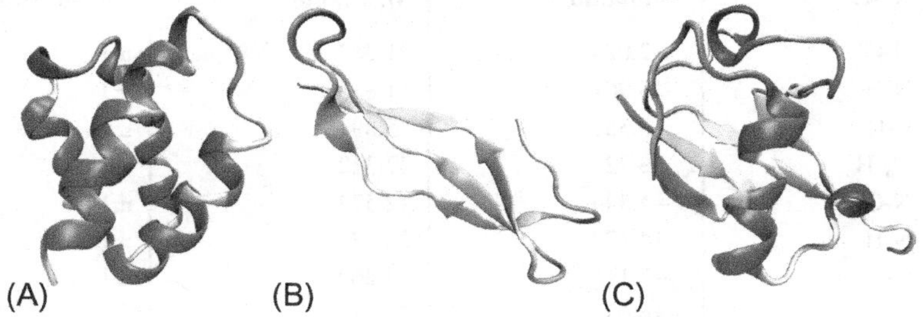

FIGURE 6.1

(A) Pf2048.1 (72 residue α protein), (B) 4OZK (49 residue β protein), and (C) 1D3Z (76 residue α/β protein).

protons, carbons and nitrogens were obtained using standard NMR methods. The resulting 1045 nuclear Overhauser effect (NOE) restraints together with torsion angle likelihood obtained from shift (TALOS) [15] backbone torsion restraints were employed to determine an experimental target structure. The computationally modeled structure of this protein that is in sufficient agreement with the experimental data is used throughout this exercise. The actual structure of this protein is currently under refinement and will soon be deposited to the Protein Data Bank [16]. The challenges in structure calculation of PF2048.1 from RDC data has been previously documented [6]. Here we use the previous results of PF2048.1 as the basis of comparison for other protein classes, and use it to further study the impact of noisy data in structure calculation of proteins using RDC data. From CATH II (β proteins) we have selected a 49-residue toxin extracted from the *Brevibacillus laterosporus* bacterium (PDB ID 4OZK). Seen in Fig. 6.1B, 4OZK contains three twisted beta strands. Finally, we have selected a 76-residue NMR structure of ubiquitin (PDB ID 1D3Z) from the CATH III class (mixed α/β proteins). This structure, seen in Fig. 6.1C, contains two beta sheets and an alpha helix.

6.2.4 SIMULATED RDC DATA

Using REDCAT (REsidual Dipolar Coupling Analysis Tool) [17,18] and the reference structures, RDCs were simulated in two alignment media using the order tensors in Table 6.1. Error of ±1 Hz was uniformly added across all RDC vectors to simulate experimental noise in the data sets. Table 6.2 summarizes the minimum and maximum values for each RDC vector corresponding to these order tensors listed in Table 6.1. The uniform distribution of ±1 Hz error left us with a variety of mildly

Table 6.1 Order Tensors Used for Synthetic RDC Calculation

	Sxx	Syy	Szz	Alpha	Beta	Gamma
M1	3×10^{-4}	5×10^{-4}	-8×10^{-4}	0	0	0
M2	-4×10^{-4}	-6×10^{-4}	10×10^{-4}	40	50	−60

Table 6.2 Columns 2 and 3 Display Minimum and Maximum RDC Values for Each Vector Set Using the Order Tensors in Table 6.1 in Two Alignment Media (M1 and M2)

	RDC	Minimum	Maximum	Added Noise (Hz)
M1	N-C	−2.029	1.287	±1
	N-H	−18.904	11.815	±1
	C-H	−3.557	5.692	±1
	C_α-H_α	−23.32	37.312	±1
M2	N-C	−1.544	2.574	±1
	N-H	−14.178	23.63	±1
	C-H	−7.115	4.269	±1
	C_α-H_α	−46.64	27.984	±1

Note: *The last column summarizes the range of uniformly distributed noise that was added to each data set.*

noisy RDCs (in the case of N-H where ±1 Hz of error is well within the total range of RDC values) to very noisy RDCs (in the case of N-C and C-H where the range of values is much smaller and ±1 Hz of error makes a considerable difference).

To establish the error tolerance of REDCRAFT in structure determination of proteins from RDC data, we have generated RDC data with varying degrees of error. In this exercise REDCAT was used to corrupt the computed RDC data with uniform error in the range of 1–6 Hz in 1 Hz increments. REDCRAFT was then deployed on each set of the data and observations were made related to the quality of the final computed structure. Results of this exercise will help in establishing the reliability of structure calculation by REDCRAFT under given noisy data conditions.

6.2.5 EVALUATION

Our evaluation in the data quantity for successful structure determination was proceeded by incremental reduction in the data quantity; maintaining the RDC data that are easiest to acquire from NMR spectroscopy. To that end, we proceeded by first eliminating C_α-H_α RDC data from both alignment media because its acquisition increases the cost of protein production and data acquisition significantly. The second phase of our investigation focused on reducing the RDC data sets from three RDCs per alignment medium, to three from the first alignment medium and one from the second alignment medium. For our last data set we reintroduce the C_α-H_α data and use it along with N-H data for a total of two RDCs from each alignment medium.

The software REDCRAFT will be utilized for our structure calculation without refinement in any other auxiliary program. Introduction of any additional refinement step could potentially introduce ambiguities to our evaluation process. We anticipated that consistent with principles of information theory, more extensive search parameters of REDCRAFT will need to be enabled as a function of reduced data sets to compensate for the absence of information.

The software packages PyMOL [19] and VMD [20] were utilized to calculate the backbone root-mean-squared deviation (bb-rmsd) between the REDCRAFT-generated structure and its respective target structures and also for visualization and rendering purposes. The measure of bb-rmsd is prevalently used to establish the structure similarity between two proteins and values under 3.5 Å and can signify the presence of structural resemblance, while values under 2 Å can be interpreted as strong structural resemblance.

The other measure that was used to evaluate the calculated structures was the RDC fitness score calculated by REDCRAFT (discussed in detail in Section 6.2.2). This fitness score provides information regarding how well the RDCs fit the final structure. A structure is considered to be of acceptable quality if its RDC score falls below the error level of the data (in our case less than 1 Hz). A lower score can be well correlated with an improved quality of the calculated structure.

6.3 RESULTS AND DISCUSSION

To evaluate the ability of REDCRAFT in calculating the correct structure of our three test proteins, five test cases were established. In each of the cases the amount of data was varied to simulate five different possible data sets. The data sets are summarized in Table 6.3.

Table 6.3 Summary of the RDCs Used in Each Experiment

Set	Medium #1 RDCs	Medium #2 RDCs
1 (4,4)	{C-N, N-H, C-H, C_α-H_α}	{C-N, N-H, C-H, C_α-H_α}
2 (4,1)	{C-N, N-H, C-H, C_α-H_α}	{N-H}
3 (3,3)	{C-N, N-H, C-H}	{C-N, N-H, C-H}
4 (3,1)	{C-N, N-H, C-H}	{N-H}
5 (2,2)	{N-H, C_α-H_α}	{N-H, C_α-H_α}

In the sections that follow we will report our findings for each of the cases in Table 6.3 to establish the feasibility of successful protein structure elucidation with the given data set.

6.3.1 STRUCTURE CALCULATION OF AN α PROTEIN

Structure calculation of PF2048 from varying quantities of RDC data using REDCRAFT has been previously reported [6]. To better facilitate comparison of results to other proteins, in this section we present a summary of the previous work on the protein PF2048.1. Structures depicted in Fig. 6.2 are the results of REDCRAFT structure calculation corresponding to each row of experimental conditions listed in Table 6.3. In addition to the five experimental conditions listed in this table, one additional experiment was also conducted that includes {C-N, N-H} RDCs from the first alignment medium and {N-H} from the second alignment medium. Table 6.4 summarizes the bb-rmsd and RDC fitness scores for each of the structures and experiments. From these results we concluded that REDCRAFT can consistently fold a protein with as much as three RDCs from two alignment media, without the need for C_α-H_α RDCs. Furthermore, REDCRAFT may successfully fold a protein with as little as two RDCs from the first alignment medium and one from the second alignment medium under some conditions. The conditions allowing for folding of proteins with less than three RDCs per alignment medium includes the availability of secondary structural restraints. In this chapter we focus on folding without these additional restraints that may or may not be available at the time of structure calculation.

6.3.2 STRUCTURE CALCULATION OF AN α/β PROTEIN

Table 6.5 describes the general configuration of REDCRAFT used throughout the experiments conducted on the protein 1D3Z. Any changes in the REDCRAFT configuration are denoted in the appropriate subsection.

Results from 4,4 — The REDCRAFT configuration file remained consistent with the general configuration shown in Table 6.5. The resulting structure, seen in Fig. 6.3A, exhibited a bb-rmsd of 1.586 Å from the target structure with the ending RDC fitness score was 1.19.

Results from 4,1 — In this case due to the reduction of data the score threshold (S.T.) was decreased to 1.2. This configuration produced a structure with 1.958 Å of structural difference with respect to the target structure and a RDC fitness score of 0.922. The corresponding structure is shown in Fig. 6.3B.

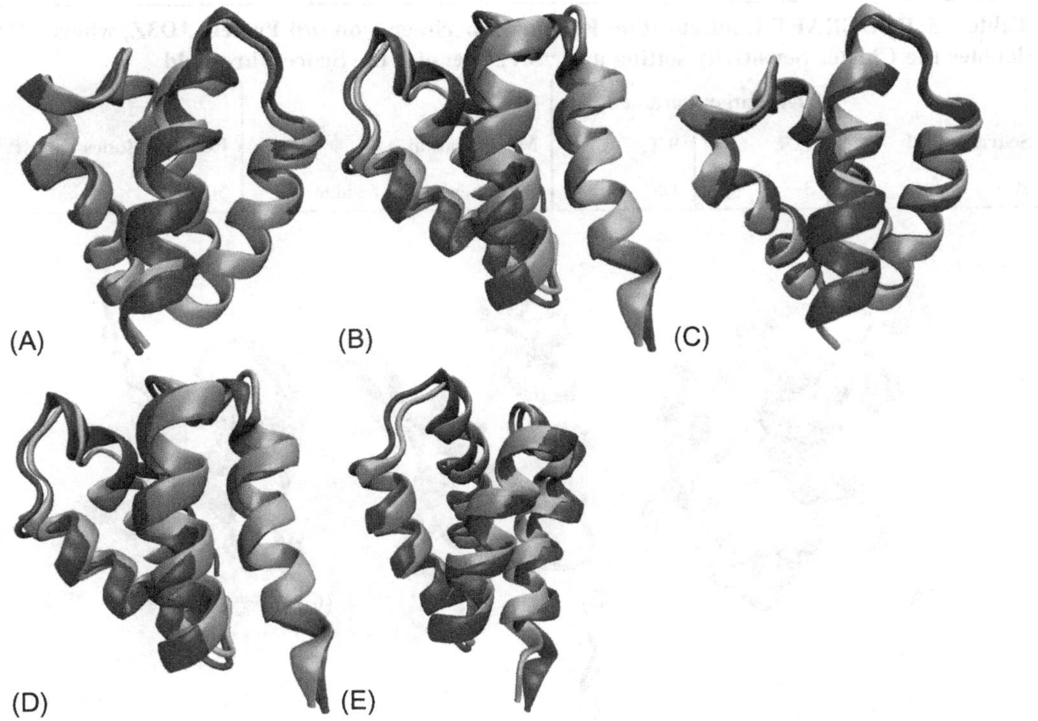

FIGURE 6.2

Each frame contains the resulting structure of an experiment (in *light grey*) superimposed onto the target structure (PF2048.1 in *dark grey*). (A) Result from 4,4, (B) result from 4,1, (C) result from 3,3, (D) result from 3,1, (E) result from 2,2.

Table 6.4 Summary of Results for PF2048.1 Experiments

Experiment	BB-RMSD (Å)	RDC Fitness Score
4,4	1.035	0.776
4,1	1.594	0.741
3,3	1.002	0.382
3,1[a]	1.594	0.741
2,2[b]	1.209	0.667

[a]*Indicates the cases where results of calculations are machine dependent.*
[b]*Indicates new results for PF2048.1 not published in our previous work.*

Table 6.5 REDCRAFT Configuration File for Experiments on α/β Protein 1D3Z, where "C.S" denotes the Cluster Sensitivity setting and "S.T." denotes the Score Threshold

	Decimation Parameters			
Search Depth	C.S.	S.T.	Minimization	Lennard Jones Cutoff
200	3	1.5	Performed every residue	50.0

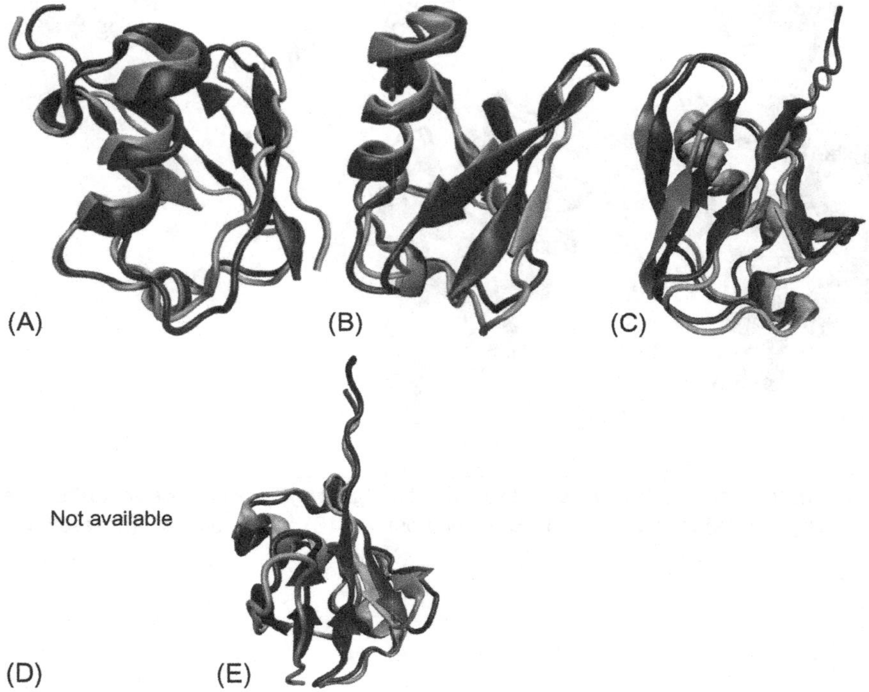

FIGURE 6.3

Each frame contains the resulting structure of a certain experiment (in *light grey*) aligned to the target structure (1D3Z in *dark grey*). (A) Result from 4,4, (B) result from 4,1, (C) result from 3,3, (D) result from 3,1, (E) result from 2,2.

Results from 3,3 — In the case of 3,3 the S.T. was set to 1.0 however, at residue 5 the contribution of decimation drops to 0. This suggests that the experiment of 3,3 requires practically no decimation to successfully fold the protein to within 2 Å of the target structure. The precise bb-rmsd to the target structure was 1.677 Å and RDC fitness score was 1.0. The resulting structure can be seen in Fig. 6.3C. It is possible with the addition of decimation parameters that this result will become even better.

Results from 3,1 — Several configurations were tried for the data set 3,1 on the α/β protein. None of these attempts were able to consistently fold the protein. The failure of this combination of RDCs is something that has not been observed and properly discussed in the past. Theoretical explanation of this pathological condition is presented in Section 6.4.

Table 6.6 Summary of Results from 1D3Z Experiments		
Experiment	**BB-RMSD (Å)**	**RDC Fitness Score**
4,4	1.586	1.19
4,1	1.958	0.992
3,3	1.710	1.00
3,1	–	–
2,2	1.790	0.919

Results from 2,2 — For the case of 2,2 the S.T. was decreased from 1.5 to 1.25. This resulted in a structure, seen in Fig. 6.3E, with a bb-rmsd of 1.79 Å from the target structure. The RDC fitness score converged to 0.919.

Summary of results for α/β protein — Fig. 6.3 shows the resulting structures for each of the experiments (excluding 3,1 since no structure was obtained) aligned to the target structure. Table 6.6 summarizes the results described above for each experiment on the α/β protein. We witness that, as in the α protein experiments, the cases using more than one RDC in the second alignment media do consistently better than the cases with a singular RDC.

6.3.3 STRUCTURE CALCULATION OF A β PROTEIN

Table 6.7 describes the general configuration of REDCRAFT used throughout the experiments conducted on the protein 4OZK. Any changes in the REDCRAFT configuration are denoted in the appropriate subsection.

Results from 4,4 — The case of 4,4 was seemingly a straightforward case to fold and required no added decimation. The final structure, seen in Fig. 6.4A, exhibited a bb-rmsd of 1.887 Å to the target structure and a RDC fitness score of 1.189. However, we postulate that with the addition of the decimation feature these scores will improve.

Results from 4,1 — The case of 4,1 required the highest S.T. (1.5) and was generally a challenging case. The final structure, seen in Fig. 6.4B, exhibited a bb-rmsd of 2.723 Å to the target structure at residue 44 and a RDC fitness score of 1.316. In the last five residues the beta strand turns on itself instead of remaining straight, causing the bb-rmsd to jump to over 5 Å in this portion. However, it is worth noting that in this same section the RDC fitness score does not show the same spike. This again points to a possible degeneracy that we will discuss in Section 6.4.

Table 6.7 REDCRAFT Parameters for Beta Protein Experiments, where "C.S." denotes the Cluster Sensitivity setting and "S.T." denotes the Score Threshold

	Decimation Parameters			
Search Depth	**C.S.**	**S.T.**	**Minimization**	**Lennard Jones Cutoff**
200	3	1.4	Performed every residue	50.0

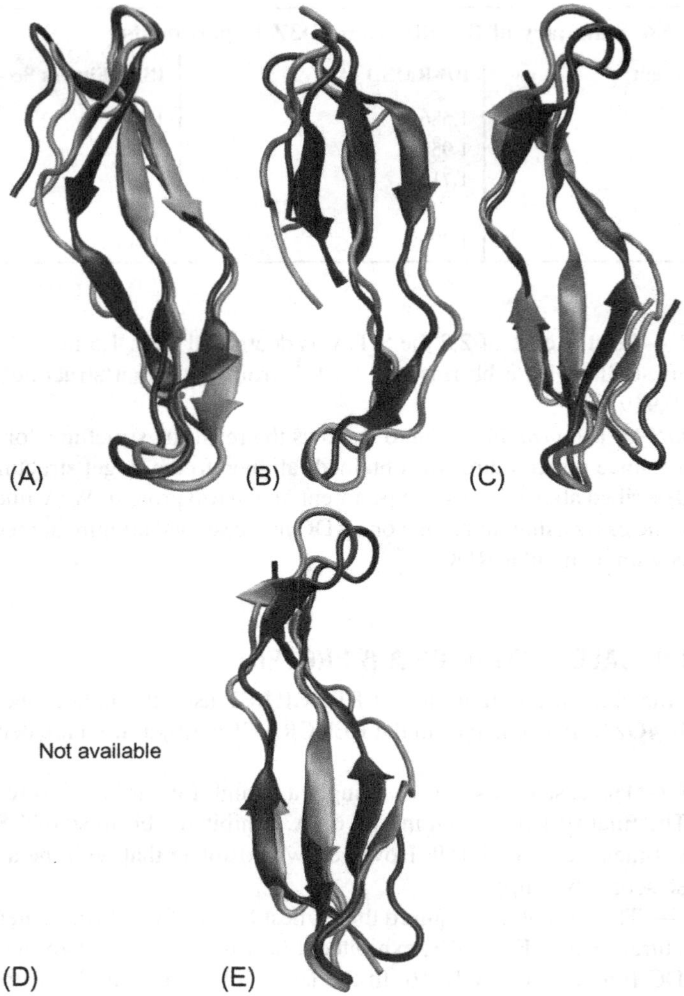

FIGURE 6.4

Each frame contains the results of a certain experiment (in *light grey*) aligned to the target structure (4OZK in *dark grey*). (A) Result from 4,4, (B) result from 4,1, (C) result from 3,3, (D) result from 3,1, (E) result from 2,2.

Results from 3,3 — In the case of 3,3 the configuration file remained the same as in Table 6.7. The resulting structure exhibited bb-rmsd of 1.892 Å to 4OZK and a RDC fitness score of 1.065. Fig. 6.4C shows the resulting structure aligned to the target structure.

Results from 3,1 — As in the case of the α/β protein, several configurations were tried for the data set 3,1 on the β protein. Again, none of these attempts were able to consistently fold the protein.

Table 6.8 Summary of Results from 4OZK Experiments

Experiment	BB-RMSD (Å)	RDC Fitness Score
4,4	1.887	1.189
4,1	2.723	1.316
3,3	1.892	1.065
3,1	–	–
2,2	1.983	0.719

Results from 2,2 — Due to the reduction in data in the case of 2,2, the S.T. was lowered to 1.0 in this experiment. The ending structure, seen in Fig. 6.4E, exhibited a bb-rmsd of 1.983 Å to the target structure. The final RDC fitness score was 0.719.

Summary of results from β protein — Fig. 6.4 shows the resulting structures for each of the experiments (excluding 3,1) aligned to the target structure. Table 6.8 summarizes the results described above for each experiment on the β protein. Our results here also confirm that experiments utilizing more than one RDC in the second alignment media do significantly better than those with singular {N-H} sets.

6.3.4 EFFECT OF ERROR IN STRUCTURE CALCULATION

To assess the effect of error in structure calculation from RDCs we selected one of the experimental configurations and iteratively added error to the data to create six separate erroneous test sets. We have selected the case of the 4,4 RDC set on PF2048.1 because of its unparalleled success in folding PF2048.1 without use of high decimation parameters or other excessive minimization approaches. The test cases span ±1 Hz to ±6 Hz of uniformly distributed error. For all of the experiments the REDCRAFT configuration file took on the parameters described in Table 6.9 with only the S.T. varying throughout the runs. These changes and the results are summarized in Table 6.10. The resulting structures from each experiment can be seen in Fig. 6.5.

As seen in Fig. 6.5, REDCRAFT was successful in reconstruction of the protein even when the RDC data included 5 Hz of added error. However, at 6 Hz of error REDCRAFT is unable to reconstruct the protein. In this experiment the structure diverges in the first loop region causing the remaining three helices to be shifted. Fig. 6.5F shows the last three helices superimposed with a bb-rmsd of 1.08 Å away from the target structure. The first helix can be seen at the bottom right of the image clearly diverging from the rest of the structure. It is likely that at this point REDCRAFT's search mechanism diverges due to lack of data and is unable to properly orient the helix. In this case, lack of data in

Table 6.9 REDCRAFT Parameters for Error Assessment Experiments

	Decimation Parameters			
Search Depth	C.S.	S.T.	Minimization	Lennard Jones Cutoff
200	3	1.0	Performed every residue	50.0

Table 6.10 Summary of Results of Error Assessment Experiments

Experiment (Hz)	Score Threshold (S.T.)	BB-RMSD (Å)	RDC Fitness Score
1	1.0	1.035	0.776
2	1.0	0.760	1.237
3	2.0	2.183	1.722
4	2.5	1.852	2.089
5	3.0	2.084	2.451
6	3.5	5.119	3.032

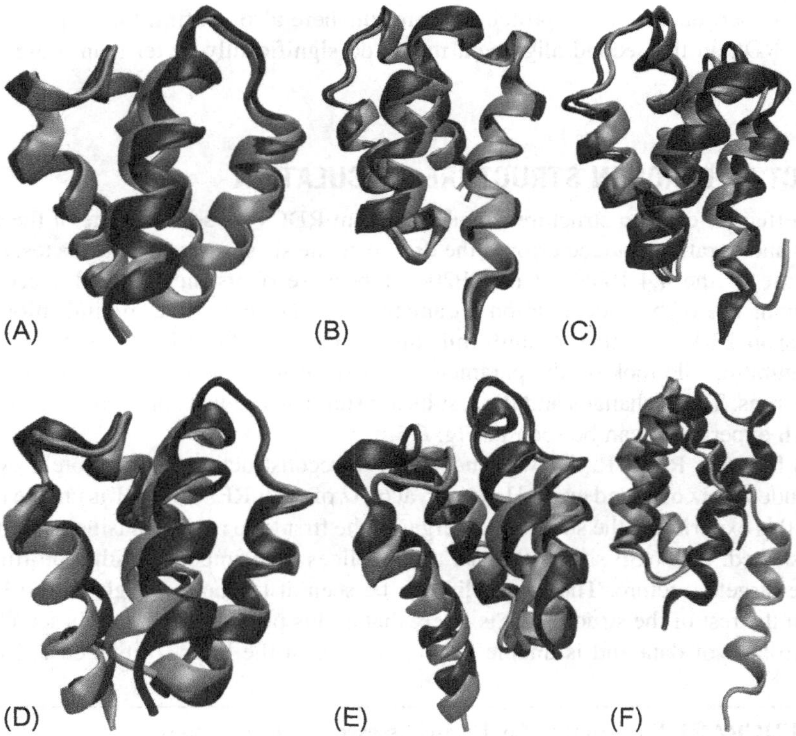

FIGURE 6.5

Each frame contains the resulting structure from a certain experiment (in *light grey*) aligned to the target structure (PF2048.1 in *dark grey*). (A) Result from 1 Hz added error, (B) result from 2 Hz added error, (C) result from 3 Hz added error, (D) result from 4 Hz added error, (E) result from 5 Hz added error, (F) result from 6 Hz added error.

the loop region is caused by the existence of a proline in which N-H and C-H vectors are missing. While this is our immediate conclusion, it is possible for alteration of REDCRAFT's other parameters to result in proper reconstruction of the structure. However, in these situations where structure is shifted tools in which structures can be aligned based on structure and not just sequence like msTALI [21] can give a much more informative assessment of structural similarity.

6.4 CONCLUSION

Exploration of the minimum data requirement is useful to establish the expected financial cost of a protein's structure determination. An exploration mechanism such as the one presented here will allow for appropriate allocation of resources as a function of a protein's medical or biological importance. This is a critical contribution to the repertoire of structure determination approaches especially in the context of personalized medicine where funds can be appropriately allocated toward culprit proteins in human diseases.

Our investigation through exploration of the five exercises listed in Section 6.3 has revealed with a high degree of certainty that structure determination of α, α/β, and β proteins can be accomplished with as little as {N-H, C_α-H_α} from two alignment media alone. However, we believe that more thorough exploration of REDCRAFT's search options, combined with addition of readily available restraints (such as dihedral restraints or scalar couplings) can reduce the needed data set further. This expectation is rooted in observations made in our previous work [6], in which data were reduced to just {C-N, N-H} from one alignment medium and {N-H} from the other. Inclusion of dihedral restraint not only helped to recover the structure of PF2048.1, but it produced the most accurate structure (to within 0.533 Å of the target protein). In this context our definition of dihedral restraints consists of whether a given residue is involved in a helix or a beta strand. This is a very generous restraint that can easily and accurately be obtained by the use of structural modeling tools such as Robetta [22] or I-TASSER [23].

Throughout our investigation of noise tolerance in structure determination with REDCRAFT we have found that successful determination of structures should be possible with errors as much as 5 Hz in the case of α proteins. While 5 Hz of error constitutes a high level of noise (approximately 25% signal noise to ratio) we believe that REDCRAFT's deep search mechanism manages to retrieve an accurate structure by utilizing the uniformity in the distribution of error. It is therefore possible for REDCRAFT to retrieve the accurate structure even with larger levels of noise. Our future work in this area will consist of similar investigations into the noise tolerance of other types of proteins (α/β and β) while optimizing the search parameters of the REDCRAFT.

Finally, we would like to address the cases in which we have encountered difficulties in folding proteins due to inherent degeneracies in RDC data. We can now affirmatively state that the cases in which only one RDC is utilized in the second alignment medium provides insufficient information to resolve the inversion degeneracies present and well documented [24] during the early part (approximately within the first 10 residues) of structure calculation. These degeneracies arise due to the fact that orientation of any collection of vectors in space are indistinguishable from a rotation of 180 degree about any of the three principal axes of the molecular alignment [24]. Therefore RDC data from a second alignment medium are required to resolve these orientational ambiguities. Because {N-H} vectors are antiparallel in beta sheets and parallel in alpha helices they cannot be used to provide an accurate estimate of the order tensor from the second alignment medium that is needed to resolve these orientational degeneracies. As a consequence, it is very unlikely to successfully fold a protein from a RDC set in which the second alignment media contains a singular RDC (as in the case of 3,1). Furthermore, it should be noted that the even though the 2,2 data set contained the same number of RDCs as 3,1 data set because of the aforementioned degeneracies, the case of 2,2 contains much more useful information than 3,1, which allows it to guide the protein to its native fold with relative ease.

ACKNOWLEDGMENTS

This work was supported by NIH Grant Numbers 1R01GM081793 and P20 RR-016461 to Dr. Homayoun Valafar.

REFERENCES

[1] Simin M, Irausquin S, Cole CA, Valafar H. Improvements to REDCRAFT: a software tool for simultaneous characterization of protein backbone structure and dynamics from residual dipolar couplings. J Biomol NMR 2014;60:241–64.
[2] Delaglio F, Kontaxis G, Bax A. Protein structure determination using molecular fragment replacement and NMR dipolar couplings. J Am Chem Soc 2000;122(9):2142–3.
[3] Hus J-C, Marion D, Blackledge M. Determination of protein backbone structure using only residual dipolar couplings. J Am Chem Soc 2001;123(7):1541–2.
[4] Andrec M, Du PC, Levy RM. Protein backbone structure determination using only residual dipolar couplings from one ordering medium. J Biomol NMR 2001;21(4):335–47.
[5] Zeng J, Boyles J, Tripathy C, Wang L, Yan A, Zhou P, et al. High-resolution protein structure determination starting with a global fold calculated from exact solutions to the RDC equations. J Biomol NMR 2009;45(3):265–81.
[6] Cole CA, Ishimaru D, Hennig M, Valafar H. An investigation of minimum data requirement for successful structure determination of Pf2048.1 with REDCRAFT. In: Proceedings of the international conference on bioinformatics & computational biology (BIOCOMP); Las Vegas, NV; 2015. p. 17–24.
[7] Bryson M, Tian F, Prestegard JH, Valafar H. REDCRAFT: a tool for simultaneous characterization of protein backbone structure and motion from RDC data. J Magn Reson 2008;191(2):322–34.
[8] Valafar H, Simin M, Irausquin S. A review of REDCRAFT: simultaneous investigation of structure and dynamics of proteins from RDC restraints. Annu Rep NMR Spectrosc 2012;76:23–66.
[9] Tian F, Valafar H, Prestegard JH. A dipolar coupling based strategy for simultaneous resonance assignment and structure determination of protein backbones. J Am Chem Soc 2001;123(47):11791–6.
[10] Shealy P, Simin M, Park SH, Opella SJ, Valafar H. Simultaneous structure and dynamics of a membrane protein using REDCRAFT: membrane-bound form of Pf1 coat protein. J Magn Reson 2010;207(1):8–16.
[11] Saupe A, Englert G. High-resolution nuclear magnetic resonance spectra of orientated molecules. Phys Rev Lett 1963;11(10):462–4.
[12] Timko E, Shealy P, Bryson M, Valafa H. Minimum data requirements and supplemental angle constraints for protein structure prediction with REDCRAFT. In: Proceedings of the international conference on bioinformatics & computational biology (BIOCOMP); Las Vegas, NV; 2008. p. 738–44.
[13] Ramachandran GN, Ramakrishnan C, Sasisekharan V. Stereochemistry of polypeptide chain configurations. J Mol Biol 1963;7(1):95–9.
[14] Orengo CA, Michie AD, Jones S, Jones DT, Swindells MB, Thornton JM. CATH — a hierarchic classification of protein domain structures. Structure 1997;5(8):1093–108.

[15] Shen Y, Delaglio F, Cornilescu G, Bax A. TALOS+: a hybrid method for predicting protein backbone torsion angles from NMR chemical shifts. J Biomol NMR 2009;44(4):213–23.
[16] Bernstein FC, Koetzle TF, Williams GJB, Meyer EF, Brice MD, Rodgers JR, et al. The protein data bank: a computer-based archival file for macromolecular structures. Arch Biochem Biophys 1978;185(2):584–91.
[17] Valafar H, Prestegard JH. REDCAT: a residual dipolar coupling analysis tool. J Magn Reson 2004;167 (2):228–41.
[18] Schmidt C, Irausquin SJ, Valafar H. Advances in the REDCAT software package. BMC Bioinf 2013;14 (1):302.
[19] DeLano WL. The PyMOL molecular graphics system. Palo Alto, CA: DeLano Sci. LLC; 2008.http//www.pymol.org.
[20] Humphrey W, Dalke A, Schulten K. VMD: visual molecular dynamics. J Mol Graph 1996;14(1):27–8. 33–8.
[21] Shealy P, Valafar H. Multiple structure alignment with msTALI. BMC Bioinf 2012;13(1):105.
[22] Kim DE, Chivian D, Baker D. Protein structure prediction and analysis using the Robetta server. Nucleic Acids Res 2004;32(Web server issue):W526–31.
[23] Wu S, Skolnick J, Zhang Y. Ab initio modeling of small proteins by iterative TASSER simulations. BMC Biol 2007;5:17.
[24] Al-Hashimi HM, Valafar H, Terrell M, Zartler ER, Eidsness MK, Prestegard JH. Variation of molecular alignment as a means of resolving orientational ambiguities in protein structures from dipolar couplings. J Magn Reson 2000;143(2):402–6.

CHAPTER

ARCHITECTURAL TOPOGRAPHY OF THE α-SUBUNIT CYTOPLASMIC LOOP IN THE $GABA_A$ RECEPTOR

7

J.L. Mustard, J.B. Worley, N.W. Seidler

Division of Basic Sciences, Laboratory of Bioinformatics and Computational Biology, Kansas City University of Medicine and Biosciences, Kansas City, MO, United States

7.1 INTRODUCTION

The highly abundant glycolytic enzyme glyceraldehyde-3-phosphate dehydrogenase (GAPDH) is known for its multifunctional properties and ability to regulate diverse cellular proteins [1]. The large array of proteins with which GAPDH interacts is thought to include a family of receptors that respond to the neurotransmitter γ-aminobutyric acid (GABA) that elicits neuronal inhibition, namely the type A class of receptors ($GABA_A$Rs). These receptors are neurotransmitter-gated chloride ion channels that mediate fast synaptic, as well as tonic, inhibitory neurotransmission. Laschet and colleagues [2] observed that GAPDH phosphorylates the $GABA_A$R, and thereby contributes to the modulation of neuronal inhibition. The phosphorylation is due to a kinase activity catalyzed by GAPDH that results in a modification of residues on the loop domain at the intracellular side of the neuronal surface membrane.

$GABA_A$R is a member of the Cys-loop superfamily of pentameric ligand-gated ion channels (often abbreviated pLGICs), including other receptor families that are gated by acetylcholine, glycine, and serotonin. Cys-loop receptors contain a characteristic disulfide bond between two highly conserved cysteines that are separated by 13 amino acid residues, creating a well-defined structural motif that is projected extracellularly. The pentameric nature of the channel refers to the annular arrangement of five distinct protein chains, or subunits, that are embedded in the neuronal surface membrane. $GABA_A$R is heteromeric, indicating that it is made up of different subunits (Fig. 7.1). The modular organization of each subunit consists of a large N-terminal extracellular ligand-binding domain followed by four α-helical transmembrane domains (TMDs), designated TM1-TM4. The stretch of amino acids that link the TM3-TM4 is a large cytoplasmic loop often referred to as the intracellular loop domain (ILD). The binding site of the native ligand GABA exists at the interface between the α- and β-subunits. The region to which GAPDH binds/phosphorylates is at the lipid bilayer surface of the ILD.

$GABA_A$Rs are found throughout the nervous system and are essential for neural signaling. Even considering the diversity of subunit subtypes (ie, total of six different subunit families, not including rho), there is thought to be a finite number of combinations of heteromeric arrangement to make up the diverse group of receptor complexes. The functional heterogeneity of the $GABA_A$Rs is due to the

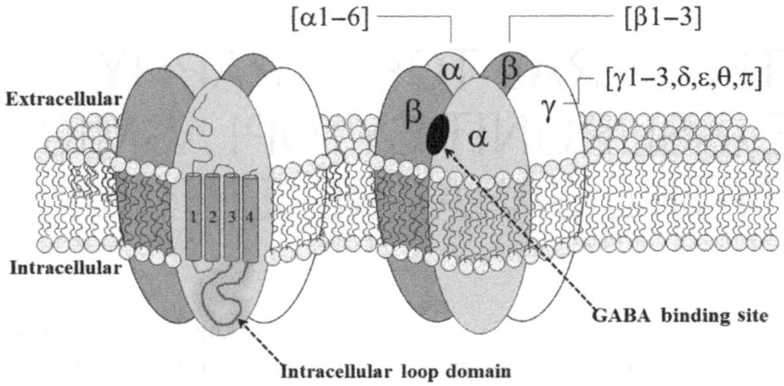

FIGURE 7.1

Illustration of the $GABA_AR$. The subunits of pLGICs share common structural features including an extracellular N-terminal domain, four TMDs, and a large cytoplasmic loop between TM3 and TM4 that is the focus of the present study. The pentameric arrangement of the subunits is illustrated showing extra- and intracellular domains *(shown above and below the lipid bilayer, respectively)* as well as the conserved TMDs. There are a total 16 different genes (not including the three rho, ρ, subunits that are omitted from this diagram because they represent a different receptor subclass; the penta-arrangement for the ρ subunits is generally homomeric yet may co-assemble heteromerically). Combinations of different subunits result in a diverse group of $GABA_AR$ subgroups. Generally, there are two α and two β subunits together with one γ or δ subunit.

differences in subunit composition. Although most neurons express several different subunit subtypes, approximately half of all $GABA_ARs$ in the adult brain contain the α-1 subunit [3].

While the structural diversity of the $GABA_ARs$ in terms of subunit composition remains to be fully elucidated, it is generally thought that the fast synaptic inhibition is due to receptor subtypes that predominately include α1, β2, and γ2 subunits [3,4]. The receptors that mediate tonic inhibition are thought to be composed primarily of α4, α5, and α6, with β1–3, and may contain a δ subunit [4,5]. $GABA_ARs$ have been shown to play a role in epilepsy, pain, and anesthesia. $GABA_AR$ also appears to regulate memory [6].

As our study shows, there is a considerable variation in sequence homology among subunit subtypes in the region ILD despite the TM3-TM4 stretches being highly conserved among the subtypes. In a 1999 review article [7], the authors indicate that channel function is clearly affected by changes in amino acid sequence within this cytoplasmic domain. Strikingly, studies point to a linkage between a naturally occurring substitution in the α6 ILD (ie, P385S) and alcoholism [8] as well as reduced response to benzodiazepine agonists [9,10], suggesting that ILD plays a key role in modulating receptor behavior. While Kash and colleagues [11] demonstrated the importance of the extracellular N-terminal domain and the TM2-TM3 extracellular domain of the α-subunits in the transduction of agonist binding, little is known about the intracellular region.

Fisher [12] reported that the TM3 region and/or the TM3-TM4 ILD influence the gating properties of this chloride channel ($GABA_AR$). In fact, the author compared receptor complexes containing either the α1 subtype or the α6. In our study, we describe salient differences between these two subtypes, including differences in the consensus site for GAPDH binding.

The TMDs create a four-helical bundle that is important for transducing pharmacological effects. The TM3 domain appears crucial in the mechanism of anesthesia. The water-filled cavity that is formed by TM2 and TM3 acts as a binding pocket for ethanol and volatile anesthetics [13]. The alteration of the four-helical bundle may have, as yet, undiscovered effects on adjacent regions that include the ILD. Researchers have implicated the regions directly adjacent to the TM3 and TM4 domains as crucial for receptor function [14,15]. Mutation of a conserved arginine (R427) at the junction between the ILD and TM4 domains affects the desensitization mechanism in a member of pLGIC superfamily, namely a serotonin-gated receptor channel. This particular residue (R427) aligns at the position of the asparagine residue (N414) in the α1 subunit of $GABA_A$Rs. It is also curious to note that this location on the α1 subunit contains the GAPDH consensus site (abbreviated GCS) that is identified as a sequence of five residues, — NXXS/TK —, where N is asparagine, X is any residue, of which there are two followed by either an S (for, serine) or T (for, threonine), which are the targets of phosphorylation, and then lastly K (for, lysine). O'Toole and Jenkins [14] identified regions, directly adjacent to the TM3 and TM4 domains, that are important in the regulation of channel function. These authors designated the regions as M3A and M4A with stretches of approximately 20 and 40 residues, respectively, noting the importance of charged residues, particularly lysine residues. Of interest to our lab group, these regions contain GCSs, but only in some of the α subunit subtypes. The ILD remains a mystery in terms of its structural orientation to the inner leaflet of the neuronal surface membrane. The recent mapping of the X-ray crystal structure of the $GABA_A$R was obtained only following the bioengineered excision of the ILD [16], suggesting that the architectural topology of the cytoplasmic loop requires an intact membrane. In our study, we used bioinformatics and computational strategies to investigate the ILD and we propose that this intracellular region exhibits a unique structural orientation, including discussion about its functional role, particularly with regards to GAPDH interaction.

7.2 METHODOLOGICAL APPROACH

We used various databases to examine the features of the α subtype subunits. Sequence information was obtained from http://www.uniprot.org, using the following entry numbers for human α1–α6: P14867, P47869, P34903, P48169, P31644, and Q16445, respectively. Corresponding gene names are GABRA1, GABRA2, GABRA3, and so on. All sequences were curated and the topological designations for domains were indicated in the website and were used in this study.

Expression data was collected from http://www.biogps.org and the probe set numbers were 206678, 207014, 207210, 208463, 206456, and 207182, for α1–α6, respectively. Select brain regions were chosen for presentation and the expression in adipocyte was given as reference.

The protein BLAST program for pairwise comparisons of sequences (available at http://www.ncbi.nlm.nih.gov) was used to compare the α1 subunit versus each of the other five α subunit subtypes (α2 through α6). Only the sequences that include the TM3, ILD, and TM4 regions were compared. Due to the large differences in size of the ILD, repeated comparisons of sequence fragments were conducted, followed by alignment scoring as described below.

The program for predicting protein regions of disorder was also employed; this was accessed at http://www.pondr.com. The VL-XT algorithm was used. The outputs represent real numbers from 0 to 1, with 0 being ideal prediction of order and 1 being the ideal prediction of *dis*order. A default threshold of 0.5 is built into the program; to eliminate ambiguity, we adjusted that threshold to 0.7, above which we purported significant disorder.

We used open access programs for secondary structure (http://www.compbio.dundee.ac.uk/jpred/; https://predictprotein.org/), providing prediction for helical versus strand configurations. Additionally, we ran Chou-Fasman predictive algorithms [17] on the α1 ILD sequence.

We built a speculative structural model using the helical wheel in examining the possibility of surface attachment of ILD helices (http://www-nmr.cabm.rutgers.edu/bioinformatics/Proteomic_tools/Helical_wheel/).

7.3 RESULTS AND DISCUSSION

By conservative estimate, there are 11 distinct receptor complex subtypes that are abundant in brain [18]. Essentially half of all $GABA_AR$ complexes in the adult brain contain the α1 subunit [3]. In the expression of the α subunits in brain, the α1, α2, and α5 were highly expressed in all regions of the brain (Table 7.1). There was one exception and that was the preferential expression of α6 in the cerebellum. As we show later in the chapter, the ILD region between α1 and α6 differs significantly. Additionally, α1 ILD contains two intact GCSs, for GAPDH-induced receptor modulation, contrasted with the α6 ILD containing no intact GCS, suggesting that regulation of neuronal inhibition in the cerebellum may differ from other brain regions.

The distribution of the various receptor subtypes is functionally divided into synaptic and nonsynaptic regions, which regulate phasic and tonic neuronal inhibition, respectively. While not an absolute

Table 7.1 Expression Levels of the α Subunit Subtypes

Tissue	1	2	3	4	5	6
Whole brain	132.60	98.30	3.85	3.00	203.85	4.95
Amygdala	82.75	321.45	4.75	3.65	691.20	6.15
Prefrontal cortex	113.70	163.65	5.65	4.35	80.40	7.50
Spinal cord	5.40	7.05	4.85	3.65	6.60	6.45
Hypothalamus	42.10	10.95	5.05	3.80	12.25	6.40
Thalamus	5.50	6.85	4.65	3.45	76.85	6.20
Caudate nucleus	4.55	33.75	4.10	4.60	106.85	5.45
Parietal lobe	137.20	94.60	4.95	3.70	10.15	7.05
Medulla oblongata	81.90	65.80	4.20	3.15	10.65	5.50
Cingulate cortex	77.20	43.80	4.70	3.50	22.95	6.25
Occipital lobe	161.40	203.55	4.10	3.50	169.15	5.40
Temporal lobe	29.95	49.85	4.20	3.15	24.10	5.70
Subthalamic nucleus	44.25	37.65	4.20	3.05	43.45	5.70
Pons	25.40	13.65	4.35	3.30	26.10	5.95
Globus pallidus	61.40	72.20	3.50	2.50	24.45	4.60
Cerebellum	13.45	7.10	3.70	2.80	5.15	49.00
Adipocyte (control)	5.05	6.35	4.50	3.40	6.10	5.85

Table 7.2 Pairwise Alignment Scoring

α1: Versus	Score	Identities	Similarities
α2	998	94	12
α3	848	79	15
α5	833	78	12
α4	470	51	9
α6	621	58	12

rule, α1–3 subunit subtypes distribute to synapses and α4–6 to nonsynaptic regions on neurons. Still, it is important to note that cellular distribution of the subunit subtypes appears to vary according to the specific location of neuronal clusters. For example, Lorenzo and colleagues [19] looked at the expression of α1–3 and α5 in abducens motor neurons, and observed that the cell body only contained the α1 subunit, while dendrites contained α1 and α2 subunits.

There are interesting observations to be found in this compilation of expression data. The brain regions showing the largest differences in expression between α1 and α5, for example, include amygdala, hypothalamus, thalamus, caudate nucleus, parietal lobe, medulla oblongata, cingulate cortex, and globus pallidus. The ratio of expression of α5/α1 in the caudate nucleus and amygdala is the highest at 21:1 and 8:1, respectively, suggesting an importance in the role of tonic inhibition in these brain regions. The sequence homology of α1 and α5 diminishes significantly in the ILD region, particularly after the stretches of residues immediately adjacent to the TMDs, TM3A, and TM4A (Table 7.2). In the region of 86 residues (reference structure α1 ILD) there are 53 identities between α1 and α2, yet only 38 identities between α1 and α5. Additionally, the TM4A GCS in α5 exhibits a small difference (—NSISK—in place of—NSVSK—, in α1) that may impact the affinity of GAPDH. These sequence variations in the ILD between α1 and α5 may provide clues about the functional differences between the two subtypes.

Only subtypes α1, α2, α3, and α5 contain GCSs that are directly adjacent to the transmembrane helices and that would be modulatable by GAPDH. The α4 subtype contains an intact GCS but it is located in the center region of the ILD sequence and consequently may have a distinct function, such as membrane trafficking. The α6 subtype is completely devoid of a GCS. Interestingly, the α4 and α6 are typically expressed at rather lower levels (Table 7.1) and are generally not found in synaptic regions.

7.3.1 SEQUENCE COMPARISON OF α SUBUNITS

In doing sequence comparison using BLAST, we met an obstacle in comparing the sequence of α1 with that of α4. While the sequences exhibited conserved residues at the TM3 and TM4 regions providing us with BLAST-derived numbers, the sequences associated with the ILD initially came up with no homologous regions. We then pared the sequences down to only those stretches of the corresponding ILDs for α1 and α4, and BLAST comparisons were performed. The regions were further pared down, omitting the just-identified similar stretches and then the remaining sequences were retested. This process was necessary due to the large disparity in ILD size between α1 and α4 (Fig. 7.3). The homologous regions were aligned and a pairwise alignment score was determined and the scores are presented in Table 7.2.

Pairwise alignment scores were computed by the following rules. For each identity and similarity, a value of 10 and 5 were given; the gap penalty was −1 for each gap. Using this scoring system allowed us to evaluate all sequence pairs.

In addition to scores, the total number of residue identities and residue similarities, as defined by the BLAST program, are also given in Table 7.2. It is important to note that the tabulated scores as well as the listed numbers of total identities and similarities represent pairwise comparisons of all three regions: TM3, ILD, and TM4. Based on these results, one can assume that the α-subunits can be subcategorized. One grouping would include α1, α2, α3, and α5 and another α4 and α6. Upon close inspection of the ILD regions on α4 and α6, we note that the ILD lengths differ greatly: 182 versus 94, respectively.

By including the TMDs (TM3 and TM4), this skews the comparisons, to some degree, as these stretches of residues are highly conserved (Figs. 7.2 and 7.3). Consider, for example, the degree to which the lysine residues have been conserved in the ILD region across these subtypes. We discuss later the proposed role of these lysine residues in the function of this region. There are 15 lysines in the 86-residue of the α1 ILD, accounting for 17.4% of the amino acids. A random percentage would be 5% (or, 1 in 20), suggesting a nonrandom event of significance. In comparing the conserved nature of these residues, we calculated that between 60% and 80% of the lysine residues are conserved among the α2, α3, and α5, relative to α1. This contrasts with the nominal 13–34% of ILD lysines conserved with α4 and α6, relative to α1.

7.3.2 SUBDOMAINS OF THE ILD

In a study on the role of the ILD [14], it was proposed that the sequences closest to the transmembrane regions are crucial to receptor function. In fact, the authors gave these regions an initial designation of M3A and M4A, referring to the adjacent residues relative to the TMDs. For the α1 subunit, the authors stated that the 20 and 40 residues from the TM3 and TM4 domains contain residues important for channel function. The α1 mutations K383E and K384E resulted in enhanced desensitization of the receptor [14]. (See accession number NP_000797; it appears that the authors [14] erred on the numbering of these residues, which should be listed as K410 and K411. Consult our Figs. 7.2 and 7.4 in this chapter for the correct numbering of these lysine residues. We assume the accuracy of the study [14] regardless of their numbering typo.)

These authors also report that mutation of the K378 (*note*: the actual location is K405) decreases chloride conductance, but that the introduction of a lysine residue at V373 (*note*: V400) did not change chloride conductance. This observation suggests that the lysines and their location in the ILD are vital to channel function.

7.3.3 SEQUENCE PATTERNS IN THE ILD

We examined the subdomains in more detail and noted several interesting features (Fig. 7.4). The pattern of lysine residues exhibits rhythmicity. In the TM3A subdomain, we find a pattern mirrored in the TM4A subdomain (Fig. 7.5, α1). This pattern exhibits a lysine singlet/doublet every five to seven residues interspersed with larger lysine groupings. TM3A and TM4A are separated by a sequence devoid of lysines in a central region of the loop that shows the highest degree of disorder.

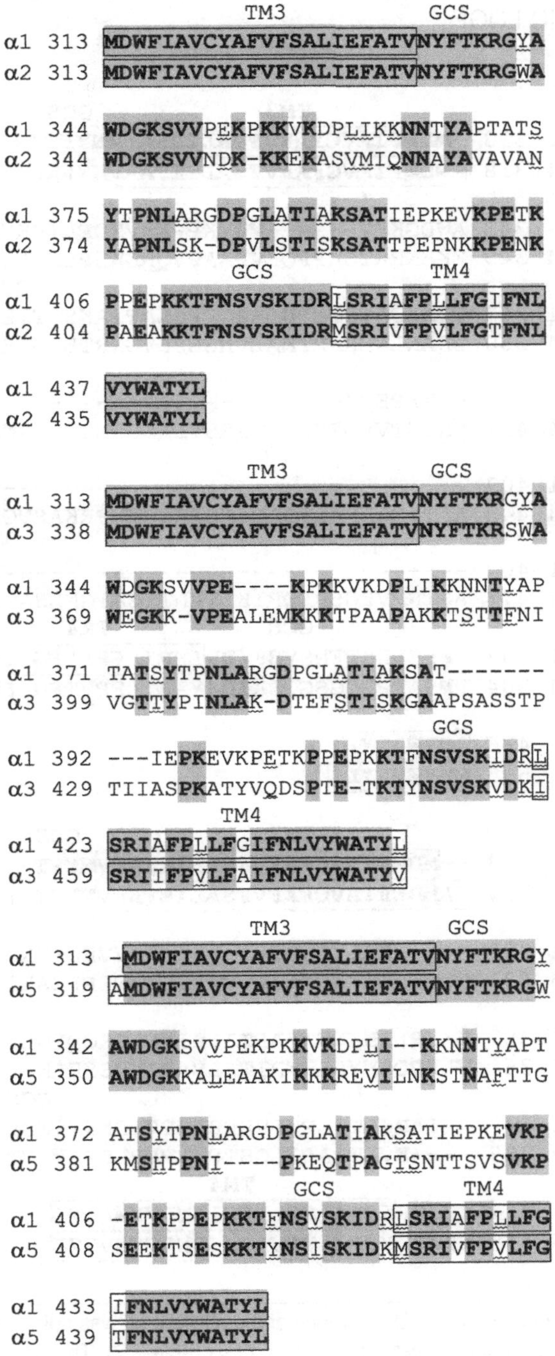

FIGURE 7.2

Sequence comparisons of conserved ILDs. The ILD sequence of the α1 subunit was compared with that of α2, α3, and α5. These comparisons gave the highest alignment scores. All of these regions contain a conserved GCS adjacent to the transmembrane domains *(shown boxed)*. Identities *(gray highlight and bolded letters)* and similarities *(squiggled underline)*.

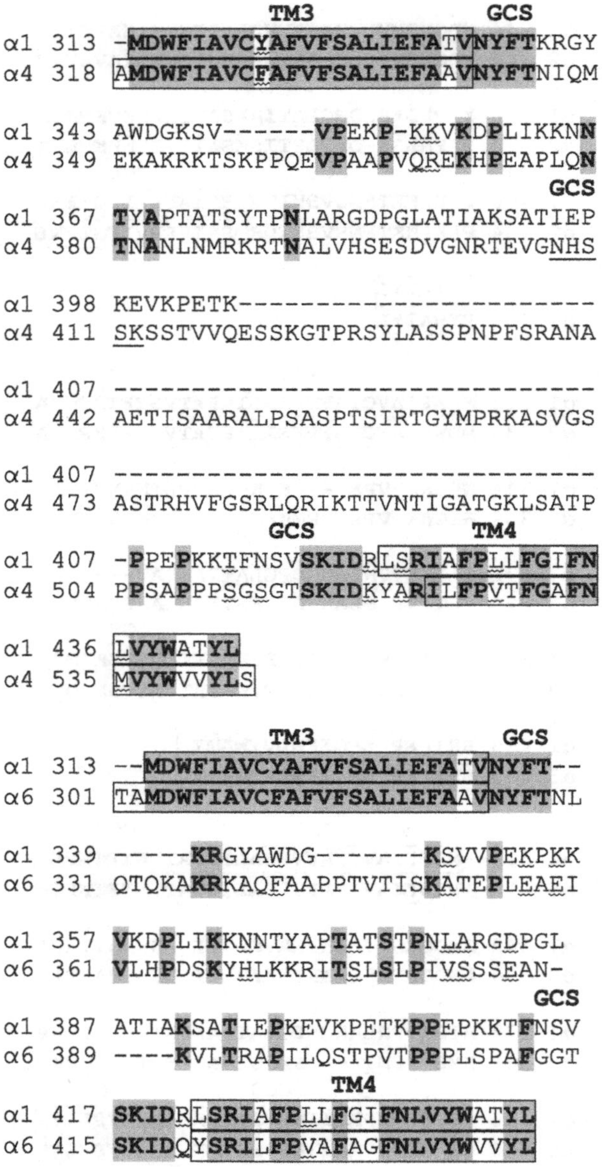

FIGURE 7.3

Comparison of less-conserved ILDs. The ILD sequence of the α1 subunit was pairwise compared with that of α4 and α6. These comparisons gave the lowest alignment scores (Table 7.2). The α4 and α6 subunits do not contain intact TM3-adjacent or TM4-adjacent GCSs. The α4 subunit interestingly exhibits an internal GCS *(underlined)*.

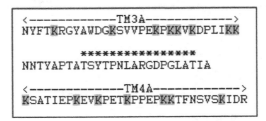

```
<-------------TM3A------------->
NYFTKRGYAWDGKSVVPEKPKKVKDPLIKK

         ******************
NNTYAPTATSYTPNLARGDPGLATIA

<--------------TM4A------------->
KSATIEPKEVKPETKPPEPKKTFNSVSKIDR
```

FIGURE 7.4

The α1 ILD sequence. The ILD sequence (335–421) from the α1 subunit is shown with the basic residue lysine (K) *highlighted in gray*. The centrally located disordered region is indicated by *asterisks* above those residues determined to have PONDR scores greater than 0.70. The sequence is presented showing two important subdomains, TM3A and TM4A, representing the residues adjacent to the TM3 and TM4, respectively.

The data in Fig. 7.5 include the TMDs (TM3 and TM4) flanking the ILD; the low PONDR® (Predictor of Naturally Disordered Regions) scores indicate their minimal disorder. The graph showing the disorder profile for the α1 subunit indicates a palindromic pattern of lysine residues with the greatest amount of disorder at the region without any lysines. This elegant palindromic feature appears partially disrupted in α2, α3, and α5 and more dramatically disrupted in α4 and α6.

7.3.4 PROTEIN ARCHITECTURE OF THE ILD

When we applied the jpred predictor for secondary structure of α1 ILD, the output indicated that only residues directly adjacent to the TMDs exhibited secondary structure (Fig. 7.6).

There are several lines of evidence showing that the peptide chains emanating from the membrane at the TM3 and TM4 domains are structurally organized in part by the physical forces provided by the phospholipid headgroups. We propose that the TM3A and TM4A chains are helical and that their periodicity is approximately six to seven residues per turn, which is reflected in the regular positioning of the lysine residues. Using the Chou-Fasman predictive algorithm [17], we computed the propensities of the TM3A and TM4A regions for forming secondary structures (Fig. 7.7).

The three-dimensional structure of the ILD is, as of now, unmapped [16]. The recent mapping of the homopentameric (all β3 subunits) $GABA_AR$ was accomplished only by removal of the ILD portion. This region appears to exhibit the capability of forming stretches of helical structure that may be stabilized by interaction with membrane components and/or other proteins, such as GAPDH. Additionally, one may speculate that the TM3A and TM4A show features that are somewhat reminiscent of the collagen helix. TM3A and TM4A contain high amounts of proline and lysine residues. The α1 ILD contains 11 proline and 15 lysine residues out of a total of 87. The periodicity of the helix would allow for the regular positioning of the lysine residue toward the lipid bilayer, permitting penetration of the positively charged side chains into the layer containing the phosphate moieties. Others have found the lysine-containing proteins bind to membrane lipid phosphates [20]. Interestingly, anesthetics disrupt this interaction and may contribute to the molecular mechanism of anesthesia [21], which is currently thought to involve the $GABA_AR$. The central region of this loop (ie, α1) appears very disordered and

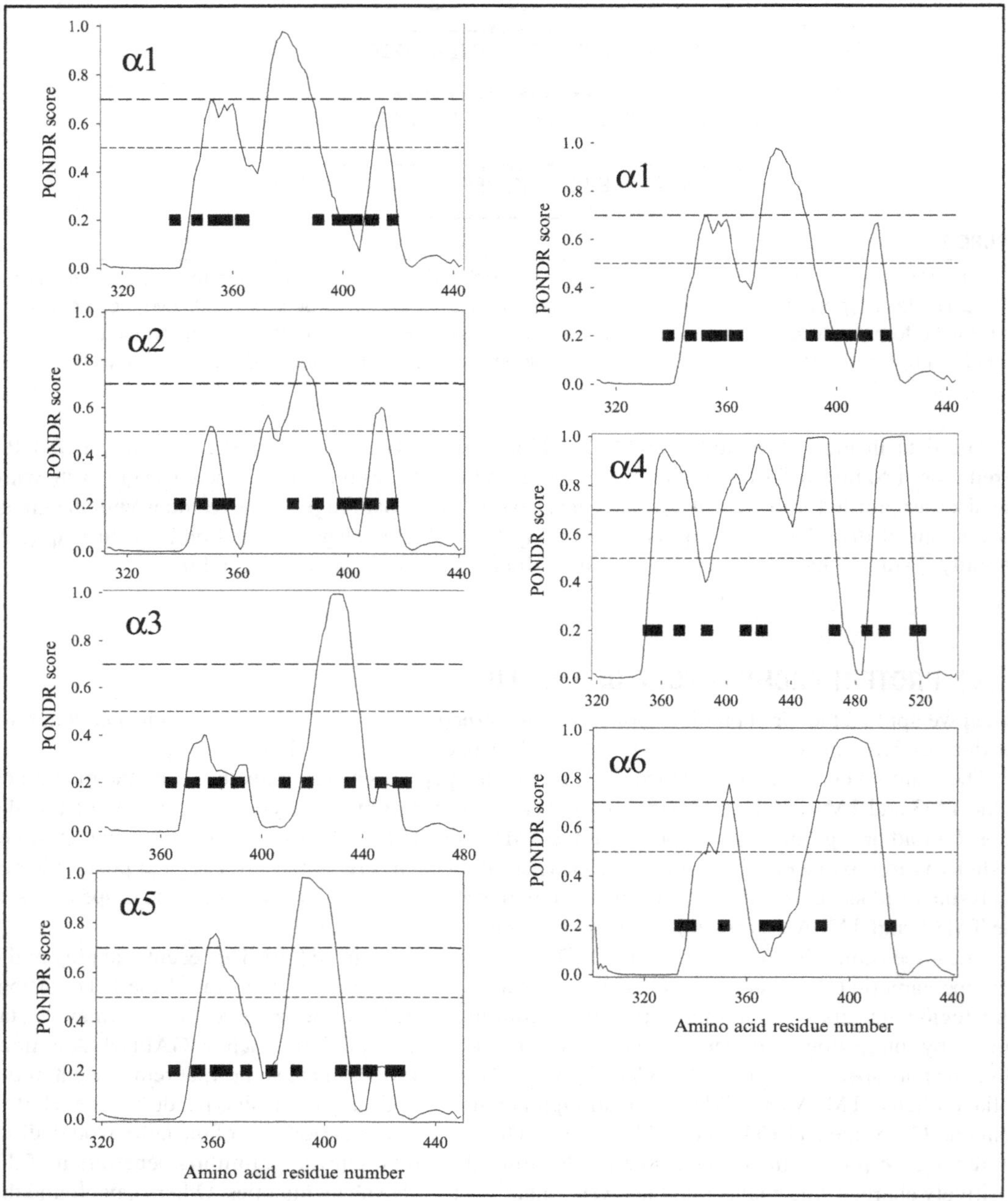

FIGURE 7.5

Comparison of order/disorder profiles. The graphs that show the predicted regions of disorder for each subunit, including TM3, TM4, and ILD sequences, were made using output data obtained from PONDR (VL-XT). The *short-* and *long-dashed* lines indicate 0.5 and 0.7 threshold levels for disorder. The *black boxes* represent the location of lysines.

```
335 NYFTK---AWD 345

417 SKIDR 421
```

FIGURE 7.6

Secondary structure prediction. The residues shown are predicted to have helical architecture. The *gray highlighted* residues represent the complete and partial GCS regions.

```
      Helical Propensity
TM3A
352 EKPKKVKDPLIKK 364
TM4A
398 KEVKPETK 405
408 EPKKTF 413
415 SVSKID 420

       Strand Propensity
TM4A
412 TFNSVS 417
```

FIGURE 7.7

Chou-Fasman results. The residues shown are predicted to have helical or strand architecture. The *gray highlighted* residues represent the partial GCS regions.

completely devoid of lysine residues, and as such, may be unencumbered enough to occupy multiple configurations that would allow this region to disengage from the inner membrane leaflet.

Based on our computational evidence, we surmise that the lysine residues form a pattern that is involved in phosphatidylserine (PS) sequestration. PS is a major annular phospholipid at the inner leaflet, surrounding the pentameric channel. There is a strong probability of an interaction between the ILD lysine residues with the phosphate boundary layer of the inner leaflet of the lipid bilayer, particularly considering that researchers were unable to crystalize this protein with the ILD. We also propose that the ILDs from neighboring channels interact and that these cooperative interactions may be facilitated by GAPDH, which contains a PS-binding site and an ILD-binding site.

7.3.5 ROLE OF THE α1 ILD IN GABA$_A$R

Approximately 50% of all GABA$_A$Rs in the adult brain contain the α1 subunit [3]. In cerebellar granule cells, Perán and colleagues [22] showed that the α1 ILD controls lateral mobility, contributing to cell surface immobilization. The authors note that immunocytochemical studies have ruled out the involvement of this region in trafficking the receptor to the cell surface. Additionally, the α2 subunit has a declustering effect in engineered synapses in HEK293 cells, compared to that of the α1 subunit [23], noting homology differences in the ILD. It was previously determined that postsynaptic localization is directed in large part by the γ subunit ILDs [24]. Clustering mechanisms that involve other binding proteins include (1) dystrophin [25], which is thought to anchor α1 (and neuroligin-2) to cortical dendrites; (2) radixin [26], which selectively anchors the α5-containing receptors to the actin cytoskeleton; and (3) gephyrin [27], which appears to bind to α1, α2, and α3 with a lowered

```
    *************
365 NNTYAPTATSYTPNLARGDPGLATIA 390
               ****************
```

FIGURE 7.8

Structure of the central ILD region. The predicted structure of the central region of the α1 ILD derived from information obtained from https://predictprotein.org. This stretch of amino acids lies between the TM3A and TM4A subdomains. The *gray highlighted* residues are predicted to be buried. The stretch of residues that is *boxed* is predicted to show strand-like secondary structure. The residues *bolded* are predicted to be protein bound. The *asterisks above* the sequence represent the binding site for gephyrin [29]. The *asterisks below* the sequence are predicted to be disordered (see Figs. 7.4 and 7.5).

affinity for the α2 subunit. The gephyrin binding site was shown to be in the α3 ILD (specifically, 396 FNIVGTTYPI405) [28] and in the α1 ILD (specifically, 361 LIKKNNTYAPTATSYT 376) with an emphasis on the phosphorylation target Thr376 (numbered 360–375 in Ref. [29]), each at a region approaching a disorder minima and a threonine-rich stretch.

Because the GAPDH enzyme binds to and phosphorylates the α1 ILD at the GCS (ie, 335 NYFTK 339 and 414 NSVSK 418, at the *underlined* residues) [2], GAPDH must form cooperative interactions with the surface membrane. Notably, GAPDH contains a PS-binding site [30]. The residues on GAPDH that bind PS are 70–94 and the near-neighbor residues are positioned at a distance of approximately 20 Å from one another in the tetrameric form of GAPDH.

The TM3A and the TM4A regions, according to the results from https://predictprotein.org, show two buried residues each, and they are located at or in close proximity to the GCSs on both ends of the ILD. This suggests that the GCS may exhibit some properties of tertiary structure, enabling it to bind GAPDH. The predictive features accessible through https://predictprotein.org allowed us to propose that the central region (ie, residues 365–390) of the α1 ILD, which is devoid of lysine residues, likely exhibits tertiary structure. The results indicate that residues T367, S374, and N378 are buried while the rest of the residues in this stretch are exposed (Fig. 7.8).

7.4 CONCLUSIONS

While the structural diversity of the $GABA_A$Rs in terms of subunit composition remains to be fully elucidated, it is generally thought that the fast synaptic inhibition is due to receptor subtypes that predominately include α1, β2, and γ2 subunits [3,4]. The $GABA_A$R that mediate tonic inhibition are thought to be composed primarily of α4, α5, and α6, with β1–3, that may contain a δ subunit [4,5]. Our study focused on the α1 subunit, particularly the ILD sequence. The six α subunit ILDs exhibit significant heterogeneity of size and sequence.

We propose that the pattern of lysine residues is involved in PS accumulation (Fig. 7.9) as the major annular phospholipid at the inner leaflet, surrounding the pentameric channel. These lysine residues likely interact with the phosphate boundary layer of the inner leaflet of the lipid bilayer. We propose that ILDs interact with neighboring ILDs and that these cooperative interactions may be facilitated by GAPDH. Moreover, GAPDH and gephyrin have a similar binding partner, dynein [31,32], which may participate in complex formation, as described previously [33].

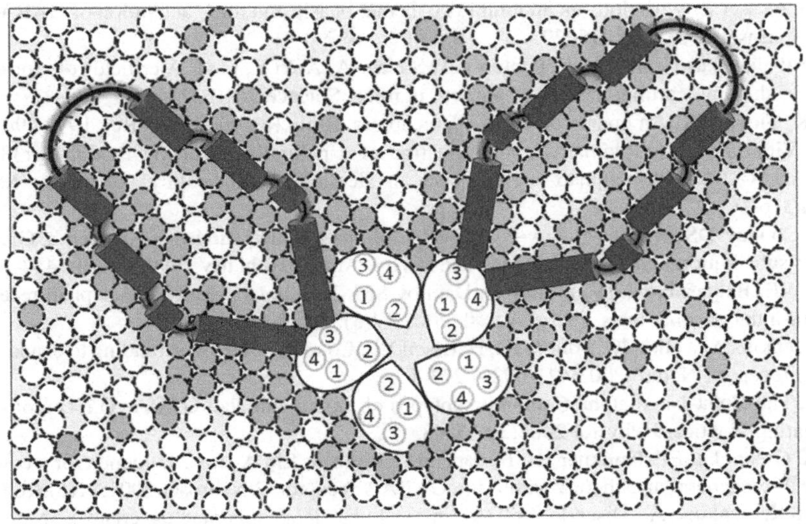

FIGURE 7.9

Architectural topography of the ILD. This illustration shows our proposed structural orientation of the ILD relative to the neuronal surface membrane. This view is from the cell interior, looking up at the inner leaflet of the lipid bilayer. The pentameric arrangement of the receptor subunits is shown with the four-helical bundle indicated by the *numbers within circles*. The complex of five subunits circumscribes a central pore of the illustrated channel. Emanating from the TM3 and TM4 helices are the cytoplasmic loops (*dark-gray* connected cylinders), which we propose adhere to the phospholipid surface through charge-charge interactions. The phospholipids are represented by *dashed circles* with the negatively charged phospholipids (such as phosphatidylserine) shown in *gray* and all other types in *white*. This diagram depicts the focal accumulation of acidic phospholipids.

Our working model of the structure of the ILD suggests the primary organizing feature is the pattern of lysine residues that interact with the phosphate layer of mainly PS phospholipids, which are further ordered by the interaction with GAPDH.

The role of GAPDH in moderating the physical orientation of $GABA_AR$ clusters suggests that modification of this protein would play a significant role in anesthesia, epilepsy, and aging-related brain disorders, such as Alzheimer's, offering a novel point of medical intervention.

REFERENCES

[1] Seidler NW. Multiple binding partners. Adv Exp Med Biol 2013;985:249–67.

[2] Laschet JJ, Minier F, Kurcewicz I, et al. Glyceraldehyde-3-phosphate dehydrogenase is a $GABA_A$ receptor kinase linking glycolysis to neuronal inhibition. J Neurosci 2004;24(35):7614–22.

[3] McKernan RM, Whiting PJ. Which GABAA-receptor subtypes really occur in the brain? Trends Neurosci 1996;19(4):139–43.

[4] Jacob TC, Moss SJ, Jurd R. GABA(A) receptor trafficking and its role in the dynamic modulation of neuronal inhibition. Nat Rev Neurosci 2008;9(5):331–43.

[5] Farrant M, Nusser Z. Variations on an inhibitory theme: phasic and tonic activation of GABA(A) receptors. Nat Rev Neurosci 2005;6(3):215–29.
[6] Shen H, Sabaliauskas N, Sherpa A, Fenton AA, Stelzer A, Aoki C, et al. A critical role for α4βδ GABAA receptors in shaping learning deficits at puberty in mice. Science 2010;327:1515–8.
[7] Mehta AK, Ticku MK. An update on GABAA receptors. Brain Res Brain Res Rev 1999;29(2–3):196–217.
[8] Iwata N, Virkkunen M, Goldman D. Identification of a naturally occurring Pro385-Ser385 substitution in the GABA(A) receptor alpha6 subunit gene in alcoholics and healthy volunteers. Mol Psychiatry 2000;5(3):316–9.
[9] Iwata N, Cowley DS, Radel M, Roy-Byrne PP, Goldman D. Relationship between a GABAA alpha 6 Pro385Ser substitution and benzodiazepine sensitivity. Am J Psychiatry 1999;156(9):1447–9.
[10] Hoffman WE, Balyasnikova IV, Mahay H, Danilov SM, Baughman VL. GABA alpha6 receptors mediate midazolam-induced anxiolysis. J Clin Anesth 2002;14(3):206–9.
[11] Kash TL, Jenkins A, Kelley JC, Trudell JR, Harrison NL. Coupling of agonist binding to channel gating in the GABA(A) receptor. Nature 2003;421(6920):272–5.
[12] Fisher JL. The alpha 1 and alpha 6 subunit subtypes of the mammalian GABA(A) receptor confer distinct channel gating kinetics. J Physiol 2004;2:433–48.
[13] Jenkins A, Greenblatt EP, Faulkner HJ, Bertaccini E, Light A, Lin A, et al. Evidence for a common binding cavity for three general anesthetics within the GABAA receptor. J Neurosci 2001;21(6):RC136.
[14] O'Toole KK, Jenkins A. Discrete M3-M4 intracellular loop subdomains control specific aspects of γ-aminobutyric acid type A receptor function. J Biol Chem 2011;286(44):37990–9.
[15] Hu XQ, Sun H, Peoples RW, Hong R, Zhang L. An interaction involving an arginine residue in the cytoplasmic domain of the 5-HT3A receptor contributes to receptor desensitization mechanism. J Biol Chem 2006;281(31):21781–8.
[16] Miller PS, Aricescu AR. Crystal structure of a human GABAA receptor. Nature 2014;512(7514):270–5.
[17] Chou PY, Fasman GD. Empirical predictions of protein conformation. Annu Rev Biochem 1978;47:251–76.
[18] Luscher B, Fuchs T, Kilpatrick CL. GABAA receptor trafficking-mediated plasticity of inhibitory synapses. Neuron 2011;70(3):385–409.
[19] Lorenzo L-E, Russier M, Barbe A, Fritschy J-M, Bras H. Differential organization of γ-aminobutyric acid type A and glycine receptors in the somatic and dendritic compartments of rat abducens motoneurons. J Comp Neurol 2007;504:112–26. doi:http://dx.doi.org/10.1002/cne.21442.
[20] Kim J, Mosior M, Chung LA, Wu H, McLaughlin S. Binding of peptides with basic residues to membranes containing acidic phospholipids. Biophys J 1991;60(1):135–48.
[21] Bangham AD, Mason W. The effect of some general anaesthetics on the surface potential of lipid monolayers. Br J Pharmacol 1979;66(2):259–65.
[22] Perán M, Hooper H, Boulaiz H, Marchal JA, Aránega A, Salas R. The M3/M4 cytoplasmic loop of the alpha1 subunit restricts GABAARs lateral mobility: a study using fluorescence recovery after photobleaching. Cell Motil Cytoskeleton 2006;63(12):747–57.
[23] Dixon C, Sah P, Lynch JW, Keramidas A. GABAA receptor α and γ subunits shape synaptic currents via different mechanisms. J Biol Chem 2014;289(9):5399–411.
[24] Alldred MJ, Mulder-Rosi J, Lingenfelter SE, Chen G, Lüscher B. Distinct gamma2 subunit domains mediate clustering and synaptic function of postsynaptic GABAA receptors and gephyrin. J Neurosci 2005;25 (3):594–603.
[25] Panzanelli P, Gunn BG, Schlatter MC, Benke D, Tyagarajan SK, Scheiffele P, et al. Distinct mechanisms regulate GABAA receptor and gephyrin clustering at perisomatic and axo-axonic synapses on CA1 pyramidal cells. J Physiol 2011;589(20):4959–80.
[26] Loebrich S, Bähring R, Katsuno T, Tsukita S, Kneussel M. Activated radixin is essential for GABAA receptor alpha5 subunit anchoring at the actin cytoskeleton. EMBO J 2006;25(5):987–99.

[27] Maric HM, Mukherjee J, Tretter V, Moss SJ, Schindelin H. Gephyrin-mediated γ-aminobutyric acid type A and glycine receptor clustering relies on a common binding site. J Biol Chem 2011;286(49):42105–14.
[28] Tretter V, Kerschner B, Milenkovic I, Ramsden SL, Ramerstorfer J, Saiepour L, et al. Molecular basis of the γ-aminobutyric acid A receptor α3 subunit interaction with the clustering protein gephyrin. J Biol Chem 2011;286(43):37702–11.
[29] Mukherjee J, Kretschmannova K, Gouzer G, Maric HM, Ramsden S, Tretter V, et al. The residence time of GABA(A)Rs at inhibitory synapses is determined by direct binding of the receptor α1 subunit to gephyrin. J Neurosci 2011;31(41):14677–87.
[30] Kaneda M, Takeuchi K, Inoue K, Umeda M. Localization of the phosphatidylserine-binding site of glyceraldehyde-3-phosphate dehydrogenase responsible for membrane fusion. J Biochem 1997;122 (6):1233–40.
[31] Tisdale EJ, Azizi F, Artalejo CR. Rab2 utilizes glyceraldehyde-3-phosphate dehydrogenase and protein kinase Cι to associate with microtubules and to recruit dynein. J Biol Chem 2009;284(9):5876–84.
[32] Garcıa-Mayoral MF, Rodrıguez-Crespo I, Bruix M. Structural models of DYNLL1 with interacting partners: African swine fever virus protein p54 and postsynaptic scaffolding protein gephyrin. FEBS Lett 2011;585(1):53–7.
[33] Montalbano AJ, Theisen CS, Fibuch EE, Seidler NW. Isoflurane enhances the moonlighting activity of GAPDH: implications for GABAA receptor trafficking. ISRN Anesthesiol 2012;2012. 970795.

CHAPTER

8

FINDING LONG-TERM INFLUENCE AND SENSITIVITY OF GENES USING PROBABILISTIC GENETIC REGULATORY NETWORKS[a]

Q.N. Tran

The University of South Dakota, Vermillion, SD, United States

8.1 INTRODUCTION

Boolean networks are well-studied discrete models of biological networks such as gene regulatory networks where DNA segments in a cell interact with each other indirectly through their RNA and protein expression products or with other substances in the cell, thereby governing the rates at which genes in the network are transcribed into mRNA. A Boolean network consists of a set of Boolean variables whose state is determined by other variables in the network. They are a particular case of discrete dynamical networks, where time and states are discrete. A Boolean network can be considered as a directed graph where the nodes represent the expression status of genes and directed edges represent the actions of genes on other genes. Each node $x_i \in \{0,1\}$, $i = 1,\ldots,n$, is a Boolean variable whose state value at time $t + 1$ is completely determined by the state values of nodes $x_{j_1}, x_{j_2}, \ldots, x_{j_l}$ for some $1 \leq l \leq n$ at time t by means of a Boolean function $f^{(i)} : \{0,1\}^l \to \{0,1\}$ when there are edges from x_{j_k} to x_i for all $k = 1,\ldots,l$. Thus, one can write $x_i(t+1) = f^{(i)}(x_{j_1}(t), x_{j_2}(t), \ldots, x_{j_l}(t))$, $i = 1,\ldots,n$.

Probabilistic Boolean genetic regulatory networks (PBNs) are probabilistic or stochastic generalizations of Boolean networks. In these models, the deterministic dynamics are replaced by probabilistic dynamics, which can be framed within the mature and well-established theory of Markov chains, for which many analytical and numerical tools have been developed. The value of node x_i at time $t + 1$ is now specified by possibly different Boolean functions and state transition probabilities

$$x_i(t+1) = \begin{cases} f_1^{(i)}(x_{j_1}(t), x_{j_2}(t), \ldots, x_{j_l}(t)) & \text{prob.}\, p_1^{(i)} \\ \ldots & \\ f_m^{(i)}(x_{j_1}(t), x_{j_2}(t), \ldots, x_{j_l}(t)) & \text{prob.}\, p_m^{(i)} \end{cases} \quad (1)$$

where $p_k^{(i)} \in [0,1]$, $1 \leq k \leq m$, and $\sum_{k=1}^{m} p_k^{(i)} = 1$.

This computational tool has been used in system biology to study biological systems from a holistic perspective to provide a comprehensive, system-level understanding of cellular behavior. PBN

[a]A preliminary version of this article was presented at the ACM-BCB 2015 conference in Atlanta, GA.

modeling can be used for the design and analysis of intervention strategies for moving the networks out of undesirable states such as those associated with diseases into the more desirable ones. PBNs have also been used to study the analysis and control of biological networks to find a method for a suitable medication that can be used for drug discovery and cancer treatment [1–11].

Boolean networks are special cases of PBNs in which state transition probabilities are either 1 or 0. The probabilistic nature of this PBN model affords flexibility and power in terms of making inferences from data, which necessarily contain uncertainty, as well as in terms of understanding the dynamical behavior of biological networks, particularly in relation to their structure. PBN is a discrete-time Markov chain in that the behavior at each point in time can be described by a discrete probabilistic choice over several possible outcomes.

Unfortunately, modeling of gene regulatory networks often leads to dynamic models with huge state space surpassing the size of any computer systems by orders of magnitude. One of the key aspects in the analysis of PBN is the investigation of their long-term behavior such as the attractors of the system, which were hypothesized to characterize cellular phenotype [12–14].

Markov chain Monte Carlo (MCMC) has been proposed for analyzing long-term behavior distribution by running the Markov chain for a sufficiently long time until convergence into the stationary distribution and observing the proportion of time the process spent in the parts of the state space that represent the information of interest such as the joint stationary distribution of several specific genes [1, 2, 7, 9]. Due to the difficulties with the assessment of the convergence rate to the long-term distribution, approximation such as the two-state Markov chain can be used to empirically determine when to stop the simulation and output estimates. Unfortunately, the actual inference step of the two-state Markov chain is challenging and to our knowledge the method has not been widely applied for the analysis of large PBNs.

One of the biggest obstacles for the existing methods to analyze the long-term behavior genes of a PBN is the requirement to compute the state transition diagram, which has 2^n nodes for a given PBN with n states. In this chapter, we propose a new method in which the state transition diagram is not needed. We utilize algebraic computation for the direct computation of the long-term influence and sensitivity of genes in a PBN. Our novel method only requires $O(n^2)$ memory space — a significant improvement in terms of space as well as time complexity. We are able to analyze the long-term behavior of genes in artificial PBNs with 500 genes within minutes on a desktop computer. We then compare our novel method with previously known methods and report experimental results to illustrate our theoretical arguments. Additionally, our method enables the calculation of likelihood of the occurrence of certain events of interest, thus allowing quantitative statements to be made about the system's behavior, expressed as probabilities or expectations of biological systems.

8.2 INFLUENCE AND SENSITIVITY FACTORS OF GENES IN PBNs

In a PBN, some genes may be more important than others in determining the value of a target gene. Finding the genes that have the most potent effect is an important task in studying the PBN. For example, if gene x_1 has the following predictors

$$x_1(t+1) = \begin{cases} f_1^{(1)}(x_1(t), x_2(t), x_3(t)) = x_2 & \text{prob. } 0.7 \\ f_2^{(1)}(x_1(t), x_2(t), x_3(t)) = x_2 + x_1 \cdot x_3 & \text{prob. } 0.3 \end{cases} \tag{2}$$

then x_2 is a more important variable in influencing gene x_1. Similarly, some genes may be more stable while other genes have little effect on it.

There are many examples of such biased regulation of genes from biologists. The cell cycle regulator gene p21, which is a potent cyclin-dependent kinase inhibitor, can be transcriptionally activated by a series of genes: p53, smad4, AP2, BRCA1, and others. Among those genes, p53 has the most potent effect [15].

In this chapter, we assume that a PBN has been built from experimental data. Much research on building a PBN can be found from recent works on building methods such as the coefficient of determination [16–19]. We will concentrate on analyzing the long-term influence and sensitivity of genes in a given PBN and will present a computational method for direct computation of the long-term influence and sensitivity of genes in a PBN.

Following the work of [10], we use the notion of partial derivatives of Boolean functions in defining the influence of a gene. Note that the expressiveness of Boolean algebras is significantly extended by Boolean differential calculus [20, 21]. The additionally defined differentials of Boolean variables, differentials, and further differential operators of Boolean functions as well as several derivative operations of Boolean functions allow to model changes of function values together with changes of the values of variables and many other properties of Boolean functions.

The partial derivatives of Boolean function $f(x)$ with respect to a variable x_j is defined as

$$\frac{\partial f(x)}{\partial x_j}=f(x_{|x_j\leftarrow 0})\oplus f(x_{|x_j\leftarrow 1})$$

where $\oplus$ is the *xor* operator and $x_{|x_j\leftarrow k}=(x_1,\ldots,x_{j-1},k,x_{j+1},\ldots,x_n)$ for $k=0,1$. Intuitively, the partial derivative of a Boolean function with respect to the jth variable indicates whether or not the function differs along the jth dimension. The partial derivative is 0 if switching the value of variable x_j does not change the value of the function and it is 1 otherwise.

The influence of variable x_j on the function $f(x)$ is further defined as the expectation of the partial derivative with respect to the distribution $D(x)$:

$$I_{x_j}(f)=E_D\left[\frac{\partial f(x)}{\partial x_j}\right]=Pr\left[\frac{\partial f(x)}{\partial x_j}=1\right]=Pr\{f(x_{|x_j\leftarrow 0})\oplus f(x_{|x_j\leftarrow 1})=1\}$$

where $Pr\{f(x_{|x_j\leftarrow 0})\oplus f(x_{|x_j\leftarrow 1})=1\}$ is the probability that a toggle of the jth variable changes the value of the function $f(x)$ [22].

8.2.1 INFLUENCE FACTOR OF GENES

Let $F_i=\{f_1^{(i)},\ldots,f_{l(i)}^{(i)}\}$ be the set of predictors for gene x_i. The influence of variable x_j on variable x_i is defined as

$$I_{x_j}(x_i)=\sum_{k=1}^{l(i)}I_{x_j}(f_k^{(i)})\cdot c_k^{(i)}.$$

Even though this intuitive formula has been used for other purposes before [22], we now construct a matrix A of influences as $A_{i,j}=I_{x_j}(x_i)$ for calculating the long-term influence of genes based upon this formula. A graph of influence can be constructed where vertices are genes. There is an edge from node j to node i if gene x_j should transfer its influence to gene x_i. For example, in Fig. 8.1 gene 1 has three outgoing edges, so it will transfer its influences to gene 1, 2, and 3. In general, if a node has k outgoing

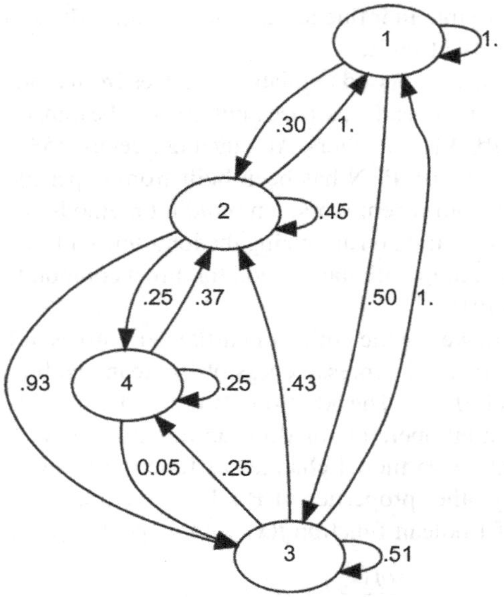

FIGURE 8.1

Influence graph for Ex.4.

edges, it will pass on its importance to each of the nodes that it links to. Hence, we will normalize each column of matrix A so that $\sum_{i=1}^{n} A_{ij} = 1$, for $j = 1,\ldots,n$. In other words, we defined a column-stochastic matrix when all of its entries are nonnegative and the entries in each column sum to one.

Conversely, gene 3 has four incoming edges, so it will be influenced by gene 1 with probability 0.50, gene 2 with probability 0.93, gene 3 with probability 0.51, and gene 4 with probability 0.05 at time $t + 1$. However, gene 1 was influenced by gene 2 with probability 1.0 at the previous time t. That said, besides the direct influence with probability 0.93 from gene 2 to gene 3 at time $t + 1$, gene 2 also indirectly influences gene 3 at the previous time through gene 1. In general, if a node has k incoming edges, it will be influenced by each of the nodes that it is linked to. From our calculation, if a gene is influenced at a higher rate then it is more sensitive to changes from other genes.

Suppose that initially the *influence factor* or sensitivity is uniformly distributed among the 4 genes, each getting 1/4. In fact, we can use any sensitivity value for the genes that we can determine at the initial time such as the normalized value of $\sum_{i=1}^{n} I_{x_j}(x_i)$ for the jth initial value. Denote by v the initial influence or sensitivity vector. Each incoming link increases the influence factor of the gene, so at time $t + 1$, we update the influence factor of each gene by adding to the current value the influence of the incoming links. This is the same as multiplying the matrix A with v. At time $t + 1$, the new influence vector is $v_1 = A \cdot v$. We can iterate the process; thus at time $t + 2$, the updated influence vector is $v_2 = A(A \cdot v) = A^2 \cdot v$. We notice that the sequences of iterates $v, A \cdot v,\ldots,A^k \cdot v$ tends to the equilibrium value. We call this the influence vector of our PBN. Clearly, our method requires only $O(n^2)$ space for matrix A and there is no need to build the transition graph of size $O(2^n)$. Notice that Step 3 in Algorithm 1 can be replaced by $A \leftarrow A^2$ as an alternative way to calculate the influence vector of genes.

ALGORITHM 1 GENEINFLUENCE

Input: a PBN
Output: influence vector of genes in the PBN
Step 1: Construct a matrix of influences A, and an initial influence or sensitivity vector, having all entries equal to $1/n$.
Step 2: Normalize A to make it a column-stochastic matrix.
Step 3: While $\|A \cdot v - v\| > \epsilon$ do $v \leftarrow A \cdot v$.
Step 4: Return v.

Lemma 1. *Algorithm geneInfluence always terminates and gives an influence vector of genes in the PBN.*

Proof. Because A is a column-stochastic square matrix, A and its transpose A^T share the same characteristic polynomial and hence have the same eigenvalues. It is easy to see that $A^T \cdot e = e$, so that 1 is an eigenvalue for A^T and hence for A where e denote an n dimensional column vector with all entries equal to 1. □

8.2.2 IMPACT FACTOR OF GENES

In the same manner, we can obtain a matrix for how a gene impacts other predictors by defining $B = A^T$. In other words, $B_{i,j} = A_{j,i}$. For example, in Fig. 8.1 gene 1 has three outgoing edges, so it will pass on its influences to gene 1, 2, and 3. Hence, in the corresponding graph for matrix B, which we call the impact graph of the PBN, the outgoing edges were reversed to become incoming edges for gene 1. In general, if a node has k incoming edges in Fig. 8.1, it is impacted by the nodes that it is linked from.

Suppose that initially the importance or *impact factor* is uniformly distributed among the 4 nodes, each getting 1/4. In fact, we can use any impact value for the genes at the initial time such as the normalized value of $\sum_{j=1}^{n} I_{x_i}(x_j)$ for the ith initial value. Denote by w the initial impact vector. Each incoming link increases the impact factor of the gene, so at time $t_0 - 1$, we update the impact factor of each gene by adding to the current value the impact of the incoming links. This is the same as multiplying matrix B with w. At time $t_0 - 1$, the new influence vector is $w_1 = B \cdot w$. We can iterate the process, thus at time $t_0 - 2$, the updated influence vector is $w_2 = B(B \cdot w) = B^2 \cdot w$. We notice that the sequences of iterates w, $B \cdot w, \ldots, B^k \cdot w$ tends to the equilibrium value. We call this the impact vector of our PBN.

8.2.3 BOOLEAN ALGEBRA

In this section, we will lay down an algebraic framework for the calculation of the partial derivatives of Boolean function. In practice, for a PBN of n genes the predictor functions have only k variables, where $k \ll n$ and k is the in-degree of the networks. In any case, the following algebraic approach will replace the need for building the truth tables for the calculation of the partial derivatives.

Boolean algebras, which were introduced by Boole in the 1850s to codify the laws of thought, have become a popular topic of research since then. The discovery in the 1930s of the duality between Boolean algebras and Boolean spaces by Stone [23–25] was a major breakthrough of the field. Stone also proved that Boolean algebras and Boolean rings are the same in the sense that one can convert from one algebraic structure to the other. In spite of its long history and elegant algebraic properties, the Boolean ring representation has rarely been used in the computational context.

Definition 2. A ring $\mathbf{K} = \langle K,+,\cdot,0,1\rangle$ is Boolean if $\mathbf{K}$ satisfies $x^2 \approx x, \forall x \in K$.

Lemma 3. *If* $\mathbf{K}$ *is a Boolean ring, then* $\mathbf{K}$ *is commutative and* $x + x \approx 0$ *[25].*

Every Boolean algebra $(K, \wedge, \vee)$ gives rise to a ring $(K,+,\cdot)$ by defining $a + b = (a \wedge \neg b) \vee (b \wedge \neg a)$ (this operation is called XOR in the case of logic) and $a \cdot b = a \wedge b$. The zero element of this ring coincides with the 0 of the Boolean algebra; the multiplicative identity element of the ring is the 1 of the Boolean algebra. Conversely, if a Boolean ring $\mathbf{K}$ is given, we can turn it into a Boolean algebra by defining $x \vee y = x + y + x \cdot y$ and $x \wedge y = x \cdot y$. Because these two sets of operations are inverses of each other, we can say that every Boolean ring arises from a Boolean algebra, and vice versa. Furthermore, a map $f: A \rightarrow B$ is a homomorphism of Boolean algebras if and only if it is a homomorphism of Boolean rings. The categories of Boolean rings and Boolean algebras are equivalent. By using these translations, there exists a Boolean polynomial for each Boolean formula and vice versa.

Since congruences on rings are associated with ideals, it follows that the same must hold for Boolean algebras. An ideal of the Boolean algebra $\mathbf{K}$ is a subset I such that $\forall x,y \in I$ we have $x \vee y \in I$ and $\forall a \in K$ we have $a \wedge x \in I$. This notion of ideal coincides with the notion of ring ideal in the Boolean ring $\mathbf{K}$. An ideal I of R is called prime if $I \neq K$ and if $a \wedge b \in I$ always implies $a \in I$ or $b \in I$. An ideal I of K is called maximal if $I \neq K$ and if the only ideal properly containing I is K itself. These notions coincide with ring theoretic ones of prime ideal and maximal ideal in the Boolean ring $\mathbf{K}$.

By using Boolean ring representation we can convert our problem of counting satisfiable solutions for $Pr\{f(x_{|x_j \leftarrow 0}) \oplus f(x_{|x_j \leftarrow 1}) = 1\}$ into finding the solutions for a Boolean polynomial with degree of at most 1 in all variables. This is the main reason why we want to use Boolean algebra in this chapter.

We now provide an example PBN and show how to build an influence graph and how to calculate the influence factor as well as the impact factor of the PBN.

Example 4. Given a PBN consisting of four genes $V = \{v_1, v_2, v_3, v_4\}$ and a set of predictors in Fig. 8.2. Notice that the probabilities have been rounded off. The actual numbers are [[1.], [.2461853940, .3784104050, .3609895426, 0.1441465845e-1], [.9319607618, 0.6803923820e-1], [1.]] for v_1, v_2, v_3, and v_4, respectively. The influence matrix of this PBN before normalization is shown in Table 8.1 and the influence graph of the PBN is shown in Fig. 8.1.

Suppose that initially the influence factor or sensitivity is uniformly distributed among the 4 genes, each getting 1/4. The long-term sensitivity or influence vector converged to [0.450595824829880, 0.207132994504042, 0.264470757717693, 0.0778004230596858]. That said, gene 4 is the least sensitive gene or in other words the most stable gene in the long run. Gene 1 is the most sensitive gene in the PBN.

$$v_1(t+1) = v_1 + v_2 + v_3 \qquad \text{prob. } 1.00$$

$$v_2(t+1) = \begin{cases} v_1 \cdot v_2 \cdot v_3 + v_1, & \text{prob. } 0.246 \\ v_2 \cdot v_3 \cdot v_4 + v_3 + v_4 + 1, & \text{prob. } 0.378 \\ v_1 \cdot v_2 \cdot v_4 + v_1 \cdot v_3 \cdot v_4 + v_2 \cdot v_3 \cdot v_4 + v_1 \cdot v_2 + v_2 \cdot v_3 + v_2 \cdot v_4 + v_3 \cdot v_4, & \text{prob. } 0.361 \\ v_1 \cdot v_2 \cdot v_4 + v_2 \cdot v_4 + v_2 & \text{prob. } 0.014 \end{cases}$$

$$v_3(t+1) = \begin{cases} v_1 \cdot v_3 + v_2 + 1, & \text{prob. } 0.932 \\ v_1 \cdot v_3 \cdot v_4 + v_3 \cdot v_4 + v_1 + v_3 + v_4 & \text{prob. } 0.068 \end{cases}$$

$$v_4(t+1) = v_2 \cdot v_3 \cdot v_4 + v_2 \cdot v_3 \qquad \text{prob. } 1.00$$

FIGURE 8.2

Set of predictors for Ex. 4.

Table 8.1 Influence Matrix for Ex. 4

1	1	1	0
0.30	0.45	0.43	0.37
0.50	0.93	0.51	0.05
0	0.25	0.25	0.25

Similarly, The long-term impact factor or impact vector converged to [0.210910910659655, 0.357142856843150, 0.292460317400817, 0.139485914740911]. That said, gene 2 is the most impacting gene in the PBN. Notice that the most stable gene of the PBN is not necessarily the most impacting gene of the networks. We have many examples showing that they are in fact not correlated.

8.3 A BIOLOGICAL CASE STUDY

To illustrate the efficiency and the accuracy of our novel algorithm, we use not only randomly generated PBNs but also the data from a human glioma gene expression data set [26]. Fig. 8.3 shows the averaged running time in seconds of our algorithm for finding the impact factor of genes in randomly generated PBNs with 20, 30, 50, 100, 250, and 500 genes. There are two sets of randomly generated PBNs, one with the in-degree of 5 and one with the in-degree of 10. Furthermore, for each data point we generated 10 PBNs and took the averaged running time. Our algorithms were implemented as a software package in Maple 2015. All experiments were performed on a workstation using an i7 CPU, 16GB of RAM and Linux Ubuntu 14.04.3 LTS.

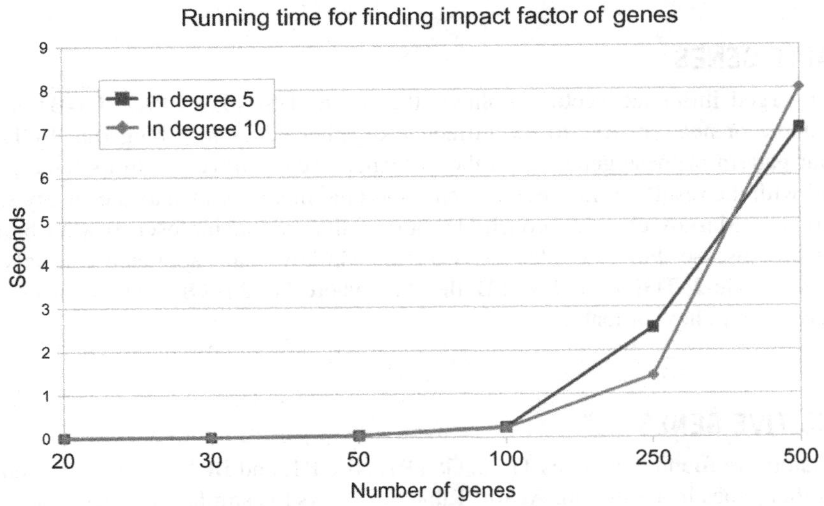

FIGURE 8.3

Experiments with randomly generated PBNs.

8.3.1 GLIOMAS CASE STUDY

Gliomas are the most common form of primary malignancies of the central nervous system (CNS) mainly affecting adults. These tumors have a histological resemblance to different types of glial cells and are categorized into astrocytomas, oligodendrogliomas, oligoastrocytomas, and ependymomas, based on the predominant cell type(s) in the respective tumor.

A PBN network of 597 genes was inferred using the coefficient of determination as in [2, 10]. A small subnet of 15 genes is shown in Fig. 8.4 with the weights on the edges representing the influences of the genes. The influence matrix of this PBN after normalization is shown in Table 8.2.

With the complexity of predictor functions, some gene influences are pretty small. To deal with many small influences we use the same idea of damping factor in Google's PageRank [27] where the influence matrix is replaced by $(1 - p) \cdot A + p \cdot T$ where T is the $n \times n$ "teleportation" matrix; that is, the matrix each of whose entries is $1/n$. We use $p = 0.10$ in our calculation.

Suppose that initially the influence factor or sensitivity is uniformly distributed among the genes. The long-term sensitivity or influence vector converged and after normalizing we have a *converged influence vector* [0.987752376216898, 0.613897953484682, 0.509838752830795, 0.163205931648281, 0.150098397974440, 0.800165646879760, 0.181809171192399, 0.656777507172725, 0.0496073065684904, 0.519537291701068, 0.369183660877093, 0.238311660580107, 0.0814175288392782, 1., 0.981858486296723] for genes Tie-2, TGFB3, ERCC1, HSP40, TDPX2, GSTP1, GNB1, NDKB, TOP2A, SCYB10, PDGFA, NKEFB, β-Actin, NKFB1, and BCL2A1, respectively. Some obvious expectation that a gene such as TOP2A should be stable and should not be sensitive to the influence of other genes can be verified from its lowest influence factor.

It is worth nothing that our novel method is not only very efficient (finishing in 0.225 s) but also capable of identifying stable genes and sensitive genes that were not known before, as we will explain the next three subsections.

8.3.2 STABLE GENES

From the converged influence vector, it shows that genes HSP40, TDPX2, GNB1, NKEFB, and β-Actin are stable or not sensitive to the influence of other genes in a long run. In Table 8.3, we see the similar pattern of these genes when the influence vector converges to its fixed point.

Compared with the results from previous computational methods such as the steady state analysis using the two-state Markov chain approach [1], our results are much closer to what biologists have known about this disease. For example, the two-state Markov chain approach can only tell us that among three genes Tie-2, TGFβ_3, and NKFB, the state where Tie-2 is OFF, TGFβ_3 is ON, and NKFB is ON will have the highest probability.

8.3.3 SENSITIVE GENES

On the other hand, we found that genes Tie-2, GSTP1, NFKB1, and BCL2A1 are very sensitive to the influence of other genes in a long run. Again, Table 8.3 shows the similar pattern of these genes when the influence vector converges to its fixed point. This finding is in line with what we have learned from biologists as [28] found that Tie2 activation was related to the up-regulation of integrin beta1 levels and

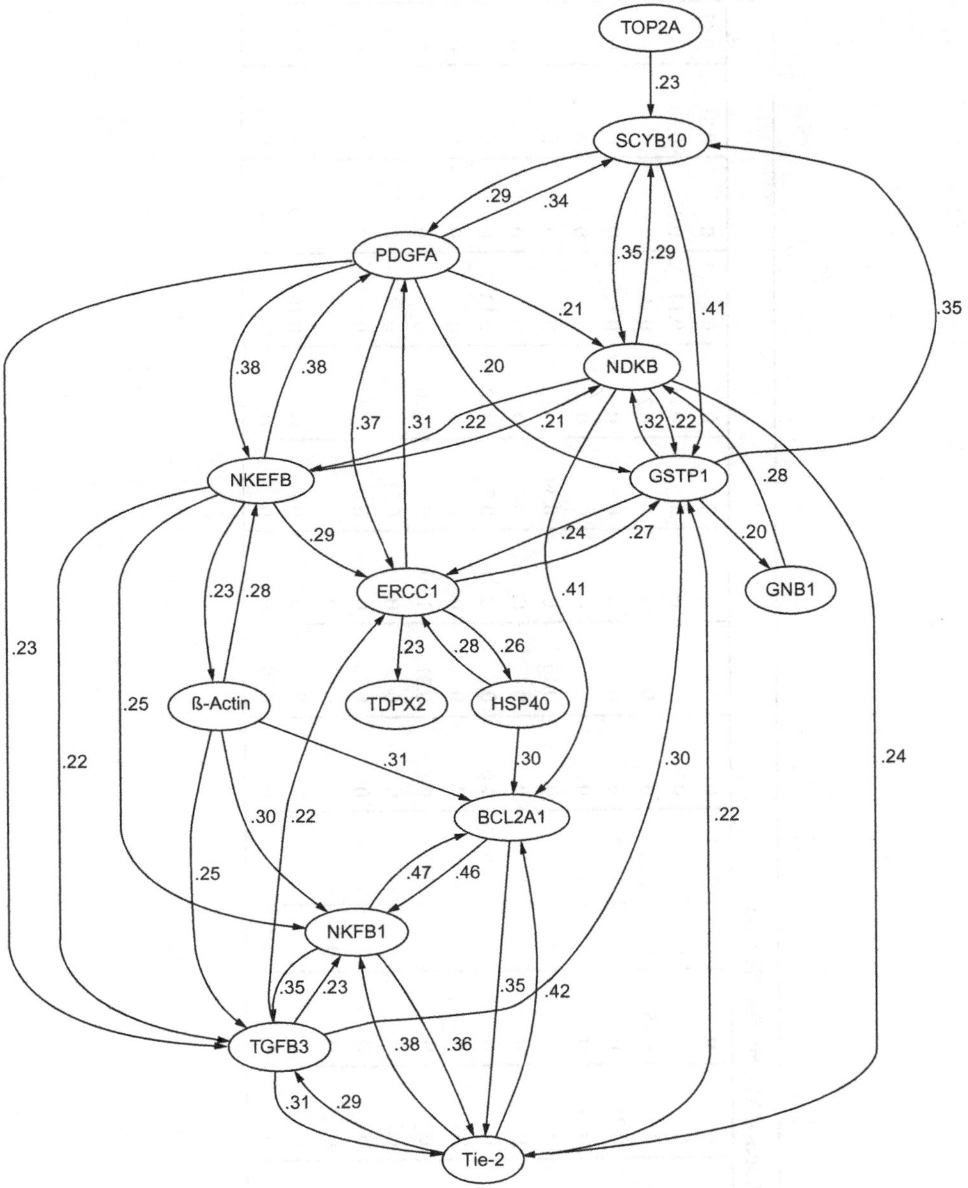

FIGURE 8.4

Influence graph for gliomas.

Table 8.2 Influence Matrix for Gliomas

0	0.29	0	0	0	0	0	0.17	0	0	0	0	0	0.31	0.43
0.22	0	0	0	0	0	0	0	0	0	0.13	0.14	0.22	0.30	0
0	0.21	0	0.48	0	0.22	0	0	0	0	0.21	0.18	0	0	0
0	0	0.24	0	0	0	0	0	0	0	0	0	0	0	0
0	0	0.21	0	0	0	0	0	0	0	0	0	0	0	0
0.17	0.28	0.25	0	0	0	0	0.16	0	0.39	0.12	0	0	0	0
0	0	0	0	0	0.18	0	0	0	0	0	0	0	0	0
0	0	0	0	0	0.29	1.00	0	0	0.33	0.12	0.13	0	0	0
0	0	0	0	0	0	0	0	0	0	0	0	0	0	0
0	0	0	0	0	0.32	0	0.21	1.00	0	0.20	0	0	0	0
0	0	0.29	0	0	0	0	0	0	0.28	0	0.24	0	0	0
0	0	0	0	0	0	0	0.16	0	0	0.22	0	0.25	0	0
0	0	0	0	0	0	0	0	0	0	0	0.15	0	0	0
0.29	0.22	0	0	0	0	0	0	0	0	0	0.16	0.26	0	0.57
0.32	0	0	0.52	0	0	0	0.30	0	0	0	0	0.27	0.40	0

Table 8.3 Convergence of Influence Factors

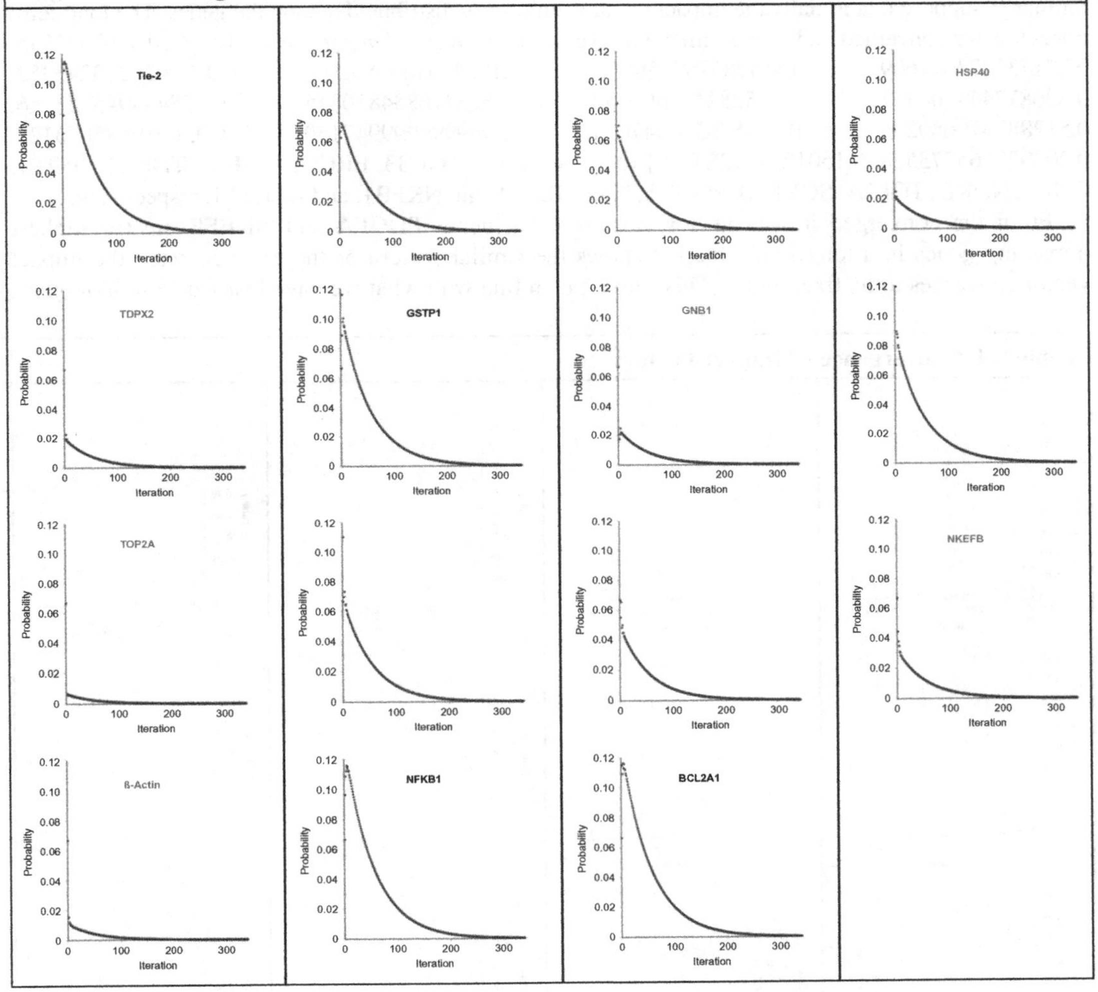

the formation of focal adhesions. Together with the fact that malignant gliomas express high levels of Ang1, biologists suggest the existence of an autocrine loop in malignant gliomas and that a Tie2-dependent pathway modulates cell-to-extracellular matrix adhesion. Furthermore, biologists also showed that Tie2 expression in the neoplastic glial cells was significantly associated with progression from a lower to the higher grade. Tie2 regulates glioma cell adhesion to the extracellular matrix, and the down-regulation of Tie2 levels by small interference RNA or the addition of soluble Tie2 abrogated the Ang1-mediated effect on cell adhesion. Our method provides a quantitative tool to verify these sensitivities of genes.

8.3.4 HI-IMPACT GENES

Similarly, suppose that initially the impact factor is uniformly distributed among the genes. The long-term impact factor converged and after normalizing we have a *converged impact vector* [0.230510562021945, 0.281733274014609, 0.554286767759576, 0.162393143989202, 0.0389022223245352, 0.496877449208407, 0.135282472604153, 0.513376834870215, 0.128454945353256, 0.512887379689246, 0.875556528547034, 0.999999999947150, 0.436019685843127, 0.200929165773528, 0.150127497384119] for genes Tie-2, TGFB3, ERCC1, HSP40, TDPX2, GSTP1, GNB1, NDKB, TOP2A, SCYB10, PDGFA, NKEFB, β-Actin, NKFB1, and BCL2A1, respectively.

From the converged impact vector, it shows that genes PDGFA and NKEFB are the highest impacting genes in a long run.Table 8.4 shows the similar pattern of these genes when the impact vector converges to its fixed point. This finding is in line with what we have learned from biologists,

Table 8.4 Convergence of Impact Factors

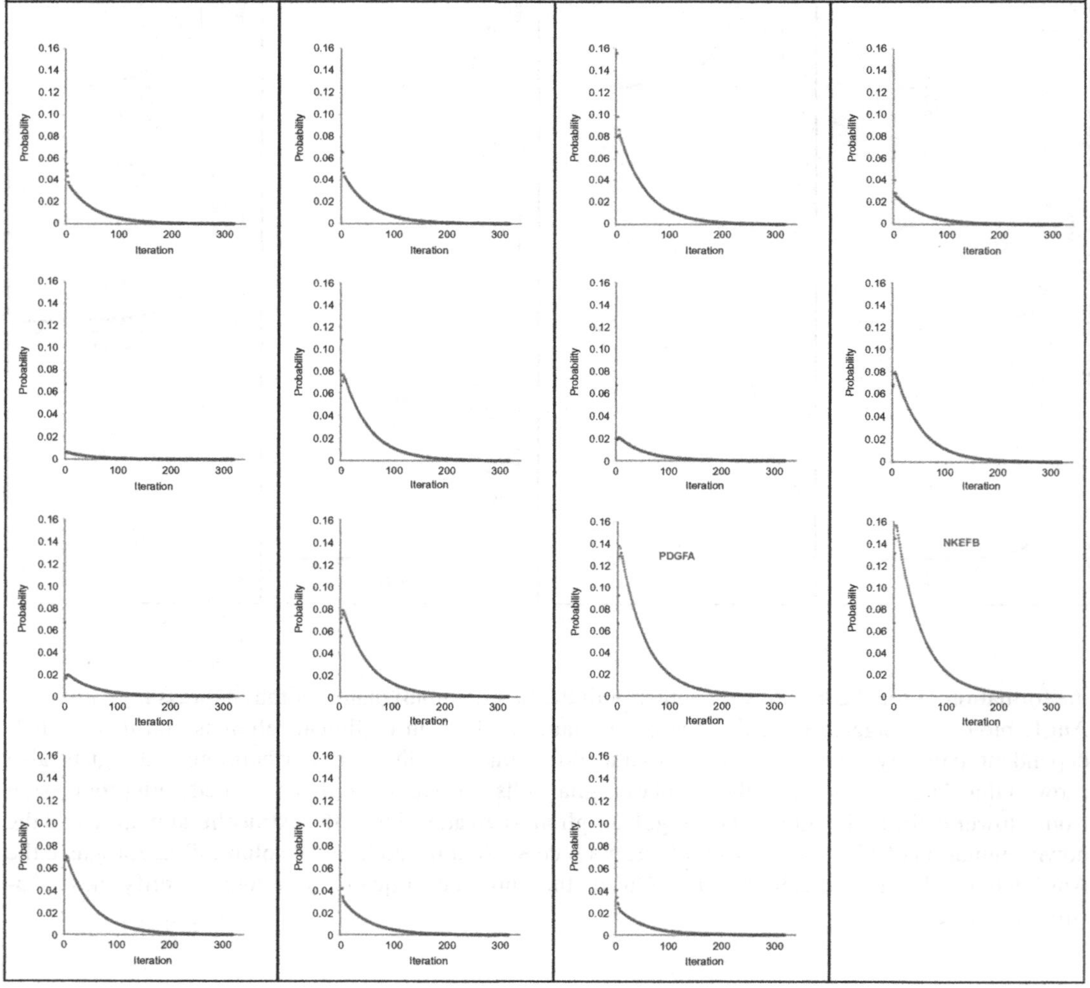

as [29] showed the family of platelet-derived growth factors (PDGFs) plays a number of critical roles in normal embryonic development, cellular differentiation, and response to tissue damage. As it is a multifaceted regulatory system, numerous pathological conditions are associated with aberrant activity of the PDGFs and their receptors. As it has been shown by [29], human gliomas, especially glioblastoma, express all PDGF ligands and both the two-cell surface receptors, PDGFR-α and -β. The cellular distribution of these proteins in tumors indicates that glial tumor cells are stimulated via PDGF/PDGFR-α autocrine and paracrine loops, while tumor vessels are stimulated via the PDGFR-β.

8.4 CONCLUSION

We presented an algebraic method for direct computation of the long-term influence and sensitivity of genes in a PBN. Our novel method only requires $O(n^2)$ memory space in contrast to other known methods in the literature that require the construction of the network's transition probability matrix with a huge size of $2^n \times 2^n$ where n is the number of genes on the PBN. We are able to analyze the long-term behavior of genes in artificial PBNs with 500 genes within minutes on a desktop computer.

Our biological case study, using PBN from a human glioma gene expression data set, showed that the long-term influence and sensitivity of genes we found in these gliomas PBN are in line with what we have learned from biologists for a long time. Compared with the results from previous computational methods such as the steady state analysis using the two-state Markov chain approach, our results are much closer to what the biologists have known about this disease. Furthermore, our results also present some knowledge that was not known before and can be used to select genes of interest as an important step before mining heterogeneous large-scale genomic data. We hope that this new finding will help to direct more wet bench research on long-term influence and sensitivity of genes.

ACKNOWLEDGMENTS

Supported in part by NSF through award CCF-1450146.

REFERENCES

[1] Brun M, Dougherty E, Shmulevich I. Steady-state probabilities for attractors in probabilistic Boolean networks. Signal Process 2005;85(10):1993–2013. http://dx.doi.org/10.1016/j.sigpro.2005.02.016.

[2] Dougherty E, Shmulevich I. Mappings between probabilistic Boolean networks. Signal Process 2003;83 (4):799–809. http://dx.doi.org/10.1016/S0165-1684(02)00480-2.

[3] Gershenson C, Kauffman S, Shmulevich I. The role of redundancy in the robustness of random Boolean networks, corr abs/nlin/0511018. http://arxiv.org/abs/nlin/0511018.

[4] Hashimoto R, Kim S, Shmulevich I, Zhang W, Bittner M, Dougherty E. Growing genetic regulatory networks from seed genes. Bioinformatics 2004;20(8):1241–7. http://dx.doi.org/10.1093/bioinformatics/bth074.

[5] Hayashida M, Tamura T, Akutsu T, Zhang S, Ching WK. Algorithms and complexity analyses for control of singleton attractors in Boolean networks. EURASIP J Bioinform Syst Biol 2008;2008:521407. http://dx.doi.org/10.1155/2008/521407.

[6] Lähdesmäki H, Hautaniemi S, Shmulevich I, Yli-Harja O. Relationships between probabilistic Boolean networks and dynamic Bayesian networks as models of gene regulatory networks. Signal Process 2006;86 (4):814–34. http://dx.doi.org/10.1016/j.sigpro.2005.06.008.

[7] Lähdesmäki H, Shmulevich I, Yli-Harja O. On learning gene regulatory networks under the Boolean network model. Mach Learn 2003;52(1–2):147–67.

[8] Liu W, Lähdesmäki H, Dougherty E, Shmulevich I. Inference of Boolean networks using sensitivity regularization. EURASIP J Bioinform Syst Biol 2008;2008:780541. http://dx.doi.org/10.1155/2008/780541.

[9] Shmulevich I, Dougherty E. Probabilistic Boolean Networks — The Modeling and Control of Gene Regulatory Networks. Philadelphia, PA: SIAM; 2010. http://www.ec-securehost.com/SIAM/OT118.html.

[10] Shmulevich I, Dougherty E, Kim S, Zhang W. Probabilistic Boolean networks: a rule-based uncertainty model for gene regulatory networks. Bioinformatics 2002;18(2):261–74. http://dx.doi.org/10.1093/bioinformatics/18.2.261.

[11] Zhang S, Hayashida M, Akutsu T, Ching WK, Ng MP. Algorithms for finding small attractors in Boolean networks. EURASIP J Bioinform Syst Biol 2007;2007:20180. http://dx.doi.org/10.1155/2007/20180.

[12] Dubrova E, Teslenko M, Martinelli A. Kauffman networks: analysis and applications. In: ICCAD '05: proceedings of the 2005 IEEE/ACM international conference on computer-aided design. Washington, DC: IEEE; 2005. p. 479–84.

[13] Kauffman S. Metabolic stability and epigenisis in randomly constructed genetic nets. J Theor Biol 1969;22:437–67.

[14] Kauffman S. The origins of order: self-organization and selection in evolution. Oxford: Oxford University Press; 1993.

[15] Gartel A, Tyner A. The role of the cyclin-dependent kinase inhibitor p21 in apoptosis. Mol Cancer Res 2002;1(8):639–49.

[16] Grimaldi M, Visintainer R, Jurman G. RegnANN: reverse engineering gene networks using artificial neural networks. PLoS ONE 2011;6(12):e28646. http://www.pubmedcentral.nih.gov/articlerender.fcgi?artid=3247226.

[17] Noman N, Iba H. Inferring gene regulatory networks using differential evolution with local search heuristics. IEEE/ACM Trans Comput Biol Bioinform 2007;4(4):634–47.

[18] Tamada Y, Bannai H, Imoto S, Katayama T, Kanehisa M, Miyano S. Utilizing evolutionary information and gene expression data for estimating gene networks with Bayesian network models. J Bioinform Comput Biol 2005;3(6):1295–314. http://dx.doi.org/10.1142/S0219720005001569.

[19] Tamada Y, Imoto S, Araki H, Nagasaki M, Print C, Charnock-Jones S, et al. Estimating genome-wide gene networks using nonparametric Bayesian network models on massively parallel computers. IEEE/ACM Trans Comput Biol Bioinform 2011;8(3):683–97. http://dx.doi.org/10.1109/TCBB.2010.68.

[20] Bochmann D, Posthoff C. Binäre Dynamische Systeme. München: R. Oldenbourg Verlag; 1981.

[21] Steinbach B, Posthoff C. Boolean differential equations, synthesis lectures on digital circuits and systems. San Rafael, CA: Morgan & Claypool Publishers; 2013.

[22] Kahn J, Kalai G, Linial N. The influence of variables on Boolean functions. In: FOCS: IEEE symposium on foundations of computer science (FOCS); 1988.

[23] Stone M. The theory of representation for Boolean algebras. Trans Am Math Soc 1936;40(1):37–111.

[24] Stone M. Applications of the theory of Boolean rings to general topology. Trans Am Math Soc 1937;41:375–481.

[25] Burris S, Sankappanavar H. A course in universal algebra. Berlin: Springer-Verlag; 1981.

[26] Fuller G, Rhee C, Hess K, Caskey L, Wang R, Bruner J, et al. Reactivation of insulin-like growth factor binding protein 2 expression in glioblastoma multiforme: a revelation by parallel gene expression profiling. Cancer Res 1999;59(17):4228–32.

[27] Brin S, Page L. The anatomy of a large-scale hypertextual web search engine. Comput Netw ISDN Syst 1998;30(1–7):107–17.

[28] Lee O, Xu J, Fueyo J, Fuller G, Aldape K, Alonso M, et al. Expression of the receptor tyrosine kinase Tie2 in neoplastic glial cells is associated with integrin beta1-dependent adhesion to the extracellular matrix. Mol Cancer Res 2006;4(12):915–26.

[29] Nazarenko I, Hede SM, He X, Hedrén A, Thompson J, Lindstroem M, et al. PDGF and PDGF receptors in glioma. Ups J Med Sci 2012;117(2):99–112.

CHAPTER

THE APPLICATION OF GRAMMAR SPACE ENTROPY IN RNA SECONDARY STRUCTURE MODELING

9

A. Manzourolajdad
National Center for Biotechnology Information, National Library of Medicine, National Institutes of Health, Bethesda, MD, United States

9.1 INTRODUCTION

Chomsky [1] initially formalized context-free grammars (CFGs) as an attempt to model languages. Since then, they have been used broadly in a variety of computer science applications. CFGs have a recursive nature and are composed of sets of rules that can drive strings of alphabets, also referred to as words. The set of words generated by a grammar is referred to as the language of that grammar. A grammar is said to be unambiguous if there is a one-to-one correspondence between the words and their descriptive derivations. Stochastic CFGs (SCFGs) assign probabilities to each rule, which in turn assigns a likelihood value to each word by multiplying the probabilities of the rules used to derive that word [2, 3]. Grenander [4], Kuich [5], Hutchins [6], Soule [7] and others have investigated important properties of CFGs and SCFGs, such as convergence of average length of derivations, capacity, or the Shannon's entropy (Shannon entropy) as defined in [8], using generating-functions techniques. The secondary structure schematic of the RNA also has a context-free nature, allowing it to be described by such grammars. RNA secondary structure was first formally described by Smith and Waterman [9]. Combinatorial features of RNA secondary structures were then explored by Stein and Waterman [10] and subsequently studied by Viennot and Vauchaussade de Chaumont [11], Hofacker et al. [12], Nebel [13], Liao and Wang [14], Doslic et al. [15] and others using generating functions and probability-generating functions.

SCFGs have had a great impact on RNA secondary structure studies [16–20]. RNA secondary structure modeling helps us make predictions about the RNA structure and its subsequent biological function, as the functions of many RNAs such as various classes of nonprotein-coding RNAs (ncRNA) are related to their structures. Typically, RNA secondary structure prediction is done by minimization of the folding energy of the sequence under a thermodynamic-based folding model such as the Boltzmann ensemble [21]. SCFGs, on the other hand, are covariance models that can imitate RNA folding with more flexibility. In the case of an SCFG-based folding model, likelihood values are assigned to all possible folding scenarios of an RNA sequence. Then, the structure having maximum likelihood (ML) value is predicted as the secondary structure of the RNA sequence. ML prediction of SCFG-based models can be done by the Cocke-Younger-Kasami (CYK) algorithm. Similar to energy minimization, the CYK algorithm is implemented through dynamic programming. The goal of model design is to obtain ML estimations that are as similar to the known RNA secondary structures as possible, thus making assignment of probabilities to rules a critical and challenging task. Rivas [20] offers a more in-depth insight into various aspects of RNA secondary structure modeling.

Current expectation maximization (EM) model training approaches generally consist of the following two steps: First, the CYK algorithm is used for structure prediction of each RNA sequence of the training set (maximization step). Second, the rule probabilities of the SCFG are reestimated based on the counts or frequencies of their occurrences in the predictions (estimation step). These estimations can be calculated either using the Laplace prior approach explained in Durbin et al. [22] or deploying similar frequency-based approaches. The iterative EM procedure can continue until the resulting rule probabilities yield desired accuracy. Model training techniques may vary, in either the definition of the ML criterion (joint vs. conditional) or in rule-probability estimation techniques [23, 24]. An SCFG-based RNA folding model can either consist of a lightweight SCFG with only a few grammar rules [23] or it can be a heavyweight grammar consisting of many rules such as super-grammars described in Rivas et al. [24].

In this work, the Shannon entropy of the SCFG, denoted here as grammar space (GS) entropy, is analytically calculated and introduced as a critical grammar feature in RNA secondary structure modeling. Presented formulations are consistent with the general form of grammars entropy known as the *derivational* entropy, and can be found in Grenander [4] and Soule [7]. In Section 9.2, a formulation is presented for calculating the Shannon entropy of the infinitely large probabilistic space of structurally unambiguous RNA-modeling grammars[1] that is consistent with the derivational entropy formulations presented in Grenander [4]. The GS entropy values of several well-established RNA folding models are then calculated under different parameter sets in Section 9.3. In Section 9.4, a criterion for SCFG-based RNA secondary structure model training is proposed based on the GS entropy. Finally, Section 9.5 consists of discussion and conclusions.

9.2 A SHANNON ENTROPY FOR THE SCFG SPACE

As previously mentioned, any SCFG refers to an infinitely large ensemble of derivations that can be generated by applying the grammar rules in a recursive fashion. In the case of unambiguous grammars, such derivations are unique and discrete random events each having their associated probability. Here, an attempt is made to compute the closed form Shannon entropy of the infinitely large probabilistic space that contains all possible derivations emanating from a given grammar. Our focus here is structurally unambiguous grammars that are designed and trained for RNA secondary structure prediction.

[1]The formulations presented in the main text focus on nonstacking grammars. In nonstacking grammars, the probability of formation of a basepair does not directly depend on nucleotide composition of the previous basepair(s). Generalization of the present formulation to stacking grammars can be done by using the appropriate basepairing probabilities matrix (see AppendixD for an example). The work here is limited to grammars that include the rules $X \rightarrow a$, $X \rightarrow aY$, $X \rightarrow Ya$, $X \rightarrow aYbZ$, $X \rightarrow YaZb$, $X \rightarrow aYb$, and $X \rightarrow \epsilon$. X, Y, and Z are nonterminals. Other representations of unambiguous grammars can also be deployed using a similar trend for calculating their entropy.

9.2.1 AN INTUITIVE EXAMPLE

SCFGs consist of terminals and nonterminals. A terminal denotes an alphabet, while a nonterminal refers to a substructure. Consider the following unambiguous grammar, denoted as Ex1, with a single alphabet, $\Sigma = \{a\}$, and the following two production rules:

$$S \rightarrow a \ (\alpha), \ \ S \rightarrow aS \ (\beta)$$

where α and β are terminal and nonterminal rule probabilities, respectively, and $\alpha + \beta = 1$. Ex1 produces an infinite number of strings s, $s \in \Sigma^*$, each of which corresponds to a unique derivation or parsing. Being exclusive events, the sum of all possible derivations converges to one in the limit of infinity, $\sum_{i=0}^{\infty} \alpha\beta^i = 1$, while the expected word length converges to the following:

$$\lim_{|\Sigma^*_{Ex1}| \rightarrow \infty} E\left[-\log p\left(\Sigma^*_{Ex1}\right)\right] = -\sum_{i=0}^{\infty} \alpha\beta^i \log\left(\alpha\beta^i\right) = -\log\alpha - (\beta/\alpha)\log\beta \tag{1}$$

where the random variable Σ^*_{Ex1} refers to the space of derivations of grammar Ex1 and $E[X]$ denotes the expectation of random variable X; $E[X] = \sum_{x \in X} p(x) \times x$.

The derived expression in Eq. (1) is *the* Shannon entropy of Ex1 GS in the limit of infinitely large number of derivations, since any ordering of the geometric summation in Eq. (1) results in the same value. This is because the summation here is absolutely convergent.[2] The Shannon entropy for Ex1 is defined for all terminal probability values α within the interval (0,1]. For the case of $\alpha = 0$, however, the entropy of Ex1 is not defined but tends toward infinity as α tends toward zero. This is in line with the intuition that as the probability of selecting a terminal, α, decreases, the expected length of derived strings increases. Fig. 9.1 depicts the Shannon entropy of Ex1 GS as a function of terminal rule probability α.

Let us consider a larger alphabet size for the grammar and its impact on entropy. Grammar Ex4 deploys rules of Ex1 but generates alphabets $\Sigma = \{\mathtt{A}, \mathtt{C}, \mathtt{G}, \mathtt{U}\}$. Ex4 generates hypothetical RNA sequences. Let us assign equal probabilities to each nucleotide given the application of a grammar rule:

$$S \rightarrow \mathrm{A|C|G|U} \ (\alpha/4), \ \ S \rightarrow \mathrm{AS|CS|GS|US} \ (\beta/4)$$

In a similar fashion, the Shannon entropy of Ex4 can be calculated in the limit of infinitely large number of derivations:

$$\lim_{|\Sigma^*_{Ex4}| \rightarrow \infty} E\left[-\log p\left(\Sigma^*_{Ex4}\right)\right] = -\log\alpha - (\beta/\alpha)\log\beta + (1/\alpha)\log 4 \tag{2}$$

It can be seen from Eq. (2) that the entropy values of grammars Ex1 and Ex4 are very similar with the only difference being an additional positive term for entropy of Ex4. Fig. 9.1 shows the degree of increase in entropy between Ex1 and Ex4. Notice how for $\alpha = 1$ the entropy of Ex4 grammar is 2 due to alphabet size 4. The additional term $+(1/\alpha)\log 4$ illustrates that rule probabilities can have a stronger impact on the entropy value than alphabet size, at least for the case of Ex1 and Ex4.

[2] If the sum of the absolute value of summands of a series is finite, it is known as an absolutely convergent series. Absolutely convergent series converge to the same value regardless of order of summation.

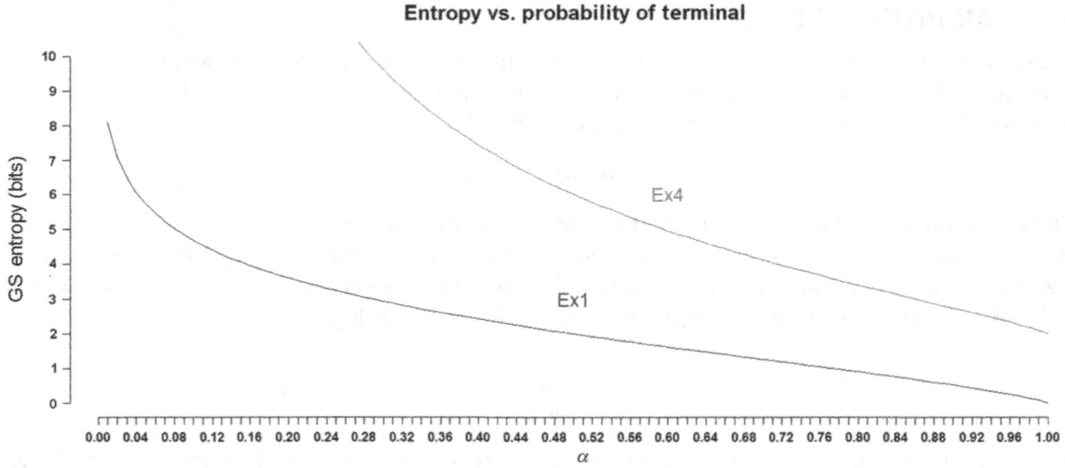

FIGURE 9.1

The Shannon entropy of grammar space of Ex1 and Ex4 as a function of terminal rule probability α. Logarithm was calculated in base 2.

Eqs. (1) and (2) were easy to derive, due to the simplicity and symmetricity of Ex1 and Ex4 grammars. Great analytical complications may arise, however, for more sophisticated grammars. In the next section, the entropy calculation is generalized to grammars having an arbitrary number of rules and nonterminals.

9.2.2 GENERALIZATION TO ALL STRUCTURALLY UNAMBIGUOUS GRAMMARS

In this section, a general method is presented for computing the GS entropy of unambiguous SCFGs regardless of the number of nonterminals, rules, and probability distributions of the rules. In doing so, various axioms applicable to the Shannon entropy were used for simplicity of expression. Rather than using the general form of representing SCFGs, notations that are more peculiar to the context of RNA structure were chosen. Applying the general formulation for the Shannon entropy of any SCFG, as done in Grenander [4] and Soule [7] through different notations, leads to the same results.

Let us use notation $H(\Pi Y|n,G,\Theta)$ for the Shannon entropy of derivations emanating from nonterminal n in GS (G,Θ), where G denotes the set of grammar rules and Θ denotes the probability vector corresponding to the rules, in the limit of infinite number of derivations:

$$H(\Pi Y|n,G,\Theta) \equiv \lim_{|\Pi Y_{(n,G,\Theta)}|\to\infty} E[-\log p(\Pi Y|n,G,\Theta)]$$

where $\Pi Y_{(n,G,\Theta)}$ is the structural space of all derivations, $(\pi,y) \in \Pi Y_{(n,G,\Theta)}$, each having probability $p(\pi,y|n,G,\Theta) = p(n \Rightarrow_\pi^* y)$. Expression n is the starting nonterminal for the generation of (π,y), y is the derived sequence, π denotes the derivation tree (secondary structure) that describes y, and operator $\Rightarrow_\pi^*$ describes the derivation tree π. Expression $H(\Pi Y|n)$ is used instead of $H(\Pi Y|n,G,\Theta)$ from here on for convenience, because G and Θ are constant throughout the GS entropy calculation. The total probability of derivation trees emanating from a given nonterminal n, $p(\Pi Y\,|n)$, can be expressed in terms of other nonterminals of the grammar by summing over the probabilities corresponding to the grammar rules that immediately emanate from the nonterminal n (see Appendix A):

$$P(\Pi Y|n) = \sum_{i\in n\rightarrow\omega} p_i \times P(\Pi Y|i_1) \times P(\Pi Y|i_2), \quad \forall n \in N \tag{3}$$

where $n \rightarrow \omega$ is any grammar rule with nonterminal n at its left-hand side, N is the number of nonterminals in the grammar, and p_i is the probability of rule i. Symbols i_1 and i_2 represent the first and second nonterminals on the right-hand side of rule i, respectively. Note, for the rules that have only one nonterminal on the right-hand side, $i_2 = \varnothing$, $P(\Pi Y\,|i_2)$ is set to one, and for rules having no nonterminals on their right-hand side, both $P(\Pi Y\,|i_1)$ and $P(\Pi Y\,|i_2)$ are set to one.

Expression $H(\Pi Y\,|n)$, can then be expressed in terms of the entropy other nonterminals in Eq. (4) by taking the entropy of the right side of Eq. (3) (see Appendix B):

$$H(\Pi Y|n) = H(\mathrm{P}_n) + \sum_{i\in n\rightarrow\omega} p_i[H(\Pi Y|i_1) + H(\Pi Y|i_2)], \quad \forall n \in N \tag{4}$$

where P_n represents the probability vector corresponding to rules emanating from nonterminal n, $\mathrm{P}_n = \{p_i | i \in n \rightarrow \omega\}$, and $H(\mathrm{P}_n)$ is the Shannon entropy of P_n, because the sum of elements of P_n equals one: $H(\mathrm{P}_n) = -\sum_{i\in n\rightarrow\omega} p_i \log p_i$.

Note, for the rules that have only one nonterminal on the right side, $i_2 = \varnothing$, $H(\Pi Y\,|i_2)$ is set to zero and for rules having no nonterminals on their right-hand side, both $H(\Pi Y\,|i_1)$ and $H(\Pi Y\,|i_2)$ are set to zero.

As a result, the Shannon entropy of nonterminals can be related to each other by N linear equations. The entropy of the SCFG space will then be equal to the entropy of the starting nonterminal S_0 (see Appendix C for an example):

$$H(\Pi Y) = H(\Pi Y|S_0) \tag{5}$$

9.3 GS ENTROPY OF RNA FOLDING MODELS

In this section, the GS entropy is calculated for various lightweight and heavyweight RNA folding models. The relationship between the GS entropy feature and model performance is then investigated. Lightweight RNA folding models were taken from Dowell and Eddy [23]. The GS entropy figures of the four structurally unambiguous grammars were calculated. Computations were repeated for all three distinct choices of model parameters. The naming of the grammars G3, G4, G5, and G6 in the mentioned work are UNA, RUN, IVO, and BJK, respectively. Three RNA secondary structure data sets by the names `mixed80`, `benchmark`, and `rfam5` were used to train each grammar model using the Conus software package [23]. Details about the grammars, the training data sets, software package, and the grammar rule probabilities are all available in Dowell and Eddy [23]. The GS entropy values of the resulting 12 SCFGs were calculated according to the presented procedure and are illustrated in Table 9.1. Symbol ∞ denotes cases where the GS entropy does not converge to a real positive number. All models trained via the `mixed80` data set have higher entropy values than those of `benchmark` and `rfam5`. Also, all `benchmark`-trained models have higher entropy values than `rfam5`-trained models, regardless of choice of grammar.

Table 9.1 GS Entropy of Structurally Unambiguous Lightweight Grammars Under Various Parameter Sets

Training Set	UNA	RUN	IVO	BJK
mixed80	∞	5448	5175	4198
benchmark	767	907	982	732
rfam5	467	533	598	452

Grammar description and parameters according to Dowell and Eddy [23]. Column Training Set *contains the name of the training set used to estimate model parameters. Logarithm was calculated in base 2.*

The performance of an SCFG-based RNA folding model is measured by its ability to correctly predict the secondary structure of the given RNA sequence. The actual structure of the RNA can be either be determined by an experiment or inferred from structural homology. Various classes of RNAs may have their unique folding features and functions, some with complicated structures difficult to predict given a simple folding model. Sensitivity and specificity (predictive positive values (PPVs)) are calculated by comparing base pairs of the model prediction to those of the real structure. The performance is then assessed by a form of averaging individual sensitivity and specificity values across a collected test set. Various classes of RNAs have different folding features and functions, some with complicated structures difficult to predict given a simple model. Models trained on the mixed80 data set were used to explore possible relationship between the GS entropy of the model and its performance in predicting RNA secondary structure. The GS entropy of grammar models trained on the mixed80 data set were plotted against average sensitivity to structures in benchmark and rfam5 test sets (average sensitivity according to Conus software [23]). GS entropy and corresponding average sensitivity values for the three BJK, RUN, and IVO grammars are shown in Fig. 9.2. The UNA grammar was excluded, because its corresponding GS entropy was not defined as a real positive number (set to ∞). The BJK grammar has lower GS entropy while having higher average sensitivity values compared to the IVO and RUN grammars. Average specificity values showed a similar pattern (data not shown).

An attempt was made to calculate the GS entropy of more recent grammars. Rivas et al. [24] described a general language, TORNADO, with which heavyweight SCFGs can be described, enabling the user to parameterize various RNA structural features such as base pair/coaxial stacking, dangles, helix/loop lengths, and so forth. Two grammar designs were chosen from the mentioned work for investigation. The first grammar is denoted as g6, which is the same as the previously described G6 or BJK model. The GS entropy of g6 was calculated using parameter sets provided by Rivas et al. [24]. The second grammar was the Basic Grammar (BG). The model BG imitates a simplified version of a folding model that is at the core of both the state-of-the-art thermodynamic model implemented in the ViennaRNA Software Package [25] and complex nearest-neighbor RNA folding models used in Do et al. [26]. Please refer to Rivas et al. [24] for further explanation.

Parameter sets for grammars g6 and BG are available for different training sets. Here, four training sets were considered. Names of training sets are shown in Table 9.2. Also, the TORNADO language enables applying different base pairing constraints on the grammars. Two of these constraints were considered here. The first constraint enforces Watson-Crick base pairing only. The second constraint

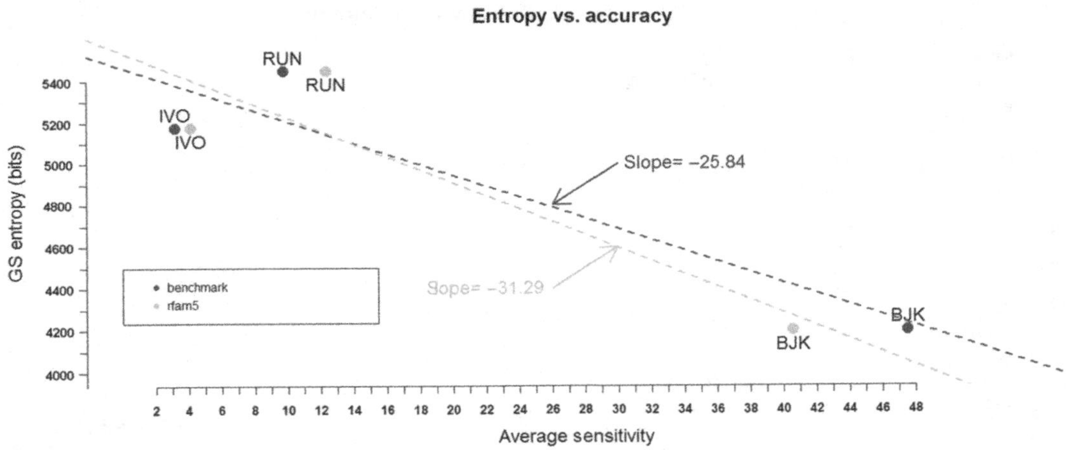

FIGURE 9.2

The GS entropy of grammar models trained on the `mixed80` data set were plotted against average sensitivity to structures in `benchmark` and `rfam5` test sets, separately. Average sensitivity according to Conus software written by Dowell and Eddy [23]. Grammar names and entropy values are according to Table 9.1. Trend lines corresponding to each test set are shown as dashed lines. Blue (dark shades) corresponds to the `benchmark` test set. Green (light shades) corresponds to the `rfam5` test set. Logarithm was calculated in base 2.

Table 9.2 GS Entropy of Structurally Unambiguous Nonstacking Grammars Under Various Parameter Sets

Training Set	BG	BGstk	BGwcx	g6	g6stk	g6wcx
TrA + 2 × TrB	37.160	37.079	35.214	378.740	377.086	357.630
TrA + TrB	47.056	46.978	44.680	412.892	411.477	390.547
TrA	73.114	73.026	69.660	469.959	468.933	446.016
TrB	14.889	14.904	13.991	243.074	240.575	228.354

Grammar description and parameters according to Rivas et al. [24]. `Basic Grammar` *denoted as BG. Extensions* `wcx` *and* `stk` *denote Watson-Crick base pairing constraint and stacking versions, respectively. Column* `Training Set` *denotes the training set used to estimate model parameters. Logarithm was calculated in base 2.*

introduces base pair dependencies derived from observed stacked base pairings. In stacked base pairing, the probability distribution of pairs varies depending on the context of surrounding pairing. An example for calculating the GS entropy values corresponding to different constraints applied on the BG model is provided in Appendix D. Extensions `wcx` and `stk` were used to denote first and second constraints on a given grammar, respectively. For instance, the stacking version of the BG grammar was denoted as BGstk. Parameter sets corresponding to different training sets and constraints are available in Rivas et al. [24]. GS entropy values corresponding to different models are shown in Table 9.2. The BG models have significantly lower GS entropy than the g6 models, regardless of training set or applied constraints. The enforcement of Watson-Crick base pairing constraint reduces the GS entropy

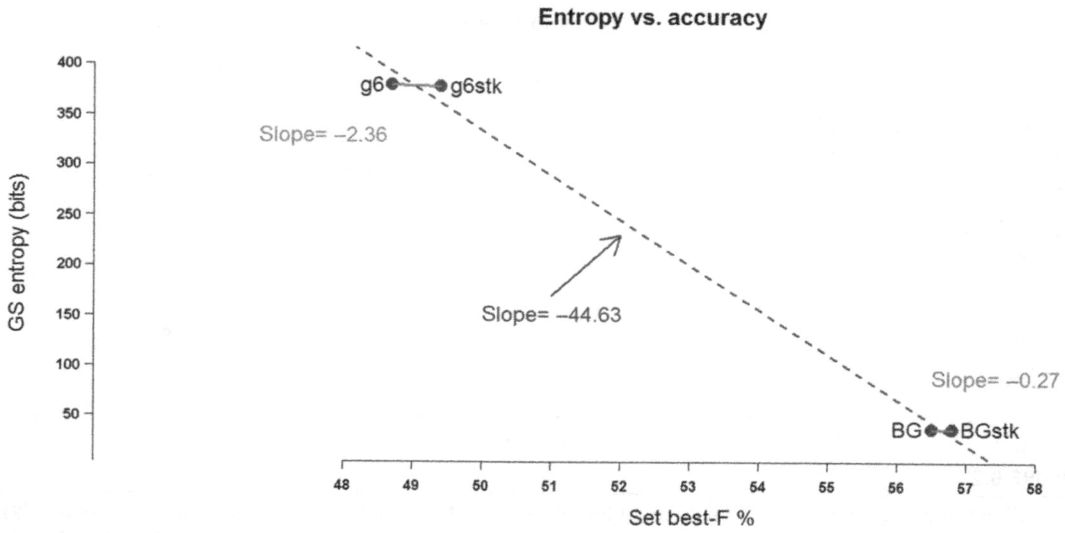

FIGURE 9.3

The GS entropy of grammar models trained on the `TrA` + 2 × `TrB` data set were plotted against best F measure values. Grammar names and entropy values are according to Table 9.2. The best F measure values were taken from Rivas et al. [24, Table 1]. The trend line is shown as a dashed line. Logarithm was calculated in base 2.

of the model for all cases of grammars and training sets. Furthermore, the application of the base pairing constraint also yields a lower GS entropy, with the exception of `TrB`-trained BG grammar. The Watson-Crick base pairing constraint has a more significant effect on the reduction of the GS entropy than the stacking constraint.

GS entropy values corresponding to the `TrA` + 2 × `TrB` training set are plotted against the best F measures of the models in Fig. 9.3. Here, F measure is the harmonic mean of the sensitivity and PPV [27]. The best F measure is used as a measure of model accuracy. Values for model accuracy are according to Rivas et al. [24, Table 1]. Similar to the lightweight models shown in Fig. 9.2, higher accuracy is generally associated with lower GS entropy. The rate of decrease in GS entropy per a unit increase in accuracy, however, is more significant between two model designs (eg, g6 vs. BG) than between a model and its stacked version (eg, g6 vs. g6stk).

9.4 THE TYPICAL SET CRITERION

As previously mentioned, current ML-based model training methods iteratively estimate rule probabilities from frequency of occurrence of corresponding rules in the predictions of RNA structures. In this section, a criterion denoted as the Typical Set Criterion (TSC) is presented to maximize the *joint* probability of the observed RNA secondary structures $\Pi Y_{\text{obs.}}$. The criterion can then be used as a constraint on probability vector Θ estimation.

Satisfying the joint maximization of all observed RNA structures is done by tuning the grammar model such that the structures become a part of the typical set[3] of structures generated by the grammar: $\Pi Y_{\text{obs.}} \subset T_\epsilon(\Pi Y)$. The typical set of structures for GS (G,Θ) with parameter ϵ can be defined as

$$T_\epsilon(\Pi Y) = \{(\pi,y) : |-\log p(\pi,y) - E[-\log p(\Pi Y)]| \leq \epsilon E[-\log p(\Pi Y)]\} \tag{6}$$

The following immediately implies for any structure in $T_\epsilon(\Pi Y)$:

$$(1-\epsilon)H(\Pi Y) \leq -\sum_i r_i(\pi,y)\log(p_i) \leq (1+\epsilon)H(\Pi Y), \quad \forall(\pi,y) \in T_\epsilon(\Pi Y) \tag{7}$$

where p_i is the probability of rule i in the model and $r_i(\pi,y)$ denotes the number of times rule i is deployed in structure (π,y). Note that the GS entropy of the model $H(\Pi Y)$ is computed according to Eq. (5).

Observed RNA secondary structures can be constrained by Eq. (7), as they are to be a subset of the typical structures generated by the given grammar. Let us refer to this constraint as the TSC for RNA secondary structure model training. To satisfy Eq. (7) for all observed structures, the grammar rule probabilities $\hat{\Theta}$ is proposed, which yields from the minimization presented in

$$\hat{\Theta} = \arg\min_{\Theta} \| -\mathrm{R}_G(\Pi Y_{\text{obs.}}) \times \log\Theta - H(\Pi Y|G,\Theta).1 \| \tag{8}$$

where function $\mathbf{R}_G(\pi,y)$ maps the structure (π,y) to a $1 \times V$ vector whose elements are $r_i(\pi,y)$ with V being the total number of rules in the grammar G. $\mathbf{R}_G(\Pi Y_{\text{obs.}})$ is then an $D \times V$ matrix with D being the total number of observed RNA secondary structures. The $\log\Theta$ is a $V \times 1$ vector containing log-likelihoods of grammar rule probabilities that are subject to the proposed minimization. Note that Eq. (8) may not be the only way to satisfy Eq. (7).

9.4.1 FUTURE WORK IN TSC-BASED MODEL TRAINING ALGORITHMS

The steps of a TSC-based model training approach can be identical to current methods with the following difference: In the probability-estimation step, the rule probability estimates are made to satisfy Eq. (8), rather than being based on Laplace prior or similar methods. The matrix $\mathbf{R}_G(\Pi Y_{\text{obs.}})$ would then contain counts of occurrences of rules in the predictions, while terms $\log\Theta$ and $H(\Pi Y\,|G,\Theta)$ are all functions of vector Θ. The ML estimates of individual structures can be done in the same manner as other methods; that is, $\max_\Theta \log p(\pi,y|G,\Theta)$.

RNA structures used for the training set are usually not representatives of all noncoding RNA structures, especially unknown structural families of noncoding RNAs. An anonymous reviewer of this work initially raised this issue and its relation to data overfitting. Regardless of the deployed model training technique, models too specific to known structures in the training set may not necessarily be effective in the discovery of novel structures. To avoid undesirably high specificity to the structures of the training set, one can select the parameter set that *minimally* reduces the GS. In other words, in the probability-estimation step, there may be more than one set of parameter sets Θ that can satisfy Eq. (8). The probability vector Θ that both satisfies Eq. (8) and yields highest GS entropy $H(\Pi Y\,|G,\Theta)$ may be

[3]The typical set is a set of sequences whose probability is close to one [28, p. 62].

more desirable. The parameter set that satisfies both criteria can then be chosen as in Eq. (9). The difference between the positive-value parameters γ_1 and γ_2 can act as a trade-off between data overfitting concerns and prediction accuracy.

$$\hat{\Theta} = \arg\max_{\Theta} [\gamma_1 H(\Pi Y|G,\Theta) - \gamma_2 \| -\mathrm{R}_G(\Pi Y) \times \log\Theta - H(\Pi Y|G,\Theta).1 \|] \tag{9}$$

9.5 DISCUSSION AND CONCLUSIONS

In this chapter, a procedure was presented for calculating the Shannon entropy of SCFGs that model RNA folding in specific. As an analytical measure of the largeness of model space, the entropy was then incorporated in a novel criterion for RNA structure model training. An earlier version of this work was presented in Manzourolajdad [29]. More rigorous mathematical proofs have been offered in the works of Grenander [4] and others. The GS entropy values for certain SCFG-based RNA folding models were calculated. An investigation into earlier lightweight models shows that the choice of training data set can have a major impact on the GS entropy value (see Table 9.1).

Lower GS entropy is generally associated with higher model accuracy. Fig. 9.2 shows that the GS entropy of the BJK model is lower than the other lightweight models while its accuracy to predict RNA secondary structure is higher. A similar conclusion about the relationship between model accuracy and GS entropy can be drawn by investigating more recent folding models. It can be seen from Table 9.2 that the GS entropy of the `TrATrBTrB`-trained `Basic Grammar` is significantly lower than that of the `TrATrBTrB`-trained BJK model (g6). Fig. 9.3 shows that the accuracy of the `Basic Grammar` is approximately 10% higher than the BJK model (from 48.7 to 56.5 best F measure [24, Table 1]).

Although the association of higher model accuracy and lower model uncertainty (here, Shannon entropy) is somewhat intuitive, significantly low GS entropy may also indicate overfitting. The entropy of the mentioned BJK model is approximately 10 times higher than that of the `Basic Grammar` (378.7 to 37.2 in Table 9.2). This implies that the folding space of the BJK model with the `TrATrBTrB`-trained parameter set can be significantly larger than the `Basic Grammar`. To get an idea of the significance in difference between the two folding spaces, consider the following argument: An approximation of an upper bound for the largeness of space S of a given probabilistic model is $2^{H(S)}$. For the two BG and g6 folding models, consider GS entropy values corresponding to the `TrB` training set and Watson-Crick constraint. The ratio of the corresponding folding spaces is in the order of $228.354 - 13.991 = 214.363$. This is actually the smallest difference between corresponding entropy values in Table 9.2. Such a significant reduction in folding space ($\approx 2^{214}$ fold) for only ~10% increase in model accuracy, here best F measure, may not be desirable. It is not clear, however, if the reduction of GS entropy of the `Basic Grammar` model is due to its specific design and architecture or the assignment of rule probabilities that are estimated by current model training approaches.

The application of stacking constraints on the models has shown to be effective in increasing its accuracy [24, Table 1]. Such increases in accuracy, however, do not lead to significant changes in the GS entropy of the model (see Fig. 9.3). Hence, the introduction of such constraints are less likely to cause data overfitting than alteration of the overall model architecture or the use of a different training set.

The TSC was proposed as a novel criterion for the current model training approaches. Eqs. (8) and (9) can be used to incorporate this criterion into the rule probability-estimation step of current model training procedures. Rivas [20] mentions a consistent performance ceiling across various model training methods, suggesting the need for other forms of information to be incorporated into model training than mere individual sequence-based folding scores. The TSC may be a suitable candidate in this regard, as it can act as a test set-independent measure of performance. It is not known, however, to what extent, TSC-based model training approaches can lead to improvements in SCFG-based RNA secondary structure modeling. For instance, an immediate concern would be the convergence of empirical entropy [30, p. 42–4] to the analytical GS entropy. As mentioned before, the GS entropy measure is only asymptotically valid for a *sufficiently large* number of structures. When is an observed set of data large enough to represent a typical set of structures corresponding to the model? What is the asymptotic behavior of the empirical entropy as the size of the data increases and at what point does it converge to the GS entropy? How does a specific grammar design (or here, folding model) impact the smallest ϵ value achievable in Eq. (6) and the subsequent optimizations? Gaining insights into such general questions as well as incorporating TSC into current EM/ML model training approaches may prove useful in improving SCFG-based RNA secondary structural modeling.

ACKNOWLEDGMENTS

This work resulted from useful conversations in the RNA-informatics lab at the University of Georgia. Communication with Robin D. Dowell regarding the Conus software was very helpful. Many thanks to Elena Rivas for helping me understand the TORNADO language and providing with various model parameters through communication. This research was supported in part by the Intramural Research Program of the NIH, National Library of Medicine. I thank Dr. John L. Spouge for his support.

APPENDIX A CALCULATING SUM OF PROBABILITIES OF DERIVATIONS IN AN SCFG

For any structurally nonambiguous grammar, each derivation $p(\pi,y)$ can be rewritten as $p(\pi)p(y|\pi)$, where derivations $p(\pi)$ correspond to a nonambiguous GS. Therefore, all derivations $p(\pi,y)$ are unique.

Let us denote $P(n{\Rightarrow}^*\Sigma^*)$ as the total probability of all derivation trees emanating from nonterminal n in the limit of infinite number of derivations:

$$P(\Pi Y|n) \equiv P(n{\Rightarrow}^*\Sigma^*) \equiv \lim_{|\Pi Y_{(n)}|\to\infty} \sum_{(\pi,y)} P(n \Rightarrow_\pi^* y)$$

For simplicity, let us consider a grammar design with the following rule types:

$$\begin{aligned} S_{r_{i_1}} &\to a \\ S_{r_{i_1}} &\to aS_{r_{i_2}} \\ S_{r_{i_1}} &\to aS_{r_{i_2}}bS_{r_{i_3}} \end{aligned} \tag{A.1}$$

where a denotes the generation of a nucleotide and $\{a,b\}$ denotes the generation of a base pair. Conditioning the probabilities of all such structures on their first left-most derivation rule gives

$$\begin{aligned} P(n{\Rightarrow}^*\Sigma^*) &= \sum_{i\in n\to\omega} p_i P(n{\Rightarrow}^*\Sigma^*|r_i) = \sum_{i\in n\to\omega} p_i P(aS_{r_{i_2}}bS_{r_{i_3}}{\Rightarrow}^*\Sigma^*) \\ &= \sum_{i\in n\to\omega} p_i P(S_{r_{i_2}}{\Rightarrow}^*\Sigma^*)\times P(S_{r_{i_3}}{\Rightarrow}^*\Sigma^*), \quad \forall n\in N \end{aligned} \tag{A.2}$$

where $S_{r_{i_2}}$ and $S_{r_{i_3}}$ can refer to an empty set of derivations $\varnothing$ depending on which rule type is deployed. In such cases, probability of one is assigned. The first equality holds because of structural unambiguity. The last equality holds because of the context-free nature of the SCFG, which implies independence between structures emanating from $S_{r_{i_2}}$ and $S_{r_{i_3}}$. In other words

$$P(aS_{r_{i_2}}bS_{r_{i_3}} \Rightarrow_\pi^* y, y_j = b) = P(aS_{r_{i_2}}b \Rightarrow_\pi^* y_1 \ldots y_j) \times P(S_{r_{i_3}} \Rightarrow_\pi^* y_{j+1} \ldots y_{n_y}), \quad \forall j, 1 \le j \le n_y, \quad \forall (\pi, y) \in \Pi Y$$

The above argument can be easily extended to other types of grammar rules such as $X \rightarrow Ya$ and $X \rightarrow YaZb$ in a similar fashion.

Eq. (A.2) results in N quadratic equations in terms of $P(\Pi Y\,|n)$s.

The solution

$$P(\Pi Y|n) = 1, \quad \forall n \in N$$

is sufficient for Eq. (A.2) to hold, because total probabilities of rules emanating from a given nonterminal is equal to one. Hence, the total probability of all derivations emanating from a given nonterminal adds up to one in the limit of infinitely large number of derivations. This enables us to define a Shannon entropy for the structurally unambiguous SCFG.

APPENDIX B COMPUTING GS ENTROPY OF AN SCFG

In this section, the GS entropy is calculated by applying the following axiom to the probability space of grammars:

Axiom Consider the four random variables $l \in L, i \in I, m \in M, n \in N$ where I partitions L into mutually exclusive sets L_is (i.e. $p(i|l) \in \{0,1\}, \forall i,l$). Furthermore, conditioning probability of l on i results in independence of probabilities of its constructing components, m and n. Hence,

$$p(l,i) = p(l) = p_i p(l|i) = p_i p(m) p(n), \quad \text{if } l \in L_i, \quad \forall l,i,m,n$$

and

$$p(l,i) = 0, \quad \text{if } l \notin L_i, \quad \forall l,i$$

Taking the entropy from both sides gives

$$H(L) = H(I) + \sum_i p_i H(L|i) = H(I) + \sum_i p_i [H(M) + H(N)] \tag{B.1}$$

Applying Eq. (B.1) on Eq. (A.2) for each nonterminal n yields

$$H(\Pi Y|n) = H(\mathrm{P}_n) + \sum_{i \in n \rightarrow \omega} p_i [H(\Pi Y|i_1) + H(\Pi Y|i_2)], \quad \forall n \in N$$

where

$$H(\mathrm{P}_n) = -\sum_{i \in n \rightarrow \omega} p_i \log p_i$$

and i_1 and i_2 represent nonterminals $S_{r_{i_2}}$ and $S_{r_{i_3}}$, respectively.

Note that the above expression is only valid in the limit of infinite derivations. If positive values are obtained for $H(\Pi Y\,|n)$s, then the Shannon entropy is absolutely convergent. In other words, if the above equations do not yield an answer to the entropy values (ie, singular matrix) or yield a negative value, then the expression `Not Defined` will be assigned to the entropy values.

APPENDIX C AN EXAMPLE OF CALCULATING THE GS ENTROPY

Consider the G4 (RUN) grammar originally developed jointly by Dowell and Eddy [23] and Graeme Mitchison:

$$\begin{aligned} S &\rightarrow aS|T|\epsilon \\ T &\rightarrow Ta|aSb|TaSb \end{aligned}$$

Probabilities corresponding to the `rfam5`-trained parameter sets using the Conus software package developed by Dowell and Eddy [23], yields

$$\begin{aligned} S &\rightarrow aS\ (0.5748)|T\ (0.3858)|\epsilon\ (0.0394) \\ T &\rightarrow Ta\ (0.4460)|aSb\ (0.5143)|TaSb\ (0.0397) \end{aligned}$$

with nucleotide probabilities `NC` being equal to [0.3320,0.1886,0.2333,0.2461] for `A`, `C`, `G`, and `U`, respectively. The base pairing probabilities `BP` are according to Table C.3.

Applying Eq. 4 on the grammar rules for nonterminals S and T yields the following two equations:

$$\begin{aligned} H(\Pi Y|S) &= H(\mathrm{P}_S) + (0.5748) \times H(\Pi Y|S) + (0.3858) \times H(\Pi Y|T) \\ H(\Pi Y|T) &= H(\mathrm{P}_T) + (0.4460) \times H(\Pi Y|T) + (0.5143) \times H(\Pi Y|S) \\ &\quad + (0.0397) \times [H(\Pi Y|T) + H(\Pi Y|S)] \end{aligned}$$

where entropy of grammar rules emanating from each nonterminal can be simplified to the following, due to independence of nucleotide and pairing probabilities from nucleotide and base pairing grammar rules, respectively:

$$\begin{aligned} H(\mathrm{P}_S) &= H([0.5748, 0.3858, 0.0394]) + (0.5748)H(\mathrm{NC}) \\ H(\mathrm{P}_T) &= H([0.4460, 0.5143, 0.0397]) + (0.4460)H(\mathrm{NC}) \\ &\quad + (0.5143 + 0.0397)H(\mathrm{BP}) \end{aligned}$$

Notations H(`NC`) and H(`BP`) are nucleotide and base pairing entropy values, respectively. Computing values in base 2 logarithm gives

Table C.3 Base Pairing Probability Distribution of the `rfam5`-Trained RUN Grammar: `BP`

	A	C	G	U
A	0.0169	0.0119	0.0143	0.1326
C	0.0127	0.0082	0.2287	0.0088
G	0.0176	0.2481	0.0153	0.0475
U	0.1553	0.0087	0.0556	0.0178

$$H(\text{NC}) = 1.970$$
$$H(\text{BP}) = 3.048$$
$$H(\text{P}_S) = 2.305$$
$$H(\text{P}_T) = 3.765$$

Substituting values yields

$$H(\Pi Y|S) = 533.25$$
$$H(\Pi Y|T) = 581.73$$

GS entropy of the above grammar is equal to the entropy of all derivations emanating from the S nonterminal:

$$H(\Pi Y) = H(\Pi Y|S) = 533.25 \text{ bits}$$

APPENDIX D GS ENTROPY OF THE BASIC GRAMMAR

The GS entropy of the `Basic Grammar` shown is calculated for parameter set corresponding to `TrainSetA` + 2 × `TrainSetB` training data set. Details of the GS entropy calculation of the nonstacking version is offered first. The Watson-Crick and base pair stacking constraints are then considered. Grammar description and parameter values were provided in TORNADO language and also through correspondence with Elena Rivas.

APPENDIX D.1 GRAMMAR DESCRIPTION

The nonstacking version of the grammar is given in TORNADO language format described in Rivas et al. [24, Supplementary Material]:

```
S → a : i e1 S(i+1,j) | F0 S | e # Start: a left base, or a left Helix, or End
F0 → a : i&j e1 F5(i+1, j-1) # Helix starts
F0 → a : i&j e2 P (i+1, j-1) # Helix (of one basepair) ends
F5 → a : i&j e3 F5(i+1, j-1) # Helix continues
F5 → a : i&j e4 P (i+1, j-1) # Helix ends
P → t-P m...m (i,j) l1 # Hairpin Loop
P → t-P m...m (i,k) l2 F0 (k+1,j) # Left Bulges
P → t-P F0 (i,k-1) m...m (k,j) l2 # Right Bulges
P → t-P d... (i, k) ...d (l, j) l3 F0 (k+1,l-1) # Internal Loops
P → t-P M2 # Multiloop
M2 → M1 M # TWO or more Helices
M → M1 M | R # ONE or more Helices
M1 → a : i e1 M1(i+1,j) | F0 # ONE Helix, possibly with single left bases
R → R (i,j-1) a : j e1 | M1 # last Helix, possibly with left/right bases
```

Parameters e1, e2, e3, e4, l1, l2, l3 are emission and loop-length probability vector symbols. Actual values can be different for each symbol depending on the given grammar rule. They can take values of vectors that are defined in grammar description. For instance, e1 in the first line is replaced by e1_1_0_0, while e1 in the second line is replaced by e1_2_0_0. Notations m...m, d..., and ...d refer to various loops. Please refer to Rivas et al. [24] for a more detailed description of transition and emission probability vectors as well as loop length probability vectors.

APPENDIX D.2 CALCULATIONS

The following notations are used: transition probability vectors are denoted as $\mathrm{P}_{NT} = \{p^1_{NT} \cdots p^N_{NT}\}$, where p^n_{NT} is the probability associated with the nth transition from the NT nonterminal. Indices of the loop-length vectors correspond to the length of the desired loop(s). For instance, $13\_2\_30\_30_{i,j}$ returns the probability having i nucleotides on one side and j nucleotides on the other, under probability distribution given by the 13_2_30_30 vector. Probability distribution vector e1_1_0_0 is used for nucleotide distribution in the loop. Expression $H(\Pi Y\ |NT)$ is shown by $H(NT)$ for simplicity.

$$H(S) = H(\mathrm{P}_S) + p^1_S \times H(\mathtt{e1\_1\_0\_0}) + p^2_S \times H(S) + p^2_S \times H(F0)$$

$$H(F0) = H(\mathrm{P}_{F0}) + p^1_{F0} \times H(\mathtt{e1\_2\_0\_0}) + p^1_{F0} \times H(F5) + p^2_{F0} \times H(\mathtt{e2\_2\_0\_0}) + p^2_{F0} \times H(P)$$

$$H(F5) = H(\mathrm{P}_{F5}) + p^1_{F5} \times H(\mathtt{e3\_2\_0\_0}) + p^1_{F5} \times H(F5) + p^2_{F5} \times H(\mathtt{e4\_2\_0\_0}) + p^2_{F5} \times H(P)$$

$$\begin{aligned}H(P) = {} & H(\mathrm{P}_P) \\ & + p^1_P \times \left[H(\mathtt{11\_3\_30\_30}) + H(\mathtt{e1\_1\_0\_0}) \times \sum_{i=3}^{30} i \times \mathtt{11\_3\_30\_30}_i \right] \\ & + p^2_P \times \left[H(\mathtt{12\_1\_30\_30}) + H(\mathtt{e1\_1\_0\_0}) \times \sum_{i=1}^{30} i \times \mathtt{12\_1\_30\_30}_i \right] \\ & + p^2_P \times H(F0) \\ & + p^3_P \times \left[H(\mathtt{12\_1\_30\_30}) + H(\mathtt{e1\_1\_0\_0}) \times \sum_{i=1}^{30} i \times \mathtt{12\_1\_30\_30}_i \right] \\ & + p^3_P \times H(F0) \\ & + p^4_P \times \left[H(\mathtt{13\_2\_30\_30}) + H(\mathtt{e1\_1\_0\_0}) \times \sum_{\substack{i=1, j=1 \\ 2 \le i+j \le 30}} i \times j \times \mathtt{13\_2\_30\_30}_{i,j} \right] \\ & + p^4_P \times H(F0) + p^5_P \times H(M2)\end{aligned}$$

$$H(M2) = H(\mathrm{P}_{M2}) + H(M1) + H(M)$$

$$H(M) = H(\mathrm{P}_M) + p^1_M \times H(M1) + p^1_M \times H(M) + p^2_M \times H(R)$$

$$H(M1) = H(\mathrm{P}_{M1}) + p^1_{M1} \times H(\mathtt{e1\_1\_0\_0}) + p^1_{M1} \times H(M1) + p^2_{M1} \times H(F0)$$

$$H(R) = H(\mathrm{P}_R) + p^1_R \times H(\mathtt{e1\_1\_0\_0}) + p^1_R \times H(R) + p^2_R \times H(M1)$$

Parameter values from file:

`TORNADO_TrATrBTrB_basic_grammar_nostack.param`

Computing values in base 2 logarithm gives

$$H(\mathtt{e1\_1\_0\_0}) = 1.948775$$
$$H(\mathtt{e1\_2\_0\_0}) = 2.484479$$
$$H(\mathtt{e2\_2\_0\_0}) = 2.472315$$
$$H(\mathtt{e3\_2\_0\_0}) = 2.456330$$
$$H(\mathtt{e4\_2\_0\_0}) = 2.391728$$
$$H(\mathtt{l1\_3\_30\_30}) = 3.213847$$
$$H(\mathtt{l2\_1\_30\_30}) = 1.983336$$
$$H(\mathtt{l3\_2\_30\_30}) = 4.502574$$
$$H(\mathrm{P}_S) = 0.9177196$$
$$H(\mathrm{P}_{F0}) = 0.5502468$$
$$H(\mathrm{P}_{F5}) = 0.8782631$$
$$H(\mathrm{P}_P) = 2.0716405$$
$$H(\mathrm{P}_{M2}) = 0$$
$$H(\mathrm{P}_M) = 0.9796935$$
$$H(\mathrm{P}_{M1}) = 0.6829725$$
$$H(\mathrm{P}_R) = 0.7453731$$

Substituting for values gives

$$H(S) = 37.1597$$
$$H(F0) = 257.4769$$
$$H(F5) = 255.8632$$
$$H(P) = 244.7208$$
$$H(M2) = 745.1210$$
$$H(M) = 475.0788$$
$$H(M1) = 270.0422$$
$$H(R) = 280.7990$$

The GS entropy is equal to the entropy corresponding to the start nonterminal:

$$H(\Pi Y) = H(\Pi Y|S) = H(S) = 37.1597 \text{ bits}$$

APPENDIX D.3 WATSON-CRICK BASE PAIRING CONSTRAINT

In the case where only Watson-Crick base pairing is allowed, base pairing probability vectors are multiplied by `wcx` and then normalized. Vector `wcx` is a binary vector containing value one for positions corresponding to Watson-Crick base pairing and zero otherwise. Resulting base pairing probabilities are calculated from original base pairing probabilities as shown in the following example:

$$\mathtt{e3\_2\_0\_0}^{\mathrm{wcx}} = \frac{\mathtt{e3\_2\_0\_0} \times \mathtt{wcx}}{\sum_{i=0}^{15} \mathtt{e3\_2\_0\_0}_i \times \mathtt{wcx}_i}$$

Reading values from file:

`TORNADO_TrATrBTrB_basic_grammar_nostack_wcx.param`

gives $H(\Pi Y) = 35.2148$ bits.

APPENDIX D.4 BASE PAIR STACKING CONSTRAINT

In the case of stacking base pairs, probability distributions are given conditioned on the base pairing context. Consider x and y as instances of context and stacked base pairings, respectively. The overall entropy of base pairing is then

$$H(XY) = H(X) + H(Y|X)$$

where the conditional entropy $H(Y|X)$ is the entropy of stacked base pairs *after* the context base pair X is generated. Each of the $H(X)$ and $H(Y|X)$ entropy values are associated with their corresponding nonterminal depending on the chronology of nonterminal generation. Generalization to higher orders of stacking can be done in a similar fashion.

The GS entropy calculations of a stacking version of the above grammar, known in TORNADO as `basic_grammar`, has the same set of equations with the following exception: the expression $H(F5)$ is replaced by the following:

$$\begin{aligned} H(F5) = H(\mathrm{P}_{F5}) &+ p_{F5}^{1} \times \sum_{i=0}^{15} \mathtt{e1\_2\_0\_0}_i \times H(\mathtt{e1\_2\_2\_}i) \\ &+ p_{F5}^{1} \times H(F5) \\ &+ p_{F5}^{2} \times \sum_{i=0}^{15} \mathtt{e2\_2\_0\_0}_i \times H(\mathtt{e2\_2\_2\_}i) \\ &+ p_{F5}^{2} \times H(P) \end{aligned}$$

where `e1_2_2_`i and `e2_2_2_`i stacking base pair probability vectors are provided in corresponding TORNADO parameter set files. Probability vectors `e1_2_0_0` and `e2_2_0_0` probability vectors are such that the nth element corresponds to the context of the respective stacking base pair probability vectors.

Reading values from file:

`TORNADO_TrATrBTrB_basic_grammar.param`

gives $H(\Pi Y) = 37.0785$ bits.

REFERENCES

[1] Chomsky N. On certain formal properties of grammars. Inform Control 1959;2(2):137–67.

[2] Booth TL, Thompson RA. Applying probability measures to abstract languages. IEEE Trans Comput 1973;C-22:442–50.

[3] Baker JK. Trainable grammars for speech recognition. J Acoust Soc Am 1979;65:S132.

[4] Grenander U. Syntax-controlled probabilities. Providence, RI: Brown University; 1967.
[5] Kuich W. On the entropy of context-free languages. Inform Control 1970;16(2):173–200.
[6] Hutchins SE. Moments of string and derivation lengths of stochastic context-free grammars. Inform Sci 1972;4(2):179–91.
[7] Soule S. Entropies of probabilistic grammars. Inform Control 1974;25(1):57–74.
[8] Shannon C. A mathematical theory of communication. Bell Syst Tech J 1948;27:379–423.
[9] Smith T, Waterman M. RNA secondary structure: a complete mathematical analysis. Math Biosci 1978;42:257–66.
[10] Stein PR, Waterman MS. On some new sequences generalizing the Catalan and Motzkin numbers. Discret Math 1979;26(3):261–72.
[11] Viennot G, Vauchaussade de Chaumont M. Enumeration of RNA secondary structures by complexity. Lecture notes in biomathematics, vol. 57. Berlin/Heidelberg: Springer; 1985; p. 360–5 [chapter 50].
[12] Hofacker I, Schuster P, Stadler P. Combinatorics of RNA secondary structures. Discret Appl Math 1998;88 (1–3):207–37.
[13] Nebel ME. Combinatorial properties of RNA secondary structures. J Comput Biol 2002;9(3):541–73.
[14] Liao B, Wang TM. General combinatorics of RNA secondary structure. Math Biosci 2004;191(1):69–81.
[15] Doslic T, Svrtan D, Veljan D. Enumerative aspects of secondary structures. Discret Math 2004;285(1–3):67–82.
[16] Eddy SR, Durbin R. RNA sequence analysis using covariance models. Nucleic Acids Res 1994;22:2079–88.
[17] Sakakibara Y, Brown M, Hughey R, Mian IS, Sjolander K, Underwood RC, et al. Stochastic context-free grammars for tRNA modeling. Nucleic Acids Res 1994;22:5112–20.
[18] Yao Z, Weinberg Z, Ruzzo WL. CMfinder — a covariance model based RNA motif finding algorithm. Bioinformatics 2006;22(4):445–52.
[19] Nawrocki EP, Eddy SR. Infernal 1.1: 100-fold faster RNA homology searches. Bioinformatics 2013;29 (22):2933–5.
[20] Rivas E. The four ingredients of single-sequence RNA secondary structure prediction. A unifying perspective. RNA Biol 2013;10(7):1185–96.
[21] Zuker M, Stiegler P. Optimal computer folding of large RNA sequences using thermodynamics and auxiliary information. Nucleic Acids Res 1981;9:133–48.
[22] Durbin R, Eddy SR, Krogh A, Mitchison G. Biological sequence analysis: probabilistic models of proteins and nucleic acids. Cambridge: Cambridge University Press; 1998.
[23] Dowell RD, Eddy SR. Evaluation of several lightweight stochastic context-free grammars for RNA secondary structure prediction. BMC Bioinformatics 2004;5:71.
[24] Rivas E, Lang R, Eddy SR. A range of complex probabilistic models for RNA secondary structure prediction that includes the nearest-neighbor model and more. RNA 2012;18(2):193–212.
[25] Hofacker IL. Vienna RNA secondary structure server. Nucleic Acids Res 2003;31(13):3429–31.
[26] Do CB, Woods DA, Batzoglou S. CONTRAfold: RNA secondary structure prediction without physics-based models. Bioinformatics 2006;22(14):e90–8.
[27] van Rijsbergen C. Information retrieval. 2nd ed. London: Butterworths; 1979.
[28] Cover TM, Thomas JA. Elements of information theory. 2nd ed. Hoboken, NJ: Wiley-Interscience; 2006.
[29] Manzourolajdad A. Shannon's entropy of the stochastic context-free grammar and an application to RNA secondary structure modeling. In: 16th International conference on bioinformatics and computational biology (BIOCOMP'15), Las Vegas, USA; 2015. p. 3–7.
[30] Lari K, Young SJ. The estimation of stochastic context-free grammars using the Inside-Outside algorithm. Comput Speech Lang 1990;4(1):35–56.

CHAPTER

10 EFFECTS OF EXCESSIVE WATER INTAKE ON BODY-FLUID HOMEOSTASIS AND THE CARDIOVASCULAR SYSTEM — A COMPUTER SIMULATION

Y. Zhang*, W.W. Liou†, V. Gupta‡

North Dakota State University, Fargo, ND, United States Western Michigan University, Kalamazoo, MI, United States†*
Borgess Medical Center, Borgess Research Institute, Kalamazoo, MI, United States‡

10.1 INTRODUCTION

Water is the principal constituent of the human body and plays a vital role in various physiological functions, such as oxygen and nutrition transports, organ functioning, and body temperature control. For a healthy human body, it is essential to keep the amounts of water and electrolyte intakes balanced with what the body needs. In normal conditions, the water ingested through both food and beverages, and the water produced as a by-product of metabolic functions are removed from the body in an equal amount, largely through urination and a smaller quantity via respiration, perspiration, and defecation. Renal elimination of the fluid, along with the waste products, is a highly regulated function of the human body. In general, to maintain a proper body-fluid homeostasis, about 2–3 L of water per day is required for healthy adults (including food water and metabolic water), in which about 1.5 L of water from drinking per day is generally recommended [1]. However, many factors, such as severe environmental conditions, strenuous exercises, diseases, and diuretic drug uses [2] may result in dehydration and the impairment of body-fluid homeostasis, leading to symptoms ranging from mild discomfort to severe health issues. Therefore, "drink before feeling thirsty" becomes a commonly accepted guideline and a large amount of water intake has been advocated by the mass media, such as the 8 × 8 rule (eight glasses of eight ounces of water per day). Recent studies, however, have raised concerns [3–7]. Although additional water intake can be therapeutic for certain patients, there seems no clear scientific evidence to support the accepted wisdom that healthy people in normal conditions could benefit from excessive water drinking.

Excessive fluid intake can affect the cardiovascular hemodynamics on both a short- and long-term basis. First, recent studies suggest that water drinking may trigger acute pressor responses, such as rapidly decreased heart rate and increased total peripheral resistance [8–10]. Drinking 480 mL of tap water was found to increase systolic pressure by up to ~30 mmHg for patients suffering from multiple system atrophy and autonomic failure [11]. The acute pressor responses are claimed to be closely related to the activation of sympathetic activity [12] and the plasma osmolality changes induced by water drinking [8]. Meanwhile, several studies suggest an instant but mild increase of blood pressure was also found in healthy subjects after a large amount of water intake [13–16].

Second, excessive water intake for a prolonged period of time may cause chronic adaptations of the body-fluid homeostasis and the blood pressure control system. Human body-fluid homeostasis and blood pressure regulation in the long-term are mediated by the renal system through its "near infinite feedback gain" [17]. While sympathetic nerve activity plays a central role in suppressing acute blood pressure changes, it almost does not affect the long-term increase of arterial pressure due to volume loading [18]. Based on the "pressure-diuresis" and the "pressure-natriuresis" mechanisms, a slight variation in blood pressure induced by the change of water and electrolyte intakes will be compensated for by a proper adaption of renal excretion. A new equilibrium point of the blood pressure will be eventually reached after changing water or electrolyte intakes due to the adaption of the nervous system. A shift in the "pressure-diuresis-natriuresis" curve is argued to be the primary reason for chronic hypertension [19]. Furthermore, this long-term adaptation may increase the probability of the genesis of other malfunctions in the cardiovascular circulations. For example, recent studies have shown the origin of atrial fibrillation has a strong correlation to the long-term stretching of left atrial wall and a chronic increase of intraatrial pressure [20–22]. Chronic congestive heart failure (CHF) and acute or chronic CHF are pathological ends to chronic fluid overload syndromes that have plagued this country and become a major public health issue [23]. The CHF population is on the rise in part due to misconceptions of fluid intake in the society. The estimated cost for taking care of chronic CHF patients is approximately 3 billion dollars annually, according to the Centers for Disease Control (CDC).

In the present study, we develop a system-level computer model to study the short- and long-term responses of the cardiovascular system and the fluid-electrolyte homeostasis to excessive water intake. In the new model, a renal system model developed by Karaaslan et al. [24] is adapted and it is coupled with an open-source hemodynamics model of human cardiovascular system — CVSim [25]. By combining the above two modified modules, the new model is capable of simulating the beat-by-beat as well as the long-term average variations in body-fluid homeostasis caused by excessive water intake. Moreover, detailed mechanical and structural properties of the different cardiovascular compartments, including the cardiac chambers, can also be obtained as outcomes of the current simulations. As clinical studies are often costly and restrictive with, for instance, securing human subjects and regulatory requirements, computer modeling will be particularly helpful for an enhanced understanding of the system-level responses of the cardiovascular system to excessive water intake. The details of the model will be described in the following section. The simulation model is then validated against clinical data. The predicted short- and long-term responses of, for example, blood pressure, heart rate, hormonal concentrations, and cardiac structural changes are presented and compared with available clinical data.

10.2 COMPUTATIONAL MODEL

An open-source model, named CVSim, has been adapted and used for the hemodynamic simulation in the present study. CVSim is based on a closed-loop circulation model for hemodynamic responses of the cardiovascular system, the total blood volume is kept constant and the body-fluid homeostasis is not simulated. For the purpose of the present study, we couple a long-term renal system model to the existing CVSim model. The hybrid model, therefore, offers the capability to simulate both the short-term response of hemodynamics and the long-term fluid-electrolyte homeostasis.

10.2.1 CARDIOVASCULAR HEMODYNAMICS: CVSim

Since 1984, CVSim has been developed and become a successful tool for teaching [25] and research [26,27]. It is a closed-loop, lumped-parameter model based on electrical circuitry analogy. As shown in Fig. 10.1, the basic unit of the model consists of resistors and capacitors, representing the afferent/efferent resistance and the reservoir functions of a modeled compartment in the human body. Voltage and currents mimic blood pressure and blood flow rate, respectively.

According to Kirchhoff's current law, a first-order ordinary differential equation can be written for a compartment:

$$\frac{P_{n-1}-P_n}{R_{n-1}}+\frac{P_{n+1}-P_n}{R_n}+\frac{d[C_n(P_{\text{ref}}-P_n)]}{dt}=0 \tag{1}$$

In the present study, the reference pressure in the interstitial space P_{ref} is assumed to be constant. Hence,

$$\frac{dP_n}{dt}=\frac{P_{n-1}-P_n}{R_{n-1}C_n}+\frac{P_{n+1}-P_n}{R_nC_n}+\frac{(P_{\text{ref}}-P_n)}{C_n}\frac{dC_n}{dt} \tag{2}$$

The capacitance, C_n, is assumed to be constant in most of the compartments, except for the four cardiac chambers and the equation is further simplified as

$$\frac{dP_n}{dt}=\frac{P_{n-1}-P_n}{R_{n-1}C_n}+\frac{P_{n+1}-P_n}{R_nC_n} \tag{3}$$

Therefore, by solving a system of first-order ordinary differential equations, the hemodynamics of the circulation system can be simulated. In the present study, a 21-comparment version of CVSim is adopted. The model includes the four cardiac chambers, pulmonary artery and vein, and other systemic arteries, veins, and microcirculations, as shown in Fig. 10.2.

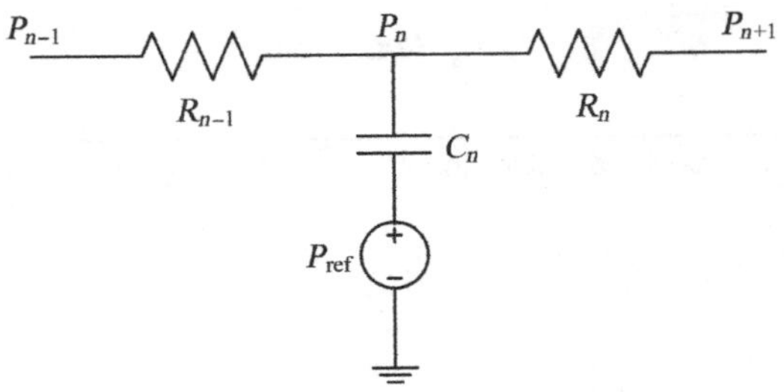

FIGURE 10.1

Electrical analog of the CVSim model.

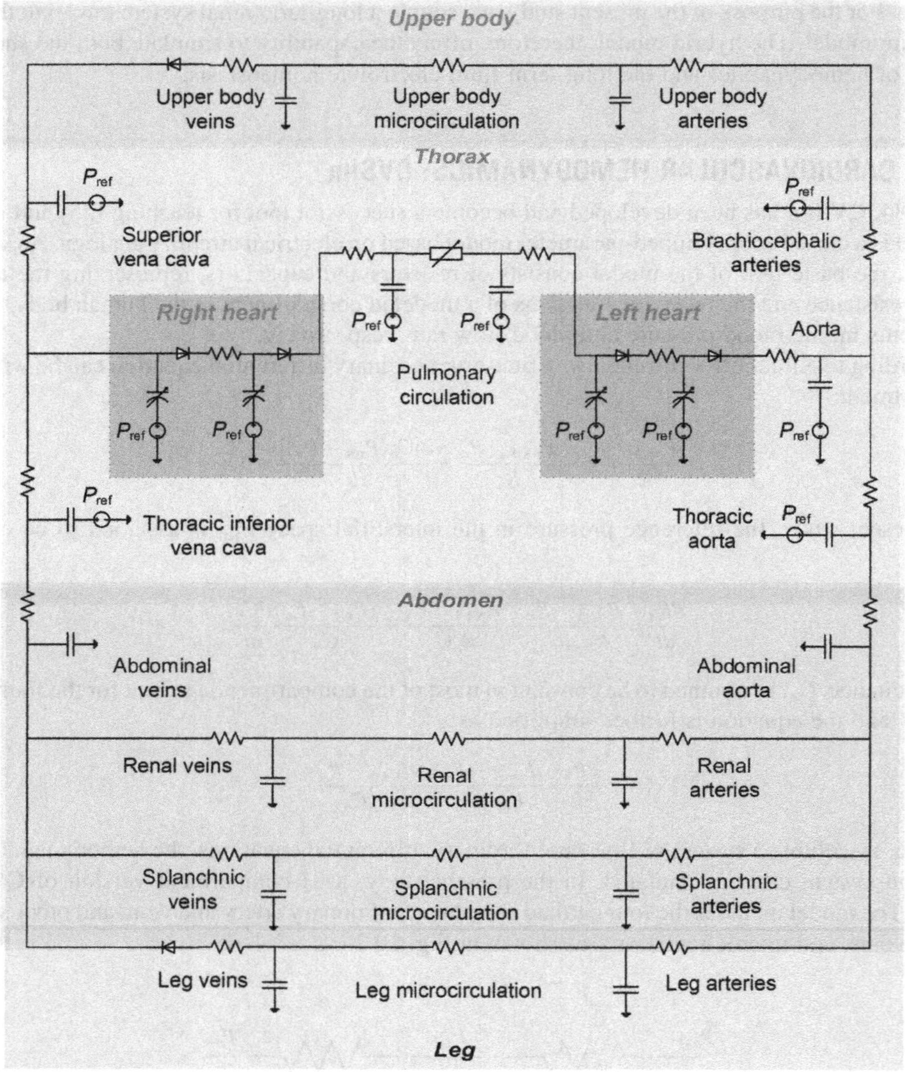

FIGURE 10.2

Structure of the 21-compartment cardiovascular model.

Modified from [28].

The pumping function of the heart is simulated by varying the elastance of the four cardiac chambers, based on the following function:

$$\frac{E(t)}{E_{es}} = \begin{cases} \frac{E_d}{E_{es}} + \frac{E_{es}-E_d}{2E_{es}}\left[1-\cos\left(\pi\frac{t}{T_s}\right)\right], & 0 \le t \le T_s \\ \frac{E_d}{E_{es}} + \frac{E_{es}-E_d}{2E_{es}}\left[1+\cos\left(2\pi\frac{t-T_s}{T_s}\right)\right], & T_s \le t \le \frac{3}{2}T_s \\ \frac{E_d}{E_{es}}, & t \ge \frac{3}{2}T_s \end{cases} \tag{4}$$

where $E(t)$ denotes the time-dependent elastance, T_s the systolic time interval for each chamber, and E_d and E_{es} the diastolic and end-systolic elastance, respectively. The modeled elastance is shown in Fig. 10.3. The time-varying capacitances of the cardiac chambers are then calculated by assuming $C(t) = 1/E(t)$. The validity of the modeled relationship has been verified by comparisons of the simulated curve with that observed in clinical studies, as can be found in Ref. [26]. The values of the resistance, capacitance, and initial volume for each compartment are assigned based on the results of clinical studies. The system of ordinary differential equations has been solved using the fourth-order Runge-Kutta method with a fixed time step of 0.001 s. A sample waveform of the left ventricular (LV), aortic, and systemic venous pressures are shown in Fig. 10.4. The assignments of the parameters and the details of the model implementations can be found in Ref. [28].

CVsim also includes modules to incorporate the cardiovascular control mechanisms. The arterial baroreflex is modeled as a set-point controller that helps to minimize the error signals arising from systematic perturbations. Specifically, the aortic arch and the carotid sinus transmural pressures are tracked using a moving average filter and then subtracted by a predefined arterial set-point pressure. The error signal is then convolved with impulse response functions and scaled by static gain values to

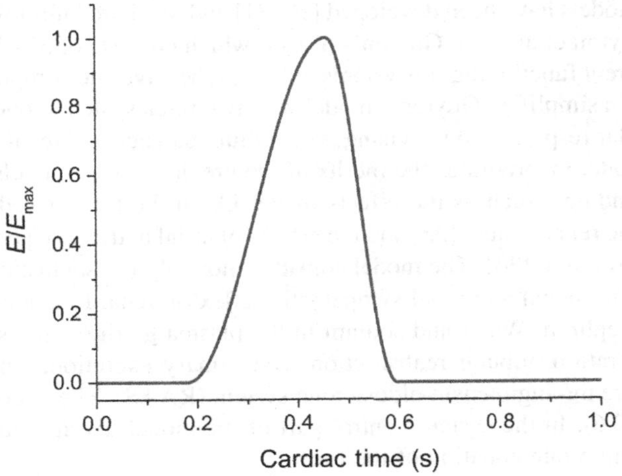

FIGURE 10.3

Time-dependent elastance.

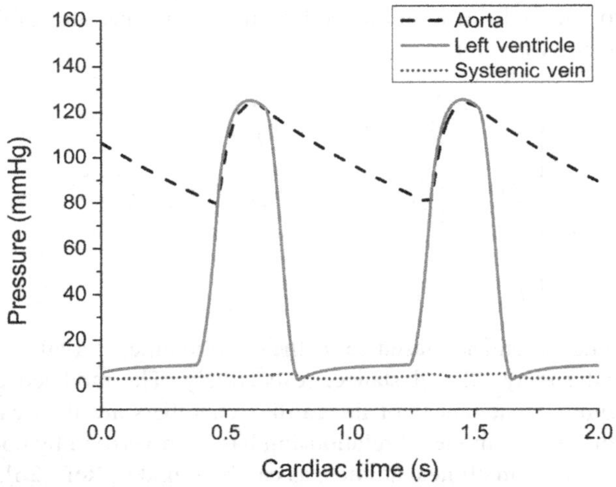

FIGURE 10.4

Pressure waveform of CVSim model.

generate an update to the efferent effector variables. The effector variables, resembling both sympathetic and parasympathetic nervous signals, are used as feedbacks to instantaneously modify the heart rate, cardiac contractility, arteriole resistance, and venous tone. The detailed mathematical formulations of the nervous control system modules and their descriptions can be found in Ref. [28] and are not elaborated here.

10.2.2 BODY-FLUID HOMEOSTASIS: A RENAL FUNCTION MODEL

Several renal system models have been developed [29–31] and most are built following the pioneering effort described by Guyton et al. [32]. Guyton's model, which consists of 354 blocks, more than 400 equations, and 18 different functioning subsystems, is comprehensive and complicated. Karaaslan et al. [24] integrated parts of a simplified Guyton's model with two renal system models [29,31] and studied long-term cardiovascular responses to the changes of sodium balance and renal sympathetic nerve activity (RSNA). The model incorporates the merits of the previous three models and incorporates the recent experimental findings, such as the effects of RSNA on the tubular sodium reabsorption and the renin secretion in the renal system [33] and the effects of atrial natriuretic peptide on the right atrial pressure and sodium excretion [34]. The model considers not only the sophisticated renal system, but also the effects of the hormonal and renal sympathetic reflex on renal functions. The renal system is simulated as a single nephron. Water and sodium in the plasma go through a sequential process, including glomerular filtration, tubular reabsorption, and urinary excretion, which are controlled by RSNA and the plasma renin-angiotensin-aldosterone system (RAAS). The structure of the model will be shown later (Fig. 10.6). In the system control part of the model, the hormone concentrations are updated based on a simple rate equation of the form

$$\frac{dC_i}{dt} = \frac{1}{\tau_i}(S_i - C_i) \tag{5}$$

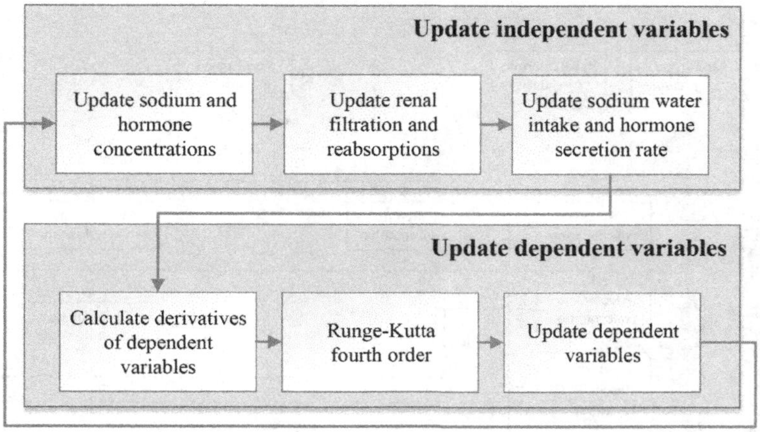

FIGURE 10.5

Implementation of the renal system model.

where C_i denotes the concentration of a specific hormone, S_i its secretion rate, and τ_i the time constant for each hormone to reach a stabilized state. Other functional blocks typically consist of equations that are based on either a curve fitting of clinical data, or a readaption from the Guyton's model. Detailed formulations, the resulting equations, and parametric assignments can be found in Ref. [24]. The entire renal system model includes 8 first-order ordinary differential equations (dependent variables) and 61 nonlinear, independent equations.

The current implementation of the renal system model is illustrated in Fig. 10.5. First, the sodium and hormone concentrations are calculated based on the values of the dependent variables (including the normal concentrations of hormones, extracellular fluid volume, total sodium amount, and baroreceptor reflex parameters) at the current time step. Second, the renal water and sodium filtration and reabsorption at each segment of the tubular system are updated. Third, water and sodium intake and hormone secretion rate are calculated. Fourth, the first-order derivatives of the dependent variables are calculated using Eq. (5). At the completion of the calculations for the current time, the dependent variables are updated using the fourth-order Runge-Kutta method. The simulation then continues to march forward in time by proceeding to the step one described earlier.

10.2.3 COUPLING OF SYSTEMS MODELS

The responses of the cardiovascular system, such as the arterial mean pressure, in the renal system model of Karaaslan et al. [24] have been modeled based on a simplified relationship among the cardiac output, mean filling pressure, and mean arterial pressure. In the present study, we use the 21-component CVSim modeling described earlier to characterize the functions of the cardiovascular system. The interactions between the renal system model and the CVSim model occur through the passing of the physiological parameters of the systems and are indicated by the *red arrowed lines* (*dark gray arrowed lines* in print version) in Fig. 10.6. Specifically, the mean (renal) arterial pressure and the right atrial pressure

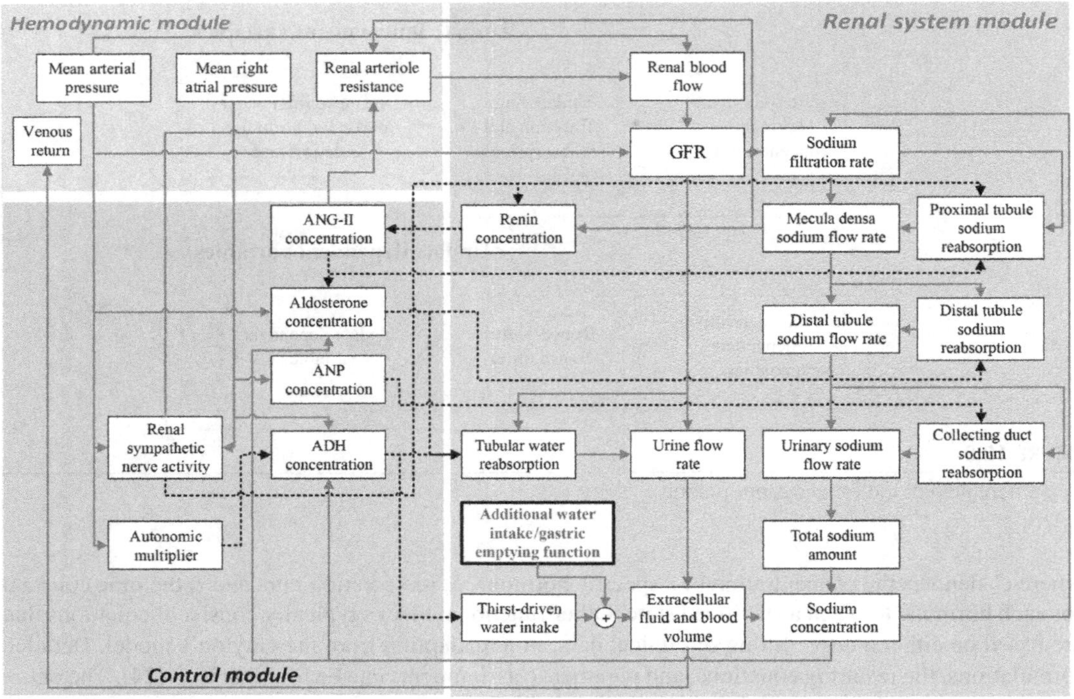

FIGURE 10.6

Structure of the new model.

are calculated in CVSim and are transmitted to the renal system model on a beat-by-beat basis. Meanwhile, the renal system model provides the changes in the blood volume and the renal arteriole resistance to the CVSim model for the calculations in the ensuing heartbeat. With this strong coupling between the two system-level models, the effects of water and sodium intakes on the hemodynamic properties of each of the modeled cardiovascular compartments, such as pressure, flow rate, and volume, can be calculated.

In the present study, the water intake module is calculated as the average amount of daily water intake for the long-term simulation. For the short-term simulations, the water intake module is modeled as a time-dependent function of the gastric emptying rate. Because the water absorption in human intestines is mainly a passive diffusion process across the osmolality gradient, it is assumed the time delay between the water consumption and the water absorption is only determined by the gastric emptying rate. Basically, liquid with low caloric density empties from the stomach much faster than the solid content and the emptying function usually resembles an exponential function [35,36]. Fig. 10.7 shows the emptying function for a diluted glucose solution provided by Calbet and Maclean [37]. An exponential function is obtained by curve fitting and has been used as the mathematical description of water intake in the current model.

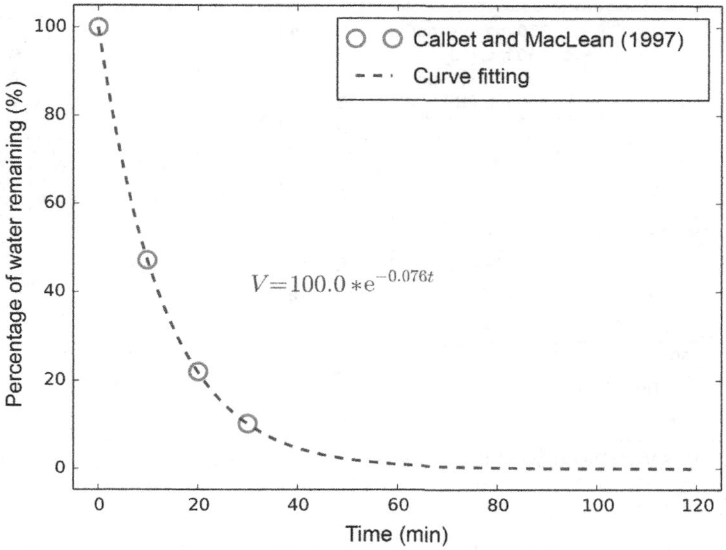

FIGURE 10.7

Gastric emptying function.

10.3 RESULTS AND VALIDATION

10.3.1 MODELING OF SHORT-TERM RESPONSES

It is known that the human renal system has the capability to produce diluted or concentrated urine in response to large osmolality variations in the plasma. With its effective tubular reabsorption and the regulation of the antidiuretic hormone (ADH) of the RAAS system, the kidney can excrete urine with a concentration as low as 50 mOsm/L [17], making it possible to maintain the balance of the fluid in the human body. In the present study, the hybrid model offers simulated systematic changes, including the body-fluid homeostasis and the cardiovascular hemodynamics, in response to a one-time water intake. In the first simulation, large amounts of water (350 and 500 mL) are given as inputs at time zero, which then enter the systems with an emptying rate as described in Fig. 10.7. The cardiovascular and renal system responses, in a matter of hours, are discussed in the following sections.

10.3.1.1 Cardiovascular responses

Fig. 10.8A compares the changes of the mean arterial pressure in response to two different amounts of water intakes used in two clinical studies, respectively. The two clinical studies cited examined healthy subjects and provided data for the blood pressure changes after water ingestions. It can be seen that the 350 and 500 mL of water intakes elicit instant, but mild, increases in the mean arterial pressure. Although the clinical data can be patient-dependent, the present simulation results follow the trend of these data well. Particularly, the peak value of the simulated blood pressure for the 350 mL case and its increases over an additional 150 mL of water intake match with that from the clinical studies, suggesting an increased amount of water intake causes an increase in the peak blood pressure. With

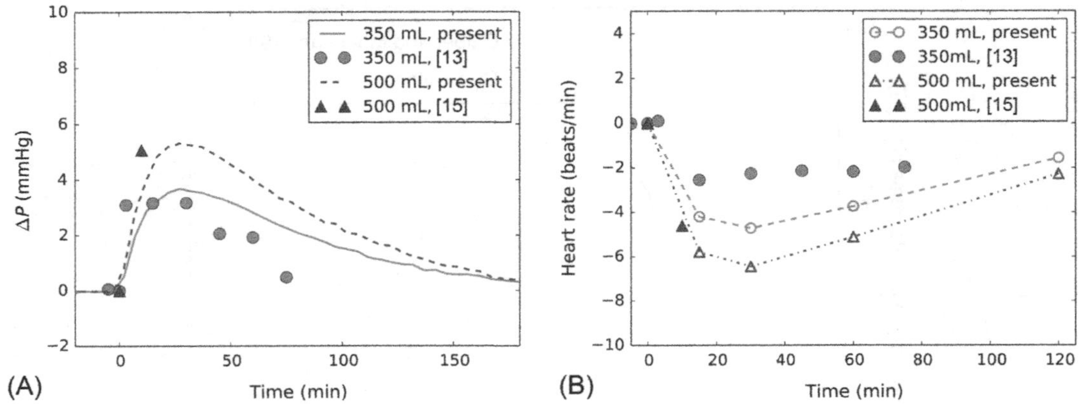

FIGURE 10.8

Cardiovascular responses to 350 and 500 mL water intake. (A) Change of mean arterial pressure and (B) change of heart rate.

time, the mean arterial pressure gradually returns to normal levels in both cases with the regulatory functioning of the renal system. Fig. 10.8B shows that the heart rate decreases slightly due to the activation of the parasympathetic nervous signals caused by an increased central venous pressure. This decreasing trend matches reasonably well with the data from the two aforementioned clinical studies. These comparisons suggest that the present hybrid model is valid in simulating the short-term responses induced by water intakes.

The current hybrid model also has the capability to simulate the mechanical functions of the heart during short-term water intake events. Fig. 10.9A shows the LV pressure-volume loops (*P-V* loop) of a

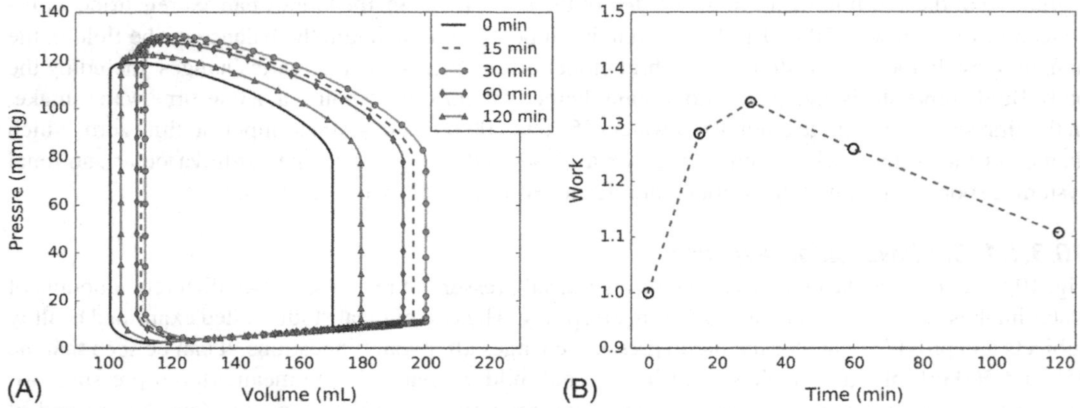

FIGURE 10.9

Left ventricular mechanical function in response to 500 mL water intake. (A) Left ventricular *P-V* loop and (B) normalized LV stroke work per heartbeat.

single heartbeat at different instances of time for the 500 mL water intake case. It is clear that due to the ingestion of water, the *P-V* loop shifts upward and to the right within 30 min of the water ingestion, suggesting increases in both the mean pressure and the volume of the left ventricle. Particularly significant is the increase in the diastolic LV volume due to the increased filling volume of water. The *P-V* loop then recovers toward the nominal shape from 60 min onward. The LV work per heartbeat is represented by the areas of the *P-V* loops. Fig. 10.9B shows the stroke work done by LV during a cardiac cycle at various instances of time (normalized by the time-zero value). The LV work increases to up to 1.35 times over that of its normal output after the water ingestion and gradually decreases after it peaks at about 30 min after the ingestion of 500 mL of water.

10.3.1.2 Body-fluid homeostasis

Fig. 10.10A shows the time history of the water input, as depicted by the gastric water emptying rate, and the urine outflow rate. The starting water emptying rate is 38 mL/min and it decreases exponentially as water gradually empties from the stomach. After the ingestion of water, the urine outflow rate increases about 3.3-fold within 30 min and gradually falls back to the normal level within a few hours. The time delay between the water intake and excretion causes a small increase of the total extracellular fluid volume in the first hour before it gradually falls back, as shown in Fig. 10.10B. Although the initial sodium excretion rate (Fig. 10.10C) also increases to about three times its normal rate with an increase of the total glomerular filtration, it returns to the normal level more quickly than the water flow. It should be noted that a sodium equilibrium is established in the simulated system prior to the water ingestion. The comparison of water and sodium excretion time history demonstrates that the urine is diluted and the kidney works to retain sodium even though the urine volume is increased. Therefore, as shown in Fig. 10.10D, the proper functioning of the renal system prevents the plasma sodium concentration from continuously decreasing and helps reestablish the sodium balance within a short period of time.

The maintenance of the body fluid and electrolyte balance discussed earlier is regulated by the ADH and the RAAS, as demonstrated by the relationships depicted in Fig. 10.6. The simulated changes of the ADH, angiotensin-II, and aldosterone hormones are present in Fig. 10.10E–H. Fig. 10.10E shows that the ADH concentration is suppressed by the decrease of plasma sodium concentration, which acts to decrease the water reabsorption in the renal tubular system. With an increased amount of glomerular filtration, the sodium flow rate at macula densa also increases, which inevitably suppresses renin and angiotensin-II concentrations, as shown in Fig. 10.10F. This actually decreases the sodium reabsorption at proximal tubules in a short period of time immediately after the water ingestion. Fig. 10.10G shows that the decrease of sodium concentration also promotes the aldosterone generation. The increase of the aldosterone concentration elevates the sodium reabsorption at distal tubules. It should be noted that a transient decrease of aldosterone is caused by the decreased level of angiotensin-II and it then increases to an above-normal level to retain sodium in the hours that follow. Because of a combined effect of the tubuloglomerular control of the renal system and the cardiovascular sympathetic activity, the renal arteriole resistance increases for a short period of time to prevent further increase of glomerular filtration and to promote sodium retention (Fig. 10.10H).

Overall, the current simulations show that, with the complex correlations among the various mechanisms modeled, this dynamic control system manages to reestablish homeostasis, after a large amount of one-time water ingestion, which resembles the real physiological responses well.

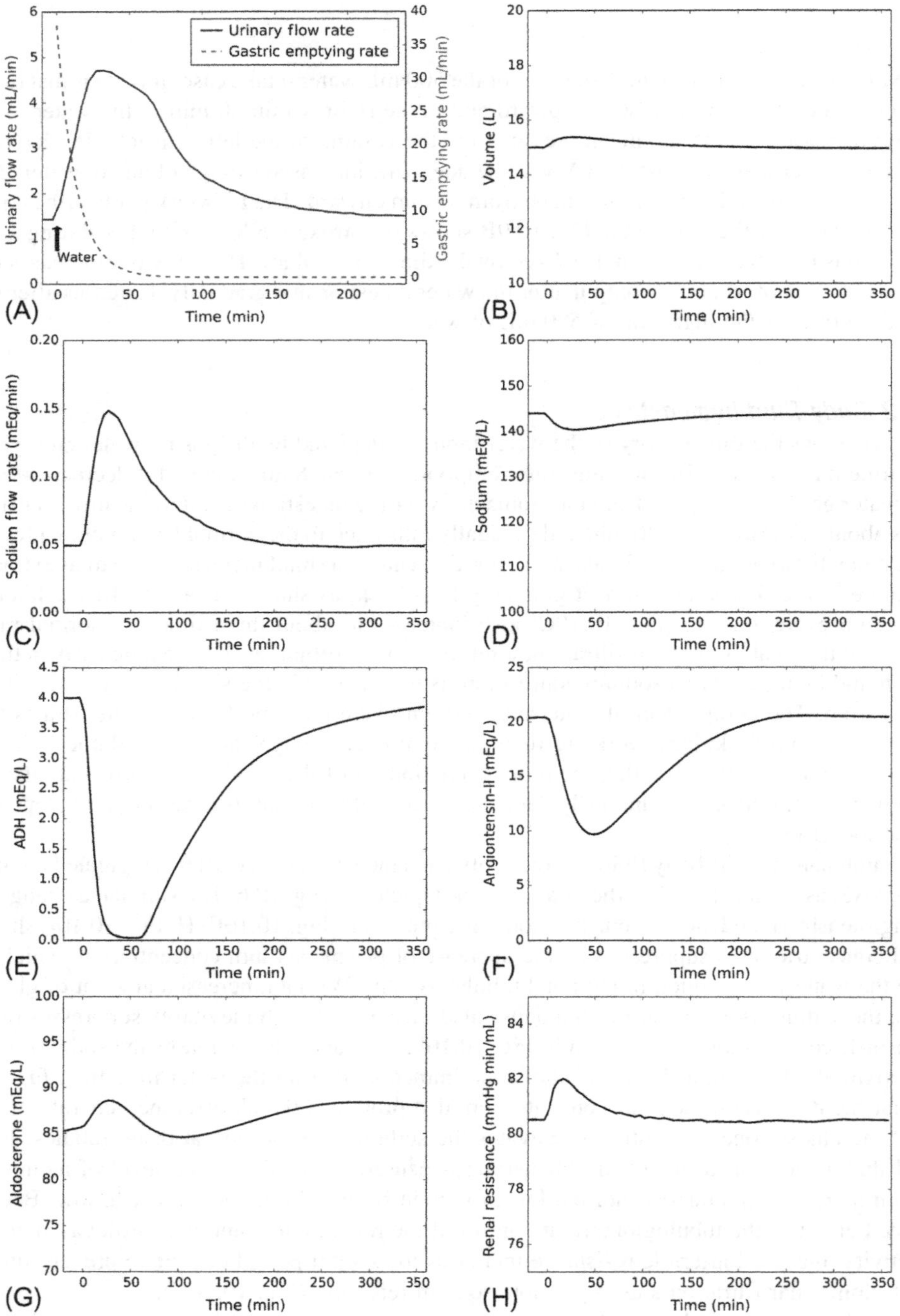

FIGURE 10.10

The responses of hormonal and renal system parameters to 500 mL water intake. (A) Urinary flow rate; (B) extracellular fluid volume; (C) urinary sodium excretion rate; (D) plasma sodium concentration; (E) ADH concentration; (F) angiotensin-II concentration; (G) aldosterone concentration; and (H) renal vascular resistance.

10.3.2 MODELING OF LONG-TERM RESPONSES TO CHRONIC EXCESSIVE WATER INTAKE

In contrast to the short-term perturbation to the systems, which can diminish quickly, a chronic change of water intake schedule may cause long-term adaptations of the cardiovascular functions and the fluid-electrolyte balance point. The shifted balances in a human body are often linked to chronic diseases, such as chronic hypertension [19]. With a long-term renal system model, the current hybrid model also has the capability to simulate long-term system responses, in terms of days, to a continued adjustment of water, or sodium, intake. Instead of using a gastric emptying function to simulate the water intake, an averaged flow rate based on a daily amount of water intake is given as the input to a long-term simulation. The arterial baroreflex control, which is active for the short-term response, is turned off in the long-term simulation.

There are few clinical data in the literature that can be used to validate the current model in terms of the simulation of the long-term effects of excessive water intakes on body-fluid homeostasis and the cardiovascular system. In our development of the current model [38], we verify the simulation methodologies by using the clinical results that studied the long-term effect of sodium intake [39]. Foods with high, intermediate, and low sodium contents (ie, 141, 106, and 64 mmol/day) were provided to two separate subject groups for 30 consecutive days. The reduction of sodium intake has been shown to result in a substantial decrease in the blood pressure in both groups. As shown in Fig. 10.11, the reduction in mean arterial pressure predicted by the current model matches well with the average value given in Ref. [39].

Prolonged increases of water intake can similarly induce chronic adaptations. In the present work, the long-term effects of different amounts of increases of water intake (ie, 2, 4, and 6 L/day) have been

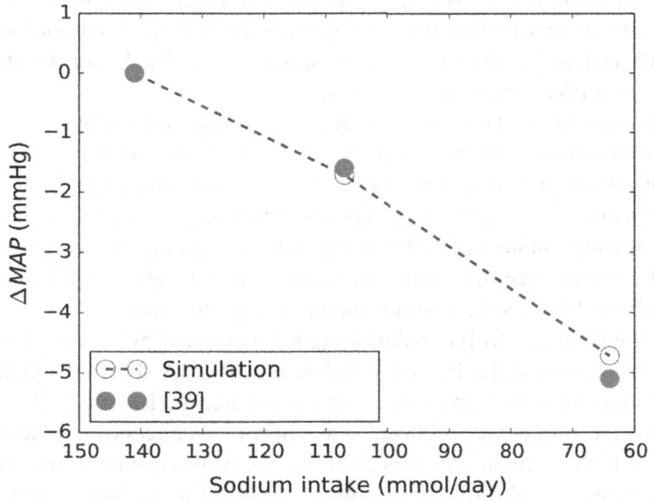

FIGURE 10.11

Mean arterial pressure changes during sodium restriction.

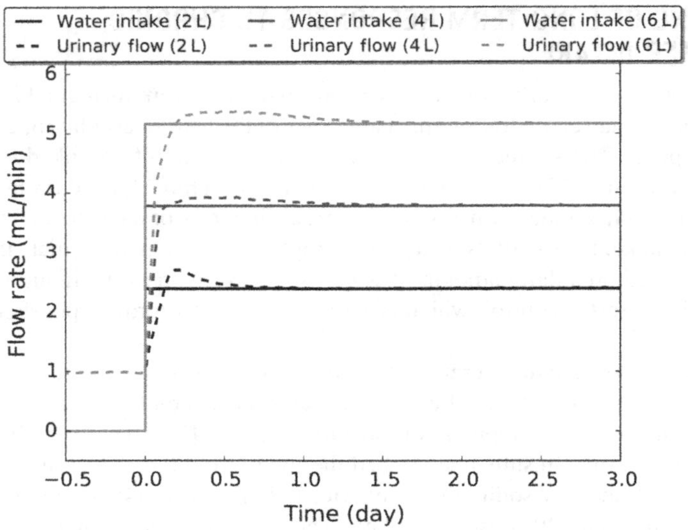

FIGURE 10.12

Changes in long-term water intake and urinary flow rate.

simulated. As shown in Fig. 10.12, prior to the water intake at day 0, the urine outflow rate is about 1 mL/min. This equals to the value of a built-in module equation that models the "thirst-driven" water intake. The state of homeostasis is used as the initial condition from which the water intake occurs, marked as day 0, in the simulation. At day 0, the daily average water intake is increased by 2, 4, and 6 L, respectively. It can be seen that the urine outflow rates first overshoot the water intake levels and then gradually fall back and adapt to the water intake values. The larger the amount of increase of water intake, the longer it takes the systems to adapt.

The continued elevation of the daily rate of water intake also causes adaptations of the extracellular fluid volume and plasma sodium concentration. The sodium intake is kept constant as 181 mEq/day in the current simulation. As demonstrated in Fig. 10.13, the fluid volume and plasma sodium concentrations change significantly during the first day and gradually asymptote to stabilized levels. For the smallest increase of water intake (2 L), the changes in these parameters are very small. For the high water intake case (6 L), the extracellular fluid volume increases by about 0.1 L and the plasma sodium concentration drops about 10%, as the sodium intake is kept constant.

These changes in the fluid-electrolyte balance are accompanied by the adaptation of the hormonal control system and the cardiovascular hemodynamics. Fig. 10.14A shows the changes of the concentrations of the various hormones in responses to the three water intake cases. The values for each case are taken at day 3 when the results are stabilized. Each hormone concentration has been normalized by its day 0 value to facilitate the comparison. It is clear that the ADH is significantly suppressed by a large increase in daily water intake and diminished almost entirely for the large water intake cases (4 and 6 L). However, the stabilized concentrations of aldosterone increase as the daily water intake increases, acting to increase the distal tubule sodium reabsorption and prevent further loss of sodium content in

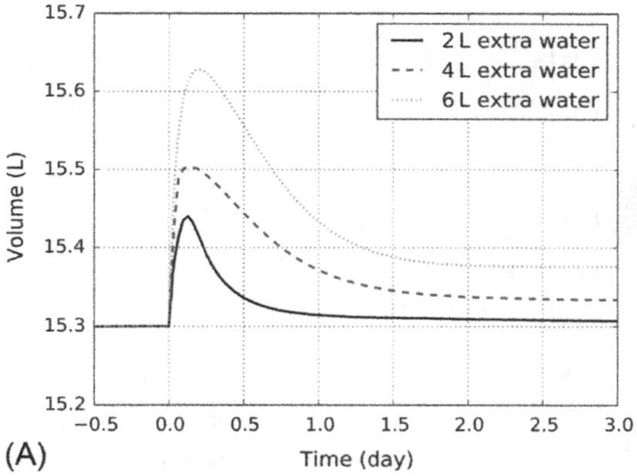

FIGURE 10.13

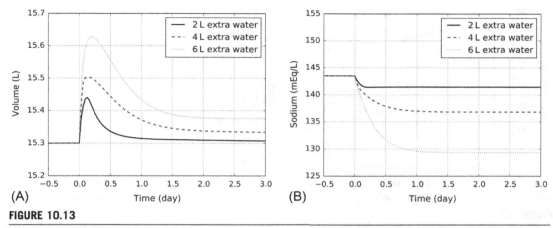

Adaptations of fluid volume and plasma sodium concentration. (A) Extracellular fluid volume and (B) plasma sodium concentration.

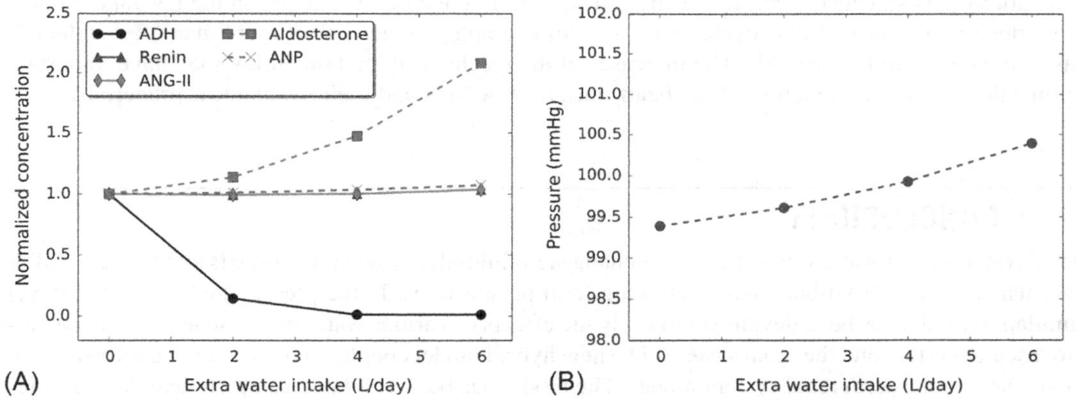

FIGURE 10.14

Adaptations of hormonal concentrations and mean arterial pressure. (A) Hormone concentrations and (B) mean arterial pressure.

the situation of a decreased plasma sodium concentration. The renin and angiotensin-II concentrations do not show significant changes, apparently as a result of the trade-off between sodium retention and the increase of the urine amount. These adaptations also result in increases of the mean arterial pressure against the increased amount of water intake, as shown in Fig. 10.14B.

The long-term adaptations of the above systematic parameters can further affect the mechanical functions of the cardiovascular systems. For example, Fig. 10.15 shows the changes in the *P-V* loop of the left ventricle as a result of the water intakes. Similar to the short-term results discussed earlier, the increase in water intake causes the *P-V* loop to shift upward and to the right (Fig. 10.15A). These

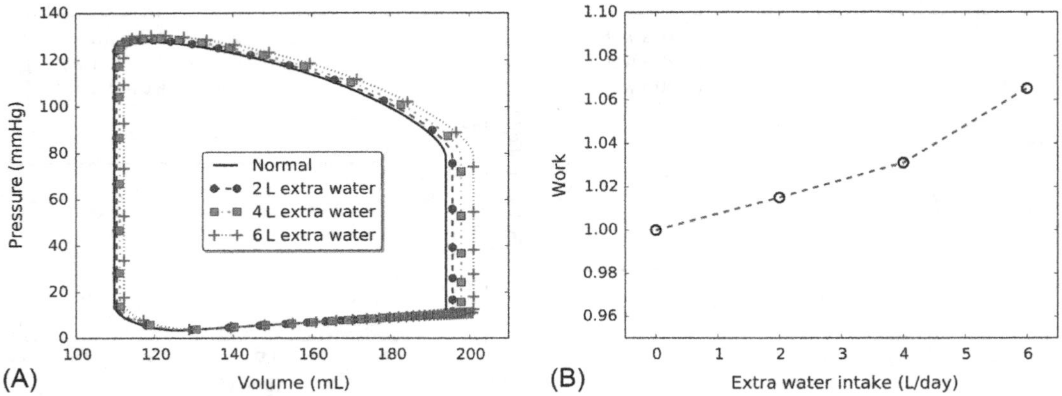

FIGURE 10.15

Adaptations of LV mechanical functions. (A) Left ventricular *P-V* relationship and (B) normalized LV stroke work per heartbeat.

adaptations persist, causing chronic changes to LV. With the chronic changes in the LV function, the work done by LV in a cardiac cycle increases. For example, an increase of more than 6% for the 6 L case can be seen in Fig. 10.15B. The increases of the mechanical loading on LV may have important implications on the remodeling of the heart muscle structures and their mechanical properties.

10.4 CONCLUSIONS

An elevated rate of water intake can cause changes in fluid-electrolyte homeostasis and trigger cardiovascular responses from both short- and long-term perspectives. In the present study, a system-level simulation model has been developed to study the effects of various water intake schedules on the cardiovascular system and the renal system. The new hybrid model couples and modifies a cardiovascular model and a long-term renal system model. The model has been validated using clinical data. The results indicate that the new model is effective in the simulation of both the short- and the long-term effects of elevated water intake.

For the simulations of acute responses, the model provides detailed time-dependent variations of the water and sodium balance after the ingestion of 500 mL water. The associated changes in the renal system, including the changes in the different hormonal concentrations, are obtained. An intake of 500 mL of water triggers instant, but mild, changes in the blood pressure and heart rate. These changes match reasonably well with data reported by the cited clinical studies. For the long-term effect simulation, the modeling results suggest that the chronic adaptations in the cardiovascular system, the renal system, and hormonal concentrations would occur, for continued excessive water intakes. Specifically, with an increase of daily water intake, the ADH concentration is suppressed and the aldosterone concentration increases significantly, which result in a slight increase in the extracellular fluid volume and a decrease in the plasma sodium concentration. These adaptations further increase the mean arterial pressure and the LV stroke work per cardiac cycle.

In summary, the current model is capable of simulating the system-level responses to excessive water intakes in both short and long time scales. The computational model represents a cost-efficient tool that can be useful to develop measures of the effects of water intake on body-fluid homeostasis and possible chronic adaptations. The current model can be further extended to consider electrophysiology and myocardium structures.

REFERENCES

[1] Jéquier E, Constant F. Water as an essential nutrient: the physiological basis of hydration. Eur J Clin Nutr 2010;64(2):115–23.

[2] Armstrong LE, Costill DL, Fink WJ. Influence of diuretic-induced dehydration on competitive running performance. Med Sci Sports Exerc 1985;17:456–61.

[3] Arnaud MJ, Noakes TD. Should humans be encouraged to drink water to excess? Eur J Clin Nutr 2011;65 (7):875.

[4] Lunn J, Foxen R. How much water do we really need? Nutr Bull 2008;33(4):336–42.

[5] Negoianu D, Goldfarb S. Just add water. J Am Soc Nephrol 2008;19(6):1041–3.

[6] Valtin H. "Drink at least eight glasses of water a day." Really? Is there scientific evidence for "8 * 8"? Am J Physiol Regul Integr Comp Physiol 2002;283:R993–R1004.

[7] Wolf R, Wolf D, Rudikoff D, Parish LC. Nutrition and water: drinking eight glasses of water a day ensures proper skin hydration-myth or reality? Clin Dermatol 2010;28(4):380–3.

[8] Brown CM, Barberini L, Dulloo AG, Montani J, Clive M. Cardiovascular responses to water drinking: does osmolality play a role? Am J Physiol Regul Integr Comp Physiol 2005;289(6):1687–92.

[9] Jordan J, Shannon JR, Grogan E, Biaggioni I, Robertson D. A potent pressor response elicited by drinking water. Lancet 1999;353(9154):723.

[10] Scott EM, Greenwood JP, Gilbey SG, Stoker JB, Mary DA. Water ingestion increases sympathetic vasoconstrictor discharge in normal human subjects. Clin Sci 2001;100(3):335–42.

[11] Jordan J, Shannon JR, Black BK, Ali Y, Farley M, Costa F, et al. The pressor response to water drinking in humans: a sympathetic reflex? Circulation 2000;101(5):504–9.

[12] Jordan J. Effect of water drinking on sympathetic nervous activity and blood pressure. Curr Hypertens Rep 2005;7(1):17–20.

[13] Ahuja KDK, Robertson IK, Ball MJ. Acute effects of food on postprandial blood pressure and measures of arterial stiffness in healthy humans. Am J Clin Nutr 2009;90(2):298–303.

[14] Callegaro CC, Moraes RS, Negrão CE, Trombetta IC, Rondon MU, Teixeira MS, et al. Acute water ingestion increases arterial blood pressure in hypertensive and normotensive subjects. J Hum Hypertens 2007;21 (7):564–70.

[15] Mendonca GV, Teixeira MS, Heffernan KS, Fernhall B. Chronotropic and pressor effects of water ingestion at rest and in response to incremental dynamic exercise. Exp Physiol 2013;98(6):1133–43.

[16] Visvanathan R, Chen R, Garcia M, Horowitz M, Chapman I. The effects of drinks made from simple sugars on blood pressure in healthy older people. Br J Nutr 2007;93(05):575–9.

[17] Hall J. Guyton and Hall — textbook of medical physiology. 12th ed. Waltham, MA: Elsevier Health Sciences; 2010.

[18] Guyton AC. Long-term arterial pressure control: an analysis from animal experiments and computer and graphic models. Am J Physiol 1990;259(5):R865–77.

[19] Hall JE, Mizelle HL, Hildebrandt DA, Brands MW. Abnormal pressure natriuresis. A cause or a consequence of hypertension? Hypertension 1990;15:547–59.

[20] Bode F, Sachs F, Franz MR. Tarantula peptide inhibits atrial fibrillation. Nature 2001;409(6816):35–6.

[21] Henry WL, Morganroth J, Pearlman AS, Clark CE, Redwood DR, Itscoitz SB, et al. Relation between echocardiographically determined left atrial size and atrial fibrillation. Circulation 1976;53(2):273–9.
[22] Kalifa J, Jalife J, Zaitsev AV, Bagwe S, Warren M, Moreno J, et al. Intra-atrial pressure increases rate and organization of waves emanating from the superior pulmonary veins during atrial fibrillation. Circulation 2003;108(6):668–71.
[23] Cotter G, Metra M, Milo-Cotter O, Dittrich HC, Gheorghiade M. Fluid overload in acute heart failure — re-distribution and other mechanisms beyond fluid accumulation. Eur J Heart Fail 2008;10(2):165–9.
[24] Karaaslan F, Denizhan Y, Kayserilioglu A, Gulcur HO. Long-term mathematical model involving renal sympathetic nerve activity, arterial pressure, and sodium excretion. Ann Biomed Eng 2005;33(11):1607–30.
[25] Heldt T, Mukkamala R. CVSim: an open-source cardiovascular simulator for teaching and research. Open Pacing Electrophysiol Ther J 2010;3:45–54.
[26] Heldt T, Shim EB, Kamm RD, Mark RG. Computational modeling of cardiovascular response to orthostatic stress. J Appl Physiol 2002;92(3):1239–54.
[27] Mukkamala R, Cohen RJ, Mark RG. A computational model-based validation of Guyton's analysis of cardiac output and venous return curves. Comput Cardiol 2002;29:561–4.
[28] Heldt T, Computational models of cardiovascular response to orthostatic stress. Ph.D. Thesis. Massachusetts Institute of Technology; 2004.
[29] Coleman TG, Hall JE. A mathematical model of renal hemodynamics and excretory function. In: Iyengar SS, editor. Structuring biological systems: a computer modelling approach. Boca Raton, FL: CRC; 1992. p. 89–124.
[30] Ikeda N, Marumo F, Shirataka M, Sato T. A model of overall regulation of body fluids. Ann Biomed Eng 1979;7:135–66.
[31] Uttamsingh RJ, Leaning MS, Bushman JA, Carson ER, Finkelstein L. Mathematical model of the human renal system. Med Biol Eng Comput 1985;23(6):525–35.
[32] Guyton AC, Coleman TG, Granger HJ. Circulation: overall regulation. Annu Rev Physiol 1972;34:13–46.
[33] DiBona GF, Kopp UC. Neural control of renal function. Physiol Rev 1997;77(1):75–179.
[34] Huang WC, Wu JN. Blunted renal responses to atrial natriuretic peptide and its reversal by unclipping in one-kidney, one clip Goldblatt hypertensive rats. J Hypertens 1997;15:181–9.
[35] Husband J, Husband P. Gastric emptying of water and glucose solutions in the newborn. Lancet 1969;294 (7617):409–11.
[36] Vist GE, Maughan RJ. The effect of osmolality and carbohydrate content on the rate of gastric emptying of liquids in man. J Physiol 1995;486(2):523–31.
[37] Calbet JAL, Maclean DA. Role of caloric content on gastric emptying in humans. J Physiol 1997;498 (2):553–9.
[38] Zhang Y, Liou WW, Gupta V. Modeling of high sodium intake effects on left ventricular hypertrophy. Comput Biol Med 2014;58:31–9.
[39] Sacks FM, Svetkey LP, Vollmer WM, Appel LJ, Bray GA, Harsha D, et al. Effects on blood pressure of reduced dietary sodium and the dietary approaches to stop hypertension (DASH) diet. N Engl J Med 2001;344(1):3–10.

CHAPTER

A DNA-BASED MIGRATION MODELING OF THE LIZARDS IN FLORIDA SCRUB HABITAT

11

R.R. Hashemi*, A.A. Bahrami†, D. Swain Jr.*, A. Schrey‡, N.R. Tyler§

Department of Computer Science, Armstrong State University, Savannah, GA, United States *IT Consultation, Savannah, GA, United States*† *Department of Biology, Armstrong State University, Savannah, GA, United States*‡ *School of Pharmacy, University of Georgia, Athens, GA, United States*§

11.1 INTRODUCTION

The ecosystem of the Florida scrub is in fact the support system for life of the scrub's plants, animals, and microscopic organisms, which in turn influences the supporting ecosystems of human life. Study of the lizards' migration is, therefore, essential in understanding some of the ecosystem attributes of the scrub [1–3]. As a result, the domain experts designated a geographical area (approximately 14,000 km^2) in Florida's scrub to study the migratory behavior of lizards. The best way to study such behavior is through building the migration model [4]. Such a model is either mathematically based or empirically based. In general, the mathematical migration models use the laws of nature to describe the behavioral patterns of species.

The empirical migration models deliver a set of migratory behavioral patterns concluded from collected data in multiobserve-record sessions of the migratory species' behavior [5]. Such a modeling approach is time-consuming, costly, and most of all it does not lend itself easily to the study of migration within a habitat. In addition, building an empirical migration model is possible only through use of tracing technologies — body heat detection, radio waves, high-resolution and ultralight tracking, and so forth — which makes the process even more costly.

As an alternative, use of data collected in one-time-test-record session reduces the observation time and cost significantly. A one-time-test-record session includes three steps of *capturing*, *evaluating*, and *releasing* the subject to its environment [6]. The first and the last steps are self-explanatory and the evaluating step includes measuring the physical attributes, biological attributes, and coordinates of the place where the subject was captured. The one-time-test-record session is highly cost-effective; however, it demands new methodologies for delivering the migration model.

We introduce a new modeling approach based on mining of data collected in one-time-test-record session of the species. The model is neither mathematical nor empirical and it is simply using the implicit data buried in the collected data. As the main component of this modeling approach, we present a new clustering technique named Expansion-CONtraction (ECON). This method is a grid-density-based clustering technique that delivers clusters with tightly close members.

The remaining organization of the chapter is as follows. Related works are covered in Section 11.2. Methodology is introduced in Section 11.3. Empirical results are discussed in Section 11.4. Conclusions and future research is the subject of Section 11.5.

11.2 RELATED WORKS

Due to the nature of migration, a geographical region population may grow or shrink. Therefore, we are after a methodology that can provide for population fluctuations (density) within the geographical regions (a grid-like structure) at the same time. In addition, if we assume that the lizards that are tightly close to each other in terms of their biological attributes make a *clan*, then the methodology must provide for partitioning of the population into a dense grid-like structure such that the members of each partition are tightly close. In summary, for extraction of the migration patterns we are in need of a grid-based [7], density-based [8] clustering methodology that delivers the clusters with tightly close members. (We refer to such clusters as tightly grid-dense (TGD) clusters.) To the best of our knowledge there is not any clustering technique that delivers TGD clusters.

We introduce the new ECON clustering method that delivers TGD clusters. ECON, therefore, lends itself easily to the extraction of migration patterns. The grid-density-based clustering method of CLustering In QUEst (CLIQUE) [9], which does not support the tight closeness of objects within the delivered clusters, is the closest clustering methodology to ECON.

CLIQUE divides each dimension of an objects' space into nonoverlapped arbitrary equal size intervals and, thus, divides the objects' space into hyperrectangles (also known as hypercells). Those hypercells in which the number of objects is above a threshold (*density* threshold) are *dense hypercells*. A dense hypercell is *maximized* (in size) by inclusion of all of its adjacent dense hypercells. Each one of the maximized dense hypercells is referred to as a *dense cluster*. Through this process CLIQUE first acts as a grid-based partitioning approach and second acts as a density-based clustering approach. In fact, CLIQUE is intended to reduce the size of the objects' space to more manageable isolated dense subspaces, whereas ECON is intended to model the migratory behaviors within a habitat. ECON deviates from CLIQUE in the following three major ways:

(a) The dimensions of the objects' space are not partitioned into arbitrary equal size intervals. In fact, partition of each dimension takes place based on the distribution of the values within the dimension.

(b) The creation of the maximized hypercells is not needed.

(c) The delivered clusters are not only a set of dense hypercells but each cell also contains tightly close objects.

In addition, the size of a dense hypercell, identified by CLIQUE, is always fixed and the size of any maximized dense hypercell is a multiple of the size of a dense hypercell regardless of the actual distribution of the objects within a maximized cell. ECON is free of these restrictions.

11.3 METHODOLOGY

In a nutshell, our methodology and its justification for discovering the lizards' migration patterns are as follows. (a) ECON is used to cluster the lizards' population based on the coordinates of the physical locations at which the lizards have been captured. The result is a set of TGD clusters representing the actual populated geographical regions within the designated scrub habitat. (b) ECON is used to cluster the lizards' population for the second time based on their DNA markers. The result is a set of TGD clusters representing the lizard clans within the scrub habitat. (c) A mapping is performed to map each clan over the geographical regions. Those geographical regions that are hosting a clan, partially or totally, make the pattern of migration for the clan. The details of the ECON clustering, discovery of the migration patterns, and analysis of the patterns are presented in the following three subsections.

11.3.1 ECON CLUSTERING

ECON clustering is composed of two phases of *expansion* and *contraction* and it adopts, to some degree, the foundation on which the CLIQUE methodology is built. To explain it further, the behavior of the CLIQUE is briefly described and points of ECON departure from CLIQUE along with their justifications are discussed.

Suppose we have a data set with two attributes of temperature and humidity. This data set represents a two-dimensional (2-D) objects' space. (The following discussion is also true when the number of dimensions is n.) Using the CLIQUE principals, both dimensions are partitioned into nonoverlapped arbitrary equal size intervals, which divide the objects' space into a number of equal size 2-D cells. If the number of objects in a given cell is above a density threshold, the cell is *dense*. Fig. 11.1A shows 35 2-D cells, among which 6 are dense. The dense 2-D cells are numbered and shown with thick boundaries.

Two dense cells are considered adjacent if they have one side in common. The maximized dense cells are generated by expanding each dense cell to include its adjacent dense cells. The projection of any dense cell on either of the dimensions has a dense one-dimensional (1-D) cell. Fig. 11.1B shows the dense 1-D cells with thick lines along with the numbered maximized dense cells with thick broken boundaries.

Suppose the actual value for the temperature and humidity of the objects in the maximized cell 2, for example, are captured in Table 11.1. Let us concentrate on the objects of cell 2. If these objects are clustered, two distinct clusters (with 100 and 90 objects, respectively) are generated. Consequently, it makes more sense to replace the temperature interval of [50–65) into two new intervals [50–53) and [59–65) and the humidity interval of [20–30) into two new intervals of [20–21] and [29–30). The reader needs to be reminded that CLIQUE ignores the two clusters and treats them as one cluster. One may conclude that although the CLIQUE delivers the dense objects' subspaces, but the objects are not clustered (ie, they are not *tightly close*). In contrast, ECON creates dense objects' subspaces that their members are tightly close.

ECON partitions each dimension based on the distribution of actual values in the dimension. Therefore, a dimension may not be partitioned in equal size intervals.

To find the actual distribution, the *expansion phase* begins in which (a) the values for the temperature are sorted in ascending order and (b) the building of the first partition starts with the first object in the sorted temperature values and expands until a *gap* is encountered [10]. (When the difference between two adjacent sorted values is larger than a threshold, it constitutes a gap.) The next partition starts with the immediate value after the gap and expands until the next gap is encountered. The expansion phase continues until the partitioning of the values for the temperature dimension is complete. All the values within any partition are tightly close but the partition is not necessarily dense. The dimension humidity also goes through the expansion phase to be partitioned.

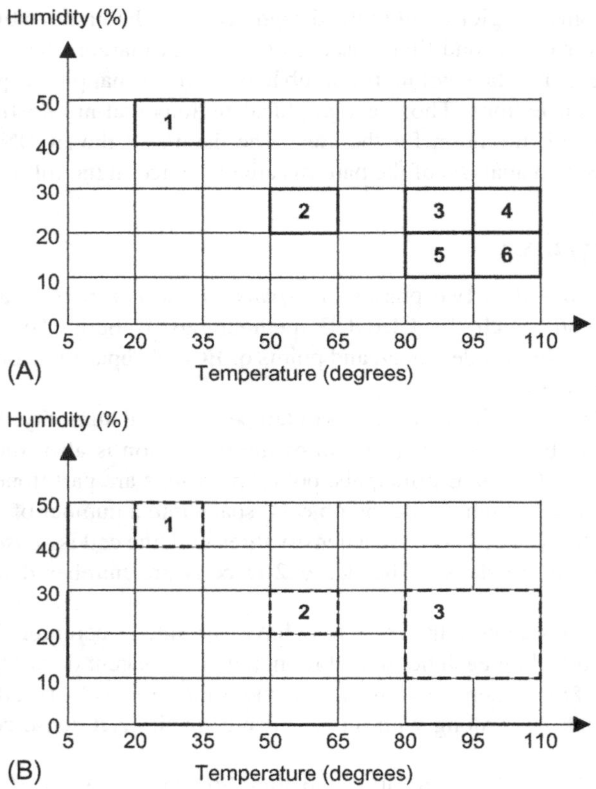

FIGURE 11.1

The nondense 2-D, dense 2-D, maximized 2-D, and projected dense 1-D cells for the object space of a data set with two dimensions of temperature and humidity: (A) thirty-five 2-D and six dense 2-D cells and (B) three maximized dense 2-D cells and five dense 1-D cells.

Table 11.1 The Details of the Objects Distribution in the Dense Maximized 2-D Cell 2 of Fig. 11.1B

Number of Objects	Range of Temperature	Range of Humidity (%)
100	[50–53)	[20–21]
90	[59–65)	[29–30)

Let us consider one of these 1-D cells on dimension temperature, say partition [85–110) in Fig. 11.2. Let the number of objects in this 1-D cell be N. That is, the N objects are scattered in an area of objects' space for which the width is the temperature partition of [85–110) and the length is the entire range of humidity, [0–50). This large area splits into five tightly close 2-D cells by the partitions of the humidity dimension. The splitting of the large area into five disjoint tightly close 2-D cells constitutes the *contraction phase* of ECON.

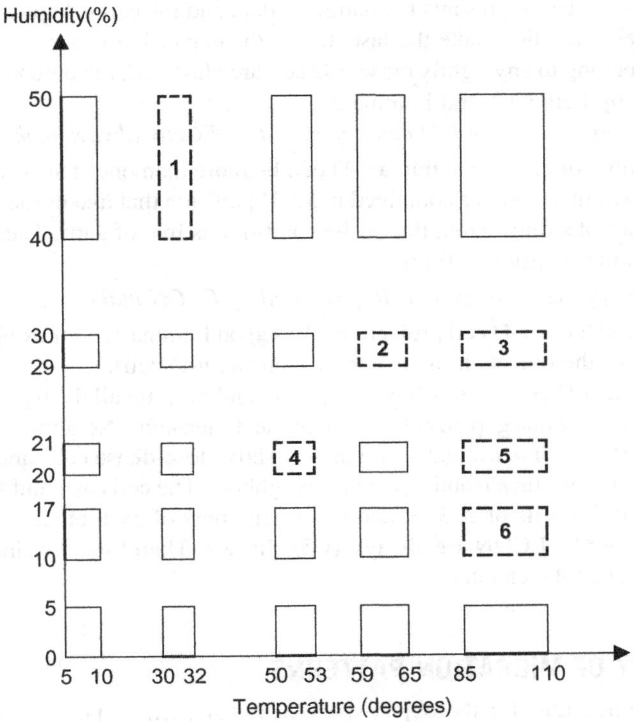

FIGURE 11.2

The partitions of the object space of Fig. 11.1 using the ECON approach.

In practice, the contraction happens between 1-D cells of two dimensions. The outcome participates in another contraction with the third dimension and this process continues until all attributes are gone through the contraction phase and n-dimensional hypercells are generated.

Among the tightly close hypercells, those for which the number of objects is greater than the density threshold are considered as the tightly close-dense hypercells. The objects' space of Fig. 11.2 is made up of 25 2-D cells with tightly close objects among which 6 of them are dense, shown by thick broken borders. As Fig. 11.2 suggests, there is always a gap between any two adjacent 1-D cells. (This is also true about the n-dimensional hypercells.) Having such openings mandate the prohibition of maximizing the tightly close-dense hypercells. The reason stems from the fact that maximized cells defy the definition of the tightly close n-D partitions.

In extreme cases, the use of partitions may generate (1) no dense 2-D cell, (2) a few small dense cells, or (3) a large dense cell with majority of objects. The first and the second cases are the result of having a large value for density threshold and/or a small value for the gap threshold, which are remedied by adjusting one or both thresholds.

The third case is the result of having a large value for the gap threshold. The problem is remedied by decreasing the gap threshold. In the case that the gap is in its lowest possible value and still there is a large dense cell, then such cell represents the nature of data and the cell is kept as is. Checking for the extreme cases and their remedies make the last step of the expansion phase.

If the objects that belong to any tightly close n-D cell are clustered, the outcome is always one cluster. Proof is provided by Lemma 1 and Lemma 2.

Lemma 1. *All the objects in any 1-D cell generated by ECON always make one cluster.*

Proof. Let the number of clusters within a 1-D cell be more than one. This is only possible if there are one or more gaps within the values contained in a 1-D partition that makes the 1-D cell. As gaps are used to partitions values of a dimension, thus, a 1-D partition is free of gaps. Therefore, having one or more gaps contradicts the partition definition. □

Lemma 2. *All the objects in any* n-D *cell generated by ECON make one cluster.*

Proof. Every n-D cell has n 1-D cell projections. Based on Lemma 1, all the objects in each 1-D cell make one cluster and so the objects in their intersection (ie, n-D cell). □

A tightly close-dense n-D cell, u, may have *neighbors* and they are all the tightly close-dense dense n-D cells separated from u by one gap on at least one of the dimensions. Neighborhood can be expanded using the *transitivity*. That is, if u, u_1, and u_2 are three tightly close-dense cells and u is the neighbor of u_1 and u_1 is the neighbor of u_2, then u and u_2 are also neighbors. The cells of 1 and 4, in Fig. 11.2, do not have any neighbors but the cells of 2, 3, 5, and 6 are neighbors of each other.

The clusters generated by ECON are always TGD clusters. Therefore, we simply refer to them as clusters through the rest of the chapter.

11.3.2 DISCOVERY OF MIGRATION PATTERNS

Let A be a set of n dimensions for the object space S. Let $A_1, \ldots, A_v$ be the subsets of A such that $A_i \cap A_j = \varnothing$ (for all i and j, where $i \neq j$) and dimensions in A_i collectively represent measurements of one property of the objects. For example, dimensions in A_i may represent the physical property measurements of the objects such as weight, length, color, and so forth. The ECON method can deliver clusters for any of the v subsets ($A_1, \ldots, A_v$) separately.

Let ECON deliver two separate sets of clusters using $A_1 = \{\text{captured location attributes}\}$ and $A_2 = \{\text{the DNA attributes}\}$, respectively. To discover the set of migration patterns out of the two separate sets, we start with introducing a number of definitions.

Definition 1. Let, $S_1 = S(A_1)$ and $S_2 = S(A_2)$ be two subspaces of $S(A)$ such that $c_1 > 0$ and $c_2 > 0$, where, $c_1 = \text{Card}(A_1)$ and $c_2 = \text{Card}(A_2)$.

Let $P = \{p_1, \ldots, p_n\}$ be the set of all c_1-D cells (clusters) in S_1 and $Q = \{q_1, \ldots, q_m\}$ be the set of all c_2-D cells in S_2 generated by ECON. Overlaying a cell, q_i, of Q over P, partitions the object space of q_i into h nonempty disjoint subpartitions ($1 \leq h \leq \text{Card}(P)$). The partitioned q_i is referred to as a *mapped partition of* q_i *over* P *with* h *spans*, or simply *a pattern over* P *with* h *spans*. Those members of P that are participating in creation of the pattern of q_i are the *underlying clusters* of pattern q_i. If M is the set of all patterns of members of Q over P, then M is the *model of* Q *over* P in object space of S and it is denoted as $M_S(Q_{S_1}|P_{S_2})$.

Definition 2. Let π_b be a pattern in $M_S(Q_{S_1}|P_{S_2})$. If the number of spans for the pattern π_b is equal to the Card(P), then π_b is a *trivial* pattern; otherwise, it is a *nontrivial* one.

If P is a set of geographical regions and Q is a set of lizard clans, then a trivial pattern means that the clan of lizards, identified by the pattern, can be found all over the geographical regions. Therefore, a trivial pattern does not signify any migratory activity and it is ignored. For the sake of simplicity, the use of the term *migration pattern* (or simply *pattern*) through the rest of the chapter means a nontrivial migration pattern unless it is expressed otherwise.

Definition 3. In model $M_S(Q_{S_1}|P_{S_2})$, let χ be the set of underlying clusters for pattern of π_b. If

(a) Card(χ) = 1 then, π_b is a *local* pattern. This pattern signifies the fact that migration of the lizards is contained within one geographical region.
(b) Card(χ) > 1 and none of the members of χ are neighbors, then π_b is a *scattered* pattern. This pattern signifies the fact that an extraordinary ecological devastation happened that scattered the clan members through several nonneighboring geographical regions.
(c) Card(χ) > 1 and all the members of χ are neighbors, then π_b is a *continuous* pattern. This pattern signifies the fact that migration of the lizards are within the neighboring geographical regions.
(d) Card(χ) > 1 and some of the members of χ transitively make one or more neighborhoods then, π_b is a *semicontinuous* pattern. Within a semicontinuous pattern may be one or more neighborhoods. Members in each neighborhood make one continuous subpattern and those members that do not belong to any neighborhood make a scattered subpattern.

Definition 4. Let $\chi = \{c_a, \ldots, c_k\}$ be the set of underlying clusters for the pattern of π_b. The *local density set* for π_b is LD_{π_b} and defined by formula (1).

$$LD_{\pi_b} = \{d_i | d_i = \text{Card}(\pi_b \cap c_i), \ \text{for } i = a \text{ to } k\} \tag{1}$$

If $d_i \le T_\Delta$ then it is *negligible* and it is removed from LD_{π_b}. (T_Δ is the local density set threshold.) The corresponding underlying cluster of a negligible local density set member is also removed from χ. The pattern π_b is a *weak pattern* if its $LD_{\pi_b} = \varnothing$. A weak pattern signifies a clan rarity and it is ignored.

Definition 5. Let $\chi = \{c_a, \ldots, c_k\}$ be the set of underlying clusters for the pattern of π_b with the corresponding LD_{π_b}. The *nonoverlapped density* (*NOD*) of π_b is defined by formula (2).

$$NOD_{\pi_b} = \text{Card}\left(\pi_b - \bigcup_{i=a}^{k} c_i\right) \tag{2}$$

The *density* of π_b is defined by formula (3).

$$d\pi_b = NOD_{\pi_b} + \sum_{i=1}^{|LD_{\pi_b}|} d_i \tag{3}$$

Definition 6. Each pattern has a *length, L*. The length of a weak pattern is zero. The length of a local pattern is one and so is the length of a scattered pattern. The length of a continuous pattern is equal to its number of pattern's spans. Length of a semicontinuous pattern is the same as the number of its subpatterns.

Fig. 11.3 illustrates a modeled objects' space; *S*. objects are shown by dots. Those clusters shown by oval shapes are the set of geographical regions, *P*, delivered by ECON only using the captured location coordinates. The clusters shown by irregular shapes (with dashed boundaries) are the set of lizards' clans, *Q*, also delivered by ECON using DNA markers. Five migration patterns are discovered by overlaying every member of *Q* on *P* and these patterns are numbered from 1 to 5. (Pattern 3 has two subpatterns and both are numbered 3.)

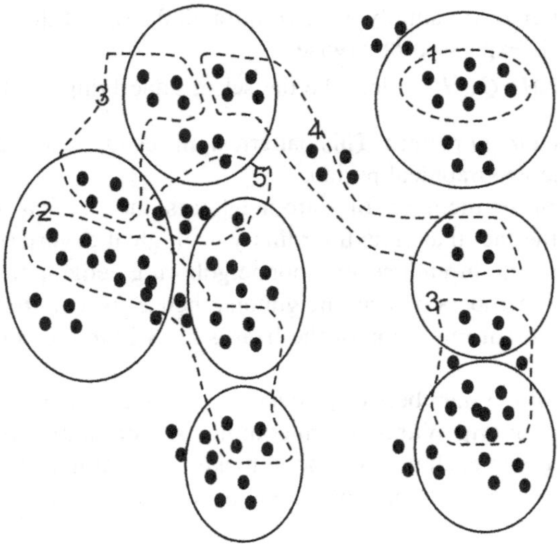

FIGURE 11.3

The $M_S(Q_{S_2}|P_{S_1})$ model.

Pattern 1 has the length of one, density of eight, *NOD* of zero, underlying clusters of one, local density set of {8}, spans of one, and it is a local pattern because it is totally encompassed by one of the clusters of *P*. Pattern 2 has the length of three, density of nineteen, *NOD* of two, underlying clusters of three, local density set of {9, 4, 4}, spans of three, and it is a continuous pattern because it has been distributed over three transitively neighbors. Pattern 3 is a semicontinuous with two disjoint subpatterns (both numbered 3). Both subpatterns are continuous and happened to have the same length of two. The *NOD* value for one is zero and for the other one is two. However, the density of one subpattern is eight and density of the other one is fourteen. The local density set for one of the subpatterns is {4, 4} and for the other one is {4,8}. Both subpatterns have two spans. Pattern 4 is a scattered pattern with the length of one, density of ten, *NOD* of two, underlying clusters of two, spans of two, and local density set of {4, 4}. Pattern 5 is a weak pattern with the length of zero, density of three, *NOD* of three, no underlying clusters, zero spans, and an empty local density set. (Pattern 5 has three negligible spans where the cardinality of each span is equal to 1.)

11.3.3 ANALYSIS OF THE MIGRATION PATTERNS

The profile of a migration pattern of π_i that is resulting from $M_S(Q_{S_2}|P_{S_1})$ is composed of the following information:

(a) *Type*: one of the values from the set {local, scattered, continuous, semicontinuous}.
(b) *Number of spans: h.*

(c) *Underlying clusters:* $\chi_{\pi_i} \subseteq P_{S_1}, (\chi_{\pi_i} = \{p_a \ldots p_h\})$.
(d) *Local density set* with respect to its underlying clusters: $LD_{\pi_i} = \{d_a \ldots d_h\}$.
(e) *Nonoverlap density:* NOD_{π_i}.
(f) *Density:* $d_{\pi_i} = d_a + \cdots + d_h + NOD_{\pi_i}$.
(g) *Length:* L_{π_i}.
(h) *Clan:* Clan_{π_i} is all the objects in $q_i \in Q_{S_2}$ before it is mapped on clusters of P_{S_1}.

Analysis of the migration patterns delivers the features of each pattern. The extracted features reveal the relative degree of willingness for migration among the clan members, relative degree of active migration among the clan members, and disclosure of possible ecosystem disasters of the past. The details are presented as a set of cases. (The above profile and its related notations are used in expressing the details.)

Case 1 (Local type patterns): Let π_i and π_j be two local patterns and let $d_{\pi_i} \gg d_{\pi_j}$. The density of the two patterns reveal the fact that the willingness for migration among the objects of Clan_{π_i} is less than the willingness for migration among the objects of Clan_{π_j}. By definition, the ratio of $\left(\text{Max}\left(d_{\pi_i}, d_{\pi_j}\right) - d_{\pi_i} + 1\right) / \left(d_{\pi_i} + d_{\pi_j}\right)$ represents the relative degree of willingness to migrate for the objects of π_i, and it is denoted as $(\alpha^{\text{w}}_{\pi_i})$. In case there are v local patterns, the relative degree of the willingness for migration for each pattern is defined by formula (4).

$$\alpha^{\text{w}}_{\pi_i} = \frac{\text{Max}\left(d_{\pi_i}, \ldots, d_{\pi_v}\right) - d_{\pi_i} + 1}{\sum_{m=1}^{v} d_{\pi_m}} \tag{4}$$

In general, the local pattern with the higher density has a lower degree of willingness for migration.

Case 2 (Continuous type patterns): Let the type for two patterns of π_i and π_j be "continuous" and let $L_{\pi_i} > L_{\pi_j}$. One may conclude that the objects of the Clan_{π_i} are more active migrant than the objects of Clan_{π_j} and the ratio of $L_{\pi_i} / \left(L_{\pi_i} + L_{\pi_j}\right)$ represents the relative degree of active migration for π_i, $(\alpha^{\text{a}}_{\pi_i})$. This conclusion makes more sense if objects of Clan_{π_i} and Clan_{π_j} have started the migration process at the same time. However, the starting of migration time is unknown. As a remedy, the $\alpha^{\text{a}}_{\pi_i}$ is divided by $\alpha^{\text{w}}_{\pi_i}$. The relative degree of active migration among v continuous patterns is calculated using formula (5):

$$\alpha^{\text{a}}_{\pi_i} = \left(\frac{1}{\alpha^{\text{w}}_{\pi_i}}\right)\left(\frac{L_{\pi_i}}{\sum_{m=1}^{v} L_{\pi_m}}\right) \tag{5}$$

Case 3 (Continuous type patterns): Let the condition $(d_a \cong \ldots \cong d_h)$ be true for the members of the set LD_{π_i}, where π_i is a continuous pattern. This means that the objects in Clan_{π_i} have reached to equilibrium in terms of migration and there is a good chance for not migrating in a near future.

Case 4 (Continuous type patterns): Let for a continuous pattern π_i, $d_{\pi_i} \gg (d_a + \cdots + d_h)$, which simply expresses that migration is currently in progress. Considering formula (3), the value of NOD_{π_i} must be extremely large. This means that the number of lizards moving in between underlying clusters is much higher than the number of lizards that reached the underlying clusters.

Case 5 (Scattered type patterns): The fact that the set of underlying clusters, χ_{π_i}, of a scattered migration pattern π_i are not neighbors reveals that a sizable environmental event has disturbed the ecosystem of the scrub. Such an event could be wildfire, tornado, hurricane, and so forth. Higher the cardinality of χ_{π_i} means a larger environmental devastation happened in the past.

Case 6 (Semicontinuous type patterns): Let π_i be a semicontinuous pattern. The type of the subpatterns and their mixture reflects the size and/or frequency of the environmental events. The devastation of the environment is considered to be the highest for the case having only one short continuous subpattern and the lowest for the case having only continuous subpatterns.

11.4 EMPIRICAL RESULTS

For each lizard captured within the designated geographical area (approximately 14,000 km^2), the values of eight microsatellite loci DNA markers (Nr 52.2, Nr 52.4, Nr 52.7, Nr 52.11, Nr 60.2, Nr 60.5, Nr 60.11, Nr 60.34) were collected. The markers are noncoding genetic elements, sometimes called STR, for simple tandem repeats (ex. GTGTGTGTGTGT) and they are highly variable. Also, the SVL (snout vent length — a measurement of length minus tail) and Universal Transverse Mercator (UTM) coordinates (UTM East and UTM North) of the location in which the lizard has been captured were recorded. As the history of the wildfire for 30 subareas within the 14,000 km^2 habitat was known, the number of wildfires along with the number of years from the last fire was assigned to each location.

The two subsets of the dimensions of the lizard's data set that we are interested in are $A_1 = \{$UTM coordinates$\}$ and $A_2 = \{$DNA markers$\}$. The dimensions in A_1 represent the measurements for one property of the lizards — *location*. The dimensions in A_2 represent the measurements for another property of the lizards — *DNA markers*. The DNA information has gone through a preprocessing step to (a) normalize the DNA data and (b) identify and remove outliers from the data set. The number of outliers in reference to the Nr 60.2 alone was 36. As a result, we totally removed the dimension Nr 60.2 from A_2. After removing the other outliers from the data set, the number of the remaining objects was 376 out of 464 objects.

Application of ECON on A_1 divided the designated habitat into nine geographical regions (location clusters). The threshold value of 2 was used for the gap size and density threshold. The size of each cluster in terms of square kilometer along with the number of lizards captured in that area and the number of wildfires are listed in Table 11.2A. Among the nine clusters, p_1, and p_2 were neighbors, p_3 did not have any neighbors, and the rest of the clusters were neighbors of each other.

Application of ECON on A_2 divided the lizard population into eight clusters (clans) using the density threshold value of 6 and the gap threshold value of 3. The later threshold value was established through a trial and error process. The eight clans (DNA clusters) along with the number of lizards for each DNA cluster are listed in Table 11.2B. (Clan q_5 was not dense and deleted.)

The model of object space using the DNA clusters and location clusters, $M_S(Q_{\text{DNA}}|P_{\text{Location}})$, was created that delivered one trivial, and seven nontrivial migration patterns (three continuous, two semicontinuous, and two scattered). The properties of all nontrivial migration patterns are given in Table 11.3.

Table 11.2 The Details of the Clusters: (A) Location Clusters and (B) DNA Clusters

(A)

Location Clusters (Geographical Regions)	Size (km^2)	# of Lizards Captured	# of Fires
p_1	1640	37	12
p_2	3150	74	7
p_3	1110	33	10
p_4	225	16	5
p_5	3285	78	10
p_6	480	24	7
p_7	2070	24	5
p_8	1080	31	6
p_9	1035	19	2

(B)

DNA Clusters (Clans)	# of Lizards
q_1	248
q_2	12
q_3	22
q_4	9
q_6	12
q_7	9
q_8	7
q_9	18

Table 11.3 The Properties of the Nontrivial Migration Patterns

Pattern	Migration Pattern Properties					
	Type	Underlying Clusters	Local Density Set	*NOD*	*d*	*L*
π_1	Continuous	p_5, p_8	{3, 4}	5	12	2
π_2	Continuous	p_5, p_6, p_8	{8, 8, 3}	3	22	3
π_3	Scattered	p_2, p_3	{2, 5}	2	9	1
π_4	Semicontinuous	p_3, p_5, p_7, p_9	{2, 2, 2, 4}	2	12	2
(π_4-Subpattern1)	Scattered	p_3	{2}	0	2	1
(π_4-Subpattern2)	Continuous	p_5, p_7, p_9	{2, 2, 4}	0	8	3
π_5	Scattered	p_2, p_3	{3, 4}	2	9	1
π_6	Continuous	p_5, p_9	{4, 2}	1	7	2
π_7	Semicontinuous	p_1, p_2, p_5, p_7, p_8	{2, 8, 2, 3, 2}	1	18	2
(π_7-Subpattern1)	Continuous	p_1, p_2	{2, 8}	0	10	2
(π_7-Subpattern2)	Continuous	p_5, p_7, p_8	{2, 3, 2}	0	7	3

11.5 CONCLUSION AND FUTURE RESEARCH

The ECON method of clustering is a tightly close grid-density-based clustering method that lends itself easily to (a) migration modeling of migratory species within their habitats and (b) handling of the migratory data collected in one-time-test-record.

The modeling of the given data set revealed seven nontrivial patterns. The number of local patterns was zero. This means that all the lizard clans have migrated. This is a typical migration behavior within a habitat. Having one trivial pattern indicates that one clan of the lizards make the predominant population within the Florida scrub habitat and their migration pattern is not discernable.

The maximum length for the continuous patterns in Table 11.3 was three and three out of the six continuous patterns and continuous subpatterns had the highest length. The continuous pattern of π_2 had the highest relative degree of willingness for migration. It makes sense because the underlying clusters of π_2 collectively had the highest number of wildfires (23).

Among the scattered patterns of π_3 and π_5, the number of wildfires for the underlying clusters suggests that both patterns had the same level of environmental devastations (17 wildfires).

The objects of the migration pattern of π_7 (a semicontinuous pattern) have been more exposed to the environmental disaster (40 wildfires in the past) than the objects of the other semicontinuous pattern. The highest relative degree of active migration belonged to the second subpattern of the semicontinuous pattern π_7. There is no indication that any of the migration patterns has reached its equilibrium.

The geographical region of p_4 does not serve in the underlying clusters of any pattern. That is, there is not a noticeable number of lizards belonging to any specific clan in p_4. Therefore, p_4 is considered a *transient region*.

The geographical region of p_5 is a *preferred region* for migration because it belongs to underlying clusters of five patterns. In other words, lizards from five different clans are present in this geographical region. It makes also sense because P_5 has the largest size. The second most popular geographical region for migration is P_2 with the second largest size.

As future research, the association analysis between (a) the DNA markers and the number of wildfires and (b) the DNA markers and the number of years from the last wildfire is in progress. The goal is to study the effects of a wildfire on DNA diversity among the DNA markers of each subject.

REFERENCES

[1] Brown TC, Bergstrom JC, Loomis JB. Defining, valuing and providing ecosystem goods and services. J Nat Resour 2007;47(2):329–76.

[2] Carpenter SR, Cole JJ, Essington TE, Hodgson JR, Houser JN, Kitchell JF, et al. Evaluating alternative explanations in ecosystem experiments. Ecosystems 1998;1(4):335–44.

[3] Southwood A, Avens L. Physiological, behavioral, and ecological aspects of migration in reptiles. J Comp Physiol B 2010;180(1):1–23.

[4] ter Braak CJF, Hanski I, Verboom J. The incidence function approach to modelling of metapopulation dynamics. In: Bascompte J, Solé RV, editors. Modelling spatio-temporal dynamics in ecology. Austin, TX: Landes Biosciences; 1998. p. 167–88.

[5] Bauer S, Klaassen M. Mechanistic models of animal migration behavior — their diversity, structure and use. J Anim Ecol 2013;82:498–508.

[6] Schrey A, Heath S, Ashton K, McCoy E, Mushinsky H. Fire alters patterns of genetic diversity among three lizard species in Florida scrub habitat. J Hered 2011;102:399–408.
[7] Grabusts P, Borisov A. Using grid-clustering methods in data classification, In: Proceedings of the IEEE international conference on parallel computing in electrical engineering (PARELEC '02), Warsaw, Poland; 2002. p. 425–6.
[8] Kriegel HP, Kröger P, Sander J, Zimek A. Density-based clustering. Wiley Interdiscip Rev Data Min Knowl Disc 2011;1(3):231–40.
[9] Agrawal R, Gehrke J, Gunopulos D, Raghavan P. Automatic subspace clustering of high dimensional data for data mining applications. In: Haas LM, Tiwary A, editors. Proceedings of the ACM international conference on management of data (SIGMOD '98). Washington: Seattle; 1998. p. 94–905.
[10] Hashemi R, LeBlanc L, Kobayashi T. Formal concept analysis in investigation of normal accidents. Int J Gen Syst 2004;33(5):469–84.

CHAPTER

RECONSTRUCTION OF GENE REGULATORY NETWORKS USING PRINCIPAL COMPONENT ANALYSIS

12

X. Wu*, B. Yang*, A. Maxwell*, W. Koh*, P. Gong†, C. Zhang*

*School of Computing, University of Southern Mississippi, Hattiesburg, MS, United States**

Environmental Laboratory, U.S. Army Engineer Research and Development Center, Vicksburg, MS, United States†

12.1 INTRODUCTION

The most critical problem in the reconstruction of genetic networks is to determine the dependencies and regulating relationships among genes. The complexity of the eukaryotic transcriptional regulation machinery makes reconstruction of gene regulatory networks (GRNs) from time series gene expression data a very challenging task. A GRN can be described by a directly connected graph in which a vertex stands for a gene and a directed edge represents a regulation relationship. In this chapter we study the methods of reconstructing GRNs from time series data of concentration of mRNAs.

Several methods have been proposed for reconstructing GRNs, such as dynamic Bayesian networks (DBNs) [1,2], probability Boolean networks (PBNs) [3], and information theory models (ITMs) [4]. In our previous work, the performance of DBN and PBN was compared using the *Drosophila* time series data and it was found that DBN outperforms PBN in most tested cases [5]. DBN and PBN are time-consuming and ITM cannot give directions of regulation relationships. A state space model (SSM) [6–10] can conquer those difficulties. SSM has almost the same inference accuracy as DBN, but it requires less computational time [11]. However, SSM still has its disadvantages. First, it needs to guess the initial values of parameters to start the iterations [8–10]. Second, it is hard to determine the gene-gene interactions in SSM.

Rangel introduced an extra direct gene-gene interaction term and used bootstrap analysis to infer GRN in SSM [8]. The bootstrap analysis can slow down the speed of SSM, which diminishes the advantage of SSM. Hirose proposed a method to extract a network from the standard SSM, but it still used a permutation method to obtain the network matrix, which needs many repeated calculations on the permutation data sets [9]. Kojima introduced a variation of SSM, which does not have an observation matrix, but it still used an iterative method and needed to guess the initial value of parameters [10]. Wu introduced the probabilistic principal component analysis to compute the values of hidden variables first, which solves the problem of determining initial values of parameters [6,7]. However, it does not address how to infer the networks. Holter used a linear model to obtain module-module interactions, but did not infer gene-gene interactions [12]. In this chapter, we develop a simplified linear model (SLM) for GRN reconstruction based on principal component analysis (PCA) and our previous work using SSMs [11]. We first use PCA to compute the values of hidden variables and the observation matrix and then use a standard linear model to fit the transformed data. After the fitting process, similar equations from Ref. [9,13] were used to extract the network without repeated calculations.

The true time series data sets such as *Yeast*, *Drosophila*, *Escherichia coli*, and *Eisenia fetida* were used for GRN reconstruction and to evaluate the performance of DBN and SSM [5,13,14]. These true data sets have only a limited number of data points and lack the flexibility to investigate the stability and sensitivity of SLM to the noise, the time intervals, and the number of time points. Simulated data generated artificially from in silico gene networks provide a "gold" standard to systematically evaluate the performance of different genetic networks inferring algorithms. In silico networks are composed of a known network topology that determines the structure and model for each of the interactions among the genes. In such simulated data, all aspects of the networks are under full control and different types of data and levels of noise are allowed. In this work, GeneNetWeaver [15] was used to generate time series data sets with respect to 20 *E. coli* networks. The simulated data sets were applied for GRN reconstruction to demonstrate the overall performance of SLM.

12.2 METHODS

12.2.1 STATE SPACE MODEL

SSM [6–10] has two kinds of variables; one is a hidden variable x_t and the other one is a measurement variable y_t. x_t and y_t are vectors, representing values at the *t*th time point. The lengths of x_t and y_t are m and k, respectively. y_t is the measurement of microarray data in time point t. As x_t is a hidden variable, its value cannot be directly measured. The purpose of introducing hidden variables is to reduce the number of parameters in this model [6–10]. If the length of the hidden variable m is less than the observed variable k, the number of parameters is decreased compared with a model that does not introduce hidden variables, such as a linear model.

The equations of linear SSM are

$$x_t = Fx_{t-1} + w_t \qquad (1)$$

$$y_t = Hx_t + v_t \qquad (2)$$

The first equation describes the transition of the hidden variable x_t, where w_t is Gaussian noise. F is the matrix introduced to let x_t be the linear combination of x_{t-1}. The second equation describes the relationship between hidden variable x_t and observed variable y_t, where v_t is Gaussian noise. y_t is a linear combination of x_t. H is an observation matrix. The transition equation (1) has a smaller number of parameters compared with a linear model because the length of x_t is less than the length of y_t. As x_t is a hidden variable, how to determine the optimum length of x_t becomes a problem. As discussed in Ref. [11], the length of m should be set to a small integer number. If m is too large, the purpose of reducing the number of parameters will be pointless, and the accuracy will be poor.

The inference process is complicated, and the analytic solution is usually not available. With a SSM, an iterative expectation maximization (EM) method was used to infer parameters [16,17] that represent the gene-gene interactions. The EM method needs the initial values of parameters to start iteration, and it is also time-consuming. After inference process, the H and F matrices can be obtained. What we intend to discover is the relationship between genes, or more specifically, the relationship between y_t and y_{t-1}. After simple derivation, one can obtain the approximate equation, $y_t = HF(H'H)^{-1}H'y_{t-1}$. The coefficient matrix C, where $C = HF(H'H)^{-1}H'$, can be used to reconstruct a GRN and then the GRN is can be compared to a realistic network [9,13]. The value of each entry in the matrix C denotes the probability of having a connection [10,13].

12.2.2 SIMPLIFIED LINEAR MODEL

The SLM can be described by the following equations:

$$y_t = Hx_t \tag{3}$$

$$x_t = Fx_{t-1} + \Omega + \sigma_t \tag{4}$$

where x_t and y_t are vectors, representing the real and observed gene expression levels at time point t. H is a transformation matrix, obtained when PCA is applied before fitting the linear model (4). F is transition matrix, obtained by fitting the linear model (4) with x_t. Ω is a constant vector, having the same length as x_t. σ_t is Gaussian noise.

PCA is used to transform the original data y_t to x_t. x_t has the same length k as y_t. This step does not introduce any loss of information. However, the first few components of x_t are the most important for the reconstruction of the original data y_t. When the first few components of x_t are retained, we successfully reduce the number of parameters. After the data dimension reduction process, the usual fit of linear model is applied to x_t.

Eqs. (3), (4) are similar to Eqs. (1), (2) in SSM. The difference is that matrix H is not a parameter in SLM; it can be determined by using PCA. Now the analytic solution of fitting linear equation (4) is available and one does not need to use an iterative method anymore. Another advantage with analytic solution is that there is no need for initial values.

Similar to SSM, the approximate relationship between y_t and y_{t-1} is $y_t = HF(H'H)^{-1} H'y_{t-1} = HFH'y_{t-1}$ [9,13]. The second equation uses the fact that H is an orthogonal matrix in SLM obtained using PCA. The network is a simpler equation compared with SSM; it does not include the inversion operation of the matrix. Moreover, in SLM, H is no longer a parameter matrix; it is only determined by the data. Because SLM has fewer parameters than SSM, the inference process is simpler and faster than SSM.

12.3 RESULTS AND DISCUSSION

As addressed in Section 12.1, GeneNetWeaver [15] was used to generate synthetic data to compare the performance of the SLM and SSM methods. The advantage of synthetic data is that the true GRN is known so we can compare the inferred GRN with the true GRN. The number of time points can be large enough that we can investigate the influence of the number of time points on inference accuracy. 20 GRNs with 30 genes and 501 time points were generated using the *E. coli* data set. The SLM and SSM methods were used to infer the 20 GRNs and compare the average accuracy. The definition of accuracy is the ratio of the number of correctly inferred edges to the total number of inferred edges. The number of edges retained in inferred GRN is set as the same as the true GRN for those two methods. The number of edges in the true GRN is usually between 30 and 60 in our examples.

As mentioned previously, Eq. (3) describes the data dimension reduction process by applying PCA. We use some examples to investigate if we can approximately reconstruct the original data by only retaining the first few components of x_t. Fig. 12.1 shows both reconstructed and original data. The number of the most important components retained in x_t is 2. It is smaller compared with the total number of genes, 30. One can see that the most important structure is still reserved, while it suddenly decreases at around the 250th time point. At the same time, the noise level of the reconstructed data is less than the original data. This is understandable, because less important components of x_t contain much high-frequency information. Here, the retained number of components of x_t is set to a small number, 2. The effects of different numbers on accuracy are discussed later.

Now we set the length of hidden variables x_t as 2 for both SSM and SLM and use this setting to test the reconstruction of 20 networks. The average accuracies for SSM and SLM are 10.8% and 9.2%. As the average accuracy of random guess is around 4.6%, SSM and SLM can capture some true regulation relationships from the time series data set. The accuracy of SSM is slightly higher than SLM, but the total calculation time for SSM and SLM is 471 s and 11 s, respectively. SLM is much faster than SSM. Because the convergence of SSM depends on the convergent criteria and initial values, the above calculation time of SSM is only a typical one; it may vary.

Fig. 12.2 shows detailed accuracies of SSM and SLM with respect to 20 different networks using the data with all 501 time points. In some cases, SSM performs better than SLM while in other cases SLM

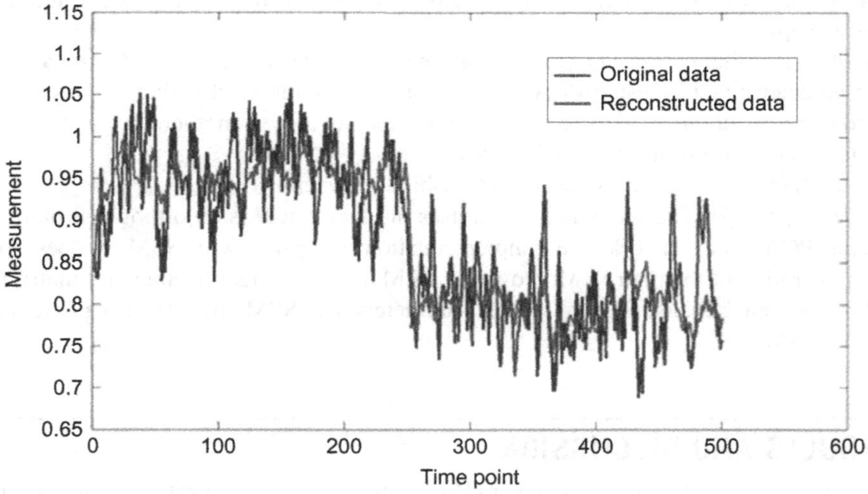

FIGURE 12.1

The original data with 30 genes and 501 time points is depicted as a black line (*blue line* in colored version). The reconstructed data retaining only two of the most important components of x_t after using PCA is depicted as a gray line (*red line* in colored version).

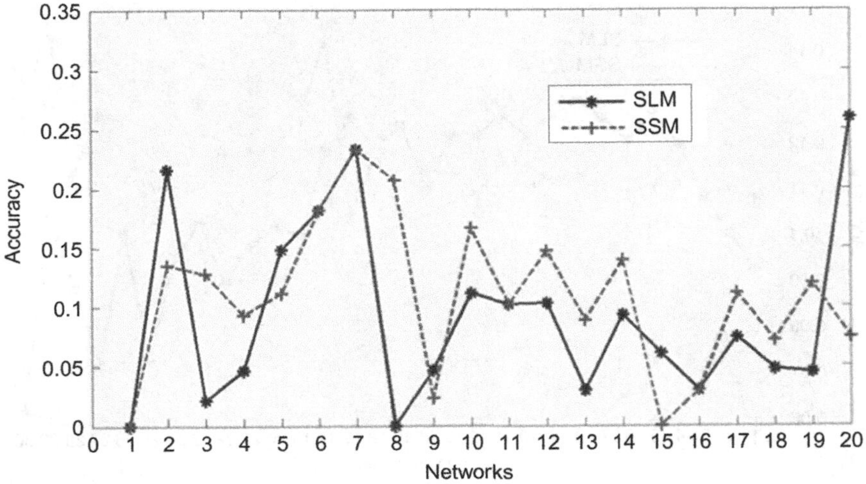

FIGURE 12.2

The detailed accuracies of 20 networks with 30 genes and 501 time points by using SSM and SLM. The length of hidden variables in both SSM and SLM is set as 2.

is better. While the performance is dependent on the specific data sets, the overall performance of SSM is slightly better than SLM.

In reality the measurement of 501 time points is not available. Usually there are only a few dozen time points, but it would be beneficial to investigate the impact of different amounts of time points (501 vs. a few dozen) on the accuracy of GRN reconstruction. These time points are indexed as 1, 2, ... 501. We can choose a subset of data that are uniformly distributed among the original data. For example, one subset of data is chosen from the original data with time points 1, 11, ... 491, 501 so that the length of interval is 10.

The data with larger intervals have the same noise level, which is how GeneNetWeaver generated those data [15]. We use different lengths of intervals, from 1 to 30, to obtain 30 different data sets. The sizes of these data sets range from 501 to 17 time points. The GRNs are inferred using these data sets with different numbers of time points. For each data set, the average accuracy is calculated based on the 20 networks. Fig. 12.3 shows the inference results (average accuracy of 20 networks) of SSM and SLM with respect to different numbers of time points. For data sets (1, 2, 3) whose sizes are from 501, 251, and 167 time points, respectively, SSM performs better than SLM. For data sets (4–17), whose sizes are from 126 to 30 time points, SLM performs better than SSM. For data sets (18–30), whose sizes are from 28 to 17, SSM performs better than SLM. For both SSM and SLM, larger sizes (number of time points) of data sets do not always lead to better performance. This is interesting and we argue that this is because those two models are linear, so a larger data set produces a less reliable fitting process. At the same time, the data set with a smaller size may cause the algorithm not to converge, so measuring a reasonable size of data is important. In our examples, a data set with more than 30 time points will be appropriate for inferring a network with 30 genes.

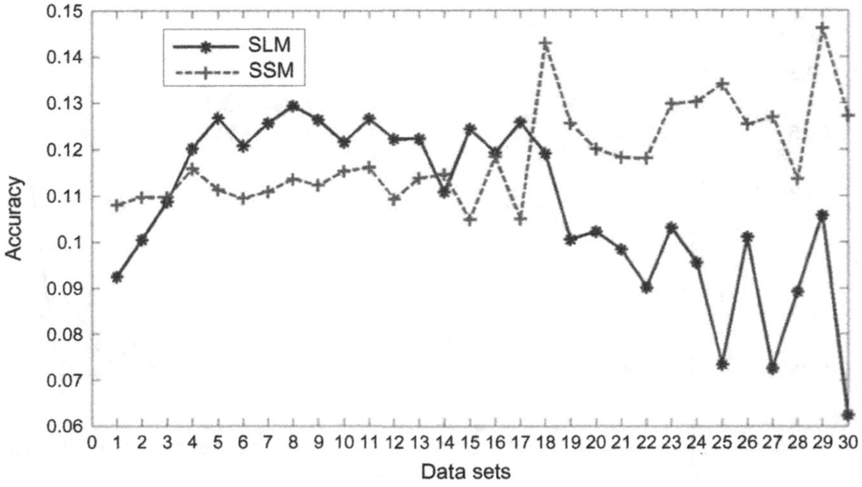

FIGURE 12.3

The average accuracies over 20 networks by using SSM and SLM. Every data set has 20 networks with a different number of time points. The length of hidden variables in both SSM and SLM is set as 2.

In the above examples, we let the length of x_t be equal to 2 for both SSM and SLM. Now we investigate the average inference accuracies when varying the length of x_t. We choose an appropriate size of data set, which has 101 time points to test. Fig. 12.4 shows that, for most lengths of x_t tested, SLM performs better than SSM. The average accuracy of SLM is stable when the length of x_t changes. In contrast, the average accuracy of SSM decreases fast when the length of x_t increases. That is understandable because a larger length of x_t means a larger number of hidden variables and the convergent results of SSM depend on how to guess initial values. A larger number of guessed initial values increase the difficulty of inferring true GRNs and results in lower accuracy in SSM.

When all 501 time points were used, the accuracy with respect to different numbers of hidden variables is shown in Fig. 12.5, in which the average accuracy of SLM is lower and it decreases fast like SSM. With 501 time points, the time interval is very small while the noise added to the measurement has the same distribution no matter what the length of time interval is. That implies that the time interval is not large enough for the measurement to have an obvious difference compared with that at the previous time points. After adding noise to those consecutive measurements without obvious differences, the data set seems to show more randomness.

The data sets with different time intervals were used to investigate if it is necessary to use PCA to reduce the dimension of a data set. Without using PCA the SLM becomes a standard linear model. Because the overfitting problem also exists in a linear model, we use data sets with different time intervals to obtain a more comprehensive result. It is similar to the test in Fig. 12.3. The difference is that the length of x_t in Fig. 12.3 is 2, and here the length is set as 30 without using PCA. Only the first 15 data sets with a larger number of time points work, as the number of parameters is large when the length of x_t equals to 30 and more data is needed for successful inference.

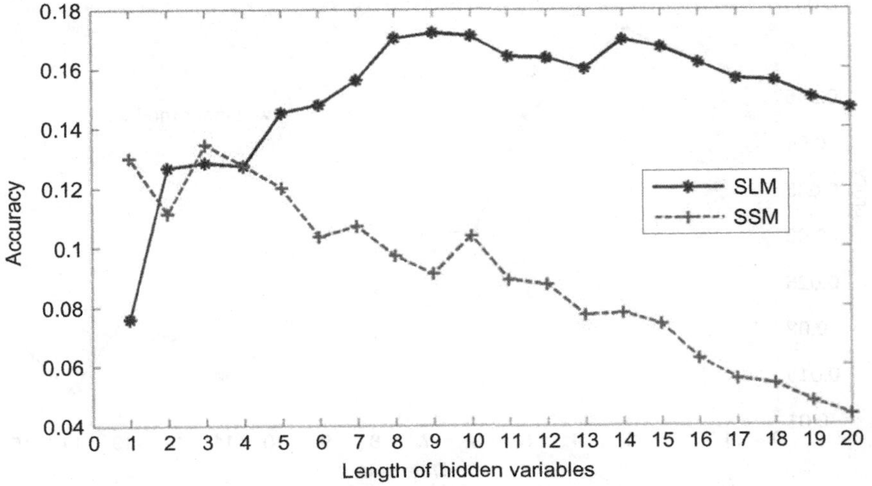

FIGURE 12.4

The average accuracies over 20 networks with 101 time points for different lengths of hidden variables using SSM and SLM.

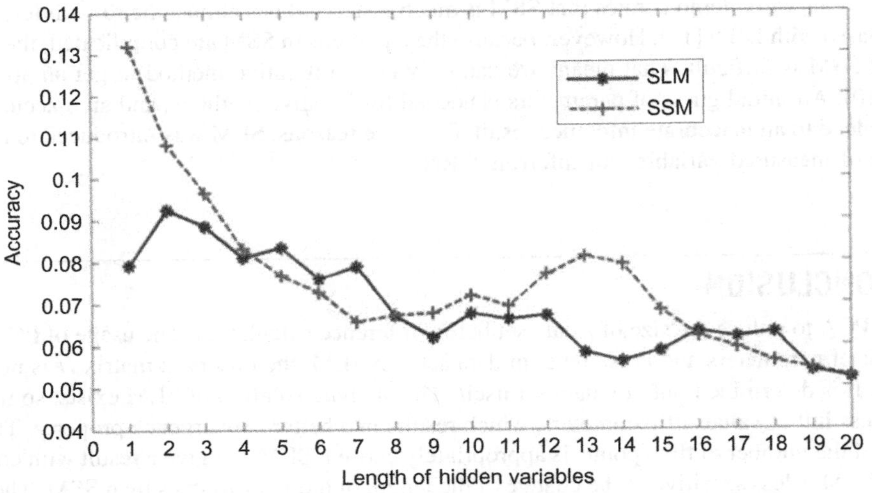

FIGURE 12.5

The average accuracies over 20 networks with 501 time points for different lengths of hidden variables using SSM and SLM.

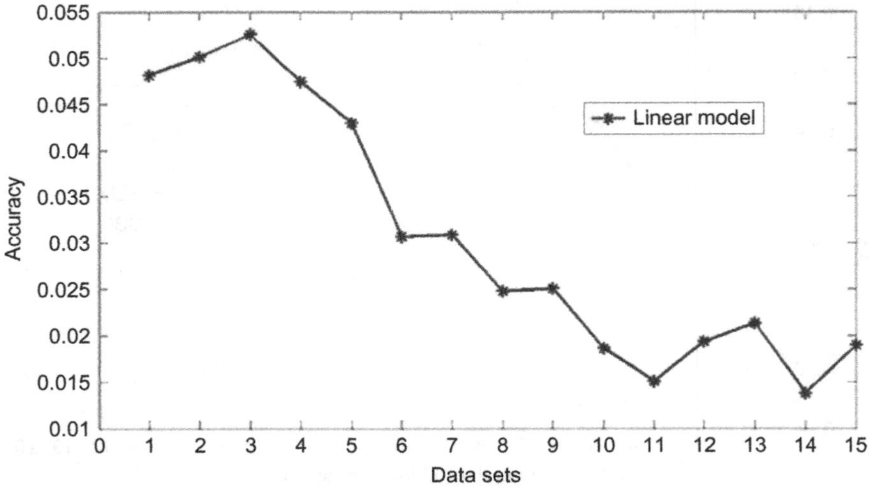

FIGURE 12.6

The average accuracies over 20 networks by using a standard linear model. Every data set has 20 networks with a different number of time points.

Fig. 12.6 shows that, due to the large number of parameters, the average accuracy is really low even if the solution of linear model exists. For most of the data sets, the average accuracy is even below the accuracy of a random guess. One of the reasons is that the noise in the data may lead to a large bias in the fitting process, which implies that the introduction of PCA is necessary and useful.

Our previous work demonstrates that SSM is much faster and has almost the same inference accuracy compared with DBN [11]. However, because the equations in SSM are complicated, the inference process of SSM is difficult. That means we can only use an iterative method to get an approximate result [8–10]. An initial guess of parameters is needed for iterative methods, and an inaccurate initial guess may lead to an inaccurate inference result. For these reasons, SLM was introduced to reduce the dimension of measured variables for inferring GRNs.

12.4 CONCLUSION

SLM uses PCA to reduce the size of a data set before inference calculation. The usage of PCA reduces the number of parameters and noise level in data sets. In SLM, the observed matrix H is no longer a parameter. It is determined only by data set itself. The analytic solution of SLM exists, so there is no need to guess initial values of parameters, which results in a better convergence property. The results show that, if the number of time points is appropriately chosen, SLM can give a result with compatible accuracy. SLM is less sensitive to the change of the length of hidden variables than SSM. The average accuracy of SSM decreases fast when the length of hidden variables grows, but SLM almost gives the same average accuracy for a large range of lengths of hidden variables. Finally, the necessity of using PCA was investigated. The results show that without using PCA, a standard linear model cannot achieve a good performance. Moreover, SLM is much simpler and faster than SSM. With the introduction of PCA, it is more convenient to take into account the *prior* knowledge of gene regulation relationships in the GRN reconstruction to improve the inference accuracy, which will be our future work.

REFERENCES

[1] Murphy K, Mian S. Modeling gene expression data using dynamic Bayesian networks: Technical report. Berkeley, CA: Computer Science Division, University of California; 1999.

[2] Zou M, Conzen S. A new dynamic Bayesian network (DBN) approach for identifying gene regulatory networks from time course microarray data. Bioinformatics 2005;21:71–9.

[3] Shmulevich F, Dougherty E, Kim S, Zhang W. Probabilistic boolean networks: a rule-based uncertainty model for gene regulatory networks. Bioinformatics 2002;18(2):261–74.

[4] Chaitankar V, Ghosh P, Perkins EJ, Gong P, Zhang C. Time lagged information theoretic approaches to the reverse engineering of gene regulatory networks. BMC Bioinformatics 2010;11(Suppl. 6):S19.

[5] Li P, Zhang C, Perkins EJ, Gong P, Deng Y. Comparison of probabilistic Boolean network and dynamic Bayesian network approaches for inferring gene regulatory networks. BMC Bioinformatics 2007;8(Suppl. 8):S13.

[6] Wu F, Zhang W, Kusalik A. Modeling gene expression from microarray expression data with state-space equations. Pac Symp Biocomput 2004;9:581–92.

[7] Wu F. Gene regulatory network modelling: a state-space approach. Int J Data Min Bioinform 2008;2(1):1–14.

[8] Rangel C, Angus J, Ghahramani Z, Lioumi M, Sotheran E, Gaiba A, et al. Modeling T-cell activation using gene expression profiling and state space modeling. Bioinformatics 2004;20(9):1361–72.

[9] Hirose O, Yoshida R, Imoto S, Yamaguchi R, Higuchi T, Charnock-Jones D, et al. Statistical inference of transcriptional module-based gene networks from time course gene expression profiles by using state space models. Bioinformatics 2008;24:932–42.

[10] Kojima K, Yamaguchi R, Imoto S, Yamauchi M, Nagasaki M, Yoshida R, et al. A state space representation of VAR models with sparse learning for dynamic gene networks. Genome Inform 2009;22:56–68.

[11] Wu X, Li P, Wang N, Gong P, Perkins E, Deng Y, et al. State space model with hidden variables for reconstruction of gene regulatory networks. BMC Syst Biol 2011;5(Suppl. 3):S3.

[12] Holter N, Maritan A, Cieplak M, Fedoroff N, Banavar J. Dynamic modeling of gene expression data. Proc Natl Acad Sci U S A 2001;98:1693–8.

[13] Li P. Inferring gene regulatory networks from time series microarray data. PhD dissertation, Mississippi: The University of Southern Mississippi; 2009.

[14] Yang Y, Maxwell A, Zhang X, Wang N, Perkins E, Zhang C, et al. Differential reconstructed gene interaction networks for deriving toxicity threshold in chemical risk assessment. BMC Bioinformatics 2013;14(Suppl. 13):S3.

[15] Marbach D, Schaffter T, Mattiussi C, Floreano D. Generating realistic in silico gene networks for performance assessment of reverse engineering methods. J Comput Biol 2009;16(2):229–39.

[16] Bishop C. Pattern recognition and machine learning. New York: Springer; 2006.

[17] Dempster A, Laird A, Rubin D. Maximum likelihood from incomplete data via the EM algorithm. J R Stat Soc Ser B 1977;39(1):1–38.

CHAPTER

*n*D-PDPA: *n*-DIMENSIONAL PROBABILITY DENSITY PROFILE ANALYSIS

13

A. Fahim, S. Irausquin, H. Valafar

Department of Computer Science and Engineering, University of South Carolina, Columbia, SC, United States

13.1 INTRODUCTION

The ultimate goal of structural genomics projects is to identify protein structures, their function, and biological significance for newly discovered sequences [1]. To achieve this goal, development of accurate methods to correctly predict the three-dimensional (3D) structure of an unknown protein is crucial. Currently, existing protein structure prediction methods can be categorized into two broad major groups: homology and ab initio modeling.

Homology modeling is based on selecting one or more frame (template) structures from protein databases that resemble the query structure's sequence [2]. The success of any template-based method is heavily dependent on completion of the protein structure databases. Statistics from Protein Data Bank (PDB) [3,4] (http://rcsb.org) indicates a total number of 109,093 (May 2015) protein structures deposited in the database. In Fig. 13.1A, it is clear that the number of novel proteins deposited has been increasing over the past decade. Moreover, no new fold family has been characterized since 2010 (Fig. 13.1B), and the number of fold families remains constant at only about 2500 despite being previously predicted as 10,000 protein fold families [5]. This indicates that traditional homology methods for identification of a novel protein structure based on sequence homology will inherently fail due to the lack of sufficient structural information. If no such template exists for a desired unknown structure within a protein library, then the 3D structure of the unknown protein may potentially be calculated from ab initio modeling [6–8] tools.

In this chapter, we present *n*-dimensional probability density profile analysis (*n*D-PDPA), an enhanced version of the previously reported 2D-PDPA for identifying and characterizing a protein structure that utilizes unassigned residual dipolar coupling (RDC) data [9,10]. RDCs are relatively rapid to obtain, and they contain orientational information about internuclear vectors relative to an arbitrarily selected molecular frame [11,12]. Utilization of a large variety of alignment media (such as PEG [alky-polyethylene glycol] and lipid bicells) [13,14] increases the practical usage of RDC data as a stand-alone source of data as well as a complement source of information to other NMR data sources such as NOE (Nuclear Overhauser Effect) and *J*-coupling in refinement of structures [15].

Recent improvements in computational modeling introduce more advanced techniques that combine different modeling methods with experimental constraints data. CS-ROSETTA [16] and RDC-ROSETTA [17] are two examples of such approaches. Although these methods may alleviate the

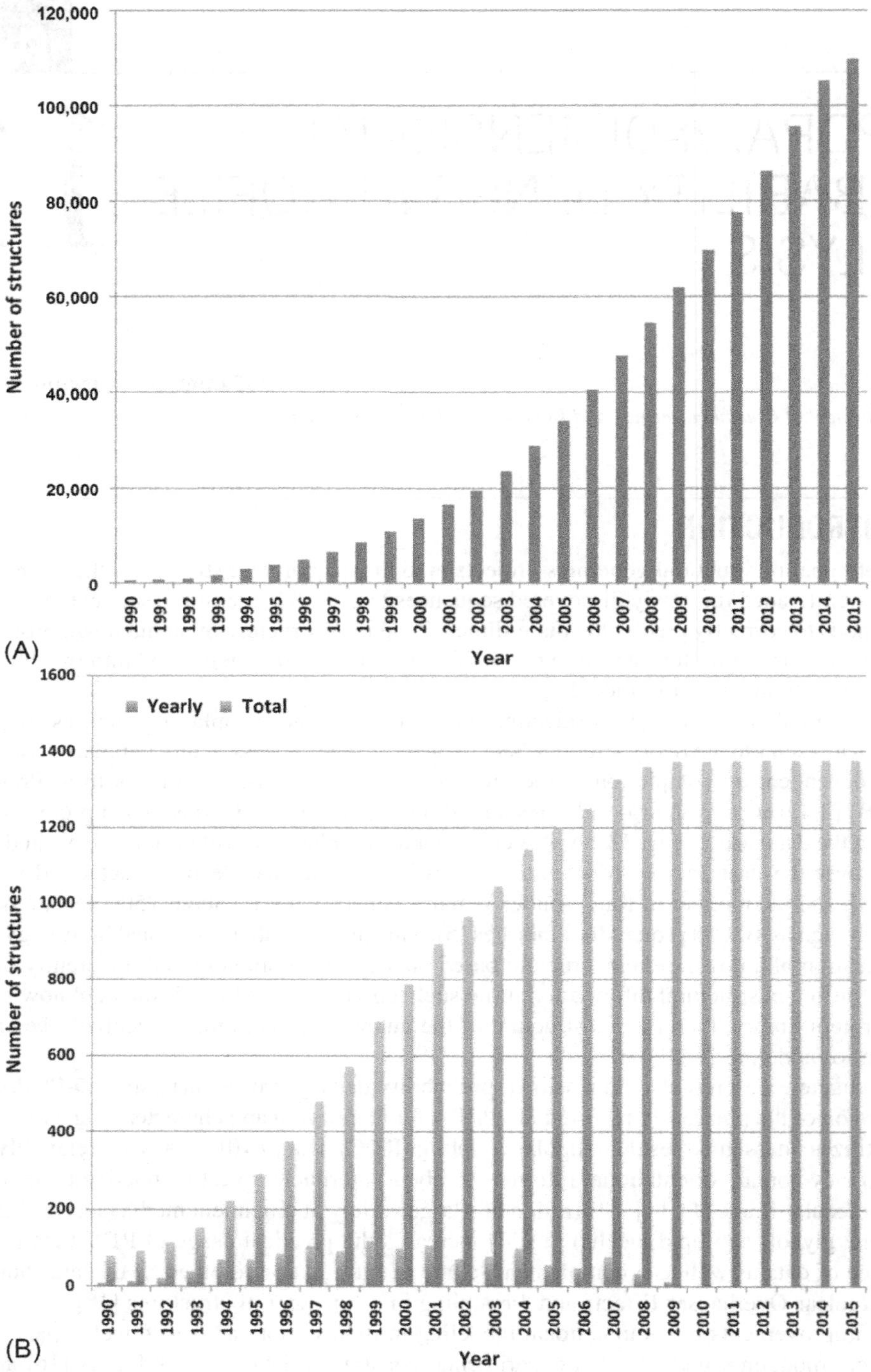

FIGURE 13.1

The deposition of protein structures in PDB (A) cumulative since 1990 and (B) based on the unique folds reported by SCOP (Structural Classification of Proteins).

problem of selecting the target template structures, they rely on assigned experimental data that is labor intensive and costly [18,19]. In PDPA however, unassigned sets of RDCs are utilized as the main source of data. The utilization of unassigned RDC sets eliminates the time-consuming assignment process. The application of 2D-PDPA method utilizing two sets of RDCs has been demonstrated previously [10]. However, the 2D-PDPA method is limited to two homogeneous sets of RDC data, usually {N-H} vectors from two different alignment media. *n*D-PDPA, on the other hand, is capable of utilizing more than two sets of unassigned RDC data from different alignment media. Moreover, the type of RDC vectors used in *n*D-PDPA are not limited to {N-H} vectors and can be the combination of different vectors such as {N-H} and {Cα-Hα}. The addition of more than two sets of RDCs from different vector types greatly increases the accuracy and selectivity of the method. However, this transition to higher dimensional data introduces new challenges such as intractable program execution time. Therefore, the core engine of the 2D-PDPA method has been revised to fulfill new requirements. The *n*D-PDPA method has been developed in C++ utilizing an object oriented paradigm and can be executed on desktop machines or Linux clusters. Execution on Linux clusters is facilitated by the use of qSub protocol. The source code for *n*D-PDPA can be obtained from our website at http://ifestos.cse.sc.edu.

In this report, the PDPA method is reviewed briefly then the result of 2D-PDPA and *n*D-PDPA are compared for accuracy, sensitivity, and measure of execution time. Finally, the *n*D-PDPA method is validated by utilizing protein structures varying in size and secondary structures with synthetic data.

13.2 RESIDUAL DIPOLAR COUPLING

The phenomena of RDCs was established for the first time in the 1960s [20]. However the practical application of RDCs to biomolecular systems emerged a decade ago for the first time [21,22]. Since then, many methods have been developed to utilize RDC data in the wide range of automated backbone resonance assignments, structure determination, protein folding to ligand protein, protein-protein interaction, and protein dynamics [23,24]. In this chapter, we will not intend to review the practical and instrumental aspect of the RDC acquisition. Instead, we concentrate on the mathematical interpretation of the RDC for our study purpose. An interested reader can be directed to [25,26] for more information.

The physical basis of RDCs is the dipole-dipole interaction between two nuclear spins. In the presence of an external magnetic field the RDC between two spins i and j is given by Eq. (1):

$$D_{ij} = \frac{-\mu_0 \gamma_i \gamma_j h}{8\pi^3 r^3} \left\langle \frac{3\cos^2\theta - 1}{2} \right\rangle \tag{1}$$

where γ_i and γ_j are the gyromagnetic ratios of given nuclei, h is Plank's constant, r is the distance between two nuclei, and θ is the angle between internuclear vector and external magnet field B_0. In an isotropic tumbling system, the RDC values average to zero and no RDC is observed. This can be treated by introducing an alignment medium to a partially aligned system for the observable RDC values.

Eq. (1) can be reformulated by algebraic manipulation suitable for computational purposes in the following:

$$D_{ij} = D_{\max} v_{ij} R(\alpha, \beta, \gamma) \begin{pmatrix} S_{xx} & 0 & 0 \\ 0 & S_{yy} & 0 \\ 0 & 0 & S_{zz} \end{pmatrix} R(\alpha, \beta, \gamma)^T v_{ij}^T \tag{2}$$

where v_{ij} is the internuclear vector between atoms i and j. $R(\alpha, \beta, \gamma)$ describes a Euler rotation of the molecule with respect to principle alignment frame. The parameters S_{xx}, S_{yy}, and S_{zz} are known as principle order parameters that describe the strength of alignment along each of the axes of alignment.

13.3 METHOD

*n*D-PDPA is an extension of the previously reported 2D-PDPA [10] that allows simultaneous analysis of more than two sets of RDC data. In principle, PDPA does not have to be limited to two sets (as in 2D-PDPA) or homogeneous data types (eg, using only {Cα-Hα} RDC sets). Normally multiple RDC data types such as {N-H} or {Cα-Hα} can be acquired in one experimental session; therefore, inclusion of which imposes no additional data acquisition time. Integration of additional data is expected to substantially increase the information content and therefore significantly improve the sensitivity and robustness of the PDPA method. The details of the PDPA method were described previously [10,27,28]. In this chapter, we provide a brief overview of the PDPA method and focus primarily on the new additions and improvements of the *n*D-PDPA. The core principle of the PDPA method is based on the fact that two similar structures should produce the same distribution patterns of RDCs, and can be used as a structural fingerprint. Therefore, measurement of the similarity between two distributions can be interpreted as the similarity of two structures.

The *n*D-PDPA algorithm is encapsulated in three functional layers. In the first layer, the experimental RDC sets are used to estimate the relative order tensors [29,30]. The number of parameters needed in this stage is a function of the number of alignment media in which RDC data are acquired. Generally for RDC data from n alignment media, $5n-3$ parameters are required to describe the relative order tensors [29]. The estimated order tensor parameters are utilized to back calculate the RDC data for a given structure. Then the n-dimensional kernel density estimation is utilized to construct the distribution map for both experimental and calculated RDC sets. The kernel density distribution is calculated based on a hyperdimensional Gaussian kernel function (described in Eq. 3) that is located at the center of each RDC data point (Fig. 13.2).

In this equation X denotes independent function parameters, M denotes a vector of RDCs that defines the center of the kernel, and Σ is covariance matrix. Both X and M vectors are of size k while the Σ is a matrix of size $k \times k$:

$$N(X \vee M, \Sigma) = (2\pi)^{-k} \left\| \sum \right\|^{-k} \exp\left[-1/2(X-M)' \sum^{-1} (X-M)\right] \tag{3}$$

The orientation of the anchor alignment medium [10,28,29] is exhaustively searched with respect to the reference structure. Therefore in the second stage the probability density profile (PDP) map is calculated for the subject structure in every possible orientation using a grid search over the Euler angles (α, β, γ) at the resolution of 5 degree. The best score is calculated from comparison of the experimental and calculated RDC distributions for all orientations, and this score is reported as the final result in the third stage. For a given library of the structures the process is repeated for every structure in the library.

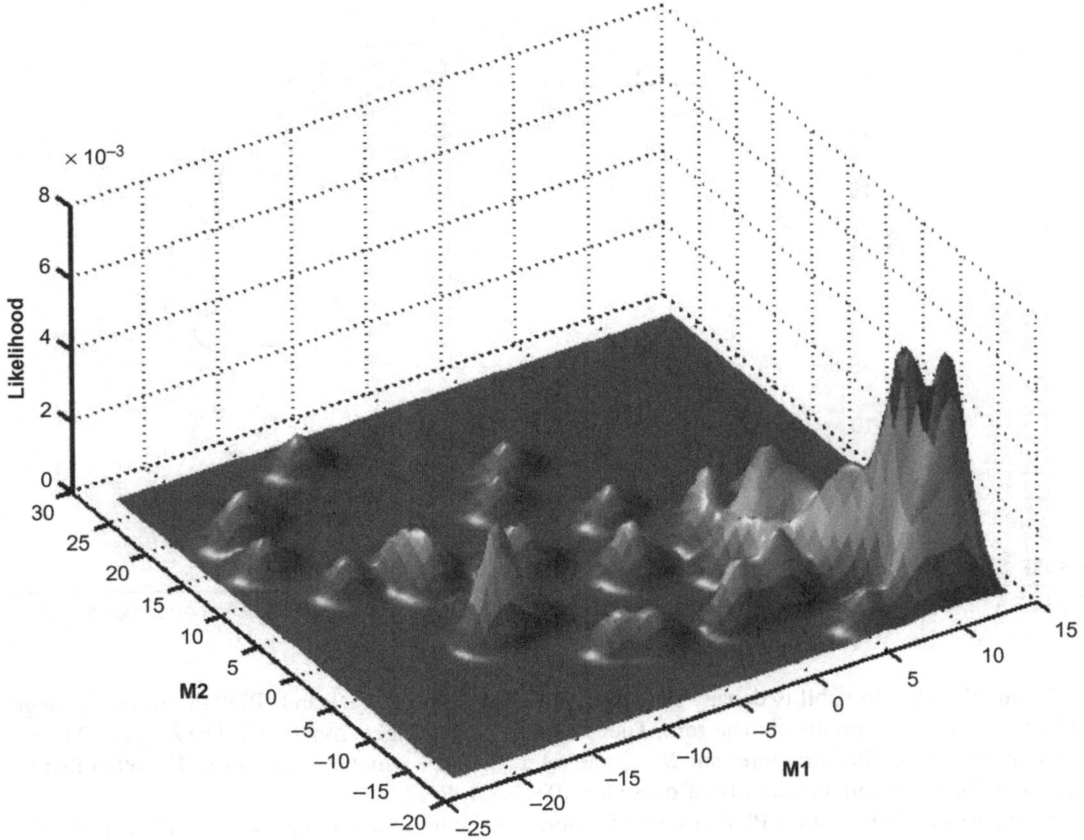

FIGURE 13.2

An example of a 2D-PDP map, using kernel density estimation. The 2D-PDP can serve as a structural fingerprint.

13.4 SCORING OF *n*D-PDPA

In 2D-PDPA Manhattan (City Block) metric [31] (shown in Eq. 4) had been utilized to compare calculated and experimental probability density distributions. In this equation B_{score} denotes the 2D-PDPA score; the summation indexes i and j cover the entire range of RDCs over alignment media M1 and M2; and $cPDP_{ij}$ (calculated PDP) and $ePDP_{ij}$ (experimental PDP) denote the likelihood of the RDC values at the location i and j. 2D-PDPA utilizes the locations of i, j that are represented by a 64×64 grid. This grid is constructed by uniformly sampling the entire range of both RDC sets for both ePDP and cPDP. Utilization of the grid guarantees the similar intervals and range (begins with minimum RDC and ends with maximum RDC values) for both cPDP and eDPD.

$$B_{score} = \sum_{Min(M2)}^{Max(M2)} \sum_{Min(M1)}^{Max(M1)} \left| cPDP_{ij} - ePDP_{ij} \right| \quad (4)$$

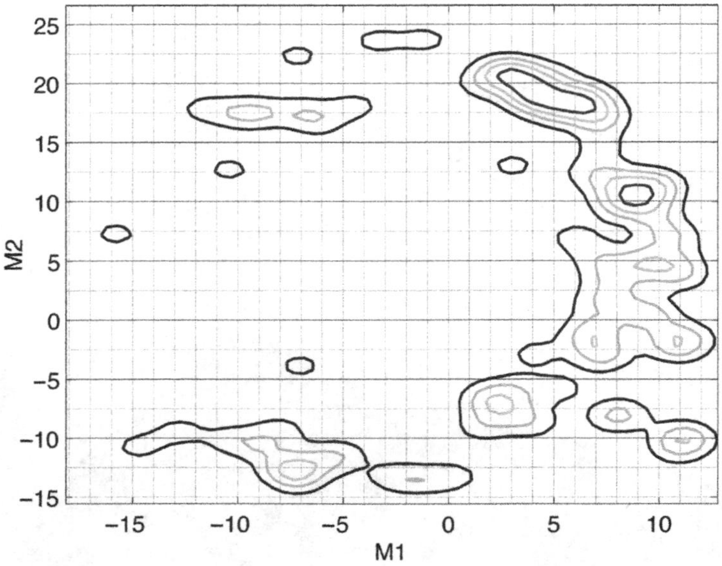

FIGURE 13.3

2D-PDPA utilizes a 64 × 64 grid for scoring. The out of boundaries area are unnecessary for comparison of distributions.

To be qualified for probability density functions, the summation of ePDP and cPDP for the entire range of RDC values are normalized to be zero. Therefore, the B_{score} ranges from 0 to 2. The B_{score} of 2 refers to completely dissimilar structures and B_{score} of 0 refers to 100% structural similarity. The other factors such as RDC error and availability of data also affects the B_{score}.

Comparison of ePDP and cPDP in a grid-fashion is the main contributing factor for the exponential time complexity of this approach. In that sense, expansion of ePDP and cPDP patterns to n-dimensions requires an exponentially increasing number of grid points (64^n if 64 points along each dimension) to serve as the location of comparisons by the factor of grid size. This quickly becomes a limiting factor for $n > 2$. Moreover, as RDC data are not uniformly distributed [27], any PDP distribution will contain large areas with the likelihood of zero or near zero. Incision of these unimportant regions for comparison of two PDPAs consumes unnecessary computational time (Fig. 13.3). The score in nD-PDPA is, on the other hand, calculated by comparison of only the information-rich regions within the distributions. By using this approach, the regions with the likelihood of zero or close to zero are not considered for calculation and, therefore, exponential contribution of the grid size is eliminated.

13.5 DATA PREPARATION

The three structures shown in Table 13.1 are used throughout our experiments. These proteins have been selected on the basis of secondary structure composition that represents the three broad structural categories of α, β, and α/β (Fig. 13.4). The atomic coordinates of the structures have been obtained

Table 13.1 The List of the Structures That Are Used for *n*D-PDPA Analysis

Protein	Secondary Structure	Number of Residues	CATH Classification
1A1Z	α	83	1.10.553.10
1OUR	β	114	2.60.120.40
1G1B	α/β	164	3.40.1410.10

The structures are obtained from Protein Data Bank.

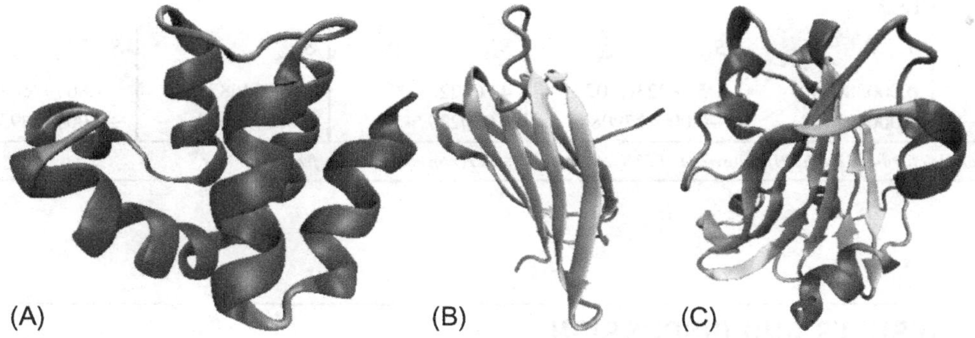

FIGURE 13.4

Cartoon representation of the proteins listed in Table 13.1. (A) Protein 1A1Z, (B) protein 1OUR, and (C) protein 1G1B.

from the PDB [3]. Three sets of RDCs, including {N-H} vectors representing first alignment medium and {N-H} and {Cα-Hα} vectors representing second alignment medium, are generated under two conditions: (1) ideal RDC sets containing no error, (2) corrupted RDC sets through the addition of ±1 Hz of uniformly distributed noise with 25% of RDCs randomly eliminated from each set to better represent pragmatic conditions. The first set (no error) that represents the ideal conditions is utilized for demonstrating the proof of concept and the second set represents more realistic conditions. To generate synthetic RDC sets the software REDCAT [32] was used with the initial relative order tensors listed in Table 13.2.

Upon completion of the data generation, the assignment information is discarded before utilization of the synthetic RDC data in *n*D-PDPA. To back calculate the order tensors two approaches were used: First the optimal order tensor is calculated using REDCAT and second estimation of the order tensors is conducted using the approximation method as described previously [30].

Estimation of the order tensor parameters is of central importance for PDPA analysis in the absence of atomic coordinates of a structure. 2D and 3D approximation software were used [30] to estimate relative order tensors that are used in PDPA analysis. In *n*D-PDPA experiments, relative order tensors are estimated utilizing approximation software when the data are synthetically corrupted by adding errors (Table 13.3).

Table 13.2 List of Initial Order Parameters Used for Generating RDC Sets in REDCAT Software

	S_{xx}	S_{yy}	S_{zz}	α	β	γ
M1	3e−4	5e−4	−8e−4	0	0	0
M2	−4e−4	−6e−4	1.00e−4	40	50	−60

Table 13.3 Order Tensor Parameters Estimation Using 2D-Approx Software for the Data in Table 13.2

	S_{xx}	S_{xy}	S_{xz}	S_{yy}	S_{yz}
M1	0.00028136	−5.38223e−07	4.70822e−07	0.000446853	1.86497e−07
M2	0.000428708	−0.000417908	0.00022974	0.000726639	−0.000129934

The data is corrupted by ±1 Hz of error and 25% of the RDCs are removed randomly from data sets.

13.6 RESULTS AND DISCUSSION

13.6.1 EXPERIMENT 1

The objective of this experiment is to establish the relation between *n*D-PDPA score and bb-rmsd. One thousand decoy structures were generated by randomly altering the φ and ψ angles with the bb-rmsd in the range of 0–8 Å distance from a reference structure (Table 13.1). The entire ensemble of the decoy structures was then subjected to evaluation by *n*D-PDPA. Finally, the scatter plot of bb-rmsd versus *n*D-PDPA scores was used to observe any significant patterns. Previously the universal funneling effect of such an exercise had been demonstrated [10] for proteins regardless of their structural characteristics. In this section we repeat the previous exercise using *n*D-PDPA engine and compare some of the results with the previous 2D-PDPA program.

In this experiment, the protein 1A1Z was selected with RDC data generated in REDCAT [32] with no added error. Fig. 13.5A shows the relationship between 2D-PDPA score and bb-rmsd for 1000 decoy structures generated from reference structure 1A1Z. The same experiment was conducted using *n*D-PDPA engine in Fig. 13.5B. As it is mentioned in Section 13.5 in *n*D-PDPA engine, the comparison for calculated and experimental PDP is based on the RDC points and not by 64 × 64 grid as it is performed in 2D-PDPA. This may reduce the sensitivity of the scoring in *n*D-PDPA compared to the 2D-PDPA (the R^2 fitness for 2D-PDPA is slightly better than R^2 in *n*D-PDPA analysis in Fig. 13.5). The lack of sensitivity can be addressed by adding more RDC sets improving the information content of the *n*D-PDPA analysis and *n*D-PDPA score fitness.

Fig. 13.6 shows the *n*D-PDPA analysis using three {N-H} RDC sets from three alignment media. The R^2 shows improvement, compared to both 2D-PDPA and *n*D-PDPA analysis using two RDC sets (Fig. 13.5A and B).

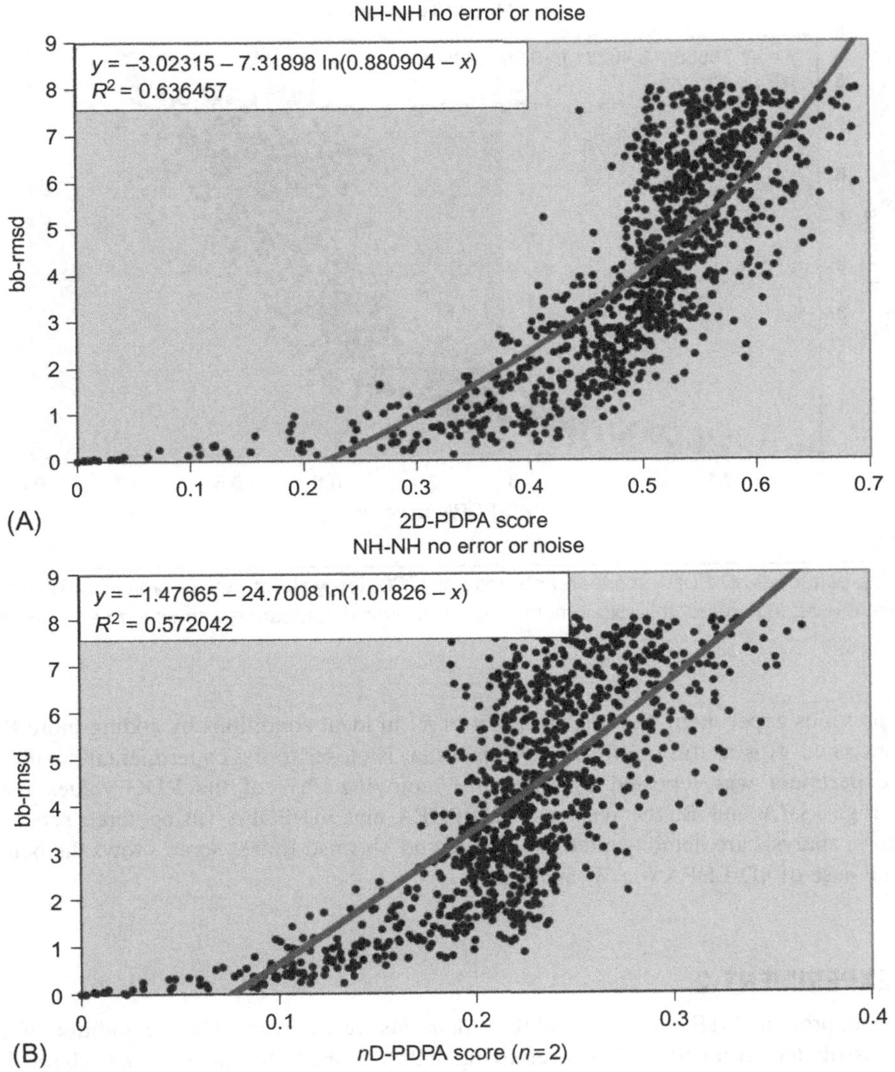

FIGURE 13.5

(A) The funneling pattern of 2D-PDPA score and bb-rmsd of 1000 decoy structures for protein 1A1Z. *Dots* in this figure represent a protein structure from decoy data set. (B) The same experiment using the similar set of RDC data sets with the *n*D-PDPA engine. *n*D-PDPA *(left)* demonstrates higher R^2 (∼0.63) due to utilization of 64 × 64 grid.

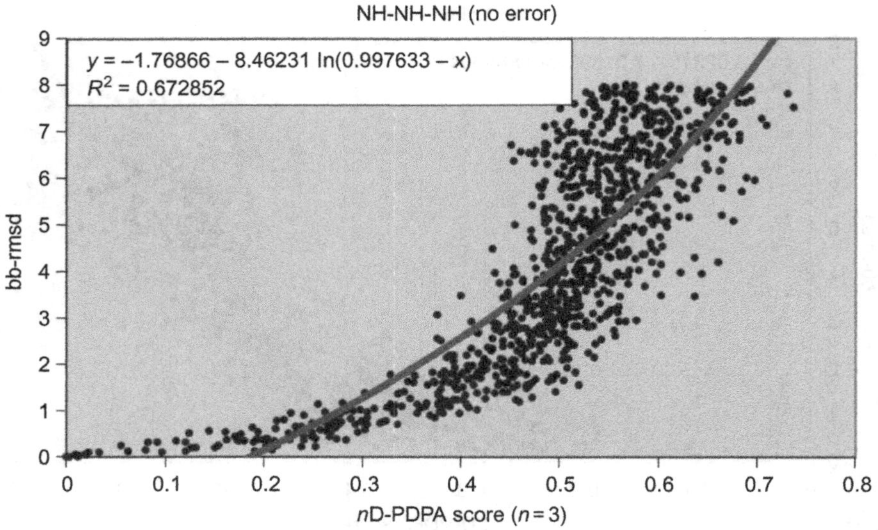

FIGURE 13.6

The funneling pattern of *n*D-PDPA score and bb-rmsd of 1000 decoy structures for protein 1A1Z. Three {N-H} RDC sets were used to conduct this experiment. The R^2 improved comparing with experiments shown in Fig. 13.5.

In the previous experiment, the improvement of R^2 in ideal conditions by adding more RDC data was demonstrated. It is useful to utilize RDC data that is closer to the experimental conditions. The previous experiment was repeated by randomly removing 25% of the RDC values for protein 1A1Z. In Fig. 13.7A and B, the results of 2D-PDPA and *n*D-PDPA (using three sets of {N-H} RDC vectors) analysis are demonstrated. The score and bb-rmsd fitness score shows the better correlation in the case of *n*D-PDPA ($n=3$) analysis.

13.6.2 EXPERIMENT 2

In this section, protein 1G1B was used, and RDC data sets were corrupted by the addition of ±1 Hz of uniformly distributed error and randomly removing of 25% of the RDC values from each set. Two hundred and fifty structures were generated by altering backbone torsion angles range from 0 to 6 Å distance from 1G1B.

In Fig. 13.8A *n*D-PDPA analysis was conducted by using two {N-H} RDC sets from two alignment media and in Fig. 13.8B the analysis was conducted by utilizing two nonhomogeneous RDC sets, {N-H} and {Cα-Hα} from two alignment media, respectively. R^2 values for both experiments are approximately similar (~0.7).

Fig. 13.9 shows the plot of *n*D-PDPA analysis for protein 1G1B by adding {Cα-Hα} as the third RDC set to the collection of two {N-H} RDC sets. The $R^2=0.8146$ indicates the improvement of *n*D-PDPA analysis fitness compared to two sets of RDCs (Fig. 13.8A and B). The experiment once again confirms the improvement of the bb-rmsd and PDPA score fitness by adding more RDC data.

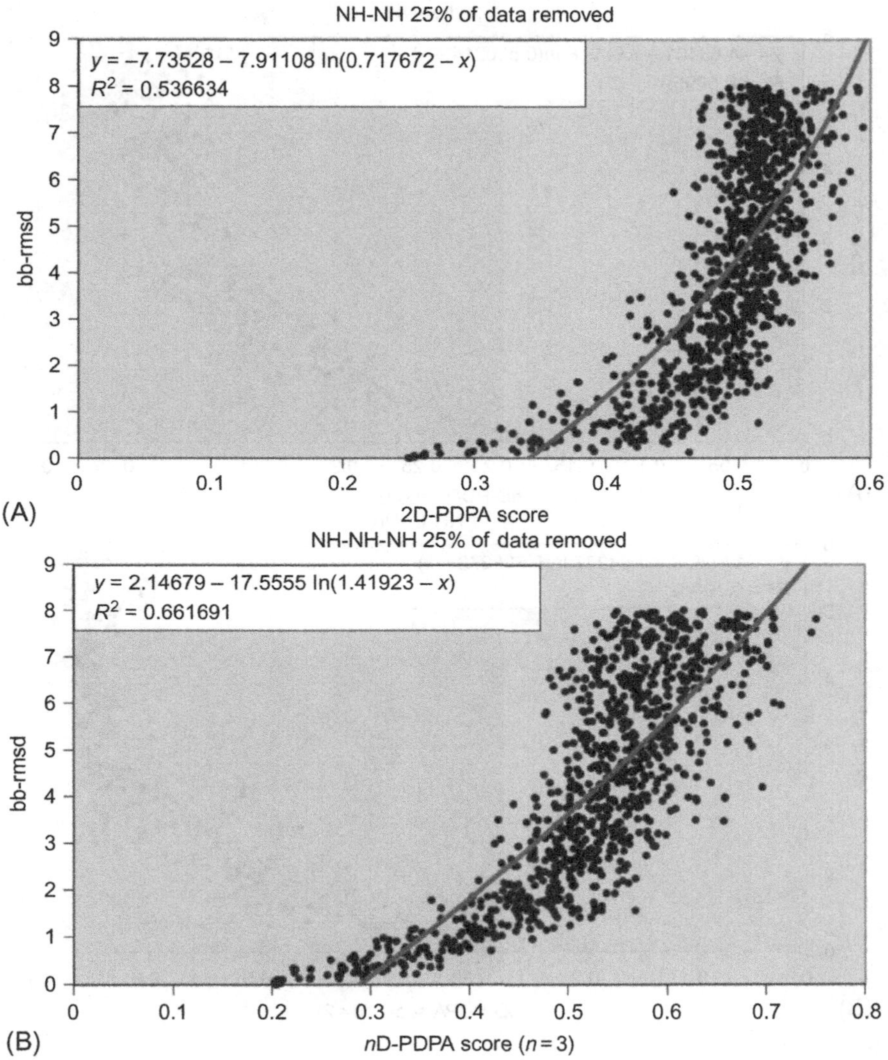

FIGURE 13.7

Two hundred and fifty decoy structures from protein 1A1Z were generated with (A) two {N-H} RDC sets. Analysis is conducted using 2D-PDPA. (B) Three sets of {N-H} RDC with 25% of the data were randomly removed from each set. *n*D-PDPA is used to conduct the experiments. The result of analysis shows improvement in R^2 when $n=3$ *(right)* by the addition of an extra RDC data set.

13.6.3 EXPERIMENT 3

Table 13.4 demonstrates the R^2 value for two of the proteins listed in Table 13.1. In Table 13.4 in all instances the value of the R^2 decreases by introducing error to the data (compare the second and third column of Table 13.4A and B). Moreover, the value of R^2 increases by adding an extra set of RDC. The

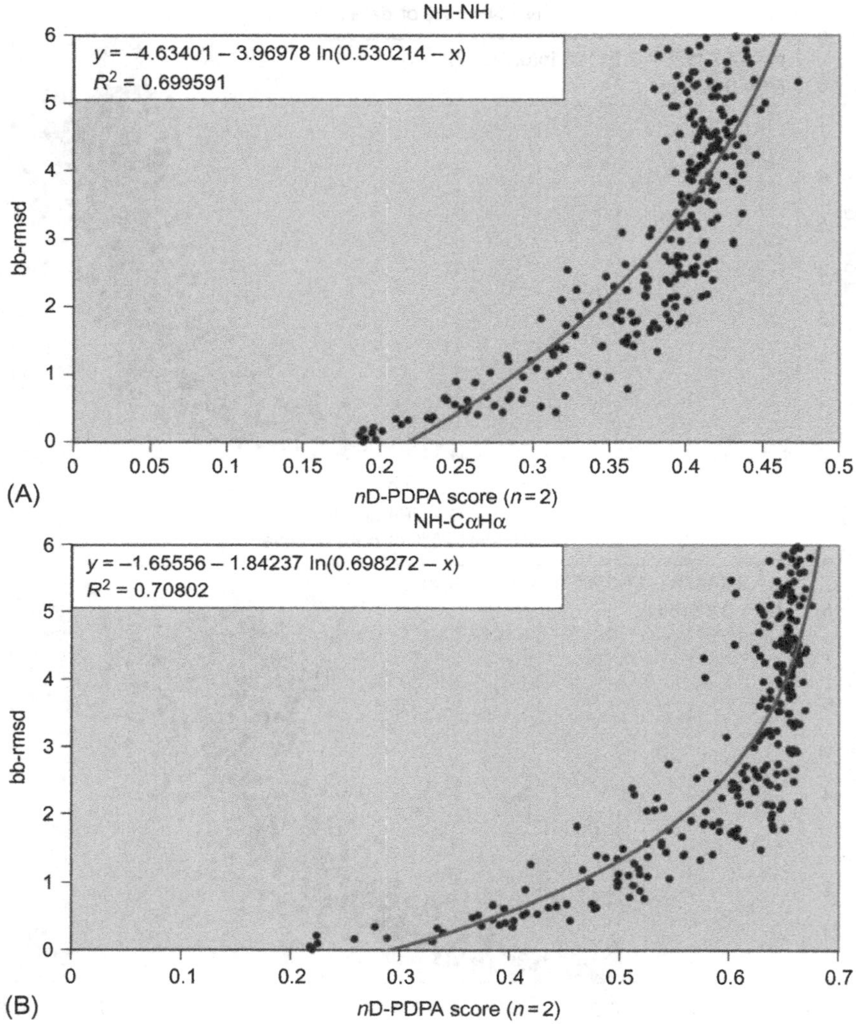

FIGURE 13.8

(A) Calculation of *n*D-PDPA scores and bb-rmsd for protein 1G1B using two {N-H} RDC sets. (B) Calculation of *n*D-PDPA scores and bb-rmsd for protein 1G1B using two {N-H (M1)} and {Cα-Hα (M2)} RDC sets.

improvement is manifested in the greater degree in the erroneous data sets. For example in Table 13.4A R^2 for three {N-H} RDC sets demonstrates about 0.35 improvement, compared to two {N-H} RDC sets (see the darker background cells in Table 13.4A).

13.6.4 EXPERIMENT 4

To benchmark the performance of the *n*D-PDPA for two or more sets of RDC, protein 1A1Z was selected, and the results were compared to 2D-PDPA results. Four synthetic {N-H} RDC sets were generated in an ideal condition. Both programs were executed on a Linux desktop with an Intel Core i7,

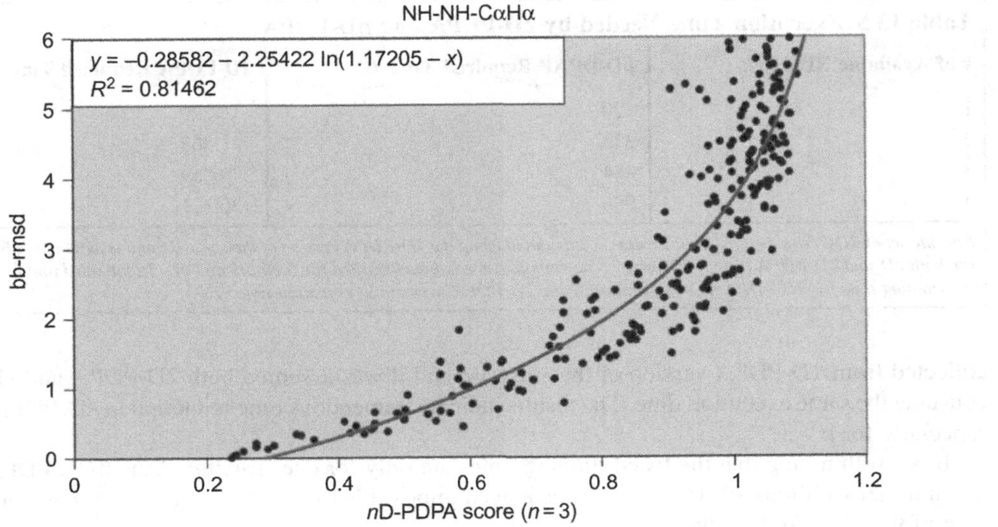

FIGURE 13.9

Calculation of *n*D-PDPA scores versus bb-rmsd for protein 1G1B utilizing three RDC sets; two of which are {N-H (M1), N-H (M2)} sets and the third one is {Cα-Hα (M2)}. R^2 value is improved in comparison to utilization of two RDC sets (Fig. 13.8).

Table 13.4 The Result of *n*D-PDPA Analysis for (A) Protein 1OUR and (B) Protein 1G1B

	R^2 No Error	R^2 With Error
(A) Protein 1OUR		
NH-NH	0.5781	0.4522
NH-CαHα	0.6797	0.4935
NH-NH-NH	0.7273	0.7026
NH-NH-CαHα	0.6873	0.6547
(B) Protein 1G1B		
NH-NH	0.6924	0.6995
NH-CαHα	0.7204	0.7080
NH-NH-NH	0.7494	0.7575
NH-NH-CαHα	0.8225	0.8146

2.67 GHz processor and 8 GB of memory. Table 13.5 shows the results of execution time for 2D-PDPA and *n*D-PDPA. Although not proven here, the asymptotic execution time of 2D-PDPA is a function of $O(C^n)$ while the execution time complexity of *n*D-PDPA is a function of $O(Cn^2)$. The 2D-PDPA is incapable of incorporating more than two RDC sets; hence the 2D-PDPA running times for the dimensions $n > 2$ were approximated using the 2D-PDPA asymptotic function. For two RDC sets, the running time was measured by executing the 2D-PDPA software. The running time for one RDC set was

Table 13.5 Execution Time Needed by 2D-PDPA and *n*D-PDPA

# of Available RDC Sets	*n*D-DPAP Required Time (s)	2D-PDPA Required Time (s)
1	20	20
2	323	363
3	484	6859
4	906	130,321

For one set of RDC (row 1) the execution time is calculated using the 1D-PDPA version of the software and is assumed to be the same for both nD and 2D-PDPA. For n=2 (row 2) the running time is benchmarked for both 2D and nD. In the third and fourth rows the running time for 2D-PDPA is approximated using 2D-PDPA asymptotic execution time.

collected from 1D-PDPA version of the software and it was assumed both 2D-PDPA and *n*D-PDPA consume the same execution time. The results indicate tremendous time reduction in *n*D-PDPA engine, especially for $n \geq 3$.

It is worth noting that the listed running times are only for one structure. Usually, a PDPA experiment utilizes a library of structures that is indeed impossible to be finished in a reasonable time in the case of the 2D-PDPA method.

13.7 CONCLUSION

Based on results from Sections 13.6.1–13.6.3 a transition from 2D-PDPA to *n*D-PDPA can be deemed advantageous for a number of reasons. First, based on availability, additional RDC data sets can be combined from multiple alignment media to increase the information content without imposing a substantial penalty in the execution time. Second, *n*D-PDPA's scope of RDC analysis is no longer limited to just {N-H} RDC data. The new improvements enable flexible inclusion of RDC data from the same or different alignment media. For example, {N-H, Cα-Hα} data from one alignment medium may be combined with {N-H} of the second and {C-N} of the third alignment medium for a total of 4D analysis of PDPA. This flexible inclusion of any available data sets from any number of alignment media can increase the information content significantly, leading to a more improved sensitivity and selectivity performance of *n*D-PDPA. Elimination of the exponential time complexity and translation of the algorithm into a polynomial time complexity is a major achievement with clear consequences in the execution time of the algorithm.

This research will be expanded in the future by utilization of experimental RDC data. It is easy to envision the application of the *n*D-PDPA method to characterize an unknown protein structure among a library of proteins from the data bank, only based on different types of unassigned RDC sets.

REFERENCES

[1] Orengo CA, Todd AE, Thornton JM. From protein structure to function. Curr Opin Struct Biol 1999;9 (3):374–82.
[2] Wood TC, Pearson WR. Evolution of protein sequences and structures. J Mol Biol 1999;291:977–95.
[3] Berman HM, Westbrook J, Feng Z, Gilliland G, Bhat TN, Weissig H, et al. The protein data bank. Nucleic Acids Res 2000;28(1):235–42.

[4] Berman HM, Kleywegt GJ, Nakamura H, Markley JL. How community has shaped the protein data bank. Structure 2013;21(9):1485–91.

[5] Grant A, Lee D, Orengo C. Progress towards mapping the universe of protein folds. Genome Biol 2004;5 (5):107.

[6] Bradley P, Misura KMS, Baker D. Toward high-resolution de novo structure prediction for small proteins. Science 2005;309(2005):1868–71.

[7] Liwo A, Khalili M, Scheraga HA. Ab initio simulations of protein-folding pathways by molecular dynamics with the united-residue model of polypeptide chains. Proc Natl Acad Sci U S A 2005;102:2362–7.

[8] Moult J, Fidelis K, Kryshtafovych A, Schwede T, Tramontano A. Critical assessment of methods of protein structure prediction (CASP) — round x. Proteins 2014;82(Suppl. 2):1–6.

[9] Fahim A, Irausquin S, Fawcett M, Valafar H. Probability density profile analysis: a method for identifying novel protein structures. In: Conference paper WorldComp; 2011.

[10] Fahim A, Mukhopadhyay R, Yandle R, Prestegard JH, Valafar H. Protein structure validation and identification from unassigned residual dipolar coupling data using 2D-PDPA. Molecules 2013;18(9):10162–88.

[11] Bolon PJ, Al-Hashimi HM, Prestegard JH. Residual dipolar coupling derived orientational constraints on ligand geometry in a 53 kDa protein-ligand complex. J Mol Biol 1999;293(1):107–15.

[12] Andrec M, Du PC, Levy RM. Protein backbone structure determination using only residual dipolar couplings from one ordering medium. J Biomol NMR 2001;21(4):335–47.

[13] Tjandra N, Omichinski JG, Gronenborn AM, Clore GM, Bax A. Use of dipolar H-1-N-15 and H-1-C-13 couplings in the structure determination of magnetically oriented macromolecules in solution. Nat Struct Biol 1997;4(9):732–8.

[14] Clore GM, Gronenborn AM, Bax A. A robust method for determining the magnitude of the fully asymmetric alignment tensor of oriented macromolecules in the absence of structural information. J Magn Reson 1998;133(1):216–21.

[15] Meiler J, Peti W, Griesinger C. DipoCoup: a versatile program for 3D-structure homology comparison based on residual dipolar couplings and pseudocontact shifts. J Biomol NMR 2000;17(4):283–94.

[16] Shen Y, Vernon R, Baker D, Bax A. De novo protein structure generation from incomplete chemical shift assignments. J Biomol NMR 2009;43(2):63–78.

[17] Rohl CA, Baker D. De novo determination of protein backbone structure from residual dipolar couplings using Rosetta. J Am Chem Soc 2002;124(11):2723–9.

[18] Jung Y-SS, Sharma M, Zweckstetter M. Simultaneous assignment and structure determination of protein backbones by using NMR dipolar couplings. Angew Chem Int Ed Engl 2004;43(26):3479–81.

[19] Shealy P, Liu Y, Simin M, Valafar H. Backbone resonance assignment and order tensor estimation using residual dipolar couplings. J Biomol NMR 2011;50(4):357–69.

[20] Saupe A, Englert G. High-resolution nuclear magnetic resonance spectra of orientated molecules. Phys Rev Lett 1963;11(10):462–4.

[21] Tolman JR, Flanagan JM, Kennedy MA, Prestegard JH. Nuclear magnetic dipole interactions in field-oriented proteins — information for structure determination in solution. Proc Natl Acad Sci U S A 1995;92(20):9279–83.

[22] Chen K, Tjandra N. The use of residual dipolar coupling in studying proteins by NMR. Top Curr Chem 2012;326:47–67.

[23] Al-Hashimi HM, Gosser Y, Gorin A, Hu W, Majumdar A, Patel DJ. Concerted motions in HIV-1 TAR RNA may allow access to bound state conformations: RNA dynamics from NMR residual dipolar couplings. J Mol Biol 2002;315(2):95–102.

[24] Wang L, Donald BR. Exact solutions for internuclear vectors and backbone dihedral angles from NH residual dipolar couplings in two media, and their application in a systematic search algorithm for determining protein backbone structure. J Biomol NMR 2004;29(3):223–42.

[25] Cavanagh J, Fairbrother WJ, Palmer III AG, Skelton NJ. Protein NMR spectroscopy: principles and practice. New York, NY: Academic Press; 1995.

[26] Levitt MH. Spin dynamics: basics of nuclear magnetic resonance. New York, NY: Wiley; 2008.
[27] Valafar H, Prestegard JH. Rapid classification of a protein fold family using a statistical analysis of dipolar couplings. Bioinformatics 2003;19(12):1549–55.
[28] Bansal S, Miao X, Adams MWW, Prestegard JH, Valafar H. Rapid classification of protein structure models using unassigned backbone RDCs and probability density profile analysis (PDPA). J Magn Reson 2008;192 (1):60–8.
[29] Miao X, Mukhopadhyay R, Valafar H. Estimation of relative order tensors, and reconstruction of vectors in space using unassigned RDC data and its application. J Magn Reson 2008;194(2):202–11.
[30] Mukhopadhyay R, Miao X, Shealy P, Valafar H. Efficient and accurate estimation of relative order tensors from lambda-maps. J Magn Reson 2009;198(2):236–47.
[31] Greshenfeld NA. The nature of mathematical modeling. Cambridge: Cambridge University Press; 1998.
[32] Valafar H, Prestegard JH. REDCAT: a residual dipolar coupling analysis tool. J Magn Reson 2004;167 (2):228–41.

CHAPTER

BIOMEMBRANES UNDER OXIDATIVE STRESS: INSIGHTS FROM MOLECULAR DYNAMICS SIMULATIONS 14

R. Miotto*, E.B. Costa*, G.G. Trellese*, A.J.P. Neto*, M.S. Baptista†, A.C. Ferraz‡, R.M. Cordeiro*

Center for Natural and Human Sciences, Federal University of ABC, Santo André, SP, Brazil Chemistry Institute, University of São Paulo, São Paulo, SP, Brazil† Physics Institute, University of São Paulo, São Paulo, SP, Brazil‡*

14.1 INTRODUCTION

Reactive oxygen species (ROS) are naturally present in the organism and participate in redox signaling pathways that are essential for the physiological control of cell function [1]. Most ROS, however, are strongly oxidizing species that need to be kept at low steady state concentrations by efficient disposal mechanisms. Increased levels of ROS are involved in deleterious processes such as aging, carcinogenesis, and neurodegenerative diseases [1–3]. When the production of ROS supersedes the antioxidant defense, oxidative stress sets in [4].

Under controlled conditions, the cell-damaging potential of oxidative stress can be explored in therapy. In the so-called *photodynamic therapy* (PDT), singlet oxygen ($^1O_2$) and other ROS are artificially generated in the biological medium by means of a photosensitizer-assisted process. Peroxidation reactions are initiated in the region exposed to light and culminates in localized cell death. In the last few years, this approach has been successfully applied as a powerful strategy for the treatment of neoplasm-related diseases [5] and is increasingly becoming a common oncological clinical practice. Other applications of PDT have also emerged, including the treatment of bacterial infections [6, 7] and tropical diseases like malaria and leishmaniasis [8].

The effects of either naturally or photodynamically generated ROS in the organism are largely influenced by their interactions with phospholipid membranes [9]. Specific reactions are compartmentalized according to the ability of ROS to cross membranes. Additionally, phospholipids are themselves very susceptible to the attack by ROS, with important consequences to membrane structure and function [10, 11]. In this sense, the knowledge of the distribution of different ROS at the biomembrane-water interface would certainly help in the understanding of reaction processes in the organism, such as lipid peroxidation and radical scavenging by membrane antioxidants. Different experimental approaches using molecular probes as fingerprints were used to provide qualitative information of ROS penetration into lipid bilayers [12–14]. However, these data are usually associated with large uncertainties as molecular probes present a high mobility and hence cannot be precisely located in the membrane [15].

Molecular dynamics (MD) simulations have become an important tool in membrane research. They provide information about atomic-level interactions that may improve the understanding of oxidative stress mechanisms. In Section 14.2, we present a short description of the method. In Section 14.3, we review its recent applications to problems related to biomembranes under oxidative stress, giving emphasis to the following case studies: permeability of biomembranes to ROS and photosensitizer-membrane interactions. In each of them, we perform a critical analysis of the simulation results, highlighting the successes, limitations, and challenges. Finally, we give examples of questions related to membranes and oxidative stress that still remain open and to which MD could offer valuable insights, such as the effects of lipid oxidation products on membrane properties.

14.2 THEORETICAL MODELING

Molecular simulations have improved in such a way that they can now be used to model the properties of complex systems. The diversity of applications has led to the development of a vast range of computational tools, specially designed to access specific properties [16]. It is important to stress that this is part of a continuous process, with tools that have been introduced in response to new advances [17]. In this sense, new computational tools have been developed to help in the understanding of multi- and interdisciplinary challenges:

1. Quantum mechanics/molecular mechanics (QM/MM): biological systems are too large to be treated explicitly with quantum methods. The idea is to describe only a small part of the system using a quantum approach, while its surroundings are treated classically [18].
2. Solvent effects in chemical reactions: first principles MD simulations allow for the study of the effects of the medium; that is, solvents, ligants, and so on, in a chemical reaction. From such simulations it is possible to obtain the potential energy surface (PES) of a given chemical reaction. Knowledge of PES is the first step in the understanding of a chemical reaction [19].
3. Mesoscopic modeling: to access very large systems, a granular description is used instead of an atomic one. In this case, a group of atoms or molecules, for example, is represented by an effective particle. The computational challenge here is the development of a method that allows the derivation of the effective interaction between these mesoscopic particles [20, 21].

One of the great advantages of numeric simulations lies in the possibility of investigating different aspects of very complex systems at a molecular level and in a systematic way. As these aspects are not easily accessed in experimental investigations, the combination of both experimental and simulation techniques will certainly contribute to the understanding of the process under investigation. In addition, numerical simulations allow for the investigation of a great variety of systems. Therefore, inviable or less applicable systems can be disregarded, reducing the number of systems to be experimentally explored.

Atomistic MD simulations are based on the stepwise solution of Newton's equations of motion for classical many-particle systems [22, 23]. There is no explicit information about the electronic degrees of freedom, meaning that interatomic interactions are described by atom-centered effective potentials. Their related parameters and functional forms, the so-called force field, are either fitted to quantum chemistry data, or empirically adjusted so as to reproduce a set of known experimental properties of the systems under study.

MD simulations have become an important tool in membrane research. Thanks to the growth of computational power in the last decade, atomistic membrane simulations can now routinely reach a timescale of a few hundreds of ns for large systems made of around 100 fully hydrated phospholipids. To generate meaningful results, MD simulations require a precise description of molecular geometry and intermolecular interactions. Force fields have been developed that accurately reproduce a large number of experimentally measurable properties of pure phospholipid membranes, including the area per lipid and the acyl chain order parameter [24, 25].

14.3 CASE STUDIES

14.3.1 PERMEABILITY OF BIOMEMBRANES TO ROS

ROS are of primary importance in biology [1, 2]. Highly reactive superoxide (O_2^-) and hydroperoxyl (HO_2) radicals are generated by the mitochondrial electron transport chain. To cope with their toxicity, the organism produces superoxide dismutases that convert O_2^- into the less reactive hydrogen peroxide (H_2O_2). However, in the presence of trace metals, H_2O_2 may generate highly toxic hydroxyl radicals (HO) via Fenton-type reactions [26, 27]. In addition, artificially generated singlet oxygen ($^1O_2$) plays a central role in PDT [5].

Simulations have offered valuable insights about the behavior of ROS at interfaces. They have shown that, in water droplets, small oxy-radicals have a tendency to accumulate at the air-water interface [28–30]. In the case of more complex biological interfaces, simulations indicated a moderate tendency of H_2O_2 to accumulate at the surface of proteins [31, 32]. Other studies showed that hydrophobic species such as O_2 and •NO concentrate at the membrane interior, but are not homogeneously distributed [33–35]. This can be explained by the fact that phospholipid bilayers are microheterogeneous environments with position-dependent properties such as dielectric constant and free volume [36]. While organic solvents are isotropically distributed and oriented in space, phospholipid acyl chains have an ordering degree. For all these reasons, solubility data based on model organic solvents are not always directly transferable to membranes.

Systematic simulation studies of the water-to-membrane partition of ROS may help to better understand how oxidative stress mechanisms operate at the molecular level. Recently, the behavior of O_2, H_2O_2 and small oxy-radicals was investigated at the membrane-water interface using MD simulations [37]. Fig. 14.1A shows the free energy profiles for ROS translocation across a 1-palmitoyl-2-oleoyl-sn-glycero-3-phosphocholine (POPC) bilayer. When hydrophobic O_2 molecules were considered, the minimum of the free energy was located at the bilayer center and the energy barrier for permeation was insignificant. In agreement with experimental findings by Subczynsky and coworkers [38], O_2 was found to be on average about 3.5 times more concentrated in the membrane interior than in bulk water. Simulations indicated that the membrane acted as a permeation barrier for all hydrophilic ROS considered. This is consistent with experimental evidence indicating that the permeation of species such as HO_2 and H_2O_2 is much lower than that observed for O_2 [9].

The activation free energy for H_2O_2 permeation was estimated to be around 33±4 kJ/mol. It is worthy pointing out that the comparison between simulated activation free energies and experimental results might be misleading, as the permeability of species such as H_2O_2 strongly depends on membrane structure and composition. Indeed, there is an order-of-magnitude variation of the permeability coefficients reported for H_2O_2 in different types of cell membranes [9].

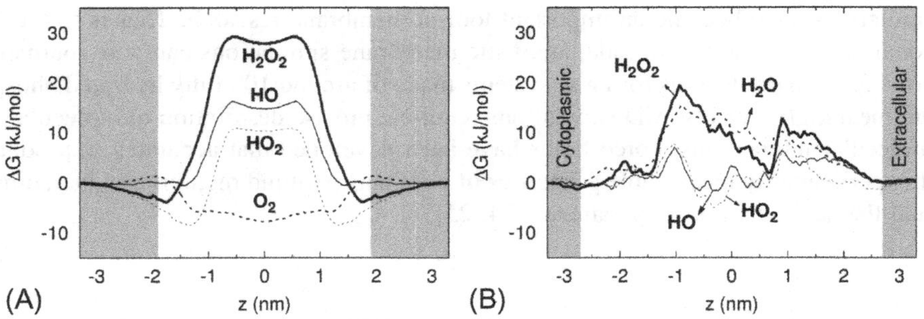

FIGURE 14.1

Free energy profiles associated to the permeation of different species through (A) a POPC bilayer [37] and (B) a plant aquaporin channel [39]. The grey area indicates the aqueous phase and the white area indicates either the membrane or the channel region.

Fig. 14.1A also shows that significantly lower barriers were found for HO and HO_2 radicals when compared to H_2O_2. In particular, the role of HO_2 in lipid peroxidation has received little attention. At physiological pH, it exists almost exclusively in the form of its conjugated base O_2^-. A free energy minimum was found for HO_2 at the membrane surface, as indicated in Fig. 14.1A. In contrast with all other ROS, HO_2 radicals were found to concentrate in the headgroups region. This can be qualitatively interpreted as a local increase of the acid/base equilibrium constant involving HO_2 and O_2^-. Further investigations testing different force fields might be necessary to quantitatively establish this fact. However, it is fair to say that our simulations suggest that HO_2 probably has an important role in both lipid peroxidation and radical scavenging by membrane antioxidants, even at physiological pH.

In Fig. 14.2 we compare the distribution of (A) ROS and (B) common antioxidants at the membrane-water interface of a hydrated POPC bilayer. From these distributions, it is clear that hydrophobic antioxidants, such as β-carotene, are more likely to access species that also accumulate in the membrane interior, such as O_2. In contrast, hydrophilic molecules like Trolox® are more likely to interact with water-soluble species. Amphiphilic molecules like α-tocopherol, are more likely to be

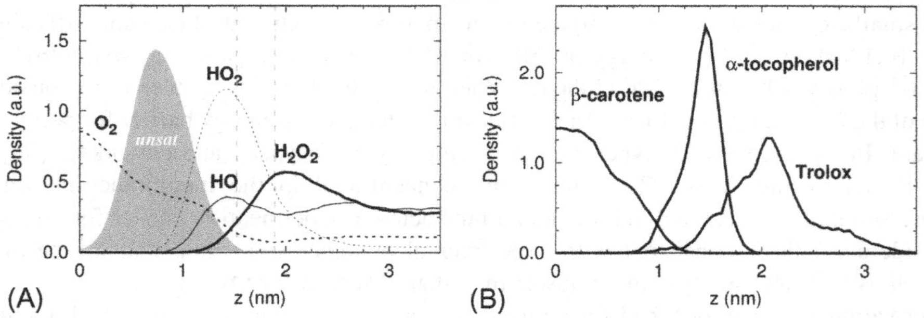

FIGURE 14.2

(A) Distribution of ROS at the membrane-water interface. The headgroups region (vertical dashed lines) and the phospholipid acyl chain unsaturations (grey area) are indicated. (B) Distribution of different antioxidants.

found in the membrane-water interface region, where they have easier access to nonionic hydrophilic ROS, especially HO_2. Therefore, our simulations clearly suggest that the individual behavior of each ROS might play a key role in the efficiency of radical scavengers. Indeed, carotenoids are known to be $^1O_2$ quenchers in biological systems, in accordance with the predictions of our simulations [40].

Data in Fig. 14.2A show a significant overlap between the distributions of HO and HO_2 radicals and the distribution of the unsaturated sites of the lipid oleoyl chains. This overlap is probably related to membrane fluidity and disorder. It means that ROS have easy access to the lipid chain unsaturations, without the need to penetrate deep in the membrane interior.

The role of membrane proteins in the transport of ROS is another important aspect that can be accessed by MD simulations [39]. Aquaporins are proteins responsible for water transport through lipid membranes. They also play a crucial role in redox signaling, mainly due to their ability to transport ROS. However, details of the mechanisms involved in such processes are still unclear, especially those at a molecular level. MD simulations were successfully applied [39] to work out the activation free energy for ROS transport through both mammalian and plant aquaporin models. The simulation results, depicted in Fig. 14.1B, indicate that aquaporins can act as hydrogen peroxide channels. In addition, HO radicals generated close to those channels might have access to their interior and hence promote the oxidation of amino acids that are essential to guarantee the pore selectivity. Biologically generated O_2^- radicals could, in principle, diffuse throughout aquaporins as their conjugated acid, the HO_2 radical.

Although simulations provided important clues about the partition and dynamics of ROS at the membrane-water interface, as well as their transport by aquaporins, attention must be called to a few limitations. Partition and permeation phenomena can be successfully studied using classical models, as clearly demonstrated in these case studies. However, because electrons are not explicitly taken into consideration in such approaches, chemical reactions cannot be properly described. This is not a critical point when relatively stable ROS, such as H_2O_2, are under analysis because their mean lifetime is usually much longer than the timescale associated with permeation. In contrast, HO radicals are very reactive [41, 42]. Therefore, classical free energy profiles can only be used to partially represent the behavior of very reactive radicals close to membranes and aquaporin channels.

14.3.2 PHOTOSENSITIZER INTERACTION WITH MEMBRANES

The mechanism of PDT action is based on the combination of a photoactive drug (photosensitizer), a light source, and molecular oxygen. The absorption of light by the photosensitizer leads to the formation of excited states, followed either by direct electron transfer to biological substrates (type I mechanism) or by energy transfer to oxygen present in the medium (type II mechanism). Type II reactions result in the formation of the short-lived and highly reactive $^1O_2$. The diffusion range of $^1O_2$ is predicted to be limited to approximately 45 nm in cellular media [43]. Its reactivity toward monounsaturated alkyl chains, on the other hand, is four orders of magnitude higher when compared to that of common oxygen [44]. Therefore, $^1O_2$ is considered to be the main cytotoxic agent in PDT, because it has the ability to react almost indiscriminately with all constituents of the cell.

To make use of the singlet oxygen cytotoxicity, the development of photosensitizers for efficient in situ generation of $^1O_2$ have attracted a great deal of attention [45]. These efforts have led to the approval of some photosensitizers for clinical use [46]. Different aspects, such as pharmacokinetic issues, stability, safety, and price must be simultaneously considered in the development of photosensitizers. From the chemical point of view, attention is given to the drug-membrane binding affinity. An amphiphilic structure is desirable because it allies the water solubility promoted by the hydrophilic part with the drug-membrane affinity provided by the hydrophobic part [47]. Engelmann et al. [48, 49] studied a series of cationic meso-(N-methyl-3-pyridinium)phenylporphyrins that present large variations in photodynamic efficiency. These differences cannot be solely ascribed to differences in their intrinsic efficiency or in their drug-membrane binding affinity. They were rather ascribed to details of molecular structure, such as relative positions and orientations of the photosensitizers at the membrane-water interface. These properties directly influence their accessibility to the hydrophobic membrane interior, where the oxygen concentration is higher than in the aqueous medium [33, 38, 49]. However, it is important to mention that the measurement of all these aspects directly in experiments is not an easy task.

Molecular modeling techniques, on the other hand, are well-suited for this purpose. They are able to provide molecular level information about the structure and interactions for chemically realistic systems. These abilities were used in several works where the computational modeling of photosensitizers at phospholipid membranes was the main subject [50]. However, there is a lack of systematic studies where a direct comparison between simulations and experimentally measured photodynamic efficiency can be made.

Recently, MD simulations were employed to model the binding between a series of cationic meso-(N-methyl-4-pyridinium)phenylporphyrins and anionic phosphatidylglycerol (PG) lipid bilayers [51]. The porphyrins studied differed both with respect to the relative number and spatial distribution of charged N-methyl-4-pyridinium (Mpyr+) groups and apolar phenyl (Phe) groups attached to the central porphyrin ring.

The chemical structures of the considered compounds [51], P2c, P2t, P3, and P4 are presented in Fig. 14.3. In all simulations, photosensitizers started at the aqueous phase and reached the membrane surface in approximately 2 ns, driven by favorable drug-membrane electrostatic interactions. The photosensitizers' immersion depth is shown in Fig. 14.4A. Simulations indicate that the central porphyrin ring of the P4 molecule stayed almost flat at the bilayer surface. The strong overlap between the distributions of the Mpyr+ groups and the Na+ membrane counterions (data not shown) indicated that the adsorption process was governed by the opposite charges of P4 and palmitoyloleoyl phosphatidylglycerol (POPG). P3 had a similar behavior, as the central ring was found to be almost parallel to the

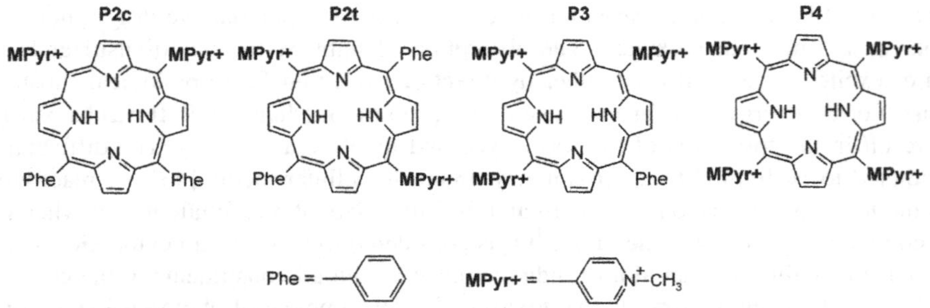

FIGURE 14.3

Chemical structures of several meso-(N-methyl-4-pyridinium)phenylporphyrins (P2t).

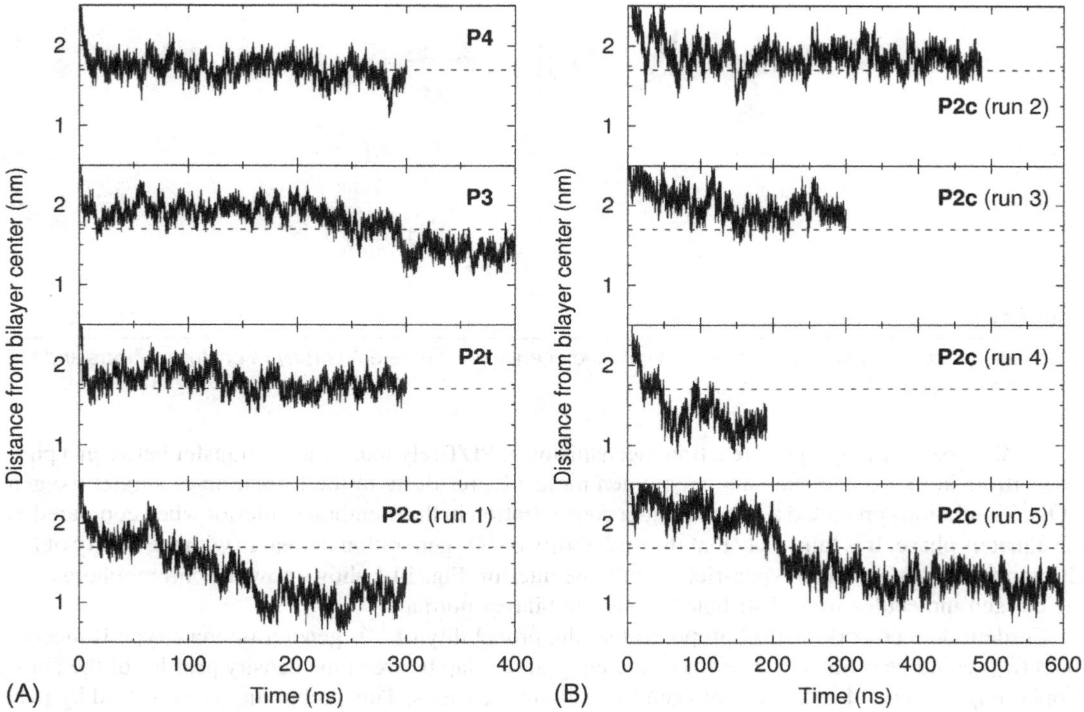

FIGURE 14.4

(A) Distance from the POPG bilayer center of different porphyrin photosensitizers as a function of simulation time. The dashed horizontal line indicates the membrane surface. (B) Distance as a function of time for P2c in different independent simulation runs.

surface, hiding its only Phe substituent in the membrane interior. P2t and P2c, on the other hand, were oriented perpendicular to the bilayer surface. For the trans isomer, simulations indicate that the molecular geometry did not allow access of both Phe rings to the membrane interior. One of the Phe groups was kept almost fully hydrated and pointing toward the aqueous phase, while the other reached the region slightly below the bilayer surface. The cis isomer presented the strongest amphiphilic character. Both Phe groups were deeply anchored in the membrane interior, while the two Mpyr+ groups remained partially hydrated at the membrane-water interface. Spatial arrangement assumed by each of the photosensitizers can be understood in the following way: each photosensitizer hid as many Phe groups as possible in the membrane interior, preserving at least partial hydration of the Mpyr+ substituents without disrupting their strong electrostatic interactions with phosphate headgroups. Therefore, Mpyr+ groups were not able to penetrate into the membrane beyond the region of the carbonylester groups.

To find out how sampling may interfere in the results, several independent simulations are compared in Fig. 14.4B. Our data indicate that penetration in the membrane may occur rather early, before 100 ns in some cases, while in other cases it is not observable even in 500 ns. Therefore, conclusions taken from simulations with a single ensemble should be treated with caution.

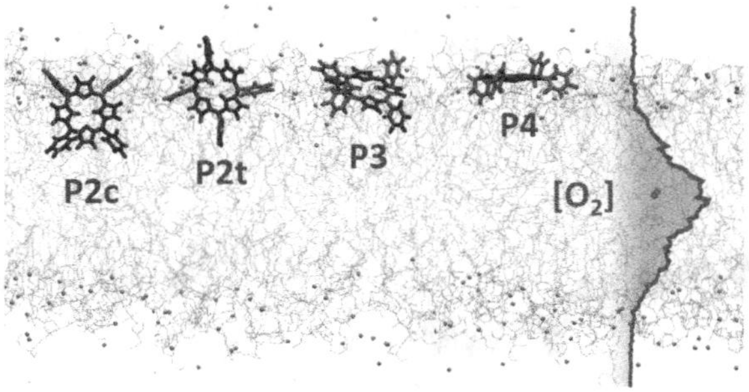

FIGURE 14.5

Schematic picture showing the immersion depth and orientation of different porphyrin photosensitizers and the distribution of O_2 at POPG membranes.

As discussed earlier, type II reaction mechanisms in PDT rely upon energy transfer between a photosensitizer in its excited state and an oxygen molecule, resulting in the formation of singlet oxygen ($^1O_2$). Simulations predicted a larger oxygen concentration in the membrane interior when compared to the aqueous phase. It is fair to say that the probability of $^1O_2$ generation increases with the ability of the chromophore to reach the oxygen-rich membrane interior. Fig. 14.5 shows how the chromophores and the oxygen molecules were distributed along the bilayer normal.

Cordeiro and coworkers [51] proposed that the probability of $^1O_2$ generation via a type II mechanism (P_{II}) could be estimated in terms of the integral overlap between the density profiles of the chromophore (ρ_{chro}) and of molecular oxygen (ρ_{O_2}) along the z axis. This probability is expressed by [51]

$$P_{II} \propto \int dz \rho_{chro}(z) \rho_{O_2}(z) \qquad (1)$$

where the integral runs over the entire system length along the z axis. In this approach, a direct correlation between photodynamic efficiency and the probability of $^1O_2$ generation, as in Eq. (1), is assumed. The relative photodynamic efficiencies for different photosensitizers derived from the overlap model are compared to experimentally derived data in Fig. 14.6B. A qualitative agreement between simulated and experimental is clearly present, see details in ref. [51]. As an illustration, the density profiles for different photosensitizers and O_2 are presented in Fig. 14.6A.

MD studies of photosensitizer interaction with membranes are not restricted to porphyrins. Results for phenothiazines, in particular methylene blue (MB) are also available. Methylene blue is a phenothiazinium dye with the following properties: strong absorbance in the range of 550–700 nm, significant quantum yield ($\phi_\Delta = 0.52$) [52], triplet with long intrinsic lifetime, low fluorescence quantum yield and lifetime, and low reduction potential [53]. Because of these characteristics, it has been used in a variety of photochemical applications including solar energy conversion [53] and PDT [54] and a recent onychomycosis clinical trial [55]. In particular, the influence of ions in the interaction of MB with dipalmitoylphosphatidylcholine (DPPC) membranes was the subject of the study of Miotto and coworkers [56]. A schematic representation of the immersion depth and orientation of MB in DPPC membrane is given in Fig. 14.7.

Fig. 14.8 shows the time evolution of the binding process of the MB in lipid bilayer. The distance between the MB and the bilayer center define the immersion depth. The results indicated that the MB

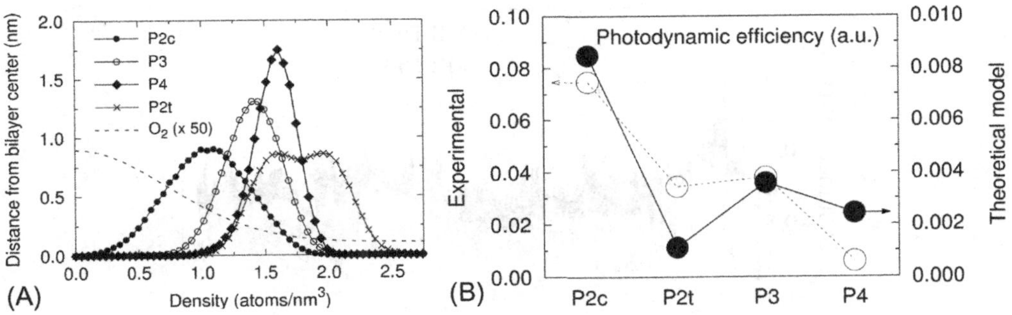

FIGURE 14.6

(A) Density profile distribution of different photosensitizers and O_2 obtained via MD simulations [51]. The concentration of O_2 was scaled up by a factor of 50 to appear in the same scale. (B) Photodynamic efficiency as estimated [51] based on the overlap between the distributions of different photosensitizers and O_2.

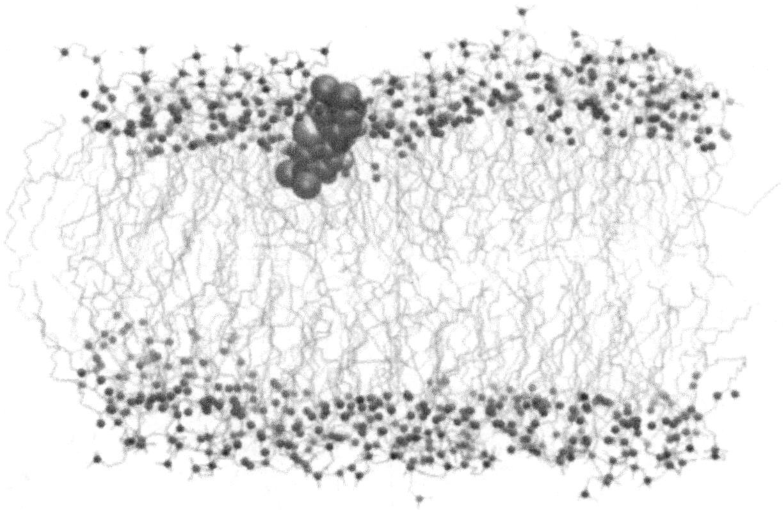

FIGURE 14.7

Schematic representation of the immersion depth and orientation of MB in DPPC membrane.

exhibited a greater immersion in DPPC in the absence of ions. Our data [56] also indicate that, in the absence of ions, MB presents a higher mobility.

For both systems, the nitrogen atoms of the AM molecule (N–N_{MB}) present a bimodal distribution (black solid lines). It is clear from Fig. 14.9 (left panel) that, in the presence of ions, the MB molecule immersion is such that one of the symmetric nitrogen atoms is in the region of the phospholipid head-group, indicated by P. When ions are not included, Fig. 14.9 (right panel), the MB molecule immersion is such that the nitrogen atom is closer to the C–C region, around the region where C=O bonds can be found.

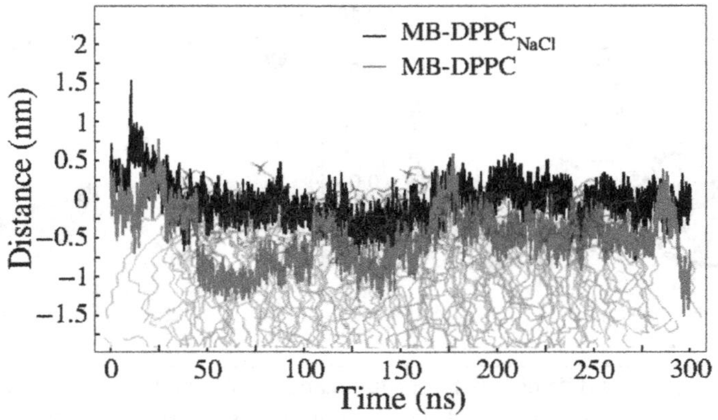

FIGURE 14.8

Temporal evolution of the drug-membrane binding process for MB. The top half of the lipid bilayer is also represented in the background.

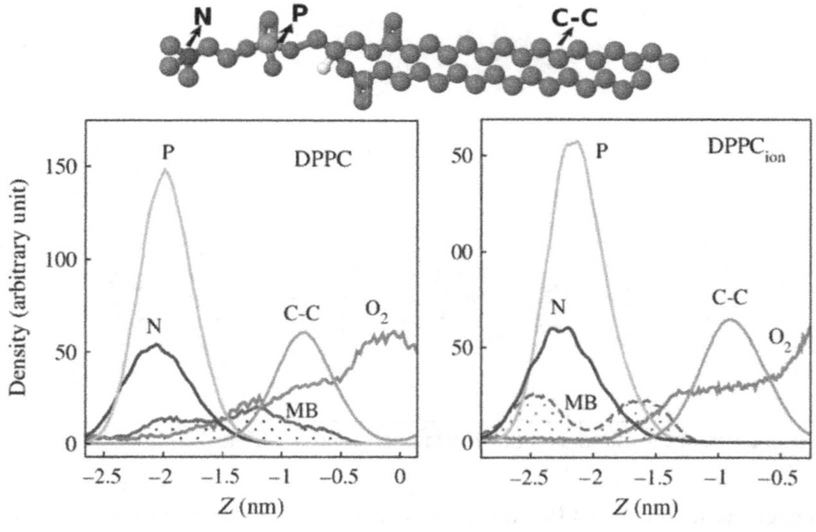

FIGURE 14.9

Density profiles, that is, spatial probability to find different molecules or functional groups along the bilayer normal. Density profiles were arbitrary scaled to allow a better visualization. Left panel: without ions; right panel: with ions.

Following the procedure proposed by Cordeiro and coworkers [51], we calculated the normalized integral overlap O_2/MB including or not explicitly considering ions in the system. The integral overlap, when ions are explicitly considered, is almost four times smaller than those obtained when ions are not considered. In other words, our results clearly indicate that the presence of ions reduces the O_2/MB superposition probability. This is in agreement with the experimental findings by Núñez and coworkers [57], who have observed a higher production of ROS in water than in 0.9% saline solution.

14.4 OUTLOOK

Despite the successes in the description of the oxidative stress in biomembranes, this field of research still has to develop new tools to investigate other oxidation mechanisms. An interesting example is the effect of lipid oxidation products on membrane properties. Nonenzymatic lipid peroxidation [58] may be initiated by free radicals. Lipids undergo hydrogen abstraction by initiating radicals, followed by oxygen capture and propagation, forming lipid hydroperoxides.

These process have just started to be explored by computer simulations with a view to offer a molecular picture of biomembranes under oxidative stress. However, the majority of these simulations have been mostly focused on phospholipid oxidation products [59–63]. The general picture that arises indicates that these products increase the membrane permeability to water and facilitate pore formation. The effect of cholesterol oxidation was considered as well [64–66]. Remarkably, coarse-grained lipid models showed that cholesterol derivatives became less effective in promoting membrane lateral domain formation as their headgroup was made more hydrophobic [67]. Recently, a drastic change in sterol orientation and membrane properties was observed in membranes containing 25-hydroxycholesterol, a side-chain oxysterol generated enzymatically [68].

So far, simulations of oxidized membranes were based on rather simplified descriptions of membrane composition. Typically, only one type of oxidation product was considered individually in each simulation [62]. However, recent experimental unpublished data obtained by our research group suggest that synergistic effects may take place in mixtures of different lipid oxidation products. In this sense, the investigation of the effect of peroxidation on multicomponent membranes composed by unsaturated phosphatidylcholines and cholesterol should be addressed and MD simulations have already proven to be a key method in the description of similar processes.

One of the challenges in the simulation of biomembranes under oxidative stress is to treat the large variety of isomeric forms of the phospholipid nitro-oxidation products. Nitro- and hydroperoxy-functional groups can be formed at various positions along the unsaturated phospholipid acyl chains. Stereocenters with different chiralities can be generated. Besides that, isomerization of the phospholipid cis-double bond may occur.

Another interesting issue is the formation of segregated membrane domains. However, spontaneous domain formation is associated with multimicrosecond timescales, which are often prohibitively long for fully atomistic simulations. A combination of atomistic MD simulations of membranes with preformed lipid domains containing nitration and oxidation products might be a good candidate to explore this problem, as it will allow the evaluation of the effect of the interactions and the thickness mismatch between different lipid phases.

The spontaneous domain formation process, on the other hand, will probably be better described by lower-resolution coarse-grained MD simulations. Coarse-grained models have been successfully employed in the simulation of lateral phase separation in membranes [69]. There are several successful strategies for the implementation of coarse-grained models in materials science [70, 71] and biology [72]. The basic idea of these models is to replace a whole molecular segment (with multiple atoms) by a single interaction center. In a structural approach, the effective potential between these interaction centers is adjusted iteratively until the structure (or the ensemble of conformations) of the coarse-grained system matches the structure of the parental fully atomistic system. Solvent molecules can even be completely removed from the coarse-grained model and considered only implicitly, meaning that their influence is incorporated into the coarse-grained potential. This leads to an improvement of several orders-of-magnitude in computational efficiency.

14.5 CONCLUSION AND SUMMARY

The use of MD simulations in the study of biomembranes under oxidative stress is critically addressed. Emphasis on permeability of biomembranes to ROS and photosensitizer-membrane interactions, including porphyrins and phenothiazines examples, are discussed. We perform a critical analysis of the simulation results, highlighting the successes, limitations, and challenges. Finally, we give examples of questions related to membranes and oxidative stress that still remain open and to which MD could offer valuable insights.

ACKNOWLEDGMENTS

The authors acknowledge financial support from CNPq and FAPESP (project 2012/50680-5).

REFERENCES

[1] Dröge W. Free radicals in the physiological control of cell function. Physiol Rev 2002;82(1):47–95.
[2] Halliwell B, Gutteridge JMC. Oxygen toxicity, oxygen radicals, transition metals and disease. Biochem J 1984;219(1):1–14.
[3] Sanz A, Pamplona R, Barja G. Is the mitochondrial free radical theory of aging intact? Antioxid Redox Signal 2006;8(3–4):582–99.
[4] Halliwell B. Free radicals and other reactive species in disease. Encyclopedia of life sciences; 2001. p. 1–7.
[5] Brown SB, Brown EA, Walker I. The present and future role of photodynamic therapy in cancer treatment. Lancet Oncol 2004;5(8):497–508.
[6] George S, Hamblin MR, Kishen A. Uptake pathways of anionic and cationic photosensitizers into bacteria. Photochem Photobiol Sci: Off J Eur Photochem Assoc Eur Soc Photobiol 2009;8(6):788–95.
[7] Wainwright M. Photodynamic antimicrobial chemotherapy (PACT). J Antimicrob Chemother 1998;42(1):13–28.
[8] Baptista MS, Wainwright M. Photodynamic antimicrobial chemotherapy (PACT) for the treatment of malaria, leishmaniasis and trypanosomiasis. Braz J Med Biol Res 2011;44(1):1–10.
[9] Möller M, Lancaster J, Denicola A. The interaction of reactive oxygen and nitrogen species with membranes. Curr Top Membr 2007;61:23–42.
[10] Mertins O, Mathews PD, Gomide AB, Baptista MS, Itri R. Effective protection of biological membranes against photo-oxidative damage: polymeric antioxidant forming a protecting shield over the membrane. Biochim Biophys Acta 2015;1848(10 Pt A):2180–7.

[11] Weber G, Charitat T, Baptista MS, Uchoa AF, Pavani C, Junqueira HC, et al. Lipid oxidation induces structural changes in biomimetic membranes. Soft Matter 2014;10(24):4241–7.
[12] Afri M, Ehrenberg B, Talmon Y, Schmidt J, Cohen Y, Frimer AA. Active oxygen chemistry within the liposomal bilayer. Part III: Locating vitamin E, ubiquinol and ubiquinone and their derivatives in the lipid bilayer. Chem Phys Lipids 2004;131(1):107–21.
[13] Fortier CA, Guan B, Cole RB, Tarr MA. Covalently bound fluorescent probes as reporters for hydroxyl radical penetration into liposomal membranes. Free Radic Biol Med 2009;46(10):1376–85.
[14] Gamliel A, Afri M, Frimer AA. Determining radical penetration of lipid bilayers with new lipophilic spin traps. Free Radic Biol Med 2008;44(7):1394–405.
[15] Kyrychenko A, Ladokhin AS. Molecular dynamics simulations of depth distribution of spin-labeled phospholipids within lipid bilayer. J Phys Chem B 2013;117(19):5875–85.
[16] Coveney PV, Fowler PW. Modelling biological complexity: a physical scientist's perspective. J R Soc Interface 2005;2(4):267–80.
[17] Levitt M. The birth of computational structural biology. Nat Struct Biol 2001;8(5):392–3.
[18] Kamerlin SCL, Haranczyk M, Warshel A. Progress in ab initio QM/MM free-energy simulations of electrostatic energies in proteins: accelerated QM/MM studies of pKa, redox reactions and solvation free energies. J Phys Chem B 2009;113(5):1253–72.
[19] Tapia O, Bertrán J. Solvent effects and chemical reactivity (understanding chemical reactivity). Amsterdam: Springer Netherlands; 2007.
[20] Ayton G, Voth GA. Bridging microscopic and mesoscopic simulations of lipid bilayers. Biophys J 2002; 83(6):3357–70.
[21] Stewart JJP. Application of the PM6 method to modeling proteins. J Mol Model 2009;15(7):765–805.
[22] Allen MP, Tildesley DJ. Computer simulation of liquids. Oxford: Oxford University Press; 1989.
[23] Frenkel D, Smit B. Understanding molecular simulation, second edition: from algorithms to applications (computational science). London: Academic Press; 2001.
[24] Poger D, Van Gunsteren WF, Mark AE. A new force field for simulating phosphatidylcholine bilayers. J Comput Chem 2010;31(6):1117–25.
[25] Poger D, Mark AE. On the validation of molecular dynamics simulations of saturated and cis-monounsaturated phosphatidylcholine lipid bilayers: a comparison with experiment. J Chem Theory Comput 2010;6(1):325–36.
[26] Prousek J. Fenton chemistry in biology and medicine. Pure Appl Chem 2007;79(12).
[27] Cheng Z, Li Y. What is responsible for the initiating chemistry of iron-mediated lipid peroxidation: an update. Chem Rev 2007;107(3):748–66.
[28] Martins-Costa MTC, Anglada JM, Francisco JS, Ruiz-Lopez MF. Reactivity of atmospherically relevant small radicals at the air-water interface. Angew Chem Int Ed Engl 2012;51(22):5413–7.
[29] Roeselová M, Vieceli J, Dang LX, Garrett BC, Tobias DJ. Hydroxyl radical at the air-water interface. J Am Chem Soc 2004;126(50):16308–9.
[30] Vácha R, Slavícek P, Mucha M, Finlayson-Pitts BJ, Jungwirth P. Adsorption of atmospherically relevant gases at the air/water interface: free energy profiles of aqueous solvation of N_2, O_2, O_3, OH, H_2O, HO_2, and H_2O_2. J Phys Chem A 2004;108(52):11573–9.
[31] Chung YH, Xia J, Margulis CJ. Diffusion and residence time of hydrogen peroxide and water in crowded protein environments. J Phys Chem B 2007;111(46):13336–44.
[32] Domínguez L, Sosa-Peinado A, Hansberg W. Catalase evolved to concentrate H2O2 at its active site. Arch Biochem Biophys 2010;500(1):82–91.
[33] Al-Abdul-Wahid MS, Yu CH, Batruch I, Evanics F, Pomès R, Prosser RS. A combined NMR and molecular dynamics study of the transmembrane solubility and diffusion rate profile of dioxygen in lipid bilayers. Biochemistry 2006;45(35):10719–28.
[34] Jedlovszky P, Mezei M. Effect of cholesterol on the properties of phospholipid membranes. 2. Free energy profile of small molecules. J Phys Chem B 2003;107(22):5322–32.

[35] Wennberg CL, van der Spoel D, Hub JS. Large influence of cholesterol on solute partitioning into lipid membranes. J Am Chem Soc 2012;134(11):5351–61.
[36] Marrink SJ, Berendsen HJC. Simulation of water transport through a lipid membrane. J Phys Chem 1994;98 (15):4155–68.
[37] Cordeiro RM. Reactive oxygen species at phospholipid bilayers: distribution, mobility and permeation. Biochim Biophys Acta 2014;1838(1 Pt B):438–44.
[38] Subczynski WK, Hyde JS, Kusumi A. Oxygen permeability of phosphatidylcholine-cholesterol membranes. Proc Natl Acad Sci U S A 1989;86(June):4474–8.
[39] Cordeiro RM. Molecular dynamics simulations of the transport of reactive oxygen species by mammalian and plant aquaporins. Biochim Biophys Acta 2015;1850(9):1786–94.
[40] Uchoa AF, Severino D, Baptista MS. Antioxidant properties of singlet oxygen suppressors. In: Natural antioxidants and biocides from wild medicinal plants; 2013. p. 65–91. CAB Direct.
[41] Davies MJ. The oxidative environment and protein damage. Biochim Biophys Acta 2005;1703(2):93–109.
[42] Buxton GV, Greenstock CL, Helman WP, Ross AB, Tsang W. Critical review of rate constants for reactions of hydrated electrons, hydrogen atoms and hydroxyl radicals (OH/O-) in aqueous solution. J Phys Chem Ref Data 1988;17(2):513.
[43] Ochsner M. Photophysical and photobiological processes in the photodynamic therapy of tumours. J Photochem Photobiol B Biol 1997;39(1):1–18.
[44] Min DB, Boff JM. Chemistry and reaction of singlet oxygen in foods. Compr Rev Food Sci Food Saf 2002;1 (2):58–72.
[45] Allison RR, Downie GH, Cuenca R, Hu XH, Childs CJ, Sibata CH. Photosensitizers in clinical PDT. Photodiagnosis Photodyn Ther 2004;1(1):27–42.
[46] Wainwright M. Dye, photodynamic therapy. Encyclopedia of color science and technology. Berlin: Springer Berlin Heidelberg; 2014. p. 1–8.
[47] Ethirajan M, Chen Y, Joshi P, Pandey RK. The role of porphyrin chemistry in tumor imaging and photodynamic therapy. Chem Soc Rev 2011;40(1):340–62.
[48] Engelmann FM, Rocha SVO, Toma HE, Araki K, Baptista MS. Determination of n-octanol/water partition and membrane binding of cationic porphyrins. Int J Pharm 2007;329(1-2):12–8.
[49] Engelmann FM, Mayer I, Gabrielli DS, Toma HE, Kowaltowski AJ, Araki K, et al. Interaction of cationic meso-porphyrins with liposomes, mitochondria and erythrocytes. J Bioenerg Biomembr 2007;39(2):175–85.
[50] O'Neil DW, Noh SY, Notman R. Computer simulations of lipid membranes and liposomes for drug delivery. In: Ouyang D, Smith SC, editors. Computational pharmaceutics: application of molecular modeling in drug delivery. Oxford: John Wiley & Sons, Inc.; 2015. p. 101–21
[51] Cordeiro RM, Miotto R, Baptista MS. Photodynamic efficiency of cationic meso-porphyrins at lipid bilayers: insights from molecular dynamics simulations. J Phys Chem B 2012;116(50):14618–27.
[52] DeRosa M. Photosensitized singlet oxygen and its applications. Coord Chem Rev 2002;233–4:351–71.
[53] Severino D, Junqueira HC, Gugliotti M, Gabrielli DS, Baptista MS. Influence of negatively charged interfaces on the ground and excited state properties of methylene blue. Photochem Photobiol 2003;77(5):459–68.
[54] Tardivo JP, Del Giglio A, Paschoal LH, Baptista MS. New photodynamic therapy protocol to treat AIDS-related Kaposi's sarcoma. Photomed Laser Surg 2006;24(4):528–31.
[55] Tardivo JP, Wainwright M, Baptista M. Small scale trial of photodynamic treatment of onychomycosis in São Paulo. J Photochem Photobiol B Biol 2015;150:66–8.
[56] Miotto R, Trellese GG, Cordeiro RM, Costa E, Ferraz AC. The influence of ions in the interaction of methylene blue with DPPC membranes. ICQNM 2014: the eight international conference on quantum, nano/bio, and micro technologies; 2014. p. 18–21.
[57] Nún-ez SCN, Garcez AS, Kato IT, Yoshimura TM, Gomes L, Baptista MS, et al. Effects of ionic strength on the antimicrobial photodynamic efficiency of methylene blue. Photochem Photobiol Sci: Off J Eur Photochem Assoc Eur Soc Photobiol 2014;13(3):595–602.

[58] Niki E, Yoshida Y, Saito Y, Noguchi N. Lipid peroxidation: mechanisms, inhibition, and biological effects. Biochem Biophys Res Commun 2005;338(1):668–76.

[59] Jarerattanachat V, Karttunen M, Wong-Ekkabut J. Molecular dynamics study of oxidized lipid bilayers in NaCl solution. J Phys Chem B 2013;117(28):8490501.

[60] Beranova L, Cwiklik L, Jurkiewicz P, Hof M, Jungwirth P. Oxidation changes physical properties of phospholipid bilayers: fluorescence spectroscopy and molecular simulations. Langmuir: ACS J Surf Colloids 2010;26(9):6140–4.

[61] Vernier PT, Levine ZA, Wu YH, Joubert V, Ziegler MJ, Mir LM, et al. Electroporating fields target oxidatively damaged areas in the cell membrane. PLoS ONE 2009;4(11):e7966.

[62] Wong-ekkabut J, Xu Z, Triampo W, Tang IM, Peter Tieleman D, Monticelli L. Effect of lipid peroxidation on the properties of lipid bilayers: a molecular dynamics study. Biophys J 2007;93(12):4225–36.

[63] Khandelia H, Mouritsen OG. Self-assembly simulations of membranes containing phospholipid oxidation products. Biophys J 2010;98(3):489a.

[64] Smondyrev AM, Berkowitz ML. Effects of oxygenated sterol on phospholipid bilayer properties: a molecular dynamics simulation. Chem Phys Lipids 2001;112(1):31–9.

[65] Stefl M, Sachl R, Olyska A, Amaro M, Savchenko D, Deyneka A, et al. Comprehensive portrait of cholesterol containing oxidized membrane. Biochim Biophys Acta 2014;1838(7):1769–76.

[66] Kulig W, Olyska A, Jurkiewicz P, Kantola AM, Komulainen S, Manna M, et al. Cholesterol under oxidative stress — how lipid membranes sense oxidation as cholesterol is being replaced by oxysterols. Free Radic Biol Med 2015;84:30–41.

[67] Perlmutter JD, Sachs JN. Inhibiting lateral domain formation in lipid bilayers: simulations of alternative steroid headgroup chemistries. J Am Chem Soc 2009;131(45):16362–3.

[68] Olsen BN, Schlesinger PH, Ory DS, Baker NA. Side-chain oxysterols: from cells to membranes to molecules. Biochim Biophys Acta 2012;1818(2):330–6.

[69] Baoukina S, Mendez-Villuendas E, Peter Tieleman D. Molecular view of phase coexistence in lipid monolayers. J Am Chem Soc 2012;134(42):17543–53.

[70] Cordeiro RM, Zschunke F, Muller-Plathe F. Mesoscale molecular dynamics simulations of the force between surfaces with grafted poly(ethylene oxide) chains derived from atomistic simulations. Macromolecules 2010;43(3):1583–91.

[71] Müller-Plathe F. Coarse-graining in polymer simulation: from the atomistic to the mesoscopic scale and back. ChemPhysChem 2002;3(9):754–69.

[72] Marrink SJ, Tieleman DP. Perspective on the Martini model. Chem Soc Rev 2013;42(16):6801–22.

CHAPTER

15 FEATURE SELECTION AND CLASSIFICATION OF MICROARRAY DATA USING MACHINE LEARNING TECHNIQUES

M. Kumar, S.K. Rath

Department of Computer Science and Engineering, National Institute of Technology Rourkela, Rourkela, India

15.1 INTRODUCTION

Accurate diagnosis of a disease like cancer is vital for successful application of any specific therapy. Even though the classification of cells into cancerous and noncancerous categories in relation to cancer diagnosis has improved quite significantly over the last decade, there is still a wide scope for enhancing the diagnosis process. This objective can be achieved with the application of less subjective models. Recent developments in diagnosis indicate that DNA microarray provides an insight into cancer classification at the gene level. This is due to their capability in measuring abundant messenger ribonucleic acid (mRNA) transcripts of thousands of genes concurrently. Basically, microarray data is obtained by four major steps that involve breaking open a cell in the initial phase, isolating the genetic contents, indentifying the genes that are turned on in that particular cell, and generating the list of the genes identified in the previous phase.

Microarray-based gene expression profiling has emerged as an efficient technique for classification, diagnosis, prognosis, and treatment purposes of various diseases [1]. Cancer diagnosis is one such vital application of microarray data analysis, as one can perform an experiment on thousands of genes concurrently.

In recent years, DNA microarray has had a great impact in determining the *informative genes* that cause cancer [2,3]. The major drawback that exists in microarray data is the curse of dimensionality problem, that is, the number of genes N by far exceeds the number of samples M (ie, $N \gg M$); this hinders the useful information of the data set, and leads to computational instability. Therefore, selecting relevant genes is a challenging task in microarray data analysis [4].

Feature (gene) selection has inspired many scientists to explore the area of functional genomics. As a consequence, numerous algorithms as well as models have evolved to achieve better diagnosis [5–7]. The main objective of feature selection (FS) is to (a) enhance classification accuracy by avoiding either overfitting or underfitting of data, (b) provide cost-effective models involving faster classification of the genes, and (c) obtain a thorough knowledge about the process involved in generating the microarray data.

There are three categories of methods to perform gene selection based on either filter methods or wrapper methods, or even using embedded methods. The intrinsic characteristics of data pertaining to the respective class labels of a gene are used in filter methods. In the case of wrapper methods, the accuracy of "learning or classification" is taken into consideration to evaluate the goodness of the gene subset by transforming the original data set into a new subset of data set. Further, in embedded methods, gene selection is embedded in the construction of the classifier.

This chapter emphasizes state-of-the-art techniques involved in pattern classification system such as the FS extraction, dimensionality reduction, and the design of a classifier.

In this report, different FS methods like t-test, F-test, Wilcoxon test, signal-to-noise ratio (SNR), χ^2-test, IG, Gini index, and Fisher score are used to select the high relevance genes. The top-ranked genes are used to classify the microarray data using various classifiers like logistic regression (LR), naive Bayes (NB), K-nearest neighbor (KNN), artificial neural network (ANN), radial basis function network (RBFN), probabilistic neural network (PNN), and support vector machine (SVM), and the results are analyzed.

The rest of the chapter is organized as follows: Section 15.2 highlights the related work in the field of microarray data classification. Section 15.3 presents the FS methodologies and the classifiers used for the analysis. Section 15.4 gives a brief idea about the various performance parameters used to evaluate the performance of classifiers (models). Section 15.5 presents the stepwise procedure for classifying the microarray data using various classifiers. It also highlights the empirical analysis, the results obtained, and interpretation drawn from the existing classifiers. This section also presents a comparative analysis for gene classification of microarray data with classifiers available in the literature. Section 15.6 concludes the chapter and considers the scope for future work.

15.2 LITERATURE REVIEW

In this section, a brief review on the work done by various authors related to microarray data is provided, and is tabulated as shown in Table 15.1. The table is subdivided into three categories: name of the author, the FS technique used by the respective author for selecting the most significant features of a sample that are responsible for causing cancer, and the last column represents the various machine learning classifiers used for classification of microarray data.

Following are the observations made from the literature survey carried out:

- Numerous FS techniques have been employed, as it plays a crucial role in selecting the most *significant features* before performing classification of the data set.
- Majority of the authors have used SVM classifier for performing microarray data classification; also, hybrid approaches have been used more frequently.
- Out of numerous data sets available in the literature survey, many authors have used data sets related to leukemia, and ovarian and breast cancer [79].

In this report, eight FS techniques (t-test, F-test, Wilcoxon test, SNR, χ^2-test, IG, Gini index, and Fisher score) in combination with seven machine learning techniques (LR, NB, KNN, ANN, RBFN, PNN, and

Table 15.1 Related Work

Author	Feature Selection	Classifier Used
Osareh et al.	Signal-to-noise ratio (SNR)	Support vector machine (SVM), *K*-nearest neighbor (KNN), and probabilistic neural network (PNN) [8]
Dina et al.	Multiple scoring gene selection technique (MGS-CM)	SVM, KNN, linear discriminant analysis (LDA) [9]
Wang et al.	*t*-Test	Fuzzy neural network (FNN), SVM [10]
Zhang and Dend	Based Bayes error filter (BBF)	SVM, KNN [11]
Xiyi Hang	Analysis of variance (ANOVA)	Sparse representation-SVM [12]
Bharathi and Natarajan	ANOVA	SVM [13]
Tang et al.	ANOVA	Discriminant kernel partial least square (PLS) [14]
Furey et al.	Signal-to-noise ratio	SVM [15]
Li et al.	Genetic algorithm	KNN [16]
Ben-Dor et al.	All genes, threshold number of misclassification (TNoM) score	Nearest neighbor, SVM with quadratic kernel, and AdaBoost [17]
Nguyen et al.	Principal component analysis (PCA)	Logistic discriminant, and quadratic discriminant [18]
Guyon et al.	Recursive feature elimination (RFE)	SVM [19]
Mundra et al.	*t*-Statistic, SVM-based *t*-statistic, SVM with RFE SVM-based *t*-statistic with RFE	SVM [20]
Lee et al.	χ^2-test	Hybrid with GA+KNN and SVM [5]
Cho et al.	SVM-RFE	Kernel Fisher discriminant analysis (KFDA) [21]
Deb and Reddy		Nondominated sorting genetic algorithm-II (NSGA-II) [22]
Lee et al.	Bayesian model	Artificial neural network (ANN), KNN, SVM [23]
Lee et al.		Multicategory SVM [24]
Paul and Iba	Probabilistic model building genetic algorithm (PMBGA)	Naive Bayes (NB), weighted voting classifier [25]
Huerta et al.	Genetic algorithm (GA)	GA-SVM [26]
Ye et al.	Uncorrelated linear discriminant analysis (ULDA)	KNN [7]
Liu et al.	GA	SVM [27]
Alba et al.	GA, particle swarm optimization (PSO)	SVM [28]
Yu et al.	Redundancy based filter (RBF)	C4.5 [29]
Ding et al.	Minimum redundancy-maximum relevance (MRMR) feature selection	NB, LDA, SVM, LR [30]
Cho and Won	Representative vector	Ensemble neural network (NN) [31]
Yang et al.	PCA	LDA [32]
Peng et al.	Fisher ratio	NB, decision tree J4.8, SVM [6]

Continued

Table 15.1 Related Work—cont'd

Author	Feature Selection	Classifier Used
Wang et al.	Information gain (IG)	Neuro-fuzzy ensemble [33]
Pang et al.	Bootstrapping consistency gene selection	KNN [34]
Li et al.	*t*-Test + partial least square (PLSDR)	KNN, SVM [35]
Yue et al.		LDA [36]
Hernandez et al.	GA	SVM [37]
Li et al.	Wilcoxon test	GA-SVM [38]
Huerta	*t*-Test	LDA-GA [39]
Yu Wang et al.	Correlation-based feature selection (CFS)	C4.5 (J4.8), NB, SMO-CFS, sequential minimum optimization (SMO)-wrapper, emerging pattern, SVM, voting machine, maximal margin linear programming (MAMA) [40]
Ruiz et al.	Best incremental ranked subset (BIRS)-BIRSw, BIRSf	NB, IB, C4.5 [41]
Zhu et al.	Univariate ranking (UR) and recursive feature elimination (RFE)	SVM, penalized logistic regression (PLR) [42]
Huynh et al.		SVD-neural network [43]
Diaz et al.	Random forest	Random forest [44]
Yeh et al.	Orthogonal array (OA)-SVM	SVM [45]
Yu et al.	SNR	PSO-SVM [46]
Chen et al.	Fisher ratio, Pearson correlation, cosine coefficient, Euclidean distance, and Spearman correlation	Ensemble with different classifier [47]
Liu et al.	Ensemble gene selection	KNN [48]
Mishra et al.	*k*-Means, SNR	SVM, KNN (*k*-means + SNR + SVM/KNN) [49]
Huerta et al.	Fuzzy logic with BSS/WSS, *t*-test, Wilcoxon test	KNN [50]
Liu et al.	Entropy	Greedy, simulated annealing (SA) [51]
Liu et al.	Mutual information (MI), *t*-test, SNR independent component analysis (ICA), PCA, and random projections (RP)	Rotation forest [52]
Cho et al.	Derivative of kernel function	kernel Fisher discriminant analysis (KFDA) [21]
Sharma et al.	Gradient LDA	KNN [53]
Sun et al.	Dynamic relevance gene selection (DRGS)	SVM, KNN, predictive analysis of microarray (PAM) [54]
J. Shim et al.	Wilcoxon test	Supervised weighted kernel clustering (SWKC) SVM [55]
Hong et al.	Pearson correlation	One vs. rest SVM (OVR SVM with NB) [56]
Chen et al.	Multiple kernel support vector machine (MK-SVM-i)	Multiple kernel support vector machine (MK-SVM-ii) [57]

Table 15.1 Related Work—cont'd

Author	Feature Selection	Classifier Used
M. Akay	*F*-score	SVM [58]
Shen et al.	Suitability score	Suitability score [59]
Yu et al.	Ant colony optimization (ACO), marker gene selection using ACO (MMACO), SNR	SVM [60]
Sun et al.	Dynamic weighted FS (DWFS)	KNN, NB [61]
Maji et al.	Maximum relevance-maximum significance	SVM, KNN [62]
Zhang et al.	Wavelet packet transforms and neighborhood rough set (WPT+NRS)	SVM [63]
Abeel et al.	Ensemble SVM-RFE	SVM [64]
Berrar et al.		PNN [65]
Guo et al.	RFE and SVM-RFE	ANN [66]
González et al.	Multivariate joint entropy guided by simulated annealing	SVM [67]
González-Navarro	MI using bootstrap	SVM, NB, KNN, LR [68]
Cai et al.	MI	SVM [69]
Wang et al.	Hybrid Huberized support vector machine (HHSVM)	SVM [70]
Bu et al.	PCA, genetic algorithm, and the floating backward search method	SVM [71]
Hong et al.	Gene boosting	SVM [72]
Hewett et al.	Boosting-based ranking algorithm (MDR)	SVM [73]
Yu et al.	Enseble technique	SVM [74]
Osareh et al.	ReliefF, correlation-based filter selection (CFS), MRMR, and general signal-to-noise ratio (GSNR), fast correlation-based filter (FCBF)	Decision tree, root based ensemble [75]
Hengpraprohm	SNR	GA-based classier [76]
Sejja et al.	SNR	SVM [77]
Kim et al.	Information gain	GA-ANN [78]

SVM) are used for carrying out the classification of samples into cancerous or noncancerous classes for leukemia, and ovarian and breast cancer data sets.

15.3 METHODOLOGY USED

15.3.1 FEATURE SELECTION METHODOLOGY

In this section, different types of FS methods are presented. In contrast to other dimensionality reduction techniques based on the concepts such as projection or compression, the FS method does not alter the data set, it only selects the subset of data from the original data set, based on certain criteria.

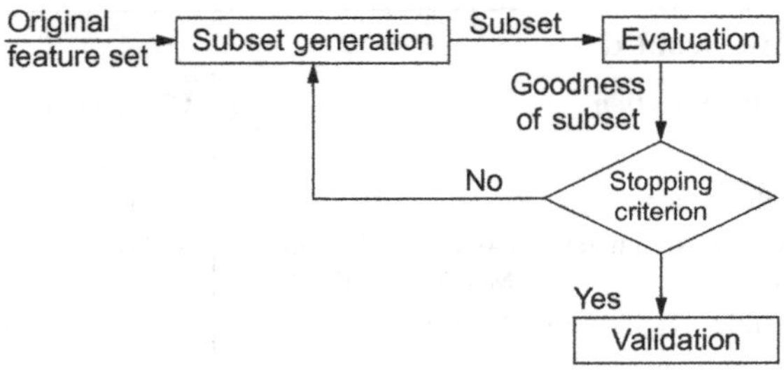

FIGURE 15.1

Key steps for feature selection/extraction.

The main objective of this review is to emphasize the benefits that FS methods provide in microarray analysis. Therefore, various FS methods are discussed with different classifiers. The main drawback of the FS method is that it does not interact with the classifier [80]. The sequence of steps followed in the FS process are shown in Fig. 15.1.

The following subsections highlight the working principle of the respective FS technique.

15.3.1.1 t-Statistic

The *t*-test is a univariate criterion, which is widely used in a filter method and is applied separately on each feature to show that there is no interaction between the features. Selecting features using "*t*-test" is to reduce the dimension of the data by finding a small set of important features that can obtain better classification performance. It is computed using Eq. (1).

$$TS(i) = \frac{\bar{X}_{i1} - \bar{X}_{i2}}{s_{X_1X_2}\sqrt{\frac{1}{n_1} + \frac{1}{n_2}}} \tag{1}$$

$$s^2_{X_1X_2} = \frac{(n_1 - 1)s^2_{X_{i1}} + (n_2 - 1)s^2_{X_{i2}}}{n_1 + n_2 - 2} \tag{2}$$

where $s_{X_1X_2}$ is an estimator of the common standard deviation of the two samples, and is calculated using Eq. (2), $\bar{X}_{ik}$ represents the *mean* of feature i of class $k \in \{1, 2\}$, and s is a standard deviation.

15.3.1.2 F-test/ANOVA/(BSS/WSS)

The analysis of variance (ANOVA) is used to compare the "multiple means" values of the data set, and visualize whether there exists any significant difference between multiple sample means. The *F*-statistic determines whether the variation between sample means is significant or not. The statistic for ANOVA is called the *F*-statistic, which is obtained from the *F*-test and can be calculated based on the following steps:

1. The variation between the group is calculated as

$$Between\ sum\ of\ squares\ (BSS) = n_1(\bar{X}_1 - \bar{X})^2 + n_2(\bar{X}_2 - \bar{X})^2 \tag{3}$$

$$Between\ mean\ squares\ (BMS) = BSS/df \tag{4}$$

2. The variation within the groups is calculated as:

$$\textit{Within sum of squares}(WSS) = (n_1 - 1)\sigma_1^2 + (n_2 - 1)\sigma_2^2 \quad (5)$$

$$\textit{Within mean squares}(WMS) = WSS/df_w \quad (6)$$

where df is the degree of freedom $df_w = (N - k)$; σ the standard deviation; N the number of samples; k the number of groups; and n_k is the number of samples in group k.

3. F-test statistic is calculated as

$$F = BMS/WMS \quad (7)$$

4. Finally, F-test value (F) is obtained.

15.3.1.3 Wilcoxon rank sum

"Wilcoxon signed rank test" is a nonparametric statistical test for testing the hypothesis based on the median values [38,81]. The hypotheses are as follows:

- Null hypothesis (H_0): the median value of the population of a feature is same, ie, $m_0 = m_1$.
- Alternate hypothesis (H_1): the median value of the population of a feature are not same, ie, $m_0 \neq m_1$.

Therefore, while selecting the important features, the null hypothesis is rejected. This implies that, there should be a significant difference between their median value, thus the alternate hypothesis is accepted. The Wilcoxon rank sum can be computed using the following equation:

$$p(g) = \sum_{i \in N_0} \sum_{j \in N_1} I\left(\left(X_j^{(g)} - X_i^{(g)}\right) \leq 0\right) \quad (8)$$

where $I = 1$, when the logical expression is true, otherwise it is 0. $X_i^{(g)}$ represents the expression value of sample i in the gene g, number of samples in different class are denoted by N_0 and N_1, and $p(g)$ represents the measurement of the expression difference of one gene in two classes. Owing that the value reaches 0 or the maximum "$N_0 \times N_1$," indicating that the corresponding gene is more important for classification. The weight of each gene is computed using Eq. (9).

$$q(g) = \max\left(s(g), N_0 \times N_1 - p(g)\right) \quad (9)$$

The high value of weight $q(g)$ signifies the most significant gene.

15.3.1.4 χ^2-test

The χ^2-test is used to test the independence between two events. It is used in FS, by measuring the occurrence of a specific term in a specific class [82]. The ranking of each term is found using Eq. (10).

$$\chi^2 = \sum_{i=1}^{n} \frac{(O_i - E_i)^2}{E_i} \quad (10)$$

The high value of χ^2 indicates the rejection of the null hypothesis, and thus these features are of very good significance; thus implying that the occurrence of the "term" and "class" are dependent.

15.3.1.5 Signal-to-noise ratio

SNR measures the relative usefulness of the feature by ranking the features [8], and is computed using Eq. (11).

$$SNR_i = \frac{|\mu_1(i) - \mu_2(i)|}{\sigma_1(i) - \sigma_2(i)} \tag{11}$$

where the saliency metric of the ith feature is represented by SNR_i, the averages of the ith feature in class 1 and class 2 are denoted by $\mu_1(i)$ and $\mu_2(i)$, and the standard deviation values of the ith feature in class 1 and class 2 are denoted by $\sigma_1(i)$ and $\sigma_2(i)$, respectively.

15.3.1.6 Information gain

IG is the expected reduction in entropy caused by partitioning the examples according to a given attribute [83]. Let X be the set of data samples with feature set A. X_v is the subset with $A = v$, and Value (A) is the set of all possible value of A, then IG is calculated as

$$IG(X, A) = Entropy(X) - \sum_{v \in Values(A)} \frac{|X_v|}{|X|} Entropy(X_v) \tag{12}$$

where $|X|$ is the cardinality of data samples X.

15.3.1.7 Fisher score

The main idea behind using Fisher score as a FS method is to select the subset of features, such that the distances between the data points in different classes are as large as possible, and the distances between data points in same classes are as small as possible. Consider μ_k^j and σ_k^j to be the mean and standard deviation of the kth class corresponding to the jth feature. The mean and the standard deviation of the whole data set corresponding to the jth feature can be denoted as μ^j and σ^j, respectively. Let c denote the total number of classes and n_k the number of samples in kth class. Then the Fisher score $F(x^j)$ of the jth feature is calculated as

$$F(x^j) = \frac{\sum_{k=1}^{c} n_k \left(\mu_k^j - \mu^j\right)^2}{(\sigma^j)^2} \tag{13}$$

where $(\sigma^j)^2 = \sum_{k=1}^{c} n_k \left(\sigma_k^j\right)^2$. The feature, which has a high Fisher score value, is considered a top-ranked feature [84].

15.3.1.8 Gini index

The Gini index is a measure of statistical dispersion intended to represent the classes of a data set. Suppose that X is a set of s samples, and that these samples consist of k different classes $(C_i, i = 1, \ldots, k)$, then based on the differences of classes, the set "X" is subdivided into k subsets as $(X_i, i = 1, \ldots, k)$. Suppose that X_i is a sample set that belongs to class C_i, and that x_i is the sample number of sets X_i; then, Gini index of set X is represented as

$$Gini(X) = 1 - \sum_{i=1}^{k} P_i^2 \tag{14}$$

where P_i is the probability that a sample belongs to C_i. If $Gini(X)$'s minimum is 0, that is, all of the members in the set belong to the same class, then it implies that maximum useful information can be obtained. When all the samples in the set are equally distributed for each class, then $Gini(S)$ is the maximum; this denotes that the minimum useful information can be obtained [85].

15.3.2 CLASSIFICATION METHODOLOGIES

From the literature review, it is observed that various supervised learning methodologies are applied in the classification of the microarray data set; out of which, some classifiers are quite frequently used. In this section, an overview of these classifiers is presented.

15.3.2.1 Logistic regression classifier

LR is a parametric form for the distribution $P(Y|X)$ where Y is a discrete value and $X = \{x_1, \ldots, x_n\}$ is a vector containing discrete or continuous values [86]. The parametric model of LR can be written as

$$P(Y=1|X) = \frac{1}{1+\exp\left(w_0 + \sum_{i=1}^{n} w_i X_i\right)} \tag{15}$$

and

$$P(Y=0|X) = \frac{\exp\left(w_0 + \sum_{i=1}^{n} w_i X_i\right)}{1+\exp\left(w_0 + \sum_{i=1}^{n} w_i X_i\right)} \tag{16}$$

The parameter W of the LR is chosen by maximizing the conditional data likelihood. It is the probability of the observed Y values in the training data. The constraint can be written as

$$W \leftarrow \arg\max_{W} \sum_{l} \ln P(Y^l|X^l, W) \tag{17}$$

15.3.2.2 Naive Bayes classifier

The NB classification algorithm relies on the Bayesian rule, with an assumption that the attributes $X_1, \ldots, X_n$ are all conditionally independent of one another for a given decision Y. The outcome of this assumption dramatically simplifies the representation of $P(X|Y)$, and the problem of estimating it from the training data [86].

Bayesian statistics, based on Bayes's theorem with some strong independent assumptions, is used in applying a probabilistic classifier, referred to as Bayes classifier. In NB classifier, the presence (or absence) of a particular feature of a class has no relevance to the presence (or absence) of any other feature.

NB classifier can be trained very efficiently in a supervised learning mode, depending on the precision of the probability model. It is observed that the method of maximum likelihood is used in estimating the parameters of the NB model. This implies that one can work with Bayes's model without giving much importance to either Bayesian probability or Bayesian methods.

It is advantageous to use NB classifier, as it uses a small amount of training data to estimate the parameters (such as means and variances of the variables) that are necessary for classification. The variance of the variables for each class needs to be determined but not the entire covariance matrix, as independent variables are assumed.

15.3.2.3 Artificial neural network

The ANN is a network of simulated neurons. It is inspired by the examination of the central nervous system. Warren in 1943 created a computational model for neural networks based on mathematical formulation and algorithms [87].

The ANN is a nonlinear data modeling tool that is usually used to model complex relationships between inputs and outputs, and to find patterns in data. This section gives a brief description of the basic structure and working of ANN technique applied for predicting the organizational performance. In general, a neuron in an ANN is:

A node having some activation function (f) that maps the input vector (X) to the output vector (Y). The neurons are connected with synapses (a signaling element) called weight vector (W). ANN architecture utilizes its computational features, which can be well applied for prediction of the outcome involved in the analysis.

The back propagation neural network (BPNN) is one of the most widely applied neural networks. It mainly involves the feed-forward network and the back propagation learning, and uses the iterative gradient algorithm to minimize the mean square error between the actual output of a multilayer feed-forward perceptron and the desired output. The BPNN can obtain the activation value by feed-forward step, and adjusts the weights, and "biases" according to the difference between the desired and actual network outputs by using the back propagation step. The execution of these two steps terminate when the network converges [88,89]. In this study, the sigmoid function is used as the activation function (f) in both the hidden and the output layer. Fig. 15.2 shows the typical architecture of a BPNN model.

15.3.2.4 Radial basis function network

The RBFN was first formulated by Broomhead and David [90] and was popularized by Moody and Darken [91]. A RBFN consists of three layers, namely the input layer, the hidden layer, and the output layer.

- Input layer: transmits the input vector to each unit in the hidden layer.
- Hidden layer: maps the input space into nonlinear space using Gaussian function. The transformation from input space to hidden space is nonlinear.
- Transformation from hidden unit space to output space is linear.

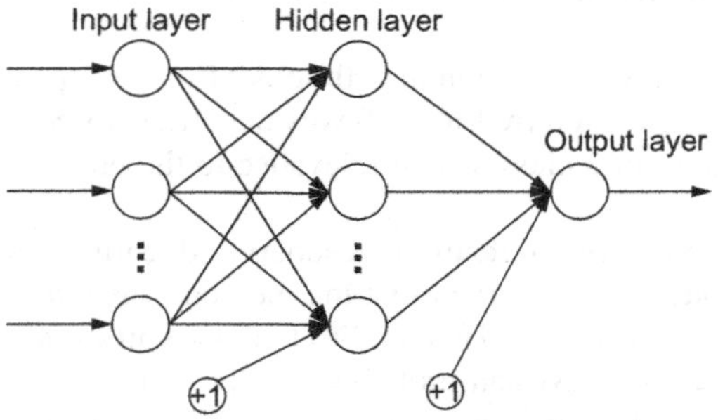

FIGURE 15.2

A typical BPNN.

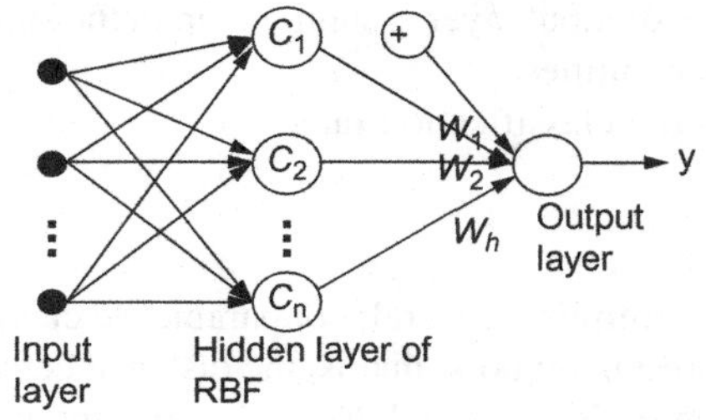

FIGURE 15.3

RBF network.

The parameters of RBFN, that is to say, centers and weight are trained using different techniques like pseudoinverse, gradient descent, and hybrid learning. In this study, hybrid learning has been used for updating the center and weights. The center is updated by applying the *k*-means algorithm, and weight is updated using the gradient descent learning method. Fig. 15.3 shows the architecture of a RBFN.

15.3.2.5 Probabilistic neural network

A PNN is a four-layered network (as shown in Fig. 15.4), consists of input, pattern, summation, and output layer that can map any input pattern to any number of classifications.

- First, the distance between input vector to training vectors is computed in the input layer.
- The second layer transforms the input space into nonlinear space using Gaussian function, and the center is determined from the training data. The Gaussian function is determined as using Eq. (18).

$$g(x) = \frac{1}{\sqrt{2\pi\sigma^2}} \sum_{k=1}^{n} \exp\left(\frac{-(x-x_k)^2}{2\sigma^2}\right) \tag{18}$$

where n, σ, x, x_k represent the number of samples from a class, smoothing parameter, testing input, and kth sample, respectively.

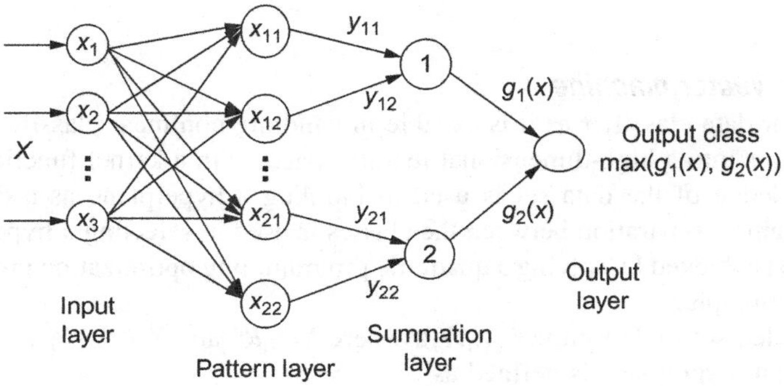

FIGURE 15.4

Basic structure of PNN.

- The contribution of each class of input layer is summed up in the summation layer, to produce a net output that is a vector of probabilities.
- The output layer determines the classification rate.

15.3.2.6 K-nearest neighbor

KNN is one of the methods for performing general, nonparametric classification. In KNN, initially the distance is measured for the nearest neighbors; that is, the distance between the test sample and all the remaining samples in the training set is computed. Next, the concept of simple majority vote is used to assign a label to a test sample over the "K" nearest neighbors.

The step-by-step working of the KNN algorithm is described in Algorithm 1.

ALGORITHM 1 *K*-NEAREST NEIGHBOR

Input: Let $D = \{(x_1, c_1), (x_2, c_2), \ldots, (x_n, c_n)\}$ be a set of n-labeled samples and x be a new instance to be classified.

Output: Classification result of new instance.

Begin

— For each labeled instance (x_i, c_i) the Euclidean distance $d(x_i, x)$ between x_i and x, where $i = 1, 2, \ldots, n$ is calculated.

— Sort $d(x_i, x)$ from lowest to highest.

— Select the K-nearest neighbor to x: D_x^K, where $K \in [1, n]$.

— Assign x to the most frequent class in the set of D_x^K.

If *(a tie occurs)* ***then***

— Sum of the distances of the neighbors in each class is computed.

If *(no tie occurs)* ***then***

— Move x into "minimum sum" class

else

— Move x into last "minimum sum" class.

endif

else

— Move x into majority class.

endif

End

15.3.2.7 Support vector machine

A SVM is a superior data classifier as it is capable in handling nonlinear classification problems by mapping input vectors into a high-dimensional feature space, with a kernel function [92].

The prior knowledge of the data set is used in building a hyperplane as a decision boundary. The maximum margin of separation between the classes is used in selecting a hyperplane. This maximization can be best achieved by solving a quadratic programming optimization problem based on the risk minimization principle.

For a given labeled set of M samples (X_i, Y_i), where $X_i \in R^d$ and $Y_i \in \{-1, +1\}$ is the associated label, the discriminant hyperplane is defined as

$$f(X) = \sum_{i=1}^{N} Y_i \alpha_i K(X, X_i) + b \qquad (19)$$

where $K(X,X_i)$ is a kernel function that maps the data set into different data space. The sign of $f(X)$ determines the membership of X. Construction of an optimal hyperplane is equivalent to find all non-zero α_i (support vectors) and a bias b. These parameters can be calculated by solving the following optimization problem:

$$\begin{aligned} &\min_{w,b,\xi} \; w^T w + C\sum_{i=1}^{N} \xi_i \\ &\text{s.t.} \;\; y_i\left(w^T \phi(x_i + b)\right) \geq 1 - \xi_i, \xi_i \geq 0 \end{aligned} \tag{20}$$

where ξ is the slack variable, $C\,(\geq 0)$ is the penalty parameter of the error term, and ϕ is the kernel function.

15.4 PERFORMANCE EVALUATION PARAMETERS

This section describes the performance parameters used for classification [93]. Table 15.2 shows the classification matrix, from which the values and performance parameters can be determined (Table 15.3).

Table 15.2 Classification Matrix

	No	Yes
No	True negative (TN)	False positive (FP)
Yes	False negative (FN)	True positive (TP)

Table 15.3 Performance Parameters

Performance Parameters	Description
$Precision = \frac{TP}{FP+TP}$	The degree to which the repeated measurements under unchanged conditions show the same results
$Precision = \frac{TP}{FN+TP}$	Indicates the number of the relevant items that are to *be identified*
$F-Measure = \frac{2 \times Precision \times Recall}{Precision + Recall}$	Combines the "precision" and "recall" numeric values to give a single score, which *is defined* as the harmonic mean of the precision and recall
$Specificity = \frac{TN}{FP+TN}$	Focuses on how *effectively* a classifier identifies negative labels
$Accuracy = \frac{TP+TN}{FP+FN+TP+TN}$	Measures the percentage of inputs in the test set that the classifier correctly labeled
Receive operating characteristic (ROC) curve	A graphical plot that illustrates the performance of a binary classifier system as its discrimination threshold is varied. It investigates and employs the relationship between "true positive rate (sensitivity)" and "false positive rate (1 − *specificity*)" of a classifier

15.5 EMPIRICAL ANALYSIS OF EXISTING TECHNIQUES

The presence of a huge number of insignificant and irrelevant features degrades the quality of analysis of a disease like "cancer." To enhance the quality, it is very essential to analyze the data set in proper perspective. This section presents the proposed approach for classification of microarray data, which consists of various phases:

- Emphasis on preprocessing the input data using various methods such as missing data imputation and normalization.
- FS is carried out using various methods like t-test, F-test, Wilcoxon test, SNR, χ^2-test, IG, Gini index, and Fisher score.
- Classification is performed using different classifiers like LR, NB, KNN, ANN, RBFN, PNN, and SVM already available in the literature.

The graphical representation of the proposed approach is depicted in Fig. 15.5.

The following steps give a brief description of the proposed approach.

1. Data collection

   The data set for classification analysis, which acts as requisite input to the models, is obtained from Kent Ridge Biomedical Data Set Repository [1].
2. Missing data imputation and normalization of data set

   Missing data of a feature (gene) of microarray data are imputed by using the *mean* value of the respective feature. Input feature values are normalized over the range [0, 1] using min-max normalization technique [94]. Let X_i be the ith feature of the data set X, and x is an element of the X_i. The normalization of the x can be calculated as

$$Normalized(x) = \frac{x - \min(X_i)}{\max(X_i) - \min(X_i)} \tag{21}$$

   where min(X_i) and max(X_i) are the minimum and maximum value for the dataset X_i, respectively. If max(X_i) is equal to min(X_i), then $Normalized(x)$ is set to 0.5.
3. FS of data set

   Different statistics methods have been applied to select the features having high relevance value and hence the curse of dimensionality issue has been reduced.
4. Division of data set

   The data set is divided into two categories such as training set and testing set.
5. Build classifier

   Different classifiers have been built to classify the microarray data set.
6. Test the model

   Model is tested using the testing data set and then the performance of the classifier is compared with various performance measuring criterion using the "10-fold cross validation (CV)" technique.

15.5.1 RESULTS AND INTERPRETATION

In this section, the obtained results are discussed for the proposed approach (Section 15.5). Three case studies, namely, leukemia [1], breast cancer [95], and ovarian cancer [96] microarray data sets are

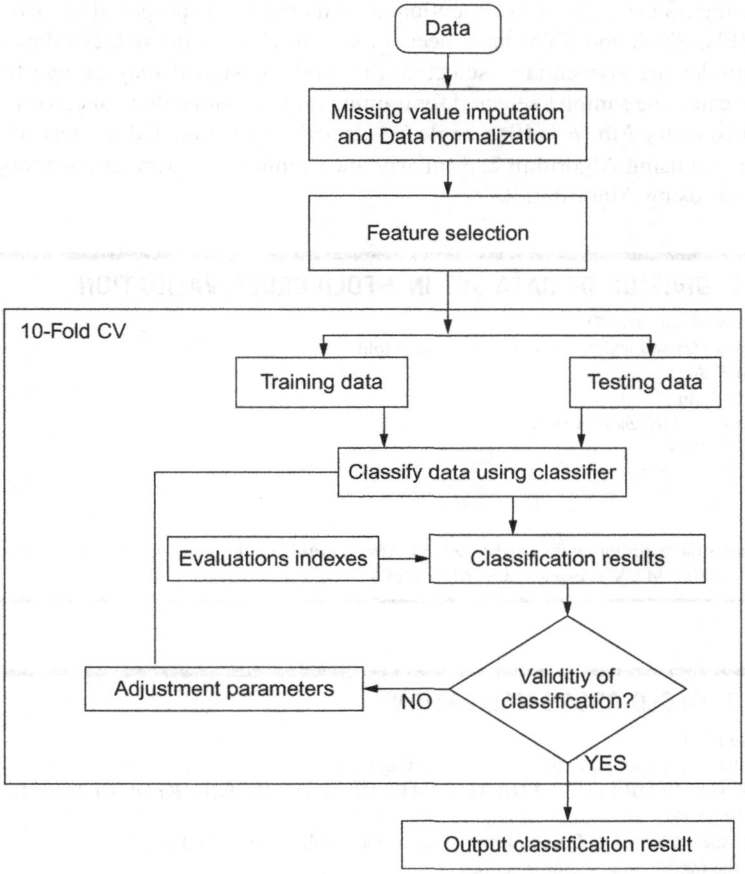

FIGURE 15.5

Stepwise procedure for microarray classification.

considered to find the classification accuracy. The classification performance is assessed using the "10-fold CV" technique for the data sets. 10-Fold CV technique provides more realistic assessment of classifiers, which generalizes significantly to unseen data.

Because the data set contains a very large number of features with irrelevant information, the FS method is applied to remove irrelevant information. FS aims at finding a feature subset that has the most discriminative information from the original feature set. This helps in selecting the features (genes) that have a high relevance score. The genes with a low relevance score are stripped off. Various statistical methods have been used to choose genes with high relevance score.

To achieve the objectives of FS (as listed in Section 15.1), the forward selection (incremental approach) method has been employed by selecting the features having high discriminative information (power) using various FS methods. Then, the top hundred features are selected in multiples of two (ie, 2, 4, …, 100).

After performing FS using the above-mentioned FS methods, the proposed classifiers like LR, NB, KNN, ANN, RBFN, PNN, and SVM have been applied to classify the reduced data set.

When the samples are sequentially selected, the model designed may be overtrained or undertrained. This is because the samples selected for training may contain either cancerous or noncancerous data. To avoid this, every Fth ($F = 10$) sample is selected for testing, and the rest of the samples are chosen as training set using Algorithm 2. Similarly, the training set is further partitioned into learning and validation sets, using Algorithm 2.

ALGORITHM 2 DIVISION OF DATA SET IN *F*-FOLD CROSS VALIDATION

Input: The array of data set (X).
Output: Training (D) and testing (T) data set for each fold.
for $i = 1$ to F **do**
  for $j = 1$ to F **do**
    $r = (i + (j - 1)N)\ mode\ size(X)$
    $T(i, j) = X(r)$
    $D(i, j) = X - T(i, j)$
  end for
end for

where i represents the partition set for the data set (X). After partitioning the data set, the model is selected by performing 10-fold CV. The 10-fold CV is discussed in Algorithm 3.

ALGORITHM 3 *F*-FOLD CROSS VALIDATION

1: ***for*** *i =1 to F* ***do***
2: Divide the data set into training set D_i and testing set T_i.
3: **WRITE THE “FOR LOOP” FOR THE VARYING PARAMETER (K) OF CLASSIFIER.**
4: **for** *j =1 to F* **do**
5: Divide the training set (D_i) into learning set (L_j) and validation set (V_j).
6: Train the model using learning set (L_j).
7: Validate the model using validation set (V_j).
8: Calculate accuracy of the model.
9: ***end for***
10: Calculate mean of accuracy of model corresponding to parameter (K_i).
11: **END THE “FOR LOOP" OF VARYING PARAMETER (*K*).**
12: Select K, corresponding to model having high accuracy (called K').
13: Train the model with training set (D_i) with K' and calculate accuracy.
14: Test the model with testing set (T_i) with K' and calculate accuracy.
15: ***end for***

The algorithm behaves differently with a different classifier; that is, for a different classifier the number of varying parameter (K) is different, for that a *for* loop is inserted in the algorithm at line number 3 and end the *for loop* at line number 11. For instance, suppose ANN is used as a classifier, for that the number of hidden nodes are varied. According to that, a *for loop* is placed at line number 3 (eg, for$K = 5:5:50$ do) and ended the for loop at line number 11 (*endfor*). Similarly, for each classifier a for loop is added, as and when required.

After performing "10-fold CV" on the data set, the predicted values of test data are collected in each of the fold and the classification matrix is designed. This analysis has been carried out on three microarray data sets by considering a varying number of features sets.

15.5.1.1 Different data sets used

To perform the classification of microarray data, three data sets, namely, leukemia, breast cancer, and ovarian cancer data sets from "Kent Ridge biomedical" repository are used [79]. The details of the data set in terms of two class problem (cancerous and noncancerous) are provided in the following subsections.

- Case study: Leukemia
  The leukemia data set consists of 7129 features (genes), categorized into two classes: acute lymphoblastic leukemia (ALL) and acute myeloid leukemia (AML). These two in combination have 72 samples. Out of 72, the data set contains 25 AML and 47 ALL samples [1].
- Case study: Breast cancer
  The breast cancer data set consists of 24,481 features (genes), categorized as "relapse" and "nonrelapse" classes, having 97 samples. Out of 97 samples, the data set contains 46 relapse and 51 nonrelapse samples [95].
- Case study: Ovarian cancer
  The ovarian cancer data set consists of 15,154 features (genes), categorized as "cancer" and "normal" classes, having 253 samples. Out of 253 samples, the data set contains 162 cancer and 91 normal samples [96].

The classifiers have been run sequentially on the varying size of feature sets [2, 100] using these microarray data sets.

15.5.1.2 Logistic regression

The results of LR have been validated using "10-fold CV" for three data sets and are tabulated in Table 15.4. The table gives the values of statistics such as the number of features (which obtained better accuracy for the respective FS method) and the accuracy obtained for the training and testing phases. In the detailed analysis, Table 15.4A-C gives the statistics for three data sets: leukemia, breast cancer, and ovarian cancer, respectively.

From the obtained result, it is observed that the LR classifier with *t*-test as a FS method achieves better accuracy of 98.61% in the testing phase for the leukemia data set for six features. Similarly, *t*-test obtained better accuracy of 80.14% and 98.81% for the breast cancer and ovarian data sets, respectively, when LR was applied. The values highlighted in bold indicate the highest accuracy obtained for the particular data set.

15.5.1.3 Naive Bayes

The classification results obtained using NB as a classifier with various FS methods are tabulated in Table 15.5. The table gives the values of statistics such as the number of features (which obtained better accuracy for the respective FS method) and the accuracy obtained for the training and testing phases. In the detailed analysis, Table 15.5A-C gives the statistics for three data sets: leukemia, breast cancer, and ovarian cancer, respectively.

Table 15.4 Result of LR With Various Feature Selection Methods

Feature Selection Methods	No. of Features	Train CV Acc. (%)	Test CV Acc. (%)
(A) Leukemia data set			
t-Test	**6**	**63.95**	**98.61**
F-test	46	81.10	97.22
Wilcoxon test	30	83.31	97.22
SNR	84	54.55	97.22
χ^2-test	48	77.64	97.22
Information gain	46	81.10	97.22
Gini index	2	65.36	72.22
Fisher score	52	74.40	97.22
(B) Breast cancer data set			
t-Test	**16**	**78.44**	**80.41**
F-test	10	81.78	79.38
Wilcoxon test	8	82.71	77.32
SNR	72	64.71	77.32
χ^2-test	82	55.00	76.29
Information gain	14	80.04	79.38
Gini index	2	77.07	76.29
Fisher score	8	82.71	77.32
(C) Ovarian data set			
t-Test	**36**	**99.52**	**98.81**
F-test	42	99.74	98.81
Wilcoxon test	48	100.00	98.81
SNR	90	99.70	97.63
χ^2-test	54	99.96	98.81
Information gain	8	97.64	98.42
Gini index	28	99.61	97.63
Fisher score	34	97.56	97.63

From the obtained result, it is clear that when *t*-test is used as a FS method, a set of six features are sufficient to achieve 98.71% of training accuracy and 98.61% of testing accuracy for the leukemia data set. Similarly, all the results can be analyzed for the breast cancer and ovarian cancer data sets. The values highlighted in bold indicate the high accuracy obtained for the particular data set.

15.5.1.4 Artificial neural network

In this study, a varying number of input nodes are considered based on the applied FS technique. In a hidden layer, selecting the number of hidden nodes is a challenging task. To overcome this issue, a varying number of hidden nodes in multiples of five in the range 5–50 are considered to design a network. Next, 10-fold CV is applied to validate the obtained results. After finding the optimal number of hidden nodes, their corresponding training and testing accuracies in each of the fold is obtained.

Table 15.5 Result of NB With Various Feature Selection Methods

Feature Selection Methods	No. of Features	Train CV Acc. (%)	Test CV Acc. (%)
(A) Leukemia data set			
t-Test	**6**	**98.71**	**98.61**
F-test	46	97.19	97.22
Wilcoxon test	30	97.19	97.22
SNR	84	97.19	97.22
χ^2-test	48	97.19	97.22
Information gain	46	97.19	97.22
Gini index	2	69.74	72.22
Fisher score	52	97.19	97.22
(B) Breast cancer data set			
t-Test	**16**	**81.03**	**80.41**
F-test	10	78.18	79.38
Wilcoxon test	8	78.56	77.32
SNR	72	78.51	77.32
χ^2-test	82	77.40	76.29
Information gain	14	78.28	79.38
Gini index	2	76.82	76.29
Fisher score	8	78.56	77.32
(C) Ovarian cancer data set			
t-Test	36	98.78	98.81
F-test	**42**	**98.82**	**98.81**
Wilcoxon test	48	98.82	98.81
SNR	90	97.65	97.63
χ^2-test	54	98.78	98.81
Information gain	40	98.78	98.81
Gini index	8	98.43	98.42
Fisher score	28	97.65	97.63

In the final model, the median of all the hidden nodes in each of the fold is considered as the optimal number of hidden nodes. The average of training and testing accuracy obtained in each of the fold are considered as the final output (accuracy) of the model.

The classification results obtained using ANN as a classifier with various FS methods is tabulated in Table 15.6. The table gives the values of statistics such as the number of features (which obtained better accuracy for the respective FS method) and the accuracy obtained for the training and testing phases. In the detailed analysis, Table 15.6A-C gives the statistics for three data sets: leukemia, breast cancer, and ovarian cancer, respectively.

From the obtained results, it is clear that when *t*-test is used as a FS method, a set of 40 features with five hidden nodes are sufficient enough to achieve 100% training accuracy and 97.22% testing accuracy for the leukemia data set. Similarly, the results can be analyzed for the other two data sets. The values highlighted in bold indicate the high accuracy obtained for the particular data set.

Table 15.6 Result of ANN With Various Feature Selection Methods

Feature Selection Methods	No. of Features	No. of Hidden Nodes	Train CV Acc. (%)	Test CV Acc. (%)
(A) Leukemia data set				
t-Test	**40**	**5**	**100.00**	**97.22**
F-test	24	5	97.18	97.22
Wilcoxon test	4	5	95.83	94.44
SNR	34	5	98.61	94.44
χ^2-test	46	5	100.00	95.83
Information gain	14	10	99.31	93.06
Gini index	4	5	95.83	94.44
Fisher score	46	5	100.00	95.83
(B) Breast cancer data set				
t-Test	**40**	**15**	**77.97**	**78.38**
F-test	12	15	80.42	74.23
Wilcoxon test	16	15	77.83	76.29
SNR	48	25	79.94	75.26
χ^2-test	52	15	77.95	75.26
Information gain	52	15	78.43	74.23
Gini index	4	10	77.90	77.32
Fisher score	4	10	77.34	76.29
(C) Ovarian cancer data set				
t-Test	44	5	99.40	100.00
F-test	**50**	**5**	**100.00**	**100.00**
Wilcoxon test	46	5	99.21	99.60
SNR	48	10	100.00	100.00
χ^2-test	50	5	99.80	100.00
Information gain	40	5	98.41	98.82
Gini index	35	10	96.56	97.87
Fisher score	42	5	95.84	97.23

15.5.1.5 Radial basis function network

There are different training schemes for updating the parameters such as the weights and center in a RBFN. In this analysis, the hybrid approach is applied to train the parameters of the network. To find the cluster centers, *k*-means clustering algorithm is used, and the weight vector is updated using a gradient descent learning algorithm. A varying number of clusters in the range from 2 to 10 are used to find the number of hidden nodes required to obtain the maximum testing accuracy. Ten-fold CV is used to validate the results. Table 15.7 shows the results of RBFN classifier using various FS methods for three data sets.

Table 15.7 gives the values of statistics such as the number of features (which obtained better accuracy for the respective FS method) and the accuracy obtained for the training and testing phases. In the detailed analysis Table 15.7A-C gives the statistics for three data sets: leukemia, breast cancer, and ovarian cancer, respectively.

Table 15.7 Result of RBFN With Various Feature Selection Methods

Feature Selection Methods	No. of Features	No. of Hidden Nodes (Clusters)	Train CV Acc. (%)	Test CV Acc. (%)
(A) Leukemia data set				
t-Test	**40**	**2**	**98.71**	**98.61**
F-test	10	5	95.07	93.06
Wilcoxon test	42	2	98.71	98.61
SNR	22	2	98.71	94.44
χ^2-test	38	2	97.43	97.22
Information gain	42	2	98.71	98.61
Gini index	2	2	88.52	90.28
Fisher score	20	2	96.62	95.83
(B) Breast cancer data set				
t-Test	**6**	**2**	**83.82**	**83.51**
F-test	42	4	79.10	77.32
Wilcoxon test	26	8	78.33	75.26
SNR	76	4	78.68	77.32
χ^2-test	2	2	72.89	71.13
Information gain	42	4	79.10	77.32
Gini index	2	2	72.89	71.13
Fisher score	16	2	79.96	81.44
(C) Ovarian cancer data set				
t-Test	14	8	98.30	98.42
F-test	50	7	98.78	98.42
Wilcoxon test	**38**	**6**	**98.82**	**98.42**
SNR	48	6	98.82	98.42
χ^2-test	46	6	98.78	98.42
Information gain	38	6	98.82	98.42
Gini index	2	2	93.29	93.28
Fisher score	42	6	98.78	98.02

From the obtained results, it is clear that when t-test is used as a FS method, a set of 40 features with two hidden nodes are sufficient enough to achieve 98.71% training accuracy and 98.61% testing accuracy for the leukemia data set. Similarly, the results can be analyzed for the other two data sets. The values highlighted in bold indicate the high accuracy obtained for the particular data set.

15.5.1.6 Probabilistic neural network

In PNN, 50% of cancerous and noncancerous classes are considered as input for hidden layers. Gaussian elimination is used as a hidden node function (Eq. 18). The summation layers sum the contribution of each class of input patterns and produce a net output that is a vector of probabilities. The output pattern having maximum summation value is classified into a respective class.

The results of PNN are evaluated by varying the value of the smoothing parameter "σ" in the range of $(0, 1]$ using "10-fold CV." The σ specifies the spread of the activation function.

The obtained results using different data sets are evaluated on various FS methods and are shown in Table 15.8. The table gives the values of statistics such as the number of features (which obtained better accuracy for the respective FS method) and accuracy obtained for the training and testing phases. In the detailed analysis, Table 15.8A-C gives the statistics for three data sets: leukemia, breast cancer, and ovarian cancer, respectively.

From the obtained results, it is clear that when *t*-test is used as a FS method, a set of 78 features with 0.2 σ value are sufficient enough to achieve 82.48% training accuracy and 84.72% testing accuracy for the leukemia data set. Similarly, the results can be analyzed for the other two data sets. The values highlighted in bold indicate the highest accuracy obtained for the particular data set.

From this result it is observed that, among all the FS methods using *t*-test, the classifier achieves better accuracy.

Table 15.8 Result of PNN With Various Feature Selection Methods

Feature Selection Methods	No. of Features	Best σ	Train CV Acc. (%)	Test CV Acc. (%)
(A) Leukemia data set				
t-Test	**78**	**0.2**	**82.48**	**84.72**
F-test	80	0.2	82.52	84.72
Wilcoxon test	42	0.1	80.98	81.94
SNR	26	0.3	77.59	80.56
χ^2-test	46	0.1	78.45	80.56
Information gain	36	0.1	78.69	79.17
Gini index	2	0.2	73.45	73.61
Fisher score	96	0.1	80.40	81.94
(B) Breast cancer data set				
t-Test	**6**	**0.3**	**71.79**	**73.20**
F-test	2	0.1	69.90	72.16
Wilcoxon test	22	0.4	66.64	69.07
SNR	82	0.4	66.97	68.04
χ^2-test	4	0.1	70.35	72.16
Information gain	14	0.1	67.96	68.04
Gini index	2	0.3	69.90	72.16
Fisher score	4	0.1	70.35	72.16
(C) Ovarian cancer data set				
t-Test	**34**	**0.3**	**98.82**	**98.81**
F-test	28	0.2	95.82	96.20
Wilcoxon test	34	0.6	98.82	98.81
SNR	100	0.1	97.08	96.84
χ^2-test	64	0.5	98.30	98.42
Information gain	32	0.1	98.39	98.42
Gini index	2	0.3	90.22	89.72
Fisher score	14	0.1	96.20	96.05

15.5.1.7 K-nearest neighbor

The KNN algorithm is used to classify the microarray data set to determine the category of the cell. Here, Euclidean distance is used to measure the distance between the training and testing samples. Table 15.9 shows the results obtained using the KNN classifier permuted with various FS methods using different microarray data sets. The results are evaluated by varying the number of nearest neighbor K in the range of $[1,n]$ with a step size of 2, where n is the number of samples in the training set. From the obtained result, it is inferred that out of 50 subsets of data set, the model with best accuracy is selected for choosing the optimal value of K. The table gives the values of statistics such as the number of features (which obtained better accuracy for the respective FS method) and accuracy obtained for the training and testing phases. In the detailed analysis, Table 15.9A-C gives the statistics for three data sets: leukemia, breast cancer, and ovarian cancer, respectively.

Table 15.9 Result of KNN With Various Feature Selection Methods

Feature Selection Methods	No. of Features	Value of "K"	Train CV Acc. (%)	Test CV Acc. (%)
(A) Leukemia data set				
t-Test	**26**	**1**	**97.19**	**97.22**
F-test	8	3	99.12	91.67
Wilcoxon test	88	3	98.21	97.22
SNR	18	1	95.95	90.28
χ^2-test	98	3	98.52	72.22
Information gain	48	1	97.19	97.22
Gini index	2	3	93.36	93.06
Fisher score	54	3	97.19	97.22
(B) Breast cancer dataset				
t-Test	**6**	**7**	**80.88**	**82.47**
F-test	48	5	82.33	78.35
Wilcoxon test	28	9	80.65	77.32
SNR	90	4	82.10	80.41
χ^2-test	2	10	74.58	71.13
Information gain	66	11	81.07	80.41
Gini index	2	10	74.58	71.13
Fisher score	82	7	80.44	77.32
(C) Ovarian cancer dataset				
t-Test	26	1	99.30	98.81
F-test	**50**	**1**	**99.39**	**98.42**
Wilcoxon test	48	1	99.39	98.42
SNR	48	1	99.39	98.42
χ^2-test	100	1	99.17	98.02
Information gain	36	1	99.35	98.42
Gini index	26	1	99.30	98.81
Fisher score	44	1	99.35	98.42

From the obtained results, it is clear that when t-test is used as a FS method, a set of 26 features with $K(=1)$ value are sufficient enough to achieve 97.19% training accuracy and 97.22% testing accuracy for the leukemia data set. Similarly, the results can be analyzed for the other two data sets. The values highlighted in bold indicate the highest accuracy obtained for the particular data set.

15.5.1.8 Support vector machine

In SVM classifier different kernel functions such as linear, polynomial, RBF (Gaussian), and tangent sigmoid are frequently used. In this analysis, RBF kernel function is used to map the input vector into high-dimensional space. The parameters of the kernel functions like *gamma*(γ) and the penalty parameter C are selected using the grid search in the range of $[2^{-5}, 2^5]$ and $[2^{-5}, 2^5]$, respectively. The results are evaluated by varying the value of kernel parameters in the specified range using "10-fold CV." Then the classifier is tested with different permutations of FS methods on three data sets. The obtained accuracy has been tabulated as shown in Table 15.10.

Table 15.10 Result of SVM With Various Feature Selection Methods

Feature Selection Methods	No. of Features	Best $\log_2\gamma$	Best $\log_2 C$	Train CV Acc. (%)	Test CV Acc. (%)
(A) Leukemia data set					
t-Test	14	5	3	99.69	100.00
F-test	32	5	0	97.99	95.83
Wilcoxon test	24	5	2	98.77	98.61
SNR	**68**	**5**	**−1**	**100.00**	**100.00**
χ^2-test	58	5	−1.5	99.69	98.61
Information gain	62	5	−1.5	100.00	98.61
Gini index	50	5	0	100.00	100.00
Fisher score	64	5	−1	100.00	98.61
(B) Breast cancer data set					
t-Test	**12**	**3.5**	**−4.5**	**83.16**	**84.54**
F-test	82	5	−2	81.67	76.29
Wilcoxon test	20	1	0	81.10	75.26
SNR	92	2.5	−2.5	82.81	74.23
χ^2-test	14	4	−5	83.40	81.44
Information gain	56	2.5	−1	81.33	76.29
Gini index	88	5	−2	81.55	77.32
Fisher score	12	3.5	−4.5	83.16	84.54
(C) Ovarian cancer data set					
t-Test	50	5	0	99.87	100.00
F-test	50	5	0	99.87	100.00
Wilcoxon test	**58**	**5**	**0**	**99.91**	**100.00**
SNR	44	5	−1	99.69	98.81
χ^2-test	68	5	−1	99.91	100.00
Information gain	40	5	−2	99.74	99.21
Gini index	2	3.5	2	94.99	95.26
Fisher score	40	5	−2	99.74	99.21

From Table 15.10, it is inferred that the number of features required corresponds to the optimal value of γ and C with their training and testing accuracy. The table gives the values of statistics such as the number of features (which obtained better accuracy for the respective FS method) and accuracy obtained for the training and testing phases. In the detailed analysis, Table 15.10A-C gives the statistics for three data sets: leukemia, breast cancer, and ovarian cancer, respectively.

From the obtained results, it is clear that when *t*-test is used as a FS method, a set of 14 features with $\gamma = 2^5, C = 2^3$ values are sufficient enough to achieve 99.69% training accuracy and 100.00% testing accuracy for the leukemia data set. Similarly, the results can be analyzed for the other two data sets. The values highlighted in bold indicate the highest accuracy obtained for the particular data set.

15.5.1.9 Comparative analysis

In this classification analysis, emphasis was placed on designing classifier models that can obtain better classification of microarray data set to categorize the cancer-causing genes into respective classes. A two-class classifier was considered, consisting of cancerous and noncancerous categories. Seven classifiers were designed with different permutations of eight FS methods. So, a comparative analysis was done to choose a better classifier among the set of designed classifiers, which involves a suitable FS method. From the obtained results, it can be inferred that among the various classifiers used in permutation with eight different FS methods, *t*-test obtained better accuracy in all the designed classifier models.

15.6 CONCLUSION

Any huge data set for a classification problem has drawbacks such as the curse of dimensionality, missing values of an attribute, presence of noise, and so forth. To overcome these pitfalls, various machine learning techniques were successfully applied for FS extraction of microarray data classification. In this chapter, an attempt was made to focus on the existing schemes available to select highly significant and relevant features in the data set for microarray in a succinct manner. Also, the work highlights the classification task carried out to classify the microarray data set using numerous machine learning techniques. The most widely used classifiers in combination with FS techniques were employed for classification. The obtained results were validated by the application of 10-fold CV. On keen observation, it is revealed that FS plays a significant role in the classification of microarray data.

The following lines highlight the future work intended to be carried out in microarray data classification. The rapid growth of diseases in the present day has led to a huge increase in the data size with respect to different categories of disease, causing enormous loss to human life. To detect a disease-causing factor of a particular class at an early stage within a large space of data is critically important. The complexity of classifying a particular disease into a particular class can be reduced by the use of the "big data" concept. This can be achieved through the use of techniques such as high performance computing, Hadoop, Spark, and so on, which minimizes the amount of time required for classifying a disease into a particular category of a class.

REFERENCES

[1] Golub TR, Slonim DK, Tamayo P, Huard C, Gaasenbeek M, Mesirov JP, et al. Molecular classification of cancer: class discovery and class prediction by gene expression monitoring. Science 1999;286(5439):531–7. doi: http://dx.doi.org/10.1126/science.286.5439.531. arXiv: http://www.sciencemag.org/content/286/5439/531.full.pdf. http://www.sciencemag.org/content/286/5439/531.abstract.

[2] Leung YF, Cavalieri D. Fundamentals of CDNA microarray data analysis. Trends Genet 2003;19(11):649–59.

[3] Flores M, Hsiao T, Chiu Y, Chuang E, Huang Y, Chen Y. Gene regulation, modulation, and their applications in gene expression data analysis. Adv Bioinformat 2013;11 [article ID 360678].

[4] Lee G, Rodriguez C, Madabhushi A. Investigating the efficacy of nonlinear dimensionality reduction schemes in classifying gene and protein expression studies. IEEE/ACM Trans Comput Biol Bioinformat 2008;5(3):368–84.

[5] Lee C-P, Leu Y. A novel hybrid feature selection method for microarray data analysis. Appl Soft Comput 2011;11(1):208–13.

[6] Peng Y, Li W, Liu Y. A hybrid approach for biomarker discovery from microarray gene expression data for cancer classification. Cancer Informat 2007;2:301–11.

[7] Ye J, Li T, Xiong T, Janardan R. Using uncorrelated discriminant analysis for tissue classification with gene expression data. IEEE/ACM Trans Comput Biol Bioinformat (TCBB) 2004;1(4):181–90.

[8] Osareh A, Shadgar B. Machine learning techniques to diagnose breast cancer. In: Proceedings of 5th international symposium on health informatics and bioinformatics (HIBIT). Antalya: IEEE; 2010. p. 114–20.

[9] Salem DA, Seoud A, Ahmed R, Ali HA. MGS-CM: a multiple scoring gene selection technique for cancer classification using microarrays. Int J Comput Appl 2011;36(6):30–7.

[10] Wang L, Chu F, Xie W. Accurate cancer classification using expressions of very few genes. IEEE/ACM Trans Comput Biol Bioinformatics (TCBB) 2007;4(1):40–53.

[11] Zhang J-G, Deng H-W. Gene selection for classification of microarray data based on the Bayes error. BMC Bioinformat 2007;8(1):370–8.

[12] Hang X. Cancer classification by sparse representation using microarray gene expression data. In: Proceedings of IEEE international conference on bioinformatics and biomeidcine workshops (BIBMW). Philadelphia, PA: IEEE; 2008. p. 174–7.

[13] Bharathi A, Natarajan A. Cancer classification of bioinformatics data using ANOVA. Int J Comput Theory Eng 2010;2(3):369–73.

[14] Tang K-l, Yao W-j, Li T-h, Li Y-x, Cao Z-W. Cancer classification from the gene expression profiles by discriminant Kernel-PLS. J Bioinformat Comput Biol 2010;8(Suppl. 01):147–60.

[15] Furey TS, Cristianini N, Duffy N, Bednarski DW, Schummer M, Haussler D. Support vector machine classification and validation of cancer tissue samples using microarray expression data. Bioinformatics 2000;16(10):906–14.

[16] Li L, Weinberg CR, Darden TA, Pedersen LG. Gene selection for sample classification based on gene expression data: study of sensitivity to choice of parameters of the GA/KNN method. Bioinformatics 2001;17(12):1131–42.

[17] Ben-Dor A, Bruhn L, Friedman N, Nachman I, Schummer M, Yakhini Z. Tissue classification with gene expression profiles. J Comput Biol 2004;7(3–4):559–83.

[18] Nguyen DV, Rocke DM. Tumor classification by partial least squares using microarray gene expression data. Bioinformatics 2002;18(1):39–50.

[19] Guyon I, Weston J, Barnhill S, Vapnik V. Gene selection for cancer classification using support vector machines. Mach Learn 2002;46(1–3):389–422.

[20] Mundra PA, Rajapakse JC. Gene and sample selection for cancer classification with support vectors based *t*-statistic. Neurocomputing 2010;73(13):2353–62.
[21] Cho J-H, Lee D, Park JH, Lee I-B. Gene selection and classification from microarray data using kernel machine. FEBS Lett 2004;571(1):93–8.
[22] Deb K, Raji Reddy A. Reliable classification of two-class cancer data using evolutionary algorithms. Biosystems 2003;72(1):111–29.
[23] Lee KE, Sha N, Dougherty ER, Vannucci M, Mallick BK. Gene selection: a Bayesian variable selection approach. Bioinformatics 2003;19(1):90–7.
[24] Lee Y, Lee C-K. Classification of multiple cancer types by multicategory support vector machines using gene expression data. Bioinformatics 2003;19(9):1132–9.
[25] Paul TK, Iba H. Selection of the most useful subset of genes for gene expression-based classification. In: Proceedings of congress on evolutionary computation (CEC), vol. 2. Portland, OR: IEEE; 2004. p. 2076–83.
[26] Huerta EB, Duval B, Hao J-K. A hybrid GA/SVM approach for gene selection and classification of microarray data. In: Giacobini M, editor. Applications of evolutionary computing. New York: Springer; 2006. p. 34–44.
[27] Liu JJ, Cutler G, Li W, Pan Z, Peng S, Hoey T, et al. Multiclass cancer classification and biomarker discovery using GA-based algorithms. Bioinformatics 2005;21(11):2691–7.
[28] Alba E, Garcia-Nieto J, Jourdan L, Talbi E-G. Gene selection in cancer classification using PSO/SVM and GA/SVM hybrid algorithms. In: IEEE congress on evolutionary computation. Singapore: IEEE; 2007. p. 284–90.
[29] Yu L, Liu H. Redundancy based feature selection for microarray data. In: Proceedings of the tenth ACM SIGKDD international conference on knowledge discovery and data mining. New York: ACM; 2004. p. 737–42.
[30] Ding C, Peng H. Minimum redundancy feature selection from microarray gene expression data. J Bioinformat Comput Biol 2005;3(02):185–205.
[31] Cho SB, Won H-H. Cancer classification using ensemble of neural networks with multiple significant gene subsets. Appl Intell 2007;26(3):243–50.
[32] Yang W-H, Dai D-Q, Yan H. Generalized discriminant analysis for tumor classification with gene expression data. In: 2006 international conference on machine learning and cybernetics. Dalian, China: IEEE; 2006. p. 4322–7.
[33] Wang Z, Palade V, Xu Y. Neuro-fuzzy ensemble approach for microarray cancer gene expression data analysis. In: International symposium on evolving fuzzy systems, 2006. Ambleside: IEEE; 2006. p. 241–6.
[34] Pang S, Havukkala I, Hu Y, Kasabov N. Classification consistency analysis for bootstrapping gene selection. Neural Comput Appl 2007;16(6):527–39.
[35] Li G-Z, Zeng X-Q, Yang JY, Yang MQ. Partial least squares based dimension reduction with gene selection for tumor classification. In: Proceedings of the 7th IEEE international conference on bioinformatics and bioengineering — BIBE 2007. Boston, MA: IEEE; 2007. p. 1439–44.
[36] Yue F, Wang K, Zuo W. Informative gene selection and tumor classification by null space LDA for microarray data. In: Yue F, et al., editors. Combinatorics, algorithms, probabilistic and experimental methodologies. New York: Springer; 2007. p. 435–46.
[37] Hernandez JCH, Duval B, Hao J-K. A genetic embedded approach for gene selection and classification of microarray data. In: Marchiori E, Moore JH, Rajapakse JC, editors. Proceedings of evolutionary computation, machine learning and data mining in bioinformatics. New York: Springer; 2007. p. 90–101.
[38] Li S, Wu X, Hu X. Gene selection using genetic algorithm and support vectors machines. Soft Comput 2008;12(7):693–8.

[39] Bonilla Huerta E, Duval B, Hao J-K. A hybrid LDA and genetic algorithm for gene selection and classification of microarray data. Neurocomputing 2010;73(13):2375–83.
[40] Wang Y, Tetko IV, Hall MA, Frank E, Facius A, Mayer KF, et al. Gene selection from microarray data for cancer classification — a machine learning approach. Comput Biol Chem 2005;29(1):37–46.
[41] Ruiz R, Riquelme JC, Aguilar-Ruiz JS. Incremental wrapper-based gene selection from microarray data for cancer classification. Pattern Recogn 2006;39(12):2383–92.
[42] Zhu J, Hastie T. Classification of gene microarrays by penalized logistic regression. Biostatistics 2004;5 (3):427–43.
[43] Huynh H, Kim J-J, Won Y. Classification study on DNA microarray with feedforward neural network trained by singular value decomposition. Int J BioSci BioTechnol 2009;1(1):17–24.
[44] Daz-Uriarte R, De Andres SA. Gene selection and classification of microarray data using random forest. BMC Bioinformat 2006;7(1):3.
[45] Yeh W-C, Yeh Y-M, Chiu C-W, Chung YY. A wrapper-based combined recursive orthogonal array and support vector machine for classification and feature selection. Mod Appl Sci 2013;8(1):11–24.
[46] Yu H, Gu G, Liu H, Shen J, Zhu C. A novel discrete particle swarm optimization algorithm for microarray data-based tumor marker gene selection. In: Proceedings of international conference on computer science and software engineering, vol. 1. Wuhan: IEEE; 2008. p. 1057–60.
[47] Chen Y, Zhao Y. A novel ensemble of classifiers for microarray data classification. Appl Soft Comput 2008;8(4):1664–9.
[48] Liu H, Liu L, Zhang H. Ensemble gene selection for cancer classification. Pattern Recogn 2010;43 (8):2763–72.
[49] Mishra D, Sahu B. Feature selection for cancer classification: a signal-to-noise ratio approach. Int J Sci Eng Res 2011;2(4):1–7.
[50] Huerta EB, Duval B, Hao J-K. Fuzzy logic for elimination of redundant information of microarray data. Genomics Proteomics Bioinformat 2008;6(2):61–73.
[51] Liu X, Krishnan A, Mondry A. An entropy-based gene selection method for cancer classification using microarray data. BMC Bioinformat 2005;6(1):76.
[52] Liu K-H, Huang D-S. Cancer classification using rotation forest. Comput Biol Med 2008;38(5):601–10.
[53] Sharma A, Paliwal KK. Cancer classification by gradient LDA technique using microarray gene expression data. Data Knowl Eng 2008;66(2):338–47.
[54] Sun X, Liu Y, Wei D, Xu M, Chen H, Han J. Selection of interdependent genes via dynamic relevance analysis for cancer diagnosis. J Biomed Inform 2012;46(2):252–8.
[55] Shim J, Sohn I, Kim S, Lee JW, Green PE, Hwang C. Selecting marker genes for cancer classification using supervised weighted kernel clustering and the support vector machine. Comput Stat Data Anal 2009;53 (5):1736–42.
[56] Hong J-H, Cho S-B. A probabilistic multi-class strategy of one-vs.-rest support vector machines for cancer classification. Neurocomputing 2008;71(16):3275–81.
[57] Chen Z, Li J, Wei L. A multiple kernel support vector machine scheme for feature selection and rule extraction from gene expression data of cancer tissue. Artif Intell Med 2007;41(2):161–75.
[58] Akay MF. Support vector machines combined with feature selection for breast cancer diagnosis. Expert Syst Appl 2009;36(2):3240–7.
[59] Shen Q, Shi W-M, Kong W. New gene selection method for multiclass tumor classification by class centroid. J Biomed Inform 2009;42(1):59–65.
[60] Yu H, Gu G, Liu H, Shen J, Zhao J. A modified ant colony optimization algorithm for tumor marker gene selection. Genomics Proteomics Bioinformat 2009;7(4):200–8.
[61] Sun X, Liu Y, Xu M, Chen H, Han J, Wang K. Feature selection using dynamic weights for classification. Knowl-Based Syst 2013;37:541–9.

[62] Maji P, Paul S. Rough set based maximum relevance-maximum significance criterion and gene selection from microarray data. Int J Approx Reason 2011;52(3):408–26.
[63] Zhang S-W, Huang D-S, Wang S-L. A method of tumor classification based on wavelet packet transforms and neighborhood rough set. Comput Biol Med 2010;40(4):430–7.
[64] Abeel T, Helleputte T, Van de Peer Y, Dupont P, Saeys Y. Robust biomarker identification for cancer diagnosis with ensemble feature selection methods. Bioinformatics 2010;26(3):392–8.
[65] Berrar DP, Downes CS, Dubitzky W. Multiclass cancer classification using gene expression profiling and probabilistic neural networks. In: Proceedings of the Pacific symposium on biocomputing, vol. 8. Singapore: World Scientific; 2002. p. 5–16.
[66] Guo P, Luo Y, Mai G, Zhang M, Wang G, Zhao M, et al. Gene expression profile based classification models of psoriasis. Genomics 2013;103(1):48–55.
[67] González F, Belanche LA. Feature selection for microarray gene expression data using simulated annealing guided by the multivariate joint entropy. Comput Syst 2014;18(2):275–93.
[68] González-Navarro FF, Belanche-Muñoz LA. Parsimonious selection of useful genes in microarray gene expression data. In: Yen N, Tran Q-N, editors. Software tools and algorithms for biological systems. New York: Springer; 2011. p. 45–55.
[69] Cai R, Hao Z, Yang X, Wen W. An efficient gene selection algorithm based on mutual information. Neurocomputing 2009;72(4):991–9.
[70] Wang L, Zhu J, Zou H. Hybrid huberized support vector machines for microarray classification and gene selection. Bioinformatics 2008;24(3):412–9.
[71] Bu H-L, Li G-Z, Zeng X-Q. Reducing error of tumor classification by using dimension reduction with feature selection. Lect Notes Oper Res 2007;7(124):232–41.
[72] Hong J-H, Cho S-B. Cancer classification with incremental gene selection based on DNA microarray data. In: IEEE symposium on computational intelligence in bioinformatics and computational biology — CIBCB'08. Sun Valley, ID: IEEE; 2008. p. 70–4.
[73] Hewett R, Kijsanayothin P. Tumor classification ranking from microarray data. BMC Genomics 2008;9 (Suppl. 2):S21.
[74] Yu H, Hong S, Yang X, Ni J, Dan Y, Qin B. Recognition of multiple imbalanced cancer types based on DNA microarray data using ensemble classifiers. BioMed Res Int 2013;2013:1–13.
[75] Osareh A, Shadgar B. An efficient ensemble learning method for gene microarray classification. BioMed Res Int 2013;doi: http://dx.doi.org/10.1155/2013/478410.
[76] Hengpraprohm S. GA-based classifier with SNR weighted features for cancer microarray data classification. Int J Sig Proces Syst 2013;1(1):29–33.
[77] KR S. Microarray data classification using support vector machine. Int J Biometr Bioinformat (IJBB) 2011;5(1):10.
[78] Kim K-J, Cho S-B. Prediction of colon cancer using an evolutionary neural network. Neurocomputing 2004;61:361–79.
[79] Li J, Liu H. Kent ridge bio-medical dataset. http://datam.i2r.a-star.edu.sg/datasets/krbd/index.html.
[80] Saeys Y, Inza I, Larrañaga P. A review of feature selection techniques in bioinformatics. Bioinformatics 2007;23(19):2507–17.
[81] Deng L, Pei J, Ma J, Lee DL. A rank sum test method for informative gene discovery. In: Proceedings of the tenth ACM SIGKDD international conference on knowledge discovery and data mining. Seattle: ACM; 2004. p. 410–9.
[82] Liu H, Setiono R. Chi2: feature selection and discretization of numeric attributes. In: 2012 IEEE 24th international conference on tools with artificial intelligence. Athens: IEEE Computer Society; 1995. p. 388–91.
[83] Ben-Bassat M. Pattern recognition and reduction of dimensionality. In: Krishnaiah P, Kanal L, editors. Handbook of statistics, vol. 2. Amsterdam: North Holland; 1982. p. 773–910.

[84] Gu Q, Li Z, Han J. Generalized fisher score for feature selection. Preprint arXiv:1202.3725.
[85] Raileanu LE, Stoffel K. Theoretical comparison between the Gini index and information gain criteria. Ann Math Artif Intell 2004;41(1):77–93.
[86] Mitchell TM. Machine learning. Burr Ridge, IL: McGraw Hill; 1997.
[87] Warren M, Walter P. A logical calculus of ideas immanent in nervous activity. Bull Math Biophys 1943;5(4):115–33.
[88] Hecht-Nielsen R. Theory of the backpropagation neural network. In: International joint conference on neural networks (IJCNN). Washington, DC: IEEE; 1989. p. 593–605.
[89] Hornik K, Stinchcombe M, White H. Multilayer feedforward networks are universal approximators. Neural Netw 1989;2(5):359–66.
[90] Broomhead DS, David L. Multivariable functional interpolation and adaptive networks. Complex Syst 1988;2(3):321–55.
[91] Moody J, Darken C. Fast learning in networks of locally-tunes processing units. Neural Comput 1989;1(2):281–94.
[92] Cortes C, Vapnik V. Support-vector networks. Mach Learn 1995;20(3):273–97.
[93] Catal C. Performance evaluation metrics for software fault prediction studies. Acta Polytech Hung 2012;9(4):193–206.
[94] Yogendra KJ, Santosh KB. Min-max normalization based data perturbation method for privacy protection. Int J Comput Commun Technol 2001;2(8):45–50.
[95] van't Veer LJ, Dai H, Van De Vijver MJ, He YD, Hart AA, Mao M, et al. Gene expression profiling predicts clinical outcome of breast cancer. Nature 2002;415(6871):530–6.
[96] Petricoin III EF, Ardekani AM, Hitt BA, Levine PJ, Fusaro VA, Steinberg SM, et al. Use of proteomic patterns in serum to identify ovarian cancer. Lancet 2002;359(9306):572–7.

CHAPTER

NEW DIRECTIONS IN DETERMINISTIC METABOLISM MODELING OF SHEEP 16

E. Black*,†, V. Rehbock†

Data Analysis Australia, Perth, WA, Australia Department of Mathematics and Statistics, Curtin University, Perth, WA, Australia†*

16.1 INTRODUCTION

Whole-body approaches to understanding and modeling animal growth and development are not commonly found in the agricultural literature. The task can seem overwhelmingly complex as there are many unanswered questions with regard to nature versus nurture, genetic predisposition, and so on. While shortcomings are inevitable, progress is not possible without some substantial baseline work. The aim of this research is to justify the effort of establishing whole-body models, and demonstrate that a modeling, optimization, and simulation approach to the understanding of the development of a single animal to maturity is possible. It opens up a promising new direction for livestock modeling where dynamic optimization can be applied to achieve a variety of objectives, using a generic sheep model as an example.

16.2 ADVANTAGES OF WHOLE-BODY METABOLISM MODELING

There have been many research studies involving sheep and livestock in general that investigate the effects of different factors on the biological and nutritional state of sheep. However, most of these studies deal with only one or two factors at a time and observe the effects of these factors in only a limited number of areas in the body. By definition, this kind of research leaves many unknowns. Whole-body metabolism modeling is a more comprehensive approach to tracking animal development. Expertise in the area of biochemistry that would allow such modeling has been available for some time. Relating to pig growth, a whole-body metabolism approach gives "fuller integration of present-day knowledge concerning growth mechanisms (than other approaches)" [1]. By integrating the underlying mechanisms of growth, it allows more complete understanding of the "important phenomena" of growth and ultimately more holistic predictions of responses in animals to a variety of factors.

As an example, while a certain type of feed may increase resistance to a certain parasite, there are also potential side effects. If a whole-body model is being used to initially test the hypothesis prior to field testing, the effects of the feed on the entire system can be investigated. If a potential side effect is identified, the experiment can be adjusted to test for this accordingly, leading to greater efficiency in field testing. Additionally, should field testing not be possible due to ethical considerations, a comprehensive metabolism model could give insight into certain outcomes that would otherwise not be possible. Another limitation of field testing is that once a sheep has been slaughtered and its components analyzed, it is clearly not able to resume further growth. A whole-body metabolism model gives the advantage of tracking the state of the sheep in continuous time, rather than at discrete intervals with an ever-decreasing sample pool.

A whole-body approach could also be used to test theories or anecdotal evidence as a base step prior to entering the field. If it is implemented into a software system, there is also the potential for new theories to be *established* using the whole-body model itself. With the advances in technology and computing power seen over the last few decades, iterative applications of inputs or controls on the model to develop new management strategies has become a reality. For example, in a scenario where the development of x kg of lean meat by y weeks of age is economically optimal, a whole-body computer model could be used to determine the feed regime or other control factors necessary to achieve this goal within specified constraints. The use of numerical techniques in solving such problems and potentially developing new approaches to livestock management provides a viable alternative in cases where an analytical approach may be too complex and time-consuming and a trial-and-error field test may be infeasible.

Enhancements in knowledge of the complex and interdependent aspects involved in energy expenditure and protein metabolism could be incorporated into a whole-body model, which could then be used to improve general animal management strategies and also to ascertain suitable genetic traits for particular environments (weather, economically viable feeds, resistance to local diseases or pests, etc.).

One such example is wool production in sheep. Wool is a major export industry in Australia worth over $2.5 billion per year (Australian Bureau of Statistics, Catalog 7503). Wool is predominantly protein and higher wool growth in sheep has been known to come at the cost of lower meat production and poor animal health. A mechanistic dynamic model of protein synthesis would help develop our understanding of the consequences of an increasing amount of protein being supplied to the skin for wool growth. The ultimate goal here would be to advise sheep breeders in how they might achieve optimal wool production while still maintaining healthy, fertile, and disease-resistant sheep.

16.3 REVIEW OF WORK TO DATE

Allometry is the study of how biological variables scale with changes in body size, and principles of basic allometry have been applied to disaggregate growth into body components as far back as the 1920s. Huxley [2] proposed the study of the relative importance of organs or chemical pools within an animal. Characterizing an animal's compartments as body protein, lipid (fat), water, and minerals (ash) was an alternative approach that grouped the organs or pools within an animal according to their chemical structure. This approach started appearing in the 1960s and 1970s, and Bastianelli and Sauvant [1] described the common conceptual framework of this approach: a feedback system, in which the body weight and composition of the animal informs the subsequent selection of feed. A component of the absorbed nutrients from the feed is a maintenance requirement (quantity of food of a given quality needed to maintain a constant body weight), and the remainder is deposited as either body lipids or protein, leading to animal growth. This framework is a reasonable approximation of the whole-body metabolism, but the nature of how these pools change and inform the change of other pools needs to be defined to complete the model.

Specific to sheep, simplistic models capturing both feed type and availability as well as body and product also appeared in the 1970s. Such environment-pasture-animal systems tracked pasture pools (seed, burrs, etc.), environmental conditions (eg, rainfall and temperature) as well as a basic representation of a sheep by its tissue and wool mass. Arnold et al. [3] examined a submodel of this system for sheep, concerned with the consumption of pasture and its use for maintenance, live weight gain, and wool production. This type of model assumes only minimal control over the feed intake of the sheep, with potential intake (relative to body weight) decreasing as the live weight increases. It is a reflection of the flock maintenance systems of the time, but is limited in its representation of experimental conditions. Including representation of how a sheep might select its own feed under different levels of pasture availability and other factors is clearly problematic. Assumptions are not only required for the diet as selected by the sheep, but also the digestibility of the feeds. Hence there is limited control over the inputs to the metabolic system. With a simplistic sheep model covering just tissue mass and wool mass, by definition the inputs need to also be simplistic. The dynamics of the model are based roughly around the relationships between the *digestible organic matter* input to the system and its effects on how close tissue and wool growth is to a predefined *maximum potential growth*, which may be dependent on the live weight of the animal or nitrogen content of the feed.

Across the 1980s and through the 1990s more sophisticated metabolism models started to emerge. It was known that differences in efficiency with which nutrients were metabolized could not be represented by simplistic models; it was dependent on the general metabolizability of the diet. The Agricultural Research Council [4] published equations for the metabolizability of different types of feed, but differences between these and the metabolizability of other feeds were still being reported in the literature, and models were limited by the availability of field research for the feed in question. Also, it was not abundantly clear *why* these differences in metabolic efficiency existed, and it became increasingly apparent that more sophisticated metabolism models were required to understand what was going on "behind the scenes." A telling example, described in Gill et al. [5] explains how there were contradictory results with regard to the impact of acetate utilization on the relationship between metabolic efficiency and crude fiber content that were reported in Armstrong and Blaxter [6] and Armstrong et al. [7], as compared to the results in Rook et al. [8] and Ørskov and Allen [9]. In attempting to reconcile this apparent discrepancy, MacRae and Lobley [10] pointed out the need to consider the glucogenic potential of the basal diet when predicting the efficiency with which acetate would be used, and in particular the amino acid supply to the tissues. Research investigating the effect of specific feed types is still ongoing, such as that of Rao and Kumar [11] with regard to general digestibility and meat traits and Sitzia et al. [12] with regard to milk production. These examples clearly demonstrate the benefit of a whole-body metabolite modeling approach, to ensure the full picture of metabolic function is being captured.

A compartmental model that simulates the metabolism of absorbed nutrients in a growing lamb was developed by Gill et al. [5]. Equations within the model were based on enzyme kinetics and the stoichiometry of the biochemical pathways involved. The model keeps track of the concentrations of different metabolites, and this information, along with parameters governing maximum rates of reactions, are the main components in the standard biochemical expressions for utilization or degradation rates of substrates (substances on which an enzyme acts; eg, glucose). Michaelis-Menton constants, coming from a standard and well-known approach to modeling enzyme kinetics as developed by Michaelis and Menton [13] are also used. These constants define the relationship between the current state and the proportion of the maximal i to j reaction velocity that will be achieved between pools at a given point in time. The general structure of these equations are described in Eq. (1), where U is the utilization rate of a substrate, s is the concentration of the substrate, V is the maximal velocity of the reaction, and K is the appropriate Michaelis-Menton constant.

$$U = V\frac{s}{K+s} = \frac{V}{1+(K/s)} \tag{1}$$

A conceptual interpretation of the Michaelis-Menton constant in this simple example is the concentration of the substrate at which the reaction velocity reaches half its maximum rate. However, there are more complex variations that take into account the common situation where utilization rates are dependent on the concentrations of multiple substrates, and here the conceptual interpretation is less straightforward. The maximal reaction velocity can also be a constant, or it can be expressed linearly with respect to substrate concentration. Gill et al. [5] model had mechanical representations of the whole-body metabolism. However, empirical relationships were used to define body fat and protein turnover. Generic expressions for body fat and protein synthesis based on biochemical knowledge would provide for a more flexible model.

Many publications relating to metabolism modeling and simulation of sheep, cows, and steers have come via the Department of Animal Science at the University of California Davis (UC Davis) and its collaborators, with similar structures and state variable definitions. Baldwin et al. [14] was a collaboration between Baldwin of UC Davis and representatives from the Animal and Grassland Research Institute in the United Kingdom, including Margaret Gill, the lead author of Gill et al. [5]. The research in Baldwin et al. [14] set up a mechanistic model for a lactating cow. It was described as a "first step in a (modeling) research programme directed toward quantitative and dynamic evaluation of current concepts, hypotheses, and data for probable adequacy as explanations of variations in partition of nutrients in lactating cows." The idea was to set up the structure and parameterize whole-animal models that could be used to evaluate a multitude of factors relating to nutrient utilization. The structure of the model was not dissimilar to that of Gill et al. [5]. Aside from the differences necessary due to the change of species and the requirement for specific representation of lactation, the notable difference between the two was the more explicit representation of rates of protein and body fat synthesis, as opposed to an empirical definition. To facilitate this, the protein pools were broken down into lean body protein, protein in viscera (internal organs), and protein in milk, rather than expressed as a total protein pool that is subsequently divided into protein types. This allowed for rates of reactions to be more specifically linked to hormonal levels, both anabolic and catabolic.

A model for growing lambs that was very similar to the lactating cow model of Baldwin et al. [14] was published in 1990 by Sainz and Wolff via the Ministry of Agriculture and Fisheries, New Zealand [15,16], and the outline of the model structure is presented in Fig. 1 of Sainz and Wolff [15,16]. The objectives of the Sainz and Wolff [15,16] research were

1. Simulation of lamb growth from 20 to 40 kg empty body weight (EBW) under varying nutritional conditions (EBW is the weight of the shorn animal, less the contents of the digestive tract, the bladder, and the fleece [17]).
2. Representation of major fundamental processes associated with growth and metabolism, aggregated to the minimal number of necessary pools.
3. Integration of current knowledge regarding biochemical transformations and metabolic regulation to the whole-animal level.

These objectives appeared to be reached, and the model was subsequently used in analyses relating to growth promotants by Sainz and Wolff themselves [15,16]. Model details are outlined further in Sainz and Wolff [15,16] and Smith [18]. The basic structure can be found in Fig. 1 of Sainz and Wolff [15,16]. State variables include circulating amino acids, glucose, acetate, and lipids, as well as separate protein pools for carcass (or lean body protein), viscera, other tissues (head, skin, etc.), and wool. Storage fat is also represented, along with an associated DNA pool for each protein pool (except wool) to govern limitations in genetic capabilities of protein growth. Other supplementary variables are also modeled, but for various reasons do not necessitate specific differential equations.

Following the publication of the Sainz and Wolff papers [15,16] there have been a number of published works in this field. Bowman et al. [19,20] developed a model of sheep on a more macro level, including elements such as stocking rates (numbers of livestock in a predefined area) and pasture availability. However, it did have more specific traits for wool, as opposed to just protein in wool, covering the industry-relevant clean wool characteristics of fiber diameter, staple length, staple strength, and vegetable matter level.

There have been a number of general reviews of existing models, many of which emphasize the need for a whole-body and mechanistic approach. These include Baldwin and Sainz's evaluation of performance and growth models based on feed intake and composition, coming out of UC Davis in 1995 [21]. Hanigan et al. [22] reviewed protein synthesis models in ruminants, concluding that a great deal of future effort is required to construct and parameterize models, and that tangible improvements at the animal level can be made. Kebreab et al. [23] takes it a step further for dairy cattle, integrating a number of models and implementing the result into a Fortran-based software. However, the specific focus is on dietary manipulation to reduce pollution from livestock. Also in 2004, McNamara of Washington State University emphasizes the advantages of mechanistic, biochemical, and dynamic models of metabolism in dairy cattle [24]. Model results are tested against observations and limitations, particularly with regard to accurate modeling of energy accumulation and energy use (most specifically in early lactation). McNamara's focus is leaning more toward research paving the way to adequate food supply for developing nations. Another publication from McNamara, this time in collaboration with Pettigrew [25], reviewed the existing mechanistic, deterministic, and dynamic models available for lactating sows.

Other examples of models published in the modern era include a more generic mammalian two-dimensional representation (mass and energy) [26,27] from New Zealand. While its structure is simplistic, it does attempt to model growth all the way from conception to maturity for mammals, and is described as having potential to be expanded to include details regarding body composition. Fox et al. [28] developed a cattle requirement model based on a combination of animal, environmental, and feed compositional information. It was a herd-level model that did not have the intricacies of an animal-level model, but did have the practical advantages of being able to represent diverse production situations and different physiological states (growth, lactation, and pregnancy). Moen and Boomer [29] from Cornell University published a model for annual energy metabolism rhythms in free-ranging mammals. While the animals were not livestock (white-tailed deer, black bears, and golden-mantled ground squirrels), it did raise the interesting issue of variation in metabolism needs according to season.

Upton [30] from the Royal Adelaide Hospital took an allometric approach to prepare organ weight and blood flow data for use in modeling the effect of drugs on the system of animals, such as sheep and pigs, in preclinical trials. The paper attempts to describe the relative components of a "standard sheep," which is then used to establish a simulated population. At the micro level, Sarnyai and Boros [31] modeled cellular energy metabolism and drug metabolism using systems biology. Their claim is that "(in order to) understand how the parts (genes, proteins, and metabolites) make up the whole organism, a systemic view is required, with genes and proteins seen more as parts of a highly interactive network with the potential to affect the network — and be affected by it — in many certain and sometimes unexpected ways, instead of as isolated entities entirely or largely determining cell function." Also at the micro level, Fleming et al. [32] looked at models for steady state metabolism for simple organisms in 2010. The work assumes time invariant reaction rates and concentration of metabolites to develop feasible reaction fluxes via constraint equations, and discusses the trade-off between imposing a multitude of physical laws and the ability to solve the resulting equations.

The Third International Symposium on Energy and Protein Metabolism and Nutrition was held in Parma, Italy, in September 2010. Proceedings of the symposium included a chapter on "Evaluation and modeling of feed value and requirements: ruminants." The proceedings contain papers from Tedeschi et al. [33] discussing the principal factors affecting the partial efficiency of the use of metabolizable energy, and from Cannas et al. [34] regarding the energy costs of maintenance of a herd. In the same proceedings, De Angelis [35] evaluates the protein and energy value of hay and wheat straw diets for lambs of four different breeds (Sarda, Appenninica, Bergamasca, and Leccese), and Oltjen et al. [36] reviews the integration of the UC Davis Sheep (UCDS), a mechanistic, dynamic model predicting lamb growth, with the small ruminant nutrition system, to predict dietary energy and protein values to input in the UCDS.

Whole-animal metabolism modeling for ruminants, and sheep in particular, is an ongoing research area. Existing models still lack flexibility. With respect to sheep, there has been a lack of published research on complex metabolism models since Sainz and Wolff's model from 1990. Sainz and Wolff's model remains the quintessential model, with mechanistic equations based on known biochemical processes, where parameters and inputs could potentially be manipulated to a multitude of conditions. However, the scope of the Sainz and Wolff model is limited to lamb growth from 20 to 40 kg, and has only very basic representation of wool. It was not known how well the model could be extended into steady state, whether issues exist relating to the representation of energy accumulation, as noted for dairy cattle by McNamara [24], or how feasible its implementation into software to assess various growth trajectories could be. Our work investigates these issues, and proposes a way forward toward an integrated whole-body sheep metabolism model that can be readily implemented in a programming environment.

16.4 OUTCOMES

Our work [18] demonstrated a feasible modeling, optimal control, and simulation approach to the understanding of the development of a single sheep to maturity. In the absence of any published refinements to the Sainz and Wolff [15,16] model since 1990, and given that previous attempts to implement the model into MISER3.3 [41] and perform optimal control computations were unsuccessful [37,38], this represents a useful step forward. With the targeted use of dynamic optimization tools, the work paves the way for further model enhancements in the future.

16.5 SUMMARY

A summary of our results [18] is given below.

- Identification of inconsistencies and errors in the presentation of rate values in the Sainz and Wolff [15,16] paper and correction thereof, where possible (eg, inconsistent rounding issues and the adjustment of incorrectly stated parameter values).

- Development of further aspects required to run the model simulation in a fully documented, reviewed, and repeatable manner, including definition of an EBW formula and the review and selection of appropriate initial conditions. This work included determining molecular weights for body proteins, wool protein, and storage fat, as well as the translation of wool protein mass into clean fleece weight and greasy fleece weight, aiding comparison of the model output to other published results.
- Identification of the sensitivities of the initial growth rates for circulating metabolites and hormonal controls with respect to the initial conditions.
- One of the more complex tasks was coding of the derivatives of the state dynamics and the objective functionals with respect to the states, system parameters, and controls (where relevant) such that errors were minimal and could reasonably be assumed to be due to fuzziness in MISER3.3's internal derivative estimates. These are needed to allow the use of gradient-based optimization tools embedded in the software. As a result, a workable optimal control and optimal parameter selection model was established.
- Replication of growth in the scope of the Sainz and Wolff [15,16] parameters (20–40 kg EBW). Extension of the time frame of the simulation and identification of limitations in the model post 40 kg.
- Use of literature results to determine a suitable feed intake structure, followed by the application of optimal parameter selections techniques to develop the model into a form that would adequately represent growth into steady state adulthood, from 2 to 3 years of age.
- Identification of several remaining shortcomings of the developed model along with suggestions for improvements (eg, definition of lactate utilization parameters and representation of growth with restricted feed intake).

16.6 FUTURE WORK

There are many potential directions for future work that are now possible due to the developments and results detailed in Smith [18]. The suggestions discussed below will require collaboration between mathematicians and researchers with biological, agricultural, and/or biochemical expertise.

With regard to the general circulation structure, as presented in Fig. 1 of Sainz and Wolff [15,16], it has been suggested that as wool growth requires energy, there should be a link between glucose and protein in wool. Similarly, including representation of the recycling of urea (from blood to the digestive system) may be necessary for a more complete model.

Initial investigations into the sensitivity of the model to lactate utilization parameters were conducted in Smith [18]. The aim of this was to simply demonstrate that the impact of the selection of these parameters on the model was not negligible, as Sainz and Wolff [15,16] had suggested. Therefore, the arbitrary selection of coefficients in the lactate dynamics may not be ideal for model accuracy. Further investigation of the effects of these coefficients on the model are needed. These were not the only parameters that appeared to have been crudely estimated. While Smith [18] investigated and adjusted a selection of parameters of the model, further consideration should be given to others. There is also the potential to allow for functions (of time, age, or other attributes of the sheep) to replace parameters that are currently assumed to be constant. An example to consider is the adaption of absorption parameters, such as for circulating lipids and acetate, to take into account the existing concentrations of these metabolites in circulating fluids.

As demonstrated in Smith [18], the model as it currently stands is limited in its ability to replicate sheep body response to periods of restricted feed intake. This is, in part, due to the simple nature of the existing DNA pool dynamics as they do not appear to respond appropriately to such conditions. There's evidence to suggest, as proposed by Wang et al. [39], that gene networks affecting fat deposition exist. However, the DNA pools in the model only relate to their respective protein pools. With regard to body degradation specifically, during certain simulations of the model very high concentrations of circulating metabolites were noted. This indicates that there are limitations in the dynamics of other state variables (not simply the DNA pools) as body degradation occurs. Conversely, the model is also limited with respect to periods of very high feed intake. The incorporation of biological mechanisms preventing sheep from eating excessively is a potential area for future research.

The definition of energy expenditure is somewhat vague in the existing model. The impact of varying levels of animal behavior is not considered. Animal behavior is, at least in part, an environmental factor. Sheep in a pen, for example, may require less feed for maintenance than those in a field or paddock. In addition, the energy requirements for thermoregulation of the body are also not explicitly considered so far.

The model is quite simplistic in the way it represents wool growth. It is only concerned with the number of moles of protein in the pool (there should perhaps be a link from circulating glucose as well), and relates directly to the number of moles of protein in the other tissues' protein pool (including, but not limited to, skin). It has been demonstrated that other attributes of the skin (see Wodzicka [40]) can influence wool growth, and it is also likely to be influenced by environmental conditions and aging. Also, other important attributes of wool, such as fiber quality, may be able to be linked with other attributes of the sheep.

As a final point, there is potential to use the model developed as a component in a sheep flock growth model, taking into account elements such as stocking rates and the types of feed available (see Bowman et al. [19,20]). This could be extended further to include other environmental conditions such as weather. In addition to the environmental factors, there are further factors at play not yet considered explicitly in this model. These include breed and genetic predispositions, disease and pests, and pregnancy and lactation.

REFERENCES

[1] Bastianelli D, Sauvant D. Modeling the mechanisms of pig growth. Livest Prod Sci 1997;51:97–107.

[2] Huxley JS. Constant differential growth ratios and their significance. Nature 1924;114:895–6.

[3] Arnold GW, Campbell NA, Galbraith KA. Mathematical relationships and computer routines for a model of food intake liveweight change and wool production in grazing sheep. Agric Syst 1977;2:209–26.

[4] Agricultural Research Council. The nutrient requirements of ruminant livestock. Farnham Royal: s.l.:Commonwealth Agricultural Bureaux; 1980.

[5] Gill M, et al. Simulation of the metabolism of absorbed energy-yielding nutriends in young sheep. Br J Nutr 1984;52:621–49.

[6] Armstrong DG, Blaxter KL. The heat increment of steam-volatile fatty acids in fasting sheep. Br J Nutr 1957;11:247–72.

[7] Armstrong DG, Blaxter KL, Graham NMcC, Wainman FW. The utilization of the enery of two mixtures of steam-volatile fatty acids by fattening sheep. Br J Nutr 1958;12:177–88.

[8] Rook JAF, Balch CC, Campling RC, Fisher LJ. The utilization of acetic propionic and butyric acids by growing heifers. Br J Nutr 1963;17:399–406.
[9] Ørskov ER, Allen DM. Utilization of salts of volatile fatty acids by growing sheep. Br J Nutr 1966;20:295–305.
[10] MacRae JC, Lobley GE. Some factors which influence thermal energy losses during the metabolism of ruminants. Livest Prod Sci 1982;9:447–56.
[11] Rao SBN, Kumar DD. Effect of substitution of soybean meal by detoxified karanja cake on diet digestibility growth, carcass and meat traits of sheep. Small Ruminant Res 2015;126:26–33.
[12] Sitzia M, et al. Feeding and management techniques to favour summer sheep milk and cheese production in the Mediterranean environment. Small Ruminant Res 2015;126:43–58.
[13] Michaelis L, Menton ML. Die kinetik der invertinwirkung. Biochem Z 1913;49:333–69.
[14] Baldwin RL, France J, Gill M. Metabolism of the lactating cow. I. Animal elements of a mechanistic model. J Dairy Res 1987;54:77–105.
[15] Sainz RD, Wolff JE. Development of a dynamic mechanistic model of lamb metabolism and growth. Anim Prod 1990;51:535–49.
[16] Sainz RD, Wolff JE. Evaluation of hypotheses regarding mechanisms of action of growth promotants and repartitioning agents using a simulation model of lamb metabolism and growth. Br Soc Anim Prod 1990;51:551–8.
[17] Butler-Hogg BW. Growth patterns in sheep: changes in the chemical composition of the empty body and its constituent parts during weight loss and compensatory growth. J Agric Sci 1984;103:17–24.
[18] Smith EC. Deterministic modelling of whole-body sheep metabolism. Perth: Curtin University; 2014.
[19] Bowman PJ, Cottle DJ, White DH, Bywater AC. Simulation of wool growth rate and fleece characteristics of Merino sheep in southern Australia. Part 1. Model description. Agric Syst 1993;43:287–99.
[20] Bowman PJ, White DH, Cottle DJ, Bywater AC. Simulation of wool growth rate and fleece characteristics of Merino sheep in southern Australia. Part 2. Assessment of biological components of the model. Agric Syst 1993;43:301–21.
[21] Baldwin RL, Sainz RD. Energy partitioning and modeling in animal nutrition. Annu Rev Nutr 1995;15:191–211.
[22] Hanigan MD, Dijkstra J, Gerrits WJJ, France J. Modeling post-absorptive protein and amino acid metabolism in the ruminant. Proc Nutr Soc 1997;56:631–43.
[23] Kebreab E, et al. An integrated mathematical model to evaluate nutrient partition in dairy cattle between the animal and its environment. Anim Feed Sci Technol 2004;112:131–54.
[24] McNamara JP. Research improvement and application of mechanistic, biochemical, dynamic models of metabolism in lactating dairy cattle. Anim Feed Sci Technol 2004;112:155–76.
[25] McNamara JP, Pettigrew JE. Protein and fat utilization in lactating sows. II. Challenging behaviour of a model of metabolism. J Anim Sci 2002;80:2452–60.
[26] Vetharaniam I, McCall DG, Fennessy PF, Garrick DJ. A model of mammalian energetics and growth: model development. Agric Syst 2001;68:55–68.
[27] Vetharaniam I, McCall DG, Fennessy PF, Garrick DJ. A model of mammalian energetics and growth: model testing (sheep). Agric Syst 2001;68:69–91.
[28] Fox DG, et al. The Cornell net carbohydrate and protein system model for evaluating herd nutrition and nutrient excretion. Anim Feed Sci Technol 2004;112:29–78.
[29] Moen AN, Boomer GS. Modeling annual energy metabolism rhythms in mammals. Ecol Model 2005;184:193–202.
[30] Upton RN. Organ weights and blood flows of sheep and pig for physiological pharmacokinetic modelling. J Pharmacol Toxicol Methods 2008;58:198–205.
[31] Sarnyai Z, Boros LG. Modeling networks of glycolysis, overall energy metabolism and drug metabolism under a systems biology approach. Annu Rep Med Chem 2008;43:329–49.

[32] Fleming RMT, Thiele I, Provan G, Nasheuer HP. Integrated stoichiometric thermodynamic and kinetic modeling of steady state metabolism. J Theor Biol 2010;264:683–92.
[33] Tedeschi LO, Fox DG, Carstens GE, Ferrell CL. The partial efficiency of use of metabolisable energy for growth in ruminants. Energy Protein Metab Nutr 2010;127:519–29.
[34] Cannas A, et al. The energetic cost of maintenance in ruminants: from classical to new concepts and prediction systems. Energy Protein Metab Nutr 2010;127:531–42.
[35] De Angelis A. Energy and protein value of lucerne hay and wheat straw diets for lambs. Energy Protein Metab Nutr 2010;127:547–8.
[36] Oltjen JW, et al. Integration of the small ruminant nutrition system and of the US Davis sheep growth model for improved predictions. Energy Protein Metab Nutr 2010;127:553–4.
[37] Hon T. Modelling protein synthesis in sheep (Honors dissertation). Perth: Curtin University of Technology; 2003.
[38] Ramsey D. Implementation of automatic differentiation code for a complex optimal control problem (mathematics project). Perth: Curtin University of Technology; 2004.
[39] Wang X, et al. Transcriptome profile analysis of adipose tissues from fat and short-tailed sheep. Gene 2014;549:252–7.
[40] Wodzicka M. Studies on the thickness and chemical composition of the skin of sheep. N Z J Agric Res 1958;1:582–91.
[41] Jennings LS, Fisher ME, Teo KL, Goh CJ. MISER3 optimal control software version 3 theory and user manual. Perth: s.l.:University of Western Australia; 2005.

CHAPTER

17 DIFFERENTIATING CANCER FROM NORMAL PROTEIN-PROTEIN INTERACTIONS THROUGH NETWORK ANALYSIS

R. Sahoo, T.S. Rani, S.D. Bhavani
SCIS University of Hyderabad, Hyderabad, Telangana, India

17.1 INTRODUCTION

Proteins play an important role in facilitating various biological processes like gene expression, cell growth, and intercellular communication in a cell. A majority of the proteins interact with each other for a specific biological activity. Hence protein-protein interactions (PPIs) are crucial for understanding biological processes. Barabasi et al. [1] indicate that cellular networks also exhibit universal laws and analysis of these interaction networks may lead to insights into disease pathways. In particular, in the case of cancer, network analysis provides us new insights into the processes involved that lead the mutations in oncogenes and tumor suppressor genes to ultimately result in abnormal cell growth. The tumor development is supposed to follow a series of steps of changes leading the normal cell to transform to a cancer cell. Hanahan et al. [2] in his seminal paper, identified six primary changes in cell physiology that collectively lead to malignant tumors that include insensitivity to inhibitory signals, evasion of apoptosis, and unrestrained replication. Our aim is to analyze the normal versus cancer networks and investigate if a cancer network structure has higher resilience in comparison to the normal network using network analysis methods like community discovery, common subgraph analysis, clique participation and so forth.

17.2 RELATED LITERATURE

Protein interaction networks (PINs), in particular, study of cancer networks has gained ground recently due to availability of pathways data, gene networks, and microarrays carrying gene expression data. Bredel et al. [3] propose an integrated approach by considering data from gene expression networks and pathway databases. Their network analysis identifies clusters of interconnected genes with common biological function relating to cell-cycle regulation in human gliomas. Wu et al. [4] continue this approach and create a functional interaction network that combines information from multiple sources such as pathway databases, PPIs, gene ontology, gene coexpression data, and so on. The authors conducted community discovery using [5] to find that cancer-related genes are indeed clustered together with the two modules containing mutated genes involved in two significant pathways, signal transduction and cell-cycle regulation, thus revealing common underlying mechanisms in the case of brain tumors.

Differential coexpression analysis carried out by Choi et al. [6] show that while interpreting changes in individual gene expression is difficult, it is fruitful to consider coexpression of pairs of genes. They show by constructing a gene coexpression network, clusters of genes that participate in protein synthesis are found in tumor-specific networks in contrast to no clusters being found in the "normal" network. Anglani et al. [7] claim that their methods are able to retrieve cancer-related genes that escape the basic differential coexpression analysis in the case of five distinct cancer types.

Huang et al. [8] conducted basic degree distribution analysis of six different tumor signaling pathways and show that all these distributions are scale free and the nodes (metabolites) having high degree are important to the underlying metabolic process. The authors stress the need to conduct a deeper analysis of the changes in the networks that occur due to cancer. Recently, Rahman et al. [9] continue this study by extracting network properties for 10 different cell-signaling pathways that participate in tumorigenesis. In the study of disease cells, they analyzed the protein interaction networks of cancer and normal state for five different tissues (bone, breast, colon, kidney, and liver) and traced notable changes and fluctuations of network parameters in cancer and normal states of the cell.

In our work, we take protein interaction data of Rahman et al. [9] to conduct a detailed analysis of proteins in a cancer state as well as a normal state. Analysis for *bone cell* is carried out and presented in this chapter. Differential coexpression network analysis reported in the literature considers basic properties of degree distribution, centrality measures like edge betweenness node based centralities, and in some cases cluster analysis [3, 6–8, 10]. We find that the networks not only contain clusters but, in fact, complete subgraphs; that is, cliques that participate significantly in cancer networks. Further, it is important to differentiate proteins that are common to normal and cancerous networks that may be related to housekeeping activities, from the proteins that appear in the cancer networks. To gain understanding of topological changes that occur in a cancer network as compared to a normal network, we conduct common subgraph analysis as well as construct bipartite graphs between the common and the other proteins. We find many interesting insights through this analysis, which is reported below.

17.3 NETWORK ANALYSIS: PROPOSED METHODS

A protein interaction network is modeled as a weighted graph $G = (V,E)$, with proteins represented as nodes V and expression values of interacting proteins are summed up to form weight of the edge shared. Edges are present between two expressed proteins and can be simply treated to constitute an unweighted network E.

We denote N as the nodes that occur in the normal network and C as the set of proteins that are present in the cancer network. Proteins that are common to both cancer and normal networks may be related to cell regulation, replication, cell growth-related signals, and so forth. It will be interesting to analyze both the common set of proteins as well as proteins that are newly recruited into a cancer network. Also, we need to study the change in dynamics that may occur due to these new proteins. Hence, the common set of proteins are retrieved and is referred to as the common set $S = N \cap C$ and the complement sets, in a normal network as O_N and in a cancer network as O_C. The induced subgraph on S is referred to as the common subgraph, which is analyzed for network properties. We construct bipartite graphs, by silencing the interactions within S,O_N and O_C and analyzing how interactions between S and O_N change to S to O_C.

The following types of analysis are carried out to differentiate normal versus cancer networks:

1. **Hub node analysis:** The networks on N and C are studied for the presence of cliques and in particular the nodes that interface multiple cliques. Brinda et al. [11] define *hubs* as those nodes that are highly connected in at both interface regions of an oligomeric structure and noninterface regions of monomeric protein. In PPI networks cliques are considered as the biological complexes formed due to complete interactions among a set of proteins. We define clique participation of a protein as the number of cliques in the network in which the protein is present. The higher the clique participation count, the greater the number of complexes formed by the protein in the cell.
2. **Centrality analysis:** Centrality of nodes in a network is computed using different centrality measures like degree centrality, betweenness centrality, eigenvector centrality, and so on. Betweenness centrality of a node v, for a given graph G for $s \neq v \neq t \in V$ is defined as

$$C_B(v) = \sum \frac{\sigma_{st}(v)}{\sigma_{st}}$$

where σ_{st} is the total number of shortest paths that pass through the nodes s and t and $\sigma_{st}(v)$ is the number of those paths passing through the node v. Community discovery is an important problem that has been addressed in social networks. Edge betweenness centrality is very popular as it is used by *Girvan – Newman edge betweenness* algorithm [5] to compute communities. Here we compute betweenness centrality to locate nodes with high betweenness centrality.
3. **Common subgraph analysis:** The induced graph on the common set of proteins is studied using degree distribution analysis and transitivity using triad analysis.
4. **Bipartite graph analysis:** The network that is obtained between the common set of proteins and the complement sets in both normal and cancer networks are studied through bipartite graph analysis.

17.3.1 DATA SET

Data set of Rahman et al. [9] deals with protein molecules involved in 10 major cancer signal transduction pathways; for example, Alpha-6-Beta-4-Integrin, Androgen Receptor, Kit Receptor, EGFR1, Hedgehog, Wnt,ID, NOTCH, TGFBR, and TNF Alpha/NF-kB. With the help of differential expression database *GeneHubs-Gepis* [12] and PPI prediction tools *PIPs* [13] and *STRING* [14], they constructed the PPI network. We have considered this PPI data for our experimentation.

Both weighted and unweighted networks can be constructed from this data. Unweighted networks are constructed similar to that of Rahman et al. [9]. G is the weighted graph denoted as $G = (V,E,W_E)$ such that V is the set of proteins (nodes) involved in the PPI network, $E \subseteq (V \times V)$ is the set of interactions (edges) involved. If i and j are two proteins and their expression values are $expr_i$ and $expr_j$ where both $expr_i$, $expr_j \neq 0$.

$$w_{ij} = expr_i + expr_j$$

where $w_{ij} \in W_E$ is the weight associated with the edge between proteins i and j. The network information for *bone cell* is given in Table 17.1.

Table 17.1 Network Information for *Bone Cell*

Network	No. of Nodes (proteins)	No. of Edges (Interactions)
Normal	192	619
Cancer	351	1783

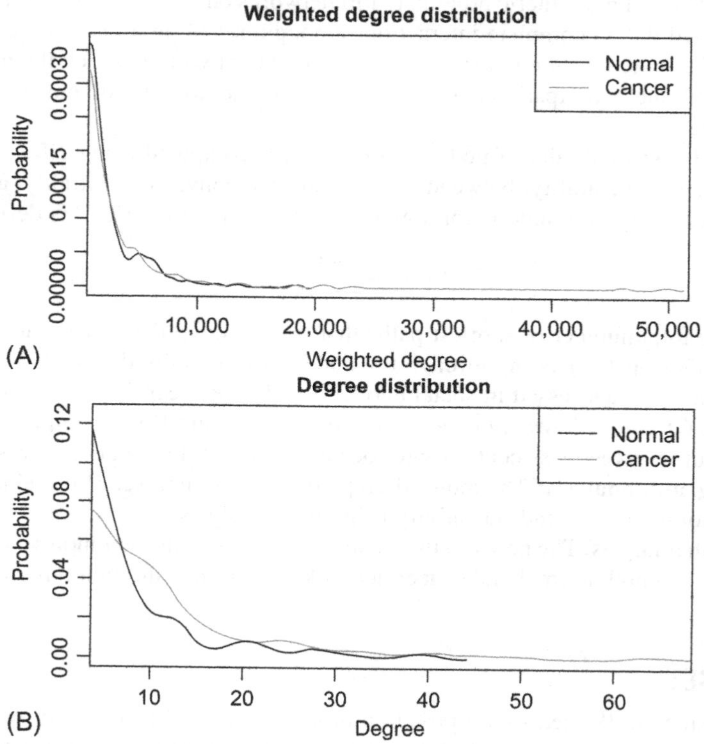

FIGURE 17.1

Analysis of degree distribution. (A) Degree distribution in weighted network; (B) Degree distribution in unweighted network.

To decide whether to consider weighted networks or unweighted networks for our analysis, we compare the degree distributions of both the networks to see if a significant difference can be observed. The degree distributions are illustrated in Fig. 17.1.

From Fig. 17.1A and B, it is observed that for both weighted and unweighted networks, the tail of the distribution is extended for cancer state as there are high degree nodes found in cancer cell.

To quantify the difference and decide whether to take weighted or unweighted network for our work, the significance test (ie, KS-test [15]) is carried out and the result is illustrated below. From Table 17.2, we observe that the distinction between normal and cancer states is more in unweighted

Table 17.2 Result for KS-Test

	D	*p*-value	Observation
Weighted	0.0951	$0.2118 > 0.05$	Same distribution
Unweighted	0.2302	$0.000038 < 0.05$	Different distribution

Table 17.3 Network Properties for Bone Cell

	Normal Network	Cancer Network
N/W density	0.034	0.029
Number of cliques	**2156**	**149,677**
Max clique size	8	15
Number of communities	**49**	**117**
Size of largest community	77	107
Diameter	7	7
Clustering coefficient	0.217	0.261
Assortativity	0.02	0.12

network as compared to weighted network. Hence unweighted PPI network is taken up for further study. We use *RStudio* [16] with *igraph* package [17] for our analysis.

17.3.2 BASIC NETWORK PROPERTIES

We have analyzed the normal and cancer protein interaction networks for bone cell as a case study.

Table 17.3 shows most of the network properties computed.

Not much difference between some of the network parameters like network density, diameter, and clustering coefficient is observed. As assortativity is higher in the cancer network, it can be concluded that preferential attachment toward similar degree nodes is higher in the cancer state than the normal state of bone cell. Other parameters like clique and community are significantly differentiating the two networks. Especially number of cliques is very high in cancer (149,677) as compared to normal (2156). So, in-depth study of these properties may give us more understanding of the behavior of the proteins in the diseased (cancer) state in comparison to the normal state.

17.4 ANALYSIS AND RESULTS

17.4.1 HUB NODE ANALYSIS

From network properties discussed in Table 17.3, clique parameter is significantly differentiating the cancer network from the normal. Clique participation of a node, defined as the number of cliques that the protein belongs to, is computed for both normal and cancer networks and is reported and its distribution illustrated in Table 17.4.

Table 17.4 Cliques in Normal and Cancer States of Bone Cell

Clique Size	Count in Normal	Count in Cancer
2	619	1783
3	575	3157
4	429	6467
5	236	13,202
6	85	22,078
7	18	28,756
8	2	29,005
9	0	22,636
10	0	13,568
11	0	6132
12	0	2019
13	0	456
14	0	63
15	0	4

From Fig. 17.2, it is observed that in the normal network, clique size ranges between 2 and 8 whereas in the *cancer network* the range falls between 2 and 14. Higher the clique size, it is observed that the number of cliques also increases up to a certain point; that is, up to clique sizes 6–8. After this point, the number of cliques decrease with increase in clique size.

Clique participation for the top 30 proteins is listed in Table 17.5 in both normal and cancer cell.

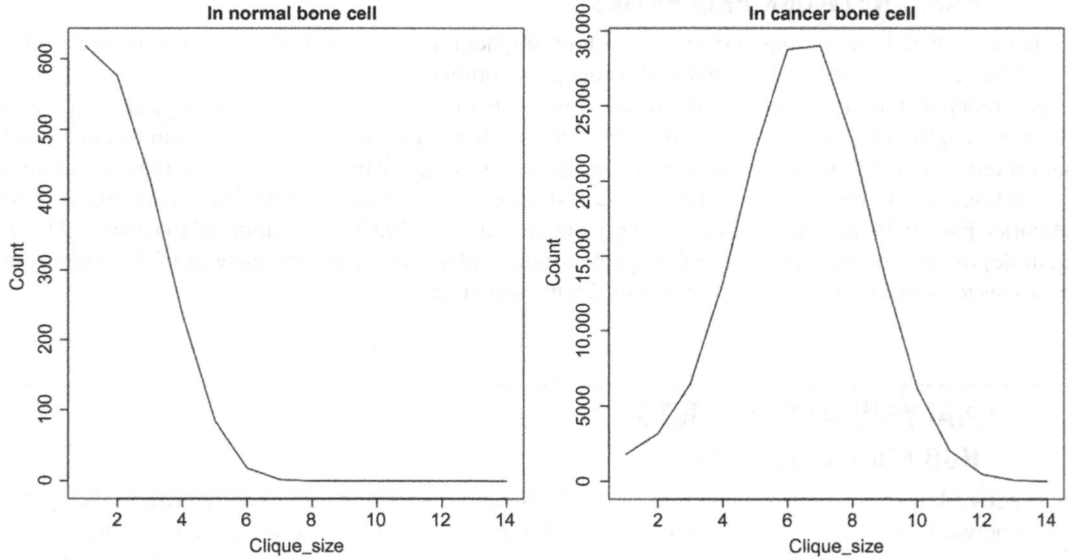

FIGURE 17.2

Clique participation of proteins.

Table 17.5 Normal Bone Cell: Proteins in Bold-face Are Common to Both Normal and Cancer Networks

Protein Name	Participation Count
FYN	461
STAT5B	461
CSK	393
STAT3	386
GRB2	337
VAV1	328
ERK1	318
SMAD3	258
PTK2	240
JUN	234
FOS	218
ABL1	214
STAT2	212
RELA	206
HDAC1	175
BRCA1	143
EPOR	128
IKBA	100
TGFBR1	83
CRK	82
JUNB	76
RAN	73
KPNA2	54
SHC1	48
CTNNB1	38
CASP3	38
NR3C1	37
HGS	36
TGFB1	35
SAM68	34

From Tables 17.5 and 17.6, it can be observed that

- Some nodes viz **ABL1**, **CRK**, **CSK**, **EPOR**, **ERK1**, **FYN**, **GRB2**, **PTK2**, **RELA**, **SAM68**, **SHC1**, **SMAD3**, **STAT2**, **STAT3**, and **STAT5B** are preserving their top positions in both the networks though their clique participations are very high in the cancer network versus the normal network.
- Some new proteins like *CBLB*, *CRKL*, *ERBB2*, *ERK2*, *GRB10*, *JAK1*, *MET*, *NCK2*, *PIK3R2*, and *WASL* are coming into the top list in the cancer network that are not found in the normal network.
- Proteins like PTPN12, which is a common protein but does not figure in the top list of the normal network, has increased participation count predominantly in the cancer network.

Table 17.6 Cancer Bone Cell: Proteins in Bold-face Are Common to Both, While Proteins in Italics Are Unique to Cancer State, Not Found in Normal State

Protein Name	Participation Count
FYN	72,781
SRC	71,878
STAT1	69,343
LYN	69,223
GRB2	66,896
STAT5B	66,390
PIK3R2	65,704
JAK1	64,854
CSK	62,413
CRKL	62,215
CBL	59,697
GRB10	56,358
STAT3	49,417
CBLB	47,126
MET	46,132
ABL1	43,848
NCK2	39,831
PTK2	23,691
EPOR	15,744
ERBB2	13,989
ERK1	11,215
CRK	5599
WASL	5322
STAT2	3271
SHC1	2089
ERK2	1214
PTPN12	1194
SMAD3	676
SAM68	642
RELA	493

17.4.2 CENTRALITY ANALYSIS

Here we compute betweenness centrality to find nodes with high centrality. We believe that high topological changes may occur in a network if these nodes are disturbed and hence are important in the context of sensitivity to dynamical changes in a network.

From Tables 17.7 and 17.8, it has been observed that

- Nearly half of the nodes are preserving their top positions though their centrality scores increase by two times in the cancer network. These are **ABL1**, **AKT1**, **CASP3**, **CSK**, **CTNNB1**, **DVL1**, **ERK1**, **FYN**, **HDAC1**, **RAN**, **RELA**, **SMAD3**, **STAT3**, and **STAT5B**.

Table 17.7 Normal Bone Cell: Proteins in Bold-face Are Common to Both Normal and Cancer Networks

Protein Name	Centrality Score
HDAC1	2588.52
CTNNB1	2412.86
SMAD3	2402.05
FYN	2179.26
ERK1	1801.79
RELA	1528.05
RAN	1310.71
DVL1	1145.25
HGS	921.73
JUN	854.19
STAT5B	718.17
SMOH	704.81
STAT3	695.57
CCND1	692.68
CSK	672.03
ABL1	648.89
NFKB1	612.03
GRB2	597.11
NR3C1	560.98
NKIRAS2	558.88
TBP	539.91
RACK1	429.85
TGFBR1	423.79
FOS	422.74
CIR	416.51
TRUSS	415.82
AKT1	385.19
ID2	379.37
CASP3	369.64
ARRB2	369.55

- Some of the high central nodes in the normal network, are losing out their centrality score due to a loss of connectivity in the cancer network, while the centrality score of nodes like CCNB1 increases predominantly due to a gain in connectivity in the cancer network as compared to the normal network.
- Some new proteins like *CBL*, *CDK2*, *HDAC2*, *HES1*, *LYN*, *MAPK14*, *MYC*, *POLR2H*, *PRKCA*, *RAC1*, *SRC*, *STAT1*, *TP53*, and *TRAF2* are coming into the top centrality list in the cancer network and are not present in the normal network.

Behavior of these proteins is discussed in detail after analyzing all the properties.

Table 17.8 Cancer Bone Cell: Proteins in Bold-face Are Common to Both, While Proteins in Italics Are Unique to Cancer State, Not Found in Normal State

Protein Name	Centrality Score
SMAD3	5720.32
FYN	4296.80
HDAC1	3850.35
CTNNB1	3676.59
STAT5B	3431.38
STAT1	3250.74
ERK1	3125.09
RELA	2903.23
DVL1	2136.38
LYN	2048.65
TP53	1977.63
STAT3	1977.52
MAPK14	1976.84
RAN	1689.89
PRKCA	1627.68
HDAC2	1521.73
CCNB1	1487.18
ABL1	1451.84
RAC1	1349.11
CDK2	1271.55
POLR2H	1257.46
AKT1	1253.07
TRAF2	1164.96
CASP3	1139.53
CBL	1137.06
CSK	1119.60
MYC	1102.78
HES1	1092.47
SRC	1061.09

17.4.3 COMMON SUBGRAPH ANALYSIS

To capture the dynamics behind a PPI network in two different states (ie, normal vs cancer state of a cell), we analyze the set of common proteins and their behavior in the network. The induced common subgraph exhibited by the common protein set and its interaction with other proteins in the network may give further insight into it. Hence, various network properties are computed for these common proteins involved in both the networks.

Comparison of different network properties between cancer and normal states will give more understanding about the network in a disease state. Hence, degree distribution analysis and triad analysis are carried out on these networks.

17.4.3.1 Degree analysis

Degree of a node is defined as the number of connections made by the node with other nodes in the network. In a PPI network, it measures the number of interactions of a protein with other proteins. Here, the change in the degree of the common set of proteins S in both normal and cancer networks is plotted in descending order of degree. From Fig. 17.3, it can be summarized that

- Degrees of the proteins in PPI networks are higher for the cancer state than the normal state. Hence, proteins in cancer state are more interactive than normal state.
- It has been observed that top high-degree proteins in both normal and cancer networks are the same proteins.

17.4.3.2 Transitivity analysis

In PPI networks, transitivity measures the average number of triads that are formed at a node, showing how well connected the neighbors of a protein are. The transitivity scores of common proteins are compared and plotted in Fig. 17.4.

From Fig. 17.4, it can be observed that

- There is a distinct difference in transitivity scores of proteins in both the states. For half of the proteins, transitivity score is high in the normal state in comparison to the cancer state, which shows that due to cancer effect there is a loss in connectivity among neighbors of proteins.
- Some proteins gain neighbor connectivity in the cancer state as their transitivity score is increasing, which may be due to the influence of new proteins coming into picture in the cancer state.
- For example, the first protein in Fig. 17.4, Human Endoglin/CD105/ENG Protein, has been regarded as an important biomarker of neovascularization, and is associated with osteogenesis in adipose-derived mesenchymal cells for skeletal regeneration. CTRP2, the first protein among the proteins in the light coloured region on the right, has no triad count at all in the normal state but has highly connected neighbors in the cancer state. This protein is related to tumor necrosis factor [18].

17.4.4 BIPARTITE GRAPH ANALYSIS

To analyze the interactions of a common set of proteins with other proteins in both cancer and normal networks, we have generated the bipartite graph ignoring the interaction within common proteins. In Figs. 17.5 and 17.6, the top of the bipartite graphs corresponds to S, the set of common nodes and bottom set of nodes is O_N and O_C, corresponding to the complement sets in the normal network and the cancer network, respectively. It has been found that interactions of common proteins are high in a cancer cell compared to a normal cell. Hence, a cancer bipartite network looks to be more dense as seen in Fig. 17.6. Degree distributions of these graphs are further studied.

Fig. 17.7 shows that in the normal network, interaction distribution for common proteins with respect to others is fluctuating while it is more stable in the cancer network making it more resilient.

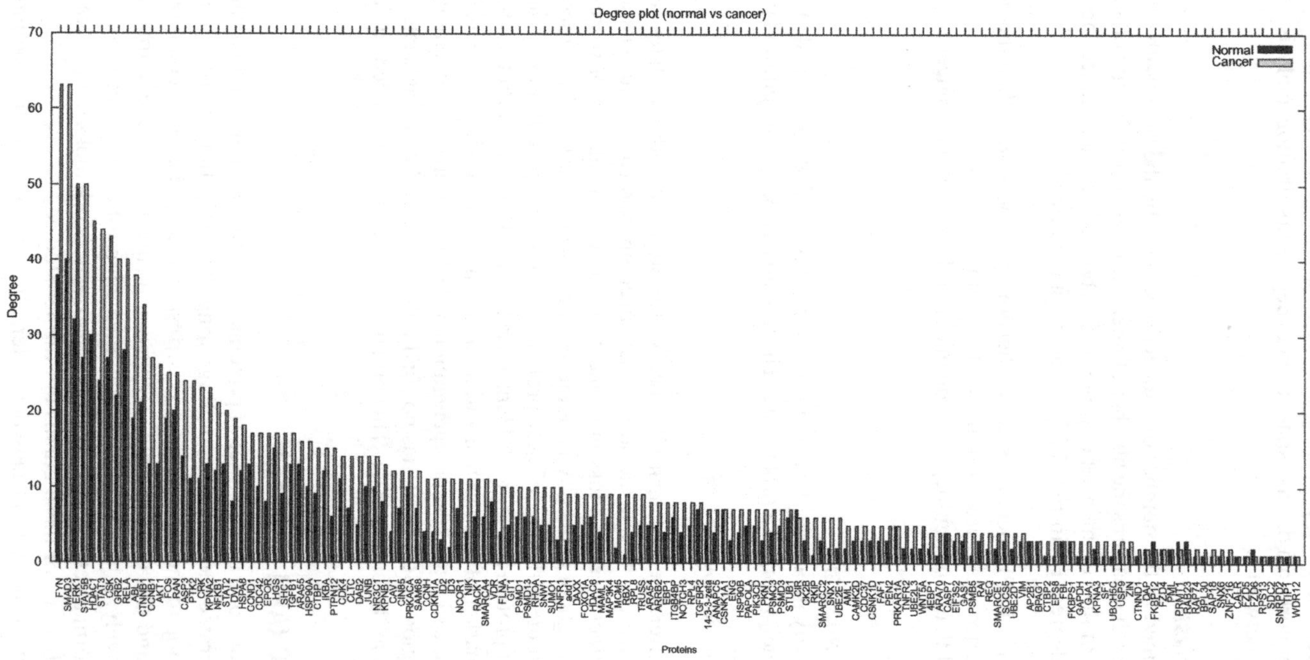

FIGURE 17.3

Degree of common proteins in normal and cancer network.

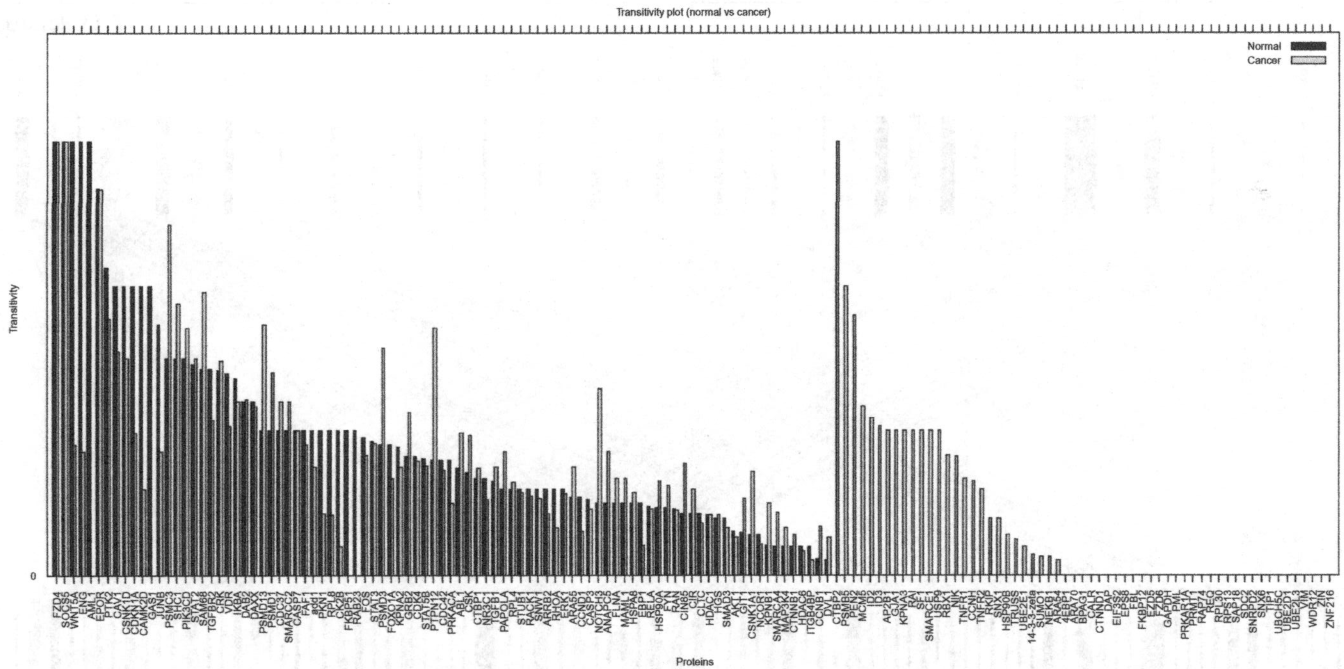

FIGURE 17.4

Transitivity score of common proteins.

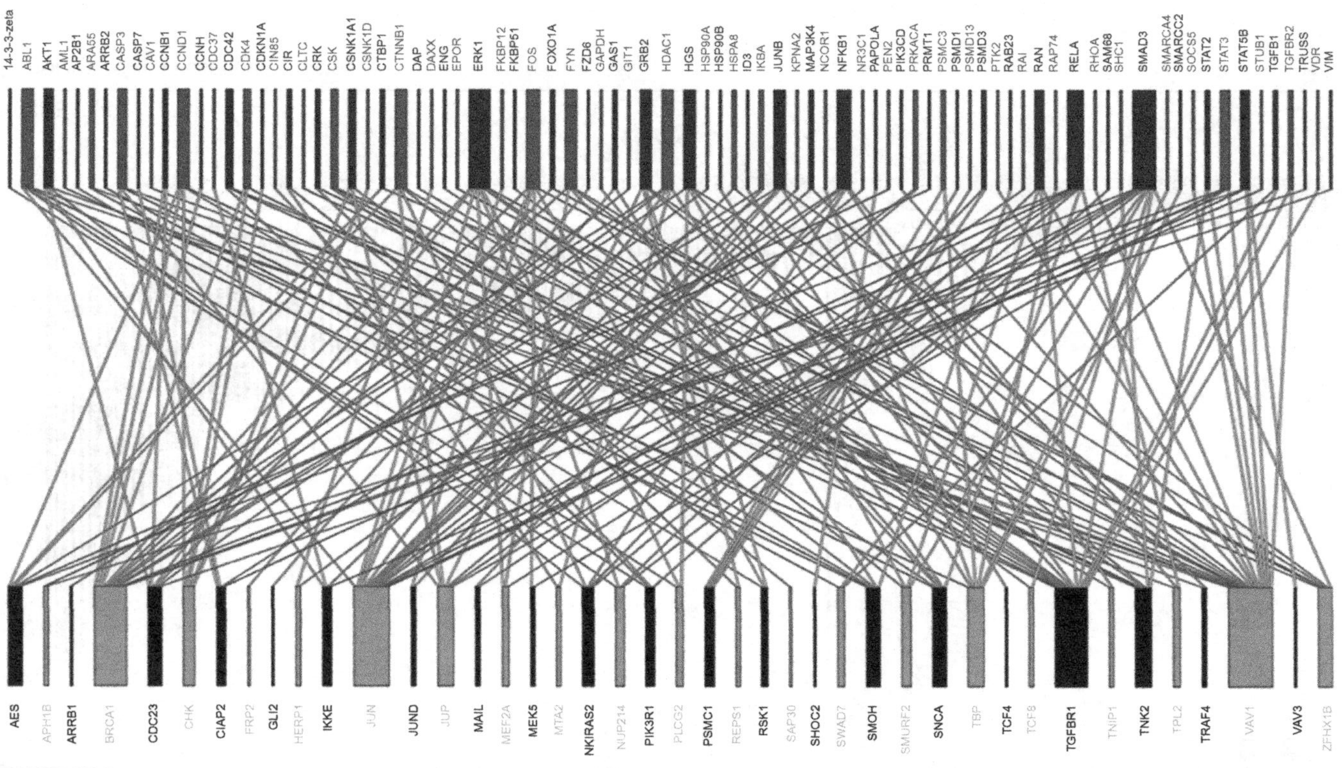

FIGURE 17.5

Interaction between common proteins versus others in normal network.

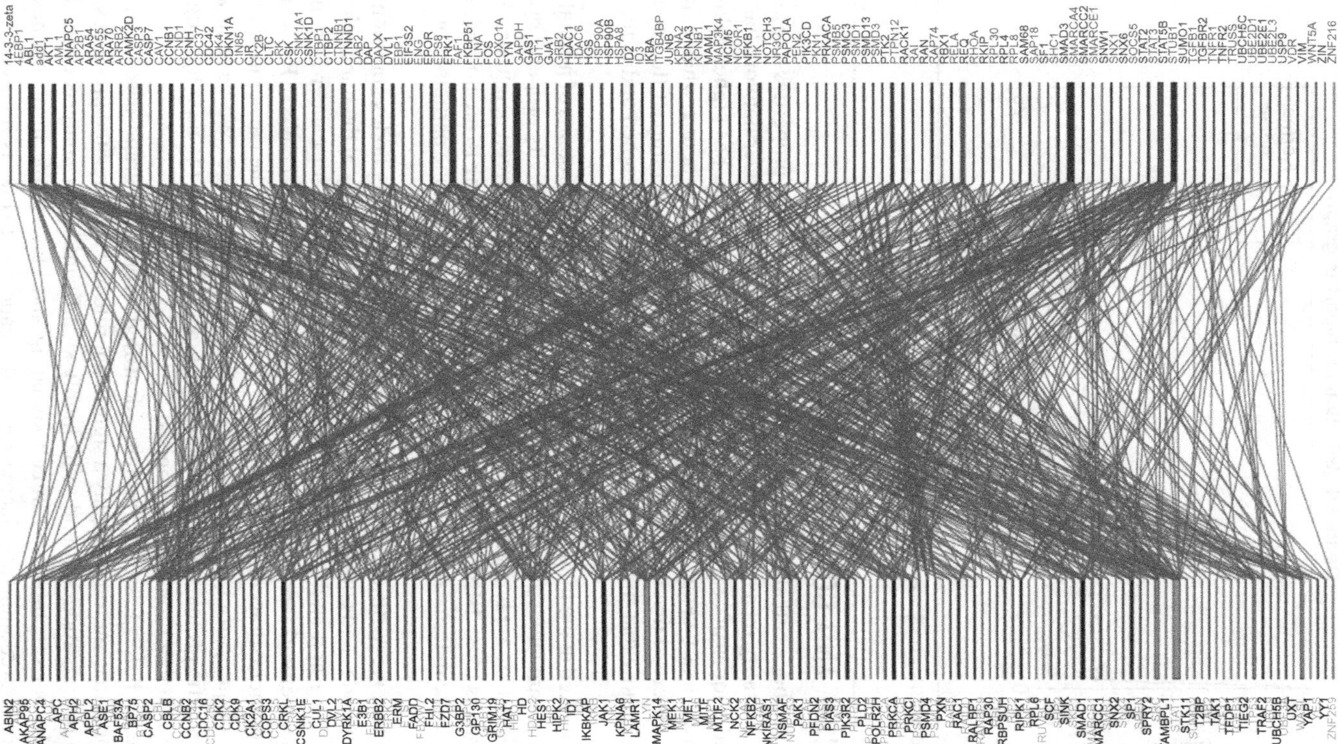

FIGURE 17.6

Interaction between common proteins versus others in cancer network.

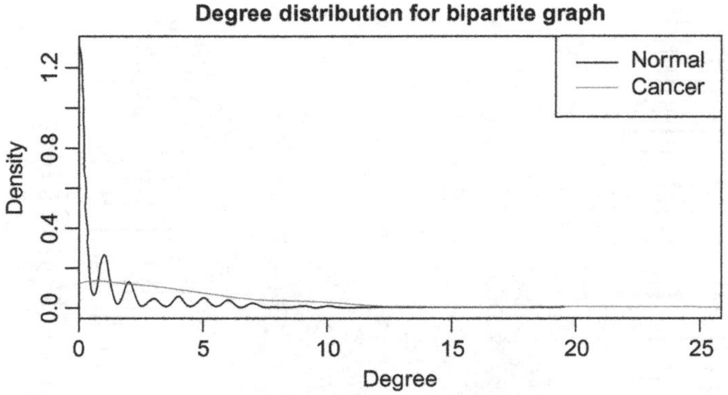

FIGURE 17.7

Degree distribution of common proteins.

17.5 DISCUSSION AND CONCLUSIONS

Unweighted networks of bone cell are built and are analyzed using various properties like assortativity, clique participation, centrality measures, and so on. It is found that the cancer network has an unusual number of cliques and cliques of large size. We find that a cancer network has higher value for assortativity as well as betweenness centrality indicating tighter community structure when compared to a normal network. It is observed that removal of high-degree nodes does not impact the topology of the cancer network, which show that the cancer network cannot be easily disrupted and is resistant to topological changes.

Further, when we looked at the induced subgraphs involving common proteins of normal and cancer networks, both have the same nodes of high degree. But the study of transitivity property reveals that in the cancer network, the triads are broken showing loss of connectivity between neighbors. We identify through our study proteins like CBLB, CRKL, and others that do not belong to the normal network but have a significant presence in terms of high betweenness centrality and clique participation count in the cancer network.

In another experiment we partitioned the nodes into two sets containing nodes common to both the networks and the other nodes and constructed a bipartite graph looking only at the interactions between these two sets. Bipartite graph analysis reveals a highly dense network for cancer in comparison to normal. In the normal network, even though the centrality scores of CTNNB1, RAN, and RELA are high, their clique participation counts are low. In a similar fashion, in the cancer network, SMAD3 and RELA have low clique participation count and a high centrality score. We have to analyze the importance of these specific proteins obtained to be significant with respect to their topological behavior from this study in collaboration with biologists.

To summarize, we list here a few of the proteins identified through the graph-based analysis of cancer and normal networks that are found to play a significant role in cancer-related processes.*PTPN12*, a protein whose clique participation is found to be highly significant in our analysis of the cancer network, is reported to be actively involved in cell signaling and plays a role in oncogenesis.*CCNB1*, whose centrality score is predominantly increasing in the cancer network, is involved in the mitosis process. Some proteins, like *SMAD3* play a role in the regulation of carcinogenesis, *FYN* control cell growth, and *RELA* is associated with multiple types of cancer are the top degree proteins found in bipartite graphs of cancer networks. This approach certainly shows promise and can be used to identify more biomarkers. An integrated view of the results obtained by the different methods will lead to a deeper understanding of the dynamics of the network topology.

ACKNOWLEDGMENTS

The authors would like to thank the UPE2 (University for Potential for Excellence), University of Hyderabad, India, for the support provided by them.

REFERENCES

[1] Barabsi AL, Oltvai ZN. Network biology: understanding the cell's functional organization. Nat Rev Genet 2004;5(12):101–13.
[2] Hanahan D, Weinberg RA. The hallmarks of cancer. Cell 2000;100(1):57–70.
[3] Bredel M, Bredel C, Juric D, Harsh GR, Vogel H, Recht BLD. Functional network analysis reveals extended gliomagenesis pathway maps and three novel MYC-interacting genes. Cancer Res 2005;65(19).
[4] Wu XG, Stein L. A human functional protein interaction network and its application to cancer data analysis. Genome Biol 2010;11(1):R53.
[5] Girvan M, Newman ME. Community structure in social and biological networks. Proc Natl Acad Sci 2002;99 (12):7821–6.
[6] Choi J, Yu U, Yoo O, Kim S. Differential coexpression analysis using microarray data and its application to human cancer. Bioinformatics 2005;21(24):4348–55.
[7] Anglani R, Creanza TM, Liuzzi VC, Panza A, Andriulli A, Ancona N. Loss of connectivity in cancer co-expression networks. PLOS ONE 2014;9(1):R53.
[8] Huang J, Zhang W. Analysis on degree distribution of tumor signaling networks. Netw Biol 2012;2 (3):95–109.
[9] Rahman KT, Islam MF, Banik RS, Honi U, Diba FS, Sumi SS, et al. Changes in protein interaction networks between normal and cancer conditions: total chaos or ordered disorder? Netw Biol 2013;3(1):15.
[10] Erjia Y, Ying D. Applying centrality measures to impact analysis: a coauthorship network analysis. J Am Soc Inf Sci Technol 2009;60(10):2107–18.
[11] Brinda KV, Vishveshwara S. Oligomeric protein structure networks: insights into protein-protein interactions. BMC Bioinformatics 2005;6:296.
[12] GeneHubs-Gepis: the differential expression database for genes. http://research-public.gene.com/Research/genentech/genehub-gepis/.
[13] Ppis: a database for human protein-protein interaction prediction. http://www.compbio.dundee.ac.uk/www-pips/.
[14] String: a database for known and predicted protein interactions. http://string.embl.de/.
[15] Sheskin DJ. The Kolmogorov-Smirnov test for two independent samples (nonparametric test employed with ordinal data). Handbook of parametric and nonparametric statistical procedures. Oxford: Chapman & Hall/CRC; 2004. p. 453–63.
[16] Rstudio: integrated tool for data analysis. http://www.rstudio.com/.
[17] Igraph for r: a package for graph theoretic analysis. http://igraph.org/r/.
[18] NCBI. http://www.ncbi.nlm.nih.gov/gene.

CHAPTER

PREDICTING THE CO-RECEPTORS OF THE VIRUSES THAT CAUSE AIDS (HIV-1) IN CD4 CELLS 18

F.J.L. Rosas*, J.C.M. Romo*, C.A. de Luna Ortega†, R.M. Gonzalez*, V.L. Rivas*, G.M. Veloz‡

Computer Science Department, Instituto Tecnologico de Aguascalientes, Aguascalientes, Mexico Universidad Politécnica de Aguascalientes, Aguascalientes, Mexico† Universidad Tecnológica del Norte de Aguascalientes, Aguascalientes, Mexico‡*

18.1 INTRODUCTION

Breast, lung, colon, and prostate cancer are the most common cancers today [1], but the frequency of cases of other types of cancer has increased; that is, cancers in blood, lymphatic system, skin, digestive system, and the urinary system. At the same time, with the existence of several types of cancer, multiple factors exist that favor the appearance of cancer in different parts of the human body; for example, blood cancer as the leukemia caused by the presence and action of a retrovirus (deltaretrovirus) and the syndrome of human immunodeficiency (AIDS) caused by the presence and action of another retrovirus known as human immunodeficiency virus (HIV) (Lentivirus), affecting the CD4 cells in the blood directly.

This work focuses specifically in the study of the cells of the blood called CD4 that are a type of lymphocytes (leukocytes). These are an important part of the immune system in humans. These cells are also called "T" cells and are attacked by retrovirus HIV.

18.2 ANTECEDENTS

In 1981, the International Committee on the Taxonomy of the Virus (ICTV) [2] proposed the following definition: "A species of the virus is a concept that will be represented normally by a group of chains of a variety of sources, or a population of chains of a particular source, that have in common a system the properties correlated that differentiate a group from other groups of chains" [2]. Today, the ICTV recognizes more than 3600 species of the virus [2].

The animal viruses are classified in six classes: I, II, III, IV, V, and VI.

18.2.1 RETROVIRUS OF THE CLASS VI

It is a group of virus of RNA that infects animals and humans.

As it can be observed in Fig. 18.1, the general structure of retrovirus is mainly formed by a lipid-protein bilayer with two protein subunits that are codified by the gene env of the virus and their own

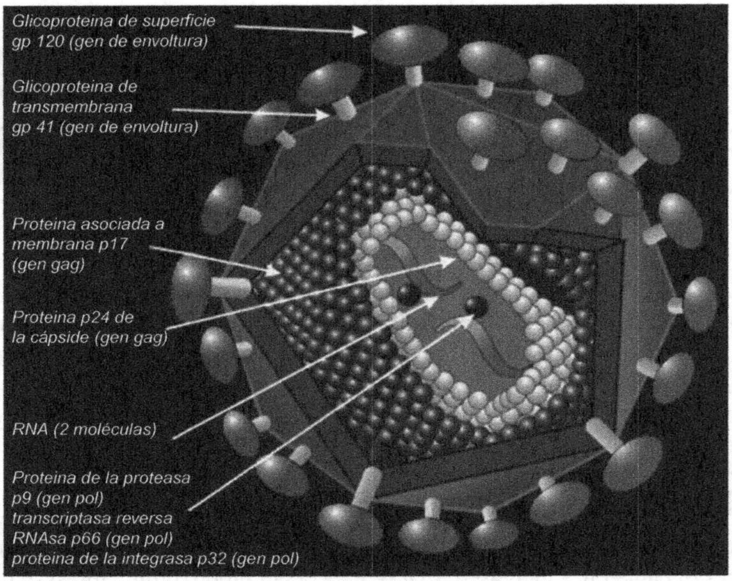

FIGURE 18.1

Retrovirus structure.

Courtesy of Stanford University School of Medicine. http://www.stanford.edu/group/nolan/tutorials/ret_6_gpedesc.html (USA-2015).

lipid and protein components of the cellular membrane. Also called specific glycoprotein that cause the infection, which contains a spherical capsid formed by three protein subunits codified by the gene gag. Inside the necessary viral enzymes for the process of viral replication are found: protease (gene pro) and inverse transcriptase and integrase, codified by the gene pol. Some retroviruses cause cancer directly, integrating genes called oncogenes in the DNA of the cell guest, causing the malignant transformation of normal cells into cancer cells; these are called virus transforming acute. Others cause cancer indirectly activating proto-oncogen of the guest, these are called virus transforming not-acute. Another important characteristic is that some retrovirus is cytotoxic for certain cells, inflating them. Most remarkable it is the virus of the syndrome of the immunodeficiency in humans that destroys the lymphocytes CD4 T that they infect.

18.2.2 CLASSIFICATION OF RETROVIRUS

Actually, retroviruses are classified in seven genera [2], as can be seen in Fig. 18.2, where the different genera are observed from retrovirus according to the family to which they belong. This is the case of HIV pertaining to the family of Lentivirus.

At the present time, the well-known and classified families by ICTV are

(a) Alpha-retrovirus, Beta-retrovirus, Epsilon-retrovirus, and Gamma-retrovirus contain simple genomes.
(b) Lentivirus, Spumavirus, and Deltaretrovirus contain complex genomes.

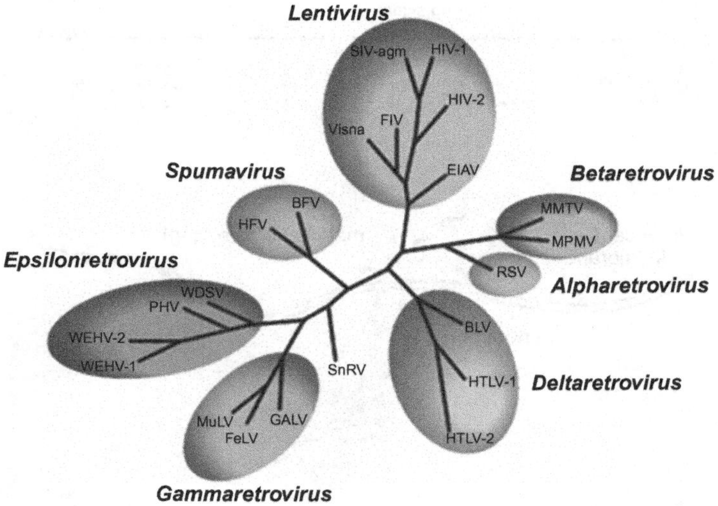

FIGURE 18.2

Filogenetic analysis of retroviruses.

Courtesy of International Committee on Taxonomy of Viruses (ICTV-2015). http://ictvonline.org/index.asp.

Only retrovirus with endogenous simple genome and spumaviruses are living in their guests; in a latent way. The Lentivirus is a citopatic retrovirus (retrovirus that damages the cell) that causes immunodeficiency syndromes fundamentally, neurological syndromes, and autoimmune diseases of slow evolution.

18.2.3 VITAL CYCLE OF RETROVIRUS

The vital cycle of retrovirus begins in the nucleus of an infected cell (upper part of Fig. 18.3), formed by the genome of the virus (genes gag, pol, env), which is contained in the membrane of the cell guest (envelope) [3].

In this stage of the vital cycle the retroviral genome is an element of the DNA integrated in the cell guest. The genome of the virus is approximately 8–12 kilobases of the DNA (it depends on the retroviral species). The genome of the virus takes advantage of elements available in the cell guest to form the capsid that locks up the heart of the virus encapsulating genes and other elements (matrix and core); immediately the virus leaves the cell guest as a free particle (central part of Fig. 18.3) and looks for other healthy cells to infect them, which is observed in the bottom part of Fig. 18.3 (target cell membrane).

18.3 RETROVIRUS MORE COMMON IN HUMANS

The HIV is a nontransforming retrovirus pertaining to the family of Lentivirus. In Fig. 18.4 the structure of retrovirus of the human immunodeficiency is appraised (HIV) [2].

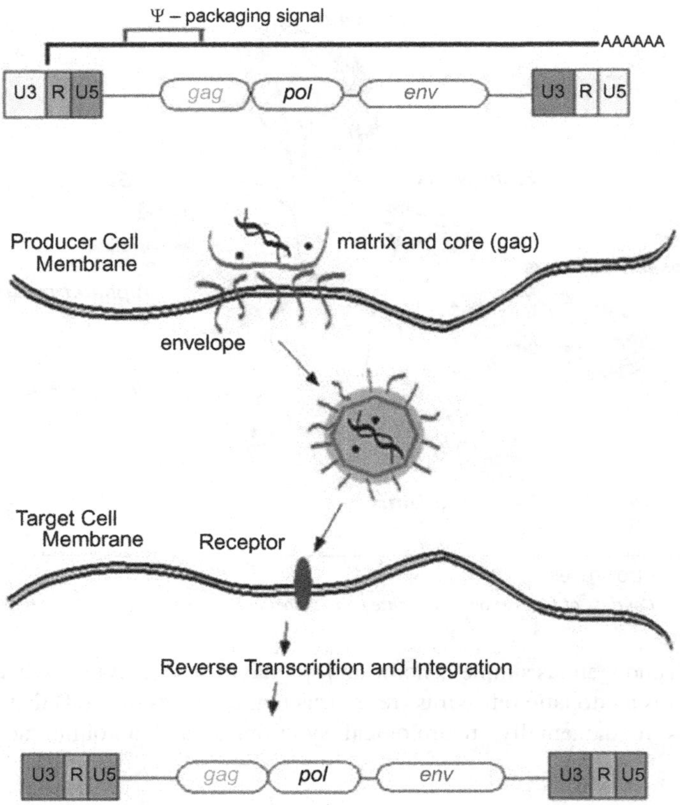

FIGURE 18.3

Vital cycle of retrovirus.

Courtesy of Stanford University School of Medicine. http://www.stanford.edu/group/nolan/tutorials/ret_6_gpedesc.html (USA-2015).

18.3.1 CELLULAR DAMAGES CAUSES BY HIV

HIV more frequency infects human CD4 cells, and when they are multiplied to fight infections, they make more copies of the HIV involuntarily. In infections prolonged by HIV, the numbers of CD4 cells are decreased. This is a sign that the immune system has been debilitated. Lower counts of CD4 cells increase the possibilities that the individual will get sick [1,2].

18.3.2 DETECTION OF THE HIV IN HUMANS

The analysis of the HIV includes tests that determine if an individual is or is not infected with the HIV that causes AIDS. Several types of analyses exist that are practiced generally on blood samples from individuals, but also other corporal fluids samples are used, including a scraped cheek [1,2].

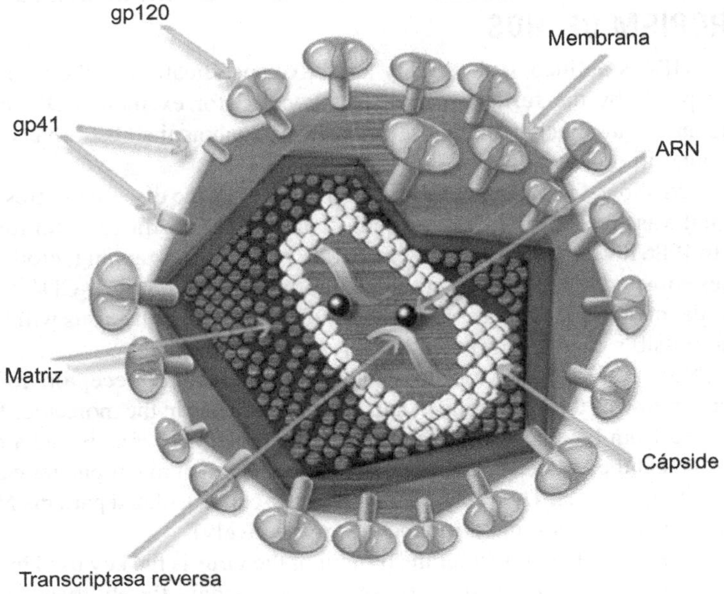

FIGURE 18.4

HIV structure.

Courtesy of Stanford University School of Medicine. http://www.stanford.edu/group/nolan/tutorials/ret_6_gpedesc.html (USA-2015).

Antibodies detection analysis. These analyses look for "antibodies" against the HIV in the blood and other corporal fluids. The antibodies are proteins produced by the immune system to fight a specific germ, in this case against HIV, which do not appear for 2 or 3 months after the organism has become infected [4].

Viral count analysis. Analysis of viral load measures the amount of HIV in the blood. Different techniques exist. The technique polymerase chain reaction (PCR) uses an enzyme to multiply the HIV in the blood sample. As soon as a chemical reaction marks the virus, the markers are measured and the amount of virus is calculated [5,6].

Analysis of CD4 cells. This analysis consists of making a count of CD4 and CD8 cells. The number of cells by cubical millimeter of blood is specified. Agreement does not exist about the normal average level of CD4 cells. The normal count of CD4 is between 500 and 1600 cells and CD8 is between 375 and 1100 cells. CD4 cells can diminish drastically in HIV+ people, and in some cases they can reach zero. Because the count of CD4 cells varies so much, the percentage of CD4 cells is also analyzed. This percentage relates to the totality of lymphocytes. If the analysis indicates that 34% of CD4 cells exist, it means that 34% of their lymphocytes are CD4 cells. The percentage is more stable than the number of CD4 cells. The normal rank is between 20% and 40%. A percentage under 14% indicates serious damage in the immune system. It is a signal of AIDS in people infected with HIV [7].

18.4 THE TROPISM OF AIDS

The tropism of the HIV is defined as the highly attractive specification of the virus toward the host tissue, determined partly by the surface markers of its cells (for example CD4 cells). The viruses develop a specific ability to attack cells in a selective way, such as the host organs and often certain cell populations found in organs of the body.

Patients with AIDS show decreasing of CD4+ lymphocytes as the disease progresses; thus, in 1984 it was believed that it was precisely the CD4 molecule that was the specific receptor for the HIV virus to enter the cell [8]. In 1986 it was shown that protein gp120, of the viral wrapping, grouped with the CD4, and both molecules co-acted as an immune complex, thus showing the gp120-CD4 union. The expression of the CD4 in the membrane is necessary but not sufficient so that the virus will fuse with the cell. The search for the possible co-receptor extended for about 10 years.

Since 1996, CCR5 and CXCR4 have been identified as the main co-receptors for the HIV, which has led to an understanding of the viral tropism and the pathogenesis in the molecular field [8]. In a few words it was observed from the beginning that all the isolated HIV-1 patients had a different tropism according to the cells that they infected. Some isolated patients infect macrophages easily while others infect line cells of T lymphocytes. Therefore, there are the so-called isolated patients M-tropics (R5X4) (the M and the T for macrophages and lymphocytes, respectively).

We could say in a sense that the gp120 of the protein of the virus is the key used by the HIV to enter the cell. The viruses R5X4 are the mutated viruses of HIV, which have the ability to attach to DNA with the co-receptor CCR5 or CXCR4, with the identification of patterns in the normal viruses such as X4 and R5 and the use of a Bayes classifier, we will be able to determine the co-receptor that the R5X4 virus will use.

18.5 MATERIALS AND METHODS

18.5.1 DATA COLLECTION

There are 149 HIV isolated sequences representing the three viral tropisms: 77 for M-tropic R5 (Table 18.1), 41 for T-tropic X4 (Table 18.2), and 31 for dual-tropic R5X4 (Table 18.3), identified by Lamers in [9] and in the National Center for Biotechnology Information (NCBI) (http://www.ncbi.nlm.nih.gov/) [10].

The DNA and the amino acids that make up the gp120 protein of each virus were obtained from the database (NCBI: http://www.ncbi.nlm.nih.gov/) [10]. Table 18.4 shows the virus category, the access number, and the amino acids of several selected viruses from each of the groups that represent the three viral tropisms (R5, X4, and R5X4).

18.5.2 GENERATION OF CHARACTERISTICS

Amino acids play central roles both as building blocks of proteins and as intermediates in metabolism. The 20 amino acids that are found within proteins convey a vast array of chemical versatility. The precise amino acid content, and the sequence of those amino acids, of a specific protein, is determined by the sequence of the bases in the gene that encodes that protein. The chemical properties of the amino

Table 18.1 Accession Numbers for Sequences of Different R5 Viruses

R5 Viruses			
AF062012	AY010852	M38429	U08453
L03698	U08670	U27443	AF307755
AF231045	U08798	U79719	AF307750
AY669778	AY669715	U04909	AY043176
U08810	U08710	U04918	AY158534
U51296	U16217	U40908	AX455917
AF407161	M26727	U08450	AY043173
AB253421	AJ418532	AF112542	AF307757
U08645	AJ418479	M63929	U08803
U08647	AJ418495	U66221	U88824
AB253429	AJ418514	AF491737	U69657
AY288084	AJ418521	U08779	AF355326
AF307753	U23487	L22084	U88826
AF411964	U04900	U27413	U08368
U08823	AF022258	AF005495	U27426
AF411965	AF258957	U52953	AJ006022
U92051	AF021477	AF321523	U08795
AF355318	U08716	L22940	
AY010759	U39259	U45485	
AY010804	AF204137	AB023804	

Table 18.2 Accession Numbers for Sequences of Different X4 Viruses

X4 Viruses			
AB014785	X01762	AF258981	U27408
AB014791	L31963	AF259003	AF411966
AB014796	U08447	AF021618	U27399
AB014810	AF355660	AF128989	U08822
U48267	AF355748	M17449	U08738
U08666	AF355742	AF075720	U08740
AF069692	AF355706	U48207	U08193
AF355319	AF180915	U72495	AF355330
AF355336	AF180903	AY189526	
M14100	AF035534	AF034375	
A04321	AF259050	AF034376	

Table 18.3 Accession Numbers for Sequences of Different R5X4 Viruses

R5X4 Viruses			
AB014795	U08445	AF259019	AF112925
AF062029	AF355674	AF259025	M17451
AF062031	AF355647	AF259021	K02007
AF062033	AF355630	AF259041	U39362
AF107771	AF355690	AF258970	AF069140
U08680	M91819	AF258978	AF458235
U08682	AF035532	AF021607	AF005494
U08444	AF035533	AF204137	

Table 18.4 Protein gp120 of Different Viruses (R5, X4, R5X4)

Viruses	Access Number	Protein (gp120)
R5X4	AB014795	VSTQLLLNGSLAEEEIIIRSENLTNNVKNIIVHLNRSV EINCTRPSNNTRTRVTLGPGRVWYRTGEIIGDIRK AYCEINGTKWNKVLTKVTEKLKGHFNKTVIFQQP
	AF062029	SFDPIPIHYCTPAGYAILKCNDKNFNGTGPCKNVS SVQCTHGIKPVVSTQLLLNGSLAEEEIIIRSENLT NNAKTIIVHLNKSVEINCTRPSNNTRTSLKIGPGQ VFYRTGDIIGNIRAAYCEINGTKWNKVLKQVTGK LEEHFKNKTIIFQPPSGGDLEITM
X4	AB014785	VSTQLLLNGSLAEEEIIIRSENLTNNVKNIVHLN RSVEINCTRPSNPTRTRITMGPGRVWYRTGEITGSIRA YCEINGTKWNKVLKQVTEKLKKHFNKTVIFQQP
	AB014791	VSTQLLLNGSLAEEEIIIRSENLTNNVKNIIVHLNRVE INCTRPSNPTRTRITMGPGRVWYRTGEITGSIKKA YCEINGTKWNKVLKQVTEKLKEHFNKTVIFQQP
R5	AF062012	AGYAILKCNDKNFNGTGPCKNVSSVQCTHGIKPVVST QLLLNGSLAEEEIIIRSENLTNNAKTIIVHLNKSVEINCTRP SNNTRTSITMGPGQVFYRTGDIIGDIRKAYCEINGTKWNE
	AY669778	VQARQLLSGIVQQQSNLLRAIEXQQHMLQLTVWGI KQLQARVLAVERYLKDQKFLGLWGCSGKIICTTAVPWNS TWSNKSFEEIWNNMTWTEWEREISNYTNQIYEILTES QNQQDRNEK DLLELDK

acids of proteins determine the biological activity of the protein. Proteins not only catalyze all (or most) of the reactions in living cells, they control virtually all cellular process. As we learn about amino acids, it is important to keep in mind that one of the more important reasons to understand amino acid structure and properties is to be able to understand protein structure and properties. The design of their own

Table 18.5 Amino Acid Properties

Amino Acid Residues	Charge	Volume (A3)	Mass (Da)	HP Scale	Surface Area	2D Structure Propensity		
						Alpha Helix	B-Strand	Turn
Alanine (A)	0	67	71.09	1.8	0.74	1.41	0.72	0.82
Arginine (I)	+1	148	156.19	−4.5	0.64	1.21	0.84	0.90
Aspargine (N)	0	96	114.11	−3.5	0.63	0.76	0.48	1.34
Aspartic acid (D)	−1	91	115.09	−3.5	0.62	0.99	0.39	1.24
Cystine (C)	0	86	103.15	2.5	0.91	0.66	1.40	0.54
Glutamine (Q)	0	114	128.14	−3.5	0.62	1.27	0.98	0.84
Glutamic acid (E)	−1	109	129.12	−3.5	0.62	1.59	0.52	1.01
Glycine (G)	0	48	57.05	−0.4	0.72	0.43	0.58	1.77
Histidine (H)	0	118	137.14	−3.2	0.78	1.05	0.8	0.81
Isoleucine (I)	0	124	113.16	4.5	0.88	1.09	1.67	0.47
Leucine (L)	0	124	113.16	3.8	0.85	1.34	1.22	0.57
Lysine (K)	+1	135	128.17	−3.9	0.52	1.23	0.69	1.07
Methionine (M)	0	124	131.19	1.9	0.85	1.30	1.14	0.52
Phenylalanine (F)	0	135	147.18	2.8	0.88	1.16	1.33	0.59
Proline (P)	0	90	97.12	−1.6	0.64	0.34	0.31	1.32
Serine (S)	0	73	87.08	−0.8	0.66	0.57	0.96	1.22
Threonine (T)	0	93	101.11	−0.7	0.7	0.76	1.17	0.90
Tryptophane (W)	0	163	186.21	−0.9	0.85	1.02	1.35	0.65
Tyrosine (Y)	0	141	163.18	−1.3	0.76	0.74	1.45	0.76
Valine (V)	0	105	99.14	4.2	0.86	0.90	1.87	0.41

Source: *Courtesy of Lamers SL, Salemi M, McGrath MS, Fogel GB. Prediction of R5, X4, and R5X4 HIV-1 coreceptor usage with evolved neural networks. IEEE/ACM Trans Comput Biol Bioinform April–June 2008;5(2).*

software in MatLab 2013, R, WEKA [11], and DNAStar [12] were used to calculate 16 general statistics from the protein gp120 of each virus; the first nine were figured out from the properties of the amino acids according to Table 18.5 with their own software (eg, amino acid type, charge, volume (A3), mass (Daltons), HP scale, surface area, alpha helix, B-strand, and turn) and the remaining properties were extracted from DNAStar (molecular weight, strongly basic (+), strongly acidic (−), the hydrophobic, polar amino acids, iso-electric point, charge at pH 7.0, etc.). The properties of amino acids were grouped later in tables (data sets) and loaded to the data mining software WEKA and R (Table 18.6) [9]. In WEKA we figured out some features such as minimum and maximum global average and standard deviation of all the viruses that belong to each category (R5, X4, and R5X4); for example, if we take the charge at pH 7.0, the standard deviation is 0.77 and the average is 9.698 for the viruses R5.

Table 18.6 DataSet of the Properties gp120 (R5X4, X4, R5)

Viruses	HP Scale	Iso-Electric Point	Charge at pH 7.0
R5X4	−16.0242859	8.49450056	2.78871235
	−16.2351317	7.45574745	2.09386078
	...	...	...
	−18.976128	4.57223777	−0.76387143
	−23.0876224	4.67223392	−0.76154492
X4	−16.5397662	−12.5715531	−5.88995583
	−8.6842059	−10.5275487	−1.92968167
	...	...	...
	−21.8430981	−11.3550309	−7.84058126
	−32.1514493	−10.7115709	−4.83229607
R5	−5.13319103	−8.1264515	29.1048261
	−8.71626002	−5.24553791	−18.4606144
	...	...	...
	−6.17507634	−8.07783669	20.3583467
	−6.03531124	−9.75213072	65.8851341

18.5.3 RESULTS

We will initially focus on the two-class case. Let ω_1, ω_2 be the two classes in which our patterns belong. In the sequel, we assume that the a priori probabilities $p(\omega_1), p(\omega_2)$ are known. This is a very reasonable assumption, because even if they are not known, they can easily be estimated from the available training feature vectors. Indeed, if N is the total number of available training patterns, and N_1, N_2 of them belong to ω_1 and ω_2, respectively, then $p(w_1) \approx N_1/N$ and $p(w_2) \approx N_2/N$.

The other statistical quantities assumed to be known are the class-conditional probability density functions (pdfs) $p(x|w_i), i = 1,2$, describing the distribution of the feature vectors in each of the classes. If these are not known, they can also be estimated from the available training data. The pdf $p(x|w_i)$ is sometimes referred to as the likelihood function of ω_i with respect to x. Here we should stress the fact that an implicit assumption has been made; that is, the feature vectors can take any value in the l-dimensional feature space. In the case that feature vectors can take only discrete values, density functions $p(x|w_i)$ become probabilities and will be denoted by $p(x|w_i)$.

Describing the Bayes rule we have [13,14]

$$p(w_i|x) = \frac{p(x|w_i)P(w_i)}{p(x)} \tag{1}$$

where each of the elements of this equation has the following meaning:

$p(\omega_i/x)$: The probability that a feature vector x, belongs to the class ω_i.
$p(x/\omega_i)$: The probability that given the class, the value of the random variable is, precisely. In other words is the pdf of the class as a random variable.
$p(w_i)$: The a priori probability of occurrence of an element of the class ω_i.

$p(x)$: The a priori probability of occurrence of an object to classify a feature vector equal to x (considered as a specific numerical vector), this element can be neglected because it has the same value for all classes.

In this way the maximum search is now focused on the values of the evaluating pdf of x [13,14].

The Bayes classification rule can now be declared as

$$\begin{array}{l} \text{If } P(\omega_1|\underline{x}) > P(\omega_2|\underline{x}) \;\; \underline{x} \rightarrow \omega_1 \;\; x \text{ is classified to } \omega_1 \\ \text{If } P(\omega_2|\underline{x}) > P(\omega_1|\underline{x}) \;\; \underline{x} \rightarrow \omega_2 \;\; x \text{ is classified to } \omega_2 \end{array} \quad (2)$$

Fig. 18.5 presents an example of two equiprobable classes and shows the variations of $P(x|\omega_i)$, $i = 1,2$, as functions of x for the simple case of a single feature ($l = 1$). The dotted line at x_0 is a threshold partitioning the feature space into two regions, R_1 and R_2. According to the Bayes decision rule, for all values of x in R_1 the classifier decides ω_1 and for all values in R_2 it decides ω_2.

However, it is obvious from the figure that decision errors are unavoidable. Indeed, there is a finite probability for an x to lie in the R_2 region at the same time it belongs in class ω_1. Then our decision is in error. The same is true for points originating from class ω_2. It does not take much thought to see that the total probability of committing a decision error is given by [14]:

$$P_e = \frac{1}{2}\int_{-\infty}^{x_0} p\left(\frac{x}{\omega_2}\right)dx + \frac{1}{2}\int_{x_0}^{+\infty} p\left(\frac{x}{\omega_1}\right)dx \quad (3)$$

As we have seen, this classifier is based on managing of the second member of the Bayes theorem:

$$p\left(\frac{w_i}{x}\right)\cdot p(w_i);\; i = 1,2,\ldots,N \quad (4)$$

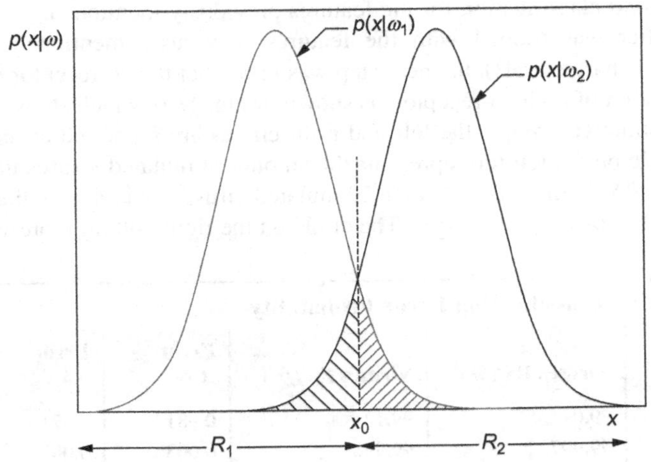

FIGURE 18.5

Example of the two regions R_1 and R_2 formed by the Bayesian classifier for the case of two equiprobable classes.
Courtesy of Theodoridis S, Koutroumbas K. Pattern recognition. *3rd ed. Academic Press; 2006.*

What is the pdf of the different classes $w_1, w_2, \ldots, w_n$? First, we will restrict our study to normal or Gaussian distributions, which occurs in the most practical cases. We begin with the case of one-dimensional distribution; for example, when we are working with a single feature. Expression of the pdf is as follows:

$$p\left(\frac{x}{w_i}\right) = \frac{1}{\sqrt{2\pi}\sigma_i} \exp^{-\frac{1}{2}\frac{(x-\mu_i)^2}{\sigma_i^2}} \tag{5}$$

where μ_i and σ_i are the average and typical standard deviation.

The multivariate generalization of a Gaussian pdf in the l-dimensional space is given by

$$p(x) = \frac{1}{(2\pi)^{1/2}|\Sigma|^{1/2}} \exp^{\left(-(1/2)(x-u)^T\Sigma^{-1}(x-u)\right)} \tag{6}$$

where $u = E[x]$ is the mean value and Σ is the lxl covariance matrix defined as

$$\Sigma = E\left[(x-u)(x-u)^T\right] \tag{7}$$

where $|\Sigma|$ denotes the determinant of Σ. It is readily seen that for $l = 1$ the multivariate Gaussian coincides with the univariate one. Sometimes, the symbol $N(u, \Sigma)$ is used to denote a Gaussian pdf with mean value u and covariance Σ.

We consider general statistics of molecular weight, iso-electric point, and charge at pH for the two categories of viruses ω_1 (R5) and ω_2 (X4), and we first got the pdf of each one of the characteristics based on its μ_i and σ_i for both types of viruses and later, we calculated the classification error (3) in the zone in which pdfs are trans lapped (see Fig. 18.5). 100,000 data that follow a normal behavior were considered to value the quality of the classifier. Table 18.7 shows the classification rate, reason of error, and optimums threshold classification for the features previously mentioned.

Once the classifier was trained with the features previously mentioned (molecular weight, iso-electric point, and charge at pH), the next step was to predict the co-receptor of the mutated virus (R5X4). The distribution of both co-receptors is shown in Fig. 18.6, which shows the mutated viruses are in one of the distinctive groups; the left and right circles are separated according to the type of co-receptor. The circle on the left top represents the amount of mutated viruses that enter exclusively in the co-receptor CCR5 (in this case from the 29 mutated viruses, only 4 have the characteristics that allow them to enter the co-receptor CCR5). The circle on the right bottom represents mutated viruses

Table 18.7 Measuring Classification Error Probability

	Viruses R5 (%)	Viruses X4 (%)	Error R5	Error X4	Optimal Threshold
Molecular weight	99.01	99.12	0.981	0.871	7.85
Hydrophobic amino acids	99.997	99.998	0.003	0.002	6.53
Iso-electric point	99.83	99.84	0.162	0.153	7.43
Charge at pH 7.0	99.97	99.99	.03	0.01	6.953

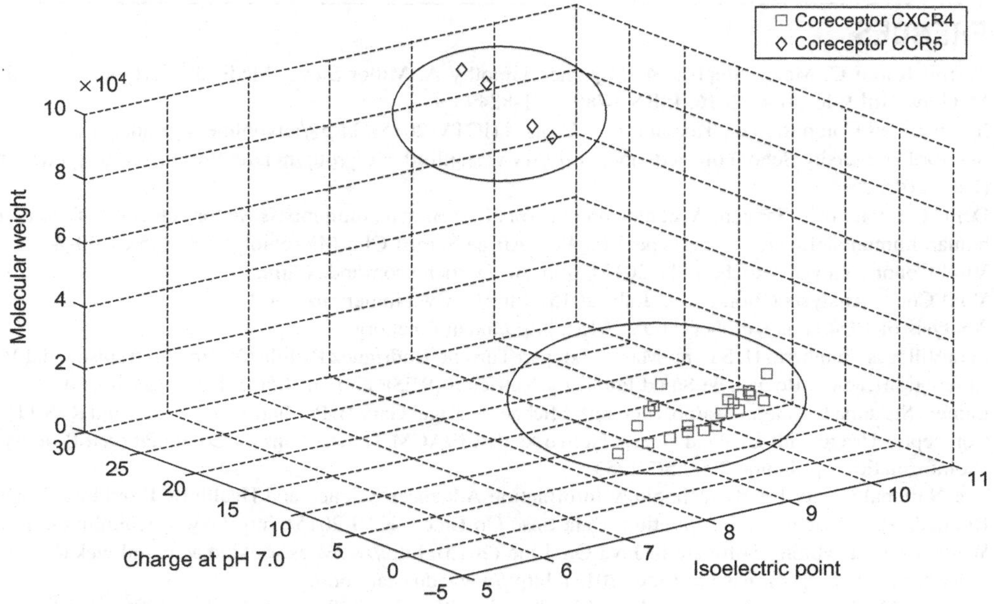

FIGURE 18.6

Predicting the co-receptors CCR5 or CXCR4 from the mutated virus (R5X4), according to its characteristics of molecular weight, charge at pH, and iso-electric point.

that have characteristics that allow them to enter to co-receptor CXCR4 (in this case, from the 29 mutated viruses 25 have this type of characteristics).

18.6 CONCLUSIONS

The infection of target cells by HIV-1 requires binding of the viral surface protein gp120 to the cellular surface protein CD4 and chemokine receptors CCR5 or CXCR4. Co-receptor usage can determine a virus's behavior both in vitro and in vivo. Viruses that utilize the CCR5 co-receptor do not induce syncytia and primarily infect macrophages, but can also infect lymphocytes. On the other hand, viruses that utilize the CXCR4 co-receptor induce syncytia in transformed CD4+ cells and have the ability to infect lymphocytes and T-cells lines. Additionally, there exists a subset of viruses that can utilize both the CCR5 and CXCR4 co-receptors and infect macrophages, as well as lymphocytes and T-cell lines; these viruses are usually identified as D-tropic.

In this chapter we observed that the viruses R5 HIV-1 use CCR5 as a co-receptor for the viral entrance, the X4 HIV-1 viruses use CXCR4, while some strange viruses known as R5X4 or D-tropic have the ability to use both co-receptors. We performed a series of experiments to implement a Bayesian classifier that allows us to identify different patterns that enables us to predict the co-receptor of the mutated virus R5X4.

REFERENCES

[1] Carroll Karen C, Morse Stephen A, Mietzner Timothy A, Miller Steve. Medical microbiology. 27th ed. McGraw-Hill Education; 2016. ISBN 9780-0-71-82498-9.
[2] International Committee on Taxonomy of Viruses (ICTV-2015). http://ictvonline.org/index.asp.
[3] Stanford University School of Medicine. http://www.stanford.edu/group/nolan/tutorials/ret_6_gpedesc.html (USA-2015).
[4] Denis F, Leonard G, Sangare A, et al. Comparison of 10 enzyme immunoassays for detection of antibody to human immunodeficiency virus type 2 in West Africa Sera. J Clin Microbiol 1988;26(5):1000–4.
[5] Viral Count Analysis (Roche Labs 2015). http://www.roche.com/index.htm.
[6] Viral Count Analysis (Biomerieux Labs 2015). http://www.biomerieux.com/.
[7] Analysis of CD4 cells (Infonet AIDS 2015). http://aidsinfonet.org/.
[8] Lara Villegas Humberto H, Salemi Marco, Ixtepan Turrent, Rodríguez Padilla Cristina. El tropismo del VIH y su fenotipificación. Revista de Salud Pública y Nutrición (RESPYN) 2004;5(4). ISBN 1870-0160.
[9] Lamers Susanna L, Salemi Marco, McGrath Michael S, Fogel Gary B. Prediction of R5, X4, and R5X4 HIV-1 Coreceptor Usage with Evolved Neural Networks. IEEE/ACM Transactions on Computational Biology and Bioinformatics April-June 2008;5(2):253.
[10] The National Center for Biotechnology Information Advances Science and Health by Providing Access to Biomedical and Genomic Information. Data Base On-Line (NCBI-2015). http://www.ncbi.nlm.nih.gov/.
[11] Weka 3.7 Data Mining Software in Java On_Line (2015). http://www.cs.waikato.ac.nz/ml/weka/.
[12] Software for Life Scientists On-Line (2015). http://www.dnastar.com/.
[13] Bishop CM. Pattern recognition and machine learning. New York: Springer-Verlag; 2006.
[14] Theodoridis S, Koutroumbas K. Pattern recognition. 4th ed. San Diego, California, USA: Academic Press is an imprint of Elsevier; 2009. p. 13–5. ISBN 978-1-59749-272-0.

SECTION

III

SYSTEMS BIOLOGY AND BIOLOGICAL PROCESSES

CHAPTER

CELLULAR AUTOMATA-BASED MODELING OF THREE-DIMENSIONAL MULTICELLULAR TISSUE GROWTH

19

B. Ben Youssef

Department of Computer Engineering, King Saud University, Riyadh, Saudi Arabia

19.1 INTRODUCTION

Cellular automata (CA) are dynamic systems, in which both space and time are discrete, consisting of a number of identical cells in a regular lattice. They were originally introduced by John von Neumann and Stanislaw Ulam as a possible idealization of biological systems with a particular purpose of modeling biological self-reproduction [1]. Each cell in the cellular space can be in a finite number of states. The next state of each cell is determined, at discrete time intervals, according to its current state, the current state of its neighboring cells, and a next-state transition rule or function. CA provide a computationally proficient technique for analyzing the collective properties of a network of interconnected cells. The use of CA in modeling various systems, including biological ones, has a number of advantages that include the fact that CA are sufficiently simple to allow detailed mathematical analysis, yet complex enough to exhibit a wide variety of complicated and emergent phenomena [2].

The development of computational and simulation models for studying biocomplexity at the cell population and tissue level can provide powerful frameworks in this area, particularly by employing systems-based approaches [3]. These approaches consider cells as system components that migrate, proliferate, and interact to generate the complex behavior observed in living systems [4]. However, employing systems-based approaches could lead to models with high complexity whose solution poses significant computational challenges [5,6]. The availability of computational models with *predictive* abilities could greatly speed up progress in this area by assisting scientists in predicting the dynamic response of cell populations to external stimuli, and by rapidly assessing the effect of various system parameters on the overall tissue growth rates. Computer simulations can thus be used to shorten the development stage by allowing researchers to quickly screen many alternatives and choose only the most promising ones for laboratory experimentation.

Because natural tissues are multicellular and have a specific three-dimensional architecture, the simulation of tissue growth consisting of more than one type of cells becomes paramount. Further, because these multiple types of cells tend to organize themselves into very specific spatial patterns, the discrete CA approach may be considered to be ideally suited to treat such problems with complicated geometry. Models with a predictive capability are also suitable for the visual and quantitative exploration of a diverse range of testable hypotheses and "what-if" query scenarios, thus providing a basis for a rational design approach [7]. This makes them a necessary prerequisite for developing systems control strategies for biotechnological processes involving the proliferation and growth of contact-inhibited cells [8].

The three-dimensional (3-D) CA model, described here, incorporates multiple cell types and covers cell motion, division, collision, and aggregation [9,10]. In particular, the model allows us to quickly evaluate the relative effect of many system parameters on the tissue growth rates including the initial density of seed cells and their spatial distribution. The rest of this chapter is organized as follows. In the next section, we present some related work in this area. Afterwards, we describe the modeling of different cellular processes involved in tissue growth. We then outline the computational model and present its corresponding algorithm. We next discuss a sample of simulation results and provide our conclusion and future directions for research.

19.2 RELATED WORK

Various modeling approaches have been used to simulate the population dynamics of proliferating cells. These models can be classified as *deterministic*, *stochastic*, and based on CA or *agents*. Deterministic models, such as the ones developed by Frame and Hu [11] and Cherry and Papoutsakis [12], provide insight into simple cell population dynamics. Such models may be useful in fitting specific quantitative results; but they give little or no topological information of the cell colonies before confluence or provide means of interpreting the parameters in terms of the biological processes involved.

Lim and Davies developed a stochastic two-dimensional (2-D) model based on a matrix of irregular polygons and using the Voronoi tessellation technique to address the issue of cell topology [13]. While this model accounted for the formation and merging of cell colonies, it made some restrictive assumptions on cell interactions and did not address cell motility. Ruaan, Tsai, and Tsao proposed another stochastic model for the simulation of density-dependent growth of anchorage-dependent cells on flat surfaces [14]. Their model included the effects of cell motion and considered that cell sizes varied with time.

A 2-D model based on CA was developed by Zygourakis et al. [15]. The model allows for contact inhibition during the proliferation process. Using the CA concept, Hawboldt et al. [16] as well as Forestell et al. [17] modeled contact-inhibited synchronous cell growth on microcarriers. Both of these models were 2-D and did not account for cell motion. Moreover, the assumption of uniform doubling time of cell populations was somewhat unrealistic in cell proliferation phenomena. Later, Lee et al. showed the importance of cell motility and cell-cell interactions in describing the cell proliferation rates [18]. This work was succeeded by another model that described the locomotion of migrating endothelial cells in two dimensions [19].

Chang and his team developed a 3-D CA-based model to describe the growth of microbial cell units [20]. This model considered the effects of bacterial cell division and cell death. Other models based on CA have also been used to solve more specific modeling problems. For instance, Kansal et al. developed a model to simulate brain tumor growth dynamics [21]. Their model utilizes a few automaton cells to represent thousands of real cells, thus reducing the computational time requirements of the model while limiting its ability to track individual cells in the cellular space. Another CA model was used by Cickovski et al. [22] as a framework to simulate morphogenesis. This model used a hybrid approach to simulate the growth of an avian limb. The cellular automaton governed cell interactions

Table 19.1 Overview of Deterministic, Stochastic, and Cellular Automata Models Used in the Simulation of Cell Proliferation Dynamics and Tissue Growth

Author(s)	Model Type	Main Features	Limitations
Frame and Hu [11]	Deterministic	• Growth rate based on cell density	• All cells assumed to be equally contact-inhibited
Cherry and Papoutsakis [12]	Deterministic	• Perimeter cell growth in cell colonies	• Assumption of circular cell colonies only • No colony mergings
Lim and Davies [13]	Stochastic	• Random cell division • Cells represented as irregular polygons	• No cell motion • Restricted cell-cell interactions
Ruann et al. [14]	Stochastic	• Density-dependent growth • Cell motility	• Restricted cell motion • Simplified cell division
Zygourakis et al. [15]	Cellular automata	• Contact-inhibited cell proliferation	• No cell motion
Forestell et al. [17]	Cellular automata	• Cell growth on microcarriers	• Restricted number of cells and their neighbors
Hawboldt et al. [16]	Cellular automata	• Cell growth for any cell line or microcarrier	• No cell motion • Synchronous growth
Lee et al. [18,19]	Cellular automata	• Cell motion and division	• One cell per square (2-D)
Kansal et al. [21]	Cellular automata	• Tumor growth • 3-D model	• No cell motion • No tracking of individual cells
Chang et al. [20]	Cellular automata	• 3-D model • Cell division and death	• No cell motion • No contact inhibition
Ben Youssef [10]	Cellular automata	• 3-D model • Cell motion, division, and collision	• Single cell type
Cickovski et al. [22]	Cellular automata	• Morphogenesis • Multiple cell types	• No cell motion
Ben Youssef and Tang [9]	Cellular automata	• Multiple cell types • Formation of multicelluar aggregates in 3-D	• Cell size does not vary

while reaction-diffusion equation solvers were used to determine the concentration levels of surrounding chemicals. In Table 19.1, we present an overview of these deterministic, stochastic, and CA models while highlighting their main features and limitations.

While our main focus here is on CA-based models, there also exist a number of agent-based lattice-free models to simulate tissue growth [23,24]. Agent-based models (ABMs) can be thought of as generalizations of CA models, where a number of individual and autonomous constituent entities (known as *agents*) interact locally to create a higher level, group behavior [5]. These models apply the dynamics of cell proliferation and death to describe tissue pattern formation and growth. Other related models are suitable for describing the locomotion of a fixed number of cells where cells move relatively slowly with respect to other processes like the diffusion of soluble substances [25]. Some of the ABMs use regular triangulation to generate the neighborhood topology for the cells, thus allowing for a continuous representation of cell sizes and locations in contrast to grid-based models [26]. Others utilize multiscale approaches to model collective phenomena in multicellular assemblies [27]. The reader is referred to the recent work by Hwang et al., which reviews a number of rule-based modeling techniques of multicellular biological systems using, among others, ABMs [5].

19.3 MODELING OF BIOLOGICAL PROCESSES

We assume that tissue growth is characterized by the following four main cellular processes: cell division, cell motion, cell collision, and cell aggregation. Fig. 19.1 provides a high-level view of these processes for two cells of different types during their mitotic cycle.

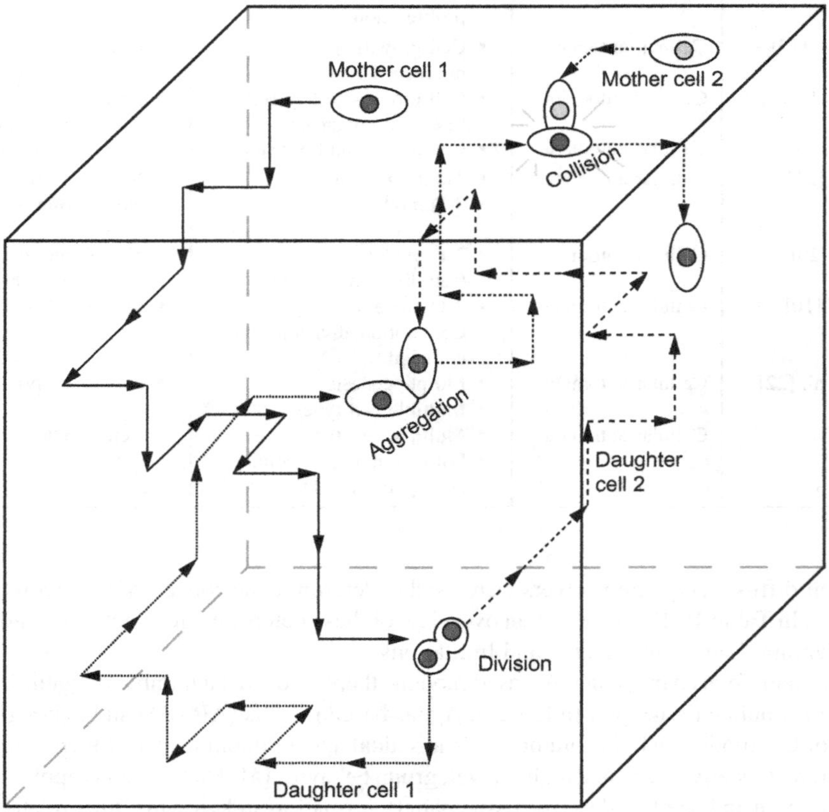

FIGURE 19.1

Persistent random walk of two mother cells of different types (1 and 2) during their division cycle. The two daughter cells move away from each other and may *aggregate* or *collide* with other cells.

19.3.1 CELL DIVISION

Mammalian cells are anchorage-dependent and require a substrate or a scaffold in which they can grow. The growth of cells is characterized by the formation of confluent layers in which neighboring cells touch one another. As cell division occurs, two newly formed daughter cells are born. Cell division continues until a cell is completely surrounded by other cells. This is known as *contact inhibition*. As confluent patches of cells form, only cells at the outer edges of the patches can divide while cells inside the patches are contact inhibited. The effects of contact inhibition can be reduced with cell motion as increased motility can significantly enhance cell proliferation rates. These two competing processes and their opposing effects complicate the dynamics of cell population [15]. We model cell division as a two-step process:

1. If there are vacant sites in a cell's neighborhood, then the cell divides and two new daughter cells are created. One daughter cell occupies the original site, and the other daughter cell occupies a vacant neighboring site.
2. Each daughter cell is assigned new parameters based on the cell population characteristics of its type.

The position for a daughter cell is chosen according to a random algorithm based on the growth probabilities. The time interval between the division of a cell and its subsequent division is called the *cell cycle time*. The cell cycle time is known to follow a wide distribution, resulting in the asynchronous proliferation of cells.

19.3.2 CELL MOTION

Cell motility is an important function of mammalian cells. It is vital for many physiological processes such as wound healing and plays an important role in counterbalancing the effects of contact inhibition [28]. To model cell motion, we must characterize the trajectories traversed by individual cells. In earlier studies concerning cell motion trajectories, the common method used was to observe the initial and final cell positions. Such approaches do not provide detailed information on how individual cells move and are incapable of evaluating the important locomotory parameters, such as individual cell speed, persistence, and so forth. Other studies have shown, however, that several cell lines execute a persistent random walk [29]. That is, cells move in a certain direction for a fixed duration of time, and then suddenly turn and move in another direction. Changes in direction can be the result of cell collision or as a response to some intracellular activity. Using these observations, Lee et al. [19] developed a Markov chain model to characterize the locomotion of endothelial cells in two dimensions. We employ this approach and extend it to three dimensions to describe the movements of individual cells in the cellular space. To characterize cell migration in a way that is suitable for a computer implementation, our discrete model incorporates the following information:

1. The speed of cell migration;
2. The expected duration of cell locomotion in a given direction;
3. The probability distribution of turning angles to determine the next direction of cell movement;
4. The frequency of cell stops; and
5. The duration of cell stops.

19.3.3 CELL COLLISION

Mammalian cells move in a certain direction for some period of time and, then, they turn and migrate in another direction. Cell collision occurs when a cell moving in a certain direction or when a cell is changing its direction and encounters another cell of a different type in its path. It was observed in Ref. [30] that cell direction changes take place either in response to some intracellular signal or when two cells collide with each other. As a result, when a cell of one type collides with a cell of a different type, the cell slows down for a period of time and then changes its direction. The duration of time a cell stays in the stationary state after a cell collision is based on its type [30]. Once the cell is ready to resume its motion, it migrates in a new direction. The modeling steps used in the cell collision process are described below:

- The cell stops for a number of steps.
- The cell changes its direction and resumes motion.

19.3.4 CELL AGGREGATION

Cell aggregation is a feature of tissue formation that allows the binding of cells of the same type. It is this specific grouping of cells that enables the tissue to perform its intended purpose. Cell aggregation is the combination of two cellular functions: cell-to-cell recognition and cell adhesion. The self-recognition quality lets cells identify cells of the same type. When cells of the same type encounter each other, they adhere to one another and form a cellular aggregate. As more cells of the same cell type encounter the cellular aggregate, the cellular aggregate becomes larger, forming a cluster of cells. The adhesion can be strengthened by aggregation factors that are sometimes secreted by the cells [31]. As a result of aggregation, the cell slows down, "sticks" to another cell of the same type, and changes its direction of motion. The basic steps used to model the process of cell aggregation are listed below:

- The two cells stop for a number of steps, thereby entering an aggregation state.
- The two cells change their direction and resume locomotion.

19.4 COMPUTATIONAL MODEL

Tissue regeneration is a highly dynamic process. When cells are seeded in a 3-D scaffold, they migrate in all directions, interact with each other, and proliferate until they completely fill the space available to them. This assumes that enough nutrients are always available to sustain cell growth everywhere in the interior of the scaffold. To model this dynamic process, we consider CA consisting of 3-D grids with N^3 total cubic computational sites [2]. Each site is a *finite automaton* that can exist in one of a finite number of states and interacts with its six immediate neighbors as shown in Fig. 19.2. That is, a site may be either

- Empty and available for a cell to move in, or
- Occupied by a cell, which is at a given point in its mitotic cycle and moves in a certain direction. No other cell can move or divide into an already occupied site.

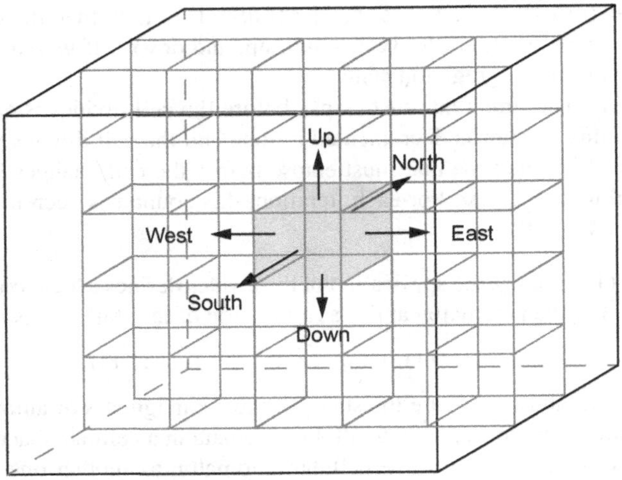

FIGURE 19.2

A cell in the cellular automaton interacts with its six immediate neighbors. This is known as the *von Neumann neighborhood* in three dimensions.

Proliferating cells execute *persistent random walks* in space [32]. This process consists of the following stages:

1. Each cell in the population moves in one direction for a certain period of time (*persistence*). At the end of this interval, the cell stops and turns to continue its migration in another direction. The persistence is a random variable whose density function can be determined experimentally.
2. When two cells *collide*, they stop for a short period of time before resuming their migration to move away from each other.
3. At the end of its cycle, a cell stops to divide into two daughter cells.
4. This process is repeated until the cell populations have completely filled the scaffold or until the cells cannot migrate and divide any further [9].

To simulate these dynamics, the state $x_j()$ of each cellular automaton takes values from a set of integer numbers that code all the required information about the cell type, its migration speed, the direction of movement, and the time remaining until the next direction change and the next cell division. Our model also considers cell *division time* as a random variable whose probability density function can be obtained experimentally using the procedure described by Lee et al. [19]. Hence, every automaton has its state evolving at discrete time steps Δt through interactions with neighboring automata. Let us consider the jth automaton that contains a cell at time t^r. Its state $x_j(r)$ is specified by the following numbers:

1. Cell type $k_{t,j}$: For each cell population, this is a unique identifier. The number of modeled cell populations is based on the number of digits used to represent $k_{t,j}$. Using a single digit, up to nine different cell populations can be simulated with each population having its own division and migratory parameters.

2. Migration index m_j ($m_j \in \{0, 1, 2, 3, 4, 5, 6, 7\}$): If $m_j = 1,2,\ldots,6$, then the cell is migrating in one of the six directions (east, north, west, south, up, and down). If $m_j = 0$, the cell is stationary. If $m_j = 7$, the cell is in the aggregation state.
3. Division counter $k_{d,j}$: The time that must elapse before the cell divides is equal to $t_d = k_{d,j}\Delta t$. For each iteration, this counter is decremented by one and the cell divides when $k_{d,j} = 0$.
4. Persistence counter $k_{p,j}$: The time that must elapse before the cell changes its direction of movement is equal to $t_p = k_{p,j}\Delta t$. For each iteration, this counter is decremented by one and the cell turns when $k_{p,j} = 0$.

For every automaton j ($1 \le j \le N^3$), the application of these rules defines a local transition function specifying the state $x_j(r+1)$ of the automaton at t^{r+1} as a function of the states of its neighbors at t^r; that is,

$$x_j(r+1) = f_j(x_j(r), x_{j+1}(r), x_{j+2}(r), \ldots, x_{j+6}(r)), \tag{1}$$

where $x_{j+1}(r), x_{j+2}(r), \ldots,$ and $x_{j+6}(r)$ are the states of the six neighbors of automaton j. The application of the local transition functions, $f_j(\ldots)$, to all the automata in a cellular space transforms a configuration $X(r) = [x_1(r), x_2(r), \ldots, x_{N^3}(r)]$ of the cellular automaton to another one $X(r+1)$ according to Eq. (1). Thus, a global transition function F acting on the entire array can be defined as follows:

$$X(r+1) = F(X(r)), \quad r = 0, 1, 2, \ldots \tag{2}$$

As a result, starting from an initial configuration $X(0)$, the cellular automaton follows a trajectory of configurations $X(1), X(2), \ldots, X(r), \ldots$ defined by the global transition function F. At each time level, the states of all the cells of an automaton are updated in parallel.

19.5 ALGORITHM

19.5.1 INITIAL CONDITION AND INPUTS

The simulation results reported in this chapter are obtained for a 200 × 200 × 200 cellular array utilizing two cell populations. Each one of these two cell populations, referred to as cell population 1 and cell population 2, respectively, has its own division and migration characteristics. The division time distributions for these two cell populations are given in Table 19.2. Cells from population 1 are considered to be fast-moving cells that migrate at 10 μm/h while cells from population 2 are slow-moving cells migrating at a speed of only 1 μm/h.

Next, the sites that will be occupied by cells at time t^0 are selected. The assignment of seed cells to the grid sites may be done either randomly (using, eg, a uniform distribution with one of the two

Table 19.2 Cell Division Time Distributions for the Two Cell Populations

	Cell Populations	
Division Times (h)	Cell Population 1 (%)	Cell Population 2 (%)
[12, 18)	64	4
[18, 24)	32	32
[24, 30)	4	64

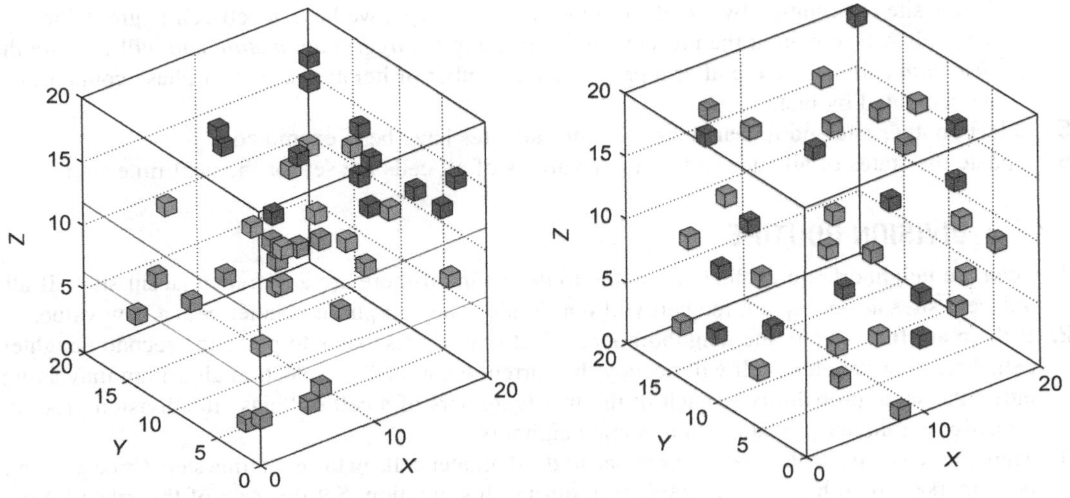

FIGURE 19.3

An example of two uniform cell-seeding distributions displaying three cell types in *segmented* (left) and *mixed* (right) seeding modes, respectively. A total of 40 cells in a 20 × 20 × 20 cellular array are seeded, yielding a 0.5% cell-seeding density.

seeding modes depicted in Fig. 19.3 below) or according to rules that emulate special cases of tissue regeneration like *wound healing* [4]. Afterwards, an initial state $x_j(0)$, at time t^0, is assigned to each occupied site j based on the population characteristics of that cell type. The migration index m_j is randomly selected, the value of the persistence counter $k_{p,j}$ is properly chosen, and the cell division counter $k_{d,j}$ is set according to the experimentally determined distribution of cell division times. As stated previously, the integer counters $k_{p,j}$ and $k_{d,j}$ will be decremented at every iteration and the cell will change its direction of movement or divide when $k_{p,j}=0$ or $k_{d,j}=0$, respectively.

19.5.2 ITERATIVE OPERATIONS

At each time step $t^r = t^{r-1} + \Delta t$, $r = 1, 2, \ldots$

1. Randomly select a computational site.
2. If this site contains a cell that is ready to divide, execute the *division routine* and go to step 5.
3. If this site contains a cell that is ready to change its direction of movement, execute the *direction change routine* and go to step 5.
4. Otherwise, try to move the cell to a neighboring site in the direction indicated by the migration index of its current state:
   a. If this site is free, *mark* it as the site that will contain the cell at the next time step and decrement the persistence and cell phase counters by one.
   b. If this site is occupied by a cell from a different cell type, we have a cell-cell collision. The cell will remain at the present site by entering the *stationary state* and will execute the *direction change* routine after a prespecified number of iterations. Its cell phase counter is decremented by one.

c. If this site is occupied by a cell from the same cell type, we have a cell-cell aggregation. The cell will remain at the present site by entering the *aggregation state* and will execute the *direction change* routine after a prespecified number of iterations. Its cell phase counter is decremented by one.

5. Select another site and repeat steps 2–4 until all sites have been examined.
6. Update the states of all sites so that the locations of all cells are set for the next time step.

19.5.3 DIVISION ROUTINE

1. Scan the neighborhood of the current site to determine if there are any free adjacent sites. If all adjacent sites are occupied, the cell will not divide. The cell phase counter gets a new value.
2. If there are free sites in the neighborhood, select one of these sites to place the second daughter cell. The other daughter cell will occupy the current location. The selection algorithm may assign either the same probability to each of the free neighbors of a cell or "bias" the division process by assigning higher probabilities to some neighbors.
3. Mark the selected site that will contain one of the daughter cells in the next time step. Once a site has been marked, no other cell can move in it during this iteration. Set the state of this site $x_j(r)$, at time step t^r, by defining the migration index as well as the persistence and cell division counters.

19.5.4 DIRECTION CHANGE ROUTINE

1. Scan the neighborhood of the current site to determine if there are any free adjacent sites. If all adjacent sites are occupied, the cell remains at the present site. The cell is also assigned a new persistence counter.
2. If there are free sites in the neighborhood, select one of these sites by using a random algorithm based on the experimentally determined state-transition probabilities.
3. Mark the selected site that will contain the cell in the next time step to prevent other cells from occupying it. Set the persistence counter to its appropriate initial value and decrement the cell phase counter by one.

19.6 CALCULATIONS OF TISSUE GROWTH RATE

Starting with a total number of seed cells that is equal to N_O, the algorithms describing the rules for cell migration and division transform the cellular array to simulate the dynamic process of tissue growth. At some time t after the start of the simulation, $N_c(t)$ sites of the 3-D grid are occupied by cells. Extending the approach described by Cheng et al. [32] to the case of multiple cell types, we can compute a measure to indicate the volume coverage at time t denoted by the cell volume fraction $k(t)$, which is defined as follows:

$$k(t) = \frac{N_c(t)}{N^3} = \frac{\sum_{i=1}^{n} N_{c_i}(t)}{N^3}, \quad \text{with } N_O = N_c(0) = \sum_{i=1}^{n} N_{c_i}(0) \tag{3}$$

where N^3 is the size of the cellular space $(= N_x \times N_y \times N_z)$, $N_{c_i}(t)$ is the number of occupied computational sites by cell type i at time t, $N_{c_i}(0)$ is the number of seed cells of type i, and n is the number of cell types ($n \geq 1$). For the uniform seeding, the cell volume fraction indicates the fraction of cells occupying the cellular space at a given time. The overall *tissue growth rate* represents the increase in volume coverage with respect to time. To this end, the tissue growth rate measure is given by the following formula:

$$\frac{dk(t)}{dt}=\frac{N_c(t)-N_c(t-\Delta t)}{\Delta t \times N^3}=\frac{\sum_{i=1}^{n}(N_{c_i}(t)-N_{c_i}(t-\Delta t))}{\Delta t \times N^3}. \quad (4)$$

Here, $k(t)$ is the cell volume fraction at time t, as given above in Eq. (3), and Δt is the time step in days. We also define the cell *heterogeneity* measure, H, to be equal to the ratio of the initially seeded number of cells from population 1 (fast cells) to that from population 2 (slow cells). That is, when $H=9$, there are nine cells from population 1 for every cell from population 2 in the cell seeding distribution. The simulation continues until all sites are occupied by cells, that is until $k(t)$ equals a prespecified *confluence* parameter, such as 99.999%.

19.7 SIMULATION RESULTS AND DISCUSSION

19.7.1 EFFECT OF CELL HETEROGENEITY ON VOLUME COVERAGE AND TISSUE GROWTH RATE

Fig. 19.4 shows the temporal evolution of volume coverage as the heterogeneity measure, H, is varied for both the segmented and mixed cell seeding distributions. In these simulation runs, the value of H is chosen from the set $\{1,3,5,7,9\}$ while the initial seeding density is maintained at 0.5%. We observe that volume coverage increases with time until it reaches confluence for all values of H and that as H is increased, full volume coverage is reached sooner. This is because an increase in the value of this ratio results in a larger number of fast cells initially seeded in the cellular space; thus, allowing these cells to dominate the proliferation process. Faster moving cells spread out in the cellular space seeking empty regions, which delays the formation of cell colonies and leads to faster proliferation by mitigating the impact of contact inhibition. This also results in an increase in the overall tissue growth rate as depicted in Fig. 19.5. Such an impact is more pronounced in the segmented distribution for values of $1<H\leq 5$.

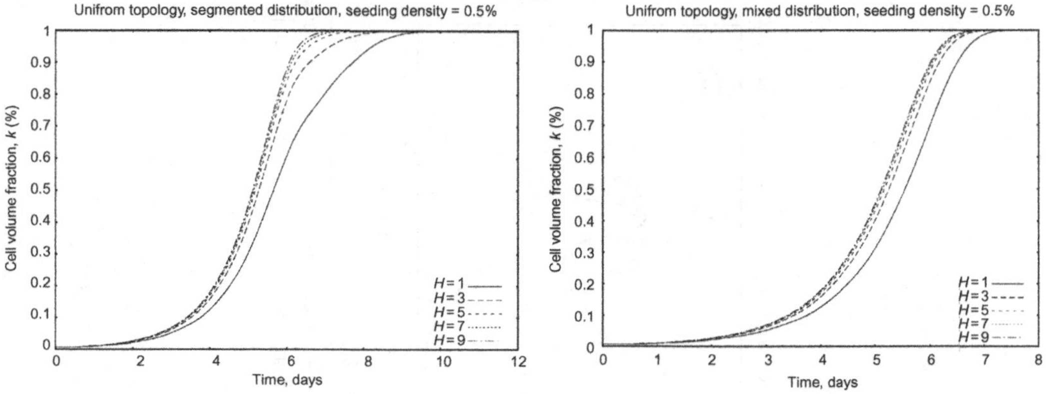

FIGURE 19.4

Effect of varying the cell heterogeneity ratio, H, on the cell volume fraction for the *segmented* (left) and *mixed* (right) cell-seeding distributions.

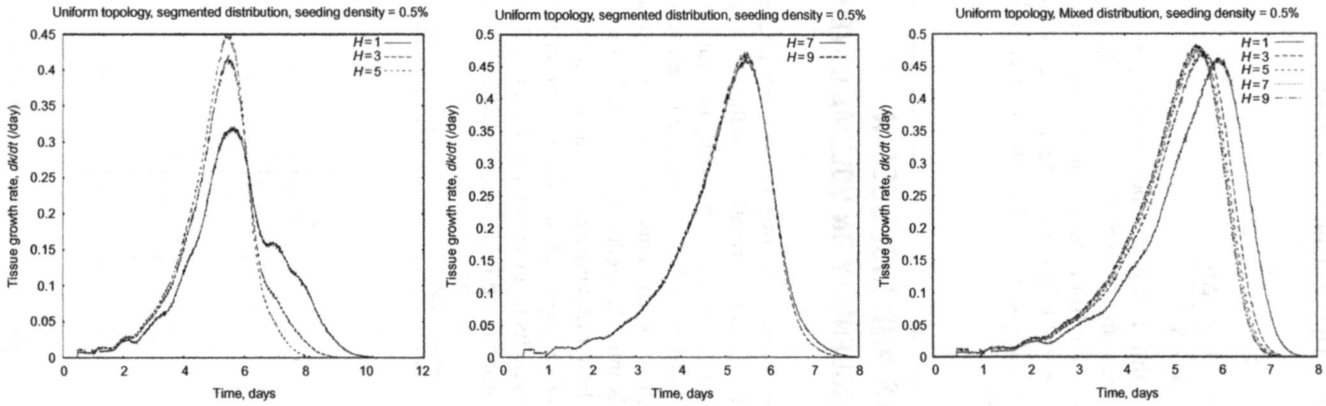

FIGURE 19.5

The overall tissue growth rate as the cell heterogeneity ratio, *H*, is varied from 1–5 (left), then 7–9 (center) for the segmented cell seeding distribution, and 1–9 for the mixed distribution (right).

This indicates that fast-moving cells tend to seek the nearby empty sites initially belonging to the cellular space segment containing the slower cells to divide. In all cases, the tissue growth rate increases initially, reaches a maximum, and then decreases as a result of contact inhibition brought about by the formation of cell colonies and other subsequent colony-merging events.

19.7.2 COMPARISON OF THE TWO UNIFORM CELL SEEDING DISTRIBUTIONS

Figs. 19.6 and 19.7 show comparisons between the cell volume fraction and tissue growth rates obtained by using the segmented and mixed uniform seeding distributions. Here, two different values of the ratio H were used, $H = 1$ and $H = 9$, respectively, with the total seeding density maintained at 0.5%. In Fig. 19.6, we observe that when $H = 1$ the mixed distribution takes less time to reach full volume coverage and yields a higher tissue growth rate. The mixed distribution also yields a higher maximum value of the tissue growth rate than the segmented one (approximately 0.46 vs. 0.32). This may be attributed to the fact that contact inhibition has less of an effect in the mixed distribution where faster cells have more nearby empty spaces to move and divide into, which in turn frees up sites for the slower-moving cells as well. Increasing the value of H to 9 shows a stronger positive impact on the time to reach confluence and the tissue growth rate in the case of the segmented distribution than the mixed one. In the segmented distribution, the increased number of faster-moving cells affords these cells the opportunity to disperse in the cellular space and eventually dominate the proliferation. This results in a similar overall tissue growth behavior for both distributions. As Fig. 19.7 clearly illustrates in this case, the distinction between the two seeding distributions becomes less apparent when the faster-moving cells constitute at least 90% of the seeded cells. Hence, we observe that when using equal proportions of seed cell types, the mixed distribution may be chosen over the segmented one. In the event that large variations in the number of seed cells are employed, the segmented distribution could be as beneficial in yielding a high tissue growth rate.

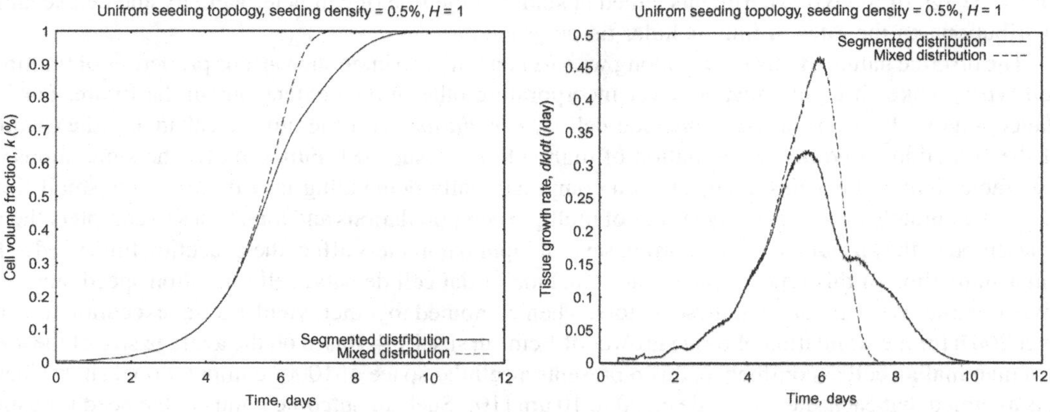

FIGURE 19.6

Comparison of the cell volume fraction (left) and the overall tissue growth rate (right) between the segmented and mixed seeding distributions for $H = 1$ and a seeding density of 0.5%.

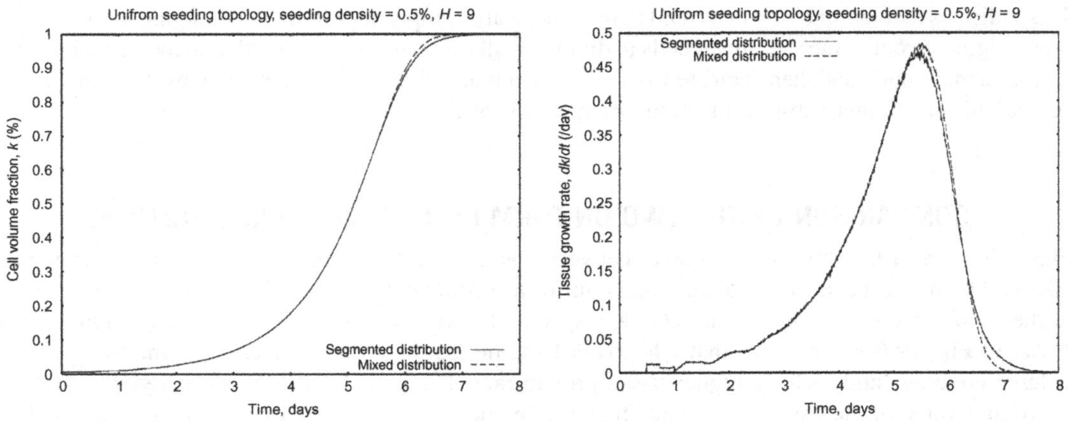

FIGURE 19.7

Comparison of the cell volume fraction (left) and the overall tissue growth rate (right) between the segmented and mixed seeding distributions for a seeding density of 0.5%, with the ratio $_{y}$ being increased to 9.

19.8 CONCLUSION AND FUTURE WORK

In this chapter, we presented the description of a 3-D computational model for the growth of multicellular tissues based on the concept of discrete CA. The model simulates many aspects of cell behavior involving cell migration, division, collision, and aggregation while incorporating multiple cell types using two different seeding distributions. The flexibility of the model allows for the exploration of the influence of many system parameters on the tissue growth rate. We reported related simulation results from the serial implementation of the model. Some of these results may have useful implications for the design of in vivo experiments aimed at studying the role of cell heterogeneity and cell seeding distributions on the rates of multicellular tissue growth.

The discrete nature of this model, along with its capability to integrate various properties of multiple cell types, makes it highly adaptable for incorporating other model extensions in the future. For instance, one such extension could include cell *differentiation* with the aim of enhancing the quality of the conditions used in the simulation of multicellular tissues [8]. Furthermore, the simulations of realizable multicellular tissue objects is a computationally demanding task that requires small time steps to accurately describe the dynamics of multiple cell populations and long times to complete them. In addition to the size of the cellular array, several input parameters affect the execution time needed to run a simulation of this type. Some of these include initial cell density, cell migration speed, and cell division time. We estimate that these factors, when combined together, yield a serial execution time of over 200 h for the simulation of tissue growth of 1 cm^3 in size [33]. Based on the average size of the area of a mammalian cell at confluence, this represents a cellular space of 1000^3 computational sites, where it is assumed that each site has a side equal to 10 μm [10]. Such an outcome points to the need for using parallel computing systems to reduce the time to obtain simulation results. To address this issue, we plan to implement the current model on many parallel systems, including distributed-memory, shared-memory, and heterogeneous parallel architectures such as multicore CPU and GPU machines [34].

Moreover, we will work on integrating a visualization solution with this simulation model to assist researchers to explore the spatial and temporal domains of tissue growth in real time and to provide them with useful means to interpret and analyze simulation data and, potentially, to compare them with experimental results. This latter component of our research program is already underway and we have recently developed a visualization prototype for the base computational model using a single cell type [35].

ACKNOWLEDGMENTS

The author would like to acknowledge the funding for this research work received from the Deanship of Scientific Research and the Research Center in the College of Computer & Information Sciences at King Saud University, Saudi Arabia (under Projects RC120920 and RC121231), as well as the past support provided by Simon Fraser University, Canada.

DEFINITIONS OF KEY TERMS

Cellular Automata Cellular automata (CA) are dynamic systems, in which both space and time are discrete, consisting of a number of identical cells in a regular lattice. They were originally introduced by John von Neumann and Stanislaw Ulam as a possible idealization of biological systems with a particular purpose of modeling biological self-reproduction. Each cell in the cellular space can be in a finite number of states. The next state of each cell is determined, at discrete time intervals, according to its current state, the current state of its neighboring cells, and a next-state transition rule or function.

Model To model is to abstract from reality a description of a dynamic system. Modeling is the process of establishing interrelationships between important entities of a system, where models are represented in terms of goals, performance criteria, and constraints. Modeling has an iterative character that is the result of many feedback loops emanating from the different stages of the modeling process.

Simulation Computer simulation is the discipline of designing a model of an actual or theoretical system, executing the model on a computer, and analyzing the execution output. Simulation embodies the principle of learning by doing as well as role playing.

Tissue From a cellular organizational level, tissues fall between cells and organisms. Thus, a tissue is a collection of cells that are from the same origin, but can be non-identical. This ensemble of cells carries out a specific (and identical) function. At a higher level, the grouping of multiple tissues forms an organ.

Agent-Based Model Agent-Based Model (ABM) is a computational model that uses agents to evaluate their effects on a given system by simulating their actions and interactions, both individually and collectively. An agent is a discrete entity that is autonomous with its own goals and behaviors including a capability to adapt and modify such behaviors. Thus, agent-based models (ABMs) can be thought of as generalizations of CA models, where a number of *agents* interact locally in order to create a higher level, group behavior.

REFERENCES

[1] Wolfram S. Cellular automata and complexity: collected papers. Reading, MA: Addison-Wesley; 1994.

[2] Deutsch A, Dormann S. Cellular automaton modeling of biological pattern formation: characterization, applications, and analysis. Boston, MA: Springer-Verlag; 2005.

[3] An G, Mi Q, Dutta-Moscato J, Vodovotz Y. Agent-based models in translational systems biology. Wiley Interdiscip Rev Syst Biol Med 2009;1(2):159–71.
[4] Majno G, Joris I. Cells, tissues and disease: principles of general pathology. Oxford, UK: Oxford University Press; 2004.
[5] Hwang M, Garbey M, Berceli SA, Tran-Son-Tay R. Rule-based simulation of multi-cellular biological systems—a review of modeling techniques. Cell Mol Bioeng 2009;2(3):285–94.
[6] Levin SA, Grenfell B, Hastings A, Perelson AS. Mathematical and computational challenges in population biology and ecosystems science. Science 1997;275(5298):334–43.
[7] Motta S, Pappalardo F. Mathematical modeling of biological systems. Brief Bioinform 2012;14(4):411–22.
[8] Azuaje F. Computational discrete models of tissue growth and regeneration. Brief Bioinform 2011;12 (1):64–77.
[9] Ben Youssef B, Tang L. Simulation of multiple cell population dynamics using a 3-D cellular automata model for tissue growth. Int J Nat Comput Res 2010;1(3):1–18.
[10] Ben Youssef B. Simulation of cell population dynamics using 3-D cellular automata. In: Proceedings of the 6th international conference on cellular automata for research and industry (ACRI'04), LNCS 3305; 2004. p. 562–71.
[11] Frame KK, Hu WS. A model for density-dependent growth of anchorage-dependent mammalian cells. Biotechnol Bioeng 1988;32:1061–6.
[12] Cherry RS, Papoutsakis ET. Modelling of contact-inhibited animal cell growth on flat surfaces and spheres. Biotechnol Bioeng 1989;33:300–5.
[13] Lim JHF, Davies GA. A stochastic model to simulate the growth of anchorage-dependent cells on flat surfaces. Biotechnol Bioeng 1990;36:547–62.
[14] Ruaan RC, Tsai GJ, Tsao GT. Monitoring and modeling density-dependent growth of anchorage-dependent cells. Biotechnol Bioeng 1993;41:380–9.
[15] Zygourakis K, Bizios R, Markenscoff P. Proliferation of anchorage-dependent contact-inhibited cells: I. Development of theoretical models based on cellular automata. Biotechnol Bioeng 1991;38(5):459–70.
[16] Hawboldt KA, Kalogerakis N, Behie LA. A cellular automaton model for microcarrier cultures. Biotechnol Bioeng 1994;43(1):90–100.
[17] Forestell SP, Milne BJ, Behie LA. A cellular automaton model for the growth of anchorage-dependent mammalian cells used in vaccine production. Chem Eng Sci 1992;47(9–11):2381–6.
[18] Lee Y, Markenscoff P, McIntire LV, Zygourakis K. Characterization of endothelial cell locomotion using a Markov chain model. Biochem Cell Biol 1995;73:461–72.
[19] Lee Y, Kouvroukoglou S, McIntire LV, Zygourakis K. A cellular automaton model for the proliferation of migrating contact-inhibited cells. Biophys J 1995;69(10):1284–98.
[20] Chang L, Gilbert ES, Eliashberg N, Keasling JD. A three-dimensional, stochastic simulation of biofilm growth and transport-related factors that affect structure. Microbiology 2003;149(10):2859–71.
[21] Kansal AR, Torquato S, Harsh IV GR, Chiocca EA, Deisboeck TS. Simulated brain tumor growth dynamics using a three-dimensional cellular automaton. J Theor Biol 2000;203(4):367–82.
[22] Cickovski TM, Huang C, Chaturvedi R, Glimm T, Hentschel HGE, Alber MS, et al. A framework for three-dimensional simulation of morphogenesis. IEEE/ACM Trans Comput Biol Bioinform 2005;2(4):273–88.
[23] Schaller G, Meyer-Hermann M. Multicellular tumor spheroid in an off-lattice Voronoi–DeLaunay cell model. Phys Rev E 2005;71(5 Pt 1):051910.
[24] Palsson E. A three-dimensional model of cell movement in multicellular systems. Futur Gener Comput Syst 2001;17:835–52.
[25] Beyer T, Meyer-Hermann M. Delauny object dynamics for tissues involving highly motile cells. In: Chauviere A, Preziosi L, Verdier C, editors. cell mechanics: from single scale-based models to multiscale modeling. Boca Raton, CA: CRC Press; 2010. p. 417–42.

[26] Beyer T, Schaller G, Deutsch A, Meyer-Hermann M. Parallel dynamic and kinetic regular triangulation in three dimensions. Comput Phys Commun 2005;172(2):86–108.
[27] Drasdo D, Jagiella N, Ramis-Conde I, Vignon-Clemental IE, Weens W. Modeling steps from benign tumor to invasive cancer: examples of intrinsically multiscale problems. In: Chauviere A, Preziosi L, Verdier C, editors. Cell mechanics: from single scale-based models to multiscale modeling. Boca Raton, CA: CRC Press; 2010. p. 379–416.
[28] Martin P. Wound healing—aiming for perfect skin regeneration. Science 1997;276:75–81.
[29] Gruler H, Bultmann BD. Analysis of cell movement. Blood Cells 1988;10(1):61–77.
[30] Lee Y, McIntire LV, Zygourakis K. Analysis of endothelial cell locomotion: differential effects of motility and contact inhibition. Biotechnol Bioeng 1994;43(7):622–34.
[31] Wolfe S. Introduction to cell biology. Belmont, CA: Wadsworth Publishing Co.; 1983
[32] Cheng G, Ben Youssef B, Markenscoff P, Zygourakis K. Cell population dynamics modulate the rates of tissue growth processes. Biophys J 2006;90(3):713–24.
[33] Ben Youssef B, Sammouda R. Pseudorandom number generation in the context of a 3D simulation model for tissue growth. In: Proceedings of the 14th international conference on computational science (ICCS 2014), Procedia-computer sciences, 29C: Elsevier; 2014. p. 2391–400.
[34] Dematté L, Prandi D. GPU computing for systems biology. Brief Bioinform 2010;2(3):323–33.
[35] Ben Youssef B. A visualization tool of 3-D time varying data for the simulation of tissue growth. Multimed Tools Appl 2014;73(3):1795–817.

CHAPTER

20 A COMBINATION OF PROTEIN-PROTEIN INTERACTION NETWORK TOPOLOGICAL AND BIOLOGICAL PROCESS FEATURES FOR MULTIPROTEIN COMPLEX DETECTION

N. Zaki*, E.A. Mohamed†

College of Information Technology, United Arab Emirates University, Al Ain, United Arab Emirates Department of Management Information Systems, College of Business Administration, Al Ain University of Science and Technology, Al Ain, United Arab Emirates†*

20.1 INTRODUCTION

The introduction of high-throughput screening methods has significantly contributed to the increasing amount of protein-protein interaction (PPI) data for humans, microbial, viral pathogens, and many model organisms [1]. It is desirable to use this wealth of data to provide insights into organizational principles of life. One issue that has received a considerable amount of attention is the detection and characterization of multiprotein complex from the PPI data. A multiprotein complex, also called protein machines, is a group of two or more associated proteins formed by interactions that are stable over time. It was shown by Vanunu et al. [2] that a protein and its high-confidence interactors are believed to form a putative multiprotein complex that is related to diseases such as prostate cancer, Alzheimer's, and diabetes.

Several methods were developed in the past to detect multiprotein complexes, as the molecular structure of a protein complex can be determined experimentally using techniques such as X-ray crystallography or nuclear magnetic resonance (NMR). However, these conventional techniques are expensive and inefficient and the reason why researchers have switched to develop computational-based methods for multiprotein complex detection. Earlier computational methods include Markov clustering (MCL) [3], restricted neighborhood search clustering (RNSC) [4], CFinder [5], and molecular complex detection (MCODE) [6]. Recent methods include maximal cliques (CMC) [7] for discovering multiprotein complexes in weighted PPI networks. CMC uses an iterative scoring method called AdjstCD to assign weights to protein pairs. The AdjstCD weight in this method indicates the reliability of the interaction between protein pairs. Nepusz et al. developed ClusterONE [8], which initiates from a single seed vertex before a greedy growth procedure begins to add or remove vertices to detect clusters of proteins in the PPI with high cohesiveness. Zaki et al. [9] developed ProRank, which ranks the importance of each protein in the network based on the interaction structure and the evolutionary relationships between proteins. The ranking process in this case proved valuable for detecting multiprotein complexes. A recent method called PEWCC [10] has showed great potential by employing the concept of weighted clustering coefficient for assessing the reliability of the interaction data and detecting the multiprotein complexes.

Most of the above-mentioned methods mainly focus on the network topological information and fail to consider information from the protein primary sequence, which is of considerable importance for multiprotein complex detection. It was mentioned by the authors of ProRank [9] that the accuracy improvement achieved by incorporating sequence similarity information to their algorithm was not significant. Therefore, to achieve a breakthrough, we need a deeper understanding of the characteristics of the proteins within the multiprotein complexes. In this chapter, we propose a supervising learning method for multiprotein complex detection by integrating network topological features and biological process information to be used in conjunction with multiclass support vector machine classifiers.

20.2 METHOD

The proposed method, which we call SVM-Net, mainly consists of four major steps, feature extraction, data preparation (preprocessing), mining patterns (classification), and postprocessing (evaluation). These steps are described in the following sections and are illustrated in Fig. 20.1.

20.2.1 FEATURES EXTRACTION

The formation of multiprotein complexes might be regulated at different levels, including transcriptional regulation. In prokaryotes for instance, a significant proportion of the genes that are co-regulated at the transcriptional level usually code for proteins that physically interact [11]. This proportion is even higher for gene groups whose co-regulation is conserved in different genomes [12]. Therefore, two sets of valuable features can be extracted. The first is the out-degree and in-degree related to transcriptional regulation interaction. This feature represents the number of outgoing or incoming links to the gene g corresponding to a protein. Links in this case are represented in terms of transcriptional regulation interactions. The second is the betweenness centrality with respect to transcriptional regulation interactions. For instance, if σ_{g1g2} denotes the total number of shortest paths between two genes σ_{g1} and σ_{g2}, then the value $\sigma_{g1g2}(g)$ can be defined as the number of shortest paths between g_1 and g_2 passing through g. The paths in this case are represented in terms of transcriptional regulation interactions. Similarly, betweenness centrality with respect to the physical interaction can also be calculated as $f(g) = \sum_{g1 \neq g \neq g2} \frac{\sigma_{g1g2}(g)}{\sigma_{g1g2}}$. The graph of protein interactions is crucial for the understanding of the global behavior of the network and therefore integrating topological properties, cellular components, and biological processes retains valuable knowledge of the characteristics of the multiprotein complexes. Hence, two informative sets of features can be extracted that include the cellular components

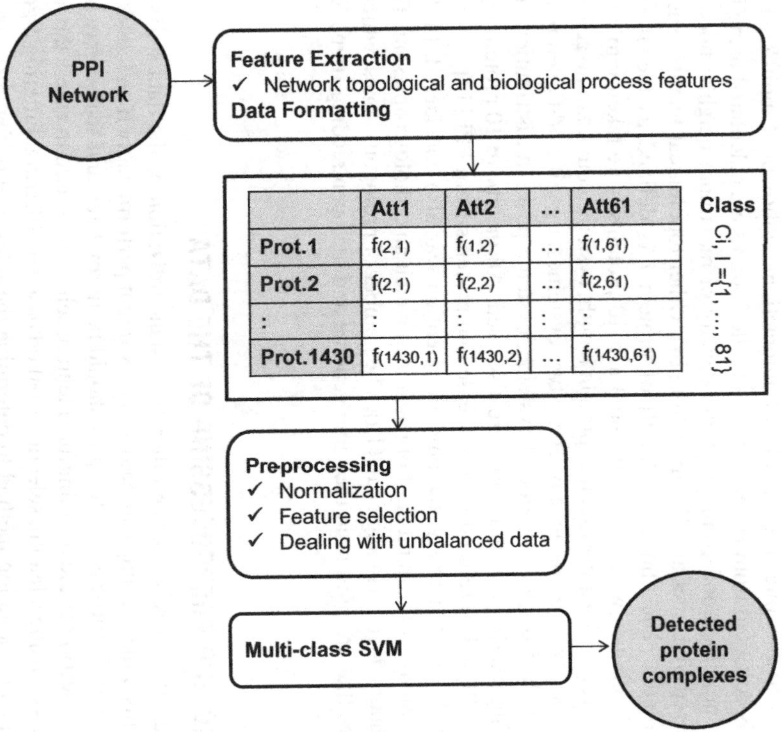

FIGURE 20.1

Overview of the proposed SVM-Net method. It consists of four major steps: feature extraction, data preparation and preprocessing, classification, and postprocessing. The input in this case is a PPI network and the output is deducted multiprotein complexes.

(cytoplasm, endoplasmic reticulum, mitochondrion, nucleus, or other localization) and biological processes (cell cycle, metabolic process, signal transduction, transcription, transport, or other process). The above-mentioned four feature sets were obtained from Acencio and Lemke [13].

PPI is often represented as a graph $G=(V,E)$, where V is a set of nodes (proteins) and E is a set of edges (interactions) connecting pairs of nodes. This representation allows us to study the network using the concepts and principles of graph theory. Therefore, two sets of features such as betweenness centrality related to integrated functional, degree related to integrated functional, maximum neighborhood component, and density of maximum neighborhood component are considered. In case of the betweenness centrality and the degree, the values are represented in terms of integrated functional with respect to physical interaction and genomic context network interactions. Following Chiou-Yi et al. [14], the network information is collected from Hu et al. [15] and the features are calculated using iGraph software [16]. Maximum neighborhood component and density of maximum neighborhood component properties were proposed by Lin et al. [17] and Chin [18]. Other topological features such as Clique level were also calculated. The clique level [19] of protein i is defined as the maximal clique containing i. Here, only cliques with sizes between 3 and 10 proteins were taken into consideration.

Sequence primary structural features such as protein length, cysteine count, amino acid occurrence, average cysteine position, average distance of every two cysteines, cysteine odd-even index, average hydrophobicity, average hydrophobicity around cysteine, cysteine position distribution, and average position specific scoring matrix of amino acid were also used. All the above 10 protein features were taken from Lin et al. [20] and were used to detect essential proteins from PPI [14].

Evolutionary related feature, namely, the phyletic retention was also considered. In this case the phyletic retention of protein i is the number of organisms in which an ortholog is present. The ortholog of each protein was obtained from Hwang et al. [19]. The number of prologous genes, which is defined as the number of genes that are present in the same genome and the open reading frame length, were also considered.

20.2.2 PREPARING AND PREPROCESSING OF THE DATA

The data extracted are often very sparse and therefore, standardization of the data set is a common requirement for many machine learning estimators as they might perform badly if an individual feature is not normally distributed. In this case all features should be normalized and scaled between 0 and 1.

To ensure that all our attributes are meaningful, a feature selection is used to assess the relevance of each attribute. We focus on using a feature selection method based on filtering. Filtering algorithms use an independent search and evaluation method to determine the relevance of features variables to the data mining task. Therefore we employed the "GainRatioAttributeEval" method available in Weka [21] to evaluate the worth of an attribute by measuring the gain ratio with respect to the class. Information gain ratio biases the classifier against considering attributes with a large number of distinct values. The distribution of proteins across complexes is obviously imbalanced and therefore, the problem can be tackled at the stage of statistical analysis using resampling method [22]. Resampling methods include oversampling the small class to a sample size comparable to the large class, and undersampling, that is, randomly drawing samples from the large class with sample size comparable to the small class. A lot of work had been done in the data mining literature on developing resampling methods, yet these techniques are rarely applied in the biology literature [23].

20.2.3 MINING PATTERNS (CLASSIFICATION)

Once the data is preprocessed a sensible data mining task must be designed to comply with the objectives of predicting proteins in the multiprotein complexes. This problem can be handled by utilizing a multiclassification technique and therefore, support vector machines (SVM) [24,25] was selected to be used. The basic idea of the SVM algorithm is to map the given training set into a possibly high-dimensional feature space and attempting to locate in that space a hyperplane that maximizes the distance separating the positive from the rest of the examples.

The SVM algorithm addresses the general problem of machine learning to discriminate between positive and negative examples of a given class of n-dimensional vectors. To discriminate between proteins across complexes, the SVM learn a classification function from a set of positive examples μ^+ and set of negative examples μ^-. The classification function takes the form

$$f(x) = \sum\nolimits_{i:x_i \in \mu+} \lambda_i K(x, x_i) - \sum\nolimits_{i:x_i \in \mu-} \lambda_i K(x, x_i) \quad (1)$$

where the nonnegative weights λ_i are computed during training by maximizing a quadratic objective function and the function $K(.,.)$ is called a kernel function. Any protein x is then predicted to be positive if the function $f(x)$ is positive. More details about how the weights λ_i are computed and the theory of SVM can be found in Refs. [24,25].

In the case of multiple classes, an appropriate multiclass method is needed. Vapnik [24] proposed to compare one class with the others taking classes together. This strategy generates n classifiers, where n is the number of classes and the final output is the class that corresponds to the SVM with the largest margin. For multiclass problems one has to determine n hyperplanes. Thus, this method requires the solution of n quadratic programming optimization problems, each of which separates one class from the remaining classes. Therefore, the dominant approach for doing so is to reduce the single multiclass problem into multiple binary classification problems.

20.2.4 POSTPROCESSING PATTERNS

Following the classification step it is important to evaluate the patterns detected by the SVM. Several evaluation measures are used in this study such as precision $\frac{TP}{TP+FP}$, recall $\frac{TP}{TP+FN}$, F1 measure $2\frac{\text{Precision}*\text{Recall}}{\text{Precision}+\text{Recall}}$, and accuracy $\frac{TP+TN}{N}$, where TP is defined as related protein classified as "related," TN is unrelated protein classified as "related," FP is related protein classified as "unrelated," FN is unrelated protein classified as "unrelated," and N is the total number of proteins in the data set.

Once all proteins are classified in groups (complexes) with reasonable classification accuracy it is important to assess the quality of the detected complexes. To evaluate the accuracy of the detected complexes, we used the Jaccard index, which is defined as follows:

$$Match(K, R) = \frac{|V_K \cap V_R|}{|V_K \cup V_R|} \quad (2)$$

where V_K and V_R are the set of proteins in complex K and R, respectively. The complex K is defined to match the complex R if $Match(K, R) \geq \alpha$ where $\alpha = 0.3$ or 0.5 (as most of the available methods were evaluated). To estimate the cumulative quality of the detection, we follow Zaki et al. [9] and compare the number of matching complexes with the number of reference complexes using recall ($RE_c = \frac{N_{MK}}{N_K}$), precision ($PR_c = \frac{N_{MR}}{N_R}$), and F_C-measure ($F_c = 2 \times \frac{PR_c \times PE_c}{PR_c + PE_c}$), where N_{MK} is a number of matching reference complexes, N_{MR} is a number of detected reference complexes, N_K is a number of reference complexes, and N_R is the number of detected complexes.

To assess the accuracy estimation of the proteins predicted in the reference and detected complexes, three further characteristics are used:

$$\text{Recall}: \ RE_N = \frac{\sum_{i=1}^{N_{MK}} |C_i|}{\sum_{i=1}^{N_K} |K_i|} \tag{3}$$

where $|C_i| = \max_{(R_j:Match(K_i,P_j) \geq \alpha)} |K_i \cap R_j|$

$$\text{Precision}: \ PR_N = \frac{\sum_{i=1}^{N_{MK}} |C_i|}{\sum_{i=1}^{N_R} |R_i|} \tag{4}$$

where $|C_i| = \max_{(K_j:Match(K_i,P_j) \geq \alpha)} |R_i \cap K_j|$

$$F_N - \text{measure}: \ \left(F_N = 2 \times \frac{PR_N \times RE_N}{PR_N + RE_N}\right) \tag{5}$$

Calculations were made of precision and recall at complex and complex protein levels. Furthermore, we evaluated the performance of our method using the maximum matching ratio (MMR), which reflects the maximal one-to-one mapping between detected and reference complexes. The algorithm to calculate the MMR is available from Nepusz et al. [8].

20.3 EXPERIMENTAL WORK AND RESULTS

The effectiveness of the proposed method is evaluated using a PPI data set that was prepared by Gavin et al. [26]. The details of the data set are summarized in Table 20.1. The network contains no isolated nodes. The reference data of complexes was created from the Munich Information Center for Protein Sequences (MIPS) [27]. In the case of MIPS, only complexes that were manually annotated from the Database of Interacting Proteins (DIP) interaction data are considered. Following Leung et al. [28], complexes of sizes less than 5 proteins are excluded and therefore, 81 complexes were considered. The data sets are available for download from http://faculty.uaeu.ac.ae/nzaki/Research.htm.

Table 20.1 Network Analysis of the PPI Dataset Prepared by Gavin et al. [26]

Simple Parameter	Value
Number of proteins	1430
Number of interactions	6531
Network density of	0.006
Average number of interactions	9.134
Network heterogeneity	1.077
Clustering coefficient	0.416
Network centralization	0.050

The experimental work started by the exploration and the preparation of the PPI data set. A total of 61 features were extracted (as explained in Section 20.2.1). The features were analyzed and the "Gain-RatioAttributeEval" method reveals that features related to organelle such as vacuole, mitochondrion, and endoplasmic reticulum are strongly linked with the detection of multiprotein complexes. Features related to amino acid occurrence and in particular "GLN," "GLY," and "LYS" are also proved valuable. Similarly, there is no evidence suggesting that organelle such as peroxisomes and the bud neck (a constriction between the mother and the daughter cell (bud) in an organism that reproduces by budding) have no strong links to the characterization of multiprotein complexes.

One other observation inferred from the data exploration as shown in Fig. 20.2 is that the distribution of proteins across multiprotein complexes is unbalanced. From a data mining point of view this data requires balancing and therefore, resampling method with random seed equal to one was used. The resampling in this case produces a random subsample of a data set using replacement.

Once the preprocessing step is completed and the data set is prepared, multiclass SVM was used. The Library for Support Vector Machines (LibSVM) implemented by Rong-En and Chih-Jen Lin [29] was used. One of the significant parameters needed to tune the SVM is the choice of the kernel function. The kernel function allows SVM to locate the hyperplane in high dimensional space that effectively separate the training data [30]. The Gaussian radial basis function was used as it allows pockets of data to be classified, which is a more powerful way than just using a linear dot product. To know how accurately our predictive model will perform in practice, cross-validation was used. Cross-validation is a model validation method for assessing generalizability of a classifier into other independent data sets. *k*-fold cross-validation is a commonly used cross-validation technique for small-size data sets to assess the performance of the classifier. In this experimental work, 10-fold cross-validation was used where the original sample is randomly partitioned into 10 equal size subsamples. Of the 10 subsamples, a single subsample is retained as the validation data for testing the model, and the remaining 9 subsamples are used as training data. The cross-validation process in this case is repeated 10 times, with each of the 10 subsamples used exactly once as the validation data. The 10 results from the folds can then be averaged (or simply combined) to produce a single estimation. The advantage of the cross-validation over repeated random subsampling is that all observations are used for both training and validation, and each observation is used for validation exactly once.

The overall classification accuracy of assigning proteins to their corresponding complex is 71.05. The classification precision, recall, and F1 measures are 0.72, 0.71, and 0.71, respectively. The list of the detected complexes was then compared to the reference complex data set (both available at http://faculty.uaeu.ac.ae/nzaki/Research.htm). The proposed method was able to impressively detect 76 complexes out of the 81 reference complexes with the value of $\alpha = 0.30$. Furthermore, we compared the performance of SVM-Net to other state-of-the-art methods for detecting multiprotein complexes. The comparison is shown in Table 20.2. More than one quality measure was used to assess the performance of each algorithm. The parameters of the methods listed in Table 20.2 were optimized to achieve the best accuracy possible.

As shown in Table 20.3, SVM-Net is able to detect more matched complexes (76 and 64 matching complexes, $\alpha = 30$ and $\alpha = 50$, respectively) than other state-of-the-art methods with higher recall and precision. The performances of ProRank [9] and ClusterONE [8] however, were particularly good when the value of $\alpha \geq 60$. ProRank and ClusterONE were able to detect 15 and 12 complexes, respectively, with similarity overlap of 90% (close to a perfect match).

The number of matched complexes ($\alpha = 30$) with respect to the number of detected complexes are shown in Fig. 20.3.

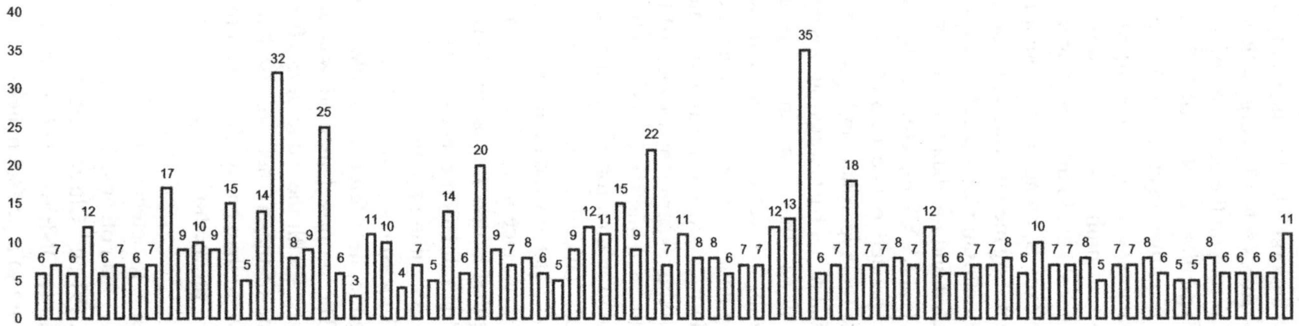

FIGURE 20.2

The distribution of proteins across complexes.

Table 20.2 Performance Comparison of SVM-Net to ClusterONE, CMC, MCode, PEWCC, and ProRank

Evaluation Measures	ClusterONE [8]	CMC [7]	MCode [6]	PEWCC [10]	ProRank [9]	SVM-Net
RE_c	0.803	0.753	0.568	0.753	0.790	0.938
PR_c	0.313	0.324	0.523	0.744	0.557	0.938
F_c	0.450	0.453	0.544	0.748	0.653	0.938
RE_N	0.694	0.558	0.355	0.604	0.556	0.541
PR_N	0.420	0.397	0.485	0.656	0.618	0.967
F_N	0.523	0.464	0.410	0.629	0.585	0.694
MMR	0.613	0.549	0.404	0.540	0.571	0.587

Table 20.3 The Number of Matched Complexes Detected by SVM-Net in Comparison to ClusterONE, CMC, MCode, PEWCC, and ProRank Using Different Values

Method	$\alpha=30$	$\alpha=50$	$\alpha=60$	$\alpha=70$	$\alpha=80$	$\alpha=90$
ClusterONE [8]	65	59	50	38	26	12
CMC [7]	61	51	36	31	21	9
MCode [6]	46	33	23	20	14	6
PEWCC [10]	61	55	37	30	23	10
ProRank [9]	64	52	41	33	25	15
SVM-Net	76	64	37	24	13	3

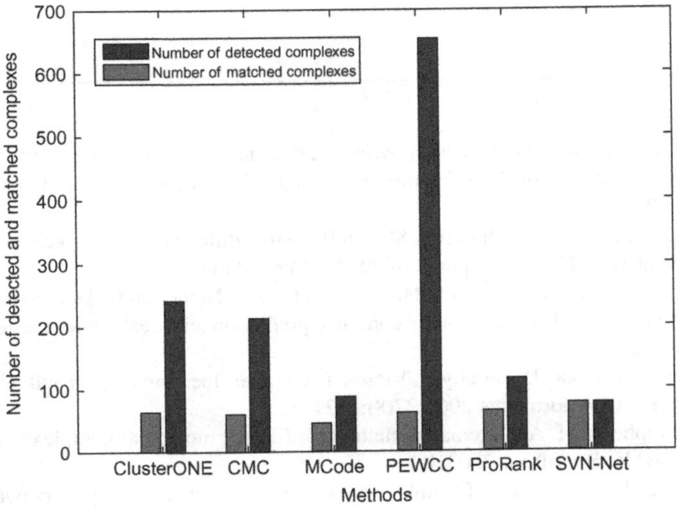

FIGURE 20.3

Matched multiprotein complexes versus detected multiprotein complexes ($\alpha=30$).

20.4 CONCLUSION

Most of the currently available methods for detecting multiprotein complexes mainly focus on topological information and fail to consider the information from protein primary structure. Another weakness is that they are dependent on the quality of the PPI data mainly produced by high-throughput experiments and not particularly the proteins (node) in the network. The high-throughput experiments are believed to be noisy and fragmented due to the limitations of the corresponding experimental techniques and the dynamic nature of protein interaction maps, which may have a negative impact on the performance of complex recognition algorithms [10]. For example, Sprinzak et al. [31] showed that the reliability of high-throughput yeast two-hybrid assays is around 50%, and that the size of the yeast interactome is estimated to be 10,000 to 16,000 interactions. Therefore, depending on interactions (links) only will not be sufficient for accurate detection of multiprotein complexes. Protein sequence information is of considerable importance for protein complex detection. Based on this observation, we introduced SVM-Net to discover multiprotein complexes from yeast PPI network. SVM-Net extracts valuable features from the protein primary structure (amino acid background frequency) and the topology of the PPI network, which is helpful for the effective detection of the multiprotein complex. The experimental works conducted on a PPI network prepared by Gavin et al. [26] and a reference data set of 81 multiprotein complex showed that SVM-Net outperforms five of the state-of-the-art protein complex detection methods. In the future, more valuable features such as gene ontology or gene expression can be incorporated.

ACKNOWLEDGMENT

The authors would like to acknowledge the assistance provided by the office of the Research and Graduate Studies at the United Arab Emirates University (Project # 31t046) and ICT (Project # 21T043-ICT).

REFERENCES

[1] Zaki NM. Multi-protein complex detection by integrating network topological features and biological process information. In: International conference on biomedical engineering and systems (ICBES'14), Prague, Czech Republic; 2014.

[2] Vanunu O, Magger O, Ruppin E, Shlomi T, Sharan R. Associating genes and protein complexes with disease via network propagation. PLoS Comput Biol 2010;1(6):e1000641.

[3] Dongen S. Graph clustering by flow simulation. Utrecht, The Netherlands: University of Utrecht; 2000.

[4] Andrew DK, Przulj N, Jurisica I. Protein complex prediction via cost-based clustering. Bioinformatics 2004;20(17):3013–20.

[5] Adamcsek B, Palla G, Farkas IJ, Derenyi I, Vicsek T. CFinder: locating cliques and overlapping modules in biological networks. Bioinformatics 2006;22(8):1021–3.

[6] Bader GD, Christopher WH. An automated method for finding molecular complexes in large protein interaction networks. BMC Bioinform 2003;4:2.

[7] Guimei L, Wong L, Chua HN. Complex discovery from weighted ppi networks. Bioinformatics 2009;25(15):1891–7.

[8] Nepusz T, Yu H, Paccanaro A. Detecting overlapping protein complexes in protein-protein interaction networks. Nat Methods 2012;9:471–2.
[9] Zaki NM, Berengueres J, Efimov D. Detection of protein complexes using a protein ranking algorithm. Proteins Struct Funct Bioinform 2012;80(10):2459–68.
[10] Zaki NM, Dmitry D, Berengueres J. Protein complex detection using inter-action reliability assessment and weighted clustering coefficient. BMC Bioinform 2013;14:163.
[11] Simonis N, Helden J, Cohen GN, Wodak SJ. Transcriptional regulation of protein complexes in yeast. Genome Biol 2004;5:R33.
[12] Huynen M, Snel B, Lathe W, Bork P. Predicting protein function by genomic context: quantitative evaluation and qualitative inferences. Genome Res 2000;10:1204–10.
[13] Acencio ML, Lemke N. Towards the prediction of essential genes by integration of network topology, cellular localization and biological process information. BMC Bioinform 2009;10:290.
[14] Chiou-Yi H, Chang-Biau Y, Zih-Jie Y, Chiou-Ting T. Prediction of protein essentiality by the support vector machine with statistical tests. Evol Bioinform 2013;9:387–416.
[15] Hu P, Janga SC, Babu M, Díaz-Mejía JJ, Butland G, Yang W, et al. Global functional atlas of escherichia coli encompassing previously uncharacterized proteins. PLoS Biol 2009;7(4):e96.
[16] Csardi G, Nepusz T. The igraph software package for complex network research. InterJournal Complex Syst 2006;1695, http://igraph.org.
[17] Lin CY, Chin CH, Wu HH, Chen SH, Ho CW, Ko MT. Hubba: hub objects analyzera framework of interactome hubs identification for network biology. Nucleic Acids Res 2008;36:438–43.
[18] Chin CH. Prediction of essential proteins and functional modules from protein-protein interaction networks. Doctoral Dissertation, Taiwan: National Central University; 2010.
[19] Hwang YC, Lin CC, Chang JY, Mori H, Juan HF, Huang HC. Predicting essential genes based on network and sequence analysis. Mol Biosyst 2009;5(12):1672–8.
[20] Lin CY, Yang CB, Hor CY, Huang KS. Disulfide bonding state prediction with SVM based on protein types, In: Proc. IEEE fifth international conference on bio-inspired computing: theories and applications, Changsha, China; 2010. p. 1436–42.
[21] Mark H, Eibe F, Geoffrey H, Pfahringer B, Reutemann P, Witten IH. The weka data mining software: an update. ACM SIGKDD Explor Newsl 2009;11(1):10–8.
[22] Estabrooks A, Jo T, Japkowicz N. A multiple resampling method for learning from imbalanced data sets. Comput Intell 2004;20:18–36.
[23] Paul HL. Resampling methods improve the predictive power of modeling in class-imbalanced datasets. Int J Environ Res Public Health 2014;11:9776–89.
[24] Vapnik VN. The nature of statistical learning theory. New York, NY: Springer-Verlag New York, Inc.; 1995
[25] Cristianini N, Shawe-Taylor J. An introduction to support vector machines: and other Kernel-based learning methods. New York, NY: Cambridge University Press; 2000.
[26] Gavin A, Aloy P, Grandi P, Krause R, Boesche M, Marzioch M, et al. Proteome survey reveals modularity of the yeast cell machinery. Nature 2006;440:631–6.
[27] Mewes HW, Frishman D, Mayer KF, Münsterkötter M, Noubibou O, Page P, et al. MIPS: analysis and annotation of proteins from whole genomes in 2005. Nucleic Acids Res 2006;34:169–72.
[28] Leung H, Xiang Q, Yiu SM, Chin F. Predicting protein complexes from ppi data: a core-attachment approach. J Comput Biol 2009;16(2):133–9.
[29] Fan R-E, Chen P-H, Lin C-J. Working set selection using second order information for training SVM. J Mach Learn Res 2005;6:1889–918.
[30] Zaki NM, Bouktif S, Lazarova-Molnar S. A combination of compositional index and genetic algorithm for predicting transmembrane helical segments. PLoS ONE 2011;6(7):e21821.
[31] Sprinzak E, Sattath S, Hargalit H. How reliable are experimental protein-protein interaction data. J Mol Biol 2003;327:919–23.

CHAPTER

INFOGENOMICS: GENOMES AS INFORMATION SOURCES

21

V. Manca[*,†]

Department of Computer Science, University of Verona, Verona, Italy[*] *Center for BioMedical Computing (CBMC), University of Verona, Verona, Italy*[†]

21.1 INTRODUCTION

In recent years concepts from information theory and computer science were fruitfully applied to the analysis of genomes, coming from algorithms [1–4], formal language theory [5–8], and linguistics [9–13]. Moreover, it was realized that *alignment-free* methods in genome analysis [2,14–16] could be very useful in discovering global properties of genomes, better than classical methods based on string alignment.

At the same time, project ENCODE (ENCyclopedia Of DNA Elements) [17] is aimed at extracting lexicons and catalogs of fragments in the human genome on the basis of their biochemical properties (see websites: http://nature.com/encode; http://epd.vital-it.ch). Infogenomics [4,18–22] intends to develop an informational annotation of genomes by considering them as information sources by applying methods coming from information theory, such as information source, discrete distribution, entropy, entropic divergence, and random processes.

21.2 BASIC NOTATION

Strings are finite sequences of symbols over a finite alphabet. In the case of genomes, the strings (contiguously) occurring in them are over the DNA alphabet $\Gamma = \{a, c, g, t\}$ (that we assume are ordered $a < c < g < t$).

Generic strings are denoted by Greek letters (possibly with subscripts) and λ indicates the empty string (useful for expressing mathematical properties of strings). The symbol occurring in string α at position i is denoted by $\alpha[i]$, and the length of α is denoted by $|\alpha|$. The string occurring in α between the positions i and j (included) is denoted $\alpha[i, j]$. Basic operations are assumed on string. Concatenation is the most important operation over strings, usually indicated by the juxtaposition $\alpha\beta$ of the two strings α and β that are concatenated.

A genome G is a string over Γ (symbols are written from left to right, according to the chemical orientation $5' - 3'$ of nucleotides represented by a, c, g, t). Strings occurring in a genome G are also called words, factors, k-mers, k-grams of G.

The set $pos_G(\alpha)$ consists of (first) positions where α occurs in G, and the (occurrence) multiplicity of α in G is denoted by $mult_G(\alpha)$. We call hapax of G a word occurring in G once, while we call repeat of G any word occurring in G at least twice. Of course, a string that includes a hapax is a hapax too, while a string included in a repeat is a repeat too. In informational genome analysis the following genomic indexes *mrl(G)*, *mhl(G)*, *mfl(G)* have a special relevance.

We denote by *mrl(G)* the *maximum repeat length*, that is, the length of the longest repeats of G, while *mhl(G)* is the *minimum hapax length*, that is, the length of the shortest hapaxes of G. Finally, *mfl(G)* is the shortest length m such that for all the lengths k smaller than m all the possible k-mers occur in G.

The overlap concatenation of the string $\alpha\gamma$ with $\gamma\beta$ is $\alpha\gamma\beta$, where γ is the maximal overlap between the two strings, that is, the longest string that is a suffix of $\alpha\gamma$ and a prefix of $\gamma\beta$.

The set Γ^k consists of all possible k-mers, while $D(G)$ consists of all words of G, and $D_k(G)= D(G)\cap\Gamma^k$ (all k-mers occurring in G). A dictionary of a genome G is a subset of $D(G)$. All set theoretic operations and relations can be applied to dictionaries, in particular, given a dictionary L, then $|L|$ is the number of its elements (with some notation overloading, because $|\alpha|$ denotes also the length of the string α).

A dictionary L of a genome G covers a set P of positions of G, or P is the L-coverage of G, when $P=\{j\in |\ G[h,k]\in L \text{ for some } h\leq j\leq k\}$. The coverage ratio of L w.r.t. G is the ratio between the length of G and the cardinality of P. This notion of coverage can be more properly called "dictionary genome coverage," while dictionary positional coverage refers to the numbers of words of L that occurs in a given position j of G, given by $|\{w\in L|\ w=G[j-h, j+k] \text{ for some } h, k\geq 0\}|$. The average positional coverage of L in G is the average of the positional coverage over all positions of G.

The problem of genome sequencing can be completely expressed in terms of genome strings, genome dictionaries, genome coverage, and positional coverage. In fact, given a dictionary L of G (whose words are usually called *reads*) the sequencing of G corresponds to the *most probable* genome G that is covered by L, with a coverage ratio close to 1. This problem is computationally complex and without a unique solution. However, it can be solved, with a good approximation, if some hypotheses are assumed about the genome coverage and positional coverage of L in G, plus some additional information to reduce the ambiguity for a correct allocation of words over genome positions.

This possibility tells us the important fact that suitable dictionaries contain all the information present in a genome. This "informational equivalence" has a great theoretical and practical impact and is one of the main intuitions inspiring the infogenomics approach.

The reader may refer to Refs. [23–25] for the basic notions of probability and information theory assumed in the following discussion. We limit ourselves to report the definition of entropy for a probability function p (or probability distribution, according to the usual terminology) defined over a set X, which is crucial in information theory:

$$H(p) = -\sum_{x\in X} p(x)\lg p(x). \tag{1}$$

21.3 RESEARCH LINES IN INFOGENOMICS

According to Shannon, an information source (X, p) is given by a set X and a probability function p, defined over X, assigning to every element $x\in X$ a probability $p(x)$ (of being emitted by the source). Now, let G be a genome and L a dictionary of G, then an information source is naturally associated to G and L, where $X=L$ and for every $\alpha\in L$, $p(\alpha)$ is the probability of α of occurring in G. In more formal terms, if $L=\{\alpha_1, \alpha_2, \ldots, \alpha_k\}$ with word multiplicities $n_1, n_2, \ldots, n_k$ and $n_1+n_2+\cdots+n_k=n$, then

$p(\alpha_1) = n/n_1, p(\alpha_2) = n/n_2, \ldots, p(\alpha_k) = n/n_k$. From this simple definition we can easily define the entropy $H_L(G)$ of a genome G, with respect to dictionary L, by setting the following equation:

$$H_L(G) = -\sum_{\alpha \in L} p(\alpha) \lg p(\alpha).$$

Given two genomes G_1 and G_2 and a common dictionary L that in G_1 has the probability function p_1 and in G_2 has the probability distribution p_2, then the Kullback-Leibler entropic divergence between G_1 and G_2, with respect to D, can be defined as

$$KL_L(G_1, G_2) = \sum_{\alpha \in L} p_1(\alpha) \lg[p_1(\alpha)/p_2(\alpha)].$$

Analogous kinds of entropic divergences can be easily applied to genomes, by using the same idea. For example, the Kullback-Leibler-Jeffrey divergence is

$$JKL_L(G_1, G_2) = -\sum_{\alpha \in L} [p_1(\alpha) - p_2(\alpha)] \lg[p_1(\alpha)/p_2(\alpha)].$$

It is easy to show that *JKLD* is symmetric but not transitive, while *KLD* is neither symmetric nor transitive, but both are reflexive, and both are always positive. Moreover, *JKLD*($G1$, $G2$) = *KLD*($G1$, $G2$) + *KLD*($G2$, $G1$).

We want to remark that a dictionary allows us to transform a genome in an information source. This explains very well why dictionaries are a key point in the informational approach to genomes. Definitions given above are very natural applications of information theoretic concepts to genomes, but several questions need to be addressed for a better understanding of their use and of their potentialities. The first question is related to the computational aspect. In fact, if dictionary L has an average word length over 20, then the computations of genomic entropies and divergences are prohibitive. For example $D_{20}(G)$, when G is the human genome, it has a size of hundreds of millions words, and any naive method of computation is unrealistic to consider. This raises the problem of defining efficient algorithms and efficient programs for these kinds of computations. In Ref. [21] an efficient software was developed, which was based on the data structure of suffix arrays [26], where genomic entropies for real genomes and very big dictionaries can be computed in a couple of hours on a personal computer.

The second question concerns the choice of good dictionaries that make these concepts interesting. For example, what means common dictionary to G_1 and G_2? Usually the simple intersection of two dictionaries does not work.

Shannon discovered basic laws of signal transmission that allow us to quantify the information passing in a communication process. But genomes surely pass biological information along the generations of individuals and in their evolution process, from early organisms to the most recent ones, along the tree of life. Therefore, the content of biological information inside genomes cannot be unrelated to the probabilistic information introduced by Shannon. In that perspective, the information of an emitted symbol is equated to $-\lg p$ if p is its emission probability. Therefore, according to Eq. (1), the entropy is the mean information emitted by the information source (X, p). This implies that the genomic entropy gives the mean information of a genome G when it is "read" with the words of L.

The general notion of "word," in terms of formal analyses of texts, has generated complex linguistic debates. For genomes, such a notion is more difficult to define, because a knowledge, comparable to the linguistic competences of humans, is not available for genomes. However, the power of computational analysis and the vastness of genomic data suggest us to reconsider the problem.

In infogenomics the integration of theoretic informational analysis with application and computation in real genomes is crucial, by means of powerful data representations, algorithms, and software. Results obtained in Refs. [4,18–21] support this approach. Moreover, inspired by a research originally applied to literary texts [27], we developed an algorithm of genomic word extraction, exclusively based on information theoretic concepts, and some computational experiments, currently in progress, seem to confirm the emergence of meaningful elements within lengths between 6 and 30 [21]. The main ingredients of this algorithm are the recurrence distance distributions of words, Bernoullian genomes, and entropic divergences for comparing and evaluating similarity and dissimilarity between different probability distributions.

Finally, informational measures of complexity were computed that are quite coherent with the phylogenesis of species (research in progress). This fact has an even wider relevance, because an understanding of information passages among genomes, along evolution pathways, could shed light in the informational organization of genomes, which has to be related to their biological functions.

In the following sections we give additional details about important key concepts of infogenomics.

21.4 RECURRENCE DISTANCE DISTRIBUTIONS

Bernoullian (or random) genomes are synthetic genomes generated by random extraction of letters in the genomic alphabet, with some assigned probabilities to the letters (without specification, they are assumed equally probable). Such genomes can be easily produced by using classical number generators, by encoding numbers by strings (in many possible ways). Moreover, apart from their generation, we know from probability theory that some phenomena in such genomes agree to very precise probability distributions. For example, under a suitable hypotheses, the number of times a given word occurs, within an interval of a given length in a random genome, agrees to a suitable Poisson distribution. Moreover, the distance occurring between two consecutive occurrences of a given word, agrees to an exponential distribution correlated with the previous one. In other words, we know very well how some random phenomena behave, or equivalently, we know which probability distributions hold over words of random genomes. This premise is important for the next discussion.

Let us consider a genome G and a word α occurring in G with the positions where its occurrences start. It was noticed, for literary texts, that if the word is semantically relevant for the text, then its occurrences tend to occur in clusters; that is, it does not follow a uniformly distributed random distribution, but is more concentrated around some places. Therefore, if we consider the distances between two consecutive occurrences of α we get a function assigning to each distance d the probability $RDD_G(\alpha, d)$ of occurring at distance d (the ratio between the number of times it recurs at distance d and the multiplicity of α in G). This function is called recurrence distance of α in G and provides a sort of profile of the behavior of α in G. In Ref. [28] recurrence distance distributions (RDDs) of many kinds of words in different genomes are reported, which show different shapes of the related curves, which are directly correlated to very specific phenomena.

As we already noticed, a RDD of k-mers has an exponential shape in Bernoullian genomes. If we compute RDDs for 3-mers we discover a clear difference with respect to pure exponential curves, and some well characterized irregularities. Moreover, these kinds of irregularities are different when distribution refers to different regions of the same genome. The most spectacular difference appears in *E. coli*, where an RDD of 3-mers has a typical shape consisting of an expected exponential curve, and a second exponential curve realized by some peaks above the first exponential one, occurring exactly with a relative distance 3 between each other. This phenomenon, which we call peak 3-periodicity, was already observed in the literature, but in a different context, and it is connected to the density of protein coding regions. In fact, it disappears in the whole human genome, but becomes clearly visible when it is applied only to the human exome. We do not provide further details here, but want to remark the biological relevance that RDDs have. If these distributions are computed for non-coding RNA of the human genome, peaks with a 3-periodicity appear again. Moreover, if RDD is applied to k-mers with $k>3$ (but $k<mfl(G)$) peaks occur even with no periodicity, but words that are inside recurrence pairs, at distances corresponding to peaks, show very regular repetitive patterns. In general, by means of RDDs, we are able to discover patterns, even when they are not exact, but approximate.

21.5 AN INFORMATIONAL MEASURE OF GENOME COMPLEXITY

What is the quantity of information contained in a genome G? An answer based on the digital nature of genomes could measure the length of G. In fact, any letter needs 2 bits to be identified within the nucleotide alphabet of 4 symbols (eg, 1 purine, 0 pyrimidine, and 01 for A, 11 for G, 00 for C, and 01 for T). In conclusion, if $|G|=n$, then $2n$ bits express its digital content. However, this analysis is too flat to be generally satisfactory. If we apply Shannon's probabilistic approach, then the average quantity of information of G is the entropy of G, with respect do a given dictionary L. But what is the appropriate dictionary for such a measure? We can answer with a second question. What is the dictionary L of G such that $H_L(G)$ reaches its maximum possible value? Lets call dictionaries with this property maximally entropic dictionaries, then they could be a good choice for answering the first question.

A necessary property for maximally entropic dictionaries can be found by applying the well-known feature of entropy, of reaching its maximum for equally distributed probability functions. Now it is easy to prove that a dictionary having the minimum number of words that are all hapaxes of G is a maximally entropic dictionary.

However, these dictionaries are very difficult to properly identify in real genomes. Therefore, we followed a different line of thought. In fact, it can be theoretically proved, and computationally tested, that, in the average, in a Bernoullian genome R, $D_m(R)$ is maximally entropic when $m=mrl(R)+1$; that is, when m is the length, incremented by 1, of the longest repeats of R. Then, essentially, omitting detailed passages, for the sake of simplicity, we evaluate this value m for a random genome having the same length of G and compute a variant of Kullback-Leibler entropic divergence between G and R, with respect to dictionary $L=D_m(G)$.

On the basis of this analysis, by introducing some approximations to improve computational efficiency, a formula was deduced, giving a measure of the "entropic distance" of a genome G from a random genome R long as G. It is not possible to give other details here about the deduction of this formula and its computation, but some values are reported in Table 21.1, where a coherence of these values with classical phylogenetic trees clearly appears. Moreover, some typical measures over genomes, such as length, CG percentage, or number of genes, are not directly related to the values

Table 21.1 Informational Complexity (*IC*) Values of Some Genomes (Rightmost Column) in Increasing Order

Species	IGI	N%	CG%	*IC*(*G*)
Nanoarchaeum equitans	0.49 Mb	0.00	31	0.011
Escherichia coli	4.93 Mb	0.00	50	0.038
Cyanidioschyzon merolae	14.9 Mb	0.00	55	0.111
Saccharomyces cerevisiae	12.0 Mb	0.00	38	0.145
Arabidopsis thaliana	119 Mb	0.16	36	0.176
Caenorhabditis elegans	100 Mb	0.00	35	0.198
Drosophila melanogaster	99 Mb	0.98	42	0.281
Oryza glaberrima	285 Mb	4.00	41	0.375
Vitis vinifera	426 Mb	2.35	35	0.655
Danio rerio	1.34 Gb	0.14	36	1.061
Macaca mulatta	2.88 Gb	11.21	42	1.552
Homo sapiens GRCh37	3.08 Gb	4.88	41	1.768

The length of genomes, the percentages of unknown letters N, and the CG percentages are also given in the other columns.

expressing this complexity, which is purely determined by means of information measures, capturing deep informational aspects of genome structures. However, the percentage of unknown nucleotides, N, surely introduces an error in the evaluation of this information complexity, which so far was not precisely determined.

Many other related issues are under investigation, to clarify technical aspects and to obtain a better interpretation and extension of the obtained results. However, a sure indication of the centrality of information theory in the analysis of genomes seems widely confirmed.

21.6 EXTRACTION OF GENOMIC DICTIONARIES

Genetic code is biologically almost universal. It tells us the letters of the texts written on genomes, but what are the "words" used for expressing biological meanings for life processes in the various species? The passage from the genetic code to genomic codes (probably different for different classes of organisms) is a necessary step toward a better comprehension of genomes. The starting point of such an investigation is the determination of meaningful words of a given genome; therefore the extraction of dictionaries. For this task, all the ingredients introduced in the previous section will be used. Therefore, RDDs, random genomes, and entropic divergences will be integrated in complex procedures, organized in consecutive phases. Namely, we start from an initial dictionary of short words called seeds (shorter than five characters). For each seed α we evaluate the entropic divergence of $RDDG(\alpha)$ with respect to the expected $RDDR(\alpha)$, where G is the genome under considerations, and R is a Bernoullian genome with the same length of G. The value of this divergence gives a sort of level significance for α.

However, if α is a subword of a larger string, for which the same or a greater significance is found, then we go on to extend (in both directions) this seed until a decreasing of significance is reached (many possible situations arise if we consider the relationship between seed elongation and length of the extracted word). In this way, we were able to extract hundreds thousands words of different lengths, in the length range 6–30, from the human genome, and many interesting phenomena were observed that deserve further analyses, biological interpretations, and validations. Of course, the outlined procedure is not so easy to realize, because it requires massive computations and many complex subprocedures.

The extracted words are firstly evaluated by considering their genome and positional coverage, their length, multiplicity, and other particular properties that clearly appear. We want only to report that it was found that less than 2000 hexamers for each human chromosome (within all the 4096 different hexamers) reach, in the average, a genome coverage around 88%. It is really surprising that a such small portions of short words can so widely cover the human genome. Moreover, a natural partition of words arises, that is, words that are subwords of other extracted words, that we call roots and words that are non subwords of other extracted words, that we call maximal morphemes.

Moreover, if we intersect all the extracted hexamers from all chromosomes, then we get a very small intersection; but if intersections are performed among specific groups of chromosomes, the situation changes dramatically, and around 90% of common extracted hexamers are found in each of four specific groups of chromosomes (apart only one, where intersection is smaller). Of course, many questions are still open, and surely a deep reflection has to be developed by using specific biological knowledge. But surely the extracted dictionaries give us elements that are informationally relevant. Semantics does not coincide with information, but surely it is based on it. Therefore, it seems that the selection of words, with such a kind of procedures, could be very useful for gaining new comprehension of the structure of genomes. When "putative words" are also biologically confirmed as relevant, we could proceed to define categories of words, and to discover their dynamics of combinations, integrations, and evolution.

21.7 CONCLUSIONS

Genomes direct the biological functions of cells. They were assembled and selected by natural selection, from primitive genomes, which initially had basic regulatory roles in the processes of biochemical transformation inside membranes. Along the way, they acquired an increasing level of specialization and efficiency that surely was based on a sophisticated internal organization. When they are viewed as information sources, the laws of information theory, its concepts and formulas can be applied, which reveal the deep structure on which *genomic codes* are based.

REFERENCES

[1] Deonier RC, Tavaré S, Waterman M. Computational genome analysis: an introduction. New York: Springer Science + Business Media; 2005.

[2] Vinga S, Almeida J. Alignment-free sequence comparison—a review. Bioinformatics 2003;19(4):513–23.

[3] Vinga S. Information theory applications for biological sequence analysis. Brief Bioinform 2013; 15(3):376–89.

[4] Manca V. Infobiotics: information in biotic systems. New York: Springer-Verlag; 2013.

[5] Head T. Formal language theory and DNA: an analysis of the generative capacity of specific recombinant behaviors. Bull Math Biol 1987;49(6):737–59.

[6] Paun G, Rozenberg G, Salomaa A. DNA computing, new computing paradigms. Heidelberg: Springer-Verlag; 1998.
[7] Manca V, Franco G. Computing by polymerase chain reaction. Math Biosci 2008;211(2):282–98.
[8] Franco G, Manca V. Algorithmic applications of XPCR. Nat Comput 2011;10:805–19.
[9] Brendel V, Busse H. Genome structure described by formal languages. Nucleic Acids Res 1984;12 (5):2561–8.
[10] Searls DB. The language of genes. Nature 2002;420(6912):211–7.
[11] Searls DB. Molecules, languages and automata. In: Grammatical inference: theoretical results and applications. Heidelberg: Springer-Verlag; 2010. p. 5–10.
[12] Puglisi A, Baronchelli A, Loreto V. Cultural route to the emergence of linguistic categories. Proc Natl Acad Sci 2008;105(23):7936–40.
[13] Gimona M. Protein linguistics—a grammar for modular protein assembly? Nat Rev Mol Cell Biol 2006;7 (1):68–73.
[14] Hao B, Qi J. Prokaryote phylogeny without sequence alignment: from avoidance signature to composition distance. J Bioinforma Comput Biol 2004;2(01):1–19.
[15] Hampikian G, Andersen T. Absent sequences: nullomers and primes. In: Pacific symposium on biocomputing, vol. 12; 2007. p. 355–66.
[16] Yin C, Chen Y, Yau SS-T. A measure of DNA sequence similarity by Fourier transform with applications on hierarchical clustering. J Theor Biol 2014;359:18–28.
[17] Consortium TEP. An integrated encyclopedia of DNA elements in the human genome. Nature 2012; 489(7414):57–72.
[18] Castellini A, Franco G, Manca V. A dictionary based informational genome analysis. BMC Genomics 2012;13(1):485.
[19] Franco G. Discrete and topological models in molecular biology. In: Jonoska N, Salto M, editors. Perspectives in computational genome analysis. Berlin Heidelberg: Springer-Verlag; 2014. p. 3–22. Ch. 1.
[20] Bonnici V. Informational and relational analysis of biological data. PhD Thesis, Department of Computer Science, University of Verona, 2015.
[21] Bonnici V, Manca V. Infogenomics tools: a computational suite for informational analysis of genomes. Bioinform Proteom Rev 2015;1(1):7–14.
[22] Manca V. Research lines in Infogenomics, 2015. Bioinform Proteom Rev 2009;1(1):1–4.
[23] Feller W. An introduction to probability theory and its applications, vol. 1. New York: John Wiley & Sons; 1968.
[24] Shannon CE. A mathematical theory of communication. Bell Syst Tech J 1948;27:379–423. 623–656.
[25] Cover TM, Thomas JA. Elements of information theory. New York: John Wiley & Sons; 1991.
[26] Abouelhoda MI, Kurtz S, Ohlebusch E. Replacing suffix trees with enhanced suffix arrays. J Discrete Algorithms 2004;2(1):53.
[27] Carpena P, Bernaola-Galván P, Hackenberg M, Coronado A, Oliver J. Level statistics of words: finding keywords in literary texts and symbolic sequences. Phys Rev E 2009;79(3):035102.
[28] Bonnici V, Manca V. Recurrence distance distributions in computational genomics. Am J Bioinform Comput Biol 2015;1(1):1–18.

SECTION

IV

DATA ANALYTICS AND NUMERICAL MODELING IN COMPUTATIONAL BIOLOGY AND BIOINFORMATICS

CHAPTER

ANALYSIS OF LARGE DATA SETS: A CAUTIONARY TALE OF THE PERILS OF BINNING DATA

22

R.W. Rumpf, J. Gonya, W.C. Ray

The Research Institute at Nationwide Children's Hospital, Columbus, OH, United States

22.1 INTRODUCTION

Bioinformaticists and computational biologists have always worked with data sets that were on the edge of computational tractability; the difference now as we enter the age of "Big Data" is that the data sets have grown to the point where they are no longer even feasibly explorable by a single individual—we have to trust our computational processes. Herein lies the danger—we should not consider analyses of this complexity to be a commodity transaction performed by black box algorithms. All too frequently algorithms written for one specific analysis can become suborned toward uses for which they were never intended.

In the case of data sets where the data is continuous but the algorithm requires discrete data, the data must be binned prior to analysis. This in itself introduces ambiguity and error into the analysis but is accepted because it is required if one wishes to analyze the data with the intended algorithm. There are undoubtedly as many binning strategies as there are data sets and scientists to analyze them. Commonly accepted practice is to place the data points into evenly sized bins based on distribution of the data over the maximum range of the data (eg, quartiles or other divisions). While this would seem to be a logical and stochastically supported approach, with an even distribution of value *ranges*, the number of data points in each bin will vary, which may lead to stochastic anomalies and/or inaccuracies.

An alternative is to create a number of bins of arbitrary size relative to the data range, each of which contains the same number of data points, resulting in bins of different range size/span but equal statistical power.

Because any downstream statistical analysis draws its power from the binning method [1], the implication is that different binning methods will result in different analysis outcomes. This can be easily demonstrated using the visual analytics tool StickWRLD [2,3] Originally designed to show coinheritance of paired residues in protein multiple sequence alignments (MSAs), StickWRLD has recently been applied to canceromics [4] data as well as continuous data from clinical health-care research [4,5]. Briefly, StickWRLD calculates the strength of the correlation between not only all variables, but all values within each variable, and presents the user with a 3-D cylindrical representation where correlated values are linked via an edge (Fig. 22.1). The user can adjust the statistical thresholds for both p and r (the residual, or *observed-expected*), effectively visually filtering the data to discover only

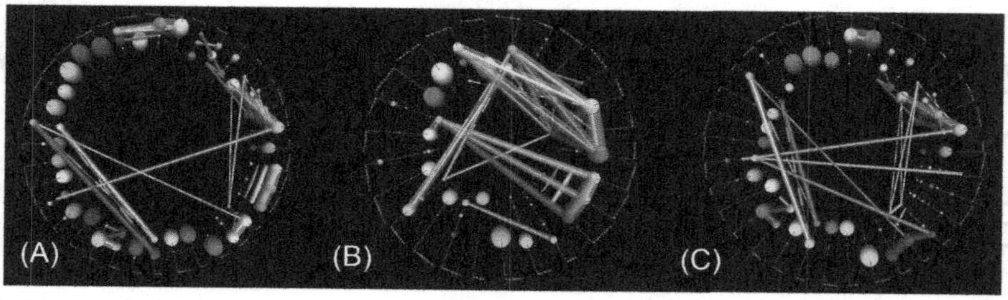

FIGURE 22.1

Differential patterns of correlation resulting from binning variations of the same data set. A clinical data set containing continuous data from a neonatal intensive care unit was binned in three different ways, resulting in different correlations seen between variables. Variables are displayed around the edge of the cylinder and are standardized to appear in the same location in all three representations; for this example the residual was standardized at 0.08 for all three representations.

Based on the clinical data set used in Rumpf RW, Gonya J, Ray WC. Visual hypothesis & correlation discovery for precision medicine. AMIA workshop on visual analytics in health care. Washington, DC: AMIA; 2014.

correlations of interest based on correlation members and strength. In the case of ordered variables, patterns of correlations may be revealed that in and of themselves may be interesting.

Because StickWRLD was originally designed to accept an MSA (which is essentially discrete data) as its input, this study had to bin the continuous clinical data prior to analysis. In the course of the analysis, three different binning strategies varying the size and number of bins were used. Each binning strategy revealed a different set of novel correlations, all of which were statistically significant.

The primary concern here is not necessarily that the statistics are rendered invalid by differential binning schemes, but rather that *significant correlations may be missed* depending on which binning scheme is used. To test this, we set out to repeat this process with another continuous data set.

22.2 METHODS

22.2.1 DATA SET

To test our hypothesis we began with a "standard" gene expression data set. The GSE1346 data set [6] was selected at random from the NCBI Gene Expression Omnibus database [7,8]. This expression array data set compares the expression of 16 genes for approximately 16,000 samples under various conditions. To facilitate comparison in StickWRLD we used a subset of this larger data set consisting of 100 samples chosen at random. For this data, StickWRLD would detect correlations between genes that shared similar response in expression levels for all treatment conditions.

22.2.2 BINNING

Two binning schemes were employed: a basic scheme, where the range of the data was divided into quartiles, and a second scheme, which divided the data points equally into six differentially sized groups such that while each bin spanned a different proportion of the data range, an equal number of data points was placed into each bin.

22.2.3 STICKWRLD ANALYSIS

Data was formatted and loaded into the PYTHON version of StickWRLD as described previously [4,5].

22.3 RESULTS

Both binning variations were loaded separately into StickWRLD. A top-down [9] approach at discovering correlations was used, where the residual was first increased until no relationships were detected, and then slowly ramped back down to see relationships of most significance. Unsurprisingly, each binning variations had a different threshold for this technique, and as expected, different relationships were seen.

22.3.1 BINNING VARIATION 1

Binning variation 1 did not display any correlations between gene expression until the residual was tuned down to 0.185. At this level, nine correlations were seen between genes (Fig. 22.2A). The correlations are listed in Table 22.1.

When the residual was tuned one increment lower (to 0.180), the number of relationships increased significantly (Fig. 22.2B). For purposes of simplicity, we limited the comparison to only those most significant relationships.

22.3.2 BINNING VARIATION 2

Binning variation 2 first displayed correlations at a residual threshold of 0.135; markedly lower than binning variation 1. At this level, seven correlations were seen between genes (Fig. 22.3A). These correlations are also listed in Table 22.1.

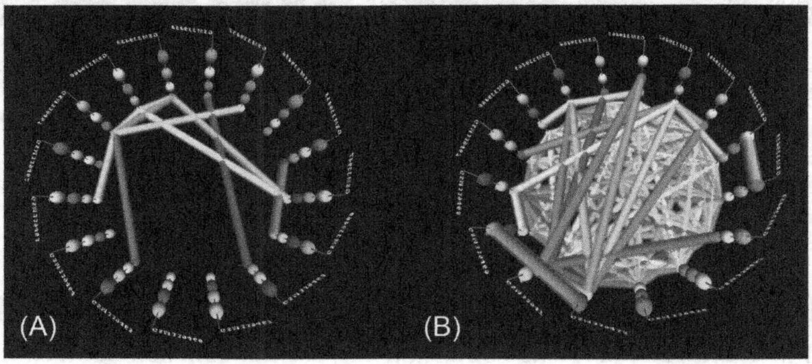

FIGURE 22.2

Correlations seen for binning variation 1. (A) With the residual threshold set to 0.185, nine correlations between genes are clearly visible. These correlations indicate genes whose change in expression level was linked for the conditions examined. (B) With the residual threshold reduced by one increment to 0.180, the number of correlations becomes difficult to process visually.

Table 22.1 Correlations Detected by Binning Variants

Binning Variation 1	Binning Variation 2	Correlations in Common
339461:339465	339459:339461	339459:339461
339461:339463	339457:339458	
339457:339461	339455:339456	
339459:339461	339463:33947	
339460:339461	339465:33947	
339460:33947	339466:33947	
339459:33947	339465:339466	
339458:339468		
339455:339469		

For each binning variation, the correlations identified at the highest threshold for residual are displayed. Only one correlation—that between genes 339459 and 339461—was seen in both binning variations.

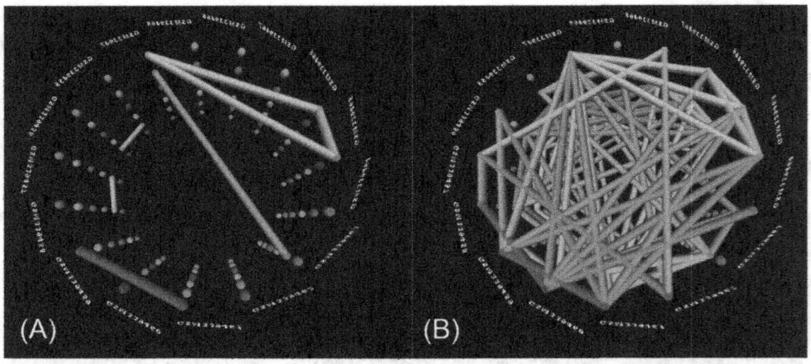

FIGURE 22.3

Correlations seen for binning variation 2. (A) The first correlations were seen with the residual tuned to 0.135; markedly lower than that for binning variation 1. Only seven correlations are seen at this threshold, only one of which was also seen in binning variation 1. (B) As before, reducing the residual threshold by one increment (to 0.0130) increased the number of correlations enough to make visual analysis challenging at best.

22.3.3 COMPARISON OF CORRELATIONS BETWEEN BINNING VARIATIONS

As can be seen in Table 22.1, only one correlation was seen in common between the two binning variations at the initial residual threshold. It was only when the residual was further reduced to 0.1 for both data sets that both binning variations discovered essentially the same set of correlations between genes (an agreement of 118/119 correlations, or 99%). At this residual threshold the actual visual display became hopelessly overwhelmed, rendering a visual analysis impossible.

22.4 DISCUSSION

As data sets become increasingly larger in this age of "big data," we are becoming more reliant on analysis methods that summarize and reduce the results to a more digestible size. As these processes tend to involve abstraction (eg, binning, or visual analytics, for example), the potential for "signal loss" is greater. Our analysis confirms that for a continuous data set, different binning algorithms can result in dramatically different high-level analysis results. Initial settings for the residual in StickWRLD results in only ~12% overlap in discovered correlations; it wasn't until a much deeper analysis was performed—deeper than would normally have been attempted for this particular visual analytic tool—that the overlap reached 99%; even then a complete identity was never achieved. This clearly indicates that the reliance on analysis tools to process large data sets, particularly those requiring data binning, must be approached with caution.

The binning methods we employed are both common approaches to working with continuous data. Both methods (quartile vs. equal distribution of data points) attempt to maximize the statistical power of the downstream analysis, but in different ways. The quartile approach divides the range of data points into four equal groups, seeking statistical significance at the logical regions of the distribution. The equal distribution method creates bins of different ranges but with an equal number of data points, seeking to maximize the statistical power of each bin. As seen in our results, the initial results (at a very high residual setting) were very different between the two sets; representative of the different statistical foci of each binning strategy. When the residual threshold was reduced sufficiently, both strategies revealed essentially the same results, yet this is not an optimal solution, particularly for a visual analytic approach such as StickWRLD. In both cases, the high-level analysis, which is the point of the visual analytic, loses potentially important correlations. And despite the overlap at lower residual thresholds, there still was not a complete identity in results.

Additional problems may be algorithm-dependent. For example, one of StickWRLD's advantages is its ability to quickly display correlations between not only variables, but between specific values within those variables. That particular capability is diminished when working with continuous data that must be binned; correlations can be drawn between bins, but not between specific values, and a comparison of differentially binned data also then becomes meaningless as the bins are not 1:1. This illustrates another concern when condensing "big" data into computationally tractable chunks: resolution is lost during binning.

22.5 CONCLUSIONS

It seems reasonable that there is, in fact, no single optimal binning strategy that will successfully identify all of the meaningful correlations in all cases. The best approach may be to use multiple binning strategies and look for correlation overlap between strategies, as we have done here. Alternately, it may be feasible to design software to enable dynamic binning strategies, much as the statistical model in StickWRLD can be dynamically updated by modifying the p and r values.

REFERENCES

[1] Virkar Y, Clauset A. Power-law distributions in binned empirical data. Ann Appl Stat 2014;8:89–119.

[2] Ray WC. MAVL/StickWRLD for protein: visualizing protein sequence families to detect non-consensus features. Nucleic Acids Res 2005;33:W315–9.

[3] Ray WC. In: A visual analytics approach to identifying protein structural constraints. IEEE VAST. IEEE; 2010.

[4] Rumpf RW, Wolock SL, Ray WC. StickWRLD as an interactive visual pre-filter for canceromics-centric expression quantitative trait locus data. Cancer Inform 2014;13:63–9.

[5] Rumpf RW, Gonya Jenn, Ray William C. Visual hypothesis & correlation discovery for precision medicine. AMIA workshop on visual analytics in health care. Washington, DC: AMIA; 2014.

[6] Bouwens M, Grootte Bromhaar M, Jansen J, Muller M, Afman LA. Postprandial dietary lipid-specific effects on human peripheral blood mononuclear cell gene expression profiles. Am J Clin Nutr 2010;91:208–17.

[7] Barrett T, Wilhite SE, Ledoux P, Evangelista C, Kim IF, Tomashevsky M, et al. NCBI GEO: archive for functional genomics data sets-update. Nucleic Acids Res 2013;41:D991–5.

[8] Edgar R, Domrachev M, Lash AE. Gene expression omnibus: NCBI gene expression and hybridization array data repository. Nucleic Acids Res 2002;30:207–10.

[9] Rumpf RW, Ray WC. Optimization of synthetic proteins: identification of interpositional dependencies indicating structurally and/or functionally linked residues. J Vis Exp 2015; e52878. http://dx.doi.org/10.3791/52878.

CHAPTER

STRUCTURAL AND PERCOLATION MODELS OF INTELLIGENCE: TO THE QUESTION OF THE REDUCTION OF THE NEURAL NETWORK

23

D. Zhukov*, I. Samoylo†, J.W. Brooks‡, V. Hodges‡
*Moscow State Technical University of Radio Engineering, Electronics and Automation "MIREA", Moscow, Russia**
I.M. Sechenov First Moscow State Medical University, Moscow, Russia†
Premier Education Group, New Haven, CT, United States‡

23.1 INTRODUCTION

It was established experimentally that the number of neural connections in a cerebral cortex of a newborn is quite small [1]. This number makes only a few percent of the neural network connections of the adult brain. However, in the process of the child's development, the number of connections between the neurons in his/her brain grows very productively and reaches its maximum by the age of 10 months old. In the subsequent stages of human development, there is a reduction in the neural network: the quantity of the synaptic links decreases and then it stabilizes. The process of the synapses' dying off and their stabilization is, probably, one of the basic mechanisms by which the obtained experience changes the structure of the brain in the course of its formation [2–5]. How much more reasonable is the process of the reduction of the synaptic connections between the neurons of the brain? What number of the synaptic connections between the neurons is sufficient for a productive intellectual activity? Let us try to find the answers to these questions with the help of the methods of numerical modeling, based on the *percolation model of human intellectual activity*.

To begin with, it is necessary to consider the basic principles of the construction and functioning of the neural network of the human brain.

According to Cajal's neuron doctrine, which is the basis of our understanding of the brain, the neuron is the main structural and functional element of the brain. The dendrites of the neuron are used to obtain signals, and axons are used to transmit signals to other neurons. Signal transmission is carried out only on the special sites, the synapses, and each neuron interacts only with certain neurons. It is important to consider that in real biological structures the number of available neurons varies from 10 to 100 billion, each of which has from 10 to 1000 connections with other nervous cells (*the multi-connectivity condition*).

The theory of the organization of the nervous system leads to the conclusion that the brain cells, neurons, are grouped in a very complex network infrastructure, thanks to which its work is carried out. The cortex functional features are determined by the distribution of cortical nerve cells (neurons) and their connections within the layers and columns. The convergence of the impulses from various sense organs is possible. According to modern ideas, similar convergence of diverse excitations is a neurophysiological mechanism of the integrative brain activity; that is, the analysis and synthesis of the reciprocal activity of an organism. The fact that neurons are summarized in complexes apparently realizing the convergence excitation results in separate neurons is of considerable importance. Ultimately, complex interactions of all parts of the brain determine the diversity of human behavior and intellectual activity.

23.2 ABILITIES OF THE BRAIN WHILE PROCESSING INFORMATION

John Griffith [6] made a rough calculation that if a person continually remembered any information with the speed of 1 bit per second throughout 70 years of their life, then 10^{14} bits of information would be accumulated in their memory; approximately equivalent to the amount of information contained in Encyclopedia Britannica. In fact, every second the human brain receives about 20 bits of information, and during 14 h, it can process 18 billion bits. To store this amount of information one needs only one-thousandth of all nerve cells of the brain. According to various estimates, the amount of information that a person can remember for a lifetime is up to 10^{21} bits. A person is able to recall the necessary information in the 10th fractions of a second, which requires the search speed of about 50 billion bits per second. It should be noted that processing such an amount of information could be provided only by a parallel operation of the nervous structures. These structures *in terms of data storage and data retrieval have a very efficient topology*.

23.3 FORMALIZED STRUCTURAL MODEL OF INTELLECTUAL ACTIVITY

The characteristic feature of the structure of the cerebral cortex is the *oriented horizontal and vertical distributions* of its constituent nerve cells (neurons) in the layers and columns. Thus, the cortical structure is notable for its spatially organized arrangement of the functioning units and connections between them.

The management of intellectual processes as well as the management of motor skills can be carried out by several hierarchically subordinated rings of the connected neurons, which among themselves distribute the roles according to the hierarchy of their abilities. One part of neurons plans only general ways of realization, and the following rings of neurons are responsible for the details of the execution. However, neurons can interact with each other not only vertically but also horizontally, forming horizontal rings. Thus, the interaction can be carried out by the principle of the branched network, where *the trajectories of the transmission of the nerve signals look like loops*: the same signal can return to the starting point several times. The main type of direct and reverse connections of the neocortex is the vertical bundles of fibers that bring the information from subcortical structures to the cortex and send it back to the cortex. Along with the vertical links, there are intracortical or horizontal bundles of associative fibers extending at various levels.

The set of neurons, their communication, and the topology of their connections while learning and saving various images and objects, form a certain subnet of knobs. Those knobs are responsible for the process that created them and, further on, it responds for the identification of the given process (or an object).

The formalized topological model of the neural network of the brain may have the form shown in Fig. 23.1: the arc-shaped lines represent nonoverlapping connections between distant neurons, and the straight segments are the connections with the nearby nerve cells.

Neurons can have both types of connections: horizontal, conditionally lying in one plane (one layer), and vertical connections between the nerve cells belonging to different layers (they are indicated in Fig. 23.1 by 1, 2, 3, 4, and 5). For example, the chain of neurons indicated as a-c-d-e-n in Fig. 23.1 can be included in one of the vertical layers, and the chain, which is indicated as o-i-p-s-m-k, can be included in a horizontal layer. *It is very important to note that the same neuron can simultaneously belong to both various horizontal and vertical layers (and the chains of the connected neurons themselves can be conditionally called horizontal and vertical rings).*

The structure shown in Fig. 23.1 can be conditionally called a random network with multiple connections between the knobs (neurons).

Let us analyze to what degree the structure represented in Fig. 23.1 corresponds to the data on the structure and operation of the human brain.

The speed of the nerve impulse is significantly less than the speed of the transmission of electrical signals at their contacts. Therefore, practically, the brain of any person loses in speed to computers, but it considerably surpasses them in its intellectual activity because of the *associativity of the brain's work*

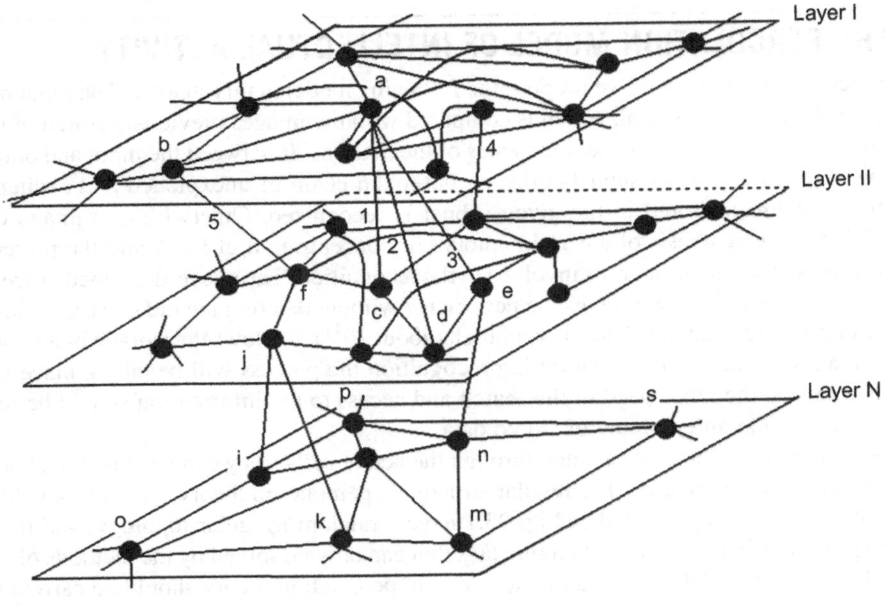

FIGURE 23.1

Formalized model of brain topology.

and almost infinite *degree of the parallelization of the information processing*. If there is an available network composed of 10–100 billion neurons with a total number of connections of 10^{12} pieces, it can be divided into subnets (eg, the size of 10^4–10^6 knobs). Given that some of the neurons or their groups can be parts of different subnets, then at a rough estimate, the number of possible combinations can be

$$C_{10^4}^{10^{12}} = \frac{10^{12}!}{10^4!(10^{12}-10^4)!};\quad C_{10^6}^{10^{12}} = \frac{10^{12}!}{10^6!(10^{12}-10^6)!}$$

It is possible to consider each of such structures as a separate processor (using computer science terminology). In this case, at a very rough estimate, there will be about 10^{11}–10^{12} units working in parallel, which is practically not achievable (even in the distant future) for a computer built on semiconductors. For the structure shown in Fig. 23.1, the increasing number of knobs and connections between them should lead to an increase in the number of possible subnets or (using the language of computer science again) parallel processors. The structure shown in Fig. 23.1 is not only multilayered, but *it is also characterized by having many different connections among its knobs*. Therefore, at the reduction of its size, a removal of one part of the structure (or leaving only a small part of it) will not affect its topological properties. If the network's work is defined also by its topological properties, then in qualitative terms, its reduction in size will not affect its work (the quantitative detection of accuracy may deteriorate or time will increase). All the above is consistent with the data proving that the localization of functions in primary areas of the brain is duplicated in such a manner that each smallest area contains the information about the whole object.

23.4 THE PERCOLATION MODEL OF INTELLECTUAL ACTIVITY

For pattern recognition purposes, we propose the following model in this chapter. The input of the neural network is the input to a signal, which is compared with the images previously stored in its subnet. This may result in some active (or excited) states of the neurons. If between the input and output layers of the network or in any of its subnetworks, an unbroken chain of unexploded and excited neurons appears, then the image stored in the given subnet is recognized. Otherwise, the image cannot be recognized. Then the synthesis of a certain amount of concentration of RNA and the protein coding information takes place in the neurons involved in the recognition. The above-described process creates one more subnet. The new subnet saves the new image without deleting the old ones. Considering that the number of possible created subnets is very high (about 10^{11}), it allows the storage of a large number of various images. Besides, given that during recognition the process will be taking place in parallel within all structures, then the speed of the search and access to the information should be reasonably high, despite a considerable volume of stored data.

It is possible to name the route created through the active cells (they can be called the knobs of the subnet) as filtering or percolation. For regular structures, percolation theory is a well-developed area. However, the structures represented in Fig. 23.1 have a random irregular topology, and the study of percolation processes in them is a challenging task that can only be solved by the methods of numerical modeling. From the point of view of a mathematician, percolation theory should be carried to probability theory on graphs. There are a large number of monographs on both theoretical and applied aspects of percolation [7–10].

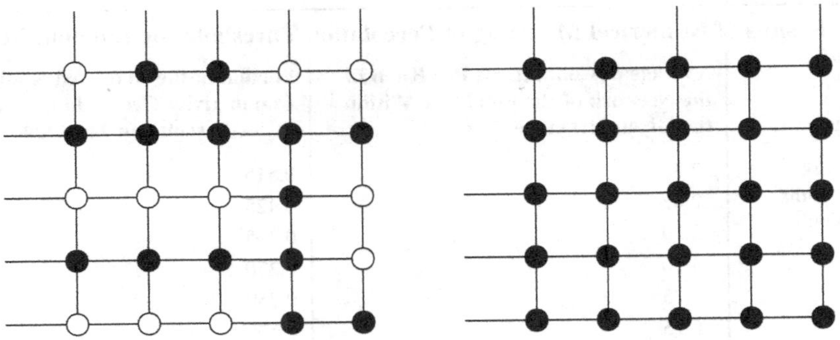

FIGURE 23.2

Percolation on a square lattice.

To explain the basic tenets of percolation theory, let us take a square network and paint over a part of the knobs in black (see Fig. 23.2).

One of the questions that can be answered by percolation theory here is: At what portion of n_c of the colored knobs does their black chain connecting the upper and lower sides of the net (the chain of connectivity) arise? For a grid of the finite size, such chains may occur at different concentration (see Fig. 23.2). However, if the size of grid L is directed to infinity, then the critical concentration becomes quite definite. Such critical concentration is called *the percolation threshold.*

The square grid is only one possible model. One can consider percolation on the triangular and hexagonal grids, trees, and three-dimensional lattices (eg, on a cubic one that is in space, with the dimension of more than three). The grid does not necessarily need to be regular; it is possible to consider the processes on random lattices.

Let us consider percolation in random networks with multiple paths between the knobs having the form shown in Fig. 23.1. We will choose on the opposite layers of the network any two knobs, A and B, and start to randomly activate certain other knobs. Obviously, if there are many activated knobs, a situation may occur between the two arbitrarily selected knobs A and B, there will be at least one "open" path (the path formed by the activated knobs). Using the methods of numerical modeling with statistical averaging of the obtained results of separate experiments, it is possible to determine at what proportion of the activated knobs (the percolation threshold) the conductivity between knobs A and B appears in the network, and how it depends on the average number of connections per single knob. Table 23.1 presents the results of numerical modeling of identifying the percolation threshold for random networks with multiple paths between the knobs (see Fig. 23.1) with a various average number of connections per knob.

Because an increase of an average number of connections per knob in the network leads to a substantial increase in time and computing resources expenses, it was decided in numerical modeling to choose the area from 2.5 to 15 connections per knob.

Fig. 23.3 shows the graphic dependence of the results introduced in Table 23.1. Fig. 23.3 demonstrates that at the increase in the average number of connections per knob in the network, the percolation threshold begins to pursue its certain minimum value. Thus, the received results suggest that there is no need to carry out numerical modeling for large values of the average number of connections per knob. Instead, it is possible to linearize the results and extrapolate them to higher values.

Table 23.1 Results of Numerical Modeling of Percolation Threshold for Random Networks

Network Type	Average of Connections Per Knob in the Network of the Final Size Within the Given Structure	Portion of the Activated Knobs, at Which Conductivity Occurs in the Network (n_c — Percolation Threshold)
Random network with multiple paths between the knobs	2.36	0.515
	2.82	0.425
	3.29	0.365
	4.70	0.270
	4.75	0.250
	6.15	0.150
	6.17	0.185
	6.75	0.175
	9.41	0.170
	10.02	0.150
	10.31	0.130
	10.69	0.135
	11.07	0.115
	13.10	0.115

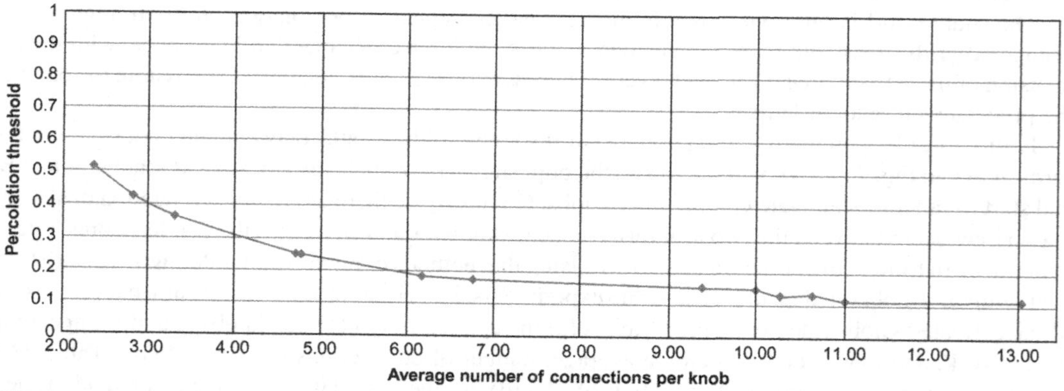

FIGURE 23.3

Dependence of the size of the percolation threshold in a random network on average number of connections per knob.

As the graphic kind of the dependence in Fig. 23.3 reminds the exponent, then it can be described by the function of the following kind:

$$P(x) = P_0(1 + e^z)$$

where $P(x)$ is the value of the percolation threshold with the average number of connections per knob equal to some value x, and $z = \frac{1}{x}$ where P_0 is the value of the percolation threshold at an infinite number

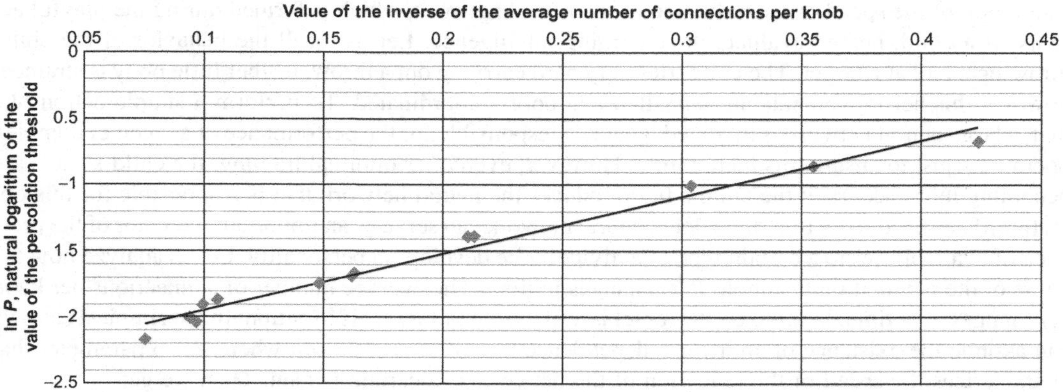

FIGURE 23.4

Dependence of the logarithm of the value of the percolation threshold on the value of the inverse of the average number of connections per knob in a random network.

of connections per knob. As Fig. 23.4 shows, the results presented in Table 23.1 are linearized well in the coordinates.

The dots in Fig. 23.4 present the experimental data and the solid line corresponds to a linear relationship $y = 4.2882z - 2.3766$, with very high correlation coefficient equal to 0.98.

At $z = \frac{1}{x} = 0$ (corresponding to the case when $x = \infty$) we get $y = \ln P_0 = -2.15$, and the value of the percolation threshold at an infinite large number of connections per knob P_0 will be equal to 0.093. Thus, for a random network with an infinite large number of connections per knob, it is enough to have an equal share of activated neurons equal to 0.093 of the total number, for the conductive chain of knobs to appear and for the network of knobs to recognize the presented image. With the average number of connections equal to 100, the percolation threshold is equal to 0.097, and at 10 it is equal to 0.143.

The obtained results show that a substantial increase in random network connections with an average of more than 10 connections per knob hardly changes the percolation threshold. From the point of view of the use of the biological resources, this type of increase is unfavorable for neural structures. Therefore, first, the reduction of the neurosynaptic redundancy of the network is an inevitable step in the formation of a neural network of the human brain, or, figuratively speaking, "that which is not in use, is dying." Secondly, offered by the authors of this chapter, the percolation model of the reduction of a neural network allows one to explain how education influences the brain. The research works of the neurosurgeons Otfrid Foerster in Germany and Wilder Penfield in Montreal marked the beginning of the theory of mental maps, according to which the subsystems of the mind are localized on the specific areas of the brain. Each of the subsystems of the brain can be considered as a random subnet with a variety of connections between the knobs (neurons). Education changes the brain structure, as well as the structure of the subnet that is responsible for a specific type of activity.

An interesting and very important issue is the problem of assessing the intellectual potential of children less than 2 years of age. The results of measurements of intelligence of young children are well correlated with the results of the IQ tests performed on the same people later in life [11]. However, such correlation in intellect is not observed with children younger than 2 years old. We believe that the estimation of the speed of the reduction of the neural network, which is formed during the playful activity of a child, helped evaluate the emerging intelligence. Let us recall the behavior of the child, throwing a ball at a target. The child tries very hard carrying out a throw, his/her little body is strained; however, his/her movements are unskilled and poorly coordinated. To perform a simple action like that, a large neural network is involved, which is responsible for the performance of a chain of complex operations just to ensure this inept throw. However, even after minimal training, the child's shots are becoming more accurate; the child's brain reduces the neural network that is responsible for this operation. The speed reduction of the local neural network can serve as an important indicator of the presence of availabilities to a certain type of activity in the developing personality. Let us analyze how the value of the percolation threshold $P(x)$ changes in time. The average number of connections per knob (x) changes over time. In this case, the cruel law of "use it or lose it" is in action. In the simplest case we can assume the existence of an inverse dependence of x of time t, $x=a/t$, where a is a parameter that characterizes the speed of the reduction of the network of a certain person. Then we get

$$P(t)=P_0\left(1+e^{\frac{t}{a}}\right)$$

and, accordingly, the speed of the reduction of the network will grow rapidly with time:

$$\frac{dP}{dt}=P_1 e^{\frac{t}{a}};\quad P_1=\frac{P_0}{a}$$

Estimation of the speed of the reduction of the local neural network opens up new possibilities for prediction, correction, and adjustment of personal development at the early stages of formation. It also contributes to the development of sensitive methods of diagnostics of neural networks of the brain in the cases of autism and hyperactivity.

REFERENCES

[1] Doidge N. The brain that changes itself. Westminster: Penguin Books; 2010. Appendix 2.
[2] Rose S. The making of memory: from molecules to mind. New York/London/Toronto/Sydney/Auckland: Anchor Books/Doubleday; 1993.
[3] Changeaux J-P, Danchin A. Selective stabilization of developing synapses as a mechanism for the specification of neuronal network. Nature 1976;264:705–12.
[4] Edelman G. Neural Darwinism: the theory of neuronal group selection. New York, NY: Basic Books; 1987.
[5] Hebb DO. The organization of behavior. New York, NY: Wiley; 1949.
[6] Griffith JS. A view of the brain. Oxford: Oxford University Press; 1967.
[7] Stauffer D, Aharony A. Introduction to percolation theory. London: Taylor and Francis; 1992.
[8] Grimmet G. Percolation. Berlin: Springer-Verlag; 1999.
[9] Kesten H. Percolation theory for mathematicians. Boston, MA: Birkhauser; 1982.
[10] Sahimi M. Percolation applications of percolation theory. London: Taylor and Francis; 1992.
[11] Stroganova TA, Tcetlin MM. Psychophysiological study of temperament in infants suffered early visual deprivation. Hum Physiol 1998;24(3):27–33.

SECTION

V

MEDICAL APPLICATIONS AND SYSTEMS

CHAPTER

ANALYZING TCGA LUNG CANCER GENOMIC AND EXPRESSION DATA USING SVM WITH EMBEDDED PARAMETER TUNING

24

H. Zhao, A. Deeter, Z.-H. Duan

Integrated Bioscience Program, Department of Computer Science, The University of Akron, Akron, OH, United States

ABBREVIATIONS

SVM	support vector machine
TCGA	The Cancer Genome Atlas
NSCLC	non-small cell lung cancers
LUAD	lung adenocarcinoma
LUSC	lung squamous cell carcinoma
RNA-seq	RNA sequencing

24.1 INTRODUCTION

High-throughput, next-generation sequencing revolutionized the genomic sequencing techniques. It allows the study of thousands of genes and even the entire exome in a given organism simultaneously [1–4]. This, as well as other high-throughput technologies such as DNA microarray, has broadened the genomic sequencing applications and changed biomedical research in a profound way [5–7]. When compared with microarray, the big data generated from next-generation sequencing is considerably more reliable [8,9]. As such, the technique has rapidly emerged as a major tool to obtain gene mutation and expression profiles of human cancers [10–15]. The availability of these big genomic data presents unique scientific challenges and opportunities. One such challenge is to understand and characterize the patterns of genomic mutation and gene expression in different cancer types presented in the data sets.

Many data mining approaches have already been developed to analyze large data sets for feature selections and sample classifications. One cancer tissue classification study using microarray data, conducted by Golub et al., involves a data set of 73 microarray samples from leukemia patients [5]. Each sample presents the expression levels of 7129 probes for 6817 genes. The study selected a list of informative genes that were used to construct a simple neighborhood analysis-based binary classifier. The results from the study confirmed the hypothesis that there was a set of genes whose expression patterns were strongly correlated with the cancer subclass distinctions. The leukemia cancer data set generated by Golub et al. has been further studied by several other researchers [16–22]. Dudoit et al. compared the performance of different discrimination methods for the classification of tumors based on the data set [16]. The methods compared include *k*-nearest neighbor classifiers, linear discriminant analysis, and classification trees. Their results reaffirmed the conclusion that the gene expression patterns from the two cancer subtypes are differentiable. On the other hand, their results also indicate that the classification results are not robust and the mean misclassification rate could go as high as about 25%.

Because mutation and gene expression profiles are noisy due to both biological and technical variations, it is clear that the effectiveness and robustness of a machine learning-based classification system significantly depends upon the nature of the input data. To enhance the stability and accuracy of a classification system, several advanced data mining methods have been deployed. Xiong and Chen developed a modified *k*-nearest neighbor classification method based on learning an adaptive distance metric in the data space [17]. The distance metric derived is data-dependent. Their results indicate the approach can substantially increase the class separability and lead to an increased performance as compared to the regular *k*-nearest neighbor classifier. Mallick et al. used several Bayesian classification techniques [18]. Antonov et al. used a maximal margin linear programming approach [19]. Dhawan et al. [20] and Sewak et al. [21] utilized assemble techniques to obtain more robust classification results. In addition, variations of support vector machine (SVM)-based algorithms as well as other wrappers, filters, and embedded methods were also used [22–26].

In this study, we propose to use SVMs with embedded parameter tuning to explore the DNA mutation and gene expression patterns in lung cancer. The embedded parameter tuning was based on data mining the training data set using validation techniques and concepts of the committee voting approach. The two independent data sets used were derived from somatic mutation data and RNA sequencing (RNA-seq) gene expression profiles of non-small cell lung cancers (NSCLC) presented at The Cancer Genome Atlas (TCGA) [27,28].

We demonstrate that classification systems based on SVMs with parameter tuning significantly improve the robustness and categorization accuracy when they are compared to SVMs with linear kernel and Gaussian kernel with default parameter setting. The approach was applied to the two data sets to explore the mutation patterns as well as the expression patterns between lung adenocarcinoma (LUAD) and lung squamous cell carcinoma (LUSC), the two most common subtypes of lung cancer. The results reveal different somatic mutation and gene expression patterns between LUAD and LUSC. Further gene ontology (GO) enrichment analysis revealed several enriched GO categories. Some of the most differentially expressed genes, as well as the top enriched GO categories, have been reportedly implicated in several pathways of the two subtypes of lung cancer [29–32]. We conclude that SVMs with embedded parameter tuning are an effective tool for analyzing somatic mutation data and gene expression profiles obtained through next-generation sequencing.

24.2 METHODS

Two data sets used in this study were obtained from TCGA data repositories [27,28]. The first set of data obtained includes somatic mutation data files from 324 lung cancer solid tissue samples in which 187 are LUAD and 137 are LUSC samples. Each sample consists of 34 attributes of heterogeneous data types including mutation locations on each chromosome as well as mutation types such as missense mutation, silent mutation, frame shift deletion, and in frame deletion. The second data set is a set of RNA-seq gene expression data from 977 specimens in which 488 are LUAD samples and 489 are LUSC samples. Each sample consists of 20,502 human genes.

To select informative features that discern the two subtypes of lung cancer, we carried out a sequence of preprocessing steps to the TCGA data to eliminate extraneous factors and simplify the input data matrix. The steps carried out to the somatic mutation data set included (1) selecting only the records with missense mutations; (2) combining mutation counts to obtain gene-specific mutation counts; and (3) retaining only the genes whose somatic mutation information were presented in both LUAD and LUSC. The resulting data from the preprocessing includes gene-specific counts of somatic mutations obtained from 135 LUAD and 137 LUSC patients. The data matrix is an integer matrix of size 14,485 (genes) by 272 (patients). We then filtered the noninformative records for which the difference between total instances of LUAD and LUSC is greater than a given threshold d_{min}. In this study, d_{min} was determined heuristically to be 6; as a result, a total 290 informative genes passed the filter (interestingly, the number of informative genes remained the same from one experiment run to another). The 290 genes are presented in Supplementary Table S1. The final data set is a 290×272 integer matrix. The normalized RNA-seq gene expression data set went through two steps of feature reduction: (1) eliminating the genes whose fold change between LUAD and LUSC is less than 2; (2) the adjusted p-values obtained from Welch's t-test for two subtypes are less than 0.01. The adjustment was done using a Bonferroni correction. The second reduced data set contains approximately 2400 genes. Although the set of genes varies from one experiment to another, most of them were selected in all 10 experiments. A total of 1933 genes are common to all 10 runs and are presented in Supplementary Table S2. To gain the biological insights of the top 290 differentially mutated as well as the top 1933 differentially expressed genes, GO enrichment analysis was conducted using the top GO package in Bioconductor [29].

SVMs are used as the classifiers in this study. A SVM is a supervised machine-learning tool and provides a nonprobabilistic binary classifier with a broad application in classification studies [30,31]. It has been widely used for solving problems in pattern recognition, classification, and regression. The SVMs work on one underlying principle, which is to insert a hyperplane between the two classes and orient it in such a way so as to keep it at the maximum distance from the nearest data points, which are defined as support vectors. The optimization problem is convex. Therefore, the optimal hyperplane can be solved using standard quadratic programming techniques. One important feature of SVM that makes it stand out from all other linear classifiers is that it can be used to convert a nonlinear classification problem into a linear problem through a kernel function. The kernel function maps two classes of data points in a lower dimensional feature space onto a high-dimensional space so that the two sets of data points can be separated using a hyperplane.

The power of a classification system depends on the distribution of the data points. While linear kernels could work very well for some applications, nonlinear kernels might be necessary for others. This study explores the robustness and accuracy of SVMs with a nonlinear kernel and embedded parameter tuning. The kernel function used is a Gaussian where $K(\boldsymbol{x}, \boldsymbol{z}) = \exp\left(\frac{-\|\boldsymbol{x}-\boldsymbol{z}\|^2}{2\sigma^2}\right), \sigma \in R - \{0\}$. To compare the performance, the linear kernel $K(\boldsymbol{x}, \boldsymbol{z}) = \langle \boldsymbol{x}, \boldsymbol{z} \rangle$ was also deployed. The embedded parameter (σ) tuning was based on techniques of data mining using cross validation and concepts of committee voting approach. The procedure is summarized in Fig. 24.1. The implementation of the procedure was done in MATLAB®.

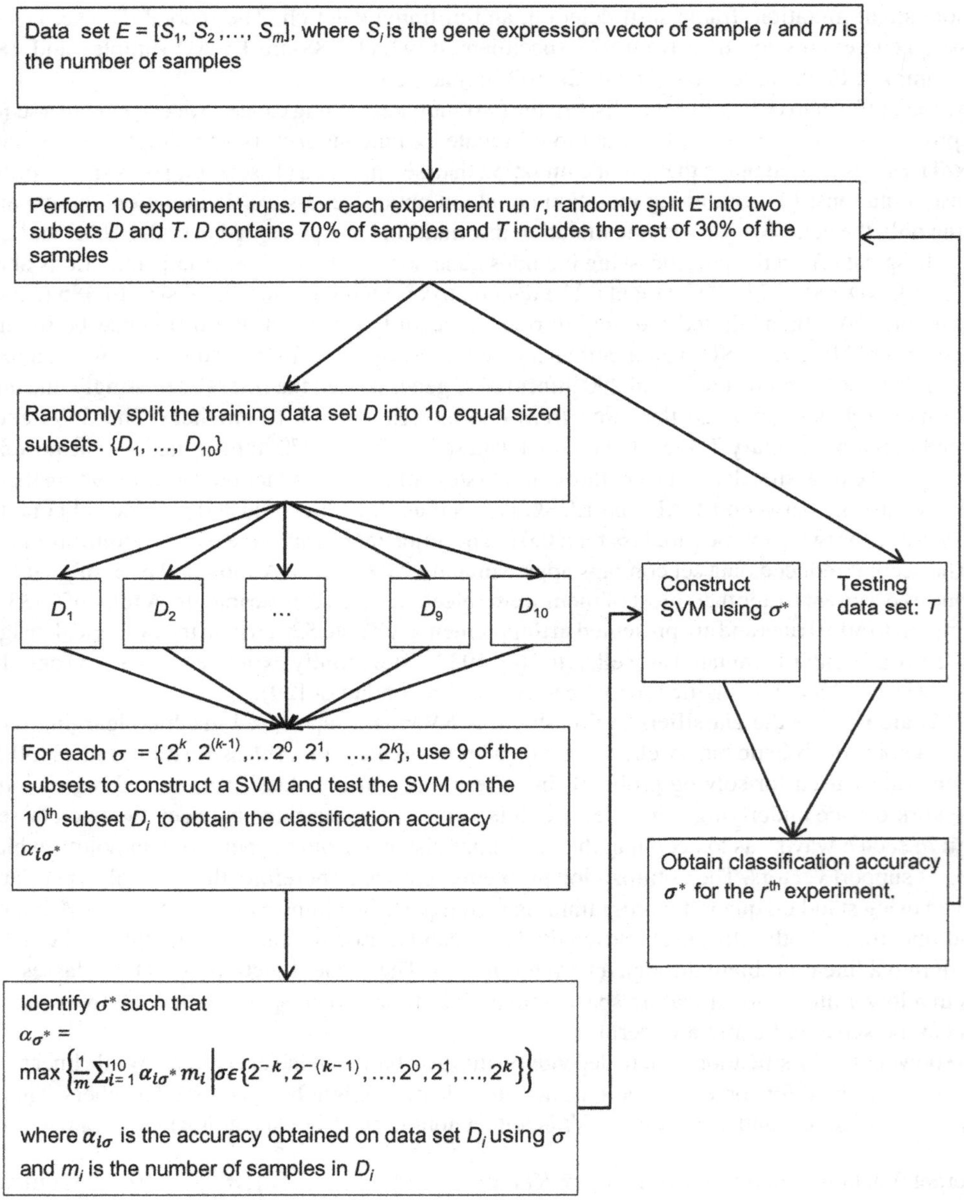

FIGURE 24.1

Parameter turning using cross validations.

24.3 RESULTS AND DISCUSSION

To demonstrate the accuracy and robustness of SVMs with embedded parameter tuning, 10 experiments were conducted on each data set using both linear kernel and Gaussian kernel, respectively. They were carried out based on the procedure outlined in Fig. 24.1. The results from the linear kernel, as well as Gaussian kernel with default parameter setting, were obtained to establish the performance control for the proposed algorithm.

The first data set is a data set of somatic mutations of lung cancer, which include mutation information for 290 informative genes in 135 LUAD and 137 LUSC patients. The training data set for each experiment consists of 95 LUAD and 96 LUSC while the testing data set consists of 40 LUAD and 41 LUSC samples. The class prediction results and accuracies based on this data set are presented in Tables 24.1 and 24.2 in the form of confusion matrices. Table 24.1 presents the class prediction results obtained from 10 experiments using SVMs with linear kernel while Table 24.2 illustrates the results from the Gaussian kernel with parameter tuning. We also conducted experiments with fixed σ values. The averages of classification accuracy and their standard errors over 20 experiments are shown in Fig. 24.2.

Table 24.1 Class Prediction Results Using the Somatic Mutations Data Set and Linear Kernel

Experiment Run	Selected Genes[a]	Actual Class	Predicted Class: LAUD	Predicted Class: LUSC	Accuracy (%)
1	290	LAUD	37	3	88.89
		LUSC	6	35	
2	290	LAUD	32	8	86.42
		LUSC	3	38	
3	290	LAUD	37	3	92.59
		LUSC	3	38	
4	290	LAUD	40	0	90.12
		LUSC	8	33	
5	290	LAUD	36	4	87.65
		LUSC	6	35	
6	290	LAUD	39	1	93.83
		LUSC	4	37	
7	290	LAUD	38	2	88.89
		LUSC	7	34	
8	290	LAUD	37	3	90.12
		LUSC	5	36	
9	290	LAUD	37	3	86.42
		LUSC	8	33	
10	290	LAUD	36	4	90.12
		LUSC	4	37	

[a]*The information of the 290 genes is presented in Supplementary Table 1.*

Table 24.2 Class Prediction Results and Accuracies Using the Somatic Mutations Data Set and Gaussian Kernel With Turned Parameter σ^*

			Predicted Class			
Experiment Run	Selected Genes[a]	Actual Class	LAUD	LUSC	Optimal σ (σ^*)	Accuracy (%)
1	290	LAUD	38	2	32	96.30
		LUSC	1	40		
2	290	LAUD	40	0	32	96.30
		LUSC	3	38		
3	290	LAUD	39	1	32	98.77
		LUSC	0	41		
4	290	LAUD	38	2	32	93.83
		LUSC	3	38		
5	290	LAUD	39	1	16	95.06
		LUSC	3	38		
6	290	LAUD	40	0	32	97.53
		LUSC	2	39		
7	290	LAUD	39	1	32	96.30
		LUSC	2	39		
8	290	LAUD	39	1	32	96.30
		LUSC	2	39		
9	290	LAUD	40	0	32	96.30
		LUSC	3	38		
10	290	LAUD	39	1	16	97.53
		LUSC	1	40		

[a]*The information of the 290 genes is presented in Supplementary Table 1.*

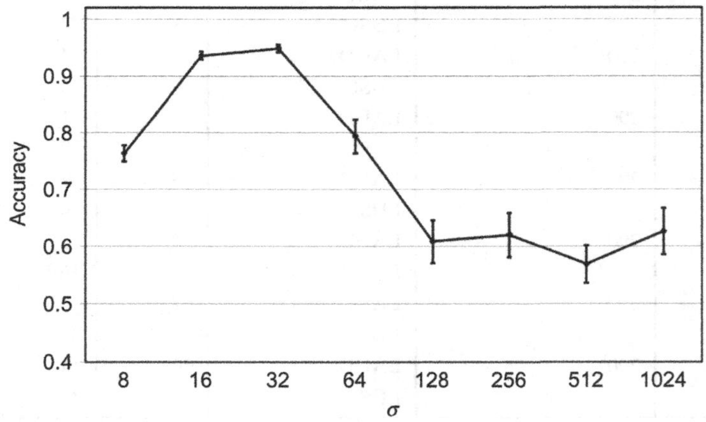

FIGURE 24.2

Classification performance using exome sequencing somatic mutation data set.

As illustrated in Tables 24.1 and 24.2, the cancer subtype prediction results from our approach show close agreement with the true subtypes of the samples for this mutation data set. Although among the misclassified samples from SVM with linear kernel, slightly more LUSC samples were misrepresented than the LUAD ones (an average of 5 versus 3), the accuracy results are relatively stable across all 10 experiments with an accuracy of 89.5 ± 2.4%. Table 24.2 illustrates that the results from the Gaussian kernel with parameter tuning are better. The accuracies are significantly improved to 94.9 ± 1.1%. The misclassified samples are again skewed slightly toward LUSC with an average of 2 misclassifications of LUSC verses less than 1 of LUAD. The optimal value of the free parameter in the Gaussian kernel is 32 for eight runs and 16 for the other two. We note that experiments were also conducted using SVM classifier with parameters $\sigma < 8$. These results were completely skewed with all LUSC being misclassified to be LUADs for all 10 experiments, indicating parameter selection is critical to develop an effective nonlinear SVM classifier.

The second data set is a collection of RNA-seq gene expression levels from 488 LUAD and 489 LUSC patients. The corresponding training subset for each experiment consists of 342 LUAD and 343 LUSC samples, respectively, while the testing subset consists of 146 LUAD and 146 LUSC samples, respectively. The class prediction results and accuracies based on the expression data set are presented in Tables 24.3 and 24.4 in the form of confusion matrices. The experimental results from 20 experiments with fixed σ values are shown in Fig. 24.3.

Table 24.3 Class Prediction Results Using the Gene Expression Data Set and a Linear Kernel

Experiment Run	Selected Genes[a]	Actual Class	Predicted Class LAUD	Predicted Class LUSC	Accuracy (%)
1	2485	LAUD	144	2	93.84
		LUSC	16	130	
2	2533	LAUD	132	14	92.81
		LUSC	7	139	
3	2454	LAUD	141	5	94.52
		LUSC	11	135	
4	2387	LAUD	138	8	94.86
		LUSC	7	139	
5	2318	LAUD	138	8	93.84
		LUSC	10	136	
6	2387	LAUD	140	6	94.86
		LUSC	9	137	
7	2385	LAUD	141	5	94.52
		LUSC	11	135	
8	2625	LAUD	133	13	91.14
		LUSC	12	134	
9	2343	LAUD	137	9	93.49
		LUSC	10	136	
10	2459	LAUD	138	8	93.15
		LUSC	12	134	

[a]*The information of the 1933 common genes is presented in Supplementary Table 2.*

Table 24.4 Class Prediction Results and Accuracies Using the Somatic Mutations Data Set and a Gaussian Kernel With Turned Parameter σ*

			Predicted Class			
Experiment Run	Selected Genes[a]	Actual Class	LAUD	LUSC	Optimal σ (σ*)	Accuracy (%)
1	2485	LAUD	142	4	128	94.18
		LUSC	11	135		
2	2362	LAUD	141	5	128	94.52
		LUSC	11	135		
3	2452	LAUD	142	4	128	94.18
		LUSC	13	133		
4	2400	LAUD	144	2	64	94.18
		LUSC	13	133		
5	2295	LAUD	143	3	64	95.21
		LUSC	11	135		
6	2384	LAUD	143	3	64	95.55
		LUSC	10	136		
7	2303	LAUD	138	8	32	94.86
		LUSC	7	139		
8	2448	LAUD	143	3	128	94.52
		LUSC	13	133		
9	2389	LAUD	145	1	64	93.84
		LUSC	13	133		
10	2484	LAUD	143	3	64	94.86
		LUSC	12	134		

[a]*The information of the 1933 common genes is presented in Supplementary Table 2.*

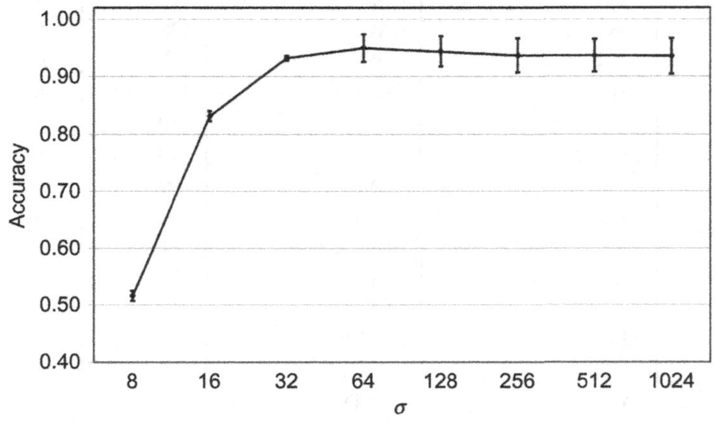

FIGURE 24.3

Classification performance using RNA-seq gene expression.

Similar results to the ones from the first data set were obtained, although the number of informative genes varies from one experiment to another. The average number of informative genes is approximately 2400. The confusion matrices obtained using a linear kernel are presented in Table 24.3, showing that SVM with linear kernel performed fairly well for this data set with an average accuracy of $93.7 \pm 1.14\%$. The misclassification rate for LUSC was 7.19% while the rate was 5.34% for LUAD. Nonetheless, the classification system with parameter tuning still overperformed the SVM with linear kernel in 9 out of 10 experimental runs. The confusion matrices and the optimal values of σ for Gaussian kernels are presented in Table 24.4. The average accuracy is $94.6 \pm 0.53\%$. The misclassification rate for LUSC was 7.81% while the rate is 2.47% for LUAD. We note that the misclassification rate of LUAD was reduced significantly but that of LUSC went up slightly.

The performance variations of SVMs with a Gaussian kernel and fixed σ values are illustrated in Figs. 24.2 and 24.3. Clearly, the classification accuracy began to improve when $\sigma = 16$ for both data sets. It reached its peak at $\sigma = 32$ for the mutation data set while the optimal value for the expression data set is $\sigma = 64$. For the mutation data set, the performance started to decrease quite dramatically when $\sigma > 32$, suggesting the critical role of the optimal σ in the performance of the SVM classification system. On the other hand, for the RNA-seq data set, the performance decline when $\sigma > 64$ is gradual. This explains why the SVM with a linear kernel performed reasonably well even though it is not the optimal classifier. In addition, Figs. 24.2 and 24.3 illustrate the increase in the standard error for both data sets for large σ, suggesting special attention needs to be paid to the robustness of the system when a large σ is adopted.

The GO enrichment analysis results of the top 290 genes that explain different mutation patterns are presented in Table 24.5 while the results from the 1933 differentially expressed genes that are common to all 10 experimental runs are shown in Table 24.6. The GO enrichment analysis reveals some very

Table 24.5 Overrepresented GO Molecular Function Terms in the Differentially Mutated Gene Set

GO ID	Term	*p*-Value
GO:0043560	Insulin receptor substrate binding	0.013
GO:0005218	Intracellular ligand-gated calcium channel activity	0.026
GO:0005219	Ryanodine-sensitive calcium-release channel activity	0.026
GO:0015278	Calcium-release channel activity	0.026
GO:0016303	1-Phosphatidylinositol-3-kinase activity	0.026
GO:0016307	Phosphatidylinositol phosphate kinase activity	0.026
GO:0019209	Kinase activator activity	0.026
GO:0030295	Protein kinase activator activity	0.026
GO:0035004	Phosphatidylinositol-3-kinase activity	0.026
GO:0035005	1-Phosphatidylinositol-4-phosphate 3-kinase activity	0.026
GO:0046934	Phosphatidylinositol-4,5-bisphosphate 3-kinase activity	0.026
GO:0048763	Calcium-induced calcium-release activity	0.026
GO:0052742	Phosphatidylinositol kinase activity	0.026
GO:0052813	Phosphatidylinositol bisphosphate kinase activity	0.026
GO:0005217	Intracellular ligand-gated ion channel activity	0.039
GO:0019207	Kinase regulator activity	0.039
GO:0019887	Protein kinase regulator activity	0.039

Table 24.6 Overrepresented GO Molecular Function Terms in the Differentially Expressed Gene Set

GO ID	Term	*p*-Value
GO:0005003	Ephrin receptor activity	8.4E−05
GO:0005149	Interleukin-1 receptor binding	0.00039
GO:0004714	Transmembrane receptor protein tyrosine kinase activity	0.0012
GO:0019199	Transmembrane receptor protein kinase activity	0.0037
GO:0004713	Protein tyrosine kinase activity	0.0051
GO:0070851	Growth factor receptor binding	0.0053
GO:0001078	RNA polymerase II core promoter proximal region sequence-specific DNA binding transcription factor activity involved in negative regulation of transcription	0.0076
GO:0005178	Integrin binding	0.0077
GO:0005005	Transmembrane-ephrin receptor activity	0.0093
GO:0005152	Interleukin-1 receptor antagonist activity	0.0093
GO:0008046	Axon guidance receptor activity	0.0093
GO:0016307	Phosphatidylinositol phosphate kinase activity	0.0093
GO:0005125	Cytokine activity	0.012
GO:0070888	E-box binding	0.014
GO:0004672	Protein kinase activity	0.022
GO:0016410	*N*-Acyltransferase activity	0.026
GO:0016790	Thiolester hydrolase activity	0.026
GO:0019215	Intermediate filament binding	0.026
GO:0030547	Receptor inhibitor activity	0.026
GO:0048019	Receptor antagonist activity	0.026
GO:0016773	Phosphotransferase activity, alcohol group as acceptor	0.029
GO:0030545	Receptor regulator activity	0.034
GO:0000287	Magnesium ion binding	0.045
GO:0001228	RNA polymerase II transcription regulatory region sequence-specific DNA binding transcription factor activity involved in positive regulation of transcription	0.046
GO:0005126	Cytokine receptor binding	0.046
GO:0050839	Cell adhesion molecule binding	0.046
GO:0001104	RNA polymerase II transcription cofactor activity	0.048
GO:0005044	Scavenger receptor activity	0.048
GO:0051213	Dioxygenase activity	0.048
GO:0072341	Modified amino acid binding	0.048
GO:0001105	RNA polymerase II transcription coactivator activity	0.049
GO:0035258	Steroid hormone receptor binding	0.049
GO:0043295	Glutathione binding	0.049
GO:1900750	Oligopeptide binding	0.049
GO:0019902	Phosphatase binding	0.049

interesting molecular function groups in which the genes show different mutation and gene expression patterns. Several of them have been reported in the literature [32–35]. Lung cancer is the second most commonly occurring noncutaneous cancer with the highest mortality rate among all cancers [36]. NSCLC contributing to about 84% of all lung cancers is a general term for several different types of lung cancer, including LUAD and LUSC [36]. Similar to that of many other cancers, the molecular basis of lung cancer is genetic mutation [37]. When mutation occurs, the expression levels of related genes and their products are altered. Unduly expressed or underexpressed genes dysregulate biochemical pathways, including metabolic and signaling pathways, which further dysregulate cell growth, division, DNA repair, and apoptosis [37]. Therefore, understanding the role of genetic and expression variations in lung cancer are essential to improve the diagnosis, treatment, and prognosis of lung cancer, shedding light on certain areas of personalized medicine development [37–42]. LUAD is the most frequent histology in NSCLC. Current genomic research of LUAD has provided encouraging new treatments to the LUAD population, which include EGFR tyrosine kinase inhibitors and ALK inhibitors that specifically target oncogenes EGFR and ALK [40,41]. On the other hand, it is unfortunate that oncogenetic mutations in LUSC are much less characterized [42]. We believe that's why protein kinase activity-related genes are so pronounced in illustrating the different mutation and expression patterns of the two subtypes, and their associated GO groups are on top of the list in Tables 24.5 and 24.6.

24.4 CONCLUSIONS

We have developed an automatic classification system based on SVMs with embedded parameter tuning. The system is validated through a sequence of experiments designed to classify two subtypes of lung cancer tissues using the exome sequencing somatic mutation and gene expression data obtained from TCGA. Through experiments, we demonstrated that our approach is significantly better than the classification systems based on SVMs with a linear kernel and Gaussian kernel with default parameter settings. The cross-validation results reaffirmed the genes identified are informative and their somatic mutations and expression levels are statistically significant for characterizing the two subtypes of lung cancer LUAD and LUSC. These genes reveal discerned somatic mutation patterns, shedding light on potential oncogenetic mutations and gene expression patterns, validating the conclusion that cancer tissues of different subtypes are differentiable at both the mutation and expression levels. Additionally, the overrepresented GO terms provide further biological insights into pulmonary tumorigenesis and cancer differentiation. We conclude that the SVM with embedded parameter tuning is an effective tool for analyzing genomic mutations and RNA-seq gene expression data.

SUPPLEMENTARY MATERIALS

Supplementary Table 1: http://www.cs.uakron.edu/~duan/SVM/SupplTable1.xlsx
Supplementary Table 2: http://www.cs.uakron.edu/~duan/SVM/SupplTable2.xlsx

COMPETING INTERESTS

The authors declare that they have no competing interests.

AUTHORS' CONTRIBUTIONS

HTZ and ZHD conceived the research idea. HTZ implemented the algorithm and performed all cross-validation experiments. AD conducted GO enrichment analysis. HTZ, AD, and ZHD interpreted the results and drafted the manuscript. All authors have read and approved the final manuscript.

ACKNOWLEDGMENT

This work was supported in part by the Choose Ohio First for Bioinformatics scholarship program.

REFERENCES

[1] Mardis ER. The impact of next-generation sequencing technology on genetics. Trends Genet 2008;24(3):133–41.
[2] Pettersson E, Lundeberg J, Ahmadian A. Generations of sequencing technologies. Genomics 2009;93(2):105–11.
[3] Wang Z, Gerstein M, Snyder M. RNA-Seq: a revolutionary tool for transcriptomics. Nat Rev Genet 2009;10 (1):57–63.
[4] Metzker ML. Sequencing technologies — the next generation. Nat Rev Genet 2010;11(1):31–46.
[5] Golub TR, Slonim DK, Tamayo P, Huard C, Gaasenbeek M, Mesirov JP, et al. Molecular classification of cancer: class discovery and class prediction by gene expression monitoring. Science 1999;286:531–7.
[6] DeRisi J, Penland L, Brown PO, Bittner ML, Meltzer PS, Ray M, et al. Use of a cDNA microarray to analyse gene expression patterns in human cancer. Nat Genet 1996;14:457–60.
[7] Hurd PJ, Nelson CJ. Advantages of next-generation sequencing versus the microarray in epigenetic research. Brief Funct Genomic Proteomic 2009;8(3):174–83.
[8] Dalman MR, Deeter A, Nimishakavi G, Duan ZH. Fold change and *p*-value cutoffs significantly alter microarray interpretations. BMC Bioinformatics 2012;13(Suppl. 2):S11.
[9] Klebanov L, Yakovlev A. How high is the level of technical noise in microarray data? Biol Direct 2007;2:9.
[10] Meldrum C, Doyle MA, Tothill RW. Next-generation sequencing for cancer diagnostics: a practical perspective. Clin Biochem Rev 2011;32(4):177–95.
[11] Thomas RK, Baker AC, Debiasi RM, et al. High-throughput oncogene mutation profiling in human cancer. Nat Genet 2007;39(3):347–51.
[12] Meyerson M, Gabriel S, Getz G. Advances in understanding cancer genomes through second-generation sequencing. Nat Rev Genet 2010;11(10):685–96.
[13] Shibata T, Aburatani H. Exploration of liver cancer genomes. Nat Rev Gastroenterol Hepatol 2014;11(6):340–9.
[14] Renkema KY, Stokman MF, Giles RH, Knoers NV. Next-generation sequencing for research and diagnostics in kidney disease. Nat Rev Nephrol 2014;10(8):433–44.

[15] Han S-S, Kim WJ, Hong Y, Hong S-H, Lee S-J, Ryu DR, et al. RNA sequencing identifies novel markers of non-small cell lung cancer. Lung Cancer 2014;84(3):229–35.
[16] Dudoit S, Fridlyand J, Speed TP. Comparison of discrimination methods for the classification of tumors using gene expression data. J Am Stat Assoc 2002;97:77–87.
[17] Xiong H, Chen X-W. Kernel-based distance metric learning for microarray data. BMC Bioinformatics 2006;7:299.
[18] Mallick BK, Ghosh D, Ghosh M. Bayesian classification of tumors by using gene expression data. J R Stat Soc Ser B 2005;67:219–34.
[19] Attonov Antonov V, Tetko IV, Mader MT, Budczies J, Mewes HW. Optimization models for cancer classification: extracting gene interaction information from microarray expression data. Bioinformatics 2004;20:644–52.
[20] Dhawan M, Selvaraja S, Duan Z-H. Application of committee kNN classifiers for gene expression profile classification. Int J Bioinform Res Appl 2010;6(4):344–52.
[21] Sewak MS, Narender PR, Duan ZH. Gene expression based leukemia sub-classification using committee neural networks. Bioinform Biol Insights 2009;3:89–98.
[22] Jose A, Mugler D, Duan ZH. A gene selection method for classifying cancer samples using 1D discrete wavelet transform. Int J Comput Biol Drug Des 2009;2(4):398–411.
[23] Ben-Dor A, Bruhn L, Friedman N, Nachman I, Schummer M, Yakhini Z. Tissue classification with gene expression profiles. J Comput Biol 2000;7(3–4):559–83.
[24] Lee Y, Lee C. Classification of multiple cancer types by multicategory support vector machines using gene expression data. Bioinformatics 2003;19:1132–9.
[25] Peng S, Xu Q, Ling XB, Peng X, Du W, Chen L. Molecular classification of cancer types from microarray data using the combination of genetic algorithms and support vector machines. FEBS Lett 2003;555:358–62.
[26] Liu B, Cui Q, Jiang T, Ma S. A combinational feature selection and ensemble neural network method for classification of gene expression data. BMC Bioinformatics 2004;5:136.
[27] Cerami E, Gao J, Dogrusoz U, Gross BE, Sumer SO, Aksoy BA, et al. The cBio cancer genomics portal: an open platform for exploring multidimensional cancer genomics data. Cancer Discov 2012;2(5):401–4 [data access on 06/04/2014].
[28] Gao J, Aksoy BA, Dogrusoz U, Dresdner G, Gross B, Sumer SO, et al. Integrative analysis of complex cancer genomics and clinical profiles using the cBioPortal. Sci Signal 2013;6:pl1.
[29] Gentleman RC, Carey VJ, Bates DM, Bolstad B, Dettling M, Dudoit S, et al. Bioconductor: open software development for computational biology and bioinformatics. Genome Biol 2004;5(10):R80.
[30] Cortes C, Vapnik V. Support-vector networks. Mach Learn 1995;20(3):273.
[31] Hsu C-W, Chang C-C, Lin C-J. A practical guide to support vector classification. Technical report, Department of Computer Science and Information Engineering, National Taiwan University; 2003. http://www.csie.ntu.edu.tw/~cjlin/papers/guide/guide.pdf.
[32] Ding L, Getz G, Wheeler DA, Mardis ER, McLellan MD, Cibulskis K, et al. Somatic mutations affect key pathways in lung adenocarcinoma. Nature 2008;455:1069–75.
[33] Elena B. Pasquale, Eph receptors and ephrins in cancer: bidirectional signaling and beyond. Nat Rev Cancer 2010;10(3):165–80.
[34] Arikkath J, Campbell KP. Auxiliary subunits: essential components of the voltage-gated calcium channel complex. Curr Opin Neurobiol 2003;13(3):298–307.
[35] Cappuzzo F, Tallini G, Finocchiaro G, et al. Insulin-like growth factor receptor 1 (IGF1R) expression and survival in surgically resected non-small-cell lung cancer (NSCLC) patients. Ann Oncol 2010;21(3):562–7. http://dx.doi.org/10.1093/annonc/mdp357.
[36] American Cancer Society. Cancer facts & figures 2014, Atlanta: American Cancer Society; 2014. http://www.cancer.org/acs/groups/content/@research/documents/webcontent/acspc-042151.pdf.

[37] Herbst RS, Heymach JV, Lippman SM. Lung cancer. N Engl J Med 2008;359(13):1367–80. http://dx.doi.org/10.1056/NEJMra0802714.

[38] Bhattacharjee A, Richards WG, Staunton J, Li C, Monti S, Vasa P, et al. Classification of human lung carcinomas by mRNA expression profiling reveals distinct adenocarcinoma subclasses. Proc Natl Acad Sci U S A 2001;98(24):13790–5.

[39] Pao W, Hutchinson KE. Chipping away at the lung cancer genome. Nat Med 2012;18(3):349–51.

[40] Lynch TJ, Bell DW, Sordella R, Gurubhagavatula S, Okimoto RA, Brannigan BW, et al. Activating mutations in the epidermal growth factor receptor underlying responsiveness of non-small-cell lung cancer to gefitinib. N Engl J Med 2004;350(21):2129–39.

[41] Soda M, Choi YL, Enomoto M, Takada S, Yamashita Y, Ishikawa S, et al. Identification of the transforming EML4-ALK fusion gene in non-small-cell lung cancer. Nature 2007;448(7153):561–6.

[42] Clinical Lung Cancer Genome Project (CLCGP), Network Genomic Medicine (NGM). A genomics-based classification of human lung tumors. Sci Transl Med 2013;5:209ra153.

CHAPTER

25 STATE-OF-THE-ART MOCK HUMAN BLOOD CIRCULATION LOOP: PROTOTYPING AND INTRODUCTION OF A NEW HEART SIMULATOR

T.B. Baturalp, A. Ertas
Department of Mechanical Engineering, Texas Tech University, Lubbock, TX, United States

25.1 INTRODUCTION

Heart disease is agreed to be the highest cause of death in the world by most health organizations. Heart disease and stroke statistics of the American Heart Association [1] state that, on the basis of 2009 death rate data, cardiovascular disease was the reason for one of every three deaths in the United States. According to other sources, 2150 Americans die because of cardiovascular disease each day, which is an average of one death every 40 s. Heart failure can be treated by medications, medical devices, and surgery. With respect to another source [2], approximately 4000 cases each year require a heart transplant; however, only less than half of them can receive one. Currently, there are about 5 million Americans who suffer because of heart failure, and over 500,000 patients are diagnosed with it each year [3]. The increasing donor shortage and limited heart transplant waiting time generates a need for a temporary solution such as an assistive device to keep the patient alive while a donor is being found. Most of the cardiac failures happen in the left side of the heart, which is the part of the heart that pumps blood to the body. Left ventricular assistive devices (LVADs) have been developed to increase the cardiac flow output of the left ventricular (LV) chamber.

While LVADs provide a solution for patients who suffer from cardiac insufficiency, valvular heart disease (VHD) is widely accepted as another significant portion of heart diseases. VHD involves problems with one or more of the valves of the heart (the aortic and mitral valves on the left and the pulmonary and tricuspid valves on the right). It can be treated by medication and generally with valve repair or artificial heart valve (AHV) replacement. In 2003, over 290,000 heart valve operations were performed worldwide with an increase of 10–12% per year. Thus, a rough estimation can be made that it will exceed 850,000 in 2050 [4]. Another study [5] shows that VHD covers a percentage between 10% and 20% of all cardiac surgical procedures in the United States. Up to the present, over four million people across the world have received an AHV [6]. Replacement of heart valves have been done for last six decades, since the first replacement performed in 1952. During the last six decades more than 50 AHVs have been designed or developed [7].

Mock circulation loops (MCLs) play an essential role not only in in vitro testing (not in a body) and development of LVADs and AHVs, but also in other circulation-related devices such as total artificial hearts, artificial lungs, vascular grafts, bioreactors for tissue engineered heart valves, and intraaortic balloon pumps. Cardiac device design procedures generally adopt MCLs before advancing to animal or clinical trials, which are much more troublesome and expensive. With respect to standards of the American Society for Artificial Internal Organs (ASAIO) and the Society of Thoracic Surgeons (STS), experimental flow loops should correctly represent significant parameters of the human circulatory system under normal and worst-case physiologic conditions [8]. Also, Clemente et al. [9] published an article that conducts the setup of technical standards for mechanical heart assist devices and the approach to problems related to technical standards for biomedical devices. Various physiological cardiac failure or operating scenarios need to be replicated in the MCL for testing, including but not limited to LVADs and heart pumps. These different scenarios require a fully automated MCL that can reproduce the necessary conditions precisely and switch between them without trouble. Based on listed essential MCL functionalities, not only MCL actuator parameters such as geometry, different movement trajectories, and elastance of ventricular wall, but also versatility of the MCL parameters such as resistance and compliance are critical and need to be developed for imitating different scenarios of human circulation in an experimental setup.

The aim of this study is to propose a novel MCL design which is fully automated, and capable of replicating wide range of cardiac operating and failure scenarios including mimicking the movements of LV chamber of the heart. The novel design of a new MCL should include several important factors. A wide literature review is presented in this chapter to seek these factors on MCLs. These factors can be listed as versatility of the hemodynamic parameters like resistance and compliance. In addition, the pump of the MCL should be more realistic than the ones in the literature, as the state-of-the-art pulsatile blood pumps are not capable to mimic torsion and wringing action of the LV, muscular dysfunctions of the heart, and more realistic shape of the chamber.

25.1.1 BACKGROUND

MCLs in the literature can be categorized into two main groups with respect to their flow types: non-pulsatile and pulsatile systems. Generally, flow type is defined by the pump or actuator of MCL. Non-pulsatile flow MCLs use continuous pumps such as centrifugal or axial pumps, while pulsatile MCLs are equipped with various pumps (piston, cam driven, diaphragm-based pumps, and pneumatically and hydraulically operated pressure chambers) in the literature. Recent developments showed that normal physiological cardiac conditions can be reproduced by using slaughterhouse pig hearts, which are used for their morphological and physiological similarities to human hearts.

The initial MCLs were mainly used on testing artificial hearts. One of the earliest MCLs was built by Kolff [10] in 1959. It included both systemic and pulmonary circulation loops, and the ventricles were activated by use of compressed air chambers. The biggest incomplete side of this design was resistance, because no resistance valve is used in this study. Another early in vitro test setup was developed by Björk et al. [11] in 1962 to examine prosthetic mitral and aortic valves. The study claims that the developed system was capable of accurately simulating various physiological conditions. The system consisted of interconnected valve-testing chambers, aortic analog, peripheral resistance, and left atrium analog. Peripheral resistance and vertical position of the reservoir were adjustable. The main contribution of this study was the usage of collapsible molded rubber sac LV. A good example for initial MCL designs with flexible tubing and cam-driven ventricle was Reul et al.'s [12] design in 1974. Their study was also one of the leading studies that used a Windkessel chamber with adjustable air volume for compliance. The downside of this study was the lack of a suitable connection for ventricular assist devices (VADs). Pennsylvania State University's mock circulation system is another example of remarkable MCL designs developed by Rosenberg et al. [13] in 1981. The MCL consisted of resistance, compliance, inertia, systemic and pulmonary circulation, VAD connections, and adjustable cardiac conditions. While the MCL represented acceptable results and provided a proper in vitro testing setup for artificial hearts, inertia values were incorrectly assumed to be equal for systemic and pulmonary circulations.

As stated previously, MCL can be categorized into two main groups as pulsatile and nonpulsatile with respect to their flow generation types. As there are many studies in the literature about MCLs, this categorization can be widened regarding the type of the mock circulation system's pumps. Many different pumping and actuation systems are used on MCLs but they can be categorized into four principal groups: biological, piston, VAD, and pressure chamber-based pump systems.

25.1.1.1 MCLs with biological pump systems

In recent years, biological pump systems began to be used in MCLs to create more realistic simulations. In most of the studies in the literature, entire explanted hearts were integrated into in vitro setups. The reason behind this approach is allowing a better preservation of the anatomical structures and at the same time not including all the physiological complexities of animal models. Other advantages of using explanted hearts are enabling the potential applications of new experimental apparatus or surgical procedures as the environment is more familiar to surgeons to operate and analyze their hemodynamic effects.

As the use of entire explanted hearts is inconvenient due to the required protocols, complexity, and cost, it had been suggested by Richards et al. [14] to use the explanted hearts as a passive structure, which means pressurizing the blood from another source and using the chamber feature of the heart. An external pulsatile pump was used in this study, and results were found to be not optimal, especially in terms of flow rates and the pressure wave forms. This study was followed by Leopaldi et al. [15] by using an entire explanted porcine heart, whose LV is pressurized by an external pumping system. Electrically conditioned latissimus dorsi muscles are also used for actuation in various studies [16–19].

Most of the whole heart mock loop designs were accomplished to maintain cardiac contractility ex vivo. The explanted working heart models were capable of reproducing the physiological ventricle pressure-volume relationship with state-of-the-art mimicking of the shape and motion of the real heart, although the complexity and costs of the related experimental protocols represented serious drawbacks. The PhysioHeart platform was developed by de Hart et al. [20] to overcome some gaps in the study of comprehensive cardiac mechanics, hemodynamics, and device interaction of MCLs. Cardiac performance of the MCL was controlled and kept at normal levels of hemodynamic performance for up to 4 h. Cardiac changes and performance of an entire heart during an explantation into the developed in vitro apparatus were investigated by Chinchoy et al. [21]. Similarly, LV ejection function of ex resuscitated pig hearts was examined by Rosenstrauch et al. [22]. LV function was restored and maintained in all six hearts for 30 min in this circuit. Although usage of explanted whole hearts has great advantages, such as reproducing the ventricular wall motion, geometry, and contraction, they have a major drawback in duration of experimentation because they don't contract more than 6 h. This drawback makes fatigue and long-term testing of cardiovascular devices impossible, which are crucial on validation of these devices.

25.1.1.2 MCLs with VAD pumps

VADs are used in MCLs not only as a testing device, but also as the main or driving pump. Naturally, those pumps are already tested and usually already available in the market. In this section, brief information will be given about MCLs that use VADs as the main pump.

One of the pioneer studies that utilize a VAD as the major pump of the MCL is researched by Schima et al. [23], who sought simple and inexpensive solutions for common problems of MCLs. Another study that measures the performance of artificial blood pumps by using them as a pump in a MCL is conducted by Knierbein et al. [24]. Also, LVADs were used to simulate LV function and aortic flow by Papaioannou et al. [25].

25.1.1.3 MCLs with piston pumps

Piston pumps are advantageous because of their mechanical simplicity, reliability, and ease of measurement of the variables of interest such as ventricular pressure and volume. They are also more controllable compared to other pumps. The downside of piston pumps can be pointed out as being hard to mimic the pulsatile flow and elastic nature of the heart and always having to be in a cylindrical shape, which is not similar to the real LV shape. In this section, MCLs from selected papers in the literature that are equipped with a piston pump as the main pump of the loop will be introduced.

In vitro reproduction of the LV and arterial tree in a mock circulatory system and interaction of them with a LVAD was examined by Ferrari et al. [26]. In another study of Ferrari et al. [27], an elastance model is used to mimic Frank Starling's law for reproducing more realistic hemodynamic values. Singh et al. [28] developed a pulsatile MCL to test the robustness of AHVs and their effects on the parameters associated with the circulatory system. In LVAD studies, not only is the design of the device important but also the control of the device is essential. For this purpose, Vaes et al. [29] designed and developed a MCL that was capable of featuring the properties of the (diseased) heart and mimicking the baroflex response of the heart.

25.1.1.4 MCLs with pressurized chambers

The need for better elastance, ventricular shape, pulsatile flow, and simulating the Frank Starling law led the authors toward the idea of using pressurized chambers for representing the ventricles of the heart. Both pneumatic and hydraulic pressurized chambers were used in the literature. In this section, a brief survey on MCLs that use pressurized chambers as heart ventricles will be introduced.

A systemic MCL was established to investigate the movements of the heart valves during pulses of the heart by Verdonck et al. [30]. In this study, atria and LV were represented by an elastic bag made of latex in a hydraulic type (water) chamber. Pantalos et al. [31] developed a MCL that was equipped with a pneumatic chamber and flexing polymer sac for testing VADs under normal, heart failure, and partial recovery test conditions. Another pneumatic pressurized chamber-type driven systemic MCL was built by Patel et al. [32] to validate LVADs under congestive heart failure, exercise, and normal conditions. Arrhythmias and diastolic function problems were focused on by Mouret et al. [33] who constructed a new systemic MCL that was driven by the dual activation simulator. Pantalos et al. [34] developed a mock circulation that behaves differently under altered physiologic conditions for testing cardiac devices. The purpose of the study was to assess the ability of the mock ventricle to mimic the Frank

Starling response of normal, heart failure, and cardiac recovery conditions. As seen in the literature of pressurized chamber pump-type MCLs, versatility for creating operating conditions and replicating ventricular geometry stands out among features of MCLs. On the other hand, there is still room for development of features like mimicking ventricular wall motion, contraction, and muscle fiber orientation and also operating conditions like muscle dysfunctions, which is one of the most common cardiovascular diseases.

25.2 NOVEL DESIGN OF MCL

A wide literature review has been conducted on MCL designs to investigate the needs to be improved in a novel MCL design. First of all, capability of mock LVs needs to be improved for replicating human LV chamber's movements and physiological parameters for different scenarios such as healthy rest, healthy exercise, various cardiovascular diseases, and failure states. Additionally, a fully automated and controllable circulation system is needed in the literature because controllable MCLs have begun to be introduced recently in the literature. One example to this kind of study was conducted by Legendre et al. [35], which was equipped with an engine-like mechanism pump system that simulates the LV. This pump system uses a piston to push a diaphragm, which enables creation of an unsteady flow. Normal healthy and pathologic state patient conditions were simulated in the tests, and their results were compared to results in the literature. The system was found accurate to simulate in vivo conditions. By current technological developments on the sensors and data acquisition systems, a fully automated and controllable MCL can be built that utilizes controllable valves for resistance, controlled air pressurized compliance chambers for compliance (also known as the reciprocal of elastance), and inertiance that can be controlled by the geometry of the tubes and properties of the system fluid, which has reasonably stable value in human circulation. These parameters will be adjusted to simulate different cardiovascular states in addition to the pump of the system. The pump of the system should be more realistic than the ones in the literature, as the pulsatile blood pumps are not capable of mimicking torsion action of the LV, muscular dysfunctions of the heart, and more the realistic shape of the chamber. An in vitro beating heart simulator should be developed, which has been seen in the literature as needed for reducing the required time to develop, test, and refine of cardiovascular instruments such as heart valves and assistive devices in general.

The ideal pulsatile pump of a MCL was defined by Knierbein et al. [24], who stated that it should be capable of replicating the dynamic properties of the physiological load as closely as possible for generating physiological flows and pressures at the intersection between the pump and the mock loop. Resistances and volumes must be variable in a range that for different pump sizes and different circulatory conditions approximates physiological conditions. Handling of the system must be simple and reliable to facilitate reproducibility of test parameters.

The fully automated systemic MCL was designed in a computer-aided design (CAD) environment, which can be seen in Fig. 25.1.

The developed MCL consists of two compliance chambers for systemic and aortic compliance values. The LV simulator, pressure and flow sensors, resistance valves, a drain container for resetting the system, signal conditioner for the flow sensor, a data acquisition device to digitize outputs of the sensors, and an atrial chamber as open air container with adjustable height to generate constant pressure are the other components of the developed MCL. Clear tygon tubing with different diameters were used

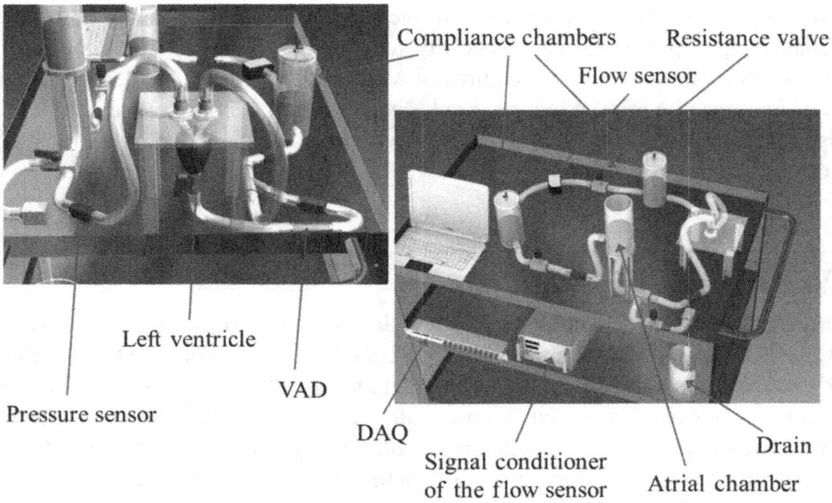

FIGURE 25.1

Developed MCL with annotations.

in the system and integrated to the CAD environment with respect to bending radius of the selected tubing. A steel cart was used to add mobility to the design. A bypass tubing from the bottom of the LV simulator to the aorta was made for mounting the LVADs to the system. This bypass tubing was considered and designed as optional by adding a valve to the bottom of the LV simulator. A pressure sensor was also added to the output of the LVAD to evaluate its performance. Clamp-on tubing type flow meters were investigated in the literature for ease of use and noninvasive features to the system, as no physical contact is required with the fluid media. Only one ultrasonic flow sensor (Transonic, ME20PXL) was selected because it is easy to relocate the flow sensor for obtaining measurements from different locations. A stand for the LV simulator was also designed to support it while not constraining its contractive motion. Another function of this stand was holding the AHVs and making the assemble/disassemble process easier to test different types of heart valves.

Measurement of pressure from various locations in a MCL is essential. Main locations to measure pressure in a systemic MCL are upstream and downstream of the compliance chambers, the outlets of the atrium and LV chamber, and the ventricular assistive device. As compliance chambers are designed with air pressure-based adjustment, air pressure transducers are also required.

The human circulatory system has two main resistances: systemic and pulmonary. The developing MCL has only systemic circulation and resistances in the sections of MCLs that are dependent on the length and cross-sectional area of the pipe. Thus, a proportional control valve to adjust the level of systemic resistance is crucial in MCL design. A computer-controlled proportional valve (Hass Manufacturing Company, Model EPV-375B) was chosen, which operates between a 1 and 5 V DC control signal, and this valve represents the total peripheral resistance of the circulatory system.

When the blood pressure in a blood vessel increases, it reacts with expanding its volume. This characteristic of blood vessels is called compliance. It can be considered as inverse to the stiffness because compliance value increases with increasing flexibility. Therefore, compliance should be considered as a controlled parameter in a fully automated MCL. For this purpose, two pressurized air type compliance chamber were included, which represents compliance of the pulmonary artery and aorta. These compliance chambers were equipped with a computer-controlled air regulator to enable the automation of MCL.

The features above are combined in a prototype experimental setup that is shown in Fig. 25.2. The whole prototyped MCL system can be seen on the left-hand side of Fig. 25.2. While the flow components were placed on the top shelf on a mobile cart, electrical and signal processing components were located on the lower shelf due to circuit protection purposes. Currently, electrical and signal processing components consist of a signal conditioner of the ultrasonic flow sensor, a data acquisition system from National Instruments Corporation, and power supplies for sensors. The flow sensor signal conditioner is connected to the data acquisition system to gather all of the input and output signals and deliver them to a desktop PC.

Two prototyped air pressure-connected compliance chambers, automated resistance valve, open air atrium chamber (located at the left upper side of the picture), holder for LV heart simulator (located at the bottom of the picture), and their connections with tygon tubing is shown in the right-hand side picture of Fig. 25.2. While all of the white plastic parts (caps and bases of the chambers and LV holder)

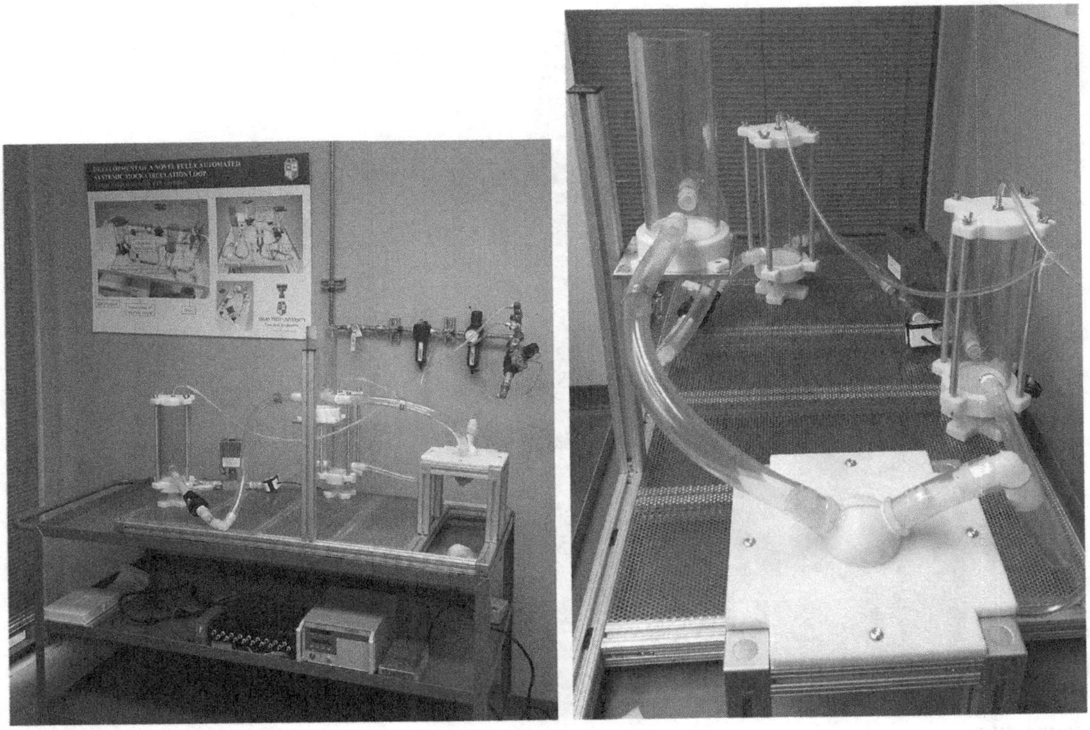

FIGURE 25.2

Prototyped MCL system (left side: whole system view; right side: high spot view of the system).

were manufactured from ABS plastic by using a 3-D printer, impact-resistant polycarbonate tubes were used for all of the circular transparent chambers.

A clearer view of the compliance chambers and automated resistance valve is given in Fig. 25.3. Also, the ultrasonic pressure sensor can be seen to right side of the automated resistance valve. All of the chambers and main components are annotated in Fig. 25.3. The atrial chamber was designed as an open air chamber as the pressure in the atrial chamber of the heart is much more stable compared to other parts. But the pressure in the prototyped atrium chamber should be adjustable because it varies with respect to different patients and operating conditions. Thus, the atrial chamber was mounted to an adjustable height aluminum t-slotted frame. Also, a manual resistance valve can also be seen at the bottom of Fig. 25.3. A t-slotted aluminum frame was used as mainframe structural material of the experimental setup due its ease of assembly and modularity.

The compliance chambers and LV heart simulator were connected to a main air duct of the building, which is shown in the right-hand side of Fig. 25.4. The pressure of the main air duct was reduced by using a manual air regulator and the main outlet was multiplied by the help of an output multiplier piping component. After obtaining three regulated air outlets, two of them were used for compliance chambers while the last one was used to supply pulsatile airflow for the LV heart simulator. A microcontroller controlled on/off type solenoid was used to achieve pulsatility for the LV heart simulator, which can be seen under the LV holder in Fig. 25.4.

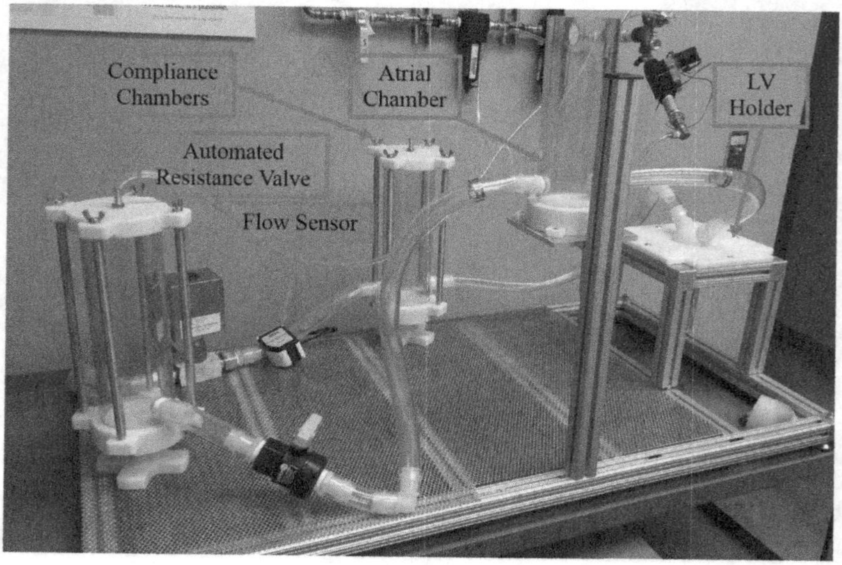

FIGURE 25.3

Prototyped MCL system (left upper side view).

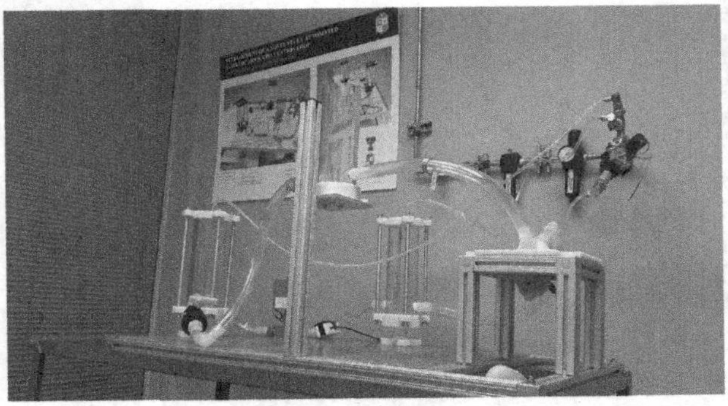

FIGURE 25.4

Prototyped MCL system (left lower side view).

25.2.1 LV HEART SIMULATOR DESIGN OF MCL

Developing a realistic mock LV chamber that mimics shape and wall movements of a real LV requires a wide investigation on not only shape and motion of LV, but also orientation and contraction of myocardial fibers. The transformation of the heart shape during its beating is found to be directly related to the pumping performance of the heart. Thus, the motion of the LV wall is essential on replication of the pumping function of the LV. In this section, some studies about LV shape, motion, myocardial fiber orientation, and torsion will be introduced and a prototyped pneumatic LV pump will be demonstrated.

LV form and geometry and impact on its function and efficiency was investigated by Buckberg et al. [36] and Sengupta et al. [37]. The effect of myocardial fiber orientation on contractility and helical ventricular myocardial band concept was revealed by Torrent-Guasp [38]. The helical ventricular myocardial band concept was an innovative new concept for understanding three-dimensional, global, and functional structure of the ventricular myocardium. Another important aspect for wall motion of LV is the twisting movement of the ventricle during systole, which was investigated in detail for the first time by Streeter et al. [39]. Accepted opinion [40,41] on the cause of the torsional movement of the LV is possible due to the helical orientation of myocardial fibers and the promising opinion on function is the creation of a suction effect to assist the diastolic filling. Additionally, the systolic twisting motion stores energy that is to be used during diastole for ventricular filling [42].

In the context of gathered information about the architecture of the LV, a pneumatic muscle-actuated mock LV prototype was manufactured. The geometry was created by lofting cross-sectional representations of the LV chamber and it was inverted in a CAD environment to obtain mold geometry. The mold consists of three different parts as seen in Fig. 25.5 and it was prototyped by using a 3-D printer. While two components of the mold were used to create the outer layer of the LV, the part in the middle creates the inner layer.

The printed mold was filled with "Dragon Skin" brand high-performance silicone, which is reasonably strong and elastic. Additionally, a second mold was designed for forming one solid band in which the custom pneumatic muscles were placed in the desired formation. After the pneumatic muscle band is created by placing three pneumatic muscle fibers together (Fig. 25.6), the band is inserted into the main mold in a helical formation as seen in Fig. 25.7, which shows the completed LV chamber. The pneumatic muscle strips are connected to a series of pressure regulators that contract the ventricle to

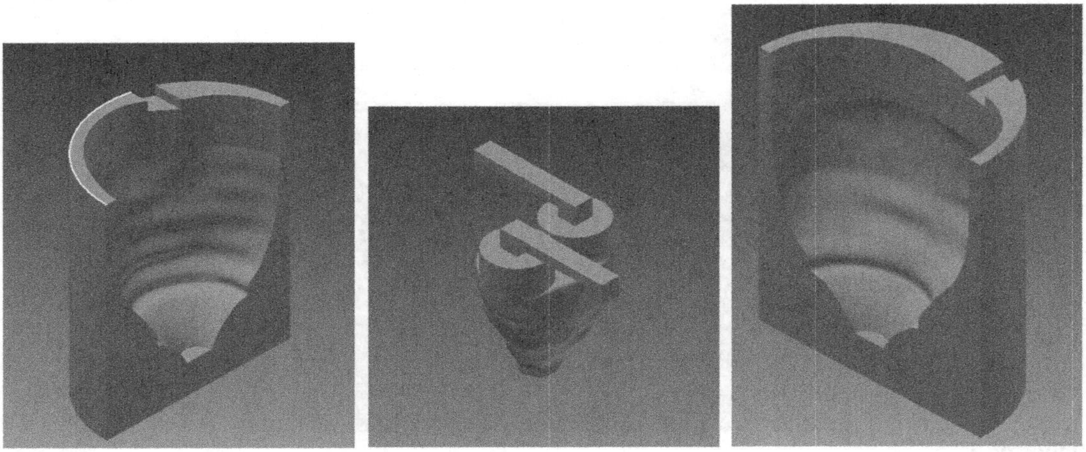

FIGURE 25.5

3-D printed mold of the LV.

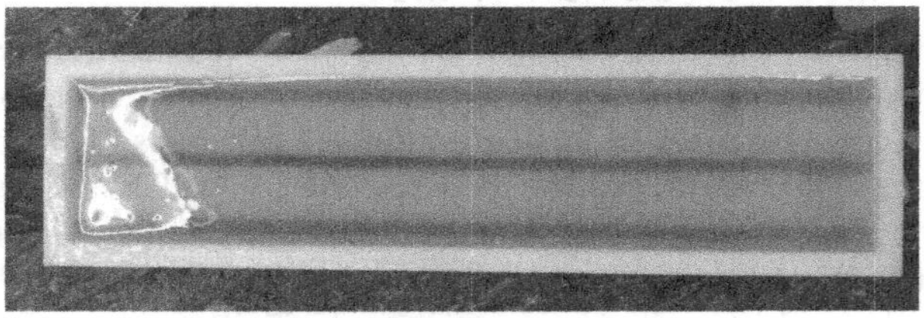

FIGURE 25.6

Pneumatic muscle band includes three pneumatic muscles and a strip of Dragon Skin.

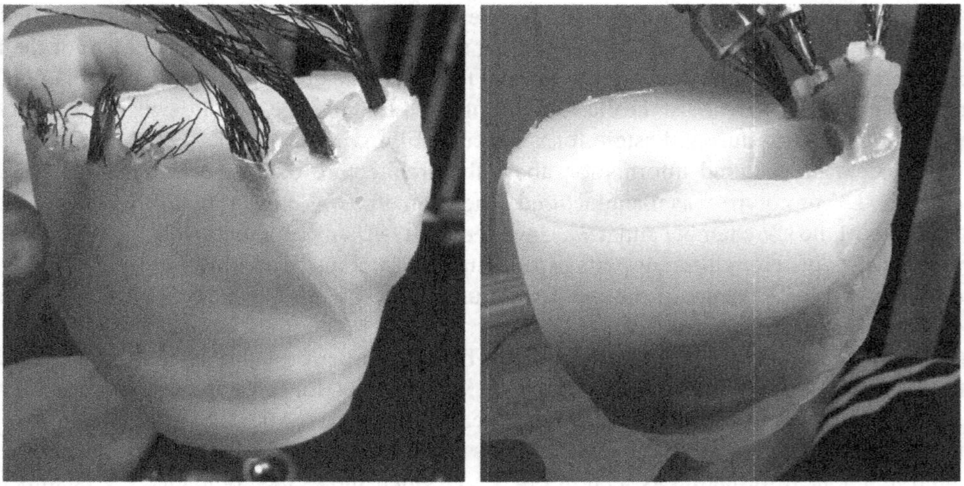

FIGURE 25.7

Silicone molded LV chamber.

produce the same effect as that of a real left ventricle. The custom-made pneumatic muscles are made from rubber tubing and black pneumatic mesh. While one end of the muscle was folded over and sealed, an inflation needle was inserted at the other end.

The result of the initial tests showed that silicon tissue is structurally strong enough because no tears or rips were seen. On the other hand, silicon LV did not deform enough due to the high thickness of the LV wall. Contraction was found to be insufficient because of air leaks on custom-made pneumatic muscles and the thickness of the tissue. However the proof of concept is considered as successful because mock LV wall motion resembles the real left ventrical wall motion. Sufficient contraction can be reached by improvements on the thickness of the tissue and the performance of pneumatic muscles. More information can be found in previous work [43].

25.3 CONCLUSIONS

Design and prototyping process of a novel, fully automated systemic MCL, and a proposed design of the LV heart simulator was described in this chapter. A wide-ranging review of current MCLs and physiological features of LV was conducted and presented. In the light of literature review findings, computer-controlled MCL design that is capable of replicating various cardiac operating conditions and able to switch between them smoothly was proposed. The prototyping process of the MCL system was also depicted. Additionally, the geometry and wall motion of the real left ventrical was attempted to be implemented on the actuator of the proposed MCL by prototyping a pneumatically actuated mock LV. The prototyped LV was found to be insufficient in terms of contraction, but the reasons for its insufficiency were found and improvements are on the way.

REFERENCES

[1] Go AS, Mozaffarian D, Roger VL, Benjamin EJ, Berry JD, Borden WB, et al. Executive summary: heart disease and stroke statistics: 2013 update: a report from the American Heart Association. Circulation 2013;127(1):143–6.

[2] Rose EA, Gelijns AC, Moskowitz AJ, Heitjan DF, Stevenson LW, Dembitsky W, et al. Long-term use of a left ventricular assist device for end-stage heart failure. N Engl J Med 2001;345(20):1435–43.

[3] Spoor MT, Bolling SF. Valve pathology in heart failure: which valves can be fixed? Heart Fail Clin 2007;3 (3):289–98.

[4] Yacoub MH, Takkenberg JJM. Will heart valve tissue engineering change the world? Nat Clin Pract Cardiovasc Med 2005;2(2):60–1.

[5] Maganti K, Rigolin VH, Enriquez Sarano M, Bonow RO. Valvular heart disease: diagnosis and management. Mayo Clin Proc 2010;85(5):483–500.

[6] Sun JCJ, Davidson MJ, Lamy A, Eikelboom JW. Antithrombotic management of patients with prosthetic heart valves: current evidence and future trends. Lancet 2009;374(9689):565–76.

[7] Dasi LP, Simon HA, Sucosky P, Yoganathan AP. Fluid mechanics of artificial heart valves. Clin Exp Pharmacol Physiol 2009;36(2):225–37.

[8] Pantalos GM, Altieri F, Berson A, Borovetz H, Butler K, Byrd G, et al. Long-term mechanical circulatory support system reliability recommendation: American Society for Artificial Internal Organs and The Society of Thoracic Surgeons: long-term mechanical circulatory support system reliability recommendation. Ann Thorac Surg 1998;66(5):1852–9.

[9] Clemente F, Ferrari GF, De Lazzari C, Tosti G. Technical standards for medical devices. Assisted circulation devices. Technol Health Care 1997;5(6):449–59.
[10] Kolff WJ. Mock circulation to test pumps designed for permanent replacement of damaged hearts. Cleve Clin Q 1959;26(4):223–6.
[11] Björk VO, Intonti F, Meissl A. A mechanical pulse duplicator for testing prosthetic mitral and aortic valves. Thorax 1962;17(3):280–3.
[12] Reul H, Tesch B, Schoenmackers J, Effert S. Hydromechanical simulation of systemic circulation. Med Biol Eng 1974;12(4):431–6.
[13] Rosenberg G, Phillips WM, Landis DL, Pierce WS. Design and evaluation of the Pennsylvania State University mock circulatory system. ASAIO J 1981;4(2):41–9.
[14] Richards AL, Cook RC, Bolotin G, Buckner GD. A dynamic heart system to facilitate the development of mitral valve repair techniques. Ann Biomed Eng 2009;37(4):651–60.
[15] Leopaldi AM, Vismara R, Lemma M, Valerio L, Cervo M, Mangini A, et al. In vitro hemodynamics and valve imaging in passive beating hearts. J Biomech 2012;45(7):1133–9.
[16] Guldner NW, Klapproth P, Großherr M, Brügge A, Sheikhzadeh A, Tölg R, et al. Biomechanical hearts muscular blood pumps, performed in a 1-step operation, and trained under support of clenbuterol. Circulation 2001;104(6):717–22.
[17] Pochettino A, Anderson DR, Hammond RL, Spanta AD, Hohenhaus E, Niinami H, et al. Skeletal muscle ventricles: a promising treatment option for heart failure. J Card Surg 1991;6(1):145–53.
[18] Mizuhara H, Koshiji T, Nishimura K, Nomoto S-i, Matsuda K, Ban T. Evaluation of a compressive-type skeletal muscle pump for cardiac assistance. Ann Thorac Surg 1999;67(1):105–11.
[19] Geddes LA, Badylak SF, Tacker WA, Janas W. Output power and metabolic input power of skeletal muscle contracting linearly to compress a pouch in a mock circulatory system. J Thorac Cardiovasc Surg 1992;104 (5):1435–42.
[20] de Hart J, de Weger A, van Tuijl S, Stijnen JM, van den Broek CN, Rutten MC, et al. An ex vivo platform to simulate cardiac physiology: a new dimension for therapy development and assessment. Int J Artif Organs 2011;34(6):495–505.
[21] Chinchoy E, Soule CL, Houlton AJ, Gallagher WJ, Hjelle MA, Laske TG, et al. Isolated four-chamber working swine heart model. Ann Thorac Surg 1607–1614;70(5):2000.
[22] Rosenstrauch D, Akay HM, Bolukoglu H, Behrens L, Bryant L, Herrera P, et al. Ex vivo resuscitation of adult pig hearts. Tex Heart Inst J 2003;30(2):121–7.
[23] Schima H, Baumgartner H, Spitaler F, Kuhn P, Wolner E. A modular mock circulation for hydromechanical studies on valves, stenoses, vascular grafts and cardiac assist devices. Int J Artif Organs 1992;15(7):417–21.
[24] Knierbein B, Reul H, Eilers R, Lange M, Kaufmann R, Rau G. Compact mock loops of the systemic and pulmonary circulation for blood pump testing. Int J Artif Organs 1992;15(1):40–8.
[25] Papaioannou TG, Mathioulakis DS, Tsangaris SG. Simulation of systolic and diastolic left ventricular dysfunction in a mock circulation: the effect of arterial compliance. J Med Eng Technol 2003;27(2):85–9.
[26] Ferrari G, De Lazzari C, Mimmo R, Ambrosi D, Tosti G. Mock circulatory system for in vitro reproduction of the left ventricle, the arterial tree and their interaction with a left ventricular assist device. J Med Eng Technol 1994;18(3):87–95.
[27] Ferrari G, De Lazzari C, Mimmo R, Tosti G, Ambrosi D, Gorczynska K. A computer controlled mock circulatory system for mono-and biventricular assist device testing. Int J Artif Organs 1998;21(1):26–36.
[28] Singh D, Singhal A. Design and fabrication of a mock circulatory system for reliability tests on aortic heart valves. In: ASME 2007 summer bioengineering conference. American Society of Mechanical Engineers; 2007. p. 753–4.
[29] Vaes M, Rutten M, van de Molengraft R, van de Vosse F. Left ventricular assist device evaluation with a model-controlled mock circulation. In: ASME 2007 summer bioengineering conference. American Society of Mechanical Engineers; 2007. p. 723–4.

[30] Verdonck P, Kleven A, Verhoeven R, Angelsen B, Vandenbogaerde J. Computer-controlled in vitro model of the human left heart. Med Biol Eng Comput 1992;30(6):656–9.

[31] Pantalos GM, Koenig SC, Gillars KJ, Ewert DL. Mock circulatory system for testing cardiovascular devices. Eng Med Biol 2002;2:1597–8.

[32] Patel S, Allaire PE, Wood HG, Adams JM, Olsen D. Design and construction of a mock human circulatory system. In: Summer bioengineering conference, Sonesta Beach Resort, Florida; 2003.

[33] Mouret F, Garitey V, Gandelheid T, Fuseri J, Rieu R. A new dual activation simulator of the left heart that reproduces physiological and pathological conditions. Med Biol Eng Comput 2000;38(5):558–61.

[34] Pantalos GM, Koenig SC, Gillars KJ, Giridharan GA, Ewert DL. Characterization of an adult mock circulation for testing cardiac support devices. ASAIO J 2004;50(1):37–46.

[35] Legendre D, Fonseca J, Andrade A, Biscegli JF, Manrique R, Guerrino D, et al. Mock circulatory system for the evaluation of left ventricular assist devices, endoluminal prostheses, and vascular diseases. Artif Organs 2008;32(6):461–7.

[36] Buckberg G, Hoffman JIE, Mahajan A, Saleh S, Coghlan C. Cardiac mechanics revisited the relationship of cardiac architecture to ventricular function. Circulation 2008;118(24):2571–87.

[37] Sengupta PP, Krishnamoorthy VK, Korinek J, Narula J, Vannan MA, Lester SJ, et al. Left ventricular form and function revisited: applied translational science to cardiovascular ultrasound imaging. J Am Soc Echocardiogr 2007;20(5):539–51.

[38] Kocica MJ, Corno AF, Carreras-Costa F, Ballester-Rodes M, Moghbel MC, Cueva CNC, et al. The helical ventricular myocardial band: global, three-dimensional, functional architecture of the ventricular myocardium. Eur J Cardiothorac Surg 2006;29(1):21–40.

[39] Streeter DD, Spotnitz HM, Patel DP, Ross J, Sonnenblick EH. Fiber orientation in the canine left ventricle during diastole and systole. Circ Res 1969;24(3):339–47.

[40] Rüssel IK, Götte MJW, Bronzwaer JG, Knaapen P, Paulus WJ, van Rossum AC. Left ventricular torsion: an expanding role in the analysis of myocardial dysfunction. JACC Cardiovasc Imaging 2009;2(5):648–55.

[41] Shaw SM, Fox DJ, Williams SG. The development of left ventricular torsion and its clinical relevance. Int J Cardiol 2008;130(3):319–25.

[42] Rothfeld JM, LeWinter MM, Tischler MD. Left ventricular systolic torsion and early diastolic filling by echocardiography in normal humans. Am J Cardiol 1998;81(12):1465–9.

[43] Baturalp TB, Ertas A. State of the art mock circulation loop and a proposed novel design. In: Proceedings of the international conference on biomedical engineering and science (BIOENG'15), July 27–30; 2015. p. 23–9.

CHAPTER

26

FRAMEWORK FOR AN INTERACTIVE ASSISTANCE IN DIAGNOSTIC PROCESSES BASED ON PROBABILISTIC MODELING OF CLINICAL PRACTICE GUIDELINES☆

P. Philipp*, Y. Fischer†, D. Hempel‡, J. Beyerer*,†

Vision and Fusion Laboratory IES, Karlsruhe Institute of Technology KIT, Karlsruhe, Germany Fraunhofer Institute of Optronics, System Technologies and Image Exploitation IOSB, Karlsruhe, Germany† Steinbeis-Transfer-Institut Klinische Hämatoonkologie, Donauwörth, Germany‡*

26.1 INTRODUCTION

A challenge of the medical diagnostic today can be seen in the reviewing and evaluation of the huge number of publications. For example, a search of the term "myelodysplastic syndrome diagnosis" in Pubmed [1] yields about 12,000 results. For a decision maker, a profound inquiry concerning a specific topic can therefore be extremely laborious. Moreover, the steady growth of published findings makes it almost impossible for individuals to keep their knowledge up-to-date [2]. With the use of clinical practice guidelines (CPGs), the consolidated medical knowledge can be condensed into general recommendations of actions. High-quality CPGs are proposed by bodies of experts with respect to the current state of research [3]. Consequently, for an individual medical practitioner, CPGs open up a scope of actions and decisions in the context of a contemporary diagnostic practice. In addition to the development and dissemination of a CPG (see Fig. 26.1), the actual implementation of recommendations by the medical practitioner plays a decisive role. The physician has to adapt a diagnostic algorithm to the given boundary conditions (eg, patient, equipment, medical experience) [4,5]. Consequently, there is a gap between theoretical knowledge and practical solutions. Additionally, barriers can arise from (for example) low acceptance of CPGs on the part of the physician. The described situation is the subject of much research [6–11]. A passive dissemination (eg, distribution via print media)

☆This chapter is an extended version of the original paper: Patrick Philipp, Yvonne Fischer, Dirk Hempel, and Jürgen Beyerer, "Modeling of clinical practice guidelines for interactive assistance in diagnostic processes," in WorldComp 2015, World Congress in Computer Science, Computer Engineering, and Applied Computing: HIMS 2015, International Conference on Health Informatics and Medical Systems, July 27–30, Las Vegas, Nevada, USA, 2015, pp. 3–9.

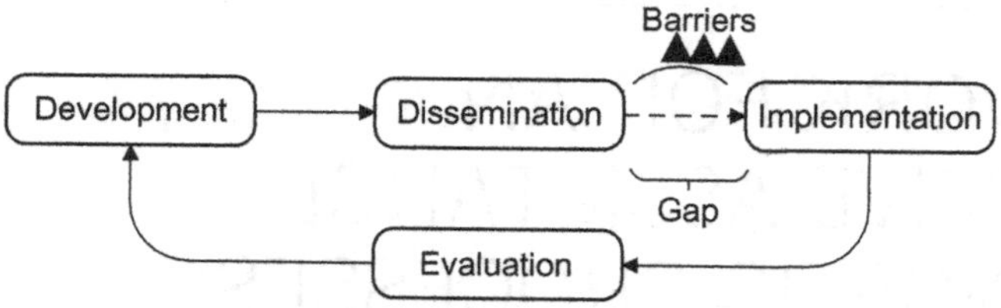

FIGURE 26.1

Stages of a clinical practice guide (CPG). The recommendations are developed and disseminated. There is a gap between theoretical knowledge and practical actions performed by the medical practitioner. Additionally, there can be barriers that have to be overcome.

has only little effect on an actual practitioner's behavior [4,5]. Therefore, we propose an interactive assistance of the practitioner during the diagnostic process, which helps to reduce the gap between theoretical knowledge and practical solutions and helps to overcome barriers. Barriers can arise from different CPG stages [12]. We are convinced that most of them could be moderated by creating the possibility to modify the recommendations by the practitioner him- or herself. This includes, for example, the reduction of fear of regimentation or short-term modifications due to medical symposia. That's why our approach of modeling medical knowledge comprises a dialogue between technical and medical domain experts as well as the modification of knowledge by the medical expert him- or herself.

26.2 APPROACH OF MODELING CPGs

Usually CPGs contain knowledge in the form of texts and schematic diagrams that cannot automatically be translated into models without further ado. We believe that the formalization of knowledge can be done via an expert dialog (see Fig. 26.2). Therefore, experts from the medical and the technical domains are necessary. Together they can develop a CPG model in the form of a Unified Modeling Language (UML) activity. Alternatively, the guideline can be interpreted by the medical expert only. This approach is useful if a practitioner wants to modify an already existing UML activity independently. This bypass could help to lower barriers during the CPG implementation. The benefit of our approach is that it is based on a UML activity. Different models representing the CPG can automatically be generated by only one given activity. Therefore, we developed translation rules. The UML activity in Fig. 26.2 serves as an interface for the actual models used for providing assistance functions. These functions propose suitable examination values to the practitioner during the diagnostic process. In [46] we introduced the automatic translation of a UML activity into a Petri net. The transformation rules are based on the work of Störrle et al. [13,14]. A new approach is used to semiautomatically translate a UML activity into a Bayesian net. What makes this translation semiautomatic is the fact that the parameters of the net (ie, conditional probabilities) have to be assessed manually once the net structure is automatically generated from the activity. In this chapter, we focus on the translation of UML activities into Bayesian nets.

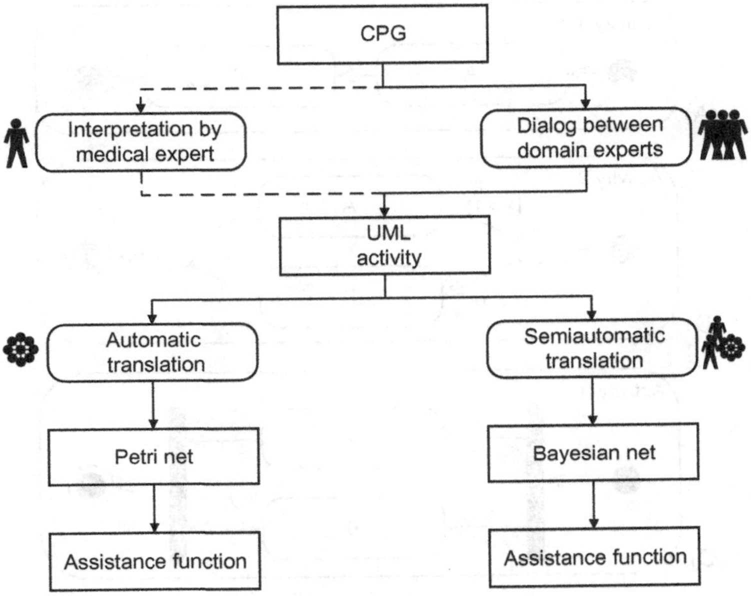

FIGURE 26.2

A CPG is transformed into a UML activity by an expert's dialog. A bypass of the procedure is introduced to allow an exclusive modification by the medical expert. The UML activity serves as an interface to the models used for providing the actual assistance functions. These models are (semi)automatically generated from the UML activity by translation rules.

26.3 CONSTRUCTION OF THE INTERFACE

UML activities have been chosen as an interface because their syntax is formalized and analyzed by various experts [15]. Furthermore, UML is accepted in the software industry worldwide [15–17]. A huge benefit of UML activities is their easy comprehensibility for the medical as well as the technical domain experts. This is a necessary precondition to make the experts' dialog work smoothly and to allow modifications by the medical expert on his or her own.

26.3.1 STATE OF THE ART

UML 2.4 comprises a total of 14 different chart types that can be divided into structural and behavioral diagrams [16]. Activity diagrams are among the latter and thus model not the static but the dynamic behavior of a system and its components. Thus, an activity answers the question of how a particular process or algorithm proceeds [16]. Control flows, object flows, actions, decisions, and forks can be used to specify such an activity [17]. Fig. 26.3 shows the typical routings that appear in the guideline models for chronic myeloid leukemia (CML) and myelodysplastic syndromes (MDS). The black dot represents the start of an activity (initial node), whereas the double circle corresponds to the end of an activity (activity final). The rounded rectangles are the actions that are to be performed, while the

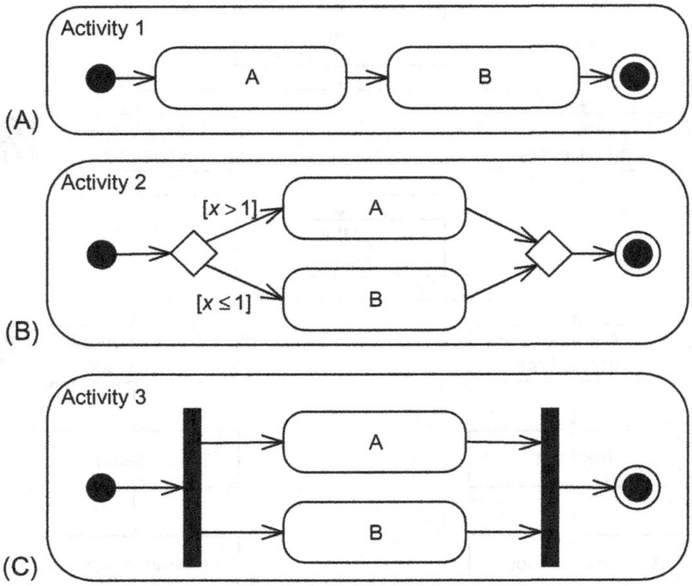

FIGURE 26.3

The figure shows the three typical routings appearing in the CPG models of CML and MDS. In (A), the actions A and B are sequentially performed (one after another). In (B), there is a decision to be made to perform either A or B. (C) shows a routing where A and B are performed concurrently. Consequently, both actions are performed in any possible order.

arrows represent the flow. Fig. 26.3A shows a case where actions are carried out one after another (sequentially). Fig. 26.3B depicts a selective routing. Only one of the two actions A and B is performed. The decision is represented by a diamond (decision node) and depends in this example on a variable x, which is either greater than 1 or not. The second diamond is called a merge node as it merges the two possible flows. Fig. 26.3C shows a case where two actions can be performed concurrently. The flow is split up by a so-called fork node (black bar). The join node on the right synchronizes the flows. As a consequence, the flow continues (ie, the activity ends) only if both actions have been performed (in any arbitrary order).

26.3.2 MODELING OF A PARTICULAR DISEASE

Fig. 26.4 shows the UML activity for CML. Due to the complexity of the CML, CPG, and the resulting size of the corresponding UML activity, the sketch emphasizes some parts of interest (magnifying glasses). Fig. 26.4A depicts a sequence of actions. The first action is "suspicion of CML." That's an important precondition, as there are different CPGs for different diseases. Consequently, the diagnosis algorithms of a CPG normally start with a specific suspicion for the disease under consideration. The second action is anamnesis (case history). During the anamnesis, the practitioner asks the patient if he or she feels bone pain, that is, the value "bone pain" is a result of the activity "anamnesis." We used a

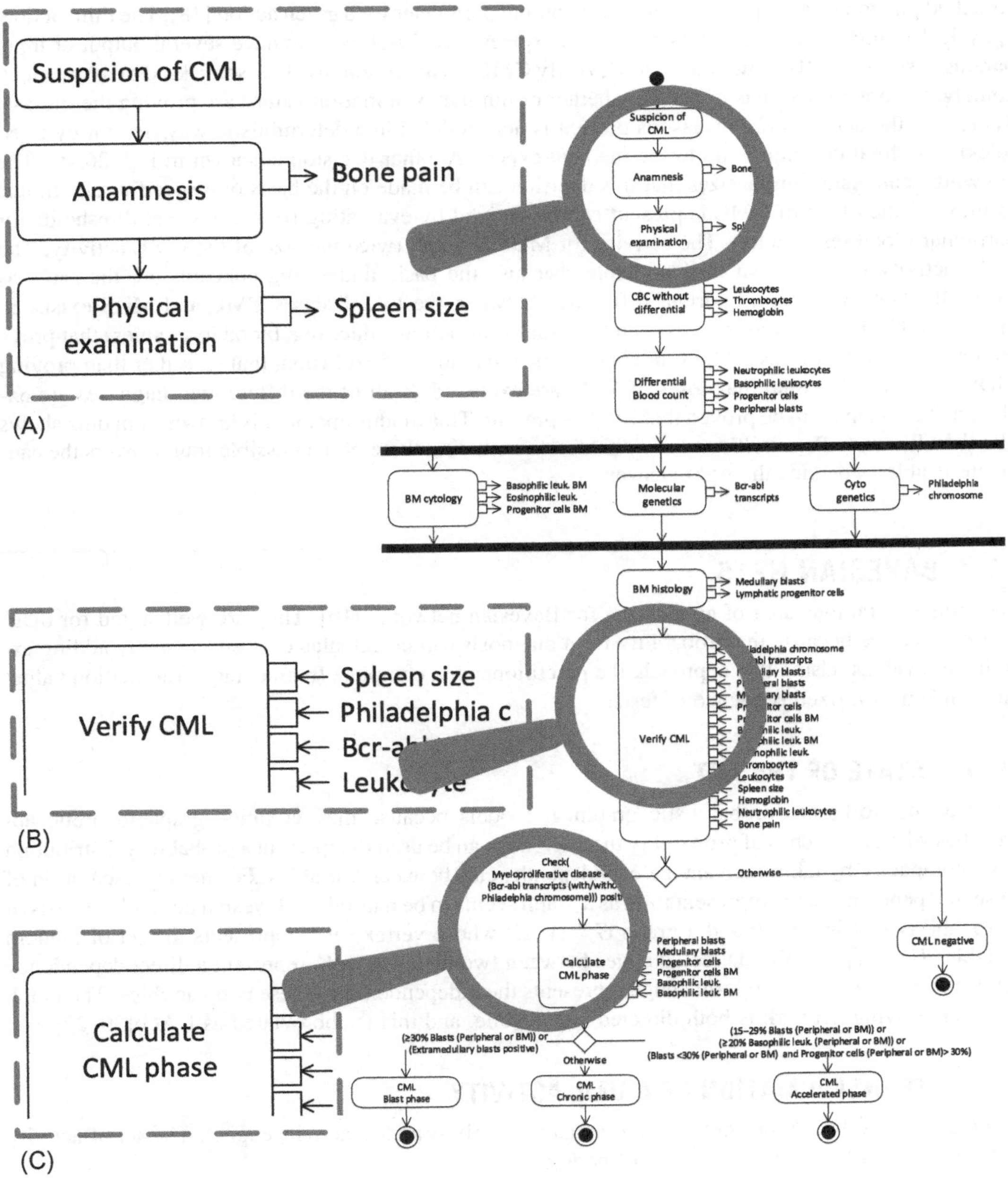

FIGURE 26.4

In the background of this figure, the UML activity for CML is shown. Because of the size of the activity, the sketch emphasizes some parts of interest (magnifying glasses). (A) shows a sequential order of actions. (B) and (C) show two different types of actions. The first one is a decision based on examination values that cannot be made by deterministic rules. Consequently, the medical expert has to decide what to do, not the model. The second action is a decision that is based on a fixed rule (eg, thresholds for particular blood test results).

so-called pin notation to specify a value as an output parameter for a given action [18]. The third action, "physical examination," generates the output "spleen size." Actions can have several output or input parameters. Fig. 26.4B shows the action "Verify CML." This action involves some kind of assessment, namely, the practitioner has to decide whether or not the examination values are proving the disease. Therefore, the decision if a disease is present is not modeled in a deterministic way (ie, not by fixed rules). The final decision is up to the medical expert. Another decision is shown in Fig. 26.4C. The keyword "calculate" emphasizes that this decision can be made on the basis of a specific rule. In this example, which type of CML is present can be derived by evaluating fixed rules (eg, thresholds for particular blood test results). The activity for MDS is about twice the size of the CML activity. The MDS activity is not shown in this chapter because the basic underlying concepts are the same as for CML. However, one important difference between the two diseases CML and MDS exists. In the case of CML, the practitioner is searching for examination values (eg, blood test values) that prove the presence of the disease. MDS, in contrast, is a diagnosis of exclusion, that is, rather than proving MDS, known differential diagnoses of MDS are excluded. If all of the differential diagnoses are excluded, it is assumed to be proven that MDS is present. This modus operandi is known from quiz shows like *Who Wants to Be a Millionaire?*—that is, by excluding three of the possible four answers the candidate is able to deduce the right answer.

26.4 BAYESIAN NETS

Medicine is a famous area of application for Bayesian networks [19]. They are well suited for diagnostic processes because the probability for a diagnosis can be calculated by successively adding examination values. Using this approach, the practitioner can complete fragmentary examination values independent of a fixed sequence of tests.

26.4.1 STATE OF THE ART

Bayesian networks are probabilistic graphical models because they combine graph theoretic approaches with approaches of probability theory. They can be used to represent a probability distribution more compactly by taking advantage of independencies between variables. For the representation of these independencies, the representation as a graph seems to be natural. A Bayesian network consists of a probability distribution P and a graph $G=(V,E)$ whose vertex set V represents the set of random variables $U=\{X_1,\ldots,X_n\}$. Directed edges between two nodes $V_i \rightarrow V_j$ represent a direct dependency between two variables—a missing edge represents the independence of these two variables. The graph to the underlying network is both directed and acyclic, and this is abbreviated as DAG [20–22].

26.4.2 TRANSFORMATION OF A UML ACTIVITY

Given a UML activity represented as a graph, $\mathcal{U}=(\text{activity nodes, activity edges})$. The set of activity nodes can be further divided into sets of nodes:

- $\mathcal{A}$: Set of actions,
- $\mathcal{S},\mathcal{E}$: Initial node and final node,
- $\mathcal{B}$: Set of decision and merge nodes (branch nodes),

- $\mathcal{C}$: Set of fork and join nodes (concurrency nodes),
- $\mathcal{O}$: Set of object nodes.

The set of object nodes is given by the set of data pins. A node that is part of one of the node sets $\mathcal{S}, \mathcal{E}, \mathcal{B}, \mathcal{C}$ is called a control node. Furthermore, the set of activity edges is given by

- $\mathcal{KF}$: Control flow, that is, activity edges between actions and control nodes as well as between them and underneath each other.
- $\mathcal{DF}$: Object flow, that is, activity edges between actions and object nodes or between control nodes and object nodes.

Formally, the translation $[\![\mathcal{U}]\!]$ of a UML activity $\mathcal{U}$ to a DAG $G = (V, E)$ of a Bayesian network is given by

$$[\![(\text{activity nodes, activity edges})]\!] = (V, E),$$

where

$$V = \{e_j | (e_i, e_j) \in \mathcal{DF},\ \ e_i \in \mathcal{O},\ e_j \in \mathcal{A}\} \tag{1}$$

$$\cup \{e_i | (e_i, e_j) \in \mathcal{DF},\ \ e_i \in \mathcal{O},\ e_j \in \mathcal{A}\} \tag{2}$$

$$\cup \{v | v \in \mathcal{A}, \text{Depth}(v) = 1\} \tag{3}$$

$$E = \{(e_j, e_i) | (e_i, e_j) \in \mathcal{DF},\ \ e_i \in \mathcal{O},\ e_j \in \mathcal{A} : e_j \text{ contains ("verify")}\} \tag{4}$$

$$\cup \{(e_i, e_j) | (e_i, e_j) \in \mathcal{DF},\ \ e_i \in \mathcal{O},\ e_j \in \mathcal{A} : e_j \text{ contains ("calculate")}\} \tag{5}$$

$$\cup \{(e_i, v) | v \in \mathcal{A} : \text{Depth}(v) = 1,\ \ e_i \in \mathcal{A} : e_i \text{ contains ("verify")}\}. \tag{6}$$

It is assumed that the nodes of the Bayesian network have a unique name. If a UML activity diagram has several activity nodes with the same name (eg, as pins of different actions), it is indeed translated several times. But because the destination node has the same name in each case, it is added to the Bayesian network only once. That's because adding an element to a set that the element is already a part of, does not alter the set. UML actions are provided with input pins representing a diagnosis, a score, or a phase of a disease. Actions are transformed to vertices of the corresponding Bayesian net (Eq. 1). The pins of these actions are transformed to vertices as well (Eq. 2). They are providing examination values for an action that can be a nondeterministic verification (diagnosis) or a deterministic calculation (score or phase of a disease due to thresholds, etc.). Because diseases cause typical test results, there is a directed edge from diagnosis to the relevant examination values (Eq. 4). This is a causal interpretation of an edge (a Bayesian net reflecting the causal structure normally reflects the expert's understanding of a domain and is therefore useful if the parameters of a net are to be assessed by a survey). The process of translation is depicted in Fig. 26.5A and B. In the case of a deterministic calculation, the direction of an edge is reversed (Eq. 5). That is, because the examination values are causing a specific score or phase. The distinction of the cases (Eqs. 4 and 5) is not given by the activity's structure. But the translation can be performed by searching for a specific keyword in the action's name. The function contains checks if a keyword is present. The keyword "verify" represents a nondeterministic verification and "calculate" represents a deterministic calculation. The translation rules (Eqs. 3 and 6) apply for a diagnosis of exclusion like MDS. In this case, we get a special network structure where all differential diagnoses become parents of the diagnosis of exclusion (see Fig. 26.5C).

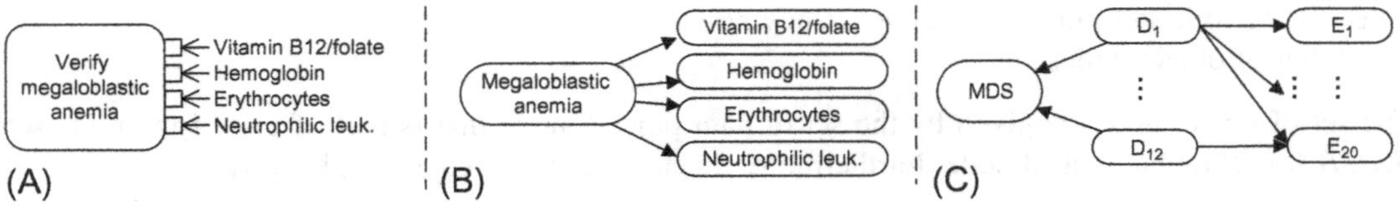

FIGURE 26.5

(A) and (B) depict the translation of a UML action. Node and pins are transformed to vertices in the Bayesian net. There are directed edges from diagnosis to examination values because diseases cause specific test results. (C) Shows the Bayesian structure for a diagnosis of exclusion like MDS.

26.4.3 NETWORK STRUCTURE

The network structure for a disease like CML follows Fig. 26.5B. For a diagnosis of exclusion like MDS, the application of translation rules generate a Bayesian network structure outlined in Fig. 26.5C. The conditional probability table (CPT) of MDS is given by

$$P(\text{MDS}|D_1,\ldots,D_{12}) = \begin{cases} 1, & \text{if MDS} = f(D_1,\ldots,D_{12}) \\ 0, & \text{otherwise} \end{cases}, \quad \text{where } f(D_1,\ldots,D_{12}) = \neg D_1 \wedge \ldots \wedge \neg D_{12}. \tag{7}$$

Because many differential diagnoses have an impact on several examination values, the corresponding examination nodes can have several parent nodes. For example, the examination node hemoglobin has 10 parents (see Fig. 26.6). Even if all these involved random variables are binary, this would lead to a hemoglobin CPT with 2^{10+1} values (half of them, ie, 2^{10}, have to be explicitly specified). To build all the CPTs in a robust fashion, we reduced the large amount of values by using some simplifications.

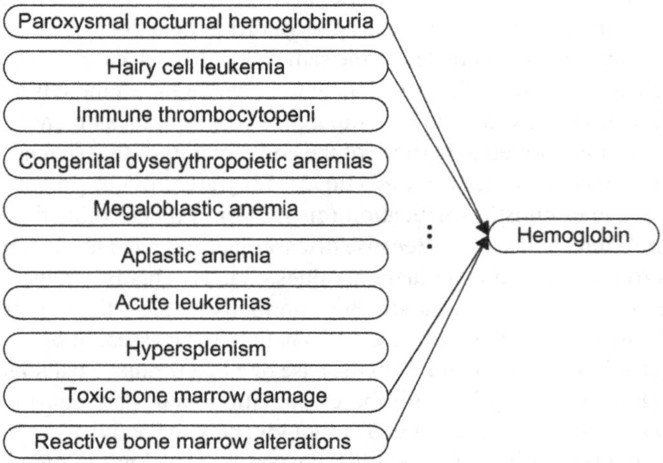

FIGURE 26.6

Examination value hemoglobin is a child of 10 different differential diagnoses. This would lead to CPT with 2^{11} parameters from which 2^{10} would have to be explicitly specified. With the use of some simplifications, the CPT of the node hemoglobin can be modeled by a noisy OR. This reduces the amount of parameters from 2^n to n.

We used noisy ORs [23] to reduce the number of parameters for binary nodes with n parents from 2^n to $2n$. Consequently, the number of parameters increases linearly with the number of parents. For random variables with more than two states, we applied the so-called noisy MAX model to reduce the number of parameters [23–25]. Using the noisy OR model, the following assumptions are made: Given a node Y with binary values $\{y, \bar{y}\}$ (ie, true or false) and a set of binary parent nodes $Pa(Y) = X_1, X_2, \ldots, X_n$: The parents $Pa(Y)$ are interpreted as causes of Y, assuming that every parent node X_i is able to independently produce Y, that is, can cause $Y = y$. Therefore, noisy ORs are associated with models dealing with the "independence of causal influence" (ICI) models. These models assume that there are no interactions among the causal mechanisms by which the parent nodes X_i influence the value of Y [26]. The noisy OR is "noisy" because a parent node X_i only produces the effect Y with a certain probability. This probability is called noisy parameter λ_i. That is, even if a parent node X_i is true ($X_i = x_i$), the effect Y might not be present. Consequently, $(1 - \lambda_i)$ represents the probability of a so-called inhibitor being present, which prevents X_i from causing $Y = y$. Fig. 26.7 illustrates the noisy OR model by introducing n auxiliary variables $Z_1, \ldots, Z_n$. Every Z_i probabilistically depends on its parent nodes X_i and indicates how likely X_i causes $Y = y$. Y results from a deterministic function f of the auxiliary variables $Z_1, \ldots, Z_n$. This function has to be commutative and associative [27]; in case of noisy OR this function is given by $f_{OR}(Z_1, \ldots, Z_i) = Z_1 \vee Z_2 \vee \ldots \vee Z_n$. The assumption of ICI models (ie, there is no interaction among the causal mechanisms represented by X_i) is reflected by the absence of the edges $X_i \rightarrow Z_j$ or $Z_i \rightarrow Z_j$ (each with $i \neq j$). Because of this assumption, there is no interaction among the inhibitors, too. Consequently, the probability $P(Y = \bar{y})$ can be calculated as the product of single inhibitor probabilities:

$$P(\bar{y}|X_1, \ldots, X_n) = \prod_{i:X_i = x_i} P(\bar{z_i}|x_i) \cdot \prod_{i:X_i = \bar{x_i}} P(\bar{z_i}|\bar{x_i}) = \prod_{i:X_i = x_i} (1 - \lambda_i). \tag{8}$$

Respectively,

$$P(y|X_1, \ldots, X_n) = 1 - \prod_{i:X_i = x_i} (1 - \lambda_i). \tag{9}$$

In practice, it is not always feasible to model all parent nodes influencing a node Y. To sum up all not explicitly modeled influences, we added a so-called leak probability [23]. It represents a low

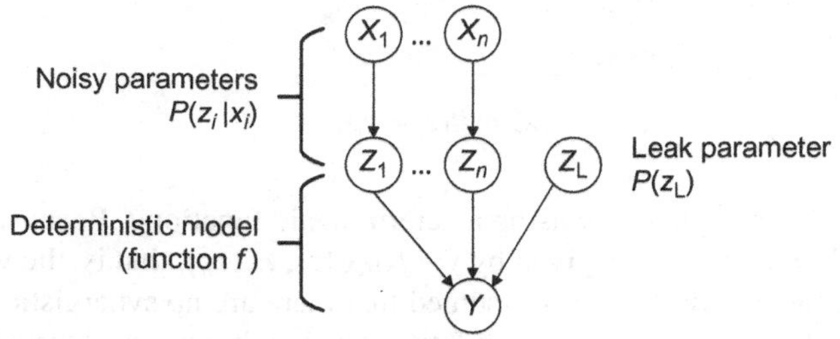

FIGURE 26.7

The noisy OR structure depicted in this figure is theoretical in nature and serves as a basis for deriving the necessary equations [26]. $Z_1, \ldots, Z_n$ indicate how likely a parent X_i causes $Y = y$. All Z_is are linked by a deterministic function $f_{OR}(Z_1, \ldots, Z_i) = Z_1 \vee Z_2 \vee \ldots \vee Z_n$.

probability $P(z_L) = \lambda_0$ that an effect Y is present although all values of the parent nodes X_i are false. Using $P(\overline{z_L}) = (1 - \lambda_0)$, Eq. (8), results in

$$P(\bar{y}|X_1,\ldots,X_n) = (1-\lambda_0) \prod_{i:X_i=x_i} (1-\lambda_i), \tag{10}$$

Respectively,

$$P(y|X_1,\ldots,X_n) = 1 - \left[(1-\lambda_0) \prod_{i:X_i=x_i} (1-\lambda_i)\right]. \tag{11}$$

If a random variable Y (eg, representing specific test results) is not binary but multivalued, the noisy OR model cannot be applied. In such a case, a noisy MAX model, which is an extension of the noisy OR model for multivalued random variables, can be used [23–26]. In accordance to [26] the binary parent nodes, X_i act as causes for a deviation of a random variable Y from its so-called neutral state. As in the case of the noisy OR model, there is no interaction among the causal mechanisms represented by X_i. In contrast to the noisy OR, model Y is not limited to binary random variables; instead, Y is given by a so-called graded variable [24]. A graded variable Y is an ordinal variable whose neutral state is the minimum of Y. The neutral state represents the absence of anomaly, whereas higher states are seen as more severe degrees of anomaly [26]. For example, an examination value like "thrombocytes" could be graded as follows: "normal," "mild decrease," "moderate decrease," "severe decrease." In our case, the binary parents X_i are graded variables, too. The state "false" represents the neutral state (disease is not present), whereas the state "true" is the next higher anomaly of the neutral state (disease is present). In the noisy MAX model, the auxiliary variables Z_i correspond to the degree of deviation from neutral state of Y, which is produced by the parents X_i. Consequently, the auxiliary variables Z_i and Y must share the same domain [26]. The noise parameter of the noisy MAX model represents the probability that a parent node X_i, taking the value x_i, raises the value of Y from the neutral state to value y. The noise parameters are given by Ref. [26]

$$\lambda_{z_i}^{x_i} = P(z_i|x_i).$$

This is equivalent to

$$\lambda_y^{x_i} = P(Z_i = y|x_i).$$

The resulting value of Y is calculated by using a deterministic function f. Because we are dealing with the noisy MAX model, this function is given by $y = f_{\mathrm{MAX}}(z_1, \ldots, z_n)$, that is, the value of Y is the maximum of the values of the Z_is. By this, it is assumed that there are no synergistic effects by the causal mechanisms by which the parent nodes X_i raise Y to y. Or, in other words, "the winner takes all" (ie, a value is raised independently of the lower states of the other causes). This is described by the definition of the noisy MAX gate, which according to Ref. [24] is given by

$$P(Y \le y|x_1,\ldots,x_n) = \prod_i P(Y \le y|X_i = x_i, X_j = \overline{x_j},\ j \ne i). \tag{12}$$

26.4.4 NETWORK PARAMETERS

After specifying the network's structure, the parameters have to be determined (ie, the λ's introduced in Section 26.4.3). The parameters could be calculated from existing data. In the case of the diagnostic process concerning CML or MDS, there might be a patient database containing diagnoses and examination values of various patients. The conditional probabilities could then be retrieved by the use of maximum likelihood estimation or the expectation maximization algorithm [28]. Due to the lack of a patient database, our structure was parameterized by the results of a survey (which is common practice in such a case [29]). However, false estimations can arise on the part of the domain expert—their avoidance is the subject of various researches [30]. An overview of suitable methods for assessing data in the context of a survey can be found in Ref. [31]. Because a domain expert could feel overburdened by expressing his/her domain-specific knowledge in the form of probabilities, there is a huge variety of methods for assessing these values in an indirect fashion [32]. This includes the "Gambling" as well as the "Fortune Wheel" method [33]. In the latter case, the expert has to divide the area of a fortune wheel into two regions (win/lose). The areas have to be set in such a way that the probability of winning is equal to the probability that was searched for (eg, suffering from cancer). A drawback of indirect methods like "Gambling" and "Fortune Wheel" is that they are time-consuming and not always easy to understand [34]. These methods seem less suitable for assessing a moderate or high number of probabilities. Consequently, a direct method was chosen. The elicitation of the expert's knowledge by the use of a direct method can be carried out in different formats. For example, the expert can be asked for probabilities, percentages, odds, relative frequencies, or natural frequencies (see Table 26.1).

These formats can have an impact on the expert assessment. One example is the well-known "Linda Problem" given by the following description [35]: "Linda is 31 years old, single, outspoken, and very bright. She majored in philosophy. As a student, she was deeply concerned with issues of discrimination and social justice, and also participated in antinuclear demonstrations"—Please check off the most likely alternative:

(1) Linda is a bank teller.
(2) Linda is a bank teller and active in the feminist movement.

In a study of Tversky and Kahneman [35], about 80% of all respondents estimated event (2) being more likely than event (1). Thereby the probability of a single event (Linda is a bank teller) is estimated less

Table 26.1 Different Methods of Expressing Chance [30]

Method	Statement About Chance
Probability	"There was a 0.08 probability of being a victim of crime in 2002."
Percentage	"There was an 8% chance of being a victim of crime in 2002."
Odds	"The odds against being a victim of crime in 2002 were 11 to 1."
Relative frequency	"1 in 12 people were victims of crime in 2002," or "80 in every 1000 people were victims of crime in 2002."
Natural frequency	"From a population of 56 million people, 4.5 million were victims of crime in 2002."

All statements are mathematically equivalent; nevertheless, the psychological equivalence may not always be given as the literature indicates.

likely than the conjunction of two events (Linda is a bank teller and active in the feminist movement). This is in contradiction with probability theory: the joint probability can never exceed the probability of one of the single events [35,36]. This kind of false estimation can be observed in many contexts—this includes the field of medicine as well [35]. According to the studies in Refs. [36,37], an improvement can be achieved by using a frequency format (eg, Given 100 women like Linda. How many are bank tellers?). With this wording, the percentage of false estimation is in the range of 10–20% only. Besides [36,37], other studies suggest that for experts it's easier to deal with the format of natural frequency rather than other formats [35,38]. As a result, we decided to use natural frequencies for the expert survey. For large Bayesian networks, the assessment of the required probability values can quickly become a challenging task. For example, for a decision support system concerning the treatment of esophageal cancer, more than 4000 conditional probabilities were elicited [39]. Even if the assessment is efficiently performed (in the sense of time), for example, by eliciting the various states of a random variable in parallel [39], a reduction of parameters is desirable. That's because the values have to be assessed in a robust fashion [22]. Consequently, we introduced a network structure using the ICI models noisy OR and noisy MAX [40] in combination with a leak probability proposed by Henrion [23], explained in Section 26.4.3. In the case of the introduction of leak probabilities, the representation of the conditional probability distributions proposed by Henrion [23] is not identical to that introduced by Diez [24] and used in course books like Ref. [22]. If Henrion's representation is used, the corresponding question for assessing a parameter is asked as follows: "What is the probability that Y is present when X_i is present and none of the other causes that we are considering explicitly in our model are present?." That corresponds to a probability $P(y|\overline{x_1}\ldots x_i \ldots \overline{x_n})$. In the case of Diez's formulation, the question is, "What is the probability that X_i produces Y if all other possible causes (explicitly modeled or not modeled) of Y are absent?" This question can be simplified to, "What is the probability of X_i causing Y?" Consequently, $P(y|x_i)$ is assessed. Both representations can be converted into each other [41]. This can become important if data using different representations have to be compared, for example, linking parameters in Henrion's formulation obtained by a database. According to Ref. [42], the suitable representation depends on the use case; that is, if the parameters are obtained by using a database, the representation introduced by Henrion is more suitable, whereas in the case of an expert survey, the representation proposed by Diez seems to be more suitable. That's why we used the latter representation for conducting our expert survey.

26.4.5 ASSISTANCE FUNCTION

In the models of CML and MDS, the diagnostic node plays a key role. It represents the probability distribution over the states of the disease under consideration. The question is which evidence can be set to make one of the variable's states as much likely as possible? Regarding a practitioner, this means which examination value leads to a situation where the decision maker can tell most certainly whether the disease is present or not? Consequently, examination values are taken that reduce uncertainty. A measure of the uncertainty of a random variable is the entropy [43]; the higher it is, the more the probability mass scatters over the states of the random variable. In the case of a uniform distribution, the entropy is maximum. With regard to the diagnostic node that means that the more likely the variable takes one of the two states "present" or "not present," the lower the entropy is. Therefore, the reduction of entropy is an essential part of the assistance function. Let A be a discrete random variable with n states $a_1,\ldots,a_n$ and $P(A)$ the probability distribution. Then the entropy eta (in bits) is given by Ref. [43]

$$H(A) = -\sum_{i=1}^{n} P(a_i)\log_2 P(a_i), \tag{13}$$

where $H(A) \in [0,\ \log_2(n)]$

The graph of the entropy for a random variable with two states can be described by a concave function (see Fig. 26.8). The function reaches its maximum value of $\log_2(2) = 1$ if both states of the random variable are equally likely. If one of the two states has a probability of 0, the entropy drops to 0 too. In this case, we removed the uncertainty about the state of the random variable. The entropy of a random variable A (eg, diagnosis) given a random variable B (eg, examination value) is given by the conditional entropy [43]:

$$H(A|B) = H(A) - I(A, B). \tag{14}$$

$I(A, B)$ is called the mutual information and represents the reduction in the uncertainty of A due to the knowledge of B. Thus, the benefit of an examination E_1 can be rated by its effect on the uncertainty of a random variable D that represents the (non)presence of a disease. Hence, Eq. (14) may be rearranged to give

$$I(D, E_1) = H(D) - H(D|E_1). \tag{15}$$

If there are several possible examinations E_i that can be performed, we would prefer the one with the highest mutual information (ie, highest reduction of uncertainty about D). Thus, a preliminary assistance function recommending an optimal examination E^* can be obtained:

$$E^* = \arg_{E_i} \max\,(H(D) - H(D|E_i)). \tag{16}$$

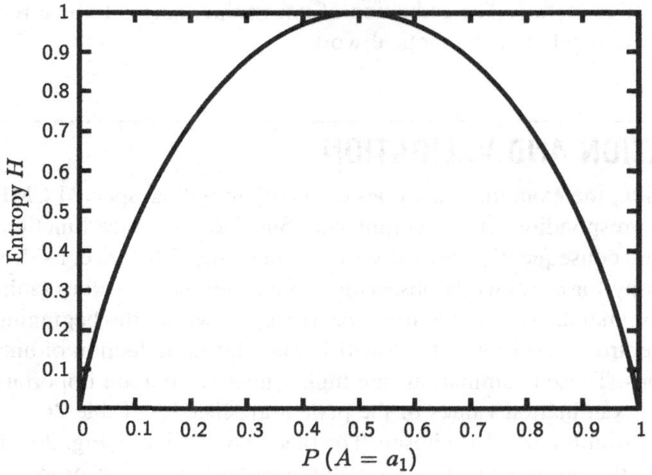

FIGURE 26.8

Entropy of a random variable A with two states a_1 and a_2. It is $P(A{=}a_2) = 1 - P(A{=}a_1)$.

Given a Bayesian net with a node representing the random variable D, the entropy $H(D)$ can be calculated by Eq. (13). The conditional entropy $H(D|E_i)$ is defined as [43,44]

$$H(D|E_i) := \sum_{j=1}^{n} P(E_i = e_j) H(D|E_i = e_j), \tag{17}$$

where $j = 1, \ldots, n$ are states of random variable E_i.

The conditioned entropy $H(D|E_i = e_j)$ in Eq. (17) is the entropy of the variable D given a certain value e_j of E_i. Thus, $H(D|E_i)$ is calculated by averaging $H(D|E_i = e_j)$ over all possible values e_j that E_i may take. In a real medical scenario, the choice of an optimal examination solely on the basis of Eq. (16) is not feasible. This would mean that an examination that is very specific for a disease would be suggested first (high benefit), regardless of whether this examination is highly invasive or costly, which might outweigh its diagnostic benefit. The order of the examinations listed in the recommendations of the CPG is a result of the consideration of different interests (costs). Among other things, the invasiveness of an examination is considered. At the beginning of the diagnostic process, the proposed examinations are less invasive than at the end of the diagnostic process when the practitioner is more convinced a disease is present or not. We propose a weighted reduction of uncertainty for integrating cost-benefit considerations during the diagnostic process into our assistance function. The decision maker has the opportunity to choose to what extent to follow the CPG recommendations or to consider a higher reduction of uncertainty during the diagnostic process:

$$\text{Recommendation}_i = (1-\alpha)(1 - k_i/m) + \alpha I(D, E_i),$$

where k_i is the depth of examination E_i in CPG, m is the overall depth of CPG, and α is the weight factor.

To allow cost-benefit considerations, the assistance function can be adjusted by the parameter alpha. For $\alpha = 1$ only the reduction of uncertainty is taken into account (benefit). Respectively, for $\alpha = 0$ the recommendation follows exactly the given CPG model (cost). The increase of the parameter alpha allows one to specify how much the practitioner wants to deviate from the CPG recommendations in favor of an uncertainty reduction. The reduction of uncertainty seems to be a realistic reason for not following a CPG recommendation in practical work.

26.5 VERIFICATION AND VALIDATION

In a first demonstration, the examination values on a patient with suspected CML are assessed in the order given by the corresponding CPG recommendation. The assistance function is therefore parameterized with $\alpha = 0$ and consequently only the costs given by the CPG are considered. Fig. 26.9 depicts the reduction of entropy for $\alpha = 0$ while observing more examination values (solid dark line). By following the CPG recommendations, the entropy decreases slowly at the beginning. With the 11th examination value the entropy has dropped below 0.1. The highest reduction of uncertainty is observed after late examinations. These examinations are highly invasive but are important for identifying the disease for sure. The examination values of the patient are listed in Table 26.2.

In a second demonstration, $\alpha = 1$ is chosen. The black dotted line in Fig. 26.9 represents the corresponding progress of the entropy. In this case the assistance function proposes examinations that maximize the reduction of uncertainty in each step. Highly risky and invasive examinations are recommended first, because they are able to reduce uncertainty the most. Instead of considering either cost

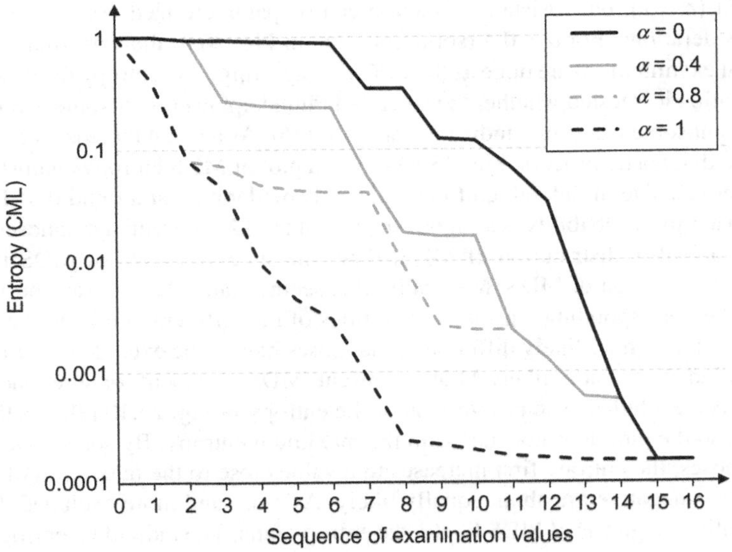

FIGURE 26.9

Entropy of the node CML versus the order of executed examinations. The first examination value obtained is assigned with sequence number 1. Table 26.2 lists the assignment of the examination values to the numbers used in the diagram for $\alpha = 0$. By following the CPG recommendations, the entropy decreases slowly at the beginning of the diagnostic process (solid black line).

Table 26.2 Patient With Suspected CML ($\alpha = 0$)

No.	Depth	Examination Value	Entropy
0	0	–	1
1	1	Bone pain negative	0.996791632
2	2	Spleen enlarged	0.937185857
3	3	Hemoglobin < 13 g/dL	0.937185857
4	3	150k/μL ≤ thrombocytes ≤ 400k/μL	0.908302337
5	3	10,000/μL < leukocytes	0.895383409
6	4	Neutrophilic leukocytes increased	0.873765252
7	4	1% ≤ basophilic leukocytes < 20%	0.346539286
8	4	Progenitor cells ≤ 30%	0.346539286
9	4	15% ≤ peripheral blasts < 30%	0.124546345
10	5	Progenitor cells bone marrow ≤ 30%	0.119056765
11	5	20% ≤ basophilic leukocytes bone marrow	0.068089434
12	5	5% < eosinophilic leukocytes	0.033581937
13	5	Philadelphia chromosome positive	0.004083213
14	5	Bcr-abl positive	0.000563717
15	6	15% ≤ medullary blasts < 30%	0.000158269
16	6	Lymphatic progenitor cell positive	0.000158269

($\alpha = 0$) or benefit ($\alpha = 1$), our assistance function can be parameterized with $\alpha \in (0, 1)$. This allows cost-benefit considerations. For $\alpha = 0.4$ (solid gray line in Fig. 26.9) the very first examinations (anamnesis, physical examination) are done as the CPG is suggesting. The entropy drops with examination 3. In this examination it is tested whether the so-called Philadelphia chromosome is present or not. The Philadelphia chromosome is a strong indicator for CML [45]. As a result there is an earlier reduction of uncertainty in the diagnostic process. Fig. 26.10 shows a plot of MDS entropy against the number of a differential diagnoses. The initial value of the entropy is moderately at around 0.5. This is due to the fact that a certain a priori probability is assigned to each of the 12 differential diagnoses of MDS, which influences the probability distribution of MDS. First, the state "present" of MDS is unlikely, even though there is the suspicion of MDS. Medically, this seems plausible and was confirmed by the expert's setting of the corresponding a priori probabilities of the differential diagnoses: Despite the suspicion of MDS, first, the more likely differential diagnoses have to be excluded. The more differential diagnoses are excluded, the more likely MDS is present. MDS is present for sure, once all differential diagnoses have been excluded. The progression of the entropy in Fig. 26.10 reflects this fact. Initially MDS is unlikely, so the plot does not start with the maximum entropy. By successively excluding the differential diagnoses, the entropy first increases to a value close to the maximum of 1. Here MDS = positive and MDS = negative are about equally likely. As more and more excluded differential diagnoses make a positive diagnosis of MDS likely, the entropy falls. The individual entropy values for $\alpha = 0$ are shown in Table 26.3.

Given now is a patient whose diagnosis has already been established. Patient data suggests that molecular genetics and bone marrow histology were actually carried out earlier during the process of diagnosis than is recommended by the guideline. The reproduction of this case in the model yields to a situation in which, according to the CPG, four differential diagnoses still have to be excluded. These are "congenital dyserythropoietic anemia," "hairy cell leukemia," "aplastic anemia," and "myeloproliferative neoplasms" (see Fig. 26.11). The assistance function proposes to exclude

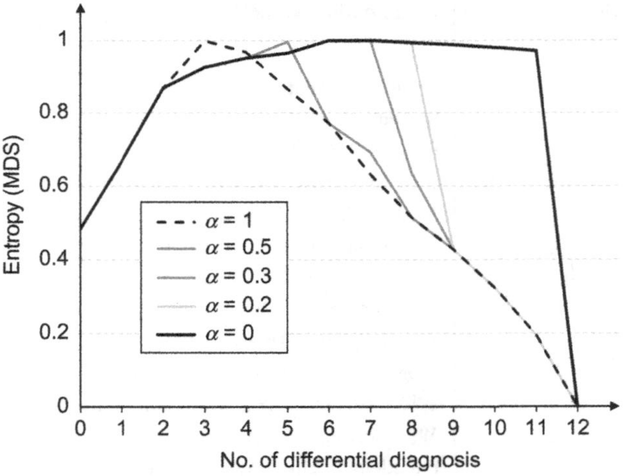

FIGURE 26.10

Entropy of the node MDS versus the order of excluded differential diagnoses for different values of α. If all differential diagnoses are excluded, MDS is present for sure—the entropy drops to 0.

Table 26.3 Patient With Suspected MDS ($\alpha = 0$)

No.	Depth	Examination Value	Entropy
0	0	–	0.483273525
1	1	Megaloblastic anemias negative	0.667357598
2	1	Reactive bone marrow alterations negative	0.869280269
3	1	Toxic bone marrow damage negative	0.926423147
4	2	Monocytosis of other etiology negative	0.951739499
5	3	Hypersplenism negative	0.965406878
6	4	Immune thrombocytopenia negative	0.999630334
7	4	Paroxysmal nocturnal hemoglobinuria negative	0.999958433
8	5	Acute leukemias negative	0.993451440
9	6	Congenital dyserythropoietic anemias negative	0.987947563
10	7	Hairy cell leukemia negative	0.980510718
11	7	Aplastic anemia negative	0.970950594
12	7	Myeloproliferative diseases negative	0

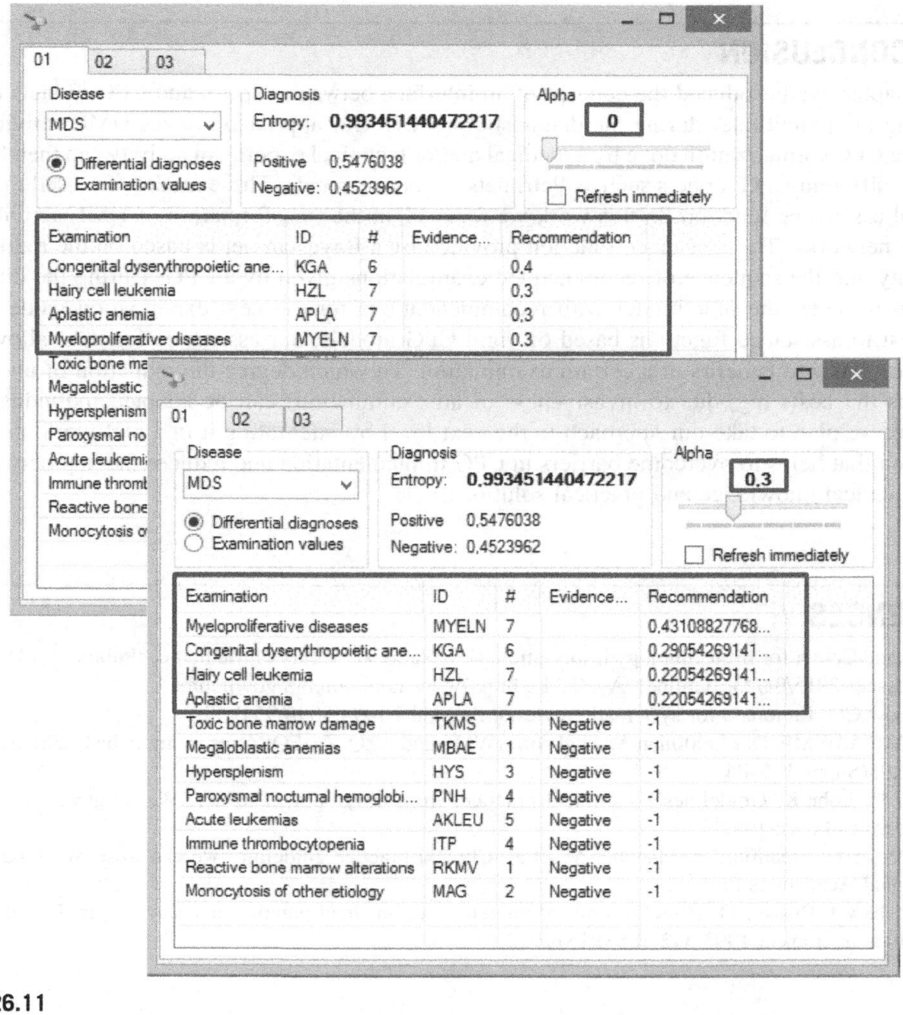

FIGURE 26.11

User interface of the assistance function. There are four differential diagnoses left.

"congenital dyserythropoietic anemia" next, because the guideline suggests to do so ($\alpha = 0$). By setting an alpha value of 0.3, it appears clear that the exclusion of myeloproliferative neoplasia in terms of the cost-benefit ratio is better than the exclusion of congenital dyserythropoietic anemia. This is exactly what happened in the real world: the practitioner recognized the higher probability of a "myeloproliferative neoplasia" because of his expertise, and decided to exclude this particular disease by molecular genetics and bone marrow histology. To sum up, it can be said that the models for CML and MDS behave as expected. They are able to describe the corresponding diagnostic process and can provide the intended assistance function. Real-world cases can be reproduced with appropriate alpha values. The parameter alpha ranges somewhere in between 0 and 1 (avoiding the extreme values 0 and 1) because medical cases are based on the consideration of the CPG recommendations as well as the reduction of uncertainty about the presence of a disease.

26.6 CONCLUSION

In this chapter, we introduced the concept of an interface between experts and CPG models used for supporting the practitioner during the diagnostic process. Our approach utilizes UML activities as a basis for a CPG formalization done by a medical and/or technical expert. An activity can then be translated into different CPG models such as Petri nets or Bayesian nets. These models are used to provide the actual assistance function. In this work we focused on the transformation of UML activities into Bayesian networks. The assistance function provided by a Bayesian net is based on the reduction of uncertainty and the sequence of recommended examinations given by a CPG. During the diagnostic process it provides the practitioner with recommendations for the next examination value to take. In contrast to assistance functions based on rigid CPG models, our assistance function allows us to weigh the costs and benefits of a certain examination. To which degree the reduction of uncertainty outweighs the costs (eg, due to invasiveness of an examination) can be adapted individually. For the future, we plan to take our approach to the next level by integrating it in a real-world diagnostic application that helps to overcome barriers in CPG implementation and reduces the gap between theoretical medical knowledge and practical solutions.

REFERENCES

[1] National Center for Biotechnology Information, U.S. National Library of Medicine, "Pubmed", March 2015, Accessed: 2015/03/23. [Online]. Available: http://www.ncbi.nlm.nih.gov/pubmed.
[2] Mulrow CD. Rationale for systematic reviews. Br Med J 1994;309(6954):597.
[3] AWMF AdWMF. Das Leitlinien-Manual von AWMF und ÄZQ. ZaeFQ: Zentrum ärztliche Qualitätssicherung 2001;95(Suppl. I):5–84.
[4] Field E, Lohr K. Guidelines for clinical practice: from development to use. Washington, DC: National Academies Press; 1992.
[5] Steinberg E, Greenfield S, Mancher M, et al. Clinical practice guidelines we can trust. Washington, DC: National Academies Press; 2011.
[6] Grimshaw J, Russell IT. Effect of clinical guidelines on medical practice: a systematic review of rigorous evaluations. Lancet 1993;342(8883):1317–22.

[7] Grimshaw J, Freemantle N, Wallace S, Russell I, Hurwitz B, Watt I, et al. Developing and implementing clinical practice guidelines. Qual Health Care 1995;4(1):55.
[8] Bero LA, Grilli R, Grimshaw JM, Harvey E, Oxman AD, Thomson MA. Closing the gap between research and practice: an overview of systematic reviews of interventions to promote the implementation of research findings. BMJ 1998;317(7156):465–8.
[9] Grimshaw J, Eccles M, Tetroe J. Implementing clinical guide- lines: current evidence and future implications. J Contin Educ Health Prof 2004;24(S1):S31–7.
[10] Alonso P, Irfan A, Solà I, Gich I, Delgado Noguera M, Rigau D, et al. The quality of clinical practice guidelines over the last two decades: a systematic review of guideline appraisal studies. Qual Saf Health Care 2010;19(6):1–7.
[11] Giguère A, Légaré F, Grimshaw J, Turcotte S, Fiander M, Grudniewicz A, et al. Printed educational materials: effects on professional practice and healthcare outcomes. Cochrane Database Syst Rev 2012;10:CD004398.
[12] Kirchner H, Fiene M, Ollenschläger G. Bewertung und Implementierung von Leitlinien. Rehabilitation 2003;42(2):74–82.
[13] Störrle H. Semantics of control-flow in UML 2.0 activities. In: 2004 IEEE Symposium on Visual Languages and Human Centric Computing; 2004. p. 235–42.
[14] Störrle H. Semantics and verification of data flow in UML 2.0 activities. Electron Notes Theor Comput Sci 2005;127(4):35–52.
[15] Kecher C. UML 2: das umfassende Handbuch. Bonn: Galileo Press; 2011.
[16] Rupp C, Queins S, et al. UML 2 glasklar. München: Carl Hanser Verlag GmbH Co KG; 2012.
[17] OMG, OMG Unified Modeling Language (OMG UML) Superstructure Version 2.4.1, 2011, Accessed: 2014/08/28. [Online]. Available: http://www.omg.org/spec/UML/2.4.1/Superstructure/PDF/.
[18] Störrle H. UML 2 für Studenten. Pearson Studium; 2005. vol. 320.
[19] Korb KB, Nicholson AE. Bayesian artificial intelligence. Boca Raton, FL: CRC Press; 2003.
[20] Pearl J. Probabilistic reasoning in intelligent systems: networks of plausible inference. San Mateo, CA: Morgan Kaufmann; 1988.
[21] Neapolitan RE. Probabilistic reasoning in expert systems: theory and algorithms. New York: Wiley; 1989.
[22] Koller D, Friedman N. Probabilistic graphical models: principles and techniques. Cambridge, MA: MIT press; 2009.
[23] Henrion M. Practical issues in constructing a Bayes belief network. Uncertain in Artif Intell 1988;3:132–9.
[24] Diez FJ. Parameter adjustment in Bayes networks. The generalized noisy OR-gate, In: Proceedings of the Ninth international conference on uncertainty in artificial intelligence; 1993. p. 99–105.
[25] Srinivas S. A generalization of the noisy-or model", In: Proceedings of the ninth international conference on uncertainty in artificial intelligence; 1993. p. 208–15.
[26] Diez FJ, Druzdzel MJ. Canonical probabilistic models for knowledge engineering. Technical report CISIAD-06-01, UNED, Madrid, Spain, Tech. Rep.; 2006.
[27] Zhang NL, Poole D. Exploiting causal independence in Bayesian network inference. J Artif Intell Res 1996;5:301–82.
[28] Dempster AP, Laird NM, Rubin DB. Maximum likelihood from incomplete data via the EM algorithm. J R Stat Soc Ser B Methodol 1977;1–38.
[29] Wiegmann DA. Developing a methodology for eliciting subjective probability estimates during expert evaluations of safety interventions: application for Bayesian belief networks. Aviation Human Factors Division, October, from http://www.humanfactors.uiuc.edu; 2005.
[30] O'Hagan A, Buck CE, Daneshkhah A, Eiser JR, Garthwaite PH, Jenkinson DJ, et al. Uncertain judgements: eliciting experts' probabilities. Chichester, UK: John Wiley & Sons; 2006.
[31] Burgman M, Fidler F, Mcbride M, Walshe T, Wintle B. Eliciting expert judgments: literature review. ACERA Australian Center of Excellence for Risk Analysis; 2006.

[32] Kjaerulff UB, Madsen AL. Bayesian networks and influence diagrams: a guide to construction and analysis: a guide to construction and analysis. New York: Springer; 2012. vol. 22.
[33] Clemen RT, Reilly T. Making hard decisions with Decision-Tools Suite; Mason, OH: South-Western; 1999.
[34] Renooij S. Probability elicitation for belief networks: issues to consider. Knowl Eng Rev 2001;16(03):255–69.
[35] Tversky A, Kahneman D. Extensional versus intuitive reasoning: the conjunction fallacy in probability judgment. Psychol Rev 1983;90(No. 4):293.
[36] Hertwig R, Gigerenzer G. Theconjunction fallacy' revisited: how intelligent inferences look like reasoning errors. J Behav Decis Mak 1999;12:275–306.
[37] Fiedler K. The dependence of the conjunction fallacy on subtle linguistic factors. Psychol Res 1988;50 (2):123–9.
[38] Schapira MM, Nattinger AB, McHorney CA. Frequency or probability? A qualitative study of risk communication formats used in health care. Med Decis Making 2001;21(6):459–67.
[39] van der Gaag LC, Renooij S, Witteman C, Aleman BM, Taal BG. Probabilities for a probabilistic network: a case study in oesophageal cancer. Artif Intell Med 2002;25(2):123–48.
[40] Pearl J. Fusion, propagation, and structuring in belief networks. Artif Intell 1986;29(3):241–88.
[41] Anand V, Downs SM. Probabilistic asthma case finding: a noisy or reformulation. AMIA Annu Symp Proc 2008;2008:6.
[42] Zagorecki A, Druzdzel MJ. An empirical study of probability elicitation under noisy-OR assumption, In: FLAIRS conference; 2004. p. 880–6.
[43] Cover TM, Thomas JA. Elements of information theory. Hoboken, NJ: John Wiley & Sons; 2006.
[44] Rish I, Brodie M, Ma S, Odintsova N, Beygelzimer A, Grabarnik G, et al. Adaptive diagnosis in distributed systems. IEEE Trans Neural Netw 2005;16(5):1088–109.
[45] Hochaus A, Baerlocher G, Brümmendorf TH, Chalandon Y, le Coutre P, Dölken G, et al. Chronische Myeloische Leukämie (CML) Leitlinie-Empfehlungen der Fachgesellschaften zur Diagnostik und Therapie hämatologischer und onkologischer Erkrankungen. Berlin: DGHO Deutsche Gesellschaft für Hämatologie und Medizinische Onkologie e.V; 2013.
[46] Philipp P, Fischer Y, Hempel D, Beyerer J. Framework for an interactive assistance in diagnostic process based on the translation of UML activities into Petri nets. In: CSCI 2015, international conference on computational science and computational intelligence: ISHI 2015, international symposium on health informatics and medical systems. December 7–9. Las Vegas, Nevada, USA: IEEE Conference Publishing Services; 2015. p. 732–7. ISBN-13: 978-1-4673-9795-7.

CHAPTER

MOTION ARTIFACTS COMPENSATION IN DCE-MRI FRAMEWORK USING ACTIVE CONTOUR MODEL

27

R. Setola*, L.M. Montoni*, B.B. Zobel†

Complex System and Security Laboratory, University Campus Bio-Medico of Rome, Rome, Italy Department of Diagnostic Imaging, University Campus Bio-Medico of Rome, Rome, Italy†*

27.1 INTRODUCTION

The development of techniques for noninvasive diagnosis is becoming more and more relevant. On one hand, the research aims to improve the existing techniques to provide to doctors more reliable tools; on the other hand, it aims to extend the noninvasive performance area to medical fields actually dominated by invasive techniques. Among the techniques of growing importance to perform the noninvasive analysis is dynamic contrast enhancement (DCE) [1–3]. The aim of the method is to determine the nature of a disease, on the base of the local vessel morphology, by analyzing how a specific contrast agent (CA) perfuses into the tissue. Specifically, a series of acquisitions of biomedical images (MRIs, CTs, echos) of the same spatial region are performed periodically in the DCE framework for a time ranging from 30 s to a few minutes and elicit diagnostic information analyzing how the CA perfusions in the region of interest (ROI). Because lesions are generally characterized by a hypervascularity, absent in a healthy parenchyma, the analysis of the dynamics of a CA allows one to characterize the affected areas. The dynamics analysis of perfusion of the CA is studied through the evolution of the intensity of the back-scattering signal as a function of time (enhancement curve (EC)). It is clear that the precision with which the EC is calculated is essential to make a correct diagnosis. Factors that may invalidate the goodness of the EC are connected to movements due to respiration or peristalsis of the organ. In their classical formulation, DCE algorithms implicitly assume that during all the acquisition sequences the ROI does not modify its shape and position. Unfortunately, it is impossible to guarantee that ROI is not subject to movement due to respiration, peristalsis, or patient's movements due to the long time requested by the acquisition procedures (up to 10 min). To overcome these difficulties it is of interest to compensate such movements [4–6]. Unfortunately, due to the peculiarity of the DCE, the development of a motion tracking algorithm is quite complex. This because not only the ROI moves over time (changing its shape and size), also because it modifies its brightness due to the perfusion CA. Notice that the changes in the brightness are generally not uniform inside each ROI and it cannot be forecast in advance. In this chapter we illustrate a technique useful to compensate artifacts in DCE induced by motion/deformation of the ROI.

Specifically, the algorithm determines for each image in the sequence the optimal contour of the ROI via active deformable contour. For each one of this ROI we determine the center of mass and the principal axes that are used to superimpose frame by frame a rototranslation compensation.

In the following, starting from the preliminarily results of [7], we illustrate the effectiveness of the proposed method to compensate artifacts induced by movements. The positive effects are more evident when the analysis, as for 2-D color maps [3], are considered.

This document has been arranged as follows:

Section 27.1. Introduction
Section 27.2. Introduction to the DCE technique
Section 27.3. Description of the active contour model
Section 27.4. Methodology and implementation of the algorithm
Section 27.5. Tracking motion
Section 27.6. Results
Section 27.7. Conclusion

27.2 DCE TECHNIQUE

The DCE technique is a noninvasive method that allows one to infer the nature of a lesion, analyzing the perfusions dynamics of a CA in the tissues [1–3]. Specifically in the case of MRI images, the underlying principle of the DCE technique is a measure of the temporal evolution of the increase of magnetic resonance signal induced in tissue masses, after the subministration of an appropriate paramagnetic CA. The presence of a paramagnetic center affects the timing of the realignment of the magnetization vector of water protons, whose resonance is measured in the MRI diagnostic purposes. Because neoplastic lesions are richer in water than the surrounding area and that the contrast medium tends to become established, it results in a sharper image. The CA, conveyed by the blood stream, reaches the ROI after a few seconds: if this presents an anomaly and the presence of excessive blood vessels, the greatest concentration and the different modes of perfusion of the CA, allowing to reveal the structure. This results in an enrichment (enhancement) of the return signal, and consequently in an increase in intensity in the image that presents a distinct coloration in the correspondence of the lesion.

The perfusion dynamics of the CA is normally described through an intensity/time curve or EC.

In the EC the abscissa shows the acquisition time of the signal and on the ordinate the value of average intensity of the signal. Specifically, considering different images belonging to a sequence it is possible to define the EC (Fig. 27.1) as

$$I(T_n, \bar{x}, \bar{y}) = [i(T_n, \bar{x}, \bar{y}) - i_0(\bar{x}, \bar{y})] \tag{1}$$

where $i(T_n, \bar{x}, \bar{y})$ is the intensity of the pixel of coordinate $(\bar{x}, \bar{y})$ at the sample time T_n; $i_0(\bar{x}, \bar{y})$ is the basal value (ie, the mean value of the intensity registered before the perfusion of the CA and assumed as background noise).

For each image pixel (x, y), corresponding to a perfused tissue position, the time series of the values $f_n(x, y)$ evaluated in each single images f_n of the temporal sequence yields the individual local time-intensity curve. Hence, the EC represents how the intensity of the backscattered signal changes in

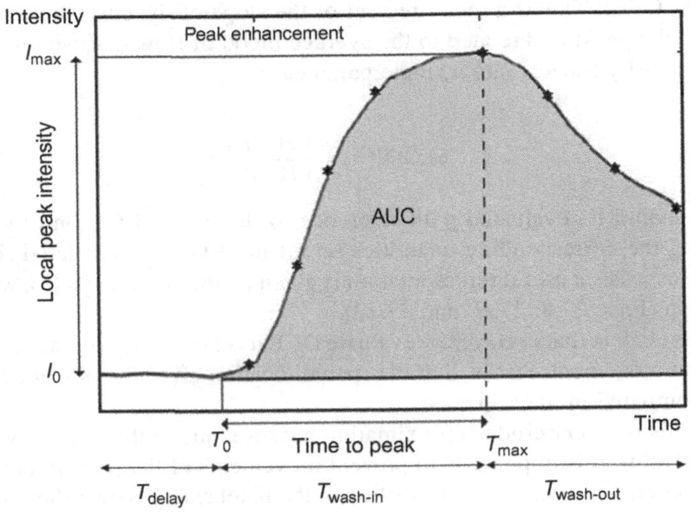

FIGURE 27.1

Enhancement curve and parameters.

function of the perfusion of the CA in correspondence of each pixel inside the ROI. Through a curve-fitting approach, four local parameters (useful for diagnoses) can be calculated from the analysis of the EC:

- Area under curve (AUC): This represents the area under the EC; it measures the quantity of CA absorbed by the region investigated; hence it yields an estimation of blood flow that diffuses into the region:

$$\mathrm{AUC}(A) = \sum_{k=1}^{M} \left\{ (T_k - T_{k-1}) \frac{1}{N} \sum_{(x,y) \in A}^{N} [i(T_k, x, y) - i_0(x, y)] \right\} \quad (2)$$

  All the quantities are referred to the ROI A that includes N pixels, and with respect to a time sequence composed by M frames.
- Local peak intensity (LPI): This is the maximum increment of the intensity with respect to the baseline intensity i_0 (pure tissue without any CA effects). This quantity gives an estimation of the maximal quantity of blood that, at a given instant, comes to the region:

$$\mathrm{LPI}(A) = \max_k \left(\max_{(x,y) \in A} [i(T_k, x, y) - i_0(x, y)] \right) \quad (3)$$

  where the max operator is evaluated with respect to all the frames into the sequences and for all pixels inside the ROI.
- Time to peak (TTP): This is the time when the intensity reaches its maximum value. It gives an indication about whether this region is directly supplied with blood or through revascularization:

$$\mathrm{TTP}(A) = T_k := [i(T_k, x, y) - i_0(x, y)] \equiv \mathrm{LPI}(A) \quad (4)$$

- Average rise (SLOPE): This is a measurement of the slope of the curve between the started rising point and the peak; it is related to the average blood of flow perfusion in the ROI and joins temporal and intensity aspects into a single parameter:

$$\mathrm{SLOPE}(A) = \frac{\mathrm{LPI}(A)}{\mathrm{TTP}(A)} \tag{5}$$

These parameters should be evaluated with reference to the whole ROI (and in this case they are estimated averaging the corresponding quantities on all the ROI) or calculated separately for each single pixel. In the last case, a useful representation is given by the color maps [3], which are explained in the results section (Figs. 27.8, 27.10 and 27.12).

From Eq. (1) it is evident that to correctly evaluate DCE it is necessary to guarantee that along all the sequence there is no movement; that is, that the spatial location $(\bar{x}, \bar{y})$ remains the same portion in all the images to be compared in the sequence.

Unfortunately, this is a very crude approximation because, due to the relatively long time of DCE procedure (up to 10 min), it is impossible to prevent movements of the patient, breathing, peristalsis, and so forth. The consequences are that the position of the pixel changes over the time; that is, we have to rewrite Eq. (1) in the following way:

$$I(T_n, \bar{x}, \bar{y}) = [i(T_n, x(T_n), y(T_n)) - i_0(\bar{x}, \bar{y})] \tag{6}$$

where $x(T_n)$ represents the abscissa (respectively, $y(T_n)$ the ordinate) of the point $(\bar{x}, \bar{y})$ at the sample time T_n as illustrated in Fig. 27.2.

In other terms, there is the need of compensating the displacement of the point $(\bar{x}, \bar{y})$ along the time to correctly calculate DCE. A simple way to reduce the effect of artifacts induced by the movements is to obtain EC with respect to a set of pixels; that is, evaluating an averaging EC on a given area or eventually on the whole ROI:

$$I_{\mathrm{ROI}}(T_k) = \frac{1}{N} \sum_{(x, y) \in \mathrm{ROI}} [i(T_k, x, y) - i_0(x, y)] \tag{7}$$

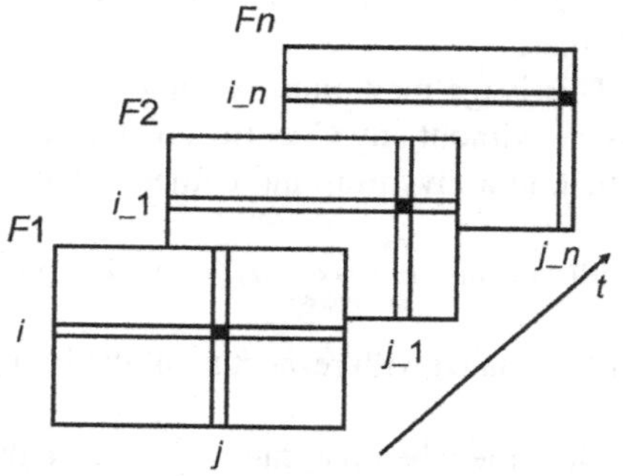

FIGURE 27.2

Temporal evaluation: the position of the pixel changes on each frame of the sequence.

In this way, small movements are partially absorbed. Unfortunately, this is a very simple method that considerably reduces the discrimination, and appears ineffective for the early analysis of cancerous lesions. To overcome such a drawback, we illustrate in the next section a strategy to compensate for artifacts without affecting the discrimination capabilities of the DCE. To this aim we exploit the capabilities of the active contours to dynamically adopt the morphological changes as a tool for "tracking" the ROI in the different images and, hence, compensate their movements.

27.3 ACTIVE CONTOUR

Active contour models (or snakes), introduced in [8] are deformable contours that have been used in many image analysis applications, including the image-based tracking of rigid and nonrigid objects, they represent a special case of the general multidimensional deformable model theory [9].

In their basic forms, the mathematical formulation draws from the theory of optimal approximation involving a functional. A traditional snake is a parametric contour embedded in the image plane $(x, y) \in \mathfrak{R}^2$. The contour is represented as a parametric curve:

$$V(s) = [X(s), Y(s)] \tag{8}$$

where $X(s)$ and $Y(s)$ are the coordinate functions and $s \in [0, 1]$ is the parametric domain. This curve is generally obtained using B-splines functions [5,6,10,11] that allow one to depict a continuous and smoothing parameterized contour. B-splines are a particular, computationally convenient representation for spline functions. In the B-spline form, a spline function $V(s)$ is constructed as a weighted sum of N_B basis functions (hence, B-splines) $B_n(s), n = 1, \ldots, N_B$; where, in the simplest (regular) case, each basis function consists of d polynomials each defined over a span of the *s-axis*, having unit length. The basic idea of the B-splines is that it is possible to obtain a contour as a combination of a set of curve as a replication of a basis function. For each basis function, $B_j(s)$, a control point $q_j = \left(q_j^x, q_j^y\right)^T$ must be defined and the curve is a weighted vector sum of those control points, written as follows:

$$V(s) = \sum_{j=1}^{N_B} B_j(s) \cdot q_j \tag{9}$$

where $B_j(s)$ is the polynomial basis function, s is the curve parameter, and $V(s) = [X(s); Y(s)]$ is a point in the 2-D image. In the presented approach, we use a simple quadratic B-spline. The first B-spline basis function $B_0(s)$ has the following form:

$$B_0(s) = \begin{cases} \dfrac{s^2}{2} & \forall s \in [0,1) \\ \dfrac{3}{4} - \left(s - \dfrac{3}{4}\right)^2 & \forall s \in [1,2) \\ \dfrac{(s-3)^2}{2} & \forall s \in [2,3) \\ 0 & \text{otherwise} \end{cases} \tag{10}$$

and the rest are mere translated copies of the first one.

One may rewrite the sum in Eq. (9), taking into account that active contours are closed lines and by using the arithmetic modular, as follows:

$$V(s) = \sum_{i=j-2}^{j} B_0(s-j) \cdot q_{1+\,\mathrm{mod}(i,N_B)} \tag{11}$$

By varying the number and the location of the control points it is possible to change the contour smoothness and its ability to fit a generic figure.

It is possible to associate to each Active Contour (AC) an energy function [8,12–14,20], which represents a measurement:

$$E^{(i)}_{\text{snake}} = E^{(i)}_{\text{internal}} - E^{(i)}_{\text{external}} \tag{12}$$

where the first term is the internal energy and the second one expresses the external energy at the ith position of the contour. The internal energy is used to control the rate of stretch and to prevent discontinuity in the contour and can be defined as follows:

$$E_{\text{int}} = \frac{1}{2}\int_0^1 \left[\alpha\left(\left|\frac{dX}{ds}\right|^2 + \left|\frac{dY}{ds}\right|^2\right) + \beta\left(\left|\frac{d^2X}{ds^2}\right|^2 + \left|\frac{d^2Y}{ds^2}\right|^2\right)\right] ds \tag{13}$$

where α and β are weighting parameters that control the snake's tension and rigidity, respectively. The first term in Eq. (13) is related to the contour elasticity, while the second term specifies the contour's strength and resistance against sudden changes.

The second term in Eq. (12) represents the external energy, which moves a snake to the feature of interest (eg, borders) in an image. This value will be minimal when the snake arrives at the features of interest. It can be defined as follows:

$$E_{\text{ext}} = \int_0^1 (f[X(s), Y(s)])ds \tag{14}$$

$$f(x,y) = -|\nabla G_\sigma(x,y) \times I(x,y)| \tag{15}$$

where $I(x,y)$ is a gray-level image and $G_\sigma(x,y)$ is a Gaussian function.

The filter effects are to make a surface uniform, eliminating spikes and ripples due to noise and to blur the image, whereas the gradient effect is to find out the edge of the image and make the external energy responsible for the attractive action toward the edges themselves [8,13].

The contour and its energy function depend only on the N_B control points location; hence, the problem is to find the best contour that approximates the edge of the ROI. From a mathematical point of view, this can be reduced to the minimization of the energy function (Eq. 12). The optimum location of the snake are searched so that the snake energy can be minimized. A snake that minimizes E_{snake} satisfies the Euler equation. With respect to Eqs. (12)–(14) one obtains

$$\frac{\delta X}{\delta \tau} = -\alpha\frac{d^2X}{ds^2} + \beta\frac{d^4X}{ds^4} - \kappa\frac{\delta f}{\delta x} \tag{16}$$

$$\frac{\delta Y}{\delta \tau} = -\alpha\frac{d^2Y}{ds^2} + \beta\frac{d^4Y}{ds^4} - \kappa\frac{\delta f}{\delta y} \tag{17}$$

The previous equations do not admit a closed-form solution. Numerical techniques, such as gradient descend method (GDM), provide a method for unconstrained minimization based on the use of search direction opposite to the gradient. A physical interpretation of Euler equations can be viewed as a force balance equation that drives the snake toward the minimum contribution of the corresponding energy by changing the coordinates of the contour according to the images characteristics.

$$F_{\text{int}} + F_{\text{ext}} = 0 \tag{18}$$

Each term of Eqs. (16), (17) is the combination of two different types of forces, internal and external, whose contributions is properly weighted by the parameters α, β, k. The internal forces can be classified as elastic and bending forces that prevent the contour from stretching and bending while the external force plays an attractive action toward the edge of the ROI. Applying the GDM, one obtains the following iterative equations, which are the discrete version of Eqs. (16), (17):

$$X^{k+1} = X^k + \left(F^k_{x(\text{elastic})} - F^k_{x(\text{bending})} + F^k_{x(\text{external})}\right)\Delta \tag{19}$$

$$Y^{k+1} = Y + \left(F^k_{y(\text{elastic})} - F^k_{y(\text{bending})} + F^k_{y(\text{external})}\right)\Delta \tag{20}$$

where X^{k+1} and Y^{k+1} collect the coordinates of the new contour while X^k and Y^k collect the same quantity for the current one; k is the iteration index and Δ is the algorithm step. Eqs. (19), (20) produce a sequence of contour point locations that minimize more and more the energy of the snake; the process is generally stopped when the next iteration does not introduce a significant change of the total energy (Eq. 12). The crucial point to guarantee the rapid convergence of the iterative equations is the need to adopt as initial contour points (ie, X_0, Y_0) belonging to a region sufficiently close to the actual contour.

27.4 METHODOLOGY AND IMPLEMENTATION

From this premise, we propose to face this problem following two steps: (1) precisely identify the contour of the ROI (organ or lesion) in a particular image and (2) establish a correspondence among the positions of such ROIs in the different images that compose a sequence.

In the following, we illustrate how active contours have been implemented and used to evaluate EC compensating the artifacts induced by movements (Fig. 27.3).

The proposed algorithm has been implemented in MATLAB R2013a environment and is composed by the following steps.

27.4.1 SELECT ROI

To realize the segmentation of an anatomical structure it is necessary to initialize a contour that contains the ROI. This is a manual activity, and we ask the medical doctor to define a contour of the ROI on one of the images of the sequence (if necessary, the first one). Specifically, the medical doctor has to click several times on the contour of the ROI.

The selected points are then interpolated to obtain an initial contour that will subsequently be subject to optimization via active contours.

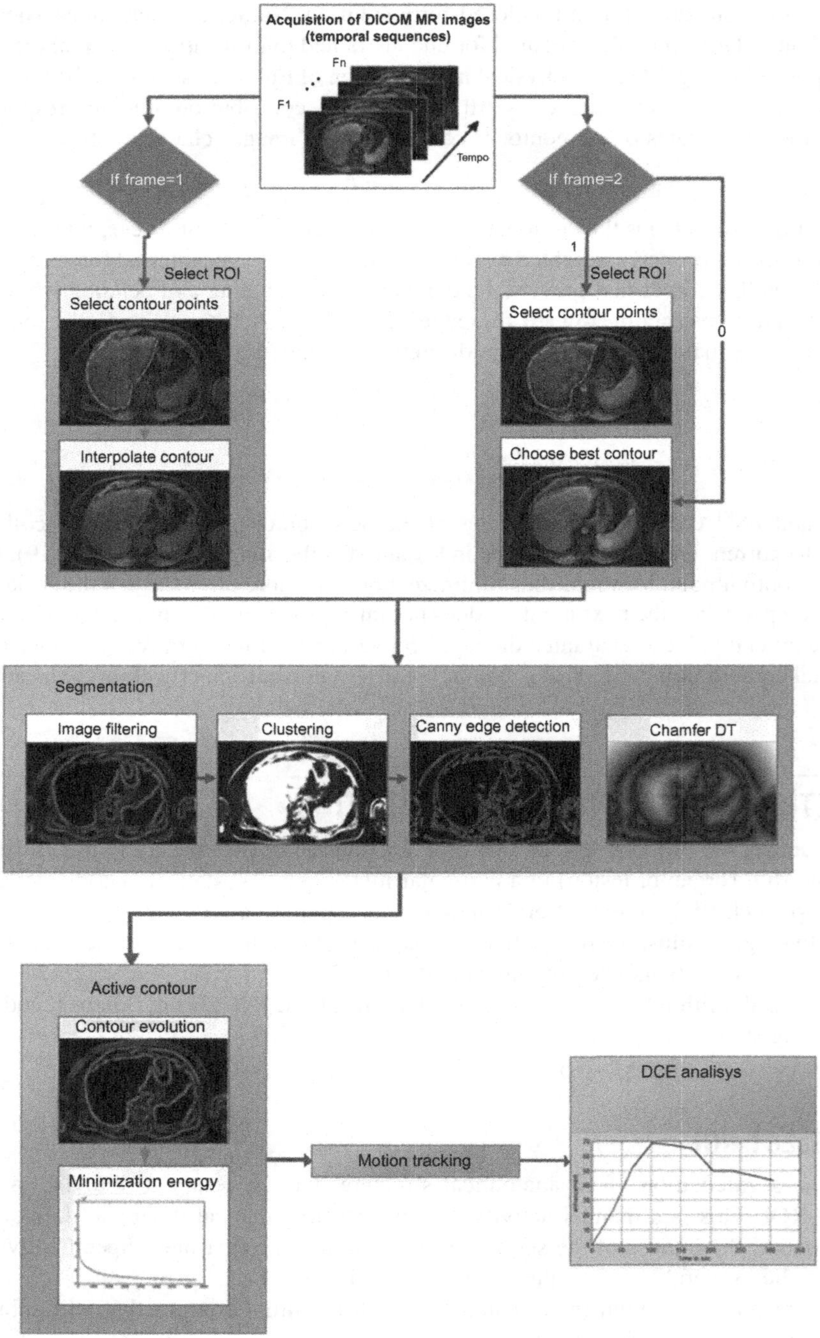

FIGURE 27.3

Flow chart algorithm.

27.4.2 IDENTIFICATION OF THE ROI

27.4.2.1 Image filtering

The external energy requires computing the gradient of the image previously convolved with a Gaussian smoothing filter. This, which corresponds to a low-pass filter, removes the high spatial frequencies allowing the removal of any peaks or ripples due to noise.

27.4.2.2 Clustering

To make more crisp and sharp contrast, and to allow an easier tracking by the snake of the edge of interest, we resorted to the use a fuzzy C-means clustering algorithm. Applying this algorithm, we obtain a matrix that returns information about the degree of membership of each object in each of the clusters where one wants to partition.

27.4.2.3 Canny edge

The Canny algorithm [15] basically finds edges where the grayscale intensity of the image changes the most. These areas are found by determining gradients of the image. It works in a multistage process. First, the image is smoothed by Gaussian convolution, then two-dimensional first derivatives are computed, and the gradient magnitude (edge strength) and gradient direction are calculated. The first-order derivative of an image $f(x,y)$ at location (x,y) is defined as the two-dimensional vector

$$G[f(x,y)] == \begin{bmatrix} G_x \\ G_y \end{bmatrix} = \begin{bmatrix} \frac{\partial f}{\partial x} \\ \frac{\partial f}{\partial y} \end{bmatrix} \tag{21}$$

The absolute gradient magnitude is given by the Euclidean distance measure

$$|G[f(x,y)]| = \left|G_x^2 + G_y^2\right|^{1/2} \tag{22}$$

where G_x and G_y are the gradients in the x- and y-directions, respectively.

The gradient direction (edge orientation) is defined as

$$\theta = \arctan\left(\frac{|G_y|}{|G_x|}\right) \tag{23}$$

Next, for each pixel we estimate the direction of the gradient, and it is classified as an edge point along this direction only if the gradient is greater than the two adjacent pixels; otherwise the value of the pixel is set to zero (*nonmaxima suppression*). Finally, using a double threshold to eliminate the pixels that have a gradient less than the low threshold (probably due to noise), and keep those that exceed the upper threshold (classified as an edge point).

The implemented Canny edge detector represents the best performance both visually and quantitatively based on the measures such as mean square distance, error edge map, and signal-to-noise ratio. The Gaussian smoothing in the Canny edge detector fulfills two purposes: first it can be used to control the amount of detail that appears in the edge image, and second it can be used to suppress noise. The image that resulted from the Canny edge detector is used to calculate the Chamfer distance transform.

27.4.2.4 Chamfer distance transform

One problem with traditional snake formulations is the limited capture range. The initial contour must, in general, be close to the true boundary; otherwise it will likely converge to the wrong result. In fact, when the initial projected contour is far from the contour of the specific organ under investigation and residing in an homogeneous region in an image, the processing time could be overlong, due to the fact that the image gradient magnitude would be zero and consequently there will be little or no edge force (f_x,f_y) able to act on the contour itself. Among the methods proposed to address this problem, we use distance potential forces (DPFs). The basic idea is to increase the capture range of the external force fields and to guide the contour toward the desired boundary. In [12] an external force model is proposed that significantly increases the capture range of a traditional snake. These external forces are the negative gradient of a potential function that is computed using a Euclidean (or Chamfer) distance. This DPF is an additional contribution to the external force, whose aim is to carry out the action on the contour attraction, making it converge toward the edge of interest, whether the region is homogeneous or not. We customized the DPF (normally computed only on binary images), referring to the mean intensity of pixels of the region taken into account, and by adding its contribution to the external force. The value of the distance map at each pixel is obtained by calculating the distance between the pixel and the closest boundary point based on Chamfer distance. The Chamfer distance transformation [16] is a very good approximation of the Euclidean distance transformation without having its high computational cost. By defining the potential energy function based on the distance map, one can obtain a potential force field that has a large attraction range. Given a computed distance map, one way to define a corresponding potential energy is as follows:

$$D(x,y) = \min_{(p,q)\in[(a,b):I(a,b)=1]}[d(x,y;p,q)] \tag{24}$$

where $d(x,y;p,q)$ is the distance between a generic point of the image (x,y) and those of coordinates (p,q). In this way a potential force field is generated such that the new coordinates of the contour are obtained by adding the following terms:

$$F_{x(\text{external})} = -\delta \times \frac{\partial D}{\partial x} \tag{25}$$

$$F_{y(\text{external})} = -\delta \times \frac{\partial D}{\partial y} \tag{26}$$

27.4.3 ACTIVE CONTOUR

Once the distance map and magnitude of the gradient image are defined, we deform the initial contour by applying forces obtained by minimizing the energy functional as mentioned above (recall that the external force is given by the sum of the force calculated on the gradient image and that calculated on the distance map). The coordinates of the snake are updated at each iteration during the evolution of the algorithm. This operation is repeated until it is deemed that an equilibrium position is attained. The solutions adopted are: verify when the distance between the current contour and the previous does not exceed a predetermined limit; and operate the same analysis in terms of energy, taking into account the values assumed by the functional.

27.4.4 EXTENDING THE BOUNDARIES OF THE ENTIRE TEMPORAL SEQUENCE

In the passage from one slice to the next, the best contour obtained by the previous slice is projected together with the boundaries of the first slice (ie, those generated from the medical doctor inputs) on the current image. Then, the algorithm evaluates the contour that best fits the ROI in the actual slice starting from both these two initial profiles. At the end of the process, the algorithm identifies on each single slice belonging to the temporal sequence of DCE the best contour that bounds the ROI.

27.5 TRACKING MOTION

As mentioned in the introduction, organs and lesions examined via the DCE procedure can change their shapes and positions over time, due to motion artifacts. Therefore, there is the need to track the motion of the ROIs along the different images that compose the DCE sequence to compensate such displacement. In our work we compensate these movements by automatically identifying the contour of the ROI on each single image in the sequence, using the AC method to capture the deformation of the ROI itself, and compensating the movement in the different images by superimposing a rototranslation [17,18]. In other words, to keep track of the ROI movement in the sequence of images, we first identify the contour of the ROI, and then we apply these quantities to compensate the artifact. In other terms, we assume in the compensation plane that the different ROI can be considered as a rigid body. Computing image-to-image coordinates of the center of mass and the rotation angle, it is possible to reconstruct the motion associated with the anatomical ROI in terms of rototranslation. The calculation of the center of mass and of the principal axes of inertia requires the knowledge of the moments of the first and second order [19]. The moments are calculated by applying the following general formula:

$$m_{p,q} = \sum_{y=0}^{M} \sum_{x=0}^{N} x^p y^q I(x, y) \tag{27}$$

The first-order moments are used for the assessment of the center of mass coordinates x_c and y_c:

$$x_c = \frac{\sum_{y=0}^{M} \sum_{x=0}^{N} xI(x, y)}{\sum_{x=0}^{M} \sum_{y=0}^{N} I(x, y)} \tag{28}$$

$$y_c = \frac{\sum_{y=0}^{M} \sum_{x=0}^{N} yI(x, y)}{\sum_{x=0}^{M} \sum_{y=0}^{N} I(x, y)} \tag{29}$$

where N and M, respectively, are the number of rows and columns that compose the desired image matrix.

The second-order moments are used for the assessment of the principal axis of inertia. The orientation of the principal axes with respect to the first slice reference framework is given by

$$\varphi = 0.5 \times \arctan\left(\frac{2 \times \mu_{11}}{\mu_{20} - \mu_{02}}\right) \tag{30}$$

where φ is the angle between the reference axis and the principal axes of inertia and where μ are the central moments

$$\mu_{20} = \sum_{y=0}^{M}\sum_{x=0}^{N}(x - x_c)^2 \times I(x, y) \tag{31}$$

$$\mu_{02} = \sum_{y=0}^{M}\sum_{x=0}^{N}(y - y_c)^2 \times I(x, y) \tag{32}$$

$$\mu_{11} = \sum_{y=0}^{M}\sum_{x=0}^{N}(x - x_c) \times (y - y_c) \times I(x, y) \tag{33}$$

Computing, image-by-image, the coordinates of the center of mass and the rotation angles, it is possible to reconstruct the movements associated with the ROI in terms of rototranslation (Fig. 27.4).

On the image on the left, we project the direct image of P_n point to emphasize the erroneous calculation that should be induced in the absence of the motion compensation. Indeed, the effective corresponding point of P_n, is the point $P_{n\to 0}$; that is, that obtained considering the corrective action.

Mathematically the generic point of the coordinate (x_n^P, y_n^P) inside to the ROI in the nth image, corresponds, in the first image, to the point of coordinates

$$P_{n\to 0} = \begin{pmatrix} x_{n\to 0}^{p} \\ y_{n\to 0}^{p} \end{pmatrix} = R_{T_n}^{T_0} P_n + \Delta_{T_n}^{T_0} \tag{34}$$

where $R_{T_n}^{T_0}$ is the rotation matrix, and $\Delta_{T_n}^{T_0}$ is the contribution in translation given by the difference between the x and y components of the centers of masses of the ROI in the nth image and first image respectively. In order to evaluate the EC curve by compensating the motion of the ROI, Eq. (1) can be rewritten as

$$I(T_n, x, y) = \left[i\left(T_n, R_{T_n}^{T_0}(x_\alpha, y_\alpha)\right) + \Delta_{T_n}^{T_0}(x_\alpha, y_\alpha)\right] - i_0(x, y) \tag{35}$$

where (x, y) are the center of mass locations on the first image, i_0 is the baseline intensity of the ROI, (x_α, y_α) is the coordinates of the generic point in the nth image, which projection, on the first image is the point (x, y).

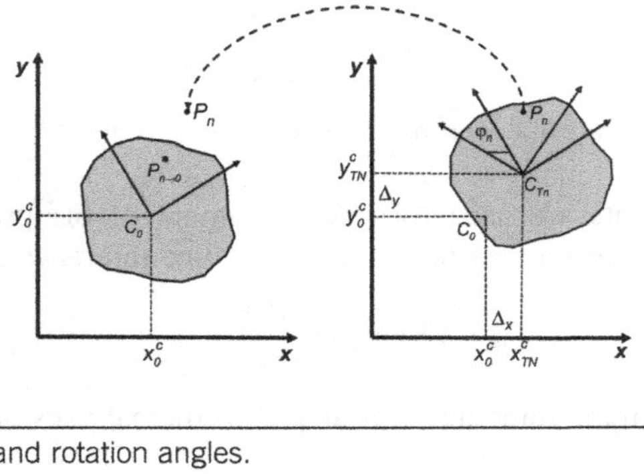

FIGURE 27.4

Center of mass displacement and rotation angles.

27.6 RESULTS

The algorithm was developed with the aim to improve the quality of postconstrastographic DCE analysis of time series using images from digital imaging and communications in medicine (DICOM) DCE-MRI. Specifically, we applied the algorithm on four types of internal organs: liver, spleen, kidney, and bowel wall, affected by disease. In Table 27.1 we report the parameters setting for different tissue objects of study in our work.

Results are reported by comparing two different approaches:

- *DCE standard*: DCE analysis without any corrective action on ROI.
- *DCE tracking motion with AC correction*: DCE analysis of rototranslated sequences through corrective actions obtained with AC segmentation.

Results are compared on an EC and color maps. For reasons of space, we report only the maps relating to AUC. The color maps AUC provides additional information on the vascularity of the diseased tissue. The more intense the color, the higher the concentration of the CA, as the presence of the lesion increases the local vascularization.

In Fig. 27.5 we superimpose in black to the liver the optimal contour identified in the first slice of the sequence. It is evident how some parts of the liver are now out of the contour; that is, the liver moved during the time. To compensate such displacement a new contour is evaluated (those represented by the white line). It is also represented, by the gray line, the correction obtained by rototranslation. The same phenomena is evident also for the kidney as shown in Fig. 27.6 and for bowel wall in Fig. 27.7.

In Figs. 27.9, 27.11, 27.13 it is shown that the EC is evaluated considering and neglecting the artifact induced by movements.

As mentioned before the net effects of errors induced by movements are more evident when the analysis is performed on a small area, as done when evaluating a 2-D color map.

Table 27.1 Parameter Setting for Different Regions: σ is the Standard Deviation; α, β, k, δ are the Weight for the Elastic, Bending, External, and Distance Potential Forces; and Δ is the Algorithm Step

	Liver	Kidneys	Spleen	Bowel Wall
Filter Dim	30 × 30	15 × 15	15 × 15	15 × 15
σ	3	2.5	2.5	3
α	0.3	0.3	0.3	0.3
β	0.03	0.02	0.03	0.02
κ	0.015	0.01	0.015	0.01
δ	0.05	0.05	0.05	0.05
Δ	0.5	0.5	0.5	0.5

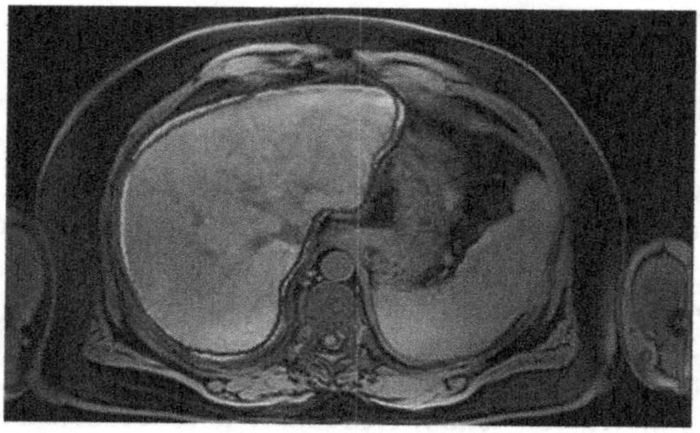

FIGURE 27.5

Liver motion: the initial contour of the specific image (black), the final optimized contour of the specific image (white), and the rototranslated contour (gray).

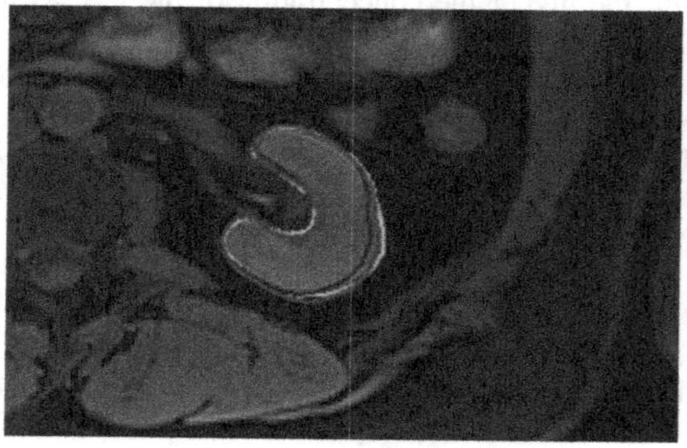

FIGURE 27.6

Kidney motion: the initial contour of the specific image (black), the final optimized contour of the specific image (white), and the rototranslated contour (gray).

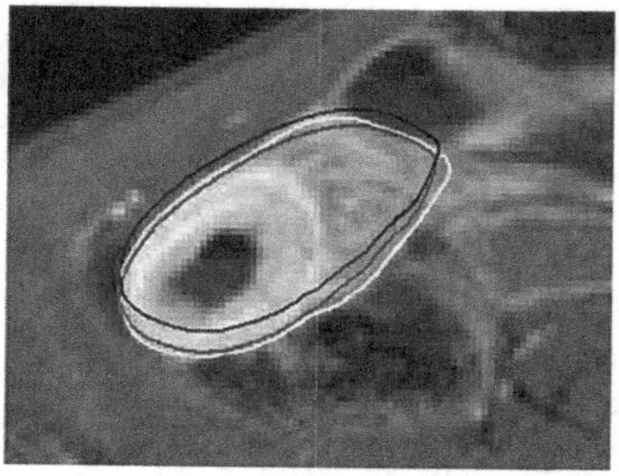

FIGURE 27.7

Bowel wall motion: the initial contour of the specific image (black), the final optimized contour of the specific image (white), and the rototranslated contour (gray).

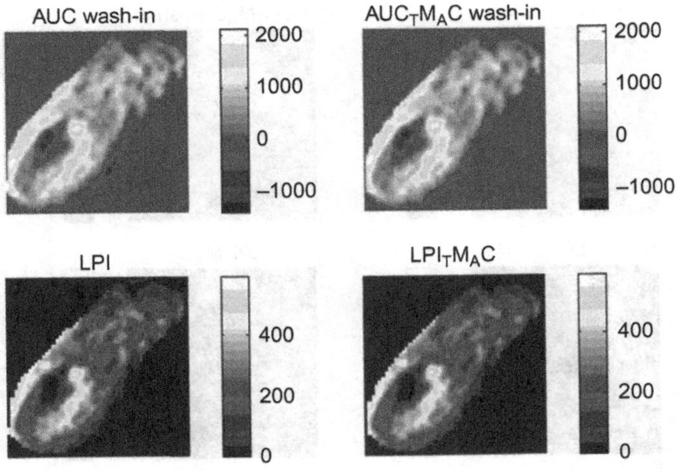

FIGURE 27.8

AUC and LPI color maps comparison: with *(left)* standard DCE analysis, and correct action by AC of bowel wall.

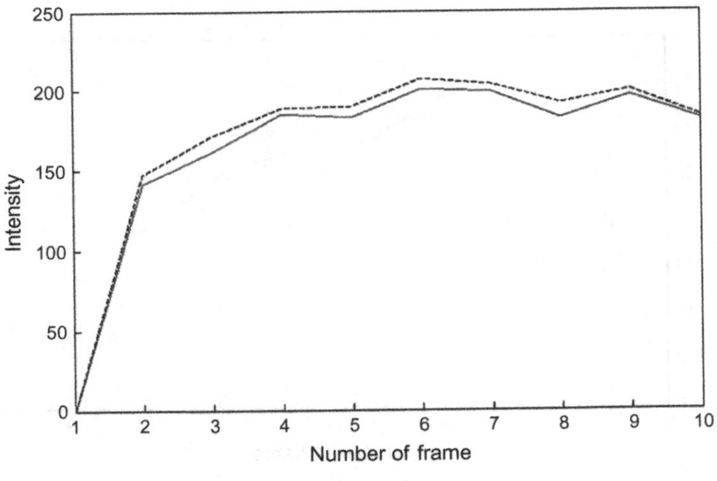

FIGURE 27.9

Enhancement curve comparison of bowel wall: before motion correction *(line)* and after motion correction *(dashed line)*.

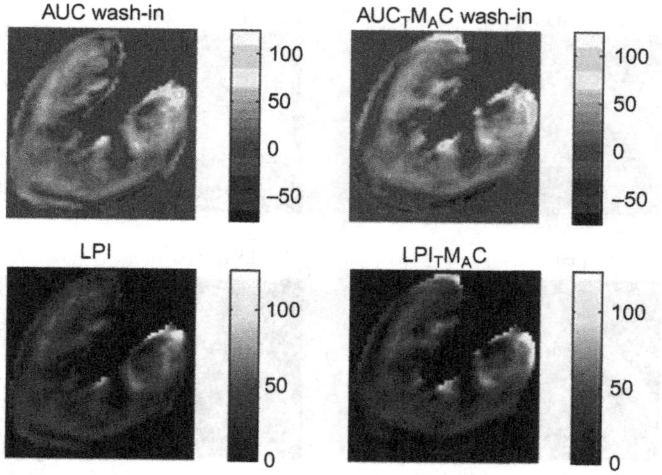

FIGURE 27.10

AUC and LPI color maps comparison: with *(left)* standard DCE analysis, and correct action by AC of left kidney.

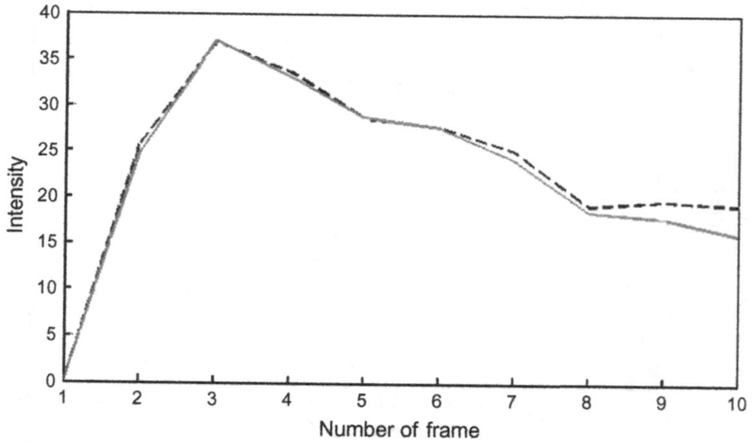

FIGURE 27.11

Enhancement curve comparison of kidney: before motion correction *(line)* and after motion correction *(dashed line)*.

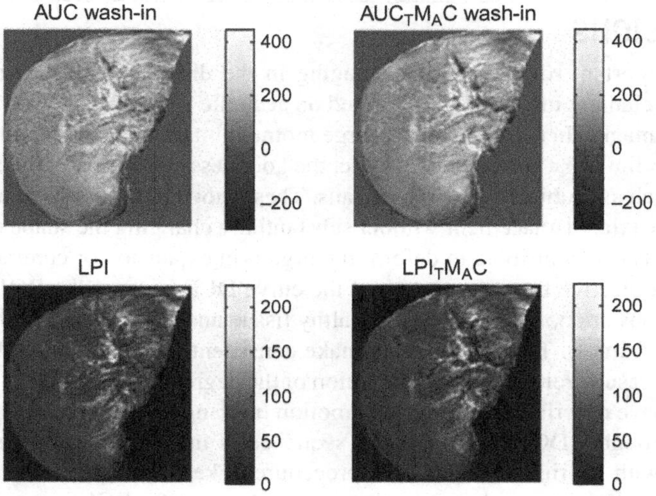

FIGURE 27.12

AUC and LPI color maps comparison: with *(left)* standard DCE analysis, and correct action by AC of liver.

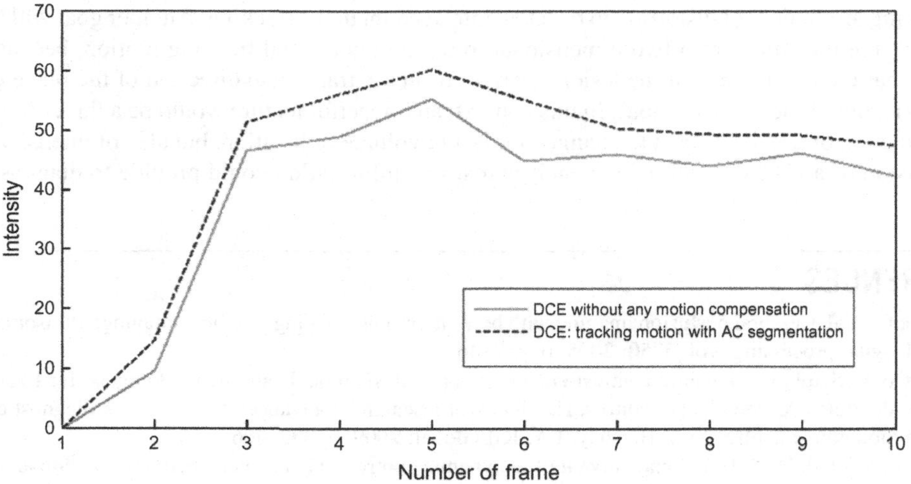

FIGURE 27.13

Enhancement curve comparison of liver: before motion correction *(line)* and after motion correction *(dashed line)*.

27.7 CONCLUSIONS

The increasingly important role of medical imaging in the diagnosis and treatment of disease has opened a number of challenging problems centered on accurate geometric models of anatomical structures from medical images. In this foreword, a large momentum has been assumed by such an invasive technique as DCE. A limit that can adversely affect the goodness evaluation of the EC is represented by the movements, which are subject to internal organs. These movements are induced by respiration and may contribute to an axial displacement without substantially changing the shape of the organ, such as peristaltic movements can contribute to deform the organ (in expansion or contraction). These movements do not make objective the construction of the curve DCE because the ROI could analyze each time the tissue portions are not correlated (ie, healthy tissue and diseased tissue that occupy the same position in different frames). The purpose is to make consistent the information they are to aggregate and then provide the results relating to the evaluation of the degree of disease of a specific organ/tissue. In this chapter, we have described an analysis of motion tracking, which consists of estimating the trajectory of a ROI through a DCE-MRI temporal sequence of images under the assumption of movements associated with a rigid body. This procedure takes advantage of applying the same movement of rototranslation to each pixel belonging to the specific ROI time sequence of images.

Using the method of active contours to define the deformation of the ROI, one can identify the center of mass and of the main axis for each frame and obtain a useful first approximation for compensating the displacement that occurs between two images. Obviously most of the human body does not conform to a rigid approximation and most of the state-of-the-art works in registration involve the development of nonrigid registration techniques for applications such as correcting soft tissue deformation during imaging.

A first improvement for the future is to relax the assumptions of rigid body motion of the lesion, introducing an element of distortion to be taken into account in the tracking. Another goal will be represented by the transition from two-dimensional to three-dimensional tracking motion, because it was noticed that the movements of the lesions also occur in the transverse direction of the plane of single section (ie, out of the plane motion). In this context, an impactful feature would be a three-dimensional reconstruction of organs subject to change, not just in volume or location, but also of intensity (related to perfusion of a CA) with all the advantages that this information could provide to diagnosis.

REFERENCES

[1] Kier C, et al. Cerebral perfusion imaging with bolus harmonic imaging. Medical imaging: ultrasonic imaging and signal processing, vol. 5750; 2005. p. 437–46.
[2] Russo V, Setola R. Dynamic contrast enhancement analysis models and methodologies. In: Exarchos TP, Papadopoulos A, Fotiadis DI, editors. Handbook of research on advanced techniques in diagnostic imaging and biomedical applications. Hershey, PA: IGI Global; 2009. p. 392–406.
[3] Russo V, et al. DyCoH: an innovative tool to dynamic contrast enhancement analysis, In: 29th annual international conference of the IEEE EMBS Lyon, France; 2007. p. 63–6.
[4] McInerney T, Terzopoulos D. Deformable models in medical image analysis: a survey. Med Image Anal 1996;1(2):91–108.
[5] Stammberger T, et al. Interobserver reproducibility of quantitative cartilage measurements: comparison of B-Spline snakes and manual segmentation. Magn Reson Imaging 1999;17(3):1033–42.

[6] Stammberger T, Rudert S, Michaelis M, Reiser M, Englmeier KH. Segmentation of MR images with B-spline snakes: a multiresolution approach using the distance transformation for model forces. In: Proceedings of the 2nd workshop on Image Processing for Medicine, BVM'98, Aachen (Germany). 1998. p. 164–8.
[7] Russo V, Setola R. Tracking motion of deformable organ in DCE framework. In: Proceeding 18th World Congress of the International Federation of Automatic Control (IFAC), vol. 18, Pt 1; 2011. p. 9627–32.
[8] Kass A, Witkin M, Terzepoulos D. Snakes: active contour models. Int J Comput Vis 1987;1(4):321–31.
[9] Terzopoulos D. On matching deformable models to images. Technical Report 60. Schlumberger Palo Alto research; 1986. Reprinted in Topical Meeting on Machine Vision, Technical Digest Series, vol. 12; 1987. p. 160–7.
[10] Lingrand D, Montagnat J. Level set and B-spline deformable model techniques for image segmentation: a pragmatic comparative study. Lect Notes Comput Sci 2005;3540:25–34.
[11] Pottmann S, Hofer M, Leopoldseder H. Approximation with active B-spline curves and surfaces. In: 10th Pacific conference on computer graphics and applications; 2002. p. 8–25.
[12] Cohen LD. On active contour model and balloons. Comput Vis Graph Image Process: Image Underst 1991;52 (2):211–8.
[13] Xu C, Prince L. Snakes, shapes and gradient vector flow. IEEE Trans Image Process 1998;7(3):259–369.
[14] Yilmaz A, Javed O, Shah M. Object tracking: a survey. ACM Comput Surv 2006;38(4):1–45.
[15] Canny J. A computational approach to edge detection. IEEE Trans Pattern Anal Mach Intell 1986; 8(6):679–98.
[16] Butt MA, Maragos P. Optimal Design of Chamfer Distance Transforms. IEEE Trans on Image Processing Oct. 1998;7(10):1477–84.
[17] Gyftakis S, Agouris P, Stefanidis A. Image-based change detection of areal objects using differential snakes. In: Proceedings of the 13th annual ACM international workshop on geographic information systems; 2005. p. 135–42.
[18] Pards M, Sayrol E. Motion estimation based tracking of active contours. Pattern Recogn Lett 2001;22 (13):1447–56.
[19] Gupta S, et al. Fast method for correcting image misregistration due to organ motion in time-series MRI data. Magn Reson Med 2003;49:506–14.
[20] Acton ST, Ray N. Biomedical Image Analysis: Tracking. In: A. C. Bovik, Ed. Morgan and Claypool: San Rafael, CA; 2006.

CHAPTER

28

PHASE III PLACEBO-CONTROLLED, RANDOMIZED CLINICAL TRIAL WITH SYNTHETIC CROHN'S DISEASE PATIENTS TO EVALUATE TREATMENT RESPONSE

V. Abedi*,[a], P. Lu*,[a], R. Hontecillas*, M. Verma*, G.A. Vess*, C.W. Philipson†, A. Carbo†, A. Leber*, N.T. Juni*, S. Hoops*, J. Bassaganya-Riera*

Nutritional Immunology and Molecular Medicine Laboratory, Virginia Bioinformatics Institute, Virginia Tech, Blacksburg, VA, United States BioTherapeutics Inc., Blacksburg, VA, United States†*

28.1 INTRODUCTION

Crohn's disease (CD) and ulcerative colitis (UC) are two clinical manifestations of inflammatory bowel disease (IBD). Current epidemiology data suggest that there are over 630,000 cases of CD in North America, with an increasing global incidence at 25% rates [1]. CD is a chronic relapsing inflammatory condition that affects mainly the gastrointestinal tract with extraintestinal manifestations caused by a combination of genetic susceptibility factors, environmental triggers, and immune dysregulation [2–5]. The current treatment for the most severe cases of this condition is the use of antitumor necrosis factor α (TNF-α) antibodies with an attempt to stimulate mucosal healing. Despite significant adverse side effects of this treatment including cancer, infection, and death, there are no effective substitutes in the market [6,7]. Thus, there is an unmet clinical need for safer and more effective CD therapeutics. Over the past decade many studies have explored the use of new therapeutics for the treatment of CD; however, even with a strong mechanism of action and promising preclinical data, clinical studies have failed [8–10]. The lack of success may be attributed to a number of factors, which includes inadequate dosing, population selection, drug inefficacy, or insufficient design optimization. Therefore, there is an urgent need to reinvent the design of preclinical studies to achieve superior results during the Phase I, II, and III clinical testing that would aid in the acceleration of New Drug Application filing. In addition, data from marginally successful clinical studies can be used to identify key

[a]These authors contributed equally to this work.

parameters and driver elements for the treatment. We have utilized data from a small-scale Phase IIa clinical trial with CD patients treated with a nutritional antiinflammatory compound; conjugated linoleic acid (CLA) [11], and a large-scale clinical trial simulation, to develop a synthetic CD population data set and a large-scale clinical trial simulation. The in silico clinical trial is used to optimize the various parameters of the design and test the new promising CD therapeutics with strong animal pharmacology packages and safety profiles acting on novel therapeutic targets (*LANCL2* and *SMAD7*).

Creating a large sample size of virtual patients for in silico clinical experimentation has been implemented successfully only in a limited number of studies [12–14]. For example, due to the high number of failed trials for Alzheimer's disease, a clinical trial simulator was recently developed and deemed reliable for future clinical trials by the U.S. Food and Drug Administration (FDA) and European Medicines Agency (EMA) [12]. The computational tools can be used to test disease-modifying effects in conjunction with randomized, parallel, placebo-controlled, or other types of trials. This tool is a successful example of the integration of patient-level and literature-based data. However, due to the complex nature of the process and accessibility to comprehensive clinical data, such studies are only beginning to emerge for other diseases, including inflammatory or immune-mediated diseases. For instance, in a recent work by Brown and colleagues [13], a computational model was constructed based on clinical data from 33 blunt trauma patients. The model was subsequently used to generate 10,000 virtual patients. Sensitivity analysis on the parameters in the model identified key elements that could provide a small survival benefit of IL-6 inhibition. Similarly, in more generalized frameworks, researchers have attempted to create synthetic electronic medical records (EMRs) to bridge the gap between novel biosurveillance algorithms operating on full EMRs and the lack of nonidentifiable EMR data [14]. One of the major concerns includes the confidentiality of patient medical information while monitoring large-scale outbreaks. In the above examples, accessibility to reliable clinical data linked to cellular and molecular markers of disease is a key factor. In addition, for modeling purposes, levels of different biomarkers, patient's disease activity, such as Crohn's Disease Activity Index (CDAI) and patient-reported outcomes (PROs), have to be measured before and after treatment. Furthermore, as the data is prone to the missing value problem, efficient methods need to be in place to address the inherent complications (see a review by Eekhout et al. [15]). Statistical methods might not always be appropriate with a small sample size. Therefore, novel computational techniques are needed to address the recurring problems that hinder the path of acceleration of development of cures for debilitating human diseases.

The task of creating large populations of diverse virtual patients for Phase II and III testing requires a balanced representative patient-level data; such that the data can be used to build deterministic or nondeterministic models. For instance, researchers used the data and literature-based information to construct an ordinary differential equation (ODE)-based model and used the model to generate instances of virtual patients [13]. In 2010, we published the first ODE-based computational model of the key immunological changes occurring in the colonic mucosa during IBD [16], and more recently we built models of CD4+ T cells differentiation to determine the modulation of mucosal immune responses by CD4+ T cell subsets during gut inflammation [17,18]. For complex diseases with a large number of parameters and limited available clinical and biomarker data for calibration, it is also possible to use advanced machine learning methods. In fact, in a recent study in modeling of CD4+ T cell heterogeneity, we have demonstrated the use of the machine learning method as a reliable alternative to large complex ODE-based models [19,20].

The predictive power of in silico simulations can provide additional insight for designing clinical trials [21] based on nutritional therapies such as CLA [11] or novel therapeutics such as those targeting SMAD7 [22] or LANCL2 [23]. For instance, based on a series of in silico, biochemical, and *in vivo* studies [23], LANCL2 has already been proposed as a novel and promising target for the discovery and development of orally active, broad-based drugs against inflammatory, immune-mediated, and chronic metabolic diseases. LANCL2 is a key mediator in inflammation and reduces the levels of proinflammatory cytokines including *TNF-α* and *IFN-γ* while increasing the antiinflammatory cytokine IL-10 [24,25]. Indeed, *TNF-α* and *IFN-γ* have been also reported as molecular markers of CD [26]. These cytokines were also measured in the clinical study on CD [11] that is used for the development of a virtual patient population. Similarly, SMAD7-targeting therapies alter the expression of regulatory signaling molecules, specifically transforming growth factor (*TGF*)-*β1*. *TGF-β1* mainly functions as a negative regulator of T cell immune responses and signals to downstream target cells via a family of *Smad* proteins. In patients with IBD, there is an overexpression of *Smad7* that further inhibits *TGF-β1* induced signaling [27]. Thus, the inhibition of Smad7 has been proposed as an investigational therapeutic for CD that favors regulatory responses. In addition, principal component analyses detect and highlight the key molecular biomarkers of CD, namely *IFN-γ* and *TNF-α*. The latter solidifies the immunological features of the synthetic CD population.

In this study, advanced machine learning methods are used to generate virtual patients based on data from clinical studies on CD. In particular Artificial Neural Network (ANN) and Random Forest (RF) models are built from clinical data and used to generate population level features. Treatment regimens are also designed based on clinical data and applied to the large virtual population to quantify and compare different treatments in the context of a randomized, placebo-controlled Phase III in silico clinical trial.

28.2 MATERIALS AND METHODS

28.2.1 STUDY DESIGN

Developing a synthetic population of healthy individual or patients from clinical data and designing in silico treatment requires a series of steps including *data extraction*, *data generation*, and *data analytics* (Fig. 28.1). During the first stage, *data extraction*, clinical data from trials on CD were extracted from publications, including clinical trials on CLA, GED-0301, and placebo. During the *data generation* stage, we predicted the missing values (including levels of biomarkers at different time points) in the original clinical trial data using supervised machine learning approaches. Based on the complete data set, we generated a large synthetic patient population data set. The latter was further utilized for an in silico randomized, placebo-controlled Phase III clinical trial using virtual treatments. During the final stage, *data analytics* and statistical analyses was performed to determine (1) statistically significant differences between effectiveness of virtual treatments and placebo, (2) statistically significant differences between different treatments, and (3) personalized treatment options based on patient's characteristics and previous or concomitant medications.

28.2.2 DATA EXTRACTION

Data from a previously published Phase IIa clinical trial [11] was used to develop a large virtual population for in silico experimentation. The clinical data incorporated deidentified patient information

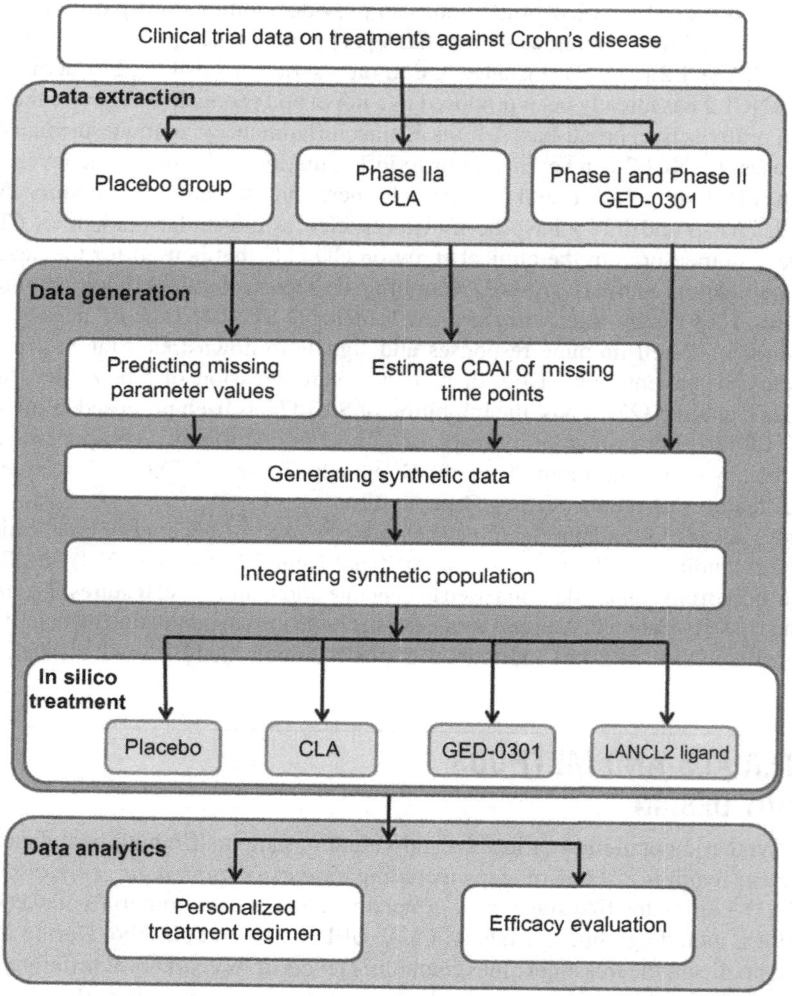

FIGURE 28.1

Study design overview. The study includes three steps: (1) Data extraction, (2) data generation, and (3) data analytics.

and CD biomarker measurements (ie, cellular and molecular immunological readouts) prior to treatment, 6 weeks and 12 weeks after treatment, as well as CDAI score at these three time points. There were 19 parameters measured during each time point. However, there were missing parameters and a relatively small number of patients (11 patients) that underwent the treatment. In addition, this initial Phase IIa clinical trial did not have a placebo group and all the patients received the treatment without discontinuation of their current treatment regime.

The second clinical data set used in this study comprised patients that received a *Smad7* inhibitor — *Mongersen* (formerly GED-0301). The study by Monteleone et al. [44] showed that a Smad7 inhibitor aided in restoring TGF-β1 signaling in chronic IBD. TGF-β1 mainly functions as a negative regulator of T cell immune responses and signals to downstream target cells via a family of *Smad* proteins. In patients with IBD, there is an overexpression of Smad7 that further inhibits TGF-β1-induced signaling [27] thereby causing an increase in production of proinflammatory cytokines such as TNF-α, a main driver underlying inflammatory processes in IBD. Smad7 intracellular protein acts by binding to the TGF-β receptor, thereby preventing TGF-β signaling, making it an attractive therapeutic target for suppressing CD. The data used for this in silico clinical study was extracted from the Phase I clinical trial [28] that involved the administration of *Mongersen* (GED0301) to 15 patients with active CD and a Phase II clinical trial [29] that was conducted to evaluate the efficacy of *Mongersen* in 166 patients for the treatment of active CD [22].

Additionally, clinical data for the placebo group was obtained from clinical trial studies on certolizumab pegol [30] and GED-0301 [22]. In the clinical trial study of certolizumab pegol, CDAI scores of patients receiving placebo were reported in terms of mean and standard deviation prior to and after treatment. In the clinical trial study of *Mongersen*, CDAIs of patients receiving placebo were reported using median and range including minimum and maximum value. The distribution of patients receiving placebo treatment in the study was biased toward lower initial CDAI scores. However, synthetic data generation was designed to create a balanced representative population by adjusting the sampling parameters.

28.2.3 DATA GENERATION

There are four main steps for the data generation procedure: (1) estimation of the missing values of parameters, (2) creation of in silico population, (3) design of the clinical trial, and (4) application of treatment to the virtual patient.

28.2.3.1 Estimating missing values

The clinical data set is high-dimensional because there are few patients (cases) and a large parameter set (variables). Using an iterative process, an ANN model was optimized to predict the missing values for all patients. The iterative process (Fig. 28.2) used a subset of parameters randomly chosen to estimate the missing value. The process was repeated 100 times and average estimates were calculated. In addition, the entire process was repeated with different model parameters (the number of hidden nodes in the ANN model) and the values were averaged with the exclusion of extreme estimations. The estimation was performed in R using the neuralnet package [31]. The method was optimized using a subset of the data set. In the optimization process, a subset of data set was selected with no missing values; 20 parameters were randomly removed and estimated using this iterative process. The mean and median differences between estimated values and expected values were 31% and 22%, respectively. Different ANN models with varying numbers of hidden nodes were able to better estimate missing values depending on the range and variation of the parameters.

28.2.3.2 Creation of a synthetic CD patient population

The data set for a real patient population enrolled in the Phase IIa clinical trial [11] was used to create the synthetic CD population. In particular, patients with mild to moderately active CD (estimated CDAI > 150 to <450) were screened for enrollment in the study. Patients were required to

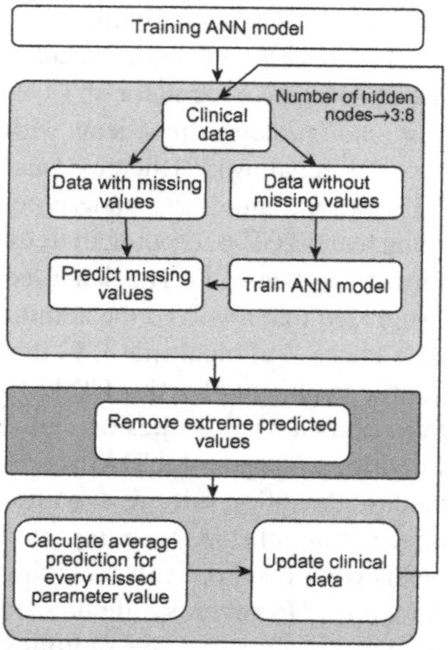

Algorithm:

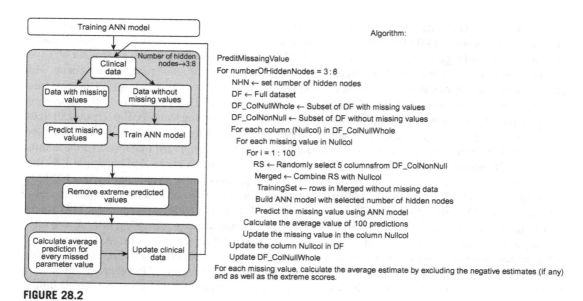

```
PreditMissaingValue
For numberOfHiddenNodes = 3 : 8
    NHN ← set number of hidden nodes
    DF ← Full dataset
    DF_ColNullWhole ← Subset of DF with missing values
    DF_ColNonNull ← Subset of DF without missing values
    For each column (Nullcol) in DF_ColNullWhole
      For each missing value in Nullcol
        For i = 1 : 100
          RS ← Randomly select 5 columnsfrom DF_ColNonNull
          Merged ← Combine RS with Nullcol
           TrainingSet ← rows in Merged without missing data
          Build ANN model with selected number of hidden nodes
          Predict the missing value using ANN model
        Calculate the average value of 100 predictions
        Update the missing value in the column Nullcol
    Update the column Nullcol in DF
    Update DF_ColNullWhole
For each missing value, calculate the average estimate by excluding the negative estimates (if any)
and as well as the extreme scores.
```

FIGURE 28.2

Flow chart and algorithm used to estimate the missing values in clinical data set.

be on stable medications 2 months prior to entry and could not be on prednisone at the time of screening. Patients were allowed to continue their baseline CD medications with the exception of oral prednisone and oral dietary supplements. The virtual patients were created to represent family members of these real patients. Specifically, synthetic patients were to some extent similar to the real patients. This strategy ensured that synthetic patients have features that are supported by clinical cases. Fig. 28.4 further explains this. The complete data set includes a range of cases: there are 30% of cases with a highest drop (>100) in the CDAI score, an additional 30% have a lower drop in the CDAI score (>50), there are 30% of cases with no significant difference in their CDAI scores after 12 weeks of treatment, and there are 10% of cases with a significant increase in CDAI score after treatment. Using each patient data as a seed entity, one parameter is randomly chosen and a random positive value (within a certain range) is added to that parameter. In addition, the remaining parameters are changed from their initial value using the relationship matrix (Fig. 28.3). Positively relevant parameters are increased (by a random percentage), while negatively relevant parameters are decreased by a random percentage. This is further explained in Fig. 28.4. The relationship matrix ensured that the random variations applied to generate the synthetic patient are biologically acceptable. For instance, a CD patient that is similar to a given real patient may more likely have a higher TNF-α and IFN-γ but lower TGF-β1; in essence, TNF-α and IFN-γ are positively correlated, while both are negatively correlated with TGF-β1. Finally 1100 virtual patients were created through this process (100 virtual patients for each real patient). The process was streamlined so the number of virtual patients could expand without any technical impediment. Unlike the real population, the virtual population has no missing values; however, the disease activity scores have to be predicted because these are not randomly generated. This is possible because clinical patient-level data that includes biomarker levels as well as CDAI scores are available

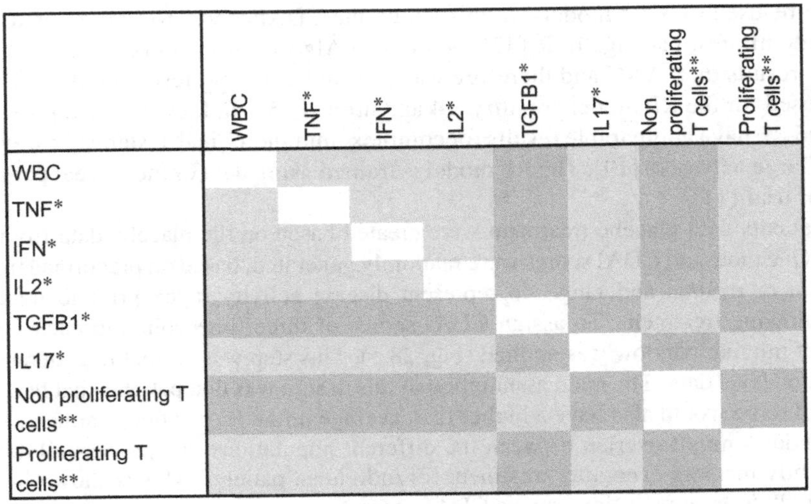

FIGURE 28.3

Parameter relationship matrix. Immunological parameters are used to create the synthetic population. The color of light gray indicates a positive relevance while the color of dark gray represents negative relevance. The matrix is designed based on expert knowledge. * indicates CD4+ and CD8+ T cells; ** indicates CD3+, CD4+, and CD8+ T cells.

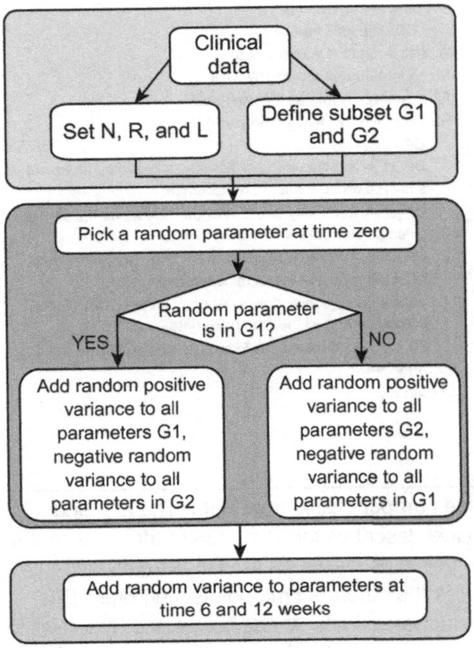

Algorithm:

```
GeneratingVirtualPatientPopulation
DF <- Clinical dataset
N <- set number of synthetic data created for each datum
R <- define the range of variance
L <- define the subset of parameters at T0
G1 <- define the subset of inflammatory parameters at T0
G2 <- define the subset of anti-inflammatory parameters at T0
SytheticPoulation <- define a matrix to save synthetic population
For i = 1 to number of row in DF
For j = 1 to N
  RS <- randomly select one parameter from L
  If RS in G1
     Random variance added to par in G1 is positive, those in G2 is negative
  else
     Random variance added to par in G1 is negative, those in G2 is positive
For each parameter in G1/G2
  Add a random variance
  Add a random variance for the same parameter at T6 and T12
```

FIGURE 28.4

Flow chart and algorithm used for generating a synthetic CD patient population based on immunological parameter relationship matrix.

[11] and can be used to build models. In this study, the CDAI scores were predicted using the RF method (randomForest package in R [32]), similar to Algorithm 1. However, in this situation RF yields better results than ANN and therefore was selected as the preferred method. The optimized parameters used for the RF model are mtry = 4 and ntree = 250. In fact, we have previously shown that ANN and RF have comparable results for complex immunological systems; however, ANN can be faster for large networks [19]. The RF model is trained using data of the 11 real patients from the CLA clinical trial [11].

Virtual patients with placebo treatment were created based on the placebo data from two clinical trial studies. One thousand CDAI scores were randomly generated, based on predefined mean and standard deviation or median and range, to represent disease activity index prior to treatment, 6 and 12 weeks following treatment. To assign CDAI scores of three time points to each virtual patient, the concept of moving window was applied (Fig. 28.5). This step was crucial to generate patient data from population level data. The main assumption in this design was that patients that had a higher than average initial score would also have a higher than average initial score after treatment. However, because the windows might overlap between the different populations, the process allowed the CDAI scores to slightly increase even after treatment for individual patients. This is shown in the five subpanels of Fig. 28.5 (treatment time versus CDAI scores).

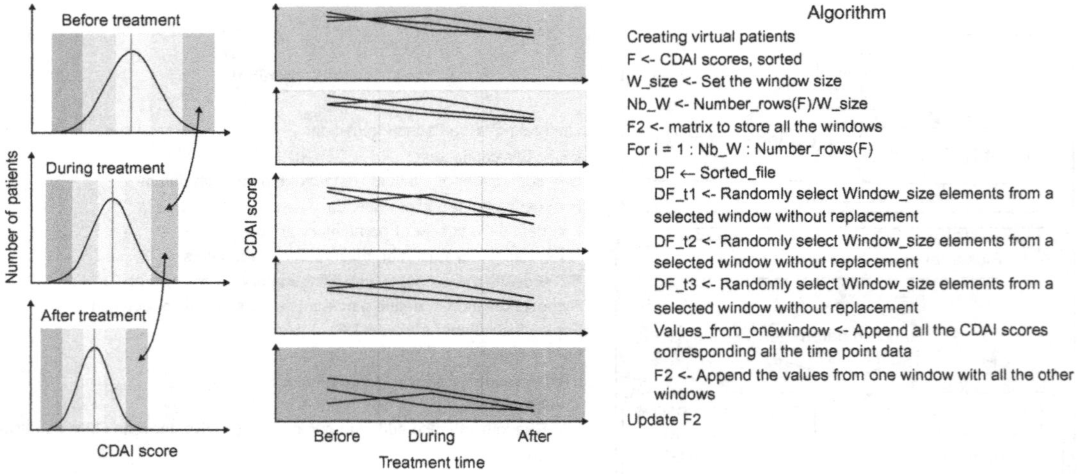

FIGURE 28.5

Assigning CDAIs at different time intervals to virtual patients based on population level data. The first and second panels show a schematic representation and the third panel describes the algorithm of the process; the code is implemented in R. The distributions at each of the time points as shown on the left were divided into the different shaded windows. These windows are matched across the different time points, and one CDAI score is randomly selected from each group as shown by the windows of similar shade connected by arrows to create a synthetic patient with three CDAI scores at their respective time points. Each connected data point on the line graph to the right represents one synthetic CD patient.

28.2.3.3 Inclusion and exclusion criteria

The inclusion and exclusion criteria were similar to the Phase IIa clinical trial [11]. In this in silico clinical trial, 80% of the patients enrolled had mild to moderately active CD (estimated CDAI >150 to <450), 10% had an estimated CDAI score CDAI >100 to <150 (symptomatic remission), and 10% had an estimated CDAI score >450 to <500 (severe/fulminant disease). Patients were on stable medications 2 months prior to entry and could not be on prednisone at the time of screening. Patients were allowed to continue their baseline CD medications with the exception of oral prednisone and oral dietary supplements.

28.2.3.4 In silico therapeutic interventions

Four treatments (placebo, CLA, GED-0301, and LANCL2 ligand) were given to 10,000 virtual patients based on the working definition of CD activity corresponding to the computational equivalent to a Phase III clinical trial. CD includes four levels: (1) *Symptomatic remission* CDAI <150; (2) *mild to moderate disease* CDAI 150–220; (3) *moderate to severe disease* CDAI 220–450; and (4) *severe/fulminant disease* CDAI >450 [33]. Initial CDAIs were randomly assigned to the 10,000 virtual patients following the ratio 1:4:4:1, for the level of CD activity. Furthermore, *IFN-γ* and *TNF-α* are considered as molecular markers of CD, which are further confirmed by the PCA analyses on the clinical data from the CLA study [11]. Thus, the efficacy of four treatments on CD could be indirectly reflected by how they could regulate *IFN-γ* and *TNF-α*, which is determined either by extracting information from publication or by predictions based on changes of CDAI scores. In the following section, the design of the four different in silico treatments is described (see Table 28.1). The simulation scores obtained following treatment were then mapped to experimental scores prior to analysis of variance (ANOVA).

Placebo

The changes of *TNF-α* and *IFN-γ* led by placebo were predicted by using CDAIs of virtual patients. Machine learning procedure is especially valuable in this design due to the lack of mechanistic understanding on the effect that the placebo could have on *TNF-α* and *IFN-γ* level. In particular, a RF model was built for prediction of the two biomarkers. The placebo treatment caused the *IFN-γ* level to decrease by 17%; however, the *TNF-α* level showed a significant increase of 58%.

Conjugated linoleic acid

The two biomarkers, *TNF-α* and *IFN-γ*, were monitored in the clinical study of CLA [11]. CLA is considered a nutritional intervention and the expected change in the levels of biomarkers could be less significant than more potent drugs. Nonetheless, the average decrease of *IFN-γ* level led by CLA is 24%; however, CLA caused an upregulation of *TNF-α* level by 25%.

Table 28.1 The Treatment Design Strategy

Treatment	TNF-α Change (t0–t6)	IFN-γ Change (t0–t6)
Placebo	−0.58	0.17
LANCL2-ligand	0.55	0.75
GED-0301	0.41	0.3
CLA	−0.25	0.24

GED-0301

The gut inflammation associated with CD is mainly characterized by the decreased activity of the immunosuppressive cytokine *TGF-β1*. The increased level of *Smad7* that inhibits the *TGF-β1* receptor contributes mainly toward the decrease. Consequently, an antisense oligonucleotide *Smad7* inhibitor GED-0301 was designed for the Phase I clinical trial wherein it was delivered primarily in the lumen of terminal ileum and right colon [28]. The study provided us with valuable data regarding the proinflammatory cytokine levels of *IFN-γ*. A decrease of 30% in *IFN-γ* expressing cells was observed. The data for *TNF-α* levels was extrapolated from the phase 2 clinical trials [22], with 40 mg of GED-0301, the same antisense oligonucleotide used for the Phase I trials. A decrease of 41% was observed in *TNF-α* expressed by the peripheral blood mononuclear cells.

LANCL2 therapeutics

LANCL2, a potentially novel therapeutic target alternative for CD, can be modulated to reduce the levels of the two proinflammatory cytokines *TNF-α* and *IFN-γ*. Data published in Ref. [25], using *LANCL2* ligands as a treatment regime on human peripheral blood mononuclear cells, showed that the *IFN-γ* levels dropped by 75% and the *TNF-α* levels dropped by 55% following the treatment.

28.2.4 DATA ANALYTICS

Statistical analyses were used to evaluate the efficacy of *LANCL2* ligands on the virtual population with different severity level of CD. Determination of statistically significant differences was made using ANOVA on changes of CDAIs, with $P < 0.05$. Two factors were considered in the ANOVA test: treatments and initial CDAIs.

28.3 RESULTS

The creation of the synthetic CD patient population from a small-scale clinical trial resulted in generating 100 patients for each seed population for a total of 1100 patients. A principal component analysis (see Fig. 28.6) verified that the key biomarkers of the disease were captured from the larger in silico population, thereby confirming the authenticity of the synthetic CD patients.

A comparative analysis was performed on the 10,000 synthetic patients treated with four alternative therapies. Overall, 20% of the patients were from initial CDAI score less than 150 or more than 450. The remaining 80% were from CDAI scores between 150 and 450. However, different treatment regimens showed different efficacy based on the initial CDAI score. In the placebo group, the patients showed significant differential response depending on their initial CDAI score. Specifically, the CDAI drop is lower for patients with moderate disease level (initial CDAI score of 150–220). See Fig. 28.7.

A two-way ANOVA was performed to analyze the effect of two factors, treatments (placebo, CLA, Smad7 therapeutics, and LANCL2 therapeutics) and initial CDAIs, on the drop in CDAI. Furthermore, the interaction effect of treatments and initial CDAIs on drop in CDAI was also evaluated. The *P*-values for both treatments and initial CDAIs were less than 0.001, indicating that treatments given to patients and the initial CDAIs of patients were both associated with how well a patient would respond to treatment. The *P*-value for the interaction between treatments and initial CDAIs was 0.03; thus, indicating that the relationship between treatments and drop in CDAIs was dependent on the initial CDAIs.

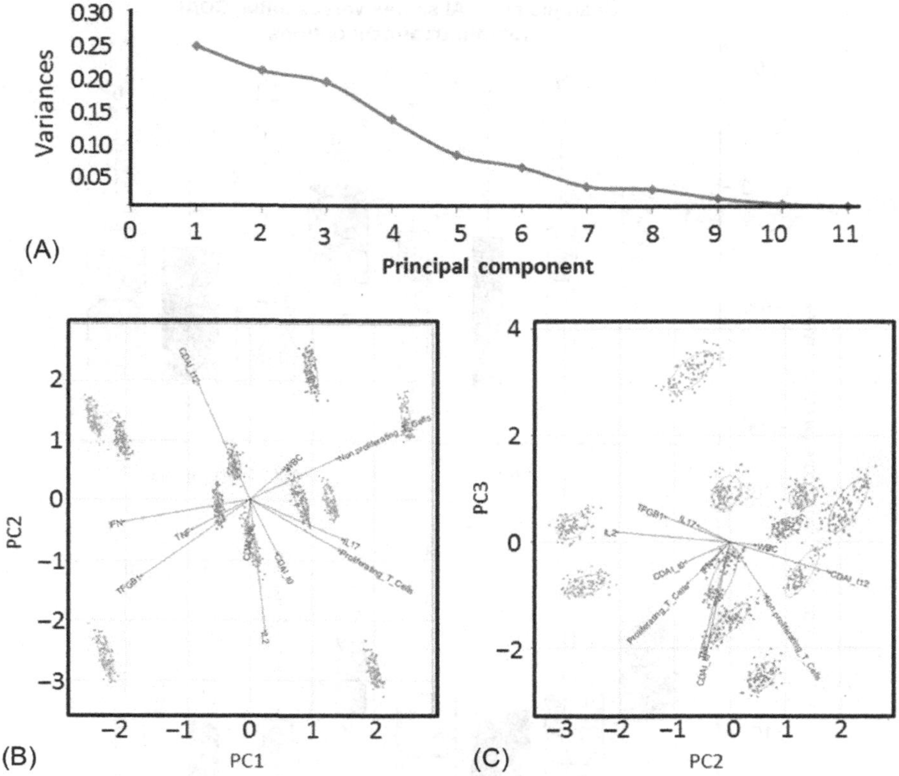

FIGURE 28.6

Principal component analysis (PCA) on a synthetic population created based on clinical data from CLA study. (A) Plot of the variances (*y*-axis) associated with the PCs (*x*-axis). (B) Biplot of PC1 and PC2. The data are projected on PC1 and PC2, which show that IFN-γ plays an important role in explaining the variation on PC1. (C) Biplot of PC2 and PC3. The data are projected on PC2 and PC3 showing that TNF-α plays an important role in explaining the variation on PC3. Clusters of data represent a synthetic CD population created from a seed patient group from the CLA clinical trial study.

Because the ANOVA test was significant for both variables (treatments and initial CDAIs) and the interaction effect between treatments and initial CDAIs was also present, a Tukey test was applied to further test the main effect and interaction effect in pairwise comparisons. The results of the Tukey test indicate that there are statistically significant ($P < 0.001$) pairwise differences between each treatment and placebo group. In addition, statistically significant ($P < 0.05$) pairwise differences also existed between higher and lower initial CDAIs groups except for 150–220 and 100–150. Tests on interaction effects showed that treatments had statistically significant differences in their effectiveness; in fact, the drop in CDAIs compared with placebo for all levels of initial CDAI ($P < 0.001$) was significant. Also, oral treatment with *LANCL2* ligand shows stronger effects than CLA and GED-0301 for patients with initial CDAIs between 150 and 220. Table 28.2 summarizes the statistical test results and shows significance between groups.

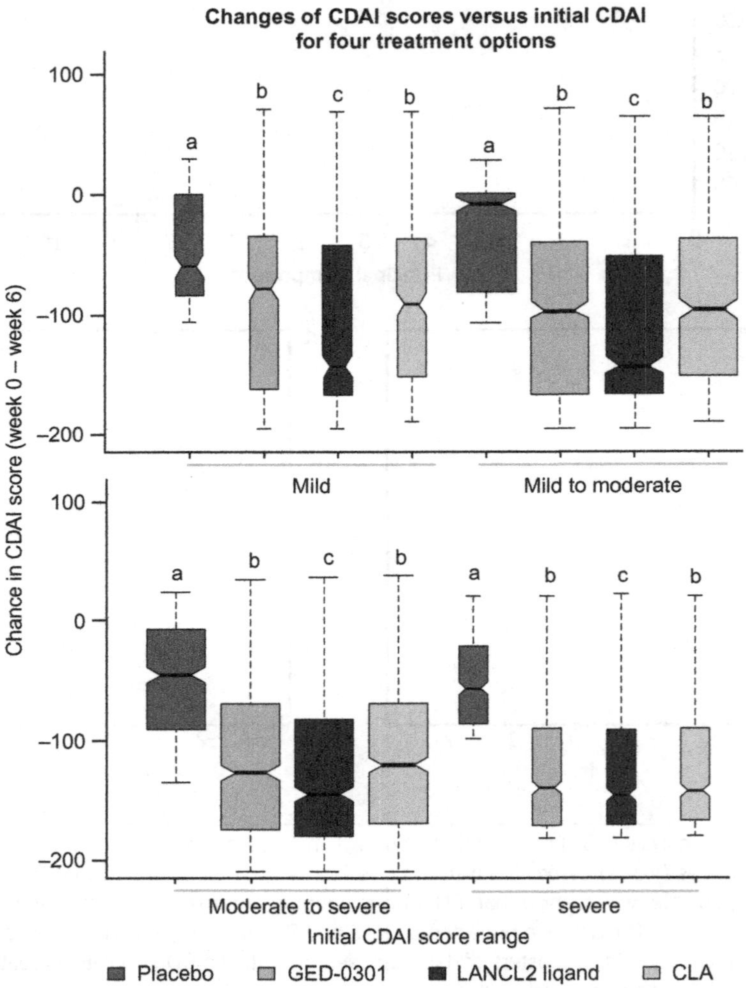

FIGURE 28.7

Changes of CDAIs during the first stage of treatment, led by four treatments strategies. Drop in CDAIs at week 6 was predicted for four treatments: LANCL2 ligand, placebo, CLA, and GED-0301. Drop of CDAIs was plotted for four groups of patients with different levels of initial CDAIs. The width of the boxes is proportional to the square roots of the number of patients in the groups. Across each CDAI range, the conditions that did and did not differ from one another are identified by subscripts. Those conditions that share a superscript letter (a, b, or c) did not differ from one another; those conditions that do not share a superscript were significantly different from one another ($P<0.05$). Table 28.2 summarizes the statistical test results and shows significance between groups.

Table 28.2 Statistical Analysis Results Comparing Different Treatment and Initial CDAI Range

Statistical Test	Significance Level (*P*-Value)
ANOVA: CDAI range	<2E−16
ANOVA: treatment	<2E−16
ANOVA (2-way): CDAI range and treatment	0.0301
Tukey multiple comparison test: GED-0301 and CLA	0.9637
Tukey multiple comparison test: LANCL2 and CLA	0.0000
Tukey multiple comparison test: placebo and CLA	0.0000
Tukey multiple comparison test: GED-0301 and LANCL2	2E−07
Tukey multiple comparison test: placebo and GED-0301	0.0000
Tukey multiple comparison test: placebo and LANCL2	0.0000

28.4 DISCUSSION

Treatment options for patients with CD show limited efficacy and significant adverse side effects. In fact, the global CD market can be divided into five segments: 5-ASA, antibiotics, biologics, corticosteroids, and immunomodulators. Even with today's aggressive treatments, still 75% of CD patients and 20–40% of UC patients cannot be effectively managed through medication and progress to needing surgery. Biologics seem to be a promising therapeutic option for severe cases of the disease; however, many clinical studies have failed to provide strong supporting evidence for further research. There is a continuous effort to provide a safer and more effective treatment that addresses the unmet clinical need of CD patients. Most clinical trials have used a 100 or 150 drop in the CDAI as a quantitative measure of effectiveness. In addition to the CDAI scores, there is the new alternative, PROs, also known as health measures, which may represent a valuable tool to better understand the quality and efficacy of a given treatment [34,35]. PRO that are derived from CDAI diary items may be appropriate for use in clinical trials for CD. This practice could also represent tools that patients as well as medical teams can use to assess and track health over time and monitor changes. We have used published information on CDAI and immunological markers of disease to create a large synthetic population of CD patients. For this Phase III clinical trial, synthetic CD patients have then been randomized to placebo, CLA, GED-0301, or LANCL2 therapeutic interventions with oral routes of administration.

GED-0301 is an inhibitor of *Smad7*, which functions by restoring the *TGF-β1* signaling in chronic IBD. The gut of patients affected with CD has high levels of *Smad7* that blocks the immune-suppressing activity of *TGF-β1*. The blockage of the immune suppressive activity thereby contributes toward increased levels of proinflammatory cytokines such as *IFN-γ* and *TNF-α*. *IFN-γ* and *TNF-α* being the major biomarkers in CD, are therefore indirectly targeted via *Smad7* inhibitor. The mechanism of action of *Mongersen* (antisense oligonucleotide—*Smad7* inhibitor) is the restoration of *TGF-β 1* signaling, thereby suppressing the inflammatory cytokine production. The Phase I and Phase II clinical trials were based on the animal studies [36] wherein *Smad7* was knockdown *in vivo* in mice with a *Smad7* antisense oligonucleotide that attenuated the experimental colitis [36]. The decrease in the percentage drops of *IFN-γ* and *TNF-α* from the human clinical studies were used in the data extraction process for this in silico clinical trial study. A recent Phase II clinical study reported that the average drop in CDAI score following full treatment regimen (84 days) with 40 mg dose was 116 points (or 122 points at maximum dose of 160 mg); however, the median and range of CDAI score prior to treatment and following treatment were [223–368] and [16–436], respectively; this highlights that the drug can increase the CDAI score significantly in some cases. The results from our placebo-controlled, randomized, Phase III in silico clinical trial at 6 weeks following the treatment shows a positive correlation between the initial disease activity score and the drop in CDAI score. This observation highlights the need for precision medicine strategies for IBD.

Oral CLA supplementation was shown to modulate immune responses in patients with mild to moderately active CD [11]. The CLA Phase IIa clinical trial was based on a small number of patients; however, the quality and availability of data facilitated this larger in silico study. CLA is a nutritional intervention with antiinflammatory properties [37,38]. However, oral CLA administration was shown to be well tolerated and suppressed the ability of peripheral blood T cells to produce proinflammatory cytokines, decreased disease activity, and increased the quality of life of patients with CD. Overall, only one patient had an increase in CDAI score following treatment (<10%). The results from in silico clinical trials at 6 weeks post treatment also highlight a positive correlation between the initial disease activity score and the drop in CDAI score. In addition, this Phase III clinical trial highlights the potential of CLA as an adjunct nutritional intervention, especially for the moderate/severe cases of CD. In fact, in the Phase IIa clinical trials, the patients that responded the best to the intervention were those with initial CDAI >220. However, the average CDAI score prior to the treatment was 245. The study could have been more successful if more severe cases had been enrolled.

IL-10 and TNF-α represent antagonistic functional behaviors during the onset of CD in the colon. IL-10 has an antiinflammatory role and has been shown to downregulate expression of MHC class II and B7 molecules, as well as IL-12 and IFN-γ production [39]. In contrast, TNF-α is a proinflammatory marker involved in systemic inflammation and activation of proinflammatory mucosal cell subsets [40]. Based on our preliminary results in mouse models of IBD, activation of the LANCL2 pathway upregulates the levels of IL-10 in the colon and suppresses TNF-α colonic levels at the gene expression and cellular level in animal models and human cells [25]. LANCL2 ligands can be a superior alternative treatment for CD patients. In fact, the results of the Phase III in silico clinical trial predict that LANCL2-based treatment can produce the significantly largest drop of CDAI scores of all treatments tested, consisting of an average drop of 126 points of CDAI for severe cases. Moreover, the results of this study suggest that the efficacy of LANCL2 therapeutics extends to all stages of disease. Thus, orally active, locally acting LANCL2-based drugs have the potential to disrupt the CD treatment paradigm.

Finally, the placebo results also show interesting and unexpected behavior. From this analysis, the placebo is most effective in patients with initial CDAI scores less than 150 or more than 220. Patients with mild to moderate disease levels tend to least benefit from the placebo effect. This is especially important as in some studies the distribution of patients in the placebo group can be biased and this may cause artifacts in the results. For instance, the number of patients with a severe disease activity could be lower than the number of patients with moderate disease activity level. Understanding the placebo effect is essential for disentangling drug effects from placebo effects, more truly capturing therapeutic efficacy in humans, and could possibly allow better designed clinical trials to maximize therapeutic outcomes and move toward informed precision medicine strategies guided by data (see a recent review [41]).

Future studies will investigate the therapeutic effects of longer-term therapeutic interventions. We will also expand the patient-level data from existing clinical trials when such data become available. Given the importance of biologics in the current treatment paradigm for CD, we will also examine the effect of treating our synthetic population with biologics such as antitumor necrosis factor α (*TNF-α*) antibodies, as well as combinatorial interventions (ie, nutritional adjuncts along with therapeutics) to the virtual patients for comparative analysis. For instance, we will identify possible interactions between diet, genetic makeup, microbiome populations, baseline medications, and response to treatment to advance personalized medicine interventions. Future studies will also apply multiscale modeling by using ENISI MSM, a high-performance computing-driven tool with scalability of 10^9–10^{10} agents [42,43], and in memory databases to integrate population level data with cellular and molecular procedural knowledge that explains response to treatment outcomes.

ACKNOWLEDGMENTS

This work was supported by funds from the Nutritional Immunology and Molecular Medicine Laboratory (https://www.nimml.org).

REFERENCES

[1] Molodecky NA, et al. Increasing incidence and prevalence of the inflammatory bowel diseases with time, based on systematic review. Gastroenterology 2012;142(1):46–54.e42. quiz e30.
[2] Baumgart DC, Sandborn WJ. Crohn's disease. Lancet 2012;380(9853):1590–605.
[3] Barrett JC, et al. Genome-wide association defines more than 30 distinct susceptibility loci for Crohn's disease. Nat Genet 2008;40(8):955–62.
[4] Papadakis KA. Chemokines in inflammatory bowel disease. Curr Allergy Asthma Rep 2004;4(1):83–9.
[5] Marks DJ. Defective innate immunity in inflammatory bowel disease: a Crohn's disease exclusivity? Curr Opin Gastroenterol 2011;27(4):328–34.
[6] Lawrance IC, et al. Serious infections in patients with inflammatory bowel disease receiving anti-tumor-necrosis-factor-alpha therapy: an Australian and New Zealand experience. J Gastroenterol Hepatol 2010;25(11):1732–8.
[7] Khan KJ, et al. Efficacy of immunosuppressive therapy for inflammatory bowel disease: a systematic review and meta-analysis. Am J Gastroenterol 2011;106(4):630–42.
[8] Auer K, et al. Translational research and efficacy of biologics in Crohn's disease: a cautionary tale. Expert Rev Clin Immunol 2014;10(2):219–29.
[9] Danese S. New therapies for inflammatory bowel disease: from the bench to the bedside. Gut 2012;61(6):918–32.
[10] Rutgeerts P, Vermeire S, Van Assche G. Biological therapies for inflammatory bowel diseases. Gastroenterology 2009;136(4):1182–97.
[11] Bassaganya-Riera J, et al. Conjugated linoleic acid modulates immune responses in patients with mild to moderately active Crohn's disease. Clin Nutr 2012;31(5):721–7.
[12] Romero K, et al. The future is now: model-based clinical trial design for Alzheimer's disease. Clin Pharmacol Ther 2015;97(3):210–4.
[13] Brown D, et al. Trauma in silico: individual-specific mathematical models and virtual clinical populations. Sci Transl Med 2015;7(285):285ra61.

[14] Buczak AL, Babin S, Moniz L. Data-driven approach for creating synthetic electronic medical records. BMC Med Inform Decis Mak 2010;10:59.
[15] Eekhout I, et al. Missing data: a systematic review of how they are reported and handled. Epidemiology 2012;23(5):729–32.
[16] Wendelsdorf K, et al. Model of colonic inflammation: immune modulatory mechanisms in inflammatory bowel disease. J Theor Biol 2010;264(4):1225–39.
[17] Carbo A, et al. Systems modeling of molecular mechanisms controlling cytokine-driven CD4+ T cell differentiation and phenotype plasticity. PLoS Comput Biol 2013;9(4):e1003027.
[18] Carbo A, et al. Computational modeling of heterogeneity and function of CD4+ T cells. Front Cell Dev Biol 2014;2:31.
[19] Lu P, et al. Supervised learning methods in modeling of CD4+ T cell heterogeneity. BioData Min 2015;8:27.
[20] Lu P, et al. Supervised learning with artificial neural network in modeling of cell differentiation process. In: Tran QN, Arabnia H, editors. Emerging trends in computational biology, bioinformatics, and systems biology. Waltham, MA: Elsevier; 2015. p. 674.
[21] Clermont G, et al. In silico design of clinical trials: a method coming of age. Crit Care Med 2004;32 (10):2061–70.
[22] Monteleone G, et al. Mongersen, an oral SMAD7 antisense oligonucleotide, and Crohn's disease. N Engl J Med 2015;372(12):1104–13.
[23] Lu P, et al. Lanthionine synthetase component C-like protein 2: a new drug target for inflammatory diseases and diabetes. Curr Drug Targets 2014;15(6):565–72.
[24] Magnone M, et al. Autocrine abscisic acid plays a key role in quartz-induced macrophage activation. FASEB J 2012;26(3):1261–71.
[25] Carbo A, Hontecillas R, Cooper J, Gandour R, Ehrich M, Bassaganya-Riera J. Lanthionine synthetase C-like receptor 2 (LANCL2): a novel therapeutic target for inflammatory bowel disease. Gastroenterology 2015;148 (4):S686–7.
[26] Plevy SE, et al. A role for TNF-alpha and mucosal T helper-1 cytokines in the pathogenesis of Crohn's disease. J Immunol 1997;159(12):6276–82.
[27] Nakao A, et al. Identification of Smad7, a TGFβ-inducible antagonist of TGF-β signalling. Nature 1997;389 (6651):631–5.
[28] Monteleone G, et al. Phase I clinical trial of Smad7 knockdown using antisense oligonucleotide in patients with active Crohn's disease. Mol Ther 2012;20(4):870–6.
[29] Magnone M, et al. Microgram amounts of abscisic acid in fruit extracts improve glucose tolerance and reduce insulinemia in rats and in humans. FASEB J 2015;29(12):4783–93.
[30] Sandborn WJ, et al. Certolizumab pegol for active Crohn's disease: a placebo-controlled, randomized trial. Clin Gastroenterol Hepatol 2011;9(8):670–678.e3.
[31] Günther F, Fritsch S. neuralnet: training of neural networks. R J 2010;2(1):30–8.
[32] Liaw A, Wiener M. Classification and regression by randomForest. R News 2002;2(3):18–22.
[33] Lichtenstein GR, Hanauer SB, Sandborn WJ. Management of Crohn's disease in adults. Am J Gastroenterol 2009;104(2):465–83.
[34] Khanna R, et al. A retrospective analysis: the development of patient reported outcome measures for the assessment of Crohn's disease activity. Aliment Pharmacol Ther 2015;41(1):77–86.
[35] Williet N, Sandborn WJ, Peyrin-Biroulet L. Patient-reported outcomes as primary end points in clinical trials of inflammatory bowel disease. Clin Gastroenterol Hepatol 2014;12(8):1246–1256.e6.
[36] Boirivant M, et al. Inhibition of Smad7 with a specific antisense oligonucleotide facilitates TGF-β1-mediated suppression of colitis. Gastroenterology 2006;131(6):1786–98.
[37] Bassaganya-Riera J, et al. Activation of PPAR gamma and delta by conjugated linoleic acid mediates protection from experimental inflammatory bowel disease. Gastroenterology 2004;127(3):777–91.

[38] Bassaganya-Riera J, Hontecillas R. CLA and n-3 PUFA differentially modulate clinical activity and colonic PPAR-responsive gene expression in a pig model of experimental IBD. Clin Nutr 2006;25(3):454–65.
[39] van Deventer SJ, Elson CO, Fedorak RN. Multiple doses of intravenous interleukin 10 in steroid-refractory Crohn's disease. Crohn's Disease Study Group. Gastroenterology 1997;113(2):383–9.
[40] Nielsen OH. New strategies for treatment of inflammatory bowel disease. Front Med (Lausanne) 2014;1:3.
[41] Colagiuri B, et al. The placebo effect: from concepts to genes. Neuroscience 2015;307:171–90.
[42] Abedi V, et al. ENISI multiscale modeling of mucosal immune responses driven by high performance computing, In: IEEE international conference on bioinformatics and biomedicine (BIBM), Washington, DC; 2015. p. 680–4.
[43] Mei Y, et al. Multiscale modeling of mucosal immune responses. BMC Bioinform 2015;16(Suppl. 12):S2.
[44] Monteleone G, Kumberova A, Croft NM, McKenzie C, Steer HW, MacDonald TT. Blocking Smad7 restores TGF-β1 signaling in chronic inflammatory bowel disease. J Clin Invest 2001;108(4):601–9.

CHAPTER

PATHOLOGICAL TISSUE PERMITTIVITY DISTRIBUTION DIFFERENCE IMAGING: NEAR-FIELD MICROWAVE TOMOGRAPHIC IMAGE FOR BREAST TUMOR VISUALIZATION

29

M. Yao*, Z. Tao†, W. Ji*, Y. Yao‡, B.D. Fleet§, E.D. Goodman§, J.R. Deller§

East China Normal University, Shanghai, China Suzhou Vocational University, Suzhou, China† Central Michigan University, Mt. Pleasant, MI, United States‡ Michigan State University, East Lansing, MI, United States§*

29.1 INTRODUCTION

Breast tumor microwave sensor system (BRATUMASS) is a breast tumor data acquisition system that uses the difference of dielectric constant and conductivity parameters between malignant tumor tissue and normal breast tissue to localize the breast tumor by detected target dielectric properties [1]. On data processing, according to the targets distance distribution, transforming the sampling signal in the time domain to the corresponding whole detection space electromagnetic property distribution is done to achieve the malignant tissues detection. However, from the aspect of microwave signal feature, how to use the intrinsic feature to detect the target and find proper signal parameters to remark the characterization of malignant breast lesions is a work of practical significance, and is also a challenge for traditional medical imaging [2].

29.2 THE SIGNALS OF BRATUMASS

Detecting points are located in the surface of the breast. The system uses a transceiver antenna, which is shown in Fig. 29.1D. The side lobe signal of the transceiver antenna is $f_p(t)$ and system noise is $N(t)$. The position of the detecting points and the structure of the antenna are shown in Fig. 29.1 [3].

The transmitting signal of BRATUMASS is

$$S(t) = rect\left(\frac{t}{T}\right) \exp\left\{j2\pi\left[f_0 t + \frac{1}{2}kt^2\right]\right\} \tag{1}$$

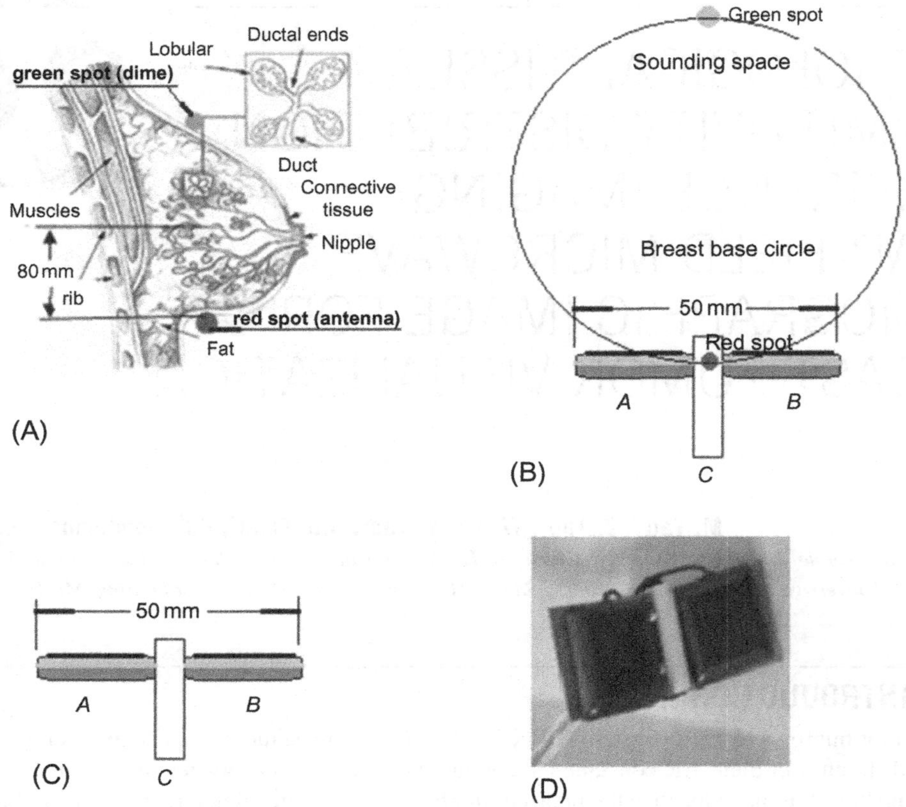

FIGURE 29.1

The position of the detecting points and the structure of the antenna. (A) The structure of the breast. (B) The schematic of the BRATUMASS detecting position; *red point* is the position of the antenna and *green point* is the position of the metal slice in (A) and (B). (C) The schematic of the transceiver antenna. A is the transmitting antenna, B is the receiving antenna, and C is the center clapboard. (D) The photo of transceiver antenna.

where $rect(t)$ is the rectangular envelope; f_0 is the initial frequency; T is the time width; and k is the frequency modulation slope.

The side lobe signal of the transceiver antenna $f_p(t)$ is

$$f_p(t) = rect\left(\frac{t-t_p}{T}\right)\exp\left\{j2\pi\left[f_0(t-t_p)+\frac{1}{2}k(t-t_p)^2\right]\right\} \quad (2)$$

where t_p is the transmission delay of the side lobe signal.

The signal obtained by the receiver antenna $S_r(t)$ chiefly includes two parts: target, $N(t)$, and $f_p(t)$. Fig. 29.2 illustrates the structure of frequency mixing. $S_f(t)$ is the output of the mixer, $S_f(n)$ is obtained from the A/D sampler.

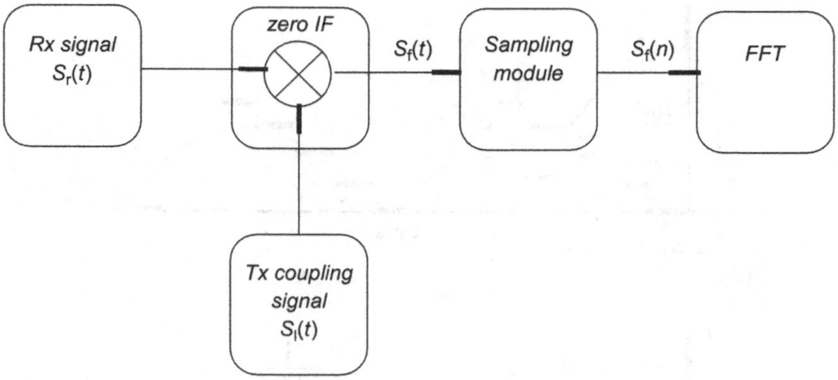

FIGURE 29.2

The structure of frequency mixing of BRATUMASS.

The output of the mixer can be expressed as

$$S_f(t) = S_r(t) \times S_L(t) \tag{3}$$

where $S_r(t)$ is the receiving signal from the receiver antenna.

$S_L(t)$ is the coupling signal from the transmitting antenna, which satisfies the requirements of frequency mixing of zero intermediate frequency (IF). Suppose γ is a coupling coefficient, and τ_0 is coupling delay. The $S_L(t)$ is

$$S_L(t) = S(t - \tau_0) \times \gamma \tag{4}$$

The status, which has no target in the detecting space, is S_0, so the receiving signals include side lobe $f_p(t)$ and noise $N(t)$. The status, which only has one target in the detecting space, is S_1, so the receiving signals obtain side lobe $f_p(t)$, noise $N(t)$, and the back wave of the single target. By analogy, S_n represents the status that has N targets in the detecting space.

In the status S_0, Eq. (4) is substituted into Eq. (3) as

$$S_f(t)|_{s_0} = \gamma \times S(t - \tau_0) \times \left(f_p(t) + N(t)\right) \tag{5}$$

$S_f(t)|_{s_0}$ is abbreviated to $S_f^0(t)$.

After Fourier transform, Eq. (5) is changed to

$$S_f^0(\omega) = A \times S(\omega) \otimes \left(F_p(\omega) + N(\omega)\right) \tag{6}$$

where $F_{di} = F^{(1)} - F^{(4)}$, $S(\omega)$, $F_p(\omega)$, and $N(\omega)$ is the Fourier transform of $S(t)$, $f_p(t)$, and $N(t)$, respectively.

In BRATUMASS, the bandwidth of slot step frequency modulation emission signal is 200 MHz, the radio frequency is 1.575 GHz, and the scanning period is 1 ms. As shown in Fig. 29.3A, the solid line stands for the transmitting signal and the dashed line for the theoretical receiving signal. The frequency of the scanning signal rises step by step. Fig. 29.3B shows the zero-IF signal output from the mixer. IF contains the information for a breast tumor (here, one target S_1) location. The transmitting signal reaches the receiving antenna and mixer after being reflected by the breast tumor, while the other

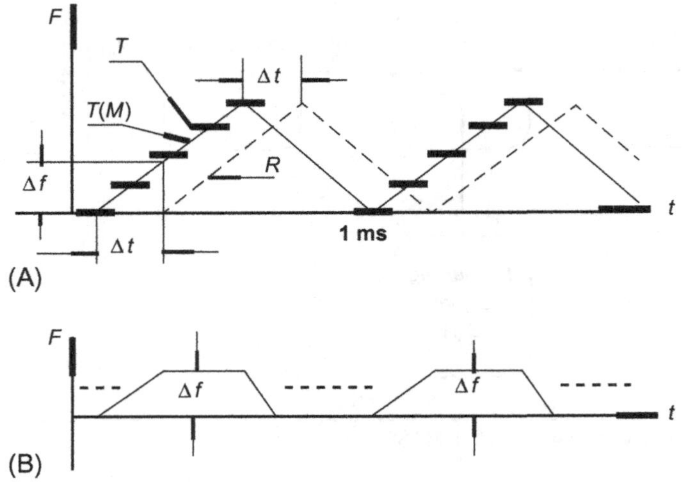

FIGURE 29.3

BRATUMASS's slot step frequency modulation signal.

part gets directly to the mixer through transmitting antenna coupling networks. The course difference of two parts, which can be deduced from zero-IF, the output of the mixer, is used to determine the distance between the antenna and the tumor.

The sampling data of a clinical case obtained by BRATUMASS is shown in Fig. 29.4 [4]. The positions of the detecting points are illustrated in Fig. 29.1B. The actual measure distance is about 150–170 mm, as patient posture is not perpendicular between the mental slice and the base circle.

29.3 FOURIER DIFFRACTION THEOREM

Microwave breast cancer detection is a kind of near-field problem, in the detection of space, no pattern, and the wave front. So, consider wave equation of the scattering field $u_s(r)$,

$$(\nabla^2 + k^2)u_s(r) = -k^2 f(r)u(r) \tag{7}$$

where $u(r)$ is the wave function of the incident wave, k is the wave number, and $f(r)$ is the characteristic function of space scattering. The right side of the equation is the source function of a homogeneous medium in the spread of the scattering field $u_s(r)$ with wave number k. This type of equation solving can use Green's function. Considering the two-dimensional situation, the source of the radiation field of free space is located in the $r_0 = (x_0, y_0)$, and Green's function is given by

$$g(r_1|r_0) = \frac{1}{4}H_0(k|r_1 - r_0|) \tag{8}$$

where H_0 is the first zero-order Hankel function (ie, the third type of Bessel function). By the principle of superposition, we can obtain the scattered field

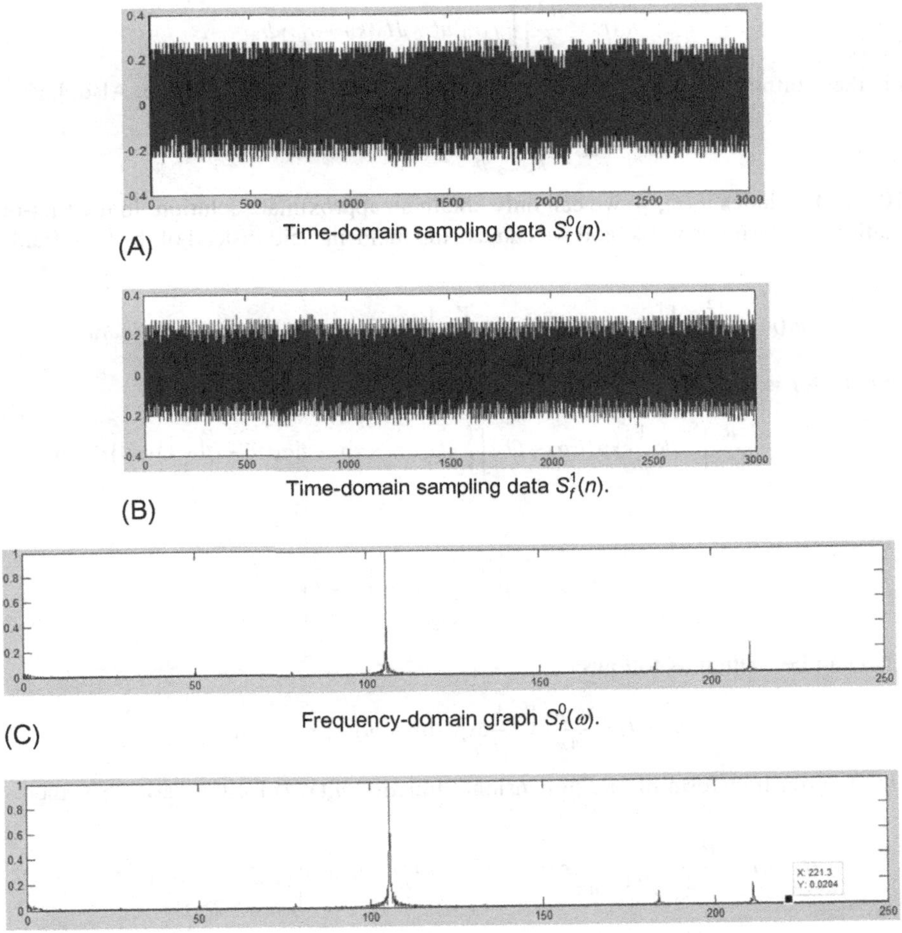

(A) Time-domain sampling data $S_f^0(n)$.

(B) Time-domain sampling data $S_f^1(n)$.

(C) Frequency-domain graph $S_f^0(\omega)$.

(D) Frequency-domain graph $S_f^1(\omega)$.

FIGURE 29.4

Sampling data of clinical case obtained by BRATUMASS. (A) The time-domain sampling data $S_f^0(n)$ when mental slice was not placed. (B) The time-domain sampling data $S_f^1(n)$ when breast surface placed a mental slice with radius 1 cm. The abscissa is the sampling ordinal, and the ordinate is the voltage level in (A) and (B). (C) The frequency-domain graph $S_f^0(\omega)$ corresponding to $S_f^0(n)$. (D) The frequency-domain graph $S_f^1(\omega)$ corresponding to $S_f^1(n)$. The abscissa is the frequency, and the ordinate is the normalized amplitude in (C) and (D).

$$u_s(r) = \frac{ik^2}{4}\iint_S f(r_0)u(r_0)H_0(k|r-r_0|)dr_0 \tag{9}$$

where S is the arbitrary area of surrounded objects cross-section in (x,y) plane. Also, has

$$H_0(k|r-r_0|) = \frac{1}{\pi}\int_{-\infty}^{\infty}\frac{1}{\beta}\exp\{i[\alpha(x-x_0)+\beta(y-y_0)]\} \tag{10}$$

In Eq. (10), $u(r)$ includes $u_s(r)$, so we can only obtain an approximate solution. In the first-order Born approximation, scattering is weak, and we can use the incident field instead of the total field. Then we can get

$$u_s(r) = \frac{ik^2u_0}{4\pi}\iint_s f(r_0)\exp(iks_0\cdot r_0)\int_{-k}^{k}\frac{1}{\beta}\exp\{i[\alpha(x-x_0)+\beta(y-y_0)]\}d\alpha dr_0 \tag{11}$$

When the detector is located in $y=l$, the detector receiving scattering field is

$$u_s(x,l) = \frac{ik^2u_0}{4\pi}\int_{-k}^{k}d\alpha\frac{1}{\beta}\exp(i(\alpha x+\beta l)]\iint_s f(x_0,y_0)\exp\{-i[\alpha(x_0)+(\beta-k)y_0)]\}dx_0dy_0 \tag{12}$$

and

$$F(\omega_1,\omega_2)\Big|_{\substack{\omega_1=\alpha\\ \omega_2=\beta-k}} = F(\alpha,\beta-k) \tag{13}$$

So, Eq. (12) can be written as follows:

$$u_s(x,l) = \frac{ik^2u_0}{4\pi}\int_{-k}^{k}\frac{1}{\beta}\exp(i(\alpha x+\beta l)]F(\alpha,\beta-k)d\alpha \tag{14}$$

$U_s(\omega)$ is the Fourier transform of one-dimensional function $u_s(x, l)$ for the variable x, then

$$U_s(\omega,l) = \frac{ik^2u_0}{2}\frac{1}{\sqrt{k^2-\omega^2}}\exp\left(i\sqrt{k^2-\omega^2}l\right)F(\omega_1,\omega_2)\Big|_{\substack{\omega_1=\omega\\ \omega_2=\sqrt{k^2-\omega^2}-k}}, \quad |\omega|<k \tag{15}$$

$F(\omega_1, \omega_2)$ is the Fourier transform of the space characteristics function $f(x, y)$. When ω_1 and ω_2 satisfy the relationship $\omega_2 = \sqrt{k^2-\omega_1{}^2}-k$, we can obtain the one-dimensional Fourier transform $U_s(\omega, \cdot)$ of scattering measured data after it is properly weighted.

29.4 TISSUE DIELECTRIC PROPERTIES AND REFLECTION COEFFICIENT

For the large difference of dielectric properties between breast tissue and malignant tumor tissue, scattering will happen in the interface of breast tissue and malignant tumor tissue. Fig. 29.5 shows the relationship of reflection and transmission at the interface of the two different mediums [5] where P_i is the incident power, P_r is the reflected power, and P_t is the transmitted power.

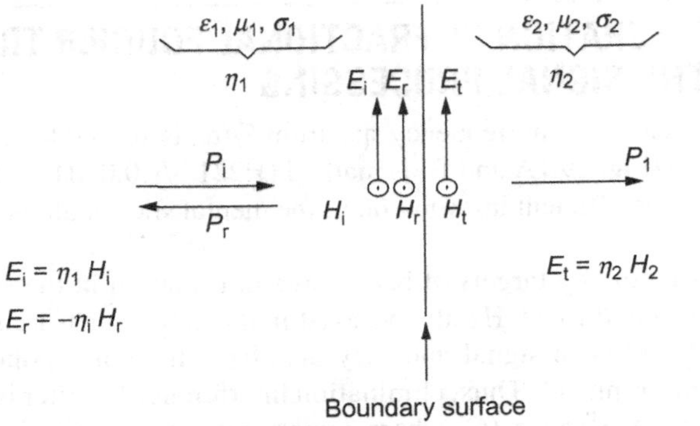

FIGURE 29.5

Reflection and transmission of a microwave wave at the two different mediums interface. P_i = incident power, P_r = reflected power, and P_t = transmitted power.

Table 29.1 Dielectric Properties of Typical Breast Tissues in 1.575 GHz

	Dielectric Properties, ε_r	Reflection Coefficient, Γ	Conductivity, σ (S/m)
Skin	36		2.64
Normal breast tissue	10		0.24
Malignant tumor tissue	50	0.49	2.8
Mammary duct	11–14	0.2018–0.49	0.45
Vascular		0.15-0.2018	

In two nonmagnetic medium interfaces, the relationship between reflection coefficient $\Gamma_{i,j}$ and dielectric properties ε_1, ε_2 is $\Gamma_{i,j} = \sqrt{\varepsilon_2} - \sqrt{\varepsilon_1}/\sqrt{\varepsilon_2} + \sqrt{\varepsilon_1}$. The ratio of incident power to reflected power is $P_r/P_i = \left|\Gamma_{i,j}\right|^2$. In each detection, the location of the target and the transceiver are relatively fixed, so the frequency components of low-frequency signal output by zero-IF mixer are relatively fixed, too. Extract the power spectrum of zero-IF output low-frequency signal to decide the target corresponding reflection coefficient (Fourier diffraction relationship).

The collection reflection coefficient $\widetilde{\Gamma}_{i,j}$ for the N layer media is

$$\widetilde{\Gamma}_{i,i+1} = R_{i,i+1} + \frac{T_{i,i+1}\widetilde{\Gamma}_{i+1,i+2}T_{i+1,i}e^{2ik_{i+1,z}(d_{i+1}-d_i)}}{1 - R_{i+1,i}\widetilde{\Gamma}_{i+1,i+2}e^{2ik_{i+1,z}(d_{i+1}-d_i)}} \quad (16)$$

Using our device parameters (radio frequency is 1.575 GHz and bandwidth is 200 MHz) to compute the parameter, we obtain dielectric properties, reflection coefficient, and conductivity of the breast tissue as shown in Table 29.1.

29.5 QUARTER OF ITERATION OF FRACTIONAL FOURIER TRANSFORMATION ALGORITHM AND THE SIGNAL PROCESSING

According to Fig. 29.4, we can see that frequency spectrum $S_f^0(\omega)$ is similar to $S_f^1(\omega)$. In Fig. 29.4D, the position of the mental slice (Fig. 29.1A and B) is marked (*x*:221.3/*y*:0.0204), 221.3 Hz corresponding to the distance 169.5 mm. The efficient information of the mental slice could not directly extract from the spectrum.

Theoretically, there are not any targets of back wave information in the status of S_0. However, spectral lines at about 105.7 and 210.6 Hz always exist in the actual measurement. Their amplitude is higher than target of back wave signal and they also have the corresponding change with the change of objective and environment. Thus, elimination interference by filter is not proper. Consider the frequency characteristic of $S_f^0(\omega)$ in (6), where a quarter iteration of the fractional Fourier transform (FRFT) algorithm is presented to enlarge amplitude of the object spectrum distribution in this chapter.

29.5.1 QUARTER OF ITERATION OF FRFT ALGORITHM

With g(*t*) and $G(\omega)$ as a Fourier transform pair, the relationship can be written by

$$G(\omega) = \frac{1}{\sqrt{2\pi}} \int_{-\infty}^{+\infty} g(t) e^{-j\omega t} dt \tag{17}$$

$$g(t) = \frac{1}{\sqrt{2\pi}} \int_{-\infty}^{+\infty} G(\omega) e^{j\omega t} d\omega \tag{18}$$

Following a brief write down for $G = F(g(t))$.

$$F(F(g(t)) = F^2(g(t)) = g(-t)$$

$$F^4(g(t)) = g(t)$$

F^n indicates that operator is used N times.

$F(\omega)$ is the Fourier transform of $f(t)$. It has the following properties: $F(\omega) = \Im(f(t))$; $\Im(F(\omega)) = \Im(\Im(f(t)) = f(-t)$. So repeating four times is a periodic repeat.

From the perspective of nonlinear dynamics, the iteration of Fourier transom is an iterated function with period 4. Use the modular $\Re$ as iterative evolution function, for accumulating the same frequency during iterative evolution and discard the phase of signal. Then,

$$|F(\omega)| = \Re(\Im(f(t))) \tag{19}$$

$$F^{(2)} = \Re(\Im(\Re(\Im(f(t))))) \tag{20}$$

$$F^{(3)} = \Re(\Im(\Re(\Im(\Re(\Im(f(t))))))) \tag{21}$$

$$F^{(n)} = \Re(\Im(\ldots\Re(\Im(\Re(\Im(\Re(\Im(f(t))))))))\ldots)) \tag{22}$$

After iterate N times, sorting frequency spectrum is obtained. Difference spectrum can be given as

$$F_{di} = F^{(1)} - F^{(n)} \tag{23}$$

29.5.2 THE INFLUENCES TO SINUSOIDAL SIGNAL STRUCTURE BY QUARTER ITERATION OF FRFT

Consider a signal $f(t) = A \sin(\omega t + \theta)$, where $\omega = 1.575$ GHz, and θ takes a random value between $-\pi$ and π. A might as well be valued at 100, sampling frequency is $10 \times \omega$, and iteration number $n = 4$. Fig. 29.6 shows the processing of quarter iteration of FRFT. The iterative result in $N = 4$ is the high-order spectrum of signal. Consequently, the location of high-order frequency in the spectrum is given.

29.5.3 PROCESSING RESULTS COMPARISON BETWEEN $S_F^0(M)$ AND $S_F^1(M)$

Comparing Fig. 29.4 $S_f^0(\omega)$ and $S_f^1(\omega)$, Fig. 29.7 demonstrates the processing result using the quarter iteration of FRFT algorithm. For the sake of convenience, the abscissa is transformed into distance, which is corresponding to frequency, with unit mm. The ordinate is normalized amplitude. Fig. 29.7A illustrates spectrum of the algorithm processing on signal S^0. In Fig. 29.7B the back wave is seen clearly at 150-170 mm, which corresponds to frequency 221.3 Hz (metal slice).

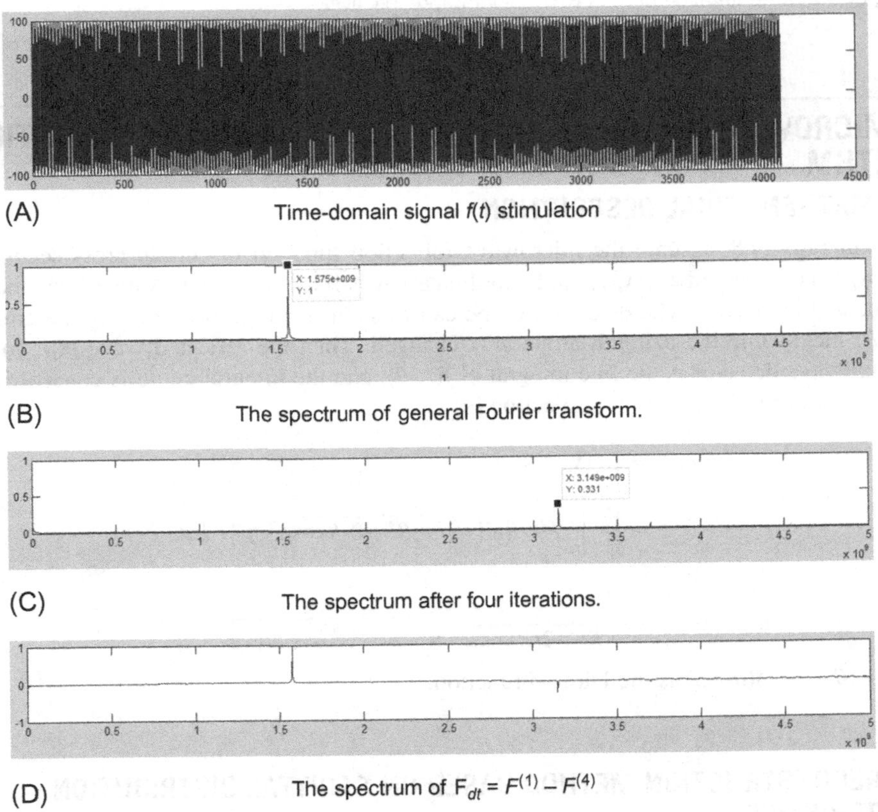

FIGURE 29.6

Sinusoidal signal structure by quarter iteration of FRFT. (A) The simulation signal $f(t)$. Its sampling depth is 4096. (B) The spectrum of normal Fourier transform, with $N=1$. (C) The spectrum after four iterations, with $N=4$. (D) The spectrum of $F_{di} = F^{(1)} - F^{(4)}$, the abscissa is frequency, and the ordinate is normalized amplitude.

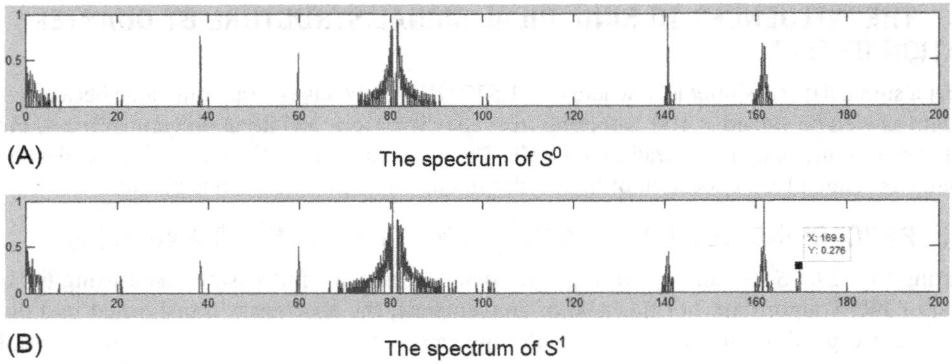

FIGURE 29.7

The result using a quarter iteration of the FRFT algorithm. (A) and (B) are the spectrums of S^0 and S^1 after separating by a quarter iteration of the FRFT algorithm, respectively.

29.6 MICROWAVE IMAGE OF SAGITTAL ITERATIVE RECONSTRUCTION ALGORITHM

29.6.1 MATHEMATICAL DESCRIPTION

As shown in Fig. 29.8, assume the microwave reflection function of certain cross sections of the imaging target is expressed as $f(x, y)$, and coordinate xoy is fixed on object. A nondirectional R/T antenna is located in (x_0, y_0). The detection probe can rotate around the object along the circle whose radius is R; meanwhile the azimuth angle φ is changed. Then the reflected wave $p(\rho, \varphi)$ received by the microwave detector is the line integral of $f(r, \theta)$, and the integral curve is concentric circular S with circle center (x_0, y_0). So the projection is

$$\begin{aligned} p(\rho, \phi) &= \int_S f(x, y) ds \\ &= \int_0^{2\pi} \int_0^{\infty} f(r, \theta) \delta\left(\sqrt{r^2 + R^3 - 2rR\cos\alpha} - \rho\right) r\,dr\,d\theta \end{aligned} \tag{24}$$

where

$$\sqrt{r^2 + R^2 - 2rR\cos\alpha} = \sqrt{(x - x_0)^2 + (y - y_0)^2} \tag{25}$$

and $\alpha = \pi - (\theta - \varphi)$. $\delta(d - \rho)$ is the Dirac-δ function.

29.6.2 RECONSTRUCTION METHOD BASED ON SAGITTAL DISTRIBUTION CHARACTERISTICS

In Fig. 29.8, collected data $p(\rho, \varphi)$ from detection point (x_0, y_0) is the accumulation of reflected wave of all points in the circular arc the center of which is the detection point and the radius is ρ. The inversion process should backfill accumulation to corresponding points according to a certain ratio; in other

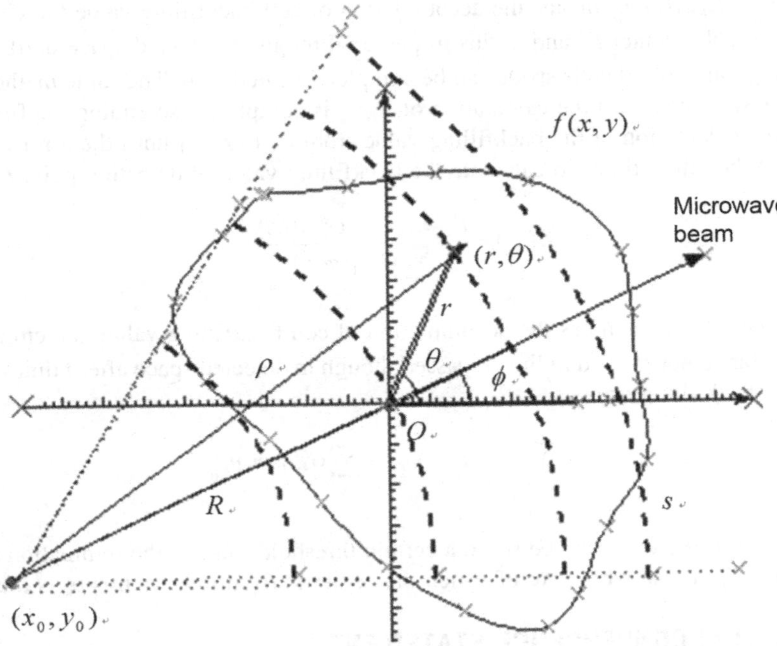

FIGURE 29.8

Sketch map of microwave reflection imaging.

words, the inversion process is a distribution process of the accumulation, which allocated $f(\rho, \varphi)$ to each point in the circle with radius ρ according to a certain ratio.

To express, the detected region is divided into $M_0 \times N_0$ parts with spatial resolution Δ. Then, reflection function $f(x, y)$ can be expressed as a discrete form; namely $f(i\Delta, j\Delta)$,

$$x = i\Delta, \quad y = j\Delta; \quad i = 1, 2, \ldots, M_0, j = 1, 2, \ldots, N_0 \tag{26}$$

It can be written as $F_{i,j}$. Test points (x_0, y_0), (x_1, y_1), … , (x_N, y_N) can be written as $P_0, P_1, \ldots, P_N$. The algorithm process is explained as follows:

Step 1 Select any point as the inversion starting point from N test points. It is sorted for $P_0, P_1, \ldots, P_N$. Any cell in the detected region is (i, j), and the distance from the center of the cell to the test point P_0 is ρ_0. $F_0(\rho_0, \varphi_0)$ indicates the projection date collecting in P_0, then the distribution value in (i, j) is $G_0(i, j) = F_0(\rho_0, \varphi_0)/n_{\rho 0}$. Where, $n_{\rho 0}$ is the number of the cell which the circular arc with the center P_0 and radium ρ_0 pass through. All cell backfilling values are calculated in the detected region like this.

Step 2 Calculate the backfilling value from P_1 to P_{N-1}. P_k is the current calculation detection point, and the $G_{k-1}(i, j)$ denotes the region value distribution after calculated P_{k-1}, then

$$G_k(i, j) = F_k(\rho_k, \varphi_k) \times \frac{G_{k-1}(i, j)}{\sum_{s_{\rho k}} G_{k-1}(m, n)} \tag{27}$$

where $\sum_{S_{\rho k}} G_{k-1}(m,n)$ means the accumulation of cell backfilling value the circular arc $S_{\rho k}$ with circular center P_k and radius ρ_k passed through in detected space until the backfilling value of all cells space can be completely calculated. The same method is applied to other test points, until the calculation of P_{N-1} is completed, so ending the first iteration.

Step 3 Repeat the calculation of the backfilling value from P_1 to P_{N-1} until the error conditions are met. When the t times to calculate the backfilling value of detection point P_k, there are

$$G_k^t(i,j) = \frac{F_k(\rho_k, \varphi_k) \times G_{k-1}^t(i,j)}{\sum_{S_{\rho k}} G_{k-1}^t(m,n)} \tag{28}$$

$\sum_{S_{\rho k}} G_{k-1}^t(m,n)$ denotes the accumulation of cell backfilling value, the circular arc $S_{\rho k}$ with circular center P_k, and radius ρ_k passed though in detected space after t times calculation. Then, the backfilling error is

$$\text{err} = \sum_{{}^{S}\sum \rho_k} \left\| F_k(\rho_k, \varphi_k) - \sum_{S_{\rho k}} G_{k-1}^t(m,n) \right\| \tag{29}$$

The backfilling error can be set to a certain threshold; that is, the remination of iteration. Where ${}^{s}\Sigma_{\rho k}$ is the whole arc of which the center is P_k and the radius ρ_k is the difference.

29.6.3 ALGORITHM CONVERGENCE STATEMENT

$x_0 \in I$ is the fixed point of interval mapping $f: I \to I$ when the derivative of f exists. When $|f'(x_0)| < 1$ (or $|f'(x_0)| > 1$), x_0 is the stable (or unstable) fixed point, it will attract (or reject) the vicinity points under the effect of iteration in the f. It is obvious that for the nearby area of the stable fixed point, the value after each iteration is always closer to the fixed point than the previous iteration value. For the nearby area of the unstable fixed point, the value after each iteration is always further from the fixed point than the previous iteration value.

The algorithm of the existing iteration fixed point is obvious. The actual reflection value is the value of the equation fixed point. The actual reflection value is $G(i, j)$ in every point (i, j). The error after particular backfill is $\Delta G_{k-1}(i,j)$, and the next iteration backfilled value is

$$G_k(i,j) = \frac{F_k(\rho_k, \varphi_k) \times (G(i,j) + \Delta G_{k-1}(i,j))}{\sum_{S_{\rho k}} G_{k-1}(m,n) = \frac{F_k(\rho_k, \varphi_k)}{\sum_{S_{\rho k}} G_{k-1}(m,n)} (G(i,j) + \Delta G_{k-1}(i,j))} \tag{30}$$

If $\Delta G_{k-1}(i,j) > 0$, then $\left| \frac{F_k(\rho_k, \varphi_k)}{\sum_{S_{\rho k}} G_{k-1}(m,n)} \right| < 1$, that is $G_k(i,j) < (G(i,j) + \Delta G_{k-1}(i,j))$. There are $\Delta G_k(i,j)) < \Delta G_{k-1}(i,j))$, and $\frac{\Delta G_k(i,j)}{\Delta G_{k-1}(i,j)} < 1$, when $\Delta G_{k-1}(i,j) > 0$, $G'(i,j) < 1$.

If $\Delta G_{k-1}(i,j) < 0$, then $\left| \frac{F_k(\rho_k, \varphi_k)}{\sum_{S_{\rho k}} G_{k-1}(m,n)} \right| > 1$, that is $G_k(i,j) > (G(i,j) + \Delta G_{k-1}(i,j))$. There are $\Delta G_k(i,j) > \Delta G_{k-1}(i,j)$ and $\frac{\Delta G_k(i,j)}{\Delta G_{k-1}(i,j)} < 1$, when $\Delta G_{k-1}(i,j) < 0$, $G'(i,j) < 1$, together $|G'(i,j)| < 1$, so the point that satisfied the stable fixed point requirement is a stable fixed point. The iteration result is always to keep close to the fixed point, which changes the fixed point to an attractor and the iterative process will eventually converge to fixed points.

29.7 BRATUMASS CLINICAL TRIALS

In Oct. 2006, we collected data of the first clinical case at the Shanghai Sixth People's Hospital (Shanghai Science and Technology Development Foundation under the project grant numbers 03JC14026). From Mar. 2009 until Sep. 2012, we collected 55 clinical cases at the Shanghai Fourth People's Hospital (Shanghai Science and Technology Development Foundation under the project grant numbers 08JC1409200). In Oct. 2013, we collected 10 clinical cases at Tumor Hospital of Xinyang Henan and The Second Affiliated Hospital of Zhengzhou University. And in Aug. 2013 at Dagang Hospital of Binhai New Area Tianjin, a clinical trial applied BRATUMASS's images to evaluate the validity for a breast tumor interventional therapeutic pattern before and after a surgical operation.

On clinical trials, we selected 16 scanning detection points, and they are arranged evenly around the bottom of the breast, as shown in Fig. 29.9A. Meantime, we also collected the normal side breast data from these 55 patients as control.

In May 2009, we collected bilateral breast data of the 13 volunteers in the normal group, and choose the 12 detection points on each side, as shown in Fig. 29.9B. We continue to prepare a microwave sounding database system to improve resolving ability of the BRATUMASS system.

In analyzed cases, diagnosis by a medical doctor after an operation determined the actual location of the tumor. Inversion results show that using the BRATUMASS imaging method can obtain dielectric properties distribution in the breast tissue. The value of dielectric properties (>50) mark the actual location of the tumor.

We used BRATUMASS to conduct clinical trials in Shanghai Fourth People's Hospital. During the experiment, the patient laid on the bed. The bottom of the breast when people stand is taken as a starting point to select 16 detection points with 15-degree intervals moving clockwise. *R/T* antenna is closed to the bottom outer edge of the breast. Zero-IF signal is obtained at the output end through the BRATUMASS. Inversion images are obtained by using a sagittal iterative reconstruction algorithm. The inversion image used cerise color to show the dielectric properties values greater than 50, red greater than 45, and yellow greater than 35.

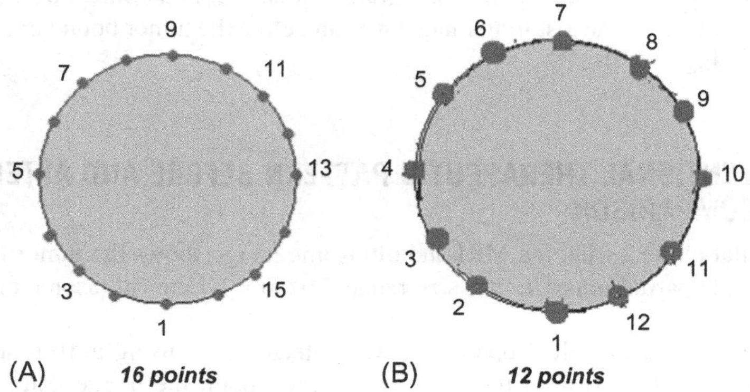

FIGURE 29.9

The location of scanning detection points: (A) 16 points and (B) 12 points.

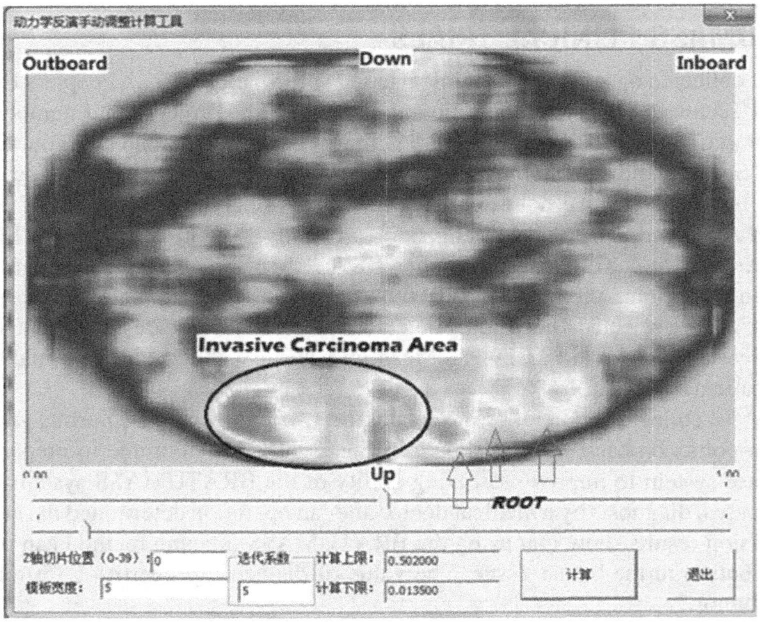

FIGURE 29.10

BRATUMASS's adjustable dynamics inversion tool box to show cancer location (outside lateral, partial upper) and the roots.

29.7.1 SCREENING AND LOCATING OF THE BREAST CANCER'S CLINICAL TRIALS CASE

Appling the sagittal iterative reconstruction algorithm, we build up BRATUMASS's adjustable dynamics inversion tool box for breast tumor tomographic imaging. In a clinical trial of invasive breast cancer cases, in practice with the resulting image, we can define the tumor boundary, and invasive root approximate range (Fig. 29.10).

29.7.2 INTERVENTIONAL THERAPEUTIC PATTERN BEFORE AND AFTER SURGICAL OPERATION'S COMPARISON

In a Dagang hospital clinical trial, the MRI and ultrasonic image shows the tumor location and size:

Left breast outside partial upper, tumor size range 3.0 cm × 1.7 cm (ultrasonic echo area), and invasive boundary.

Before an interventional surgical operation, we collected data using a 16-scan detecting point method. After surgery, we also used the same method to obtain the image data. The fourth layer and the ninth layer images are shown in Figs. 29.11 and 29.12.

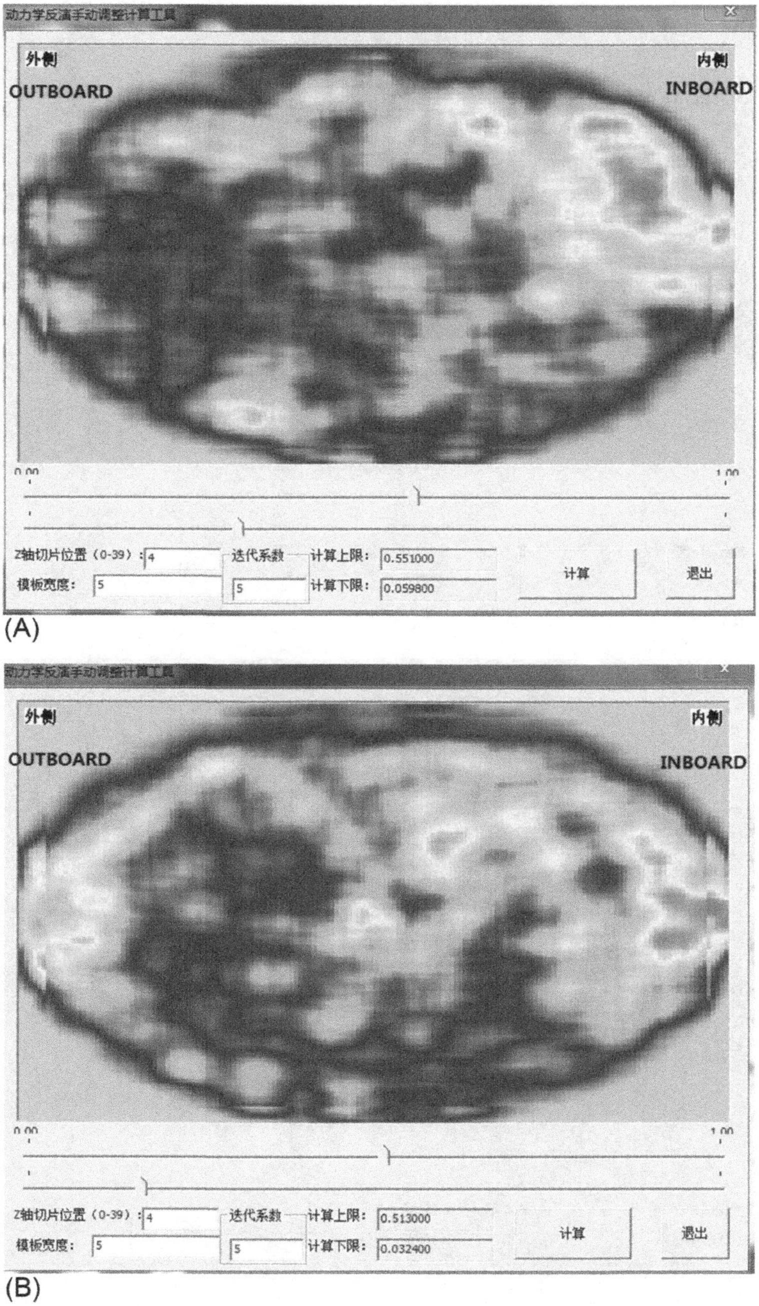

FIGURE 29.11

BRATUMASS's adjustable dynamics inversion tool box to image the fourth layer section from the breast bottom (each layer section of 2 mm). (A) Before surgical operation. (B) After surgical operation (7 days later).

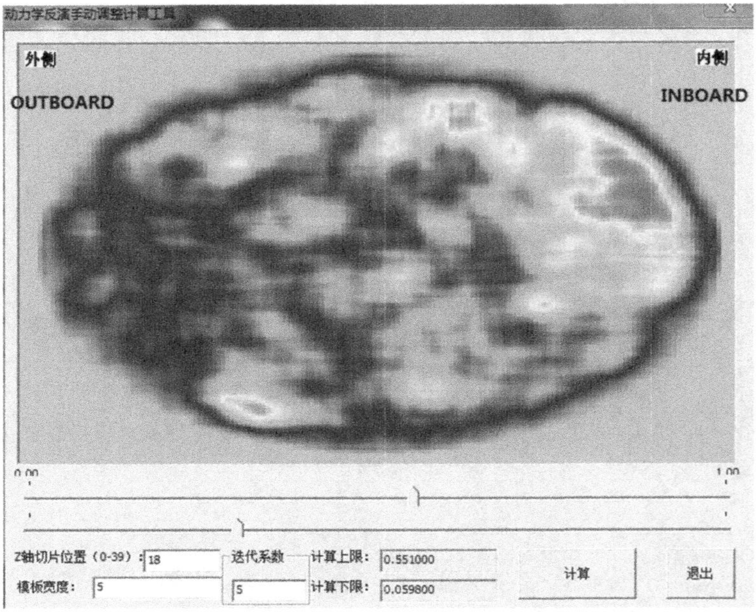

(A)

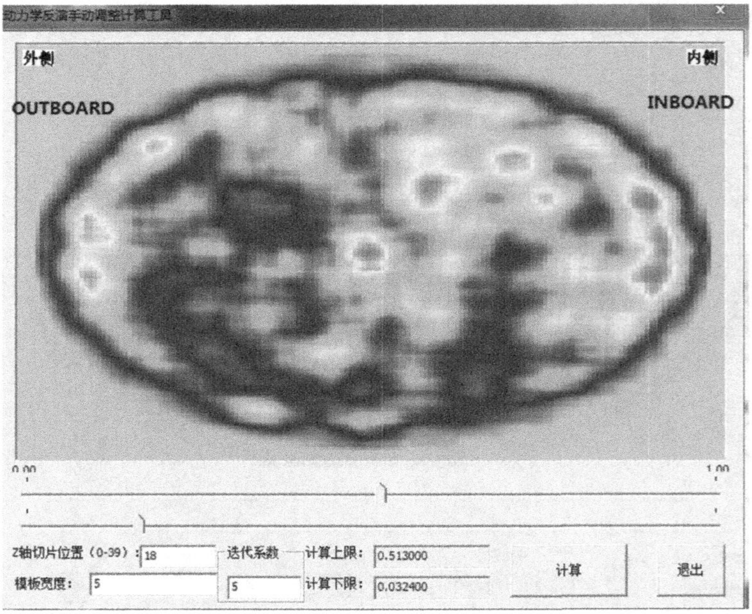

(B)

FIGURE 29.12

BRATUMASS's adjustable dynamics inversion tool box to image the ninth layer section from the breast bottom (each layer section of 2 mm). (A) Before surgical operation. (B) After surgical operation (7 days later).

29.8 CONCLUSIONS

A time domain signal of zero-IF output is obtained by BRATUMASS in clinical trial practice. The objective's hierarchical information is characterized by all frequency components in signal. Relevant objective dielectric properties are characterized by energy distribution of each frequency in signal. We used a sagittal iterative reconstruction algorithm to invert the permittivity distribution in breast tissue and used permittivity to reconstruct the breast tumor. In the inversion process, we used two reconstruction algorithms: a two-dimensional linear superposition reconstruction algorithm and a sagittal iterative reconstruction algorithm. Among these, a sagittal iterative reconstruction algorithm can be more accurate to calculate the dielectric properties distribution in the breast tissue.

The tumor location determined in the surgery can clearly be found by the corresponding dielectric properties values in the inversion image. But, a false-alarm signal may appear in a case where there is no tumor. The error leading to reconstruction region dielectric properties distribution comes from:

1. The antenna unit is handheld in clinical trial data collection, so that detection points cannot be accurately located. It brings great influence to spatial positioning accuracy in the inversion.
2. The target geometric size has a big difference with the medical measurement definition.
3. The detection case is not adequate in a clinical trial and the detection points are not enough.
4. It is difficult to ensure the antenna remains at the same detection plane and it cannot obtain exactly the same sagittal.

In addition, multivalue data in the inversion and divergence detection method cannot gather data into a certain point field, resulting in false-alarm signal generation.

In practice, there are many problems that need to be researched, such as the problem to image breast, mammary gland, and other living tissues as well as precision problems to image tumor tissues with small zenith diameter.

ACKNOWLEDGMENT

This work was performed while Prof. M. Yao was a visiting professor and PI in NSF Beacon Center Michigan State University, thanks to a visiting research program from Prof. Erik D. Goodman. M. Yao would also like to acknowledge the support of the Shanghai Science and Technology Development Foundation under the project grant numbers 03JC14026 and 08JC1409200, as well as the support of TI Co. Ltd through the TI (China) Innovation Foundation.

REFERENCES

[1] Tao Z-f, et al. Biopsy back wave preprocessing research of BRATUMASS system based on applications of fractional Fourier transform. In: Proceedings of the 2010 international conference on bioinformatics & computational biology, vol. II, July 12; 2010.
[2] Nikolova NK. Microwave imaging for breast cancer. IEEE Microw Mag 2011;12:78–94.

[3] Yao M, Tao Z-f, Pan Q-f. Application of quantum genetic algorithm on breast tumor imaging with microwave. In: Proceedings of the 11th annual conference companion on genetic and evolutionary computation conference, GECCO '09, July 2009; 2685–8.
[4] Zheng S. Breast tumor imaging method investigation in UWB near-field microwave environment. Master Thesis, East China Normal University. p. 34–5.
[5] Barnes FS, Greenebaum B. Handbook of biological effects of electromagnetic fields: Bioengineering and biophysical aspects of electromagnetic fields. 3rd ed. Boca Raton, FL: CRC Press; 2007.

CHAPTER

A SYSTEM FOR THE ANALYSIS OF EEG DATA AND BRAIN STATE MODELING

30

S. Subedi*, Y. Li†, C. Early‡, A. Chan§, J. Garza*, G. Schreiber¶, Y. Chang*, H. Lin*

Department of Computer Science and Engineering Technology, University of Houston-Downtown, Houston, TX, United States Department of Mathematics, Illinois State University, Normal, IL, United States† Department of Science and Engineering Technology, University of Houston-Clear Lake, Houston, TX, United States‡ Department of Statistics, University of California, Los Angeles, CA, United States§ Chevron-Phillips Chemical Company, Houston, TX, United States¶*

30.1 INTRODUCTION

Renowned scientist and philosopher Galvani was the first person to discover electrical activity in a living organism in the 18th century [1]. Later, the electrophysiologist Hans Berger successfully recorded electrical activity from the human brain using electroencephalography (EEG), which measures voltage oscillations due to ions flow in the neurons of the brain [1]. Today, EEG is one of the popular noninvasive techniques to record brain activity in clinical and research settings, and there is a wide range of applications for the analysis and interpretation of these measurements. The development of EEG devices, for example, EPOC from Emotiv (http://www.emotiv.com) and NeuroSky (http://www.neurosky.com), and increasing interest in EEG data analysis is evident. EEG data carries an immense potential in its usability in various areas including human-computer interaction, psychology, and neurological sciences. Therefore, it is a valuable endeavor to design an application that applies various analytical techniques to EEG data and predicts the state of the brain from which the data was acquired.

There are five major waves recorded by EEG devices (Table 30.1). Beta and gamma waves are linked with mechanism of consciousness, while alpha waves are associated with disengagement [2]. Similarly, inefficiency and daydreaming occurs during theta waves, and finally, delta waves are associated with low activity and sleeping [2]. There are numerous studies aimed at deciphering the complex relationship among consciousness of the brain, the underlying pattern of its activity, and the generation of waves, using mathematical models and computing technology. Yang et al. [3] have proposed some novel feature extraction methods using harmonic wavelet transform and bispectrum for EEG signals to be used in a brain-computer interface (BCI) system to classify left- and right-hand motor imagery. The experimental results have shown that the separation of the classes extracted by the proposed method achieved recognition accuracy of 90%. Similarly, in a different study, the spectrum analysis of brain waves using specific music stimulus has been successfully completed utilizing various statistical models [4]. The research group found that the upper alpha wave was entrained under the special

Table 30.1 Major Brainwave Frequencies

Brainwave Type	Frequency Range (Hz)	Mental States and Conditions
Delta	0.1–3	Deep, dreamless sleep, non-REM sleep, unconscious
Theta	4–7	Intuitive, creative, recall, fantasy, imaginary, dream
Alpha	8–12	Relaxed, but not drowsy, tranquil, conscious
Low beta	12–15	Formerly SMR, relaxed yet focused, integrated
Midrange beta	16–20	Thinking, aware of self and surroundings
High beta	21–30	Alertness, agitation
Gamma	30–100	Peak focus, super consciousness

brainwave stimulus. This study showed the positive correlation between upper alpha wave generation and memory formation in the brain.

The EEG is also being used to develop innovative systems in healthcare and biomedical research. A recent study has been reported to discover links between emotional states of patients and their brain activity using machine learning algorithms [5]. The research group analyzed EEG data collected during various emotional states from 40 Parkinson's disease patients and healthy subjects using a bispectrum feature and concluded that the higher frequency bands such as alpha, beta, and gamma played an important role in determining emotional states compared to lower frequency bands, delta and theta. In a different study, Direito and group [6] have designed a model to identify the different states of the epileptic brain using topographic mapping relative to delta, theta, alpha, beta, and gamma frequencies. The method achieved 89% accuracy in predicting abnormal versus normal brain states. These studies have reported that variability in analysis occurs due to two major reasons: the first based on the feature extraction method implemented, and the second being the prediction of the model is directly proportional with the increase in the constant variables associated with the modeling equation. This, overall, underscores the complexity of applying mathematical models to a natural phenomenon such as brain activity [5,6].

Brain state modeling research can be divided into two major models: statistical models and micro models. For example, statistical models are built by applying statistical analysis to collected data from meditation practitioners, while micro models try to catch physiological features of the brain state under examination. The current literature shows that both methods are used in the study of complementary and alternative medicine, which includes meditation as one of the methods. One approach is to study finite differences within the minds of those practicing meditation, and those who do not. Such an endeavor is an avenue toward modeling a wide range of brain states [7]. Loizzo et al. [8] performed a 20-week contemplative self-healing program study, which showed that a contemplative self-healing program can be effective in significantly reducing distress and disability among the testers. Habermann et al. [9], on the other hand, performed a long-term (5–20 years) project to investigate the use of complementary and alternative medicine and its effects on the testers' health. Comparisons across different groups of people are also found. For example, in a 6-week mindfulness-based stress reduction program, subjects assigned to the program demonstrated significant improvements in psychological status and quality of life compared with usual care [10]. In another study a group of Qigong practitioners were compared to a control group and positive impact on the quality of life of cancer patients was observed using EEG technologies [11].

In this chapter we focus on statistical classification methods to build a model, and any new data can then be analyzed, compared to the model, and assigned to a particular class. Thus, we can see that this process involves two discrete phases: (1) data modeling and (2) data classification. It is then our proposal that through EEG data collection and machine learning techniques, it should be possible to implement a wide range of specific applications that can provide useful functions to the user. One conceived implementation is an embedded system that would be capable of performing a real-time analysis of EEG data, as it is collected. A device such as this, when given unclassified EEG data, would then be able to classify the brain state of the user into one of a number of different classes, depending on the particular models available to the system, and how these models were trained. As the data is classified, the system would provide an indication to the user of which brain state the incoming data most closely resembles.

30.2 SYSTEM FOR EEG DATA COLLECTION, STORAGE, AND VISUALIZATION

A platform for comprehensive EEG data storage, processing, and analysis is desirable to promote applications of using EEG tools in both physiological (eg, clinical uses, sleep evaluation, fatigue detection, etc.) and psychological (cognitive sciences, BCI, etc.) scopes. Such a platform consists of EEG data collection devices (viz., EEG headset), communication channels (eg, smart phones), an online database for EEG data storage and processing, a web interface for users to access stored EEG data and activate data analysis and classification algorithms, and a forum for users to collaborate with each other while using the system. Fig. 30.1 shows a general outline of the proposed system. A valuable aspect of web-based systems is that most users find a well-designed system to be easy to use without a steep learning curve [12], primarily because of the ubiquity and widespread use of modern web-based applications. Ultimately, this means that nontechnical users can more easily focus on the analysis of the data without spending too much time learning how to use the system.

The various technologies involved in using the web for visualization purposes have been analyzed before. The Holmberg group performed a study on interactive web-based visualization in which they developed a framework to categorize different web-based technologies for 2D and 3D visualization [13]. DHTML/AJAX, or Dynamic Hypertext Markup Language with Asynchronous JavaScript and XML, consists of a combination of HTML and JavaScript and performs well under most conditions,

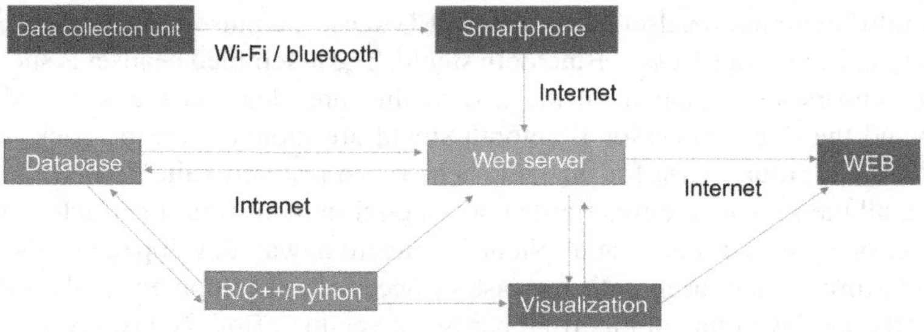

FIGURE 30.1

EEG data analysis system architecture.

with certain disadvantages related to limited communication with servers at the time of this writing. Another point made by Holmberg et al. is the popular use of this technology in commonly used platforms such as Google Maps, Facebook, and many more. Furthermore, a distinct advantage of the use of DHTML/AJAX is the fact that it is not a plugin that users must install but is rather built natively into the web browser. This means that clients do not need to install any special software to run the visualization software under this implementation. Aside from Adobe's Flash, JavaScript is the only widely used and highly compatible solution for executing client-side code, such as the code that allows a static HTML page to spring to life.

Another study, done by the Poliakov group found that a major advantage, among others, in a server-client system setup is that the client's hardware does not need to be particularly powerful as most of the processing and analysis of large data is done by the server [14]. This is desirable for our purposes, partly because servers tend to be more powerful than personal computers. This affords a decrease in execution time, as well as time spent transferring data. Another important factor with regard to server hardware is the increasingly common inclusion of more than one CPU. This makes it possible to execute data processing methods in parallel, consequently reducing the overall processing time of large amounts of data. This becomes crucial in the execution of machine learning algorithms, some of which can require large amounts of processing time, depending on the amount of data. The choice to implement our algorithms on the server side means that the majority of the work is done by the server, reducing both the load on the client as well as the amount of data that must be transferred between the server and the client.

JSON (JavaScript Object Notation) has been shown to be a viable way to transmit data from a server to a client's browser. Many common programming languages aside from JavaScript currently offer support for the JSON format. This provides convenience when developing using a combination of languages, such as with the use of PHP on the server side and JavaScript on the client side. Web-based systems have also shown that it is not only possible, but also desirable to display multiple records of data together, allowing users to better compare interpersonal differences and similarities between different records [14]. This provides a deeper level of analysis than what is possible when merely displaying individual records alone.

30.2.1 EEG DATA COLLECTION AND STORAGE

30.2.1.1 EEG headset

We briefly describe how a simple EEG headset can be built using commonly available materials. Our prototype multifunctional headset includes an EEG sensor, a pulse sensor, a temperature sensor, a microprocessor, and a microprocessor Bluetooth shield. The assembled headset is shown in Fig. 30.2, where the three sensors are mounted on the tips of the three legs on the forehead supports. The microprocessor and the microprocessor Bluetooth shield are mounted on the back, and the earlobe is used as an electrical ground base for the EEG sensor. To test and validate that the headset works properly and that all the sensors are functioning, a test environment was constructed. To approximate a real-world environment, a mobile smartphone application was developed on the Apple iPhone platform. This platform was chosen both for ease of access to development tools and also the wide availability of software development kits from hardware vendors. Both NeuroSky and Red Bear Labs included sample applications that were then transferred to a custom application that uses a simple view to display feedback from the various sensors.

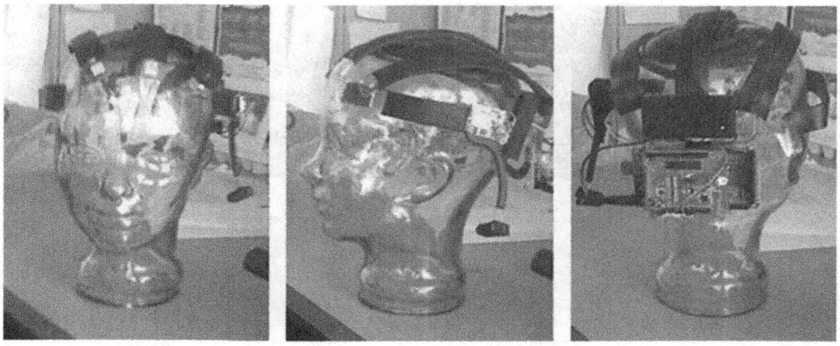

FIGURE 30.2

Prototype of the custom developed headset.

30.2.1.2 Data storage

To provide a reliable storage option that can handle the large amount of incoming data from EEG recording sessions, we store the data in a relational database. The database itself is hosted on a web server. The EEG data is stored in its own separate tables apart from other tables necessary for the basic functionality of the website. This is partly for security reasons, but mostly for clarity and ease of distinction between the EEG data and more general data. When in use, the NeuroSky headset produces a comma separated values (CSV) file that can be quite large for about 3 min of data collection. On average, the resulting file is 8–9 MB in size. These files were manually imported into the database initially, a process that requires that the data file first be transferred to the server and then imported directly into the database. To make this process simpler, we have implemented an interface that allows users to easily and seamlessly upload EEG data files.

After a user logs in to the system, they are given the option to upload a new file. The user can then select the local file they want to upload and provide a unique name for the data sets. At this point, the system will upload the file in the background, while displaying visual feedback to the user in the form of a progress bar (Fig. 30.3). Once the upload has been completed successfully, the file is stored in an upload folder and then immediately parsed into a new table in the database with the name given. Once completed, the EEG data is ready for immediate analysis through the website. If the upload fails for any reason, the user receives an appropriate message and the corrupt data is removed, thereby ensuring consistency.

30.2.1.3 Web visualization of EEG data

Once a repository of EEG data exists, it is necessary that a method exists to review and visualize the stored data. With this purpose in mind, we developed the following web-based visual and statistical review methods. The web server provides a user interface that allows users to view EEG data stored in the database and perform analysis on this data. Fig. 30.4 shows the web interface as it is displaying data that is rendered in waveform mode and statistical mode, respectively. The waveform rendering seen in Fig. 30.4 is generated dynamically within the user's browser. This allows the graph to be zoomed in or moved around, so as to focus on a specific section of the graph.

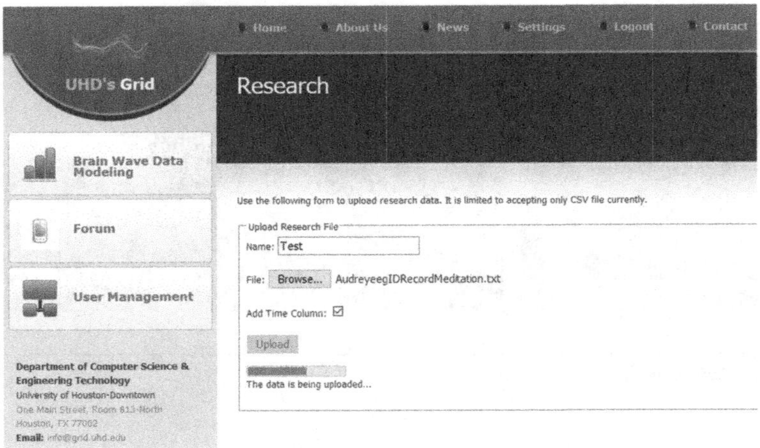

FIGURE 30.3

EEG data upload interface.

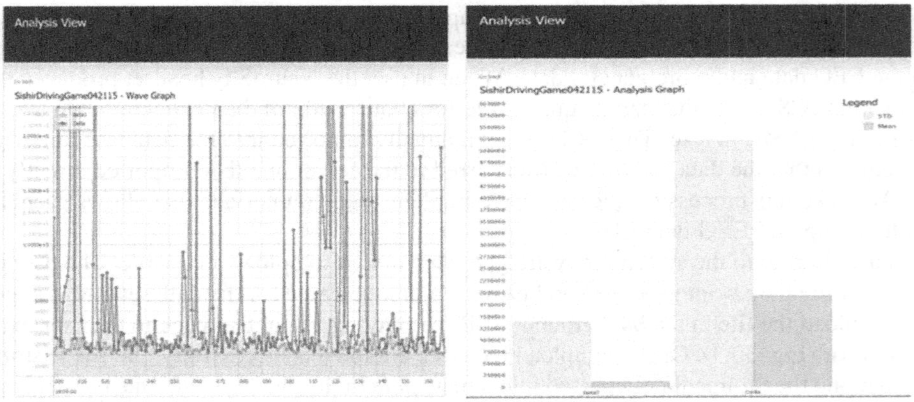

FIGURE 30.4

EEG wave analysis rendered by web interface.

30.2.1.4 Data modeling interface

Once the EEG data has been collected and stored in a standard format, it can be analyzed and modeled. In this section we present first a basic description of the way in which EEG data is measured and quantified. Next we describe the implementation of a variety of machine learning classification algorithms. The inclusion of these analysis methods is central to the overall web-based storage and analysis system, because they allow the user to analyze and test data from various subjects and collection times through a centralized interface. The current version of our toolkit includes the following classification algorithms: K-nearest neighbors (KNN), support vector machine (SVM), boosting, randomized aggregated decision trees (random forest), as well as a naïve Bayesian classifier. To implement this range of analytic methods, we have used multiple different languages and techniques. For example, our preliminary analysis and modeling of the characteristics of EEG data was done in the statistical language R and Python. Meanwhile, the machine learning algorithms available through the web interface are written in C++, and rely on the open source OpenCV package.

More specifically, to construct a model that can distinguish between two classes each algorithm requires at least two sets of data, one from each class. These data sets are arbitrarily labeled as either 1 or 0, which corresponds to the result that is output by the testing phase. In the case of EEG data classification, the data sets consist of the previously mentioned power spectrum values for the five frequency ranges listed. These values are obtained from a data table stored in the EEG data repository and are assigned to either class 0 or class 1, based on the user's selection. The data is then used by the algorithm in question to train a new model, which can then be tested against other sets of data. The training phase of the classification process is very processor intensive. Because of this, almost all of the actual computation involved in the classification process is deferred to the server, leaving to the client only the task of displaying the results. This means that to construct a model or perform a classification test, the entire data set need not be transferred from the server at all. Instead, the data remains on the server, where the classification is performed, after which the results are communicated to the client.

The classification interface (Fig. 30.5) allows the user to first select a classification algorithm. Then, the user is prompted to select either "Train" or "Test," as desired. Based on this choice, the user is either given the option of selecting multiple tables from the database with which to construct a model,

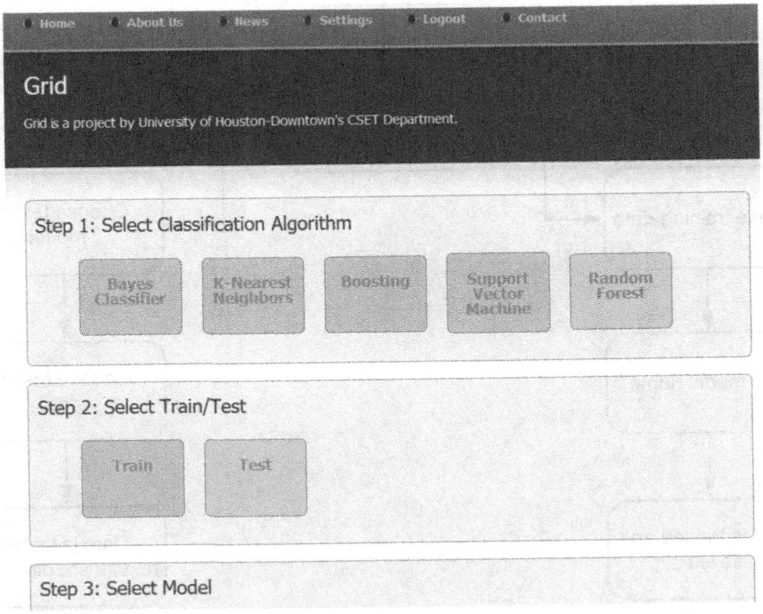

FIGURE 30.5

Algorithm selection pane.

or alternatively the option of selecting a preexisting model against which to test another table from the database. The training process then prompts the user for a name to give the new model, after which the model is trained and stored on the server. A record of this model is added to the database, so that it can be accessed in the future.

Fig. 30.6 describes the algorithm selection pane where the front-end interface is written in HTML, PHP, CSS, and JavaScript. PHP is responsible for the preprocessing and generation of the HTML pages, which use CSS to define the layout and graphical representation of the interface. Meanwhile, JavaScript is also used on the front-end for the purpose of live form handling and submission. Once the form is submitted, the server-side backend takes over. The user's selected options are passed to a PHP processing script that is responsible for executing the desired machine learning algorithm and passing the names of the chosen tables to the algorithms. The classification algorithms themselves are

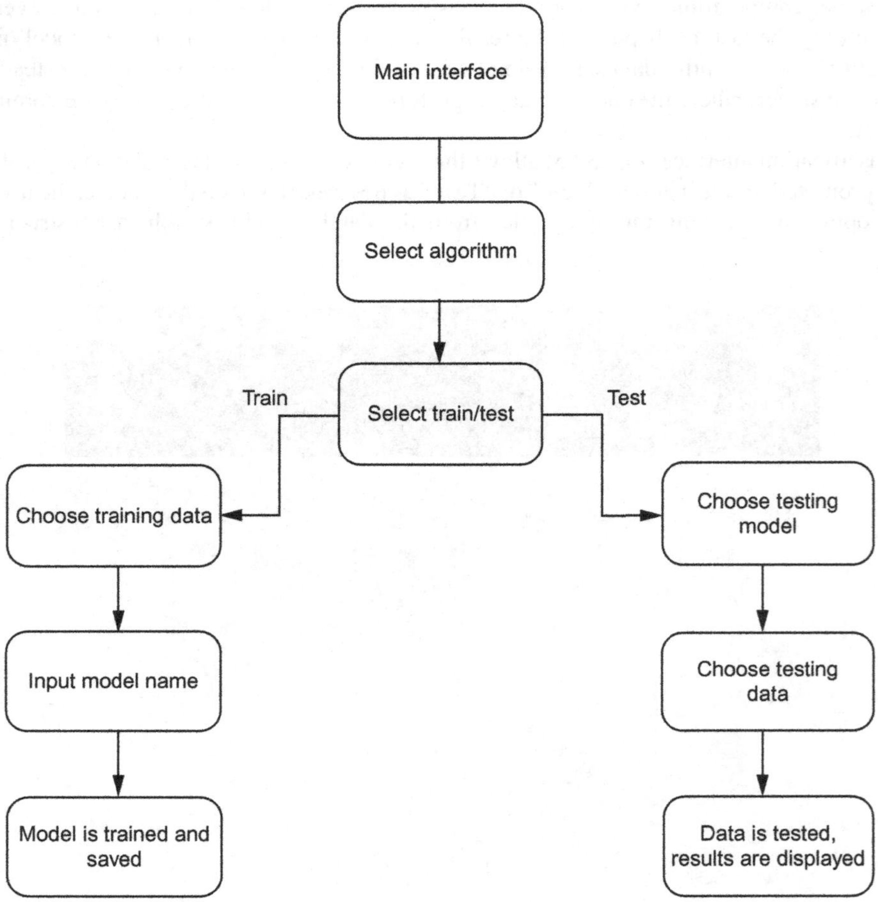

FIGURE 30.6

Algorithm selection pane model.

implemented in C++, and each is split into a separate training and testing executable. After the selected program is run, the results are reported back to the waiting PHP script, which encodes the values into an HTML page and sends it to the user's browser.

30.3 DATA ANALYSIS

The data was collected using the Neurosky Mindwave Mobile headset collected with the EEG ID Android application. For each test, the conditions were tightly controlled, in that each subject sat in the same location, in the same environment, for each sample collection. EEG data was collected for 5 min each in all cases, and so each individual sample consists of 5 min of "Active" data for playing video game, and 5 min of "Idle" data for relaxing with closed eyes. Component frequencies, including five major brain waves: delta (1–3 Hz), theta (4–7 Hz), alpha low (8–9 Hz), alpha high (10–12 Hz), beta low (13–17 Hz), beta high (18–30 Hz), gamma low (31–40 Hz), and gamma mid (41–50 Hz) were extracted from the raw data set using a feature extraction application provided by the Neurosky headset. These frequencies represent specific brain states including deep meditation and high anxiety.

30.3.1 DATA ANALYSIS ON RAW DATA SETS

The testing procedure involves varying not only the number of data sets included in the modeling phase, but also the percentage of each data sets used and the combination of different test subjects' data as presented in the architecture diagram (Fig. 30.7). There are three types of models in our study. The simplest type of model comprises only a single- subject's data, from a single collection time. A more interesting and complex case is when a model is constructed using data from multiple subjects. As the next logical step after single-subject models, we chose to train models that are composed of data from two different subjects (hereafter referred to as "bipartite" models.) Another case is a variation of the two-subject models, wherein the data is taken from the same subjects (homogenous), but the collection is from two separate times. Next, the number of subjects included in each model was then increased to three. We refer to this as a "tripartite" model. This was done to determine whether a good general model could be constructed. Additionally, we also constructed larger models, based on 12, 18, and 24 data sets, respectively. With these models, each of the three subjects provided a third of the data.

For each of these algorithms, an implementation was written in C++ using libraries from the OpenCV machine learning package. The implementations of these algorithms were designed to be run in two discrete phases: training and classification. The training phase takes at least one data file from each class as its input, and outputs a trained model. Similarly, the input for the classification or testing phase is a pre-trained model and at least one data file comprising the test data. The output of the classification phase is a confusion matrix, which shows how many samples from each class were correctly and incorrectly classified. Based on these results, a misclassification rate can be computed, or equivalently percentage values representing the portion of correct classifications. For each set common machine learning algorithms: KNN, SVM, random forest, Bayes, and boosting were chosen with an approach to include representative algorithms based on distance, tree, probability, and hypothesis, respectively.

The analysis of the result obtained on test data sets from same subject as well as different subjects showed that the random forest algorithm provides the highest percentage of correct classifications (Figs. 30.8 and 30.9). The highest accuracy level reached by random forest was 84%, which occurs

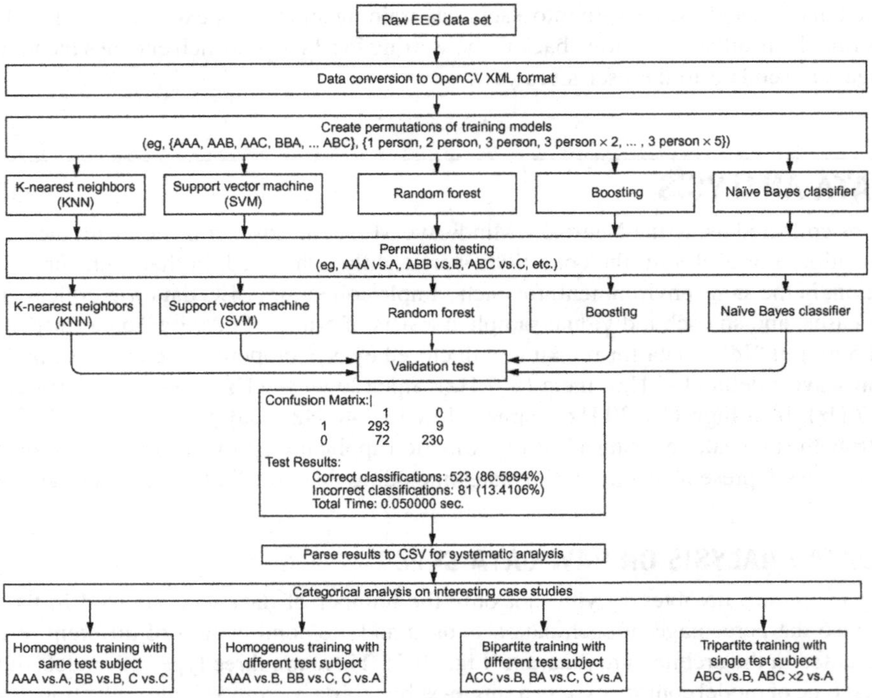

FIGURE 30.7

Architecture of systematic testing and analysis.

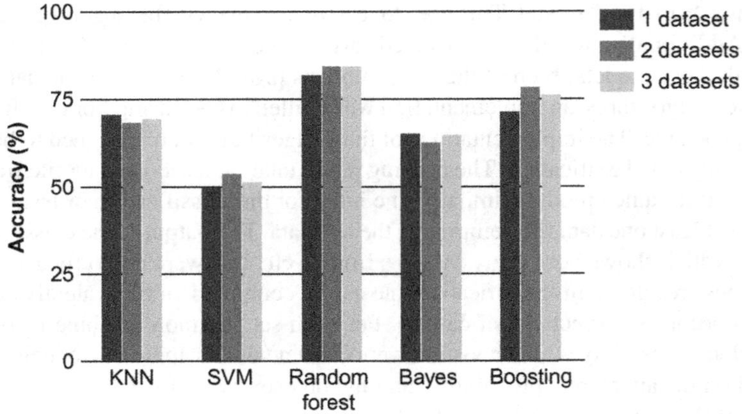

FIGURE 30.8

Test result comparison from same-subject tests.

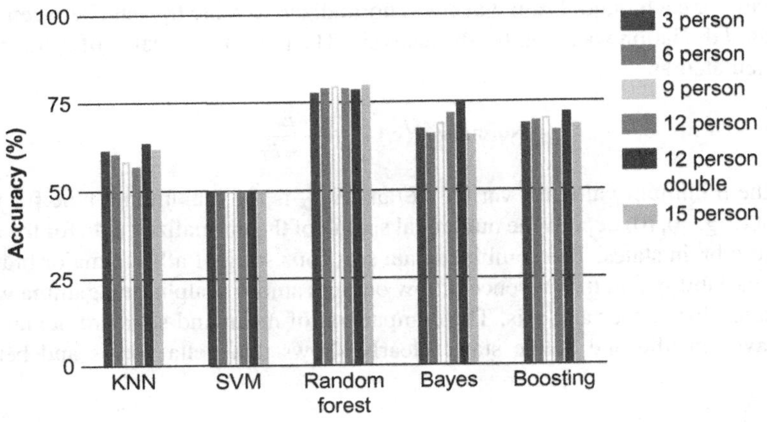

FIGURE 30.9

Test result comparison from tripartite models.

in the cases where a model was trained using three data sets from the same subject and then tested against data sets from the same subject. The results from our tests of the boosting method were the second most accurate, after random forest. Homogeneous training models incorporating data from two unique data sets seem to provide the highest accuracy rates (78%) for boosting, followed closely (76%) by the homogeneous models that were trained with three data sets.

In certain cases, the naïve Bayes classifier also produced relatively accurate results (Figs. 30.8 and 30.9). When using a tripartite training model composed of four data sets from each subject, the accuracy of Bayes reached an average of 75%. When compared to the 68% accuracy of the tripartite models trained with only one data set from each subject, it is tempting to conclude that the addition of more unique training data to a tripartite Bayes model will result in an increased accuracy; however, the accuracy level actually goes down when increasing from 1 to 2 data sets from each subject, and again when increasing from 4 to 5.

The accuracy of KNN ranged from 57% at the lowest, to 70% at the highest (Figs. 30.8 and 30.9). The lowest results were produced in the bipartite tests against a nonincluded subject, and also in the tripartite (×4) tests. KNN achieved the most accurate results in the single-person, single-data set tests. SVM consistently output results hovering around 50%, a rate that could be achieved by random guessing. Our suspicion is that SVM is not well suited to the classification of our brainwave data, possibly due to our selection of parameters. We tested the SVM algorithm with four different kernel types: linear, polynomial, sigmoid, and radial basis function. The variation of the kernel had no effect on the accuracy level of SVM's classifications, which remained firmly at 50% in all cases.

30.3.2 DATA ANALYSIS ON NORMALIZED MEAN

Another approach of understanding the structure and pattern of the data sets is by applying the machine learning techniques on inherited features of the data sets, such as the central tendency and deviation. Here, we compared the performances of the algorithms on normalized mean data sets alongside the raw analysis. The data for each major brain wave was normalized to scale the data between 0 and 1, and its mean and standard deviation was used for the analysis. The normalized value of e_i for variable E in the ith row was calculated as

$$\text{Normalized}(e_i) = \frac{e_i - E_{\min}}{E_{\max} - E_{\min}}$$

where $E_{\min}$ is the minimum value for variable E and $E_{\max}$ is the maximum value for variable E.

The box plot (Fig. 30.10) depicts the numerical spread of the normalized data for the all brain waves for active and idle brain states. The combined data sets consisting of all five major brain waves show analogous data variability and the presence of few outliers amongst alpha and gamma waves. The outliers are eliminated for further analysis. The comparison of mean and standard deviation among different brain waves in idle and active states clearly shows that delta waves and beta waves have

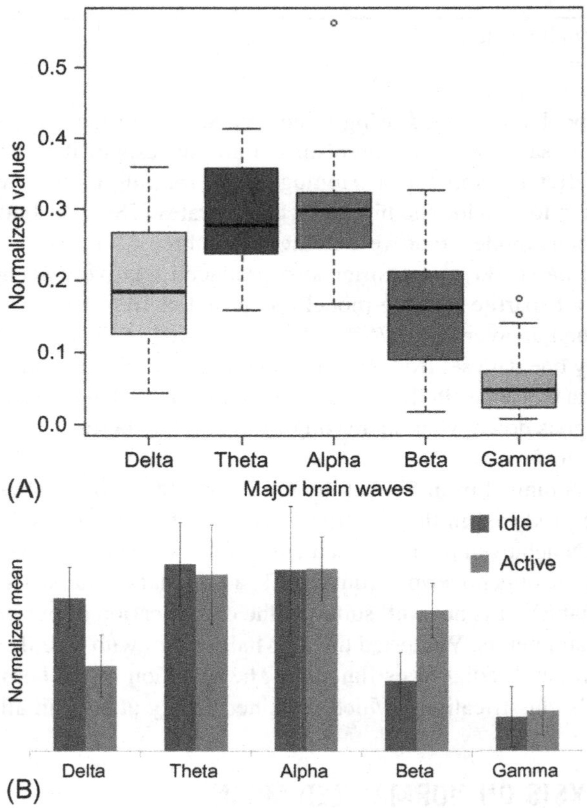

FIGURE 30.10

Visualization of normalized data sets using box plot for brain waves (A), comparison of mean and standard deviation among the brain waves in idle and active brain state (B).

Table 30.2 Correlation Analysis of the Major Brain Waves

	Delta	Theta	Alpha	Beta	Gamma
Delta	1				
Theta	0.53	1			
Alpha	−0.53	−0.50	1		
Beta	−0.75	−0.63	0.08	1	
Gamma	−0.36	−0.51	−0.07	0.35	1

significant differences (Fig. 30.10). Delta waves are clustered at higher values in idle states while beta waves are clustered at lower values, and vice versa in the active brain state. Correlation analysis corroborates that there exists a negative correlation between delta and beta waves during active and idle brain states (Table 30.2). This negative correlation can also be visualized using scatter plot (Fig. 30.11) where idle brain waves tend to cover higher x-axis coordinates while active waves were found more in higher y-axis coordinates.

Delta wave (0–3 Hz) is a dominant wave for idle state and beta wave (12–20 Hz) is a dominant wave of active state. The result also showed an interesting significant difference between these two waves. To further investigate this, we decided to focus on these two representative waves for active and idle state, respectively. Also, the understanding of the pattern of the dominant waves, delta and beta waves, for idle and active states will be an important step in deciphering the complexity of brain waves in different states. The density graphs (Fig. 30.11) further supports the idea that there exists a different pattern of delta and beta waves during active and idle states. To understand these dissimilar features of delta and beta waves, we decided to utilize the statistical machine learning techniques to explore any deep inherent differences.

A classification-based machine learning algorithm was implemented to survey the best algorithm to predict the brain states utilizing only delta and beta waves. The main challenge in this process was the problem of data separation for each brain wave at different brain states. Generally, the brain waves data from different states tend to cluster together, which becomes difficult for classification algorithms to draw a best fitting separation line. Because we were interested in comparing the performances of each algorithm in terms of the correct prediction rate, all 14 samples were used to train the algorithm and cross-validation technique was used to test the error rate of the model. Table 30.3 shows that out of the seven machine learning algorithms used, random forest showed a 4% error rate, while boosting and KNN with $n=4$, showed less than a 20% error. Similarly, SVM, naïve Bayes, neuralnet, and logistic regression showed higher error rates (Fig. 30.12).

The data analysis result demonstrates that the brain waves data performed better with tree-based algorithm random forest, while for other algorithms such as probability-based naïve Bayes and entropy-based neuralnet, the data did not achieve competitive error rate. Boosting and KNN model performed almost equivalently in predicting brain states (Fig. 30.12). KNN correctly predicted 24 out of 28 brain states while for SVM the number of incorrect prediction was slightly lower to 22 out of 28 brain sates (Fig. 30.13). These observations might be different for large sample sizes; however, the analysis does convey a finding that the tree-based model such as random forest learning algorithms are efficient in predicting brain states by analyzing EEG brain waves data for both raw and normalized mean data sets.

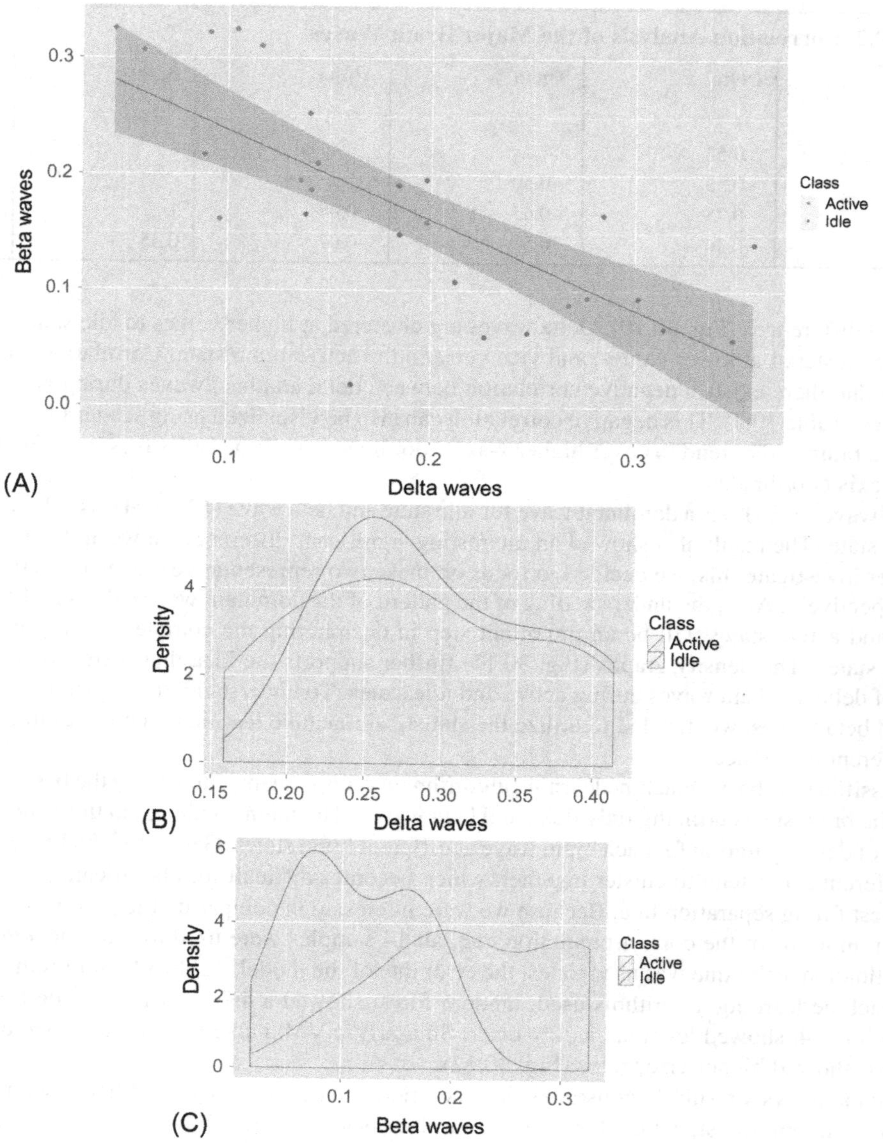

FIGURE 30.11

Scatter plot for major brain waves in active and idle brain states (A). Density graph of delta waves (0.1–3 Hz) (B) and beta waves (13–30 Hz) (C) during active and idle brain states.

Table 30.3 Summary of Classification-Based Prediction Scores

	Model							
	Train	Logit Reg	KNN	SVM	Naïve Bayes	Random Forest	Boost	Neural Net
Idle	14	11	13	11	11	14	13	13
Active	14	3	11	11	11	13	11	5
Error rate	0.00	0.50	0.14	0.21	0.21	0.04	0.14	0.36

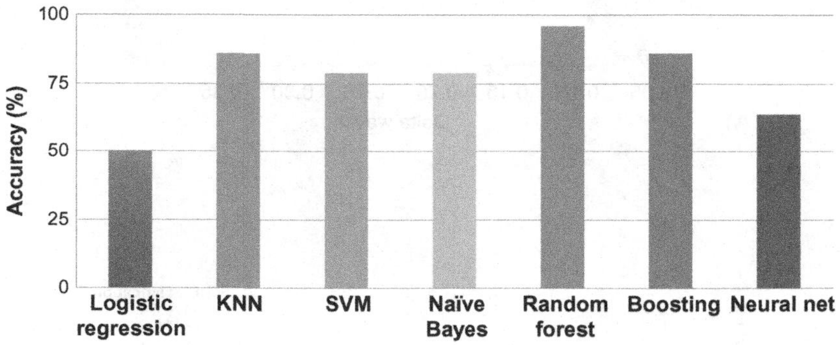

FIGURE 30.12

Comparison of common machine learning algorithms on test data sets.

Fig. 30.14 shows the comparison of all tested machine learning algorithms on normalized mean versus raw data sets. Random forest algorithm showed the lowest misclassification rate. This similarity in the performance of different algorithms with both raw and normalized mean data sets suggests that the pattern of brain waves are conserved from lower raw values to higher level of mean analysis. The overall higher values for normalized data sets might have resulted due to the test on model using the cross-validation technique on trained data sets, while for raw data sets separate train and test data sets were used. The inconsistency shown with the SVM algorithm requires further investigation as the accuracy of SVM depends to a great degree on the type of kernel used by the algorithm, and the values of the parameters passed to the algorithm during the training phase. A combination of a certain kernel and a set of parameters may have resulted in inconsistent misclassification rates.

In addition to the classification-based prediction model, it is also imperative to understand the natural structure and pattern of brain waves data in different states. One of the techniques used in analyzing organization of the data was clustering algorithm. Here, we used both *k*-means algorithm as well as hierarchical algorithm. The analysis showed that the performance of *k*-means and hierarchical clustering were similar (Fig. 30.15). Both algorithms assigned 22 out of 28 data points in the correct states while 6 of them were assigned to the wrong state. For *k*-means analysis, 28 iterations were used to incorporate all data points and 2 clusters were used to separate data points to assign each cluster to active and idle brain states. Similarly, for hierarchical clustering, dendrogram was drawn with two cuts to separate data points into two different states.

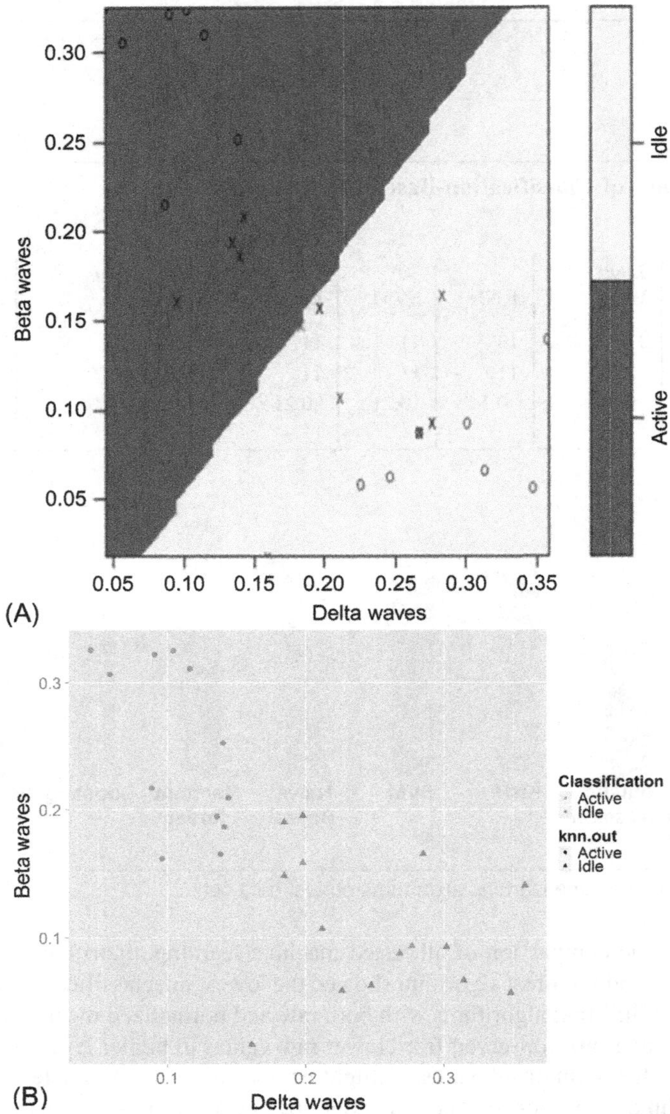

FIGURE 30.13

Prediction of active and idle brain states using SVM (A) and KNN (B) models.

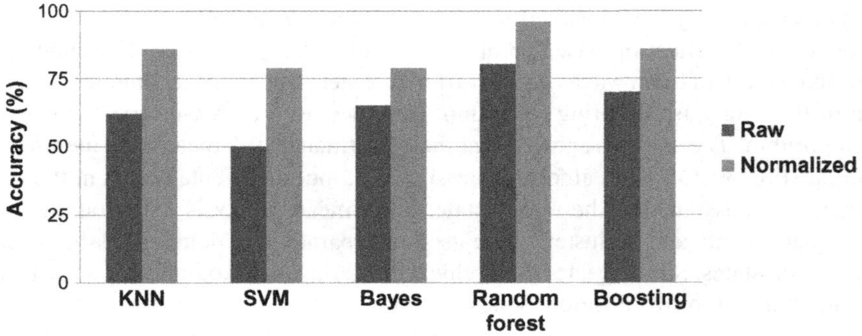

FIGURE 30.14

Comparison of algorithms performance on raw and normalized data sets.

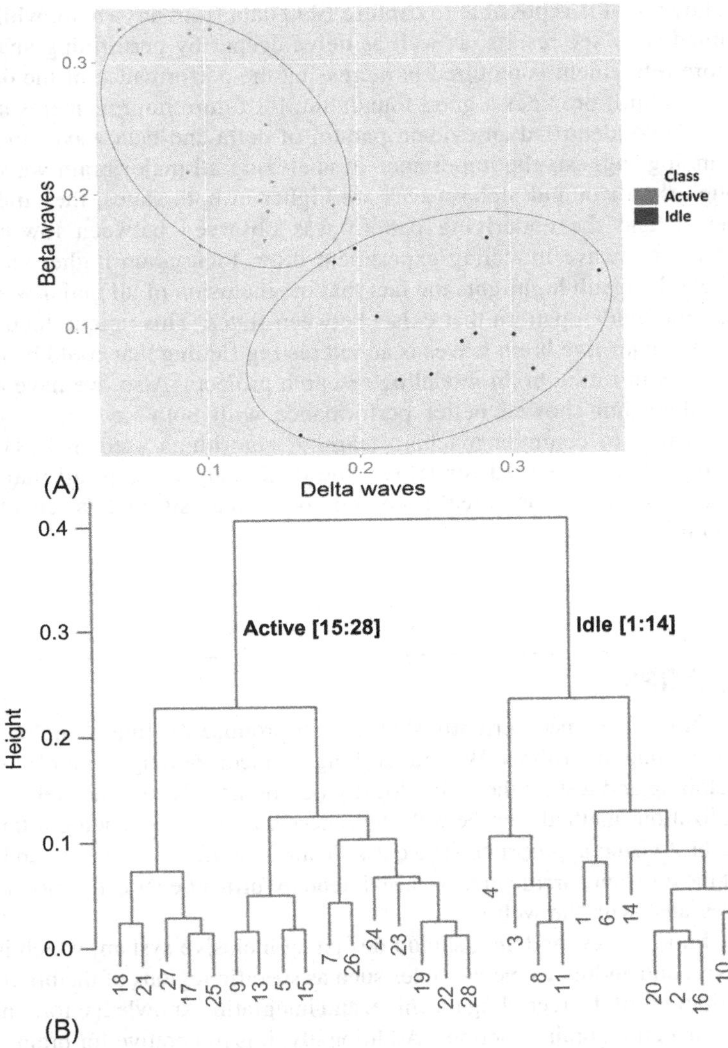

FIGURE 30.15

Cluster analysis: *k*-means (A) and hierarchical (B) for delta and beta brain waves.

30.4 CONCLUSION

In this study we provide a proof of concept for an EEG data analysis system using an EEG headset, mobile application, web server, and web interface with analytics. Additionally, the classification interface provides a way for users to test out various algorithms using different combinations of data for the purpose of constructing training models and testing new data sets on them.

Overall, we have shown that it is possible to capture EEG data from anywhere, while on the move, and be able to immediately see results, as well as delve deeper by performing analysis remotely. Although much more refinement is required in increasing the performance of the data capture and analysis, the system as built provides a good foundation for future improvements and expansions.

Additionally, we have identified an evident pattern of delta and beta waves in idle and active brain states. The finding suggests the importance of analyzing all major brain waves in each state because even though the theta and alpha waves are higher in both states, they did not show any significant difference, and the underlying pattern was observed between low-numbered delta and beta waves. The brainwave modeling experiment often focuses on higher values and single dominant waves; here the result highlights the fact that the inclusion of all major waves in the analysis could delineate the hidden pattern that exists between states. This unique feature of delta and beta waves among the major five brain waves is an interesting finding that could be implemented in recognizing brain states in future brain modeling research projects. Also, we have discovered that the random forest algorithm showed better performance with both raw and normalized mean data sets when compared to common machine learning algorithms used in EEG data analysis. This finding can now be implemented for large-scale data analysis using all major brain waves with increased sample size to conduct a real-time brain wave analysis on data sets utilizing parallel computing architecture.

30.5 FUTURE WORK

The system that we have developed currently shows great promise for future implementation of the additional machine learning algorithms. We are working on incorporating more of those analysis algorithms after developing and testing them first locally before inclusion on the website. We will also develop more visualizations methods for the website as necessary for different algorithms so as to represent results in the best visual appropriate. The classification interface will be expanded to allow the user to alter each of the relevant parameters. We also intend to further develop the mobile application to be more tightly integrated with the website.

The prospective brain waves modeling should design an inclusive system, which incorporates all the major brain waves, and addresses the variables such as specific regions of the brain, inconsistency within samples, limitations of the recording machine, and integrating knowledge form neurobiology in terms of understanding certain brain functions. Additionally, it is imperative for brain wave modeling studies to contemplate the rigorous time-series analysis of brain waves to decipher trends, irregularities, cycles, seasonality, and other variations among waves during different states. Therefore, an improvised advanced machine learning modeling system that includes all major brain waves rather than just dominant representative waves will be implemented on large data sets. The project aims to address the complexity of classification of brain waves data by modeling the major brain waves independently with clinically significant brain regions combined with the feature extraction and time-series analysis. This will achieve an efficient and predictable brain wave modeling system that has potential application in hospitality and clinical industry for self-controlled deep brain relaxation and early diagnosis of various brain abnormalities, respectively.

ACKNOWLEDGMENTS

This work is partially supported by NSF UGI-CSTEM (Grant# 0965952) and NSF Summer REU (Grant# 1262928) and National Computational Science Institute Blue Waters Student Internship program.

REFERENCES

[1] Kropotov J. Quantitative EEG, event-related potentials and neurotherapy. San Diego, CA: Elsevier; 2009.

[2] Larsen E. Classification of EEG signals in a brain-computer interface system [Ph.D. thesis]. Trondheim: Norwegian University of Science and Technology; 2011.

[3] Yang R, Song A, Xu B. Feature extraction of motor imagery EEG based on wavelet transform and higher-order statistics. Int J Wavelets Multiresolution Inf Process 2010;8(3):373–84.

[4] Zhuang T, Zhao H, Tang Z. A study of brainwave entrainment based on EEG brain dynamics. Comput Inf Sci 2009;2(2):80–6.

[5] Yuvaraj R, Murugappan M, Ibrahim N, Sundaraj K, Omar M, Mohamad K, et al. Optimal set of EEG features for emotional state classification and trajectory visualization in Parkinson's disease. Int J Psychophysiol 2014;94(3):482–95.

[6] Direito B, Teixeira C, Ribeiro B, Branco M, Sales F, Dourado A. Modeling epileptic brain states using EEG spectral analysis and topographic mapping. J Neurosci Methods 2012;210(2):220–9.

[7] Lin H. Measurable meditation, In: Proceedings of the international symposium on science 2.0 and expansion of science (S2ES 2010), the 14th world multiconference on systemics, cybernetics and informatics (WMSCI 2010), Orlando, FLorida, June 29–July 2; 2010. p. 56–61.

[8] Loizzo J, Peterson J, Charlson M, Wolf E, Altemus M, Briggs W, et al. The effect of a contemplative self-healing program on quality of life in women with breast and gynecologic cancers. Altern Ther Health Med 2010;16(3):30–7.

[9] Habermann T, Thompson C, LaPlant B, Bauer B, Janney C, Clark M, et al. Complementary and alternative medicine use among long-term lymphoma survivors: a pilot study. Am J Hematol 2009;84(12):795–8.

[10] Lengacher C, Johnson-Mallard V, Post-White J, Moscoso M, Jacobsen P, Klein T, et al. Randomized controlled trial of mindfulness-based stress reduction (MBSR) for survivors of breast cancer. Psychology 2009;18(12):1261–72.

[11] Oh B, Butow P, Mullan B, Clarke S. Medical Qigong for cancer patients: pilot study of impact on quality of life, side effects of treatment and inflammation. Am J Chin Med 2008;36(3):459–72.

[12] Lourenço A, Plácido da Silva H, Carreiras C, Alves A, Fred A. A web-based platform for biosignal visualization and annotation. Multimed Tools Appl 2014;70(1):433–60.

[13] Holmberg N, Wunsche B, Tempero E. A framework for interactive web-based visualization, In: AUIC '06 proceedings of the 7th Australasian user interface conference, vol. 50, JanuarySydney: Australian Computer Society; 2006.

[14] Poliakov A, Albright E, Hinshaw K, Corina D, Ojemann G, Martin R, et al. Server-based approach to web visualization of integrated three-dimensional brain imaging data. J Am Med Inform Assoc 2005;12(2):140–51. doi:http://dx.doi.org/10.1197/jamia.M1671.

CHAPTER

USING TEMPORAL LOGIC TO VERIFY THE BLOOD SUPPLY CHAIN SAFETY

31

N. Hazzazi*, J. Albasri†, B. Yu*, D. Wijesekera*, P. Costa‡

*Department of Computer Science, George Mason University, Fairfax, VA, United States**

Prince Sultan Military Medical City, Riyadh, Saudi Arabia† Department of Systems Engineering and Operations Research, George Mason University, Fairfax, VA, United States‡

31.1 INTRODUCTION

Blood transfusion is a procedure administered on patients during major surgeries, injuries, or illnesses such as hemolytic anemia. Transfusions are administered in 137 countries serving a population of 3.1 billion worldwide [1]. Each year, almost five million Americans need a blood transfusion [2]. The health care industry faces increasing challenges for ensuring safe, quality blood transfusions, including

- Risk of transmission of infection through unsafe blood or blood products, especially during the donors window period (ie, the time between when an infectious agent enters the donor body and when it becomes detectable to laboratory tests).
- Technical and clerical errors in the processing and testing of blood.
- Errors in the administration of blood or blood derivatives.

The Food and Drug Administration (FDA), in its strategy for blood safety and availability for improving patient health and saving lives, says that cumulatively 58% of transfusion fatalities are caused by transfusion errors and related issues [3]. In 2013, the FDA reported that there were 65 fatalities in the USA due to causes such as microbial infection, hemolytic transfusion reaction (HTR), transfusion-related acute lung injury (TRALI), and others. Transfusing blood is the end result of a long, well-regulated supply chain that consists of collecting blood from donors; testing and separating whole blood into components such as red blood cells, platelets, and so on, preserving them in regulated conditions (eg, adding preservatives and refrigeration); and conducting the transfusion based on physicians' orders and evidence-based guidelines. Not adhering to the mandated requirements in this complex supply chain may cause unsafe blood transfusions.

In past decades, many researchers and organizations changed their efforts and resources from creating standards to adopting new IT technologies that would improve blood transfusion safety. For example, the World Health Organization (WHO) [1] and the AABB [4], among others, have defined blood safety standards. In the USA, blood banks are mandated to follow FDA blood safety standards [5]. Many health organizations are using information technology tools and computerized systems for blood bank systems, such as the TANGO Automated Blood Bank System, SIBAS [6] to make the transfusion chain safer. In transfusions, adverse effects are closely examined and routinely appropriate corrective actions are taken.

In most countries, blood product safety still relies on manual documentation that is not linked together, such as paper-based or computerized forms scattered throughout the blood supply chain. Blood bank systems have moved from manual documentation to complex systems with improved functionality such as inventory control and policy management [7, 8]. However, current systems assist in collecting the necessary documentation in electronic formats but do not provide electronically verifiable safety assurance in each step. Also, current systems do not provide verifiable safety for the supply chain as a whole as specified by each locality's safety standards. We are unaware of any system that uses safety-verified workflows in administering blood products. Providing a method for doing so is the objective of this chapter.

Observed errors committed by blood bank staff, especially by limited staff members working during night shifts who nonetheless handle normal workload [9], compels electronically enforceable blood safety verification. This chapter extends our proposed work from Hazzazi et al. [10] by introducing a safety verification method that can be built into existing electronic medical record and blood bank systems using established engineering practices. It provides a refined and detailed version of our approach discussed in [10]. It includes formally modeling the supply chain of blood as a workflow, specifying the safety regulations in a logical syntax and verifying that the appropriate components of the entire supply chain satisfy applicable FDA and AABB safety regulations and creating more descriptive properties that capture more refined safety requirements than those discussed in [10].

The rest of the chapter is organized as follows. Sections 31.2 and 31.3 describe our process for verifying the safety of the supply chain of blood, which starts with modeling the supply chain as a workflow system. Our workflows are modeled as a choreographed collection of state-full processes. These processes change state due to participants — or processes working on behalf of them — executing input/output operations that result in a process state transforming into a specified collection of succeeding states as shown in Fig. 31.3. We then used an automated tool to translate the workflows to a temporal logic model checker, with some of our own updates. This is described in Section 31.4. Then, we manually parsed the safety standards mandated by FDA and AABB and manually modeled them as temporal logic statements that have to hold in particular states of the blood processing supply chain. This procedure is described in Section 31.5. Section 31.6 shows how we implemented this entire process transparent to an EMR system using an open source tool. Finally, Section 31.7 describes related work and Section 31.8 concludes the chapter.

31.2 FORMALLY MODELING BLOOD BANK WORKFLOWS

This section describes the steps taken to model blood bank workflows. First, we gathered the information about processes used in blood banks from the FDA regulations and AABB standards. Then, one author of this chapter received a month-long training from blood bank professionals while shadowing and documenting each task carried out throughout the blood supply chain. We then modeled the workflows used in blood banks using the XML-based workflow modeling language YAWL [11]. YAWL facilitates graphically representing hierarchical workflows and provides a workflow engine that can execute syntactically validated workflows. Each workflow in YAWL consists of a beginning (►), end (■), tasks (□), subworkflows (complex tasks), and arcs (→) for transitions from one task to another.

Fig. 31.1 shows the highest level workflow (so-called main net in YAWL) of the first models we created. It consists of all the main subworkflows required of any blood bank process that models each

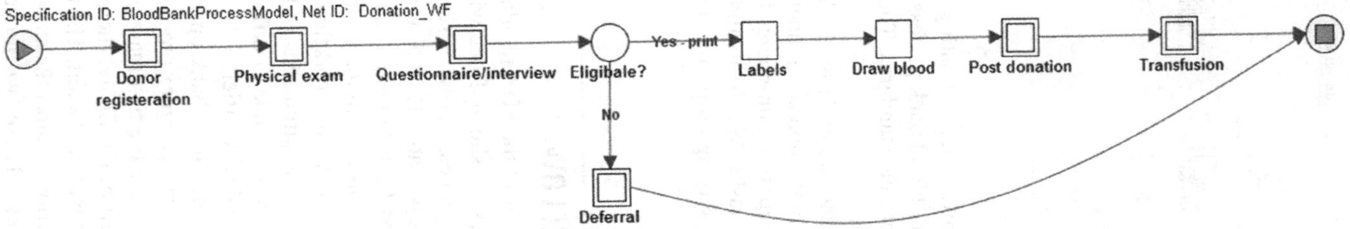

FIGURE 31.1

Main net: first version created.

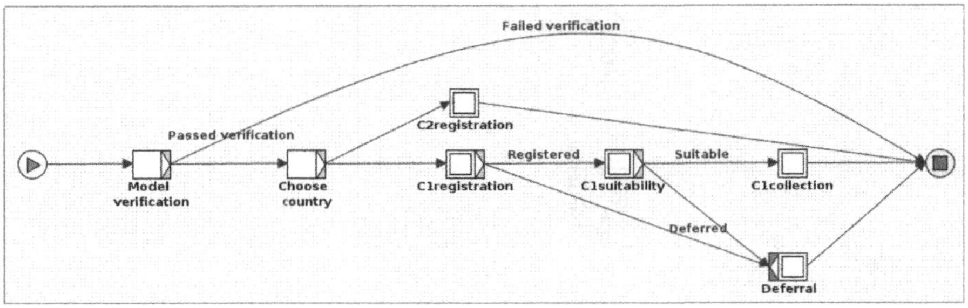

FIGURE 31.2

Main net: most updated version.

one of the complex tasks as a subworkflow. After validating the accuracy of FDA- and AABB-mandated steps of our workflow models with blood bank professionals, we updated the model to capture the processes and mandated requirements and standards. The validation process leads to updating workflows in our initial model.

Fig. 31.2 shows the main workflow (called the *main net* in YAWL) of an updated model. These updates resulted in adding more transitions in the updated model to meet the realistic task transitions based on the user input. Also, we included safety requirements based on the FDA and AABB specifications in each of the atomic and complex tasks. We then validated the attachment of the safety requirements with the states of the workflow, relying on professionals to ensure the correctness of our interpretation of the safety mandates.

31.3 THE BLOOD SAFETY WORKFLOW

This section covers the updated high-level view of the FDA regulations and AABB standards as shown in Fig. 31.3. In this figure, complex processes are shown filled with grey or black color, with their associated decomposition below them. Each process shows a set of requirements below it in bullet form. As the diagram shows, the main processes are (1) Registration, (2) Suitability/Physical Exam, (3) Deferral, (4) Collection/Draw Blood, (5) Post Donation, and (6) Transfusion. As an extension of our work, we modeled apheresis workflow throughout the main processes described. Also, updated our model and all processes variables to reflect the actual workflow. All processes — from beginning of donation until transfusion — abide by the safety requirements set forth by the FDA and AABB. To the best of our knowledge, there is no published blood bank workflow that has been verified against the FDA and AABB requirements using a mechanical verifier.

In addition to the main processes that define blood bank operations following FDA- and AABB-mandated requirements, Fig. 31.3 includes various complex processes that model the overall workflow of the blood bank operations. For example, before the first main process for the blood bank workflow that is modeled by the third box at the top left of the figure, there are two complex processes are so-called meta processes shown in the first two boxes on the left. The first models the process in which the user is required to verify the end-to-end workflow against the standard requirements, while the second captures the country-specific donation process. These two processes are not part of the allocation

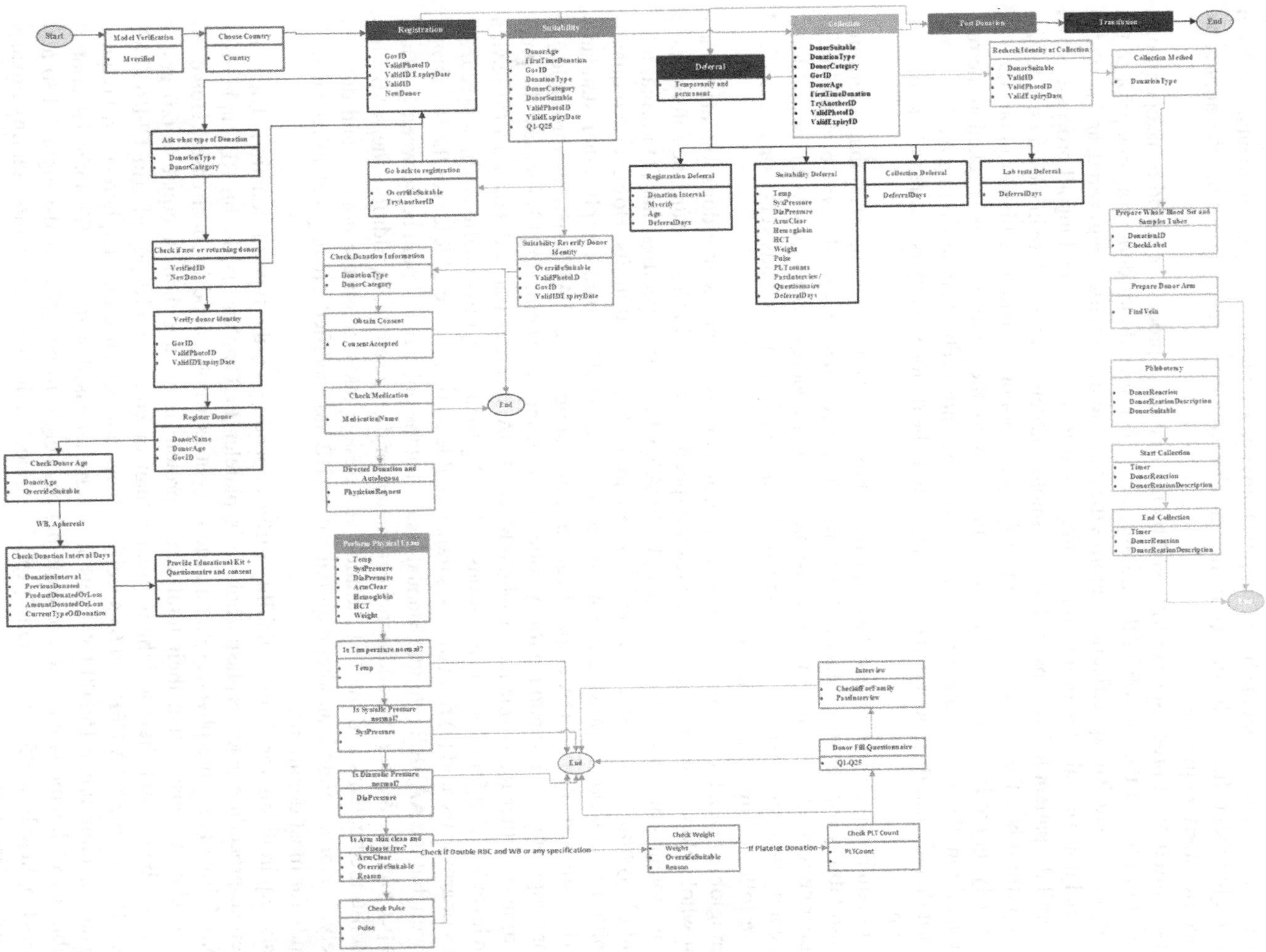

FIGURE 31.3

High-level view of the updated model + FDA regulations requirements.

processes of the blood supply chain that were verified by us, but are meta-processes that check the application processes (that model the blood supply chain) against blood safety requirements. The latter models the requirement that each country name must be known, so as to determine the applicable location-specific safety requirements.

These two initial meta-processes are followed by the first main process of blood bank operations, Registration (third box at the top left of the figure), which captures donor demographics prior to the mandated physical exam. The specification requires the donor to be identified, registered, and provided with educational material, all stemming from a safety measure mandate of tracking all processes from registration until the patient follow-ups [12]. For example, the detailed procedure in the *Identify & Verify Donor* step (third box from top) involves identifying the donor by matching his/her photo ID with the person, verifying the ID expiration date and validity. Also, the donor's age is checked at the registration. In addition, the interdonation time interval of the donor is checked depending on the type of donation, past donation, and amount donated to ensure that the donor's safety is assured after donating blood this time.

The next main process is the physical exam (fourth box at the top left in Fig. 31.3) that determines the donor's suitability for donating blood. This composite process depends on the type of donation, as there are separate regulatory requirements for whole blood or apheresis donations. All types of donations require a written consent signed by the donor, his/her medication, and answers to a standardized questionnaire followed up with an interview.

The hemoglobin level, blood pressure, temperature, arm diseases, and the interdonation interval are checked for whole blood donors. These measures are specified by the FDA to assure the safety of the donor and the donated blood sample. For example, FDA's CFR 640.3 specifies that (1) normal temperature and (2) systolic and diastolic blood pressures are within normal limits. However, no quantifiable definition of *normal* is provided. For this reason, many blood banks apply other standards (eg, AABB) in support of the FDA's specification. For example, the AABB defines thresholds of $\leq$37.5°C for temperature, $\leq$180 mm Hg for systolic pressure, and $\leq$100 mm Hg [13] for diastolic pressure. Regarding the other requirements for whole blood, FDA specifies that a donor must (a) have a hemoglobin level $\geq$12.5 g for allogenic donations and $\geq$11 g for autologous donations, (b) be free from skin diseases or arm scars, and (c) from diseases transmissible by blood. The CFR leaves the *(4) normal pulse rate* open, but the AABB Technical Manual states that the pulse rate should be between $\geq$50 and $\leq$100 beats per minute. We use this additional parameter for the pulse rate. In addition, the AABB has defined specific medications and the last duration and dosage taken to ensure donor's and donated blood's safety. Donor's weight is another requirement AABB has specified it to be greater than or equal to 110 pounds for most donations.

Apheresis requirements for donor suitability differ depending on the type of donation. There are several apheresis procedures such as plasma apheresis, platelet (PLT) apheresis, double RBC apheresis. All donations follow the same physical exam requirement as whole blood in most cases. However, donors are checked to ensure that their total serum protein is greater than or equal to 6.0 grams per milliliters of blood and their weight is greater than or equal to 110 pounds (in CFR640.63, section C5). Although the FDA CFR 640.63 specified these requirements, Plateletpheresis will require the donor to have a minimum of 150,000 platelets per microliter based on the AABB standard to control safety. Double RBC donations will require male donors height to be $\geq$5′1" and weight $\geq$130 and female donors height to be $\geq$5′5" and weight $\geq$150. We modeled the physical exam/suitability process based on these requirements.

Once eligibility is established, the donor is ready for the collection process (sixth box at the top left in Fig. 31.3). Collections also have specific requirements for regular donations (whole blood) and apheresis, which covers aspects such as unit identification, donor arm preparation, and unit temperature control (5.3.2, 5.6.3.2, in [4]). Whole blood and apheresis require each unit to be linked to a donor via his/her donor ID. FDA's CFR 640.4 states that the skin of the donor at the site of phlebotomy shall be prepared thoroughly and carefully by a method that gives maximum assurance of a sterile container of blood and a proper donor arm preparation to prevent blood contamination. Controlling the temperature of the blood bag after the collection is another requirement that the FDA specifies as collected blood to be placed in storage at a temperature between 1°C and 6°C or 21°C and 24°C immediately after whole blood collections depending on the component preparation. The FDA CFRs 640.4, 640.14, 640.22, and 640.32 provide information about whole blood collection but are not as specific on either apheresis collection or the volume of blood collected. For this reason, we used AABB specification for the volume of blood required on whole blood and apheresis collections (5.6.4 and 5.5.3.5, respectively, in [4]). The donor is monitored for any reactions during collection and once a collection is completed the system sets donation interval time depending on the type of donation collected. The step after collection is post donation, consisting of blood processing and donor monitoring (seventh box at the top left in Fig. 31.3). As stated by blood bank professionals, the donor is monitored to assure he/she does not develop any adverse reactions to ensure his/her own safety. It is mandated by the FDA in CFR 640.5 to collect extra samples of the donated blood unit at the time of collection for testing (modeled in Fig. 31.3). CFR 640.5 states that all laboratory tests shall be made on a specimen of blood taken from the donor at collection time.

CFR 640.5 also specifies the main tests that are required in processing the blood unit and their acceptable results. These include a serological test for syphilis, blood grouping, and Rh tests. In Fig. 31.3 we model the FDA-mandated requirement for the method used for blood grouping. This is stated in CFR640.5 part (b) as *at least two blood group tests shall be made and the unit shall not be issued until grouping tests by different methods or with different lots of antiserums are in agreement.* Regarding Rh grouping, most blood banks currently carry out both the blood grouping and Rh tests in parallel, which we model following them.

Further tests must be done for sterility, blood unit inspection, and test for communicable disease based on CFR 640.5 (Sections d, e, f). All donated blood shall be visually inspected and the FDA states that it should be inspected at storage and prior to using. The list of communicable diseases required to check is covered in CFR 610.40 and are included in our model.

Once blood is collected, tested, and stored, the next step is transfusion (eighth box on the top left in Fig. 31.3), in which an authorized health professional requests blood transfusion, transfuses the compatible blood, and monitors the patient. The AABB have specified the details required to request for blood transfusion (AABB standard parts 5.11.1.1 and 5.28.2 [4]) and for checking blood group ABO/Rh (AABB standard parts 5.12 and 5.12.1 [4]), which are both modeled as processes shown in Fig. 31.3.

Not meeting any of the blood safety requirements will defer the donation. There are different deferral types that depends on registration, suitability, collection, postdonation, and transfusion deferral (fifth box at the top left shown in Fig. 31.3). AABB specify deferral requirements for each of allogenic, autologous, and apheresis donations (AABB standard 5.4.4.3, 5.4.4.4, 5.5.3.4.3, 5.5.3.5.1) [4]. For this chapter, we are covering high-level deferral to ensure any process not meeting the safety requirement is deferred. Our ongoing work models the details of deferrals.

31.4 UPDATING THE YAWL2DVE TRANSLATOR

We use Divine to verify safety mandates in our blood supply chain [14]. Divine is a model checker for linear temporal logic (LTL) properties. Divine expects two inputs, a model with processes written in Divine Language `.dve` and LTL property `.ltl`. The model checker then verifies that the model against the LTL properties and outputs if the properties hold, along with standard details of model checking such as reachability, number of edges, and other metric information (max-memory, max-time, etc.). YAWL2DVE is a translator that translates YAWL specification (model) into `.dve`, which then can be used in Divine model checker.

The `YAWL2DVE` translator was created in 2010 by Fazle Rabbi, which helped us translate YAWL specification to Divine (`.DVE`) model checker language [15]. This section describes the updates we made to `YAWL2DVE` to extend its capabilities. To refine the usage of YAWL specification compared to [10] for the created blood supply change, there was a need to update and extend some of `YAWL2DVE` capabilities to ensure Divine will process any integer or string. `YAWL2DVE` extensions are (1) replace $=$ with $==$, (2) replace $;==$ with $;=$, (3) replace $\leq=$ with $\leq$, (4) replace $\geq=$ with $\geq$, (5) replace $!==$ with $!=$, (6) replace \\ with `%`, and (7) string to integer mapping.

The string to integer mapping was created to overcome Divine's limitations in string processing. Also, to create refined models that capture real-life data without encoding them in integers, we needed to have strings as data. To implement these changes, we created an algorithm (Algorithm 1) that maps data structures to regular expressions. Algorithm 1 uses the concept of a *map* that maintains a collection of key value pair associations where the key is unique in the collection. Map operations include adding, removing, and modifying key value pairs as well as looking up a value by its key. The first map (MAP1) holds variable names VAR of type string by checking all variables and their type. This ensures only expressions involving string type VAR will be modified. Regular expressions parse predicates P and expressions E. In Algorithm 1, line 5 parses predicate p_i around *and* and *or* to get expressions e_is. Line 9 parses e_i to obtain VAR, OP, and $CONST$ representing variable name, operation, and string literal, respectively. Line 11 of Algorithm 1 uses only VAR that are in MAP1. The second map (MAP2) stores $CONST$ to $INTEGER$ value pairs. $CONST$ in the right side of the expressions are replaced with a randomly generated $INTEGER$ as shown in Algorithm 1, line 13. A check is made to use the same $INTEGER$ if a $CONST$ appears more than once, as shown in Algorithm 1 line 12. Finally reconstructing the expression to replace $CONST$ with $INTEGER$ as shown in Algorithm 1, line 16. At line 19 the modified set of predicates, P', is returned where expressions involving string types are modified.

ALGORITHM 1 YAWL TO DVE PREDICATE TRANSFORMER

```
1: //Input: Set of predicates P, MAP1
2: //Output: Set of predicates P'
3: for each p_i ∈ {P} do
4:   //get set of expressions E from p_i
5:   E = regex(p_i, "( and ) | ( or )")
6:   for each e_i ∈ {E} do
7:     // Get left and right side of expression
8:     // Note: e_i = VAR + OP + CONST
9:     VAR, OP, CONST
```

```
           = regex(e_i,"(==)|(≥)| (≤)|(!=)")
    if VAR ∈ MAP1 then
      if CONST ∉ MAP2 then
         //Add generated random integer to MAP2 to CONST
         INTEGER = randomGenerate()
      end if
      e'_i = VAR + OP + INTEGER
    end if
  end for
  return P'
end for
```

31.5 VERIFYING BLOOD BANK WORKFLOWS AGAINST SAFETY REQUIREMENTS

In this section, we show how we translate FDA and AABB mandated safety requirements into LTL statements and used these statements to verify blood safety. Specifying mandated safety requirements consists of defining the predicates, states, and properties using LTL syntax to specify and verify safety requirements for modeled blood processing workflows. We start this step by translating the FDA and AABB safety requirements into LTL statements.

31.5.1 SYNTAX

In order to specify LTL syntax, let $VAR = \{\vec{x_i}; i \geq 0\}$ be a set of variables, $CONST = \{\vec{c_i}; i \geq 0\}$ be a set of constants, and $\Phi = \{p_i : i \geq 1\}$ be a set of atomic predicate symbols.

We say that $p_i(\vec{x_{i_j}})$, $p_i(\vec{x_{i_j}}) \wedge p_k(\vec{x_{k_j}})$, $p_i(\vec{x_{i_j}}) \vee p_k(\vec{x_{k_j}})$, $\neg p_i(\vec{x_{i_j}}$, $p_i(\vec{x_{i_j}})$, $\exists \vec{x_{i_j}}\, p_i(\vec{x_{i_j}})$, $\forall \vec{x_{i_j}}\, p_i(\vec{x_{i_j}})$, $p_i(\vec{x_{i_j}}) \rightarrow p_k(\vec{x_{k_j}})$, and $\Diamond p_i(\vec{x_{i_j}})$, $\Box p_i(\vec{x_{i_j}})$, $\mathcal{X} p_i(\vec{x_{i_j}})$ (sometimes this next-time operator $\mathcal{X}$ is written as $\bigcirc p_i(\vec{x_{i_j}})$) are predicates. Following standard convention, a fully instantiated predicate is one in which all variables are replaced by constants where we write $p_i(\vec{c_{i_k}})\,\vec{x_{i_j}}$ to indicate that the variables $\vec{x_{i_j}}$ in $p_i(\vec{x_{i_j}})$ have been replaced with constants $\vec{c_{i_k}}$.

31.5.2 SEMANTICS

We now summarize the commonly used semantics of temporal logic. Let $S = \{s_i : i \geq 0\}$ be a collection of states (sometimes referred to as worlds) and an accessibility relation among states as $R \subseteq S \times S$. We assume that there is a mapping (referred to as an assignment of the fully instantiated instances of the predicate symbols), say $Inst = \{inst_k k \geq 0\}$ with the mapping $AtMap = M : Inst \mapsto \wp(S)$. Then we define the satisfaction relations for the predicates in the states as follows:

- $s_i \models inst_k$ if $s_i \in AtMap(in_k)$.
- $s_i \models inst_k \wedge inst_j$ if $s_i \models inst_k$ and $s_i \models inst_j$.
- $s_i \models \neg inst_k$ if $s_i \models inst_k$.
- $s_i \models inst_k \vee inst_j$ if $s_i \models inst_k$ or $s_i \models inst_j$.
- $s_i \models \forall x\, p_k$ if $s_i \models inst_k$ for every instance $inst_k$ of p_k and the only free variable of p_k is x.
- $s_i \models \exists x\, p_k$ if $s_i \models inst_k$ for some instance $inst_k$ of p_k and the only free variable of p_k is x.

- $s_i \models \Diamond inst_k$ if $s_i' \models inst_k$ for some $s_i' \in R^*(s_i)$, where R^* is the reflexive transitive closure of R.
- $s_i \models \Box inst_k$ if $s_i' \models inst_k$ for every $s_i' \in R^*(s_i)$, where R^* is as stated above.
- $s_i \models \mathcal{X} inst_k$ if $s_i' \models inst_k$ for some $s_i' \in R^*(s_i)$.

Through the updates made to the translator and model, the sample version expanded to nine states $S = \{s_1, s_2, \ldots, s_9\}$, 152 predicates labeled $P = \{t_1, t_2, \ldots, t_{152}\}$, and 56 constants. Our model checker uses X for $\circ$. Sample safety requirements that are shown do not use the connective $\Box$. We show verification related to the registration, donor suitability, and the main workflow.

31.5.3 MAPPING SAFETY REQUIREMENTS AS ASSERTIONS IN STATES AND STATE TRANSITIONS

We describe the state transitions and safety properties that must be satisfied by state transitions to verify FDA and AABB safety requirements. Given the complexity of the process, we modeled the workflow as consisting of subworkflows. This design choice results in having hierarchical states and safety assertions associated with transitions between them, which we write as temporal logic formulas and verify using the Divine model checker. For the purpose of this chapter, we described sample state transitions, how we decomposed FDA and AABB requirements into LTL assertions about hierarchical states, and how we verified them. Tables 31.1 and 31.2 provides a summary of our assertions.

As shown in Fig. 31.4, the first state is S_1. Safety properties we use are shown in Table 31.1.

- S_1: The user starts the workflow by entering *start* into the system. On trigger t_1 (the user entering start) a transition n_1 takes the system from S_1 to S_2 as shown in Fig. 31.4.
- S_2: The system checks the model and looks for this output the requirement [mVerified]. It is a property added for future use to fully automating the verification. If the model is verified the workflow will start or else it will terminate. Currently, the requirement in LTL is entered manually. On trigger of t_{59} a transition n_2 to start the verified workflow or n_3 to stop the workflow as it did not pass the verification.
- S_3: The user enters the country. Based on the requirement [countryN], the system routes the user on trigger of t_{58} a transition n_4 and n_{56} between *C1registration* or *C2 registration*. (This chapter covers only *C1registration* and *C1suitability* and *C1collection* and *Deferral* that corresponds to the registration process in country 1, modeled by states S_4, S_5, S_6, and S_7). On trigger of t_{57} (it passes the country such as Canada, USA, New Zealand, Saudi Arabia, China, etc.), the state in transition n_4 from S_3 to S_7.
- S_4: In this composite state, the system checks the donor demographic information and registers the donor. It decomposes the subworkflow (into $S_{4.1}$-$S_{4.6}$) and outputs a String, Integer or Boolean flag *govID*, *idPhoto*, *idExpiry*, *productDonated*, *donationInterval*, *donationTypeSpecific*, and *donorAge*. The transition is modeled as n_5 that on trigger $t_8, t_9, t_{10}, t_{11}, \ldots, t_{19}$ (user identify and verify the donor ID) transition from S_4 to S_5. Conversely, if the donor ID is not verified or donation interval did not meet the standard, transition n_{40} takes S_4 to S_7, as shown in Fig. 31.4.
- S_5: In this composite state, the system checks if the donor is suitable for the donation and outputs a Boolean flag *govID*, *idPhoto*, and *idExpiry*. This state decomposes the tasks into subworkflows (going from states $S_{5.1}$ to $S_{5.13}$) and outputs a String or Integer or Boolean flag *medication*, *consent*, *lastDosageDays*, *temp*, *hgb*, *weight*, *pulse*, *systolic pressure*, or *diastolic pressure* indicating

Table 31.1 States, Property (1 & 2), and Predicates Summary

State	Property in English	Property in Predicates	Property in LTL Syntax
S1	Check if the model is verified and direct the user to the country specified. Also, direct users that did not pass the registration or suitability or collection to deferral.	/TopWF/mVerifiedN/text() $\neq\perp$ and /TopWF/countryN/text() =‘SA’ and ((/TopWF/productDonated/text() =‘PLT’ and number(/TopWF/donationInterval/text()) $\geq$ 2) or (/TopWF/productDonated/text() =‘PLA’ and number(/TopWF/donationInterval/text()) $\geq$ 28) or (/TopWF/productDonated/text() =‘RBC’ and number(/TopWF/donationInterval/text()) $\geq$ 56) or (/TopWF/productDonated/text() =‘DRBC’ and number (/TopWF/donationInterval/text()) $\geq$ 112) or (/TopWF/productDonated/text() =‘non’ and number(/TopWF/donationInterval/text()) =0)) and (/TopWF/govID/text() $\neq\perp$ and /TopWF/idPhoto/text() $\neq\perp$ and /TopWF/idExpiry/text() $\neq\perp$) and (/TopWF/donationTypeSpecific/text() =‘allogenic’ and number (/TopWF/donorAgeTW/text()) $\geq$ 17) and /TopWF/consentN/text() $\neq\perp$ and ((/TopWF/medicationN/text() =‘finasteride’ and number(/TopWF/lastDosageDaysN/text()) $\geq$ 30) or (/TopWF/medicationN/text() =‘isotretinoin’ and number (/TopWF/lastDosageDaysN/text()) $\geq$ 180) or (/TopWF/medicationN/text() =‘dutasteride’ and number(/TopWF/lastDosageDaysN/text()) $\geq$ 180) or (/TopWF/medicationN/text() =‘acitretin’ and number (/TopWF/lastDosageDaysN/text()) $\geq$ 1095) or (/TopWF/medicationN/text() =‘aspirin’ and number (/TopWF/lastDosageDaysN/text()) $\geq$ 2) or (/TopWF/medicationN/text() =‘piroxicam’ and number (/TopWF/lastDosageDaysN/text()) $\geq$ 2) or (/TopWF/medicationN/text() =‘prasugrel’ and number(/TopWF/lastDosageDaysN/text()) $\geq$ 7) or (/TopWF/medicationN/text() =‘ticagrelor’ and number(/TopWF/lastDosageDaysN/text()) $\geq$ 7) or (/TopWF/medicationN/text() =‘clopidogrel’ and number(/TopWF/lastDosageDaysN/text()) $\geq$ 14) or (/TopWF/	• In the Model Checker $t_1\&\&X(t_{59}\&\&X\, t_{57}\&\&XX((t_{11}\&\&t_{16})\Vert(t_{12}\&\&t_{17})\Vert(t_{13}\&\&t_{18})\Vert(t_{14}\&\&t_{19})\Vert(t_{15}\&\&t_{147}))\&\&(t_8\&\&t_9\&\&t_{10})\&\&(t_2\&\&t_{54})\&\&XXX(t_{41}\&\&((t_{26}\&\&t_{19})\Vert(t_{27}\&\&t_{23})\Vert(t_{28}\&\&t_{23})\Vert(t_{29}\&\&t_{25})\Vert(t_{30}\&\&t_{20})\Vert(t_{31}\&\&t_{20})\Vert(t_{32}\&\&t_{21})\Vert(t_{33}\&\&t_{21})\Vert(t_{34}\&\&t_{22})\Vert(t_{35}\&\&t_{22})\Vert(t_{36}\&\&t_{21})\Vert(t_{37}\&\&t_{21})\Vert(t_{38}\&\&t_{21})\Vert(t_{39}\&\&t_{21})\Vert(t_{40}\&\&t_{24}))\&\&t_{42}\&\&(t_{148}\&\&t_{46})\Vert(t_2\&\&t_{45}))\&\&t_{47}\&\&t_{48}\&\&(t_9\&\&t_{10}\&\&t_8)\&\&(t_3\&\&t_{52}\&\&t_{49})\Vert(t_3\&\&t_{53}\&\&t_{50})\Vert(t_4\&\&t_{52}\&\&t_{51})\Vert(t_5\&\&t_{52}\&\&t_{51})\Vert(t_6\&\&t_{52}\&\&t_{51})\Vert(t_7\&\&t_{52}\&\&t_{51})\Vert(t_4\&\&t_{53}\&\&t_{51})\Vert(t_5\&\&t_{53}\&\&t_{51})\Vert(t_6\&\&t_{53}\&\&t_{51})\Vert(t_7\&\&t_{53}\&\&t_{51}))$ • In LTL$t_1\&\&\bigcirc(t_{59}\&\&\bigcirc\, t_{57}\&\&\bigcirc\bigcirc((t_{11}\&\&t_{16})\Vert(t_{12}\&\&t_{17})\Vert(t_{13}\&\&t_{18})\Vert(t_{14}\&\&t_{19})\Vert(t_{15}\&\&t_{147}))\&\&(t_8\&\&t_9\&\&t_{10})\&\&(t_2\&\&t_{54})\&\&\bigcirc\bigcirc\bigcirc(t_{41}\&\&((t_{26}\&\&t_{19})\Vert(t_{27}\&\&t_{23})\Vert(t_{28}\&\&t_{23})\Vert(t_{29}\&\&t_{25})\Vert(t_{30}\&\&t_{20})\Vert(t_{31}\&\&t_{20})\Vert(t_{32}\&\&t_{21})\Vert(t_{33}\&\&t_{21})\Vert(t_{34}\&\&t_{22})\Vert(t_{35}\&\&t_{22})\Vert(t_{36}\&\&t_{21})\Vert(t_{37}\&\&t_{21})\Vert(t_{38}\&\&t_{21})\Vert(t_{39}\&\&t_{21})\Vert(t_{40}\&\&t_{24}))\&\&t_{42}\&\&(t_{148}\&\&t_{46})\Vert(t_2\&\&t_{45}))\&\&t_{47}\&\&t_{48}\&\&(t_9\&\&t_{10}\&\&t_8)\&\&(t_3\&\&t_{52}\&\&t_{49})\Vert(t_3\&\&t_{53}\&\&t_{50})\Vert(t_4\&\&t_{52}\&\&t_{51})\Vert(t_5\&\&t_{52}\&\&t_{51})\Vert(t_6\&\&t_{52}\&\&t_{51})\Vert(t_7\&\&t_{52}\&\&t_{51})\Vert(t_4\&\&t_{53}\&\&t_{51})\Vert(t_5\&\&t_{53}\&\&t_{51})\Vert(t_6\&\&t_{53}\&\&t_{51})\Vert(t_7\&\&t_{53}\&\&t_{51}))$

Continued

Table 31.1 States, Property (1 & 2), and Predicates Summary—cont'd

State	Property in English	Property in Predicates	Property in LTL Syntax
		medicationN/text() = 'ticlopidine' and number (/TopWF/lastDosageDaysN/text()) $\geq$ 14) or (/TopWF/ medicationN/text() = 'warfarin' and number(/TopWF/ lastDosageDaysN/text()) $\geq$ 7) or (/TopWF/ medicationN/text() = 'heparin' and number(/TopWF/ lastDosageDaysN/text()) $\geq$ 7) or (/TopWF/ medicationN/text() = 'dabigatran' and number (/TopWF/lastDosageDaysN/text()) $\geq$ 7) or (/TopWF/ medicationN/text() = 'rivaroxaban' and number (/TopWF/lastDosageDaysN/text()) $\geq$ 7) or (/TopWF/ medicationN/text() = 'Hepatitis B Immune Globulin' and number(/TopWF/lastDosageDaysN/text()) $\geq$ 260)) and number(/TopWF/tempN/text()) $\leq$ 37.5 and ((/TopWF/donationTypeSpecific/text() = 'autologous' and number(/TopWF/hgbTN/text()) $\geq$ 11) or (/TopWF/ donationTypeSpecific/text() = 'allogenic' and number (/TopWF/hgbTN/text()) $\geq$ 12.5)) and number(/ TopWF/systolicPressureTN/text()) $\leq$ 180 and number (/TopWF/diastolicPressureTN/text()) $\leq$ 100 and (/ TopWF/idPhoto/text() $\neq\perp$ and /TopWF/idExpiry/text () $\neq\perp$ and /TopWF/govID/text() $\neq\perp$) and (/TopWF/ donationType/text() = 'DRBC' and /TopWF/SexTN/ text() = 'male' and number(/TopWF/weightTN/text()) $\geq$ 130) or (/TopWF/donationType/text() = 'DRBC' and /TopWF/SexTN/text() = 'female' and number(/ TopWF/weightTN/text()) $\geq$ 150) or (/TopWF/ donationType/text() = 'RBC' and /TopWF/SexTN/text () = 'male' and number(/TopWF/weightTN/text()) $\geq$ 110) or (/TopWF/donationType/text() = 'PLT' and / TopWF/SexTN/text() = 'male' and number(/TopWF/ weightTN/text()) $\geq$ 110) or (/TopWF/donationType/ text() = 'PLA' and /TopWF/SexTN/text() = 'male' and number(/TopWF/weightTN/text()) $\geq$ 110) or (/ TopWF/donationType/text() = 'WB' and /TopWF/ SexTN/text() = 'male' and number(/TopWF/ weightTN/text()) $\geq$ 110) or (/TopWF/donationType/ text() = 'RBC' and /TopWF/SexTN/text() = 'female'	

		and number(/TopWF/weightTN/text()) $\geq$ 110) or (/TopWF/donationType/text() =‘PLT’ and /TopWF/SexTN/text() =‘female’ and number(/TopWF/weightTN/text()) $\geq$ 110) or (/TopWF/donationType/text() =‘PLA’ and /TopWF/SexTN/text() =‘female’ and numbe(/TopWF/weightTN/text()) $\geq$ 110) or (/TopWF/donationType/text() =‘WB’ and /TopWF/SexTN/text() =‘female’ and number(/TopWF/weightTN/text()) $\geq$ 110)	
S4.1	Gather information about the type of donation, specific donation type. Verify the donor identity, donor age (based on the type of donation); the donor is deferred if not verified. The donor is then registered and checks if any previous donations. Donor with previous donations should be checked against donation interval to ensure it is safe to donate for the donor and the blood unit donated.	(/C1registration/govIDR/text() $\neq\perp$ and /C1registration/idPhotoR/text() $\neq\perp$ and /C1registration/idExpiryR/text() $\neq\perp$) and (/C1registration/donationTypeSpecificR/text() =‘allogenic’ and number(/C1registration/donorAgeR/text()) $\geq$ 17) and next /C1registration/previouslyDonatedR/text() $\neq\perp$ and two states next (/C1registration/productDonatedR/text() = PLT’ and number(/C1registration/donationIntervalR/text()) $\geq$ 2) or (/C1registration/productDonatedR/text() =‘PLA’ and number(/C1registration/donationIntervalR/text()) $\geq$ 28) or (/C1registration/productDonatedR/text() =‘RBC’ and number(/C1registration/donationIntervalR/text()) $\geq$ 56) or (/C1registration/productDonatedR/text() =‘DRBC’ and number(/C1registration/donationIntervalR/text()) $\geq$ 112)	• In the Model Checker $X(t_{126}$ && $X\ t_{129}$ && $X((t_{130}$ && $t_{134})$ || $(t_{131}$ && $t_{135})$ || $(t_{132}$ && $t_{136})$ || $(t_{133}$ && $t_{137})))$ • In LTL $\bigcirc(t_{126}$ && $\bigcirc\ t_{129}$ && $\bigcirc((t_{130}$ && $t_{134})$ || $(t_{131}$ && $t_{135})$ || $(t_{132}$ && $t_{136})$ || $(t_{133}$ && $t_{137})))$

Table 31.2 States, Property (3 & 4 & 5), and Predicates Summary

State	Property in English	Property in Predicates	Property in LTL Syntax
S5.1	Validating the donor's suitable for through reverifying the identity, obtaining consent, checking medication, last dosage taken, ensuring that directed or autologous donors have a physician's request, and check donor vitals such as temperature, hemoglobin, systolic pressure, diastolic pressure, pulse, weight, and the platelet count.	Next state /C1suitability/govID/text() $\neq\perp$ and /C1suitability/idPhoto/text() $\neq\perp$ and /C1suitability/idExpiry/text() $\neq\perp$ and next two states /C1suitability/consent/text() $\neq\perp$ and after three states (/C1suitability/medicationN/text() = 'finasteride' and number(/C1suitability/lastDosageDays/text()) $\geq$ 30) or (/C1suitability/medicationN/text() = 'isotretinoin' and number (/C1suitability/lastDosageDays/text()) $\geq$ 180) or (/C1suitability/medicationN/text() = 'dutasteride' and number (/C1suitability/lastDosageDays/text()) $\geq$ 180) or (/C1suitability/medicationN/text() = 'acitretin' and number(/C1suitability/lastDosageDays/text()) $\geq$ 1095) or (/C1suitability/medicationN/text() = 'aspirin' and number(/C1suitability/lastDosageDays/text()) $\geq$ 2) or (/C1suitability/medicationN/text() = 'piroxicam' and number(/C1suitability/lastDosageDays/text()) $\geq$ 2) or (/C1suitability/medicationN/text() = 'prasugrel' and number(/C1suitability/lastDosageDays/text()) $\geq$ 7) or (/C1suitability/medicationN/text() = 'ticagrelor'	• In the Model Checker #property $X(t_{109}\&\&t_{110}\&\&t_{111}\&\& X\, t_{112}\&\&XXX((t_{149}\ \&\&\ t_{150}) \vert\vert (t_{85}\ \&\&\ t_{102}) \vert\vert (t_{86}\ \&\&\ t_{102}) \vert\vert (t_{87}\ \&\&\ t_{104}) \vert\vert (t_{88}\ \&\&\ t_{99}) \vert\vert (t_{89}\ \&\&\ t_{99}) \vert\vert (t_{90}\ \&\&\ t_{100}) \vert\vert (t_{91}\ \&\&\ t_{100}) \vert\vert (t_{92}\ \&\&\ t_{101}) \vert\vert (t_{93}\ \&\&\ t_{101}) \vert\vert (t_{94}\ \&\&\ t_{100}) \vert\vert (t_{95}\ \&\&\ t_{100}) \vert\vert (t_{96}\ \&\&\ t_{100}) \vert\vert (t_{97}\ \&\&\ t_{100}) \vert\vert (t_{98}\ \&\&\ t_{103}) \vert\vert (t_{151}\ \&\&\ t_{152})\ \&\&\ X((t_{81}\vert\vert t_{82})\ \&\&\ X\, t_{114}\&\&\ X\, t_{113}) \vert\vert X\, t_{113}\ \&\&\ XX((t_{82}\ \&\&\ t_{123}) \vert\vert (t_{83}\ \&\&\ t_{124}))\ \&\&\ X\, t_{115}\ \&\&XX\, t_{116}\&\&XXX\, t_{117}\ \&\&\ XXXX(t_{118}\ \&\&\ t_{119}))\&\&XXXX((t_{78}\ \&\&\ t_{120}) \vert\vert (t_{79}\ \&\&\ t_{108}\ \&\&\ t_{120}) \vert\vert (t_{77}\ \&\&\ t_{108}\ \&\&\ t_{120}) \vert\vert (t_{80}\ \&\&\ t_{108}\ \&\&\ t_{120}) \vert\vert (t_{79}\ \&\&\ t_{107}\ \&\&\ t_{120}) \vert\vert (t_{77}\ \&\&\ t_{107}\ \&\&\ t_{120}) \vert\vert (t_{80}\ \&\&\ t_{107}\ \&\&\ t_{120}) \vert\vert (t_{76}\ \&\&\ t_{108}\ \&\&\ t_{121}) \vert\vert (t_{76}\ \&\&\ t_{107}\ \&\&\ t_{122})))$ • In LTL $\bigcirc(t_{109}\&\&t_{110}\&\&t_{111}\&\&\bigcirc t_{112}\&\&\bigcirc\bigcirc\bigcirc((t_{149}\ \&\&\ t_{150}) \vert\vert (t_{85}\ \&\&\ t_{102}) \vert\vert (t_{86}\ \&\&\ t_{102}) \vert\vert (t_{87}\ \&\&\ t_{104}) \vert\vert (t_{88}\ \&\&\ t_{99}) \vert\vert (t_{89}\ \&\&\ t_{99}) \vert\vert (t_{90}\ \&\&\ t_{100}) \vert\vert (t_{91}\ \&\&\ t_{100}) \vert\vert (t_{92}\ \&\&\ t_{101}) \vert\vert (t_{93}\ \&\&\ t_{101}) \vert\vert (t_{94}\ \&\&\ t_{100}) \vert\vert (t_{95}\ \&\&\ t_{100}) \vert\vert (t_{96}\ \&\&\ t_{100}) \vert\vert (t_{97}\ \&\&\ t_{100}) \vert\vert (t_{98}\ \&\&\ t_{103}) \vert\vert (t_{151}\ \&\&\ t_{152})\ \&\&\ \bigcirc((t_{81}\vert\vert t_{82})\ \&\&\ \bigcirc t_{114}\&\&\ \bigcirc t_{113}) \vert\vert \bigcirc t_{113}\ \&\&\ \bigcirc\bigcirc((t_{82}\ \&\&\ t_{123}) \vert\vert (t_{83}\ \&\&\ t_{124}))\&\&\ \bigcirc t_{115}\ \&\&\bigcirc\bigcirc t_{116}\&\&\bigcirc\bigcirc\bigcirc t_{117}\ \&\&\ \bigcirc\bigcirc\bigcirc\bigcirc(t_{118}\ \&\&\ t_{119}))\&\&\bigcirc\bigcirc\bigcirc\bigcirc((t_{78}\ \&\&\ t_{120}) \vert\vert (t_{79}\ \&\&\ t_{108}\ \&\&\ t_{120}) \vert\vert (t_{77}\ \&\&\ t_{108}\ \&\&\ t_{120}) \vert\vert (t_{80}\ \&\&\ t_{108}\ \&\&\ t_{120}) \vert\vert (t_{79}\ \&\&\ t_{107}\ \&\&\ t_{120}) \vert\vert (t_{77}\ \&\&\ t_{107}\ \&\&\ t_{120}) \vert\vert (t_{80}\ \&\&\ t_{107}\ \&\&\ t_{120}) \vert\vert (t_{76}\ \&\&\ t_{108}\ \&\&\ t_{121}) \vert\vert (t_{76}\ \&\&\ t_{107}\ \&\&\ t_{122})))$

		and number(/C1suitability/lastDosageDays/text()) ≥ 7) or (/C1suitability/medicationN/text() =‘clopidogrel’ and number(/C1suitability/lastDosageDays/text()) ≥ 14) or (/C1suitability/medicationN/text() =‘ticlopidine’ and number(/C1suitability/lastDosageDays/text()) ≥ 14) or (/C1suitability/medicationN/text() =‘warfarin’ and number(/C1suitability/lastDosageDays/text()) ≥ 7) or (/C1suitability/medicationN/text() =‘heparin’ and number(/C1suitability/lastDosageDays/text()) ≥ 7) or (/C1suitability/medicationN/text() =‘dabigatran’ and number(/C1suitability/lastDosageDays/text()) ≥ 7) or (/C1suitability/medicationN/text() =‘rivaroxaban’ and number(/C1suitability/lastDosageDays/text()) ≥ 7) or (/C1suitability/medicationN/text() =‘Hepatitis B Immune Globulin’ and number(/C1suitability/lastDosageDays/text()) ≥ 360) or (/C1suitability/medicationN/text() =‘non’ and number(/C1suitability/lastDosageDays/text()) ≤ 1) and after four states (/C1suitability/donationTypeSpecific/text() =‘directed’ or /C1suitability/donationTypeSpecific/text() =‘autologous’ and next state /C1suitability/physicianrequest/text() ≠⊥ and sixth state number(/C1suitability/tempN/text()) ≤ 37.5) or next five states (number(/C1suitability/tempN/text()) ≤ 37.5) and state after (/C1suitability/donationTypeSpecific/text() =‘autologous’ and number(/C1suitability/hgb/text()) ≥ 11) or (/C1suitability/donationTypeSpecific/text() =‘allogenic’ and number(/C1suitability/hgb/text()) ≥ 12.5) and state after number(/C1suitability/systolicPressure/text()) ≤ 180 and state	

Continued

Table 31.2 States, Property (3 & 4 & 5), and Predicates Summary—cont'd

State	Property in English	Property in Predicates	Property in LTL Syntax
		after number(/C1suitability/diastolicPressure/text()) $\leq$ 100 and state after /C1suitability/armSkinDiseaseFree/text() $\neq\perp$ and next state after number(/C1suitability/pulse/text()) $\geq$ 50 and number(/C1suitability/pulse/text()) $\leq$ 100 and next state after (/C1suitability/donationTypeN/text() ='PLA' and /C1suitability/Sex/text() ='male' and number(/C1suitability/weight/text()) $\geq$ 110) or (/C1suitability/donationTypeN/text() ='RBC' and /C1suitability/Sex/text() ='male' and number(/C1suitability/weight/text()) $\geq$ 110) or (/C1suitability/donationTypeN/text() ='WB' and /C1suitability/Sex/text() ='male' and number(/C1suitability/weight/text()) $\geq$ 110) or (/C1suitability/donationTypeN/text() ='PLA' and /C1suitability/Sex/text() ='female' and number(/C1suitability/weight/text()) $\geq$ 110) or (/C1suitability/donationTypeN/text() ='RBC' and /C1suitability/Sex/text() ='female' and number(/C1suitability/weight/text()) $\geq$ 110) or (/C1suitability/donationTypeN/text() ='WB' and /C1suitability/Sex/text() ='female' and number(/C1suitability/weight/text()) $\geq$ 110) or (/C1suitability/donationTypeN/text() ='DRBC' and /C1suitability/Sex/text() ='male' and number(/C1suitability/weight/text()) $\geq$ 130) or (/C1suitability/donationTypeN/text() ='DRBC' and /C1suitability/Sex/text() ='female' and number(/C1suitability/weight/text()) $\geq$ 150) or /C1suitability/donationTypeN/text() ='PLT' and number(/C1suitability/weight/text())$\geq$ 110	

S6.1	Recheck the donor identity by checking the ID, ID Expiry Date, and Valid Photo. Ensure the right blood unit set is used and prepare donor arm thoroughly while monitoring beginning and end of the collection.	Next state /C1collection/govID/text() $\neq\perp$ and /C1collection/idPhoto/text() $\neq\perp$ and /C1collection/idExpiry/text() $\neq\perp$ and next state after (/C1collection/donationTypeN/text() ='WB' or /C1collection/donationTypeN/text() ='PLA' or /C1collection/donationTypeN/text() ='PLT') and next state after /C1collection/FindVeinT/text() $\neq\perp$ and /C1collection/armScrubT/text() $\neq\perp$	• In the Model Checker$X$ (t_{142} && t_{143} && t_{144}) && XX ($t_{139}\|\|t_{140}\|\|t_{141}$) && XXXX(t_{145} && t_{146}) • In LTL$\bigcirc$ (t_{142} && t_{143} && t_{144}) && $\bigcirc\bigcirc$ ($t_{139}\|\|t_{140}\|\|t_{141}$) && $\bigcirc\bigcirc\bigcirc\bigcirc$(t_{145} && t_{146})
S7.1	This property checks the type of deferral if it is registration deferral or collection deferral, depending on any process that did not meet the standard	/Deferral/govID/text() $\neq\top$ or /Deferral/idPhoto/text() $\neq\top$ or /Deferral/idExpiry/text() $\neq\top$ or /Deferral/findVein/text() $\neq\top$ or /Deferral/armScrub/text() $\neq\top$	• In the Model Checker X($t_{74}\|\|t_{75}$) $\|\|t_{71}\|\|t_{72}\|\|t_{73}$ • In LTL$\bigcirc$($t_{74}\|\|t_{75}$) $\|\|t_{71}\|\|t_{72}\|\|t_{73}$

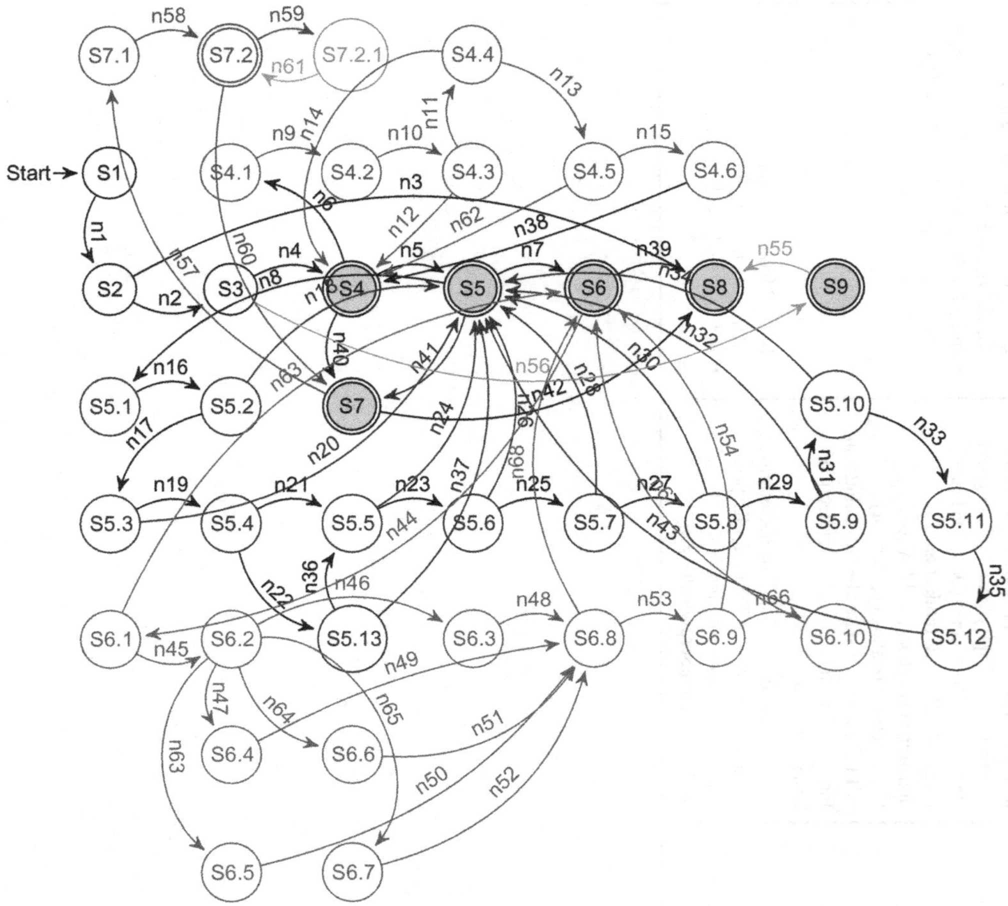

FIGURE 31.4

Full state diagram.

the donor passing the physical exam. It is modeled as transition n_7 that on trigger t_8, t_9, t_{10}, …, t_{53} (user identify the donor suitability) transition from state S_5 to S_6, as shown in Fig. 31.4.

- S_6: In this composite state, the system checks if the collection processes safety controls have been applied such as reverifying the donor, finding a clear vein, thoroughly scrubbing the arm, and maintaining time of collection and end of collection. This state outputs a Boolean flag *govID*, *idPhoto*, *idExpiry*, *FindVein*, *armScrub*, and *donationType*. This state decomposes the task into substates as shown in Fig. 31.4 from states $S_{6.1}$ to $S_{5.9}$. On trigger of t_8, t_9, t_{10}, t_3, …, t_7, t_{55}, t_{56} transitions n_{39} to state S_8.
- S_7: In this composite state, the system routes the deferrals based on the type of deferral as specified by the safety controls and standards. This chapter covers only registration and collection deferrals, which are shown in Fig. 31.4 as transitions n_{40} and n_{42}. The composite states consists of $S_{7.1}$ to $S_{7.2}$.

Now we briefly describe the decomposition of a few sample composite states. The composite state *State 4* in Fig. 31.4 is decomposed into six substates ($S_{4.1}$ to $S_{4.6}$), but we describe only three states in this chapter. The second row in Table 31.1 shows the safety property of validating the ID of a new donor should hold in state $S_{4.1}$. In the beginning state of subworkflow, the system requires the user to enter the type of donation and donation specific [donationType, donationTypeSpecific]. When the donor is successfully verified, transition n_{11} takes the system from $S_{4.3}$ to $S_{4.4}$, as shown in Fig. 31.4. We show the decomposition of composite state `State 5` in Fig. 31.4 where the safety property associated with the first row of Table 31.1 holds in state $S_{5.1}$. Because $S_{5.1}$ is the beginning state of subworkflow where the system imports the donation type and donation specific [donationTypeN, donationTypeSpecific] starts in state S_4. The decomposition takes the system through 13 subsequent states numbered $S_{5.1}$ through $S_{5.13}$ of which we describe `State 13`. It is modeled as transition n_5 that is triggered by action `start` and goes from state S_4 to S_5 in Fig. 31.4. We only describe 13 states of this sub-subworkflow and associated safety properties.

We show the decomposition of composite state in `State 5` in Fig. 31.4 with the third property holding at $S_{5.1}$ explained in Table 31.2:

- $S_{5.1}$: The start state of the subworkflow, where the completion of S_4 trigger to S_5 starts only if the donor passes the registration based on the conditions explained above. This transition, n_5, takes the system from state S_5 to state $S_{5.1}$. The user is required to reverify the donor through a Boolean of [govID, idPhoto, idExpiry]. Only if the donor passes the verification is there a transition to $S_{5.2}$ n_{16}. If not, then the user is transitioned back to states S_5 through n_{18}.
- $S_{5.2}$: This state is entered if the system received blood donation consent from the donor [consent], modeled as the transition n_{17} that takes the system from state $S_{5.2}$ to state $S_{5.3}$ triggered by the action t_{112}.
- $S_{5.3}$: The user enters [medication and lastDosageDays] to proceed. It is modeled as transition n_{19} taking the system from state $S_{5.3}$ to state $S_{5.4}$ triggered by actions $t_{84}, \ldots, t_{104}$.
- $S_{5.4}$: The system imports the donation type and its details that are specified in state $S_{4.1}$ [donationType and donationTypeSpecific] and checks if the donation type specific is a *directed or autologous* donation. This is modeled as transition n_{22} that takes the system from state $S_{5.4}$ to state $S_{5.13}$ automatically. If not, other types of donations will transition triggered by action n_{21} to $S_{5.5}$.
- $S_{5.5}$: The user or blood technician will check the donor's temperature and enter it in [temp]. The system then automatically transitions the user to state $S_{5.6}$ triggered by the action t_{113}. If not, then the system will automatically transition to state S_5 due to action n_{24}.
- $S_{5.6}$: The system will import [donationTypeSpecific] from the $S_{4.1}$ using transition n_5. The user is also required to enter the hemoglobin level [hgb]. The system then automatically transitions the user to state $S_{5.7}$ triggered by $t_{80}, \ldots, t_{83}$, t_{123}, and t_{124}. If not, then the system state transitions to S_5 due to transition n_{26}.
- $S_{5.7}$: The user will check and enter the donor [systolicPressure] to the system. Only if the condition in t_{115} is satisfied does a transition of n_{27} to the next state S_8 occur. If not, then the transition n_{28} will change the system state to S_5.
- $S_{5.8}$: The user will check and enter the donor [diastolicPressure]. If the condition in t_{116} is satisfied, the transition n_{29} will take the system to state S_9. If not, then the transition n_{30} takes the system to state S_5.

- $S_{5.9}$: The user will check and enter the donor [armSkinDiseaseFree] to the system. If the condition in t_{117} is satisfied, a transition of n_{31} to the next state S_{10} occurs. Else, a transition of n_{32} to S_5 occurs.
- $S_{5.10}$: The user will check and enter the donor [weight, sex, donationType] to the system. If the conditions in $t_{120},\ldots,t_{122}$, t_{107}, t_{108} are satisfied, a transition n_{33} takes the system to state $S_{5.11}$. If not, the transition n_{34} takes the system state to S_5.
- $S_{5.11}$: The user will check and enter the donor [PLTcount] to the system. If the condition in t_{26} is satisfied the transition n_{35} takes the system to state S_5.
- $S_{5.13}$: The user will check and enter if the donor received [physicianRequest] to the system. If the condition in t_{114} is satisfied transition n_{36} takes the system to state $S_{5.5}$. If not, transition n_{37} takes the system to state S_5.

We show the decomposition of composite state in `State 6` in Fig. 31.4 with the fourth property holding at $S_{6.1}$ explained in Table 31.2:

- $S_{6.1}$: The user is required to reverify the donor's identity using attributes modeled as Booleans [govID, idPhoto, idExpiry]. Only if the donor passes the verification, on trigger of t_{142}, t_{143}, t_{144} a transition to $S_{6.2}$ n_{45} occurs. If not, then the user is transitioned back to S_6 through n_{61} occurs.
- $S_{6.2}$: The system will route the user to the correct blood unit set depending on the type of donation through [donationType]. On trigger of t_{139}, t_{140}, t_{141} a transition to states $S_{6.3}$ through n_{48}, $S_{6.4}$ through n_{47}, $S_{6.5}$ through n_{63}, $S_{6.6}$ through n_{64} or to $S_{6.7}$ through n_{65} occurs depending on the type of the donation.
- $S_{6.3}, \ldots, S_{6.7}$: States $S_{6.3}, \ldots, S_{6.7}$ require the user to enter attributes [lotNo, unitBagVolume, anticoagulant, CheckLabel, donationID]. Once the information is entered, based on the donation type, the following transitions occur: n_{48}, n_{49}, n_{50}, n_{51}, and n_{52} to state $S_{6.8}$.
- $S_{6.8}$: The user has to enter attributes [FindVein, armScrub]. On trigger of t_{145} and t_{146} the system state transitions to $S_{6.9}$ through n_{53}. Otherwise, the system state transitions to states S_6 through n_{68} to defer the donor.
- $S_{6.9}$: The user monitors the donor and enters the following [donorReaction, donorReactionDescr, collectionStartTime]. As a consequence, the system transitions n_{66} to state $S_{6.10}$.
- $S_{6.10}$: The user monitors the donor and enters the following [donorReaction, donorReactionDescr, collectionEndtTime]. As a consequence, the system transitions n_{67} to state S_6.

31.6 IMPLEMENTATION

This section describes the system we implemented as shown in Fig. 31.5, extending our work [10, 16] by adding a workflow specification verification component. Our extended system consists of the following components: (1) electronic medical record system (EMRS), (2) workflow management system (WFMS), and (3) safety specification verification system (SSVS)

- EMRS provides a safe blood supply chain.
- WFMS: designs and executes workflow models, consisting of a workflow editor, workflow run-time engine, and other components such as a workflow task handler that enforces the completion of a specific task.
- SSVS verifies the created workflow.

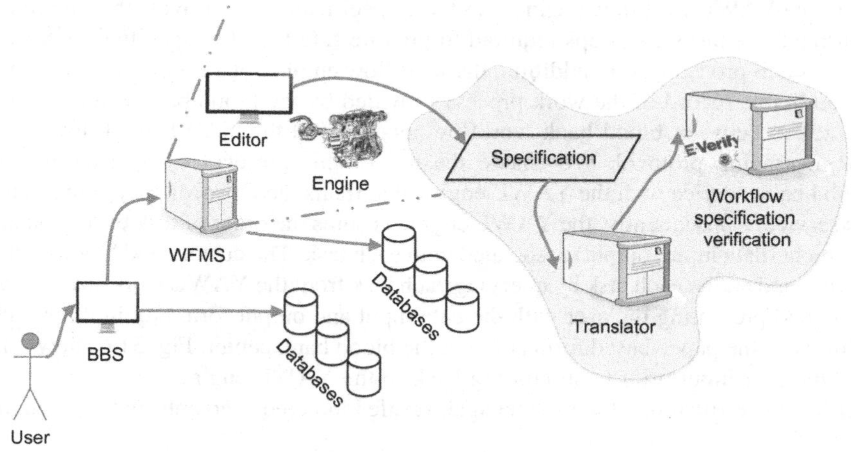

FIGURE 31.5

Implementation architecture.

We implemented our design using an open-source EMRS, OpenMRS[17], as our EMRS component. We created the user interface (UI) for blood bank systems operations. Users, such as blood bank technician, blood bank staff, phlebotomist, physician, and so forth, interact with the system via our well-designed UI. Additionally, all donors' information is stored in OpenMRS databases. We use YAWL as a loadable module in OpenMRS [10] as our workflow engine. YAWL's workflow editor models the comprehensive, completed blood bank workflow that we created for collecting and administering blood products.

YAWL's workflow engine runs and enforces the specified workflows that takes blood bank professionals through safety verified processes when collecting and administering blood products. We did so for many key reasons as mentioned in our previous publication [16, 18]. First, the YAWL workflow system has been used to implement many workflows in industry and academia [11]. Second, YAWL uses a domain independent syntax to specify workflows, and provides an editor and a runtime engine that can enforce workflows specified in YAWL syntax for any application. Therefore our models can be audited and verified against ground reality by third parties for the accuracy of the workflows. Third, YAWL is an open sourced software. Last, many research projects have used YAWL as a workflow-modeling tool in the recent past.

For SSVS, it contains the two main components, which are highlighted in yellow in Fig. 31.5. We use the workflow specification translator and the Divine model checker. The workflow specification translator creates Divine (DVE) syntax of the workflow specifications. Our model checker Divine verifies the model for safety requirements specified as LTL properties. As stated previously, we encode FDA and AABB blood safety requirements to ensure that our workflow model is compliant.

Finally, the verified blood bank workflow specification for collecting and administering blood products is stored in WFMS databases and used by the workflow engine. The UI of the blood bank workflow is represented as its own tab in the patient dashboard of OpenMRS and incorporates the blood bank center's organizational and operational knowledge of the blood bank process as a YAWL specification. The YAWL workflow engine uses these specifications to provide the caregivers the ability to step through the tasks and steps required to provide safe blood as specified by the blood bank center's policies and procedures. In addition, the workflow engine logs every incident into a database creating the auditable record of the work process provided by the blood bank center.

The interaction between blood bank workflow module and the YAWL workflow engine uses a XML/HTTP messaging protocol. We enable the use of this protocol by registering our custom-designed blood bank service with the YAWL engine that treats the OpenMRS system as an externally controllable service. Consequently, the YAWL engine ensures the order of task execution and the data flow management (data input, output) associated with each task. The customized blood bank workflow service enforces and audits each task by querying each task from the YAWL workflow engine, dynamically creating and presenting the user with the data input and output form required for each task that look very similar to the paper-based forms used in the blood bank center. Fig. 31.6 shows an example, but validates the user input prior to submitting back to the YAWL engine.

We describe the verification of our model against safe blood requirements, highlighted in yellow or grey in Fig. 31.5.

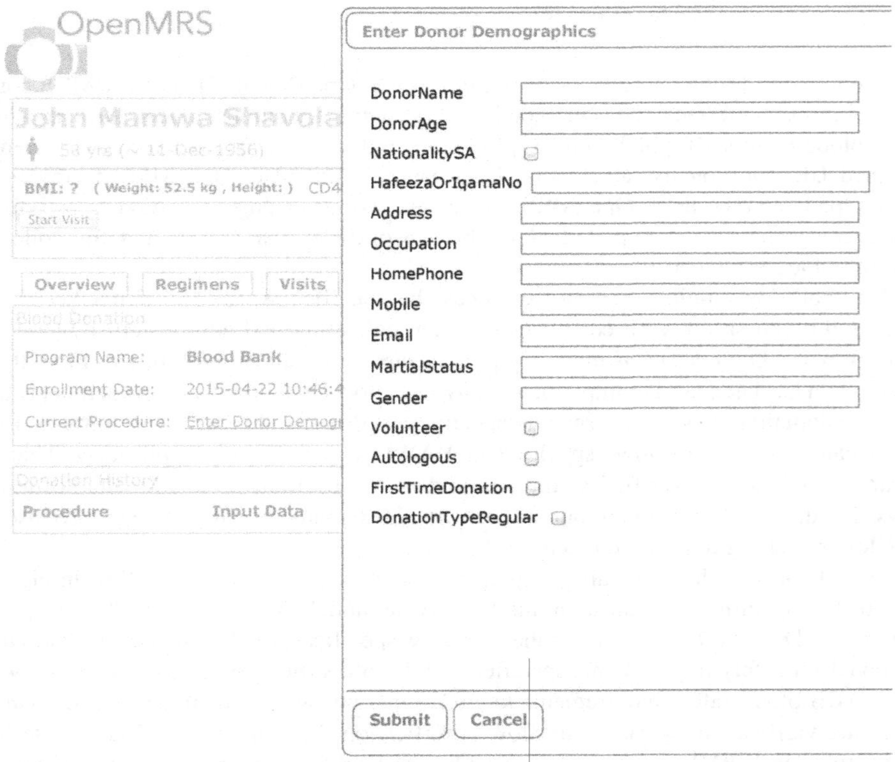

FIGURE 31.6

A workflow generated GUI.

31.7 RELATED WORK

Formally modeling and verifying models has been practiced for many years by software engineers. There have been several papers published modeling medical processes or guidelines to be verified through utilizing different types of modeling and verification tools. Each tool has been claimed to provide superior functionality in describing and verifying the model and properties. In this section we will cover related work that shows some of the methods that have been used for modeling and verification.

Although this practice has been used prior to the year 2006, [19] models Jaundice protocol (a disease that affects newborns) though using Asbru [20, 21]. Asbru uses a hierarchical plan to represent the model through defining intentions, plan body, and conditions. Also, Asbru allows the user to define processes that are sequential, unordered, parallel, and in any order. The paper also used the Karlsruhe Interactive Verifier (KIV) tool [22]. The paper provides details of translating the natural language to the model and then the verification protocol. Although the natural languages are very descriptive, translating the language to the modeling tool can be a tedious job that is not fully automatizeable.

In 2008 [23], Chen et al. modeled standard blood transfusion processes. Their model captured a subset of the blood transfusion processes and utilized nursing references of checklist. The paper identified using LittleJIL and FLAVERS & SPIN as a method for modeling and verification. It is stated that Little-JIL is mainly used as the tool precisely defined in finite-state automata. Also, the tool is scalable, clear, can specify parallelism, and can deal with exceptional conditions and defining iterations. The Little-JIL modeling tool uses a hierarchical representation. The paper stated that gaps in the model have been identified. Also, a great amount of effort has been made to formally define processes correctly as the translation process is not fully automated.

Mery et al. [24] models medical protocols of a case study involving an electrocardiogram (ECG) case for several types of heart diseases. The work utilizes the number of signals received from the ECG to evaluate the patient's condition. This paper utilized EVENT B [25] modeling language and RODIN [26]. EVENT B provides a hierarchical representation of the model. The authors state that the verification tool required some level of interaction to complete a remaining 42% of the proof.

The three related works above have shown a great amount of effort in modeling and verifying their models. However, our work has been shown to answer some of the limitations they were facing, such as automatically translating the model, and modeling a realistic workflow of current practice, and verifying the workflow against mandated federal safety requirements.

Systems such as SCC Soft Computer, MAK-system, and many others [27, 28] are currently utilized systems by many blood bank centers. These systems have shown to be hard coded and do not formally model and verify blood safety requirements. Instead, they validate safety by using FDA-specified validation guidelines as shown in the FDA 510(k) Blood Establishment Computer Software [29]. This differs from our work as the system used cannot be verified against formally modeled blood bank standards. Our work shows that our modeled blood bank workflow is verifiable and enforceable to an EMR (or blood bank system).

Ruan et al. [30, 31] specify an agent-based alarm system as properties in logic, verified against formally modeled palliative care therapeutics. They created their agent-based alarms using a subset of detailed palliative workflows, checked against norms set by palliative care providers using a first-order LTL-based model checker [30]. The paper focuses more on defining the properties used for verification modeled in palliative care. The model is created using YAWL, but the properties are defined using first-order logic, temporal logic, and description logic. Our work captures much more than a subset of blood bank workflow, and models the details of the so called *vein-to-vein* blood workflow. Also, we check the properties by extracting and translating mandated FDA and AABB safety requirements.

Kristensen et al. [32] utilize a workflow management tool and LTL to verify some specified properties using so-called *sweep-lines* in model-driven architectural design. They focused more on solving the standard problem of state space explosion that occurs in model checkers, but also discussed the use of checking if all properties hold in specific states. Our work differs as we focus toward ensuring blood bank regulations are checked in specific states to ensure all properties hold to meet the safety requirements utilizing the same model. Also, we enforce the same verified model in an EMR system.

Bottrighi et al. [33] set forth approaches to verify clinical guideline properties that are verified by a formal tool such as Divine. Their work focuses on using LTL and Promela [34] to check for consistency of clinical guidelines in ischemic stroke prevention and management. Our work, by contrast, addresses blood workflow safety by enforcing compliance with governmental regulations and standards throughout the whole blood bank workflow.

Our work also differs from what was listed in related work also by adding automated verification to ensure that practiced blood supply chains satisfy regulatory mandates. In addition, we show how EMRS can use these verified, safe workflows to provide seamless blood-related services transparent to the caregiver.

31.8 CONCLUSIONS

We have proposed and partly built what we believe to be the first system that uses a generic workflow management to drive blood collection and administration system processes. We have also used blood bank workflows to create a method to verify that the workflow steps satisfy the safety requirements mandated by governing authorities such as the FDA and the AABB. Our prototype shows that our methodology is sufficiently generic to model FDA mandates and AABB recommendations.

Blood safety requirements are dynamic (subjected to change due to regulatory changes) and, consequently, continual changes in mandates require updating the FDA regulations and AABB standards. Our system accepts these changes because the methodology we use is generic and, thus, can be used to specify changing safety standards and newer workflows. For example, hemovigilance started in 1994 as a means to further increase blood safety [35]. Hemovigilance attempts to track donation and transfusion processes to decrease the number of unwanted occurrences or events. We are in the process of building verification systems for hemovigilance.

ACKNOWLEDGMENTS

This work is sponsored in part by the Saudi Arabian Cultural Mission (SACM) and King Abdulaziz University (KAU). The views and conclusions contained herein are those of the authors and should not be interpreted as necessarily representing the official policies or endorsements, either expressed or implied, by the Government of the Kingdom of Saudi Arabia. We acknowledge James H. Pope's help and technical assistance in developing the translator.

REFERENCES

[1] WHO. Blood safety and availability. http://goo.gl/MBZqhf.
[2] The Patient Education Institute, Inc. Blood transfusion; 2013. www.patient-education.com/bloodtransfusionpdf.
[3] U.S. Food and Drug Administration. Fatalities reported to FDA following blood collection and transfusion: annual summary for fiscal year; 2013. http://goo.gl/kra0UK.
[4] American Association of Blood Banks and Standards Program Committee. Standards for blood banks and transfusion services. Bethesda, MD: American Association of Blood Banks; 2014.
[5] FDA. Code of federal regulations; 2013. http://goo.gl/m2a7fy.
[6] CBER. Substantially Equivalent 510(k) Device Information — TANGO Automated Blood Bank Analyzer System. http://goo.gl/FSnryq.
[7] Jennings JB. Blood bank inventory control. Manage Sci 1973;19(6):637–45.
[8] Cohen MA, Pierskalla WP. Management policies for a regional blood bank. Transfusion 1975;15(1):58–67.
[9] Cheng YW, Wilkinson JM. An experience of the introduction of a blood bank automation system (Ortho AutoVue Innova) in a regional acute hospital. Transfus Apher Sci 2015;53(1):58–63.
[10] Hazzazi N, Yu B, Wijesekera D, Costa P. Proceedings of the 2015 international conference on health informatics and medical systems (HIMS 2015); 2015. http://worldcomp-proceedings.com/proc/p2015/HIM6164.pdf.
[11] YAWL Foundation. YAWL – user manual; 2012. http://yawlfoundation.org/manuals/YAWLUserManual2.3.pdf.
[12] Definition of Haemovigilance: IHN — International Haemovigilance Network. http://goo.gl/5esCiQ.
[13] Roback JD. American Association of Blood Banks. Technical manual. Bethesda, MD: American Association of Blood Banks; 2008. p. 161–3.
[14] Barnat J, Brim L, Havel V, Havlicek J, Kriho J, Lenco M, et al. DiVinE 3.0 — an explicit-state model checker for multithreaded C & C++ programs. In: Computer aided verification (CAV 2013). LNCS, vol. 8044. Berlin: Springer; 2013. p. 863–8.
[15] Rabbi F, Wang H, MacCaull W. YAWL2dve: an automated translator for workflow verification. In: 2010 Fourth international conference on secure software integration and reliability improvement (SSIRI); 2010. p. 53–9.
[16] Yu B, Wijesekera D. Building dialysis workflows into EMRs. Proc Technol 2013;9:985–95.
[17] OpenMRS Developer Guide. https://wiki.openmrs.org/display/docs/Developer+Guide.
[18] Hazzazi N, Wijesekera D, Hindawi S. Formalizing and verifying workflows used in blood banks, Proc Technol 2014;16:1271–80. http://www.sciencedirect.com/science/article/pii/S2212017314003703.
[19] ten Teije A, Marcos M, Balser M, van Croonenborg J, Duelli C, van Harmelen F, et al. Improving medical protocols by formal methods. Artif Intell Med 2006;36(3):193–209.
[20] Seyfang A, Kosara R, Miksch S. Asbru's Reference Manual, Asbru Version 7.3. Technical repoart: 2002.
[21] Balser M, Duelli C, Reif W, Schmitt J, Balser M, Duelli C, et al. Universitat augsburg formal semantics of Asbru' v2.12.
[22] Balser M, Reif W, Schellhorn G, Stenzel K, Thums A. Formal system development with kiv. In: Proceedings of the third international conference on fundamental approaches to software engineering: held as part of the European joint conferences on the theory and practice of software, ETAPS 2000, FASE '00. London, UK: Springer-Verlag; 2000. p. 363–6.
[23] Chen B, Avrunin G, Henneman E, Clarke L, Osterweil L, Henneman P. Analyzing medical processes. In: ACM/IEEE 30th international conference on software engineering, 2008. ICSE '08; 2008. p. 623–32.
[24] Mery D, Singh N. Medical protocol diagnosis using formal methods. In: Liu Z, Wassyng A, editors. Foundations of health informatics engineering and systems. Lecture notes in computer science, vol. 7151. Berlin: Springer Berlin Heidelberg; 2012. p. 1–20.

[25] Abrial JR. Modeling in event-B: system and software engineering. 1st ed. New York, NY: Cambridge University Press; 2010.
[26] Coleman J, Jones C, Oliver I, Romanovsky A, Troubitsyna E. Rodin (rigorous open development environment for complex systems). Project number ist 2004-511599. In: Fifth European dependable computing conference: EDCC-5 supplementary volume; 2005. p. 23–6.
[27] MAK-SYSTEM International Group; 2010. http://www.mak-system.net/.
[28] SCC Soft Computer. SoftBank. http://www.softcomputer.com/products-services/blood-services/softbank/.
[29] Substantially Equivalent 510(k) Device Information — 510(k) Blood Establishment Computer Software. http://goo.gl/V93MPk.
[30] Ruan J, MacCaull W. Data-aware monitoring for healthcare workflows using formal methods. In: Proceedings of the second workshop knowledge representation for health care KR4HC 2010, Lisbon, Portugal; 2010. p. 51–60.
[31] Ruan J, MacCaull W, Jewers H. Agent-based careflow for patient-centred palliative care. In: Szomszor M, Kostkova P, editors. Electronic healthcare. Lecture notes of the institute for computer sciences, social informatics and telecommunications engineering. vol. 69. Berlin: Springer Berlin Heidelberg; 2012. p. 285–94.
[32] Kristensen LM, Lamo Y, MacCaull W, Rabbi F, Rutle A. On exploiting progress for memory-efficient verification of diagrammatic workflows; 2013. http://cs.ioc.ee/nwpt13/abstracts-book/paper14.pdf.
[33] Bottrighi A, Giordano L, Molino G, Montani S, Terenziani P, Torchio M. Adopting model checking techniques for clinical guidelines verification. Artif Intell Med 2010;48(1):1–19.
[34] Holzmann GJ. The spin model checker: primer and reference manual. 4th ed. Boston, MA: Addison-Wesley; 2008.
[35] Jain A, Kaur R. Hemovigilance and blood safety. Asian J Transfus Sci 2012;6(2):137–8.

CHAPTER

EVALUATION OF WINDOW PARAMETERS OF CT BRAIN IMAGES WITH STATISTICAL CENTRAL MOMENTS

32

K.S. Sim, M.E. Nia, C.S. Ta, C.P. Tso, T.K. Kho, C.S. Ee
Multimedia University, Melaka, Malaysia

32.1 INTRODUCTION

Stroke is one of the leading causes of death in the world. In 2004, stroke caused 9.7% of the cases of death in the world, and it is predicted to increase to 12.1% by 2030. In 2008, stroke was the third leading cause of death in the United States; out of approximately 550,000 strokes, about 150,000 cases were fatal. Stroke is basically due to a blood flow disruption in the brain. Ischemic stroke occurs when there is blockage of a blood vessel that supplies blood to the brain, while hemorrhagic stroke occurs when there is rupture of a blood vessel, causing a leak of blood into the brain [1–3].

In stroke evaluation, two techniques used in medical imaging are magnetic resonance (MR) and computed tomography (CT). CT is more widely used and is more sensitive to ischemic stroke because it has better contrast resolution to detect different types of brain tissues. MR is more limited in patient intolerance. The National Electrical Manufacturers Association (NEMA) and the American College of Radiology (ACR) developed a standard format of imaging known as Digital Imaging and Communications in Medicine (DICOM) that shares medical images along with associated information [4–7].

In DICOM format, the images do not go through any contrast enhancement, image processing, or other techniques that can change the properties of the image. DICOM images are always read as a 12-bit grayscale image in computer vision.

The window setting that can be performed on DICOM images is specified by an attenuation unit called the Hounsfield unit (HU) or the CT number [8]. The images will be displayed with normal gray scale with only a certain range of HUs. In CT, the two parameters window center (C) and the window width (W), measured in HUs, influence both lesion conspicuity and diagnostic accuracy. Window center refers to the center value of images while window width refers to the range of displayed HUs [9].

Low window center and narrow window width are preferred to contrast small differences in attenuation of brain tissues for ischemic stroke detection [10]. Compared to the standard window center of 20 HU and window width 80 HU, the setting with window center 32 HU and window width 8 HU is better in contrasting the normal and ischemic gray matter (GM) and white matter (WM) [11]. Two new enhanced settings were introduced for optimization of signal distribution and wavelike transform with window center 30 HU and window width 40 HU; window center 25 HU and window width 3 HU [12].

Furthermore, window center 45–50 HU and window width 50 HU is proposed by [13] for better contrast. However, these parameters are adjusted or set based on the experiments of radiologists and no criterion can prove their validity. Although there are improvements for detection, some brain tissues could not be detected, as will be discussed in the next section. Furthermore, incomplete and imperfect brain scans will cause the voxels (containing infarct tissues) to have attenuation that is higher than usual. In this study, the relationship between the width and the contrast of the window images is investigated using a unique new contrast formula.

32.2 WINDOW SETTING

A voxel is like a pixel in an image. With the average attenuation of the tissues, the HU of the voxel is determined [5]. Fig. 32.1 shows the sample HU for various types of structures. The HU range is varied from −1000 HU to +1000 HU. However, the HU can be as large as +6000 HU in some cases [14,15].

In computer vision, DICOM is read as a 16-bit unsigned image (12 bits for visual and 4 bits for storage) [8,16]. Eq. (1) is used to find the HU of a voxel at the pixel location (i, j) and X is the pixel intensity value in a DICOM image. In the header of CT volume data, the rescaled slope (m) is tagged with (0028, 1053) and rescaled intercept (a) is tagged with (0028, 1052) [17]. In addition, rescaled slope (m) is set to 1 and rescale intercept is set to 1 or −1024.

$$\mathrm{HU}(i,j) = mX(i,j) + a \quad (1)$$

The display of a DICOM image does not delineate the brain area in computer vision. For ischemic stroke, the region of interest is the area of soft tissues in which the HU range is small. Therefore, the value of window setting is important to visualize the DICOM image [18]. To make the grayscale visible, K_{max} is normally defined in 256 gray level or 8 bit [8]. The window width (W) and window center (C) are set based on the radiologist's experience. Hence, the grayscale level (K) is located where the pixel is located at point (i, j) and maximum level of new grayscale range, K_{max} as Eq. (2). If the HU

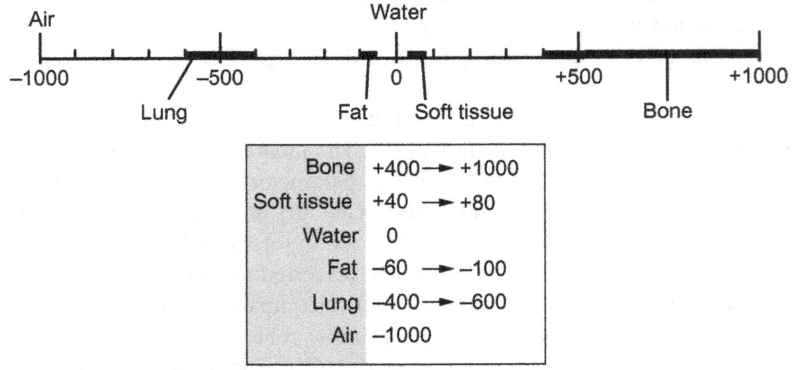

FIGURE 32.1

Sample HU for various types of structures [14].

is larger than the upper boundary or smaller than the lower boundary of the grayscale range, the HU value of the pixel will be assigned to 0.

$$\begin{cases} K = \dfrac{\left(\mathrm{HU} - \left(C - \frac{W}{2}\right)\right)}{W} \times K_{\max} \\ \left(C - \frac{W}{2}\right) \leq \mathrm{HU} \leq \left(C + \frac{W}{2}\right) \end{cases} \tag{2}$$

32.3 MATHEMATICAL DESCRIPTION OF CENTRAL MOMENTS

In mathematics, a moment is a quantitative measurement from a set of points or data. Table 32.1 shows the description of statistical mathematical moments. The first moment is known as mean or expected value. The mean normally describes the measurement of central tendency of a distribution of $x_i$as shown in Eq. (3). The mean has poor coverage when the histogram shows broad "tails." Eq. (4) shows the mean of a discrete random variable in the distribution and Eq. (5) shows the mean of a continuous random variable in the distribution [19,20].

$$\bar{x} = \frac{1}{n}\sum_{i=1}^{n} x_i \tag{3}$$

$$E(x) = x_i P_i \tag{4}$$

$$\mu(x) = \int_{-\infty}^{\infty} f(x)dx \tag{5}$$

The second moment is known as variance and is usually denoted as σ^2. It describes whether the distribution is clustered closed to the mean and is the average of the squared difference from the mean as shown in Eq. (6). However, variance is based on squared deviations of the points from the mean. If the variance is zero, it indicates that all the values in the distribution are identical to each other. A small variance indicates that the points of the distribution are close to the mean, and viceversa. Eq. (7) illustrates the variance of a discrete random variable in the distribution and Eq. (8) illustrates the variance of a continuous random variable in the distribution [19,20].

$$\sigma^2 = \frac{1}{n-1}\sum\nolimits_{i=1}^{n} (x_i - \bar{x})^2 \tag{6}$$

$$Var(x) = E\left[x^2\right] - (E[x])^2 \tag{7}$$

Table 32.1 Description of the Present Statistical Parameters

Statistical parameter	Description
First moment or mean	Measures the expected value
Second moment or variance	Measures the spread dispersion
Third moment or skewness	Measures the asymmetry
Fourth moment or kurtosis	Measures the peakedness

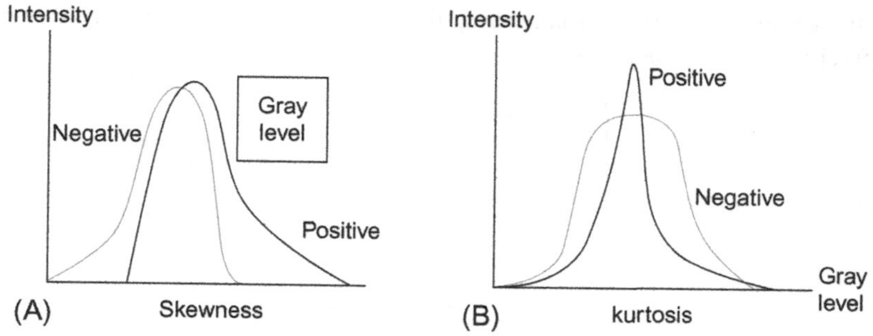

FIGURE 32.2

(A) Plot of skewness and (B) plot of kurtosis.

$$Var(x) = \int_{-\infty}^{\infty} (x-\mu)^2 f(x)dx \tag{8}$$

The third moment is also known as skewness or asymmetry and is defined in Eq. (9) and shown in Fig. 32.2A. If the distribution is symmetric, the left side and right side of the distribution are the same, corresponding to the center point. Skewness can be positive or negative or even an undefined number. A positive skewness indicates that the "tail" of the distribution tends to extend to the right side of the curve. On the other hand, a negative skewness indicates that the "tail" of the distribution tends to extend to the left side of the curve. A symmetrical distribution occurs when the variance is zero [19,20].

$$\text{Skewness} = \frac{1}{n}\sum_{i=1}^{n}(x_i - \bar{x})^3 \tag{9}$$

The fourth moment or kurtosis measures, shown in Eq. (10), the peakedness or flatness relative to a normal distribution. A positive kurtosis of a distribution is known as a leptokurtic distribution and a negative kurtosis of a distribution is known as a platykurtic distribution. An in-between distribution is termed a mesokurtic distribution. Fig. 32.2B illustrates the above three distributions [19,20].

$$\text{Kurtosis} = \frac{1}{n}\sum_{i=1}^{n}(x_i - \bar{x})^4 \tag{10}$$

The third moment and the fourth moment are used as an indicator for setting the HU. The results are based on 100 sets of brain images.

32.4 RESULTS AND DISCUSSION

We used sample brain images to run experiments on HU selection. The procedure is shown in Fig. 32.3. Fig. 32.4 shows the results of four experiments on the relationship between four mathematical moments versus the window width. Fig. 32.5 shows various brain images with their corresponding window widths. The window width is set from the range of 0 to 145 HU.

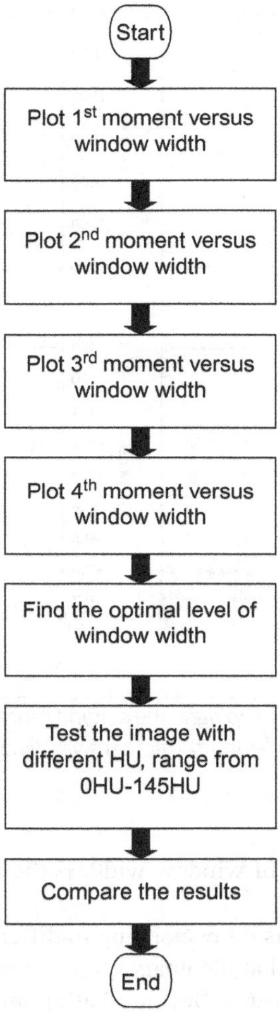

FIGURE 32.3

Flow chart of testing brain images.

From the investigation the first moment and the second moment (mean and variance, respectively) are directly proportional to the window width, while the third and the fourth moments (skewness and kurtosis, respectively) are inversely proportional to the window width. In the first and the second moments, no relation can be found through the experiments, but some clues can be found through the relationship between the third and the fourth moment with the setting of window width. From the kurtosis and skewness graphs as shown in Fig. 32.4 the window width reaches a certain level and moments become almost constant. The moments become constant when the window width reaches the range of 50–60 HU. Beyond that, there is no further information that is obtained from

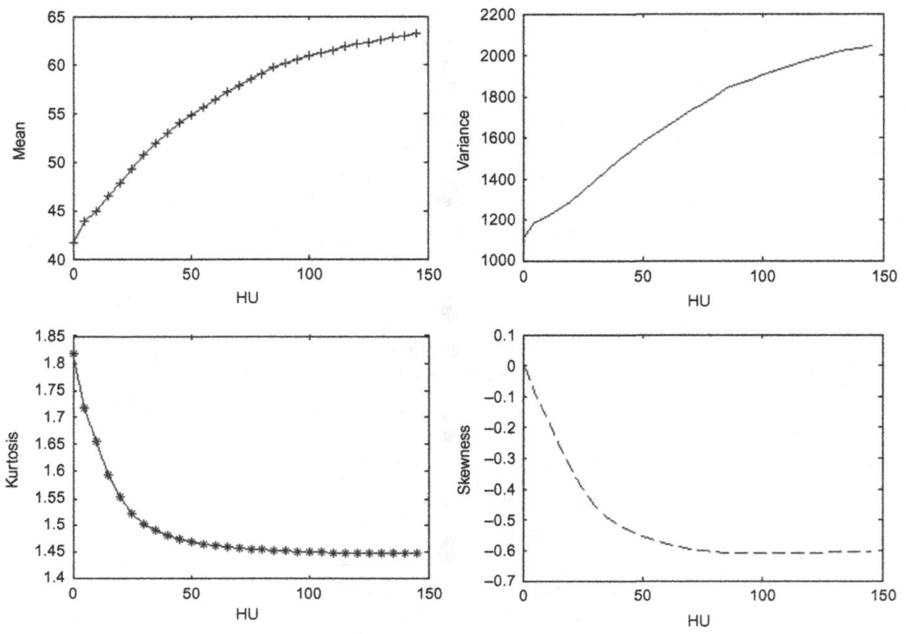

FIGURE 32.4

Top left: the first moment vs. window width; *Top right*: the second moment vs. window width; *Bottom left*: the third moment vs. window width; *Bottom right*: the fourth moment vs. window width.

the images. Hence, the optimal level of window width is the range of 50–60 HU for this particular brain image.

Fig. 32.5 shows the different results corresponding to different window widths, ranging from 0 to 145 HU. With these results, it is seen that the images that fall onto optimal level of window width are the most clear in visibility of brain tissues. Beyond that optimal level, the brain tissues become less visible. 100 sets of brain images have been found with similar findings.

Eqs. (11), (12) show the formulas of the third moment and the fourth moment, respectively, corresponding with the optimal level of window width.

$$\text{Window width}_{50\text{HU}} \le \text{Skewness}_{\text{optimal}} \le \text{Window width}_{60\text{HU}} \tag{11}$$

$$\text{Window width}_{50\text{HU}} \le \text{Kurtosis}_{\text{optimal}} \le \text{Window width}_{60\text{HU}} \tag{12}$$

There are four fundamental numbers used in the identification of test condition; namely, true positive, true negative, false positive, and false negative. There are eight basic ratios: sensitivity, specificity, positive predictive value, negative predictive value, type I error, type II error, false discovery rate, and false omission rate. There are four types of ratios: likelihood ratio for positive test, likelihood ratio for negative test, likelihood ratio for positive subject, and likelihood ratio for negative subject.

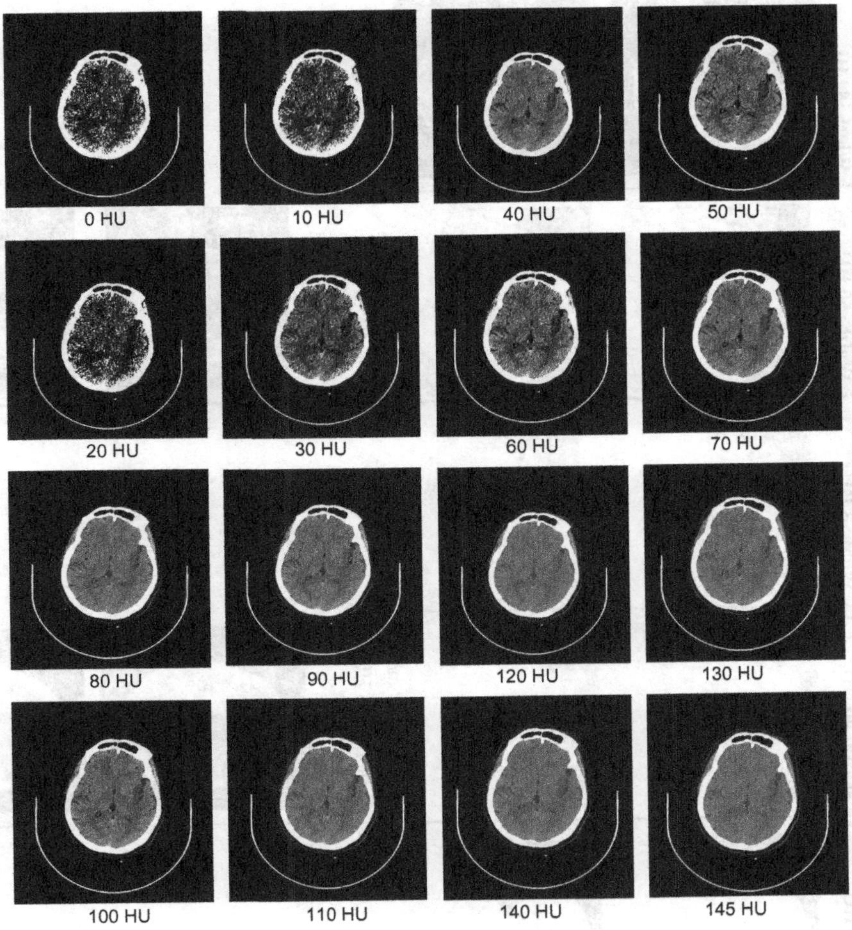

FIGURE 32.5

Test results from 0 to 145 HU.

32.5 COMPARISONS

We have compared the various settings used by various researchers [10,11,13] as well as the setting from Melaka General Hospital. The results are in Table 32.2. From the 100 sets of brain images obtained, two images were selected for the discussion.

Table 32.2 shows the comparison of the results. The first indicator was set at window center 20 HU and window width 80 HU [10]. The second indicator was set with window center 32 HU and window width 8 HU [11]. We used the method developed by Przelaskowski et al. (n.d.) as the third indicator, with window center 30 HU and window width 40 HU. The fourth indicator has the window center

Table 32.2 Comparison of Various Indicators

	Gregory et al.	Lev et al.	Przlaskowski et al.		Gadda et al.	Hospital Indicator
	Center, 20 HU Width, 80 HU	Center, 32 HU Width, 8 HU	Center, 30 HU Width, 40 HU	Center, 25 HU Width, 3 HU	Center, 50 HU Width, 50 HU	Center, 1064 HU Width, 80 HU
Image A	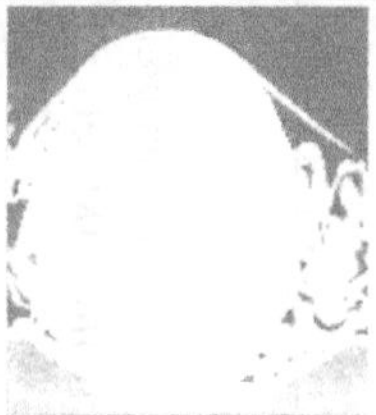				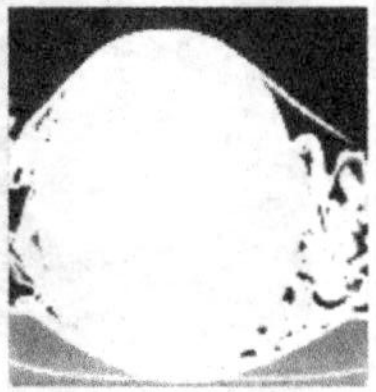	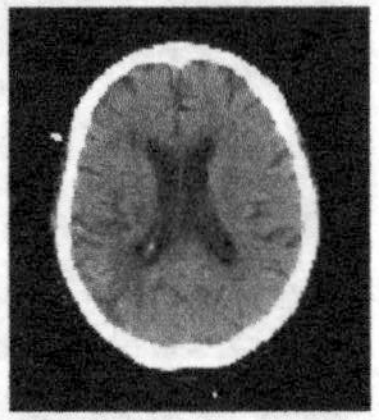
Image B	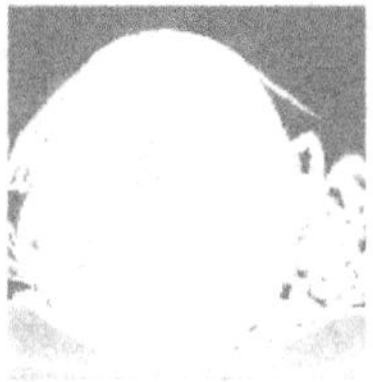				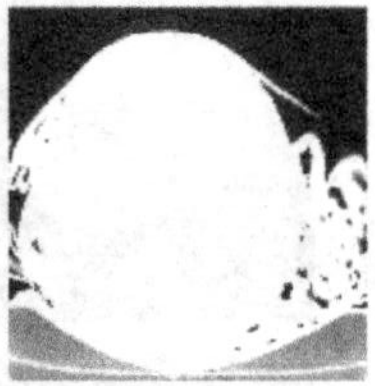	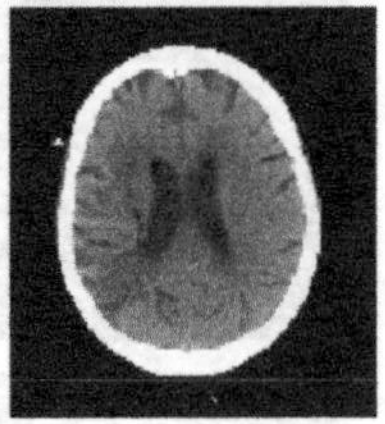
	Hospital indicator Center, 1064 HU Width, 80 HU		Proposed indicator Center, 1064 HU Width, 50 HU		Expert evaluation	
Image A	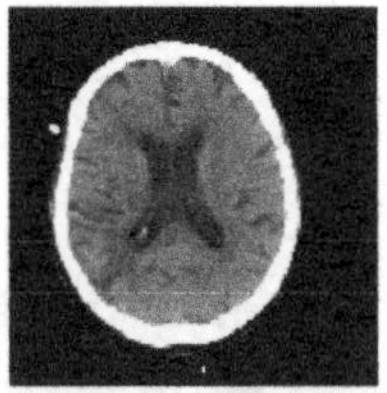		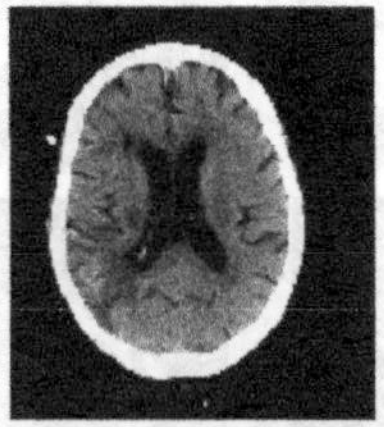		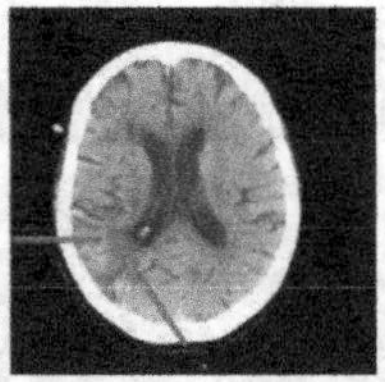	
Image B	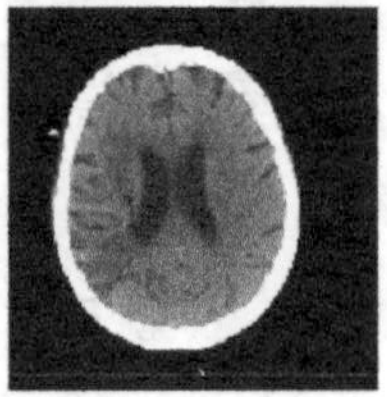		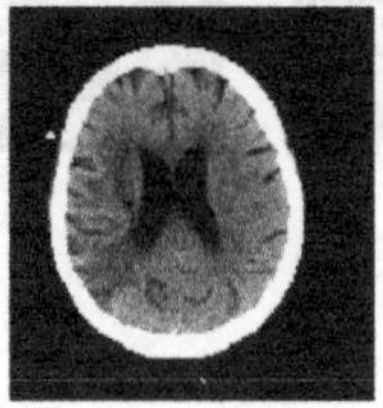		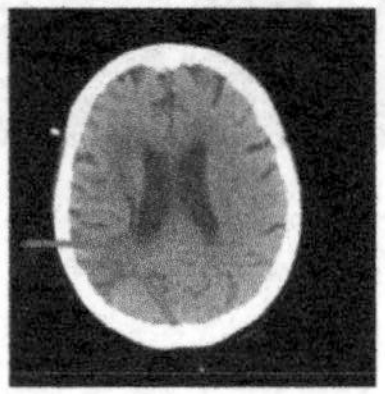	

25 HU and window width 3 HU (Przelaskowski et al., n.d.). The fifth indicator has window center 45–50 HU and window width 50 HU [13]. The sixth indicator has window center of 1064 HU and window width of 80 HU (hospital indicator).

In Image A, the brain image is not shown clearly at the proposed settings of Gregory et al. [10], Przelaskowski et al. (n.d.), and Gadda et al. [13]. However, the brain image can be shown clearly with the present indicator similarly for Image B. Hence, to have a clear vision of comparison, we use the hospital indicator, proposed indicator, and results verified by expert evaluation from the hospital.

The comparison between two indicators and expert evaluation are shown in the last three rows of Table 32.2. The first indicator is the hospital indicator. The hospital indicator is with window center 1064 HU and window width 80 HU. The second indicator is the proposed indicator with window center 1064 HU and window width 50 HU. The expert evaluation is the brain images with the exact location that is indicated by the specialist doctor from Melaka General Hospital. The arrow shows the confirmed location of infarct.

In Image A, the location of the infarct is at the right parietal lobe and right occipital lobe. The image in the hospital indicator cannot show clearly the exact location, compared with the proposed indicator, which can clearly show the location of the infarct, which is around the right parietal lobe and right occipital lobe. The experts confirm the location.

In Image B, the location of the infarct is similar to that in Image A, at the right parietal lobe and right occipital lobe. Through the proposed indicator, the location of infarct is seen more clearly than the hospital indicator. The experts confirm the location of infarct.

From the results of experiments the statistical definitions, basic ratios, and ratios of ratios are obtained. The results of 10 candidates are then presented. These results are based on 12 different cases out of 100 images with window width 80 HU (Melaka General Hospital setting). Based on the experiments the score of candidate 1 to candidate 10 are 77.78%, 75.00%, 65.28%, 61.11%, 70.83%, 66.67%, 59.72%, 66.67%, 66.67%, and 66.67%, respectively. In another experiment, the results of 10 candidates based on 12 different cases out of 100 images with window width 50 HU (proposed setting in this research) were analyzed. From the experimental results, the score of candidate 1 to candidate 10 are 88.89%, 76.39%, 70.83%, 65.28%, 72.22%, 66.67%, 62.50%, 69.44%, 69.44%, and 68.06%, respectively. Tables 32.3 and 32.4 show the results and comparison of basic ratios between 80 and 50 HU. The results in Tables 32.2 and 32.4 show that there are improvements of sensitivity,

Table 32.3 Comparison of Basic Ratios Between 80 and 50 HU

Basic Ratios	Window Width 80 HU (%)	Window Width 50 HU (%)	Improvement (%)
Sensitivity	77.38	81.40	4.02
Specificity	57.51	59.88	2.38
Positive prediction value	65.44	68.33	2.89
Negative prediction value	70.98	75.18	4.20
Type I error	42.49	40.11	−2.38
Type II error	22.62	18.60	−4.02
False discovery rate	34.56	31.67	−2.89
False omission rate	29.02	24.82	−4.20

Table 32.4 Comparison of Ratios of Ratios

	Window Width 80 HU	Window Width 50 HU
Likelihood ratio for positive test	1.82	2.03
Likelihood ratio for negative test	0.39	0.31
Likelihood ratio for positive subject	2.25	2.75
Likelihood ratio for negative subject	0.49	0.42

specificity, positive predictive value, and negative predictive value of 4.02%, 2.38%, 2.89%, and 4.20%, respectively. On the other hand, there are reductions of type I error, type II error, false discovery rate, and false omission rate of −2.38%, −4.02%, −2.89%, and −4.20%, respectively.

32.6 CONCLUSION

Window center and window width are the parameters in window setting for CT imaging. This study is more focused on window width at a fixed center of 1064 HU. Previous parameters and the current hospital parameter (used in Melaka Hospital) are tested and compared [10,11,13] (Przelaskowski et al., n.d.). In the experiment, none of the previous research parameters can detect the brain tissues clearly. The current hospital parameter can show the brain tissues. The four mathematical central moments applied show that first and second moments are directly proportional to window width. Third and fourth moments are inversely proportional to window width. With the aid of third and fourth moments, the most suitable window width level is found to be 50–60 HU, for detecting brain tissues and ischemic strokes.

ACKNOWLEDGMENT

The authors would like to thank Malacca General Hospital, Malaysia, for assistance and support in this research.

REFERENCES

[1] De Lucas EM, Sánchez E, Gutiérrez A, Mandly AG, Ruiz E, Flórez AF, et al. CT protocol for acute stroke: tips and tricks for general radiologists. Radiographics 2008;28(6):1673–87.

[2] World Health Organization, van Lerberghe W. The World Health report 2008. World Health Organization; 2008.

[3] Zaret BL, Moser M, Cohen LS. Yale university school of medicine heart book. New York: William Morrow and Co; 1992.

[4] Adams HP, Zoppo G, Alberts MJ, Bhatt DL, Brass L, Furlan A, et al. Guidelines for the early management of adults with ischemic stroke: a guideline from the American Heart Association/American Stroke Association Stroke Council, Clinical Cardiology Council, Cardiovascular Radiology and Intervention Council, and the Atherosclerotic Peripheral Vascular Disease and Quality of Care Outcomes in Research Interdisciplinary Working Groups: The American Academy of Neurology affirms the value of this guideline as an educational tool for neurologists. Circulation 2007;115:e478–534.

[5] Holmes EJ, Forrest-Hay AC, Misra RR. Interpretation of emergency head CT. Cambridge: Cambridge University Press; 2008.
[6] Mustra M, Delac K, Grgic M. Overview of the DICOM standard. In: Proceedings of international ELMAR symposium 1; 2008. p. 39–44.
[7] Tomandl BF, Klotz E, Handschu R, Stemper B, Reinhardt F, Huk WJ, et al. Comprehensive imaging of ischemic stroke with multisection CT. Radiographics 2003;23:565–92.
[8] Hounsfield GN. Computed Medical Imaging: nobel lecture in physiology or medicine 1971–1980. In: Lindsten J, editor; 1979. p. 568–86.
[9] Hsieh J. Computed tomography: principles, design, artifacts, and recent advances. 2nd ed. Bellingham: Wiley; 2009.
[10] Gregory BA, Snow RD, Brogdon BG. Value of bone window images in routine brain CT: examinations beyond trauma. Appl Radiol 1997;26:26–38.
[11] Lev MH, Farkas J, Gemmete JJ, Hossain ST, Hunter GJ, Koroshetz WJ, et al. Acute stroke: improved nonenhanced CT detection — benefits of soft-copy interpretation by using variable window width and center level settings. Radiology 1999;213:150–5.
[12] Przelaskowski A, Walecki J, Szerewicz K, Bargiel P. Acute stroke detection in unenhanced CT exams: perception enhancement by multi-scale approach. In: National conference on physics and engineering in the present Medicine and Health Carethe challenges to Poland as a New European Union Member. Warsaw; 2005. p. 94–5.
[13] Gadda D, Vannucchi L, Niccolai F, Neri AT, Carmignani L, Pacini P. CT in acute stroke: improved detection of dense intracranial arteries by varying window parameters and performing a thin-slice helical scan. Neuroradiology 2002;44:900–6.
[14] Ge Y, Grossman RI, Babb JS, Rabin ML, Mannon LJ, Kolson DL. Age-related total gray matter and white matter changes in normal adult brain. Part I: volumetric MR imaging analysis. AJNR — Am J Neuroradiol 2002;23:1327–33.
[15] Bushong SC. Computed tomography (essentials of medical imaging). New York: McGraw-Hill Medical; 2000.
[16] Bushberg JT, Seibert JA, Leidholdt ED, Boone JM. The essential physics of medical imaging. 3rd ed. North American Edition, LWW; 2011.
[17] Locke C, Zavgorodni S. Vega library for processing DICOM data required in Monte Carlo verification of radiotherapy treatment plans. Australas Phys Eng Sci Med 2008;31:290–9.
[18] Romans LE. Computed tomography for technologists: exam review. Philadelphia: LWW; 2010.
[19] Krishnamoorthy K. Handbook of statistical distributions with applications (statistics: a series of textbooks and monographs). Chapman and Hall/CRC; 2006.
[20] Press WH, Teukolsky SA, Vetterling WT. Numerical recipes: the art of scientific computing. 3rd ed. Cambridge: Cambridge University Press; 2007.

CHAPTER

AN IMPROVED BALLOON SNAKE ALGORITHM FOR ULTRASONIC IMAGE SEGMENTATION

33

M. Shen*, Q. Zhang†,‡, B. Zheng‡

Shantou Polytechnic, Shantou, Guangdong, PR China Shantou University Medical College, Shantou, Guangdong, PR China† Shantou University, Shantou, Guangdong, PR China‡*

33.1 INTRODUCTION

Cancer remains a major public health problem in the world. For instance, breast cancer has become the leading cause of death among women. The National Cancer Institute estimates that one out of eight women in the United States will develop breast cancer [1]. However, if detected at an early stage, more than 92% of breast cancers can be cured [2]. Hence, early detection of cancerous lesions is crucial for successful treatment and cure.

Ultrasound imaging has been employed for diagnosis of breast cancer, liver tumors, and so on. To facilitate early detection, many methods have been developed for ultrasonic lesion detection [3–5]. In all these methods, extracting the lesion area from the background is an essential step that provides significant clinical information to discriminate between malignant and benign tumors and thus contribute to reducing the unnecessary operations such as fine needle aspiration and biopsy. Unfortunately, the speckle brightness variations inherent in ultrasonic imaging, the low contrast of ultrasound images and the variance in shape, introduce significant difficulties in the extraction of lesions and human interpretation. This makes ultrasound image lesion segmentation a challenging task. To solve this problem, many approaches have been developed, including the support vector machine (SVM) algorithm and the region growing procedure. Region growing is a simple yet widely used algorithm, but it produces satisfactory segmentation only when lesions have clear edges [6–9]. SVM is a powerful classification technique, which is popular for lesion segmentation and detection [10,11]. For example, SVM with RBF kernels was applied to the lesion segmentation of ultrasound images [10]. However, the algorithm suffers from the interference of speckle noise.

Active contour models (also called snakes) have also been widely applied to extract the boundaries in various ultrasound images such as ovarian follicles [12], brain cortex [13], and left-ventricular edges [14]. These models used a curve that is defined by partial differential equations to evolve toward the local optimum, with respect to an objective function usually called energy. Because inherent speckle interference obscures the ultrasound images, ordinary snakes have poor convergence to lesion boundary concavity and thus cannot segment the irregular-shaped malignant lesions accurately. A lot of modified models were proposed to try to resolve the problem mentioned above, such as balloon snake [15,16], gradient vector flow (GVF) snake [17], and vector field convolution (VFC) snake [18].

The balloon snake makes the model less sensitive to initial contour and increases its capture range. However, the balloon snake model suffers from the unidirectional movement property of the balloon force; that is to say, only when the snake is initialized inside or outside the edges completely can the model perform well. Moreover, the model easily causes leaking when dealing with the weak edges because the pressure force may push the snake curves out of the object boundary.

Bidirectional movement of the balloon snake is important to allow for good segmentation at weak edges. A snake model based on hypothesized magnetic interactions between the active contour and object boundaries is proposed in Ref. [19] to impose bidirectional movement of the snake, resulting in significant improvement on capturing complex geometries and dealing with difficult initializations, weak edges, and broken boundaries. It is shown in our preliminary study [20] that this model can also be generalized and formulated explicitly as a balloon snake model with bidirectional movement caused by adaptive balloon forces that are related to but not exactly the same as the hypothesized magnetic force described in Ref. [19]. For simplicity of presentation, we term this modified magnetostatic active contour (MAC) model as an adaptive magnetostatic bidirectional balloon snake (AMBBS) model because the balloon force varies adaptively to pull and push the balloon to the object boundary.

In this chapter, the AMBBS approach is adopted for the segmentation of lesions in clinical ultrasound images, and its capability for recovering broken boundaries is theoretically analyzed. Simulated experiments are first performed to demonstrate the superior performance of AMBBS on images with noise and broken or weak edges. Then, the AMBBS approach is applied to clinical ultrasound images with fibroadenoma or fibrocystic lesions contaminated by speckle noise. Experimental results show that the AMBBS model is robust to speckle noise and can converge to complex geometries and weak edges successfully. Qualitative and quantitative comparisons with two well-known state-of-the-art approaches proposed by Kotropoulos et al. [10] and Xu et al. [21] demonstrate superior performance of the proposed AMBBS approach on lesion segmentation for medical ultrasound images.

The remainder of this chapter is organized as follows. Section 33.2 presents the method, including the proposed generalized AMBBS model and a theoretical analysis on its capability of recovering broken boundaries, followed by an introduction to the balloon snake model and the MAC model. Experimental results on the simulated images and real clinical ultrasound images are presented in Sections 33.3 and 33.4, respectively. Finally, concluding remarks are addressed in Section 33.5.

33.2 METHODS

33.2.1 BALLOON SNAKE MODEL

A traditional snake is defined as a parametric curve [22]

$$X(s) = (x(s), y(s)), \quad s \in [0, 1] \tag{1}$$

where s is the arc length of the snake contour, which moves through the spatial domain of an image to minimize the following energy function:

$$E = \int_0^1 \frac{1}{2}\left[\alpha|X'(s)|^2 + \beta|X''(s)|^2\right] + E_{\text{ext}}(X(s))ds \tag{2}$$

where $X'(s)$ and $X''(s)$ represent the first and the second derivatives of $X(s)$ with respect to s, respectively. α and β denote weighting parameters that control the elasticity and rigidity of the snake curves.

The external energy function E_{ext} is calculated from the image so that it takes on its smaller values at the features of interest, such as boundaries. Given a gray level image $I(x,y)$, the typical external energy function E_{ext} is designed to lead snakes toward the object boundary, such as the following two examples:

$$E_{\text{ext}} = -|\nabla[G_\sigma(x,y)*I(x,y)]|^2 \tag{3}$$

$$E_{\text{ext}} = G_\sigma(x,y)*I(x,y) \tag{4}$$

where G_σ denotes a two-dimensional Gaussian function with standard deviation σ and ∇ represents the gradient operator.

To improve the performance of the traditional snake, Cohen [15] proposed the famous balloon snake model through simulating the motion principle of a balloon, which makes the snake search in a larger area than the original one. The balloon force is defined as

$$F_{\text{B}}(X) = k_{\text{B}}\vec{N}(X) \tag{5}$$

where $\vec{N}$ denotes the unit inward normal of the evolving contour X and k_{B} is a constant. The balloon force inflates and pushes the active contour outwards when k_{B} is negative, whereas it shrinks and pulls the active contour inwards when k_{B} is positive. Then, the energy function becomes

$$E = \int_0^1 \frac{1}{2}\left[\alpha|X'(s)|^2 + \beta|X''(s)|^2\right] + E_{\text{ext}}(X(s))ds + \iint F_{\text{B}}dxdy \tag{6}$$

Using variational calculus and applying the Euler-Lagrange differential equation, its force balance equation can be obtained as follows:

$$\frac{dX(s)}{dt} = \alpha X^{(2)}(s) + \beta X^{(4)}(s) - \nabla E_{\text{ext}} + F_{\text{B}} \tag{7}$$

Fig. 33.1 shows an object with a complex shape to examine the original balloon snake model's convergence capability. Setting the initial contour (indicated by a small circle) inside the object boundary (see Fig. 33.1A) and k_{B} negative, the model could detect the edges accurately (shown by the outline curve in Fig. 33.1A). When the initial contour was placed outside the object boundary (see Fig. 33.1B), and let k_{B} be positive, the model also succeeded. However, when initialized across the object boundary (see Fig. 33.1C), the snake contour could not converge to the edges accurately because the balloon force is not adaptive. Furthermore, as shown in Fig. 33.1D, the original balloon model fell in dealing with the blurred object boundary as well.

The defects of this traditional balloon snake greatly restrain its application in the segmentation of lesions in medical ultrasound images because there are often weak edges, and it is difficult for radiologists to place the initial contour inside or outside completely.

33.2.2 THE MAC MODEL

The problem of the balloon model shown above is due to the fact that the balloon force is unidirectional. An adaptive bidirectional force may resolve the problem. In Ref. [19], a MAC model is proposed to allow for bidirectional movement of the snake. According to the concept of the external force field, it is hypothesized that electric currents flow through both the object boundary and the active contour, as

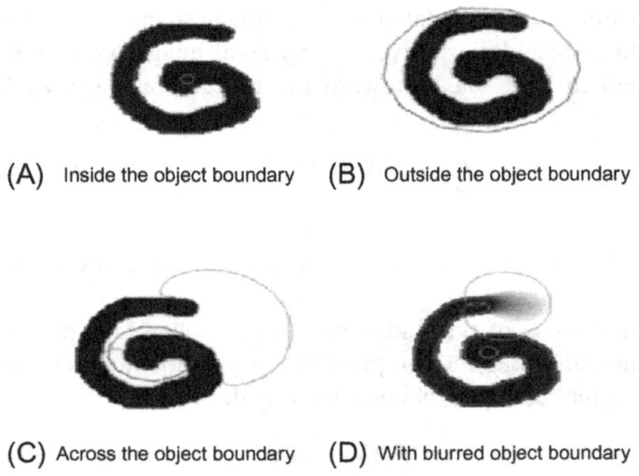

FIGURE 33.1

The results of balloon snake model with different initializations.

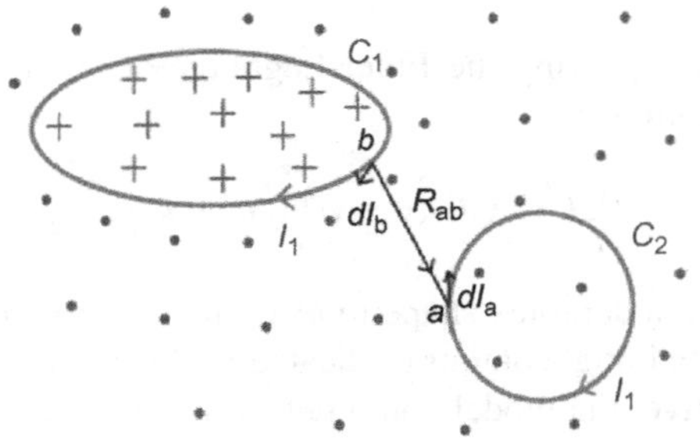

FIGURE 33.2

The magnetic field generated by C_1.

shown in Fig. 33.2. A magnetostatic field is then generated by the currents in the object boundary C_1, as shown in Fig. 33.2 with symbols "+" and ".", and a force is induced on the active contour C_2 to make it move adaptively to the object boundary C_1.

Consider infinitesimal current segments dl_b at point b on C_1, in the generated magnetic field (without considering the field generated by C_2). The magnetic flux density B at point a can be computed as Eq. (8) using the Biôt-Savart Law [23]:

$$B(a) = \frac{\mu_0}{4\pi} I_1 \int_{C_1} dl_b \times \frac{\vec{R}_{ba}}{R_{ba}^2} \tag{8}$$

where μ_0 represents the permeability constant, R_{ba} denotes the distance between point a and b, $\vec{R}_{ba}$ is the unit distance vector, and "$\times$" denotes the cross product. Let the strength of the local current I_1, dI_b proportional to the local gradient $f(n)$, and denote this local current in the 3-D space as

$$K(n) = [f(n)\Gamma(n), 0] \tag{9}$$

where $\Gamma(n)$ is the unit direction of the current in the 2-D plane.

Therefore, according to Eq. (8), the overall magnetic flux density at point a can be computed as

$$B(a) = \frac{\mu_0}{4\pi} \sum_{n \in f(n)} K(n) \times \frac{\vec{R}_{na}}{R_{na}^2} \tag{10}$$

Because many images, such as medical ultrasound images considered in this chapter, may be seriously corrupted by speckle noise, anisotropic diffusion based on Refs. [24] and [25] is employed to refine the magnetic field $\mathfrak{B}(x)$ using the following diffusion function

$$\frac{\partial \mathfrak{B}(x)}{\partial t} = r(B(x))\mathrm{div}(\mathfrak{B}) - (1 - r(B(x)))(\mathfrak{B}(x) - B(x)) \tag{11}$$

$$r(B(x)) = \mathrm{e}^{-\frac{|B(x)|f(x)}{w}} \tag{12}$$

where $\mathfrak{B}(x)$ is initialized to $B(x)$ and w denotes a fixed parameter. The diffusion term $r[B(x)]$ exhibits higher values of diffusion in the homogeneous regions.

Given the current I_2 applied to the active contour, the force at point a due to the magnetic field $B(a)$ is

$$F_{\mathrm{DB}}(a) = I_2 \gamma(a) \times B(a) \tag{13}$$

where $\gamma(a)$ denotes the electric current vector on the active contour position a. Driven by this force, the snake model can be given as

$$\frac{\partial X}{\partial t} = \left(F_{\mathrm{DB}}(x) \cdot \vec{N}\right)\vec{N} \tag{14}$$

To further smooth the contour, the standard curvature flow is employed and the contour evolution formulation can be rewritten as

$$\frac{\partial C}{\partial t} = \alpha g(x)\kappa\vec{N} + (1-\alpha)\left(F_{\mathrm{DB}}(x) \cdot \vec{N}\right)\vec{N} \tag{15}$$

where $g(x)$ represents the stopping function. Given a gray image $I(x, y)$, $g(x)$ can be obtained as [26]

$$f(x) = |\nabla(\mathrm{Gauss} * I(x))| \text{ and } g(x) = \frac{1}{1 + f(x)} \tag{16}$$

Using the level set method, the level set representation of (15) is formulated as

$$\frac{\partial \phi}{\partial t} = \alpha g(x)\nabla \cdot \left(\frac{\nabla\phi}{|\nabla\phi|}\right)|\nabla\phi| - (1-\alpha)F_{\mathrm{DB}}(x) \cdot \nabla\phi \tag{17}$$

where ϕ denotes the level set function. The numerical implementation of (17) can be found in Ref. [27].

33.2.3 GENERALIZED AMBBS MODEL

According to Eq. (13), the force imposed on the active contour in the MAC model always points to the normal (inward or outward) of the active contour; that is,

$$F_{DB}(x) = k_{DB}(x)\vec{N}(x) \tag{18}$$

Comparing Eqs. (5) and (18), it is obvious that the MAC model can be considered as a balloon model with adaptive balloon force that varies in both magnitude and direction. This variable balloon force makes the snake contour be able to move adaptively. Therefore, it can also be considered an AMBBS model. The modified balloon force has the ability to dynamically update itself with the contour evolving, which is significantly different from the original balloon force.

Furthermore, though the force (Eq. (18)) is derived from the hypothesized current in the object boundary according to electromagnetic theory, we propose to use a generalized balloon force that is related to the magnetic field generated by the object boundary but does not necessarily obey the electromagnetic theory.

In this chapter, we propose to use a generalized magnetic balloon force with the property that when the contour is far away from the objective boundary it moves to the object boundary rapidly while it moves slowly near the edge to avoid oversegmentation. This is a desired property that does not exist in the original MAC model. For this purpose, the generalized balloon force is defined as Eq. (18) with k_{DB} set as

$$k_{DB}(x) = \lambda_B(x)[1 - \beta_B(x)] \cdot e^{|B|^{-1}} \tag{19}$$

$$\lambda_B(x) = \begin{cases} 1 & \text{if } B(x) > \Pi \\ 0 & \text{else} \\ -1 & \text{if } B(x) < -\Pi \end{cases} \tag{20}$$

$$\beta_B(x) = \begin{cases} 1 & \text{if } B(x) = 0 \\ 0 & \text{else} \end{cases} \tag{21}$$

where Π is the threshold value.

When the snake contour is placed far away from the object boundary, the magnetic flux density is too weak, whereas $e^{|B|^{-1}}$ is large enough to keep the snake moving toward the object edges rapidly. When near the object boundary, $e^{|B|^{-1}}$ becomes small and drives the snake toward the edges slowly, effectively avoiding oversegmentation. Furthermore, $\lambda_B(x)$ is employed to control the snake curve to inflate or deflate adaptively. Besides, $[1 - \beta_B(x)]$ is used to avoid the snake to quiver when the snake contour is close to the object edges. The operation of this generalized AMBBS model can be illustrated in the following using an example of gray image shown in Fig. 33.3.

Fig. 33.4 shows the distribution of the resulting magnetic flux density B exerted by the object boundary in Fig. 33.3, where the X-Y plane denotes the image plane, and Z axis is perpendicular to the image plane. The magnitude of B at pixels near the edges is large and decreases rapidly with increasing distance between the point and the edges.

Figs. 33.5 and 33.6 show the corresponding λ_B and k_{DB} of the magnetic field in Fig. 33.4 respectively. It is seen that when inside the object boundary the value of λ_B is negative, whereas when outside the object boundary the value of λ_B is positive as shown in Fig. 33.5. It can also be observed from

FIGURE 33.3

An example gray image.

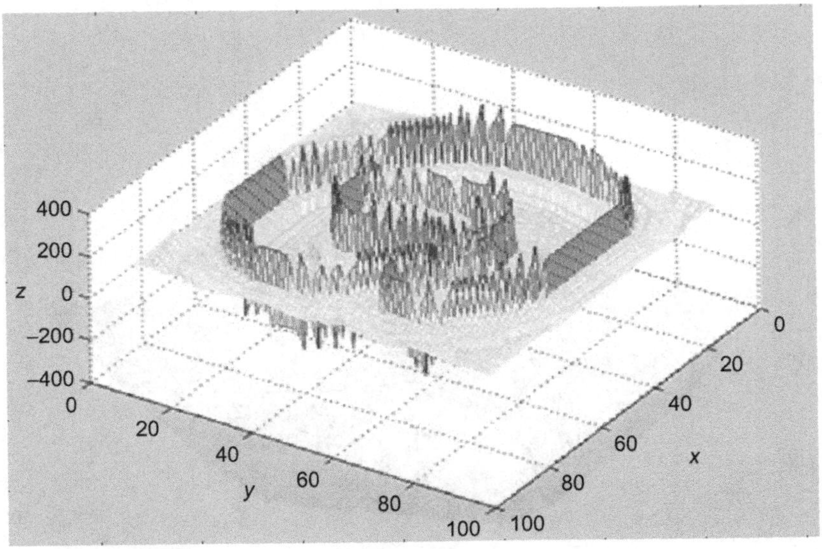

FIGURE 33.4

The distribution of the resulting magnetic flux density of Fig. 33.3.

Fig. 33.6 that k_{DB} has a large value when the snake is far away from the object boundary, meaning the balloon force is also large. With the evolution of the active contour, the curve gradually approaches the object boundary, and k_{DB} is reducing, which means that the balloon force becomes weak gradually at a more and more low speed until the snake finally stops at the object boundary.

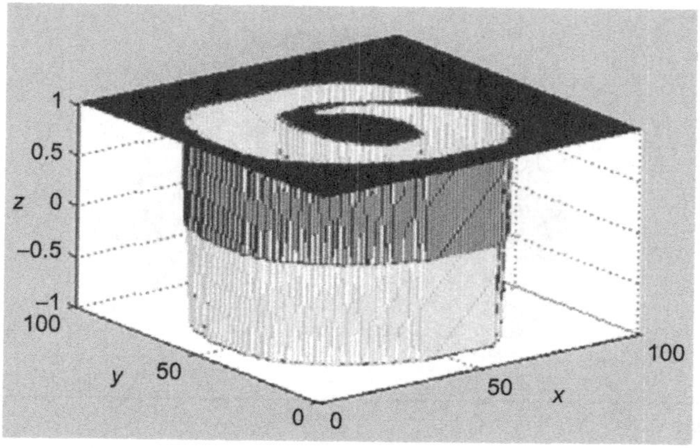

FIGURE 33.5

The corresponding λ_B of the magnetic field in Fig. 33.4 (*top view*).

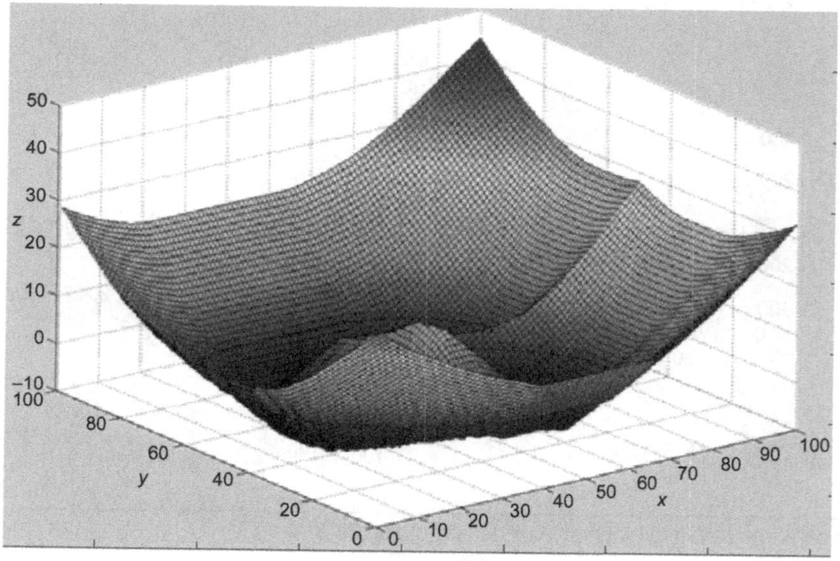

FIGURE 33.6

k_{DB} of the magnetic field in Fig. 33.4.

33.2.4 THE ANALYSIS OF THE RECOVERY OF BROKEN BOUNDARY

Different from the traditional edge-based active contour methods, the stopping function of the MAC model and the proposed generalized AMBBS model is based on the distribution of magnetic field originated by the currents on the object boundary. According to Eq. (10), we can find that the magnetic flux density at each pixel in the image plane is determined by the vectors from pixels on the object boundary to the pixel and by the electric current vector at corresponding pixels on the object edges. Thus, the magnetic field in the broken region still exists, which suggests that the AMBBS method can do well with blurred images. The details are given as follows.

Assuming that I_b is a blurred boundary with currents as shown in Fig. 33.7, where the region inside the curve denotes the blurred region. From Eq. (10), it is clear that the magnetic flux density is inversely proportional to the square of the distance between the pixel in the image plane and pixels on the object boundary. With the distance increasing, the magnetic flux density reduces rapidly. Thus, we can consider that the magnetic flux density at each pixel in the blurred region is approximately determined by the vector from the nearest pixel on the object boundary to the pixel and by the electric current vector at the nearest pixel on the object edge. Using the Biôt-Savart law, the amplitude of the magnetic flux density at each point (such as pixel a) can be stated as

$$B_a = \frac{u_0 dI_b \cdot \sin\theta}{4\pi \vec{R}_{ba}^2} \tag{22}$$

where b represents the pixel at the boundary nearest to a and θ denotes the angle between the electric current vector at b and the vector from b to a.

According to the Ampere's right-handed rule, the orientation of the magnetic field at a is related to the direction of pivoting the electric current vector dI_b to the vector $\vec{R}_{ba}$. When the direction is clockwise, the corresponding magnetic field at point a is perpendicular inside to the image plane, whereas when the rotation direction is counterclockwise, the corresponding magnetic field at point a is then always perpendicular outside, as shown in Fig. 33.7. Symbols "+" denote perpendicular inside to the image plane, and symbols " · " denote perpendicular outside to the image plane. It is worth noticing that when dI_b is parallel to $\vec{R}_{ba}$, namely, the direction is zero, and the magnetic flux density at a becomes 0 because $\theta = 0$. According to the theory of the magnetic field, we can know that the magnetic flux density on the real object boundary is zero ($B = 0$). Naturally, in the blurred region, the pixel with $B = 0$ is considered as the pixel on the object boundary. Then, the curve with $B = 0$ is obtained, which is denoted as the dash dot line in Fig. 33.7. It is observed that the curve connects the broken object boundaries together, which is called the analog object boundary. Thus, when evolving into the red region, the

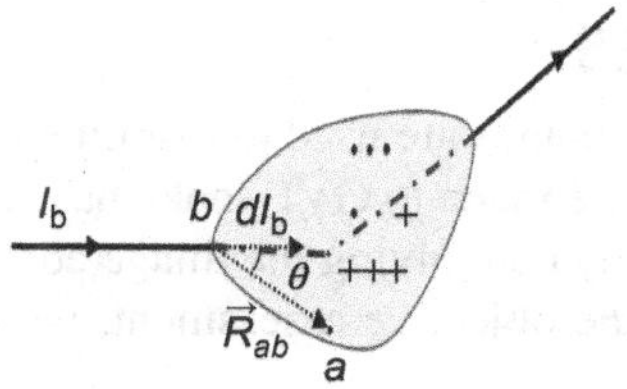

FIGURE 33.7

The magnetic field in the region of broken edge.

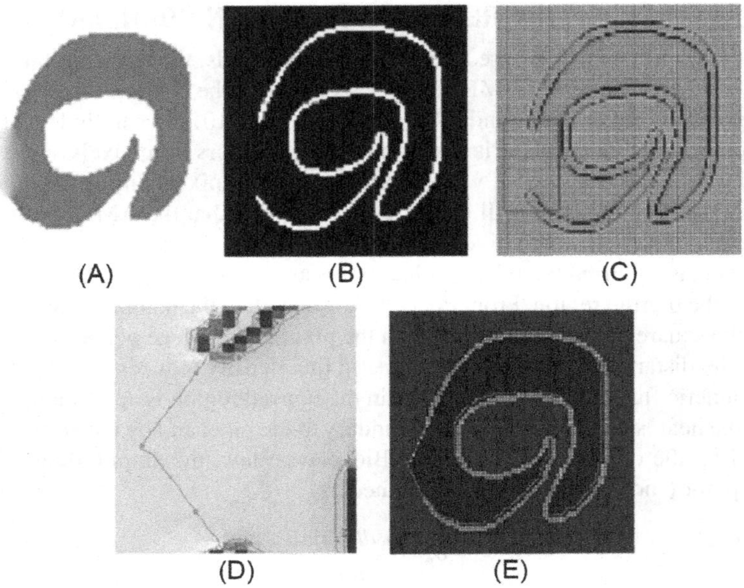

FIGURE 33.8

An example. (A) the object with a blurred boundary; (B) boundaries of the object; (C) magnitude of the magnetic field; (D) local enlargement of the red rectangle in (C); and (E) the magnitude of λ_B.

snake will stop in the analog object boundary avoiding the edge leaking. An example is given for further explanations as follows.

Fig. 33.8A shows the object with a partially blurred boundary segment. It is seen from Fig. 33.8B that the blurred boundary is unable to be detected. Computing the magnetic field, the distribution of the magnetic flux density can be then obtained as shown in Fig. 33.8C. To observe the distribution of the magnetic flux density in the blurred region, we enlarge the rectangle region in Fig. 33.8C and draw up the equipotential curve (see Fig. 33.8D). It is clear to see that there is a zero equipotential curve in the blurred region; namely, the analog object boundary mentioned above. Fig. 33.8E shows the distribution of λ_B using Eq. (20). Apparently, λ_B divides the blurred region into the regions of targets and backgrounds.

33.3 SIMULATION STUDIES

In this section, a series of simulated images are used to examine the performance of the proposed generalized AMBBS, and comparisons are made to GVF snake based on the diffusion of the gradient vectors of an edge map and VFC snake by convolving the image edge map with a vector field kernel. The relative error (RE) is employed as the objective assessment, which is defined as

$$\mathrm{RE}(\%) = \frac{n_e}{n_a} \times 100\% \tag{23}$$

where n_e represents the area of the image wrongly classified and n_a denotes the total area of the image.

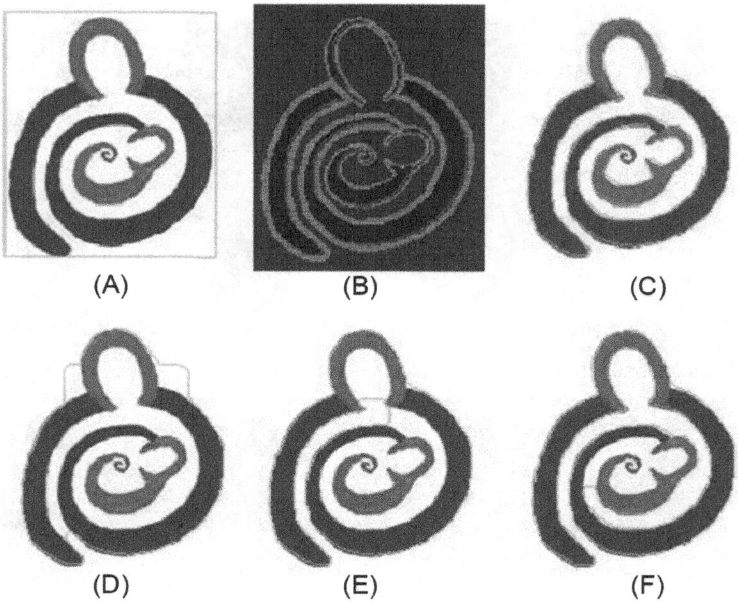

FIGURE 33.9

Handling complex shape. (A) original image with an initial curve; (B) the corresponding magnetic field; (C) the final segmentation result; and (D–F) evolution of the curve after 5, 35, and 65 iterations, respectively.

33.3.1 CAPTURING COMPLEX GEOMETRIES

To examine the convergence ability of the proposed generalized AMBBS, we consider the case in which a complex synthetic image is constructed with size 128 × 156 (see Fig. 33.9A). The green rectangle denotes the initial contour. The corresponding magnetic field is calculated as shown in Fig. 33.9B. Based on the magnetic field, the bidirectional balloon force is then constructed to drive the snakes toward the object boundary. Fig. 33.9D–F shows the evolution of the snake contour with successive iterations, and the final segmentation result can be found in Fig. 33.9C. It is clear to see that AMBBS successfully segments the complex boundary.

33.3.2 RESILIENCE TO ARBITRARY INITIALIZATIONS

In this part, an acute concavity is used to test the resilience of the proposed generalized AMBBS to arbitrary initialization as shown in Fig. 33.10 where the rectangle denotes the initial contour. Fig. 33.10A-C shows the recovered shapes obtained by GVF snakes, VFC snakes, and AMBBS, respectively. From Fig. 33.10A and B it can be seen that GVF and VFC snakes cannot segment the object successfully because their stationary vector force field exhibit saddle and stationary points that prevent the snake from converging to the object edges. For instance, there is a saddle point appearing at the entrance of the concave shape as shown in Fig. 33.11A, which is denoted as the small rectangle.

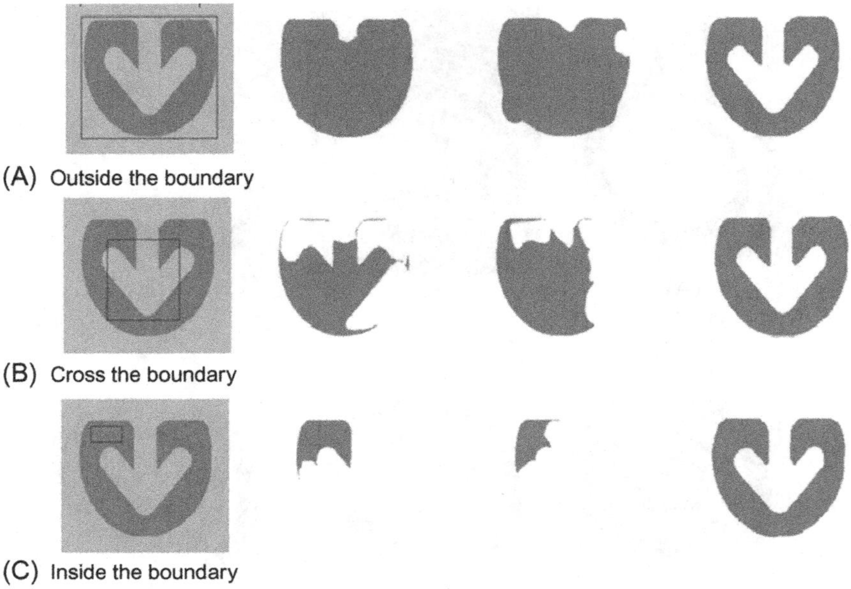

FIGURE 33.10

Arbitrary initialization. (A) results of GVFsnake; (B) results of VFCsnake; and (C) results of AMBBS.

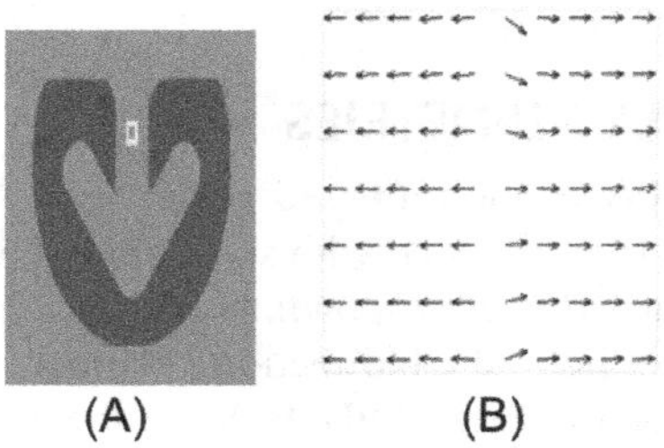

FIGURE 33.11

(A) Saddle point and (B) the GVF force map at the saddle point.

The GVF force map at the saddle point can be found in Fig. 33.11B. When evolving at this saddle point, the snake contour is tangent to the force field and thus leads the snake to stop at the entrance of the concave shape. However, only AMBBS has satisfactory results (see Fig. 33.10C) with very low REs of 1.25%, 1.77%, and 1.45%, respectively. Apparently, AMBBS achieves a significant improvement in initialization invariance.

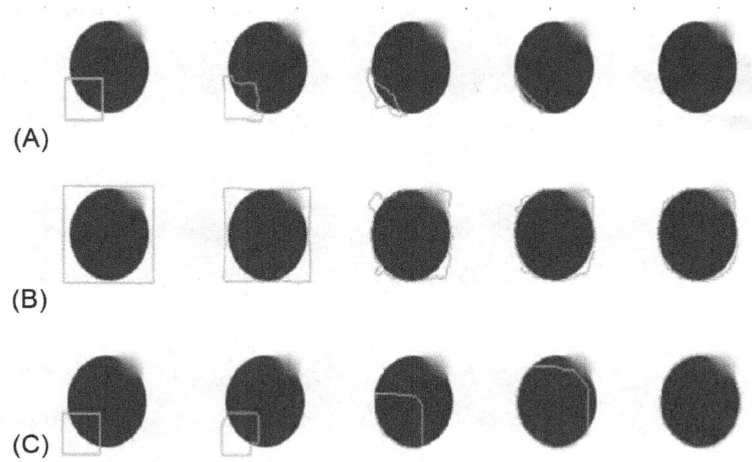

FIGURE 33.12

The convergence to an object with weak edges. (A) the results of GVF snake; (B) the results of VFC snake; and (C) the results of AMBBS.

33.3.3 CONVERGENCE ON WEAK EDGES

To test the convergence on weak edges, a circular object with a partially blurred boundary segment is carried out as shown in Fig. 33.12, commonly used for weak-edge analysis. Generally speaking, the GVF snake can converge to the blurred edge with specified initialization. However, a more arbitrary initialization as seen in Fig. 33.12A causes the snake to collapse resulting in failure. Like GVF snakes, the VFC snake also requires a specified initialization. When adopting the same initialization as the GVF snake, the VFC snake converges to a point. For comparison, the VFC snake is initialized outside the object and as close as possible to the object boundary (see Fig. 33.12B). The result shows that the VFC snake approximately contoured the object boundary, but there appears to be leaking through the blurred boundary segment. For AMBBS, the magnetic field still exists in the broken region, which can drive the snake contour to converge to the analog object boundary and thus can accurately extract the object boundary in the blurred region as shown in Fig. 33.12C.

33.3.4 RECOVERING NOISE IMAGES

Next, the simulated image is corrupted by an adaptive Gaussian white noise with respect to different noise variances, which have a peak signal-to-noise ratio (PSNR) ranging from 8.55 dB to 10.59 dB. These noise-corrupted images are employed to examine the noise sensitivity of AMBBS as seen in Fig. 33.13A, where the rectangle curve in the second column denotes the initial snake. The comparative results obtained by GVF snake, VFC snake, and AMBBS are shown in Fig. 33.13B–D. With the noise level increased, the results of GVF snake and VFC snake become greatly worse as they are sensitive to the noise. However, only our proposed method can accurately extract the object boundaries and keep relative low error rates of 2.76%, 3.12%, and 4.23% for noise-corrupted images with PSNR = 10.59 dB, 9.46 dB, and 8.55 dB, respectively.

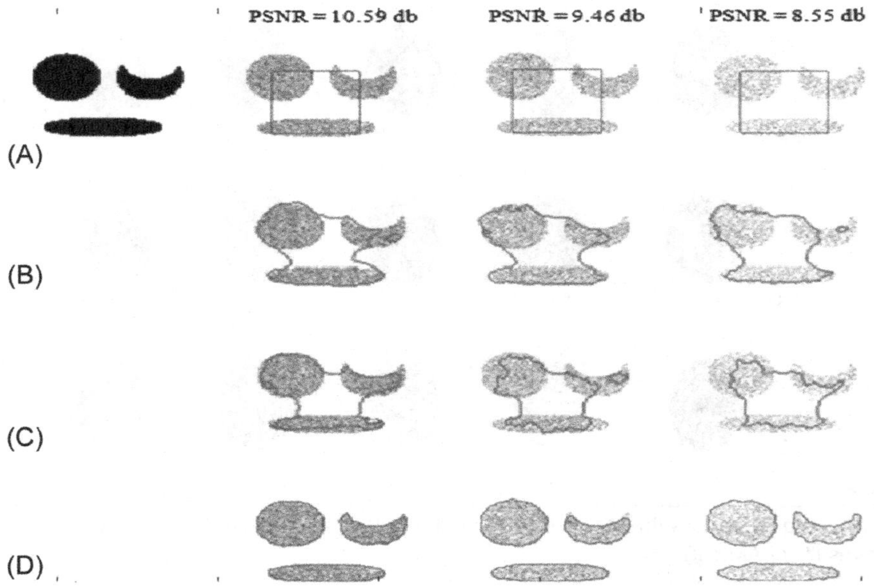

FIGURE 33.13

Recovering an object with noise. (A) the noise-corrupted images and the corressponding initial snake; (B) the results of GVF snake; (C) the results of VFC snake; and (D) the results of AMBBS.

33.4 EXPERIMENTAL RESULTS

In this section, several ultrasound images were used to test AMBBS. The images were collected from GE Healthcare [28]. Each ultrasound image has an in-plane resolution of 500×500. To evaluate AMBBS, two other state-of-the-art methods were employed for comparison. One is the adaptive level set method proposed by Xu et al. [21]. The other one is the RBF-SVMs method proposed by Kotropoulos et al. [10]. For further evaluation, a common assessment of RE shown in Eq. (23) is employed, where n_e is the difference area between the tumor area measured by the methods and the tumor area furnished by the experts. n_a is the total area of the region of interest (ROI).

Fig. 33.14A and B shows the original fibroadenoma and fibrocystic lesion in ultrasound images, common diseases of the breast, respectively. The rectangular boxes superimposed on the images are the regions of interest (ROIs). Initially, the snake contours of the adaptive level set method and the AMBBS method are initialized as the white rectangle as shown in Figs. 33.15A and 33.16A. 2000 samples from ROIs are randomly chosen as the training data of the RBF-SVMs method, with a block size of 7×7. Figs. 33.15B–D and 33.16B–D show the comparative results of the three methods, with the comparison of the corresponding REs as seen in Fig. 33.17. Although the adaptive level set method improved the active contour model by combining the boundary statistics and global statistics, the inherent limitations of the active contour still exist, such as the sensibility to the initial condition, caused the method to be instable and thus could not extract the fibroadenoma or fibrocystic lesion

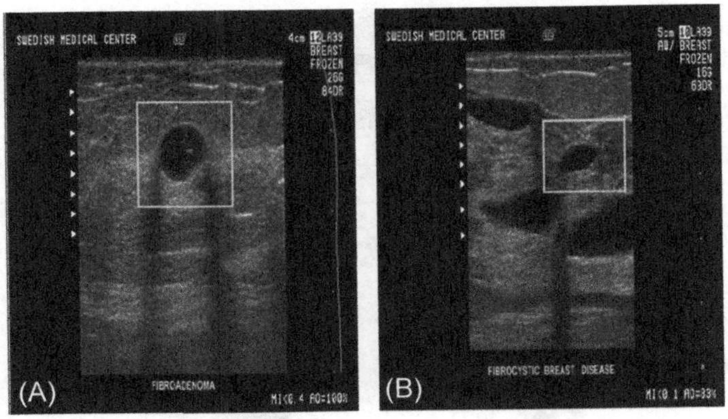

FIGURE 33.14

(A) Fibroadenoma of breast and (B) fibrocystic lesion of breast.

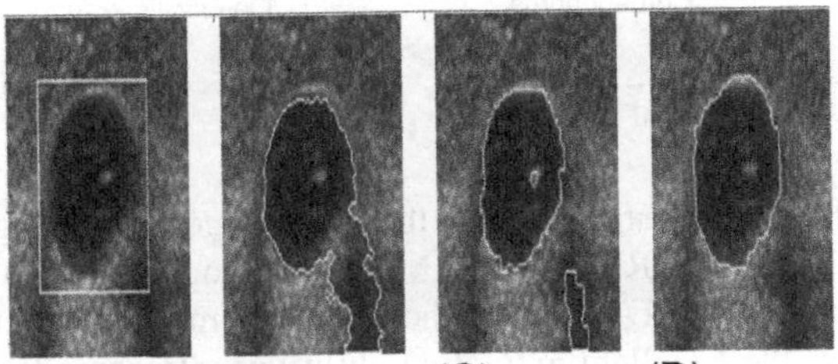

(A) (B) (C) (D)

FIGURE 33.15

(A) Fibroadenoma; (B) the adaptive level set method; (C) the RBF-SVMs method; and (D) the AMBBS method.

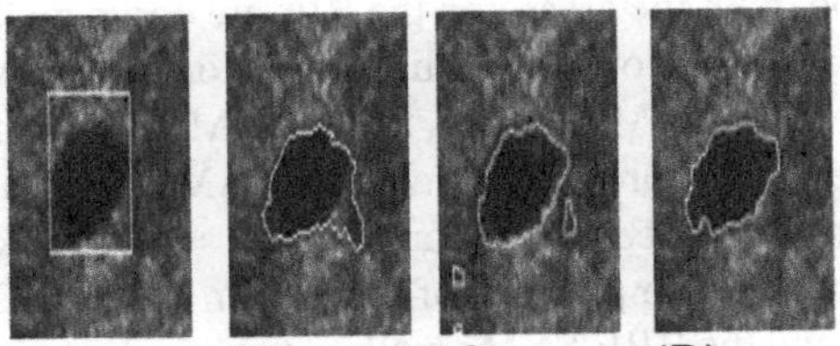

(A) (B) (C) (D)

FIGURE 33.16

(A) Fibrocystic lesion; (B) the adaptive level set method; (C) the RBF-SVMs method; and (D) the AMBBS method.

boundaries successfully (as shown in Figs. 33.15B and 33.16B). As for the RBF-SVMs method, the performance of the method is determined by the accuracy of the feature extraction. However, the features are extracted from the original image plane directly and seriously interferred by the inherent speckle noise, and thus the method has the poor performance for segmentation of ultrasound images. The segmented results by the RBF-SVMs method are shown in Figs. 33.15C and 33.16C. Apparently,

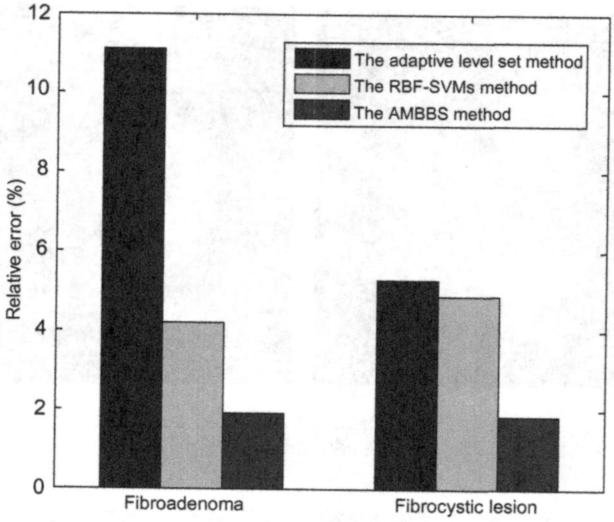

FIGURE 33.17

The comparison of the RE using different methods.

only our proposed method can successfully extract the lesion edges (see in Figs. 33.15D and 33.16D). It is observed from Fig. 33.17 that the REs of the AMBBS method are obviously less than those of the adaptive level set method and the RBF-SVMs method. Thus, compared with two other recent methods, the AMBBS method shows the excellent extracting ability of ultrasonic lesions.

The extraction of the lesions provides significant information to aid clinical diagnosis, such as the area and perimeter of the lesions. Here, the different characteristics of the lesions are tabulated in Table 33.1. The lesions can be quantitatively investigated. However, the reliability of the information depends on the accuracy of segmentation results. Thus, to prove the reliability of the information supported by the AMBBS method, both the areas and the REs are compared, as shown in Table 33.2. The first row is the areas information based on the manual extraction by the experts. The areas based on the adaptive level set method, the RBF-SVMs method, and the AMBBS method are listed from the second row to the fourth row. Apparently, the areas obtained by the AMBBS method are very close to those of the experts, and the minimum difference can be found in the segmentation of fibroadenoma with 188 pixels. The last three rows show the comparisons of REs. From Table 33.2, it can be observed that both the adaptive level set method and the RBF-SVMs method have high error rates, especially the adaptive level set method with the highest error rate of 11.10%. However, the AMBBS method always keeps a

Table 33.1 Different Characteristics of Lesions Based on the AMBBS Method

Sample	Area (Pixels)	Major Axis Length (Pixel)	Minor Axis Length (Pixel)	Circularity	Perimeter (Pixel)
Fibroadenoma	3717	74	63	0.82	239
Fibrocystic lesion	1270	61	27	0.59	165

Table 33.2 Comparisons of Areas and REs Based on Three Methods

Sample	Fibroadenoma	Fibrocystic Lesion
Expert area (pixels)	3529	1347
Adaptive level set method area (pixels)	4897	1507
RBF-SVMs method area (pixels)	3750	1457
AMBBS method area (pixels)	3717	1270
RE (%) (adaptive level set)	11.10	5.30
RE (%) (RBF-SVMs)	4.20	4.90
RE (%) (AMBBS)	1.92	1.85

very low RE rate, and the lowest error rate is only 1.85%. Thus, the AMBBS method significantly outperforms the level set method and the RBF-SVMs method. Furthermore, the information obtained from the AMBBS method is reliable and useful.

33.5 CONCLUSION

In this chapter, based on the MAC model, we have proposed a generalized AMBBS model for segmentation of ultrasonic lesions. The AMBBS overcomes the inherent limitations of the traditional balloon, such as leaking at weak boundaries due to unidirectional movement of the contour. Furthermore, theoretical analysis shows that the proposed AMBBS method is practical and feasible to the lesion extraction in medical ultrasound images. Simulated studies show that compared with GVF and VFC snake, AMBBS achieves significant improvement in capturing complex geometries and dealing with difficult initializations and weak edges. Moreover, the experimental results with clinical ultrasound images suggest that in comparison to two other state-of-the-art methods the AMBBS method shows excellent segmentation capability for ultrasonic lesions with low error rates.

ACKNOWLEDGEMENTS

This work is supported by the Specific Discipline Construction Fund of Guangdong (No.cgzhzd1105) and the Science and Technology Planning Project of Guangdong Province (No. 2012B050300024, 2012A080203004), the National Natural Science Foundation of China (No. 61302049) and the Natural Science Foundation of Guangdong (No. S2013040011786), the Open Fund of Guangdong Provincial Key Laboratory of Digital Signal, and the Image Processing Techniques and Science and Technology Planning Project of Shantou City.

REFERENCES

[1] Wun LM, Merril RM, Feuer EJ. Estimating lifetime and age-conditional probabilities of developing cancer. Lifetime Data Anal 1998;4(2):169–86.

[2] Breast cancer stages survival rate. Kanika, 2010, software available at http://www.buzzle.com/articles/breast-cancer-stages-survival-rate.html.

[3] Drukker K, Sennett CA, Giger ML. Automated method for improving system performance of computer-aided diagnosis in breast ultrasound. IEEE Trans Med Imaging 2009;28(1):122–8.

[4] Gómez W, Leija L, Pereira WCA, Infantosi AFC. Semiautomatic contour detection of breast lesions in ultrasonic images with morphological operators and average radial derivative function. Phys Procedia 2010; 3(1):373–80.
[5] Krishnamurthy C, Rodriguez JJ, Gillies RJ. Snake-based liver lesion segmentation. In: Proceedings of 6th IEEE southwest symposium on image analysis and interpretation; 2004. p. 187–91.
[6] Madabhushi A, Metaxas DN. Combining low-, high-level and empirical domain knowledge for automated segmentation of ultrasonic breast lesions. IEEE Trans Med Imaging 2003;22(2):155–69.
[7] Venkatachalam PA, Mohd AF, Ngah UK, Lim EE. Processing of abdominal ultrasound images using seed based region growing method. Intelligent sensing and information processing, 2004. Proceedings of international conference on. p. 57–62.
[8] Jung IS, Thapa D, Wang GN. Automatic segmentation and diagnosis of breast lesions using morphology method based on ultrasound. Fuzzy systems and knowledge discovery 2005;1079–88.
[9] Shan J, Cheng HD, Wang Y. A completely automatic segmentation method for breast ultrasound images using region growing. In: Proceedings of the 9th international conference on computer vision, pattern recognition, and image processing; 2008.
[10] Kotropoulos C, Pitas I. Segmentation of ultrasonic images using support vector machines. Pattern Recogn Lett 2003;24(4):715–27.
[11] Ferrari RJ, Wei X, Zhang Y. Segmentation of multiple sclerosis lesions using support vector machines. In: Proc. SPIE, vol. 5032; 2003.
[12] Muzzolini R, Yang YH, Pierson R. Multiresolution texture segmentation with application to diagnostic ultrasound images. IEEE Trans Med Imaging 1993;1(1):108–23.
[13] Davatzikos C, Bryan RN. Using a deformable surface model to obtain a shape representation of the cortex. IEEE Trans Med Imaging 1996;15(6):785–95.
[14] Chalana V, Linker DT, Haynor DR, Kim Y. A multiple active contour model for cardiac boundary detectionon echocardiographic sequences. IEEE Trans Med Imaging 1996;15(3):290–8.
[15] Cohen LD. Note: on active contour models and balloons. CVGIP: Image Understanding 1991;53(2): 211–8.
[16] Cohen LD, Cohen I. Finite-element methods for active contour models and balloons for 2D and 3D images. IEEE Trans Pattern Anal Mach Intell 1993;15(11):1131–47.
[17] Xu C, Prince JL. Gradient vector flow: a new external forces for snakes. In: Proceedings of IEEE CVPR; 1997. p. 66–71.
[18] Li B, Acton ST. Active contour external force using vector field convolution for image segmentation. IEEE Trans Image Process 2007;16(8):2096–106.
[19] Xie X, Mirmehdi M. MAC: magnetostatic active contour model. IEEE Trans Pattern Anal Mach Intell 2008;30(4):632–46.
[20] Shen M, Zheng B, Chen J. Image segmentation based on novel adaptive bidirectional balloon force model. In: Proceedings of IEEE I2MTC, Austin, May 3–6; 2010.
[21] Xu J, Chen K, Yang X, Wu D. Adaptive level set method for segmentation of liver tumors in minimally invasive surgery using ultrasound images. Proc Int Con Bioinform Biomed Eng 2007;1091–1094:.
[22] Kass M, Witkin A, Terzopoulous D. Snakes: active contour models. Int J Comput Vis 1988;1(4):321–32.
[23] Wolf D. Essentials of electromagnetics for engineering. Cambridge, United Kingdom: Cambridge University Press; 2001;90–140.
[24] Xu C, Prince J. Generalized gradient vector flow external forces for active contours. Signal Process 1998; 71(2):131–9.
[25] Xu C, Prince J. Snakes, shapes, and gradient vector flow. IEEE Trans Image Process 1998;7(3):359–69.
[26] Xie X, Mirmehdi M. RAGS: region-aided geometric snake. IEEE Trans Image Process 2004;13(5):640–52.
[27] Osher S, Sethian JA. Fronts propagating with curvature dependent speed: algorithms based on Hamilton–Jacobi formulations. J Comput Phys 1988;79(1):12–49.
[28] GE healthcare, software available at http://www.gehealthcare.com/usen/education/proff_leadership/products/msucmebr.html.

CHAPTER

BRAIN VENTRICLE DETECTION USING HAUSDORFF DISTANCE 34

K.S. Sim, M.E. Nia, C.P. Tso, T.K. Kho
Multimedia University, Melaka, Malaysia

34.1 INTRODUCTION

The ventricular system is a set of four communicating structures in the brain. It contains the cerebral spinal fluid and is continuous with the central canal of the spinal cord. The system comprises four ventricles: the left and right lateral ventricles, the third ventricle, and the fourth ventricle. A space-occupying lesion will most likely result in a midline shift, causing the ventricles to be compressed. A damaging aspect of most brain traumas is an elevated intracranial pressure. An increase in intracranial pressure may also result in a midline shift, which will also compress the ventricles. Fig. 34.1 shows a few examples of lesions and brain injuries that result in the compression of the ventricles. In such a situation, the ventricles become imbalanced, and the imbalance or asymmetry of the ventricles (comparing the right and left ventricles) is usually used as a guide during diagnosis procedures. Therefore, detecting the ventricles in a brain scan is important, and further processing the ventricle images may provide helpful information in aiding the diagnosis.

We propose the detection of the ventricles using Hausdorff distance, which measures the extent to which each point of a "model" set lies near some point of an "image" set and vice versa. The degree of resemblance is determined by this distance. The model is first generated by finding the boundary values of a ventricle. Other brain scans form the "image" set and are converted to binary images with appropriate threshold values. Boundary sets of the binary image are then compared against the "model" set using the Hausdorff distance to find the ventricles. The ventricles are considered detected if the corresponding boundary set has a Hausdorff distance that is below a certain threshold.

34.2 THE HAUSDORFF DISTANCE

There are many modified Hausdorff distances proposed to improve its efficiency and accuracy [1,2]. However, the classic Hausdorff distance (CHD) is sufficient for the detection of ventricles. Given two finite point sets $A=\{a_1, \ldots, a_p\}$ and $B=\{b_1, \ldots, b_q\}$, the CHD is defined as

$$H(A,B) = \max\left(h(A,B), h(B,A)\right) \tag{1}$$

$$h(A,B) = \max_{a \in A}\left(\min_{b \in B}(d(a,b))\right) \tag{2}$$

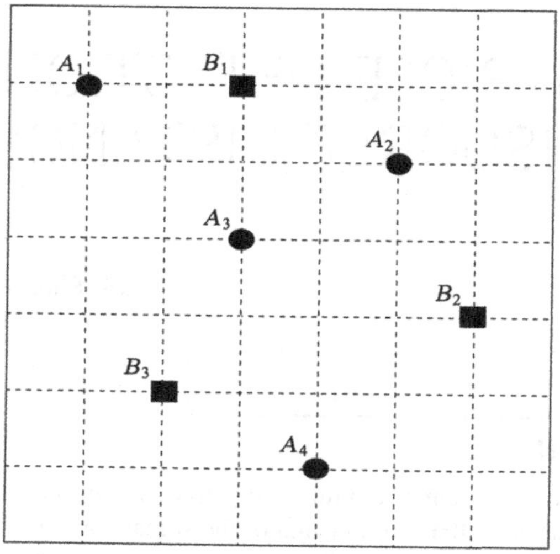

FIGURE 34.1

2 sets of points, *A* and *B*.

$$h(B, A) = \max_{b \in B}\left(\min_{a \in A}(d(b, a))\right) \tag{3}$$

where $d(a, b)$ is the Euclidean distance between a and b. The function $h(A, B)$ is called the directed Hausdorff distance from A to B, which identifies the point $a \in A$ that is farthest from any point of B and measures the distance from a to its nearest neighbor in B. This means that $h(A, B)$ first looks for the nearest point in B for every point in A, and then the largest of these values are taken as the distance, which is the most mismatched point of A. Subsequently, the Hausdorff distance $H(A, B)$ is the maximum of $h(A, B)$ and $h(B, A)$. Consequently, it is able to measure the degree of mismatch between two sets from the distance of the point of A that is farthest from any point of B, and vice versa [1,2]. For further illustration of the CHD, Fig. 34.1 and Table 34.1 show some basic calculations.

Table 34.1 shows the Euclidean distance between every point in A to every point in B. The directed Hausdorff distance is in bold, which is the maximum distance. The $h(A, B)$ is found to be 2.24, while $h(B, A)$ is also 2.24 in this case. Subsequently, the Hausdorff distance, obtained by using Eq. (1), is 2.24.

Table 34.1 Euclidean Distance Between Set *A* and *B*

$d(a, b)$	B_1	B_2	B_3	$\min(d(a, b))$
A_1	2.00	5.83	4.12	*2.00*
A_2	2.24	2.24	4.24	*2.24*
A_3	2.00	3.16	2.24	*2.00*
A_4	5.10	2.83	2.24	***2.24***
$\min(d(b, a))$	*2.00*	*2.24*	***2.24***	

With this, it can be said that every point in A is within a distance of 2.24 to a point in B. There is a pair of points with the exact distance of 2.24, which are the most mismatched points between the two sets.

The Hausdorff distance and its derivatives have been used in many pattern recognition-based applications. Edge eigenface weighted Hausdorff distance (EEWHD) method was proposed [2] for face recognition with higher recognition rate compared to other Hausdorff distance-based face recognition algorithms. Pedestrian detection for video surveillance application has also been reported to be successful when the Hausdorff distance approach was used with a generic human shape as a model [3].

Iris recognition insensitive to lighting condition is also possible with a Hausdorff distance-based method, with comparable results to other iris recognition algorithms [4]. A combination of least-trimmed square Hausdorff distance and particle swarm optimization was proposed by [5] for image registration, which is to exactly match the features of a source and target image over a series of spatial transform. Hausdorff distance was used by Ref. [6] in palm print matching, while the weighted Hausdorff distance was used for word image matching in both English and Chinese documents [7]. The detection and identification of the ventricles of the brain will add to this ever growing list of Hausdorff distance applications.

34.3 THE PROPOSED METHOD

34.3.1 CREATING THE MODEL

Various methods can be used to create the template or model for later use in the Hausdorff distance method. An outline similar to the ventricle shape can be drawn at the center of a 512×512 pixels image (this size is used because most computed tomography (CT) cranial scans come in this fixed size). The boundary or the coordinates of this line is then stored as an $m \times 2$ matrix, with each row containing $[x, y]$ coordinates, respectively. Another method, which is used in this chapter, is to use a normal brain scan's ventricles as the template. Care has to be taken that the scan chosen should be of a perfectly healthy brain, with the brain situated at the center of the image, and not tilted in any direction. These factors will allow better Hausdorff distance calculation in the later parts. The following flow chart depicts the steps involved in creating a ventricle template out of a normal brain scan as shown in Fig. 34.2.

Digital imaging and communications in medicine (DICOM) is the format of CT images. After reading the CT image from DICOM format, it is converted to a grayscale image by using the default window width and window center, as included in the DICOM format. The window width and window center are special attributes unique to DICOM image format, which allows the focus of desired data. The window width will determine the range of values shown on the gray scale, while those values above and below this range will be clipped and shown as black or white. The window center will determine where the center of this range is situated. For example, the typical window width for a cranial CT scan is 80, with a window center of 40. This means that only pixels with values ranging from 0 (0 corresponds to (window center − window width)/2, which is (40 − 80)/2)) to 80 (80 corresponds to (window center + window width)/2, which is (40 + 80)/2)) in the original DICOM format are shown in the gray scale when these two attributes are used. CT scans have values ranging from −1000 to 1000 (these values are also known as the Hounsfield unit). Therefore, those pixels with values below 0 are shown as black, while those above 80 are shown as white. The result of this windowing is the typical CT cranial scans that we see, as shown in Fig. 34.3A.

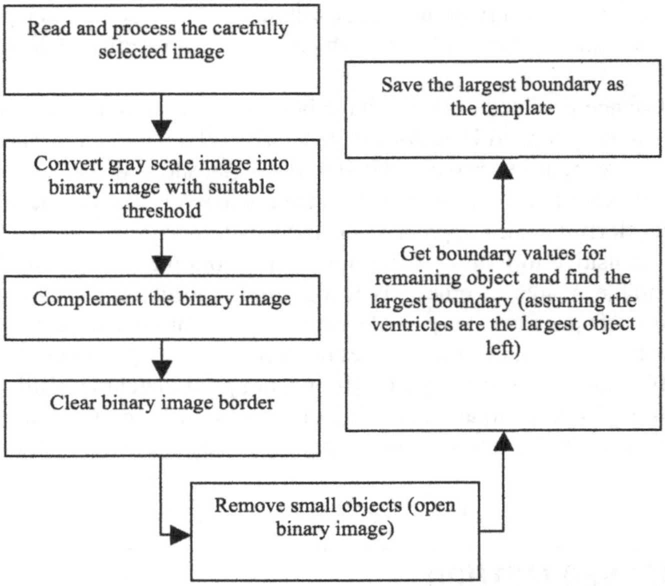

FIGURE 34.2

Step-by-step description of creating the template.

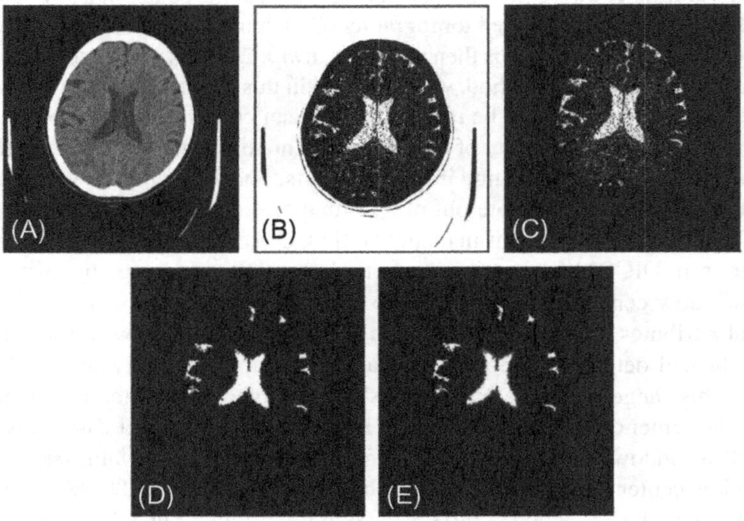

FIGURE 34.3

Steps in obtaining the template of a ventricle from a real CT scan. (A) Original CT scan with clear ventricles, (B) complementary binary image of (A), (C) results after clearing the boundary, (D) after opening the binary image, and (E) outlined in gray at the center, is the boundary with the largest size, which is also the ventricle.

The resulting image will be converted to a binary image with a suitable threshold. The conversion to binary image should leave the ventricles black, and the surrounding brain matter as white. This binary image should be complemented so that the ventricles are white (the object). Clearing the border of the complemented image will give a good background (black). Small objects (small white dots) are cleared by opening the binary image. The remaining objects will include the ventricles, and possibly some other smaller noise objects.

The boundary values for all these objects are obtained with the assumption that the ventricles are the largest object left; the boundary with the largest size is considered as the template of the ventricle and is saved for later use.

34.3.2 VENTRICLES DETECTION WITH THE TEMPLATE PRODUCED

For the actual detection of the ventricles, some image processing is first done on the CT scan. This processing is almost similar to the steps in creating the template. The full process is described in the flow chart in Fig. 34.4.

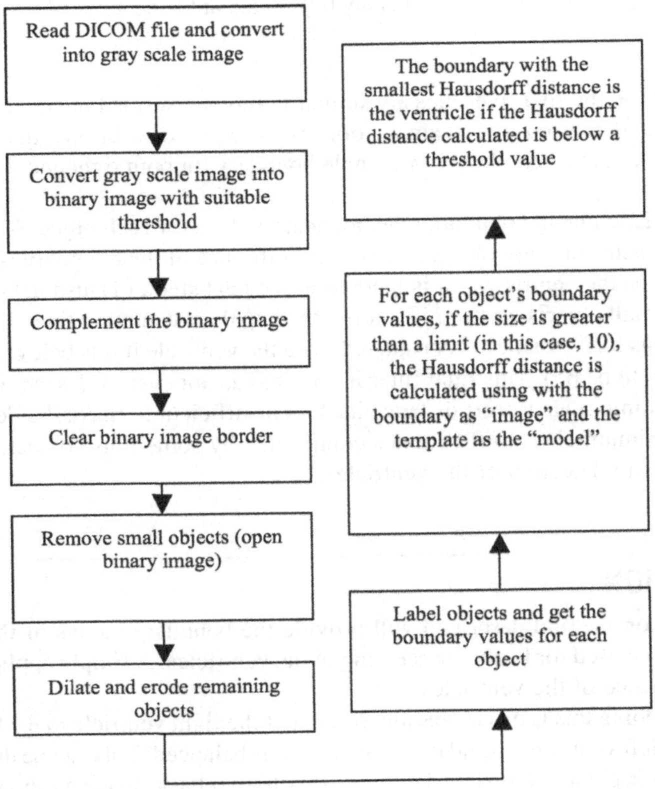

FIGURE 34.4

Detecting the ventricles using the Hausdorff distance.

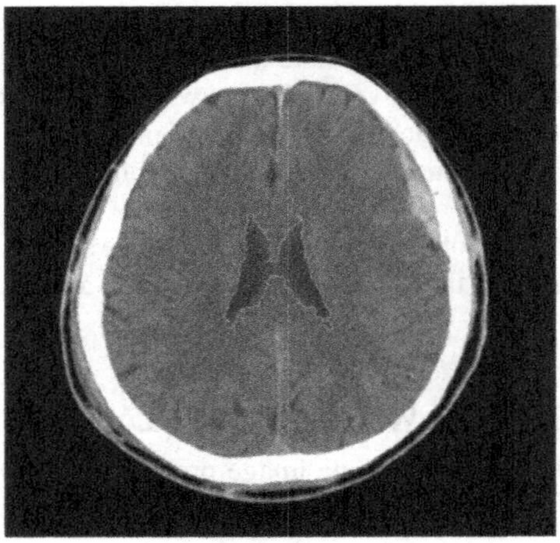

FIGURE 34.5

Successful auto detection of the ventricles (boundary highlighted at the center).

As seen in Fig. 34.4, the first five steps are similar to those described in creating the ventricle template. The dilation and erosion of remaining objects is required to ensure that both right and left ventricles are "joined," as the template is one single boundary for both right and left ventricles (as seen in Fig. 34.3E).

The next step of labeling and obtaining the boundary values for each object is to accommodate the possibility of the presence of noise objects. However, if the size of the boundary is less than 10 (meaning it is too small to be the ventricles), it is ignored in the next step of Hausdorff distance calculation. The elimination of small objects will significantly speed up the calculation time. Finally, the boundary with the smallest Hausdorff distance is considered to be the ventricle if it is below a threshold value (in this case, it is chosen to be 65). This final filter is required as not every CT scan may contain the ventricles, hence the minimum Hausdorff distance itself is insufficient to make the decision, as every CT scan will have a minimum Hausdorff distance contributed by some noise object. Fig. 34.5 shows an example of a successful detection of the ventricles.

34.4 DISCUSSION

The ventricle detection method described will provide the boundary values of the ventricles. These boundary values can be used for further processing of the ventricles. A simple application is to quantify the balance or imbalance of the ventricles.

A simple way of doing this is by comparing the area of the right ventricle to the left. The ratio of the right ventricle to the left ventricle should be close to 1 if it is balanced. This can be done by first splitting the ventricles into the right and left side. The ventricles have a basic shape as shown in Fig. 34.6. The ventricles can be split intuitively by connecting the two points shown by the red arrows. To do this, each boundary value is compared to the previous in the clockwise direction, starting at a random point. Point

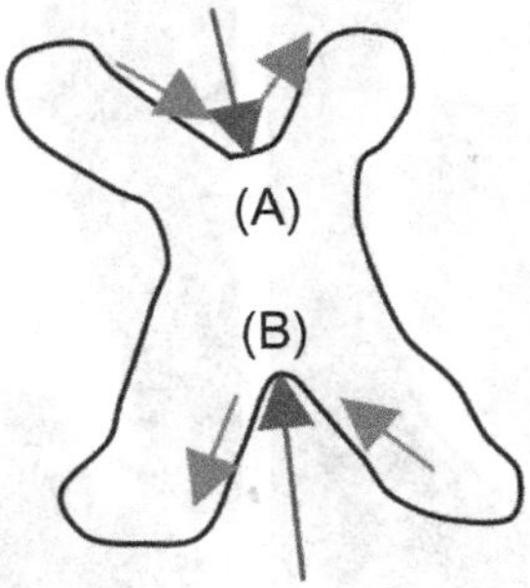

FIGURE 34.6

Basic shape of the detected ventricles. Points (A) and (B) show the 2 points required to split the ventricles to the left and right halves.

(a) should be the only point where there is a "down-up" (green arrows) situation happening from left to right, while point (b) should be the only point where there is an "up-down" situation happening from right to left. Using these unique properties of these two points, they can be located easily. Checking for a real "down" or a real "up" by inspecting the next 10 or 20 subsequent boundary values will highly increase the accuracy of the algorithm. In case of a plateau, the center point of the plateau is considered as the point of interest.

When these two points are identified, a straight line can be drawn through them by using the very basic linear graph equation of

$$y = mx + c \tag{4}$$

where m = slope of the straight line, c = y-intercept.

Fig. 34.7 shows an example of a successful split of the ventricles using this technique. Fig. 34.8 shows more examples of different ventricles that are split successfully, and a few cases in which the splitting was less than perfect.

With the successful splitting of the ventricles, the area of the right and left ventricles can easily be calculated. A ratio between the two (right:left) will quantify how balanced/imbalanced the ventricles are and aid medical personnel in the diagnosis process. There are many types of brain lesion that can be visually detected on a CT scan and magnetic resonance (MR) image. They may appear to be hypodense (darker regions) or hyperdense (brighter regions) compared to other normal cells and tissues.

The detection of brain lesion is often problematic and cannot be done by a simple gray scale to binary method because of structures such as the skull (which appears as white in CT scans) and also the ventricles (which appear to be darker). These structures contribute to extra pixels on the extreme ends. By detecting these structures through the Hausdorff method, they can be eliminated rather easily. For example, in Fig. 34.7A, the ventricle can be detected, and all the pixels within the boundary can be changed to something that is bright. This will enable the detection of hypodense lesions to be done with ease, as there are no more dark-region pixels left apart from those contributed by the lesion. A similar method can be applied to remove the skull to detect hyperdense lesions.

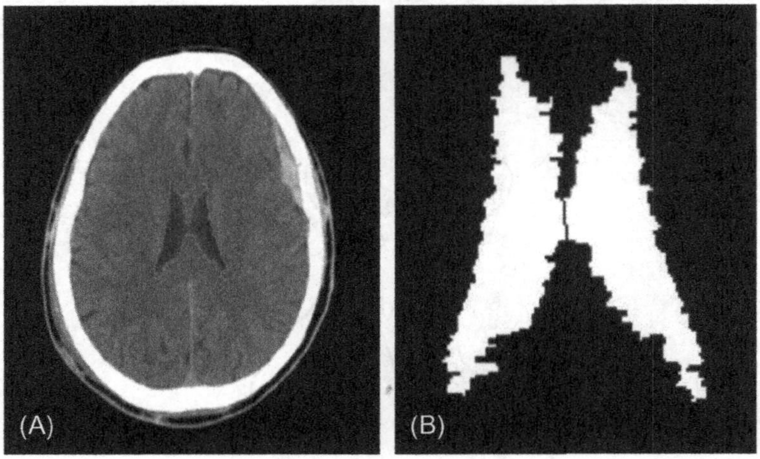

FIGURE 34.7

Splitting the ventricles. (A) The original ventricle in the CT scan is detected and (B) the ventricle is split into its right and left counterparts.

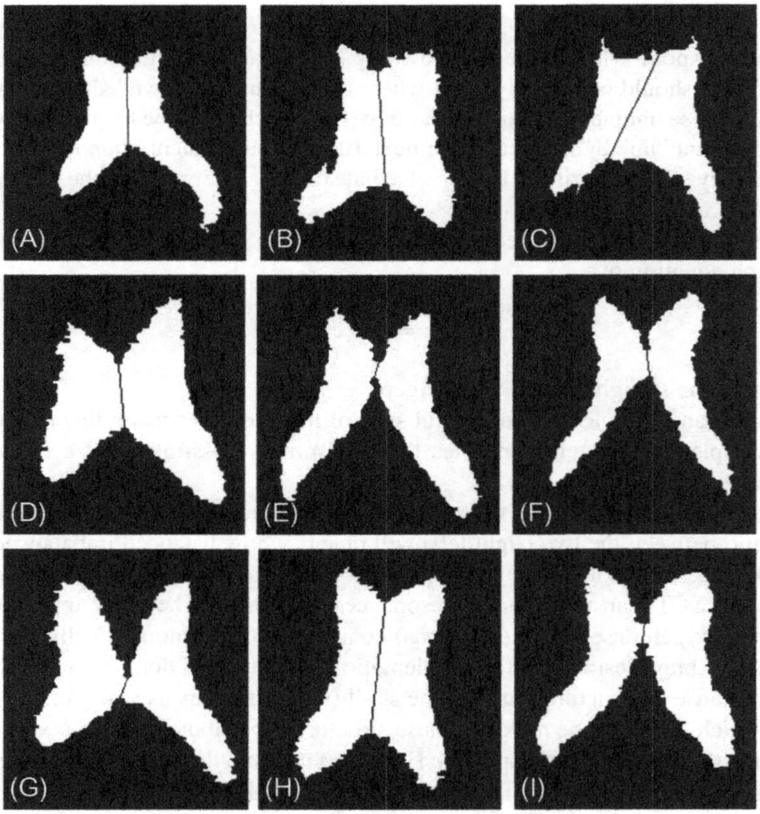

FIGURE 34.8

Different patients' ventricles were separated successfully, except Patient 3, whose ventricles were of irregular shape, (A) Patient 1 (old infarct), (B) Patient 2 (early infarct case), (C) Patient 3 (no infarct, imperfect separation), (D) Patient 4 (early infarct case), (E) Patient 5 (early infarct case), (F) Patient 6 (no infarct), (G) Patient 7 (old infarct), (H) Patient 8 (early infarct case), and (I) Patient 9 (early infarct case).

34.5 CONCLUSION

The Hausdorff method is known to be efficient in image comparison due to its simplicity and its tolerance to small perturbations. Though the CHD is not translation invariant and rotation invariant, these are not major problems in the detection of the ventricles, as cranial CT scans or MR images are rather similar for all cases in terms of the positioning of the brain in the image. Therefore, using the Hausdorff distance is an effective method to detect various brain structures, especially the ventricles. The method has potential to be applied to other cases in image analysis and diagnosis.

REFERENCES

[1] Huttenlocher DP, Klanderman Ga, Rucklidge WJ. Comparing images using the Hausdorff distance. IEEE Trans Pattern Anal Mach Intell 1993;15(9):850–63.

[2] Tan H, Zhang Y-J. Computing eigenface from edge images for face recognition based on Hausdorff distance. In: Fourth international conference on image and graphics (ICIG 2007); 2007. p. 639–44.

[3] Gastaldo P, Zunino R. Hausdorff distance for target detection. In: 2002 IEEE international symposium on circuits and systems. Proceedings, Scottsdale, USA, vol. 5; 2002. p. 661–4.

[4] Sudha N, Wong YHK. Hausdorff distance for iris recognition. In: 2007 IEEE 22nd international symposium on intelligent control. Singapore: IEEE; 2007. p. 614–9.

[5] Li H, Lin Y, Wang A. An medical image registration approach using improved Hausdorff distance combined with particle swarm optimization. In: 2008 fourth international conference on natural computation. Jinan, China: IEEE; 2008. p. 428–32.

[6] Li F, Leung MKH. Palmprint matching using pairwise relative angle based Hausdorff distance, In: 2009 IEEE 13th international symposium on consumer electronics. Kyoto, Japan: IEEE; 2009. p. 550–3.

[7] Lu Y, Chew LT, Weihua H, Liying F. An approach to word image matching based on weighted Hausdorff distance. In: Proceedings of sixth international conference on document analysis and recognition. IEEE Comput. Soc. 2001. p. 921–5.

CHAPTER

35 TUMOR GROWTH EMERGENT BEHAVIOR ANALYSIS BASED ON CANCER HALLMARKS AND IN A CANCER STEM CELL CONTEXT

J. Santos, Á. Monteagudo
Department of Computer Science, University of A Coruña, A Coruña, Spain

35.1 INTRODUCTION

Cancer is a complex collection of distinct genetic diseases united by different hallmarks (traits that govern the transformation of normal cells to malignant cells). Hanahan and Weinberg described these hallmarks in their 2000 article [1] and its update in 2011 [2]. In these articles the authors described six essential alterations: self-sufficiency in growth signals, insensitivity to growth-inhibitory (antigrowth) signals, evasion of programmed cell death (apoptosis), limitless replicative potential, sustained angiogenesis, and tissue invasion. In the update [2] the authors included two more hallmarks: reprogramming of energy metabolism and evasion of immune destruction, that emerged as critical capabilities of cancer cells. Moreover, the authors described two enabling characteristics or properties of neoplastic cells that facilitate acquisition of hallmark capabilities: genome instability and tumor-promoting inflammation (mediated by immune system cells recruited to the tumor site).

The traditional approach was to use differential equations to describe tumor growth [3]. Nevertheless, these approaches tend to represent tumor cells collectively by a single proliferation term and a death term, including more optional specialized functionalities like interaction of tumor cells with their local environment [4]. Moreover, many models presuppose that all cancer cells have acquired the same hallmarks.

The interaction among cells generates an emergent behavior; that is, a behavior present in systems whose elements interact locally, providing a global behavior that is not possible to explain from the behavior of a single element, but rather from the interactions of the group [5]. Cellular automata (CA) were the most used tool in artificial life to study and characterize the emergent behavior [6, 7]. A cellular automaton is defined by a set of rules that establishes the next state of each of the sites of a grid environment given the previous state of this site and the states of its defined neighborhood, where the states can be associated with the cell states in the intended simulations of tumor growth.

Thus, with respect to the classical models based on the use of differential equations, the approaches relying on cellular automata models or agent-based models make easy the modeling at a cellular level, where the state of each cell is described by its local environment. Previous works have used the CA capabilities for different purposes in tumor growth modeling [8–11]. Some authors used simulations focused on particular cancer types. For example, Bankhead and Heckendorn [12] used CA to specifically model ductal carcinoma in situ (DCIS), a common form of noninvasive breast cancer. Other works were focused on tumor simulation aspects rather than a particular cancer type. For instance, Gerlee and Anderson [9] proposed a cellular automaton model in which each cell is equipped with a microenvironment response network that determined the behavior of the cell based on the local environment and to investigate the prevascular stage of invasive tumor growth, whereas Gevertz et al. [10] used a cellular automaton algorithm, originally designed to simulate spherically symmetric tumor growth, generalizing it to incorporate the effects of tissue shape and structure.

On the contrary, fewer previous works have used CA models based on the presence of hallmarks. For example, Abbott et al. [13] and Spencer et al. [14] investigated the dynamics and interactions of the hallmarks in a CA model in which the main interest of the authors was to describe the likely sequences of precancerous mutations or pathways that end in cancer. They were interested in what sequences of mutations are most likely and the dependence of pathways on various parameters associated with the hallmarks. Basanta et al. [15] used a CA model based on the Hanahan and Weinberg hallmarks, focusing their work on analyzing the effect of different environmental conditions on the sequence of acquisition of phenotypic traits. We also used CA to model the behavior of cells when the hallmarks are present and in the avascular phase, with a different aim to those previous works, as we focused on the study of the multicellular system dynamics in terms of emergent behaviors that can be obtained, analyzing the relative importance of different hallmarks [16, 17] and the capability of cancer stem cells (CSCs) and hallmarks to generate tumor growth and regrowth in different conditions [18, 19].

The implications of CSCs [20] in the resultant behavior are shown here, taking into account the effects of different treatments against different cell types. In the next section we briefly summarize the relevant aspects of our model based on the presence of the hallmarks. In Section 35.3.1 we detail different scenarios to show different behavioral regimes that can be obtained when different hallmarks are acquired in different situations. In Section 35.3.2 we explain the implication of CSCs in the resultant behavior obtained, whereas in Section 35.4 we expose the conclusions about the simulations.

35.2 METHODS

We followed the event model used by Abbott et al. [13] in their study of the likely sequences of precancerous mutations that end in cancer, to simulate the behavior of cells when different hallmarks are acquired, as previously exposed in more detail in our previous works [17, 19].

In the simulation each cell resides in a site in a 3-D lattice and has an artificial "genome" that indicates if any of five different hallmarks are activated as a consequence of mutations. The mutations occur when a cell divides: a hallmark is acquired with a hallmark mutation rate ($1/m$) defined by the parameter m (default value $m = 100{,}000$ as in [13–15]). We have considered five hallmarks: *self-growth (SG)*, *ignore growth inhibit (IGI)*, *evasion of apoptosis (EA)*, *effective immortality (EI)*, and *genetic instability (GI)*.

Although Abbott et al. [13] considered the hallmark angiogenesis (ability to stimulate blood vessel construction), in our work metastasis (cancer cells invade other tissues and spread to other organs) and angiogenesis are not considered, as we are interested in the first avascular phases of tumorigenesis. Thus, every cell has its genome, which consists of five binary hallmarks (SG, IGI, EA, EI, and GI) plus two parameters particular to each cell: Parameters *telomere length* and *hallmark mutation rate*

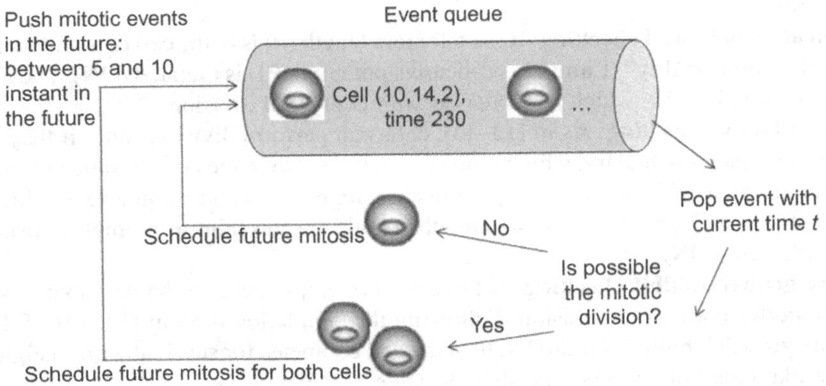

FIGURE 35.1

Scheme of the event model used in the simulation.

can change their values in a particular cell over time. The cell's genome is inherited by the daughter cells when a mitotic division occurs.

In the modeling mitoses are scheduled between 5 and 10 time iterations in the future for simulating the variable duration of the cell life cycle (between 15 and 24 h) as indicated in Fig. 35.1. Taking into account these time intervals, each iteration represents an average time of 2.6 h, so, for example, every 1000 iterations in the simulation imply an average time of 15.5 weeks.

The main aspects of the model can be summarized in the following steps:

Start: The simulation can begin with only one healthy cell at the center of the grid, as in most previous works [11, 13, 15, 21] or with the grid full of healthy cells. Mitoses are scheduled for the initial cells (push a mitotic event in an event queue between 5 and 10 time iterations in the future).

After the new daughter cells are created, mitosis is scheduled for each of them, and so on. Each mitotic division is carried out by copying the genetic information (the hallmark status and associated parameters) of the cell to an unoccupied adjacent space in the grid. Random errors occur in this copying process, so some hallmarks can be activated, taking into account that once a hallmark is activated in a cell, it will never be repaired by another mutation [13].

In terms of complex systems, the emergent growth behaviors are independent of the initial condition regarding the initial number of healthy cells, with the only difference of the required iterations [16, 17].

Pop event: The events are ordered on event time. Pop event from the event queue with the highest priority (the nearest in time).

Random cell death test: Cells undergo random cell death with low probability ($1/a$ chance of death, default value $a = 1000$) because of several causes.

Genetic damage test: The larger the number of hallmark mutations, the greater the probability of cell death (n/e, being n the number of hallmarks acquired and e a parameter with default value 10). If "Evade apoptosis" (EA) is ON, death as consequence of the genetic damage is not applied.

Mitosis tests:

1. **Replicative potential checking**: If the telomere length (*tl*) is 0, the cell dies, unless the hallmark "Effective immortality" (Limitless replicative potential, EI) is mutated (ON). The initial default telomere length is 50, which is decreased with every cell division.
2. **Growth factor checking**: As in [13–15], cells can perform divisions only if they are within a predefined spatial boundary, which represents a threshold in the concentration of growth factor; beyond this area (95% of the inner space in each dimension in our simulations, which represents 85.7% of the 3-D grid inner space) growth signals are too faint to prompt mitosis (unless hallmark SG is ON).
3. **Ignore growth inhibit checking**: If there are not empty cells in the neighborhood, the cell cannot perform a mitotic division. Following the simulation used in [13, 14], if the hallmark "Ignore growth inhibit" (IGI) is ON, then the cell competes for survival with a neighbor cell and with a likelihood of success ($1/g$, default value $g = 30$).

If the three tests indicate possibility of mitosis,

- Increase the hallmark mutation rate ($1/m$) if genetic instability (GI) is ON, by a factor i (default value $i = 100$ as in [13, 15]).
- Add mutations to the new cells according to hallmark mutation rate ($1/m$).
- Decrease (one unit) telomere length in both cells.
- Push events. Schedule mitotic events (push in event queue) for both cells: mother and daughter, with the random times in the future.

If mitosis cannot be applied,

- Schedule a mitotic event (in queue) for mother cell.

35.3 RESULTS

35.3.1 EMERGENT BEHAVIORS AND RELATED HALLMARKS

First, we can analyze the resultant emergent behaviors in different representative scenarios that determine the predominance of different hallmarks. We used in all the examples a grid of 125,000 cell sites (50 sites in each dimension), as in [13, 14]. In most of the examples, the simulations begin with the grid full of healthy cells.

We considered for the analysis three representative situations obtained with concrete parameter sets. In the first case (Fig. 35.2) we used a high hallmark mutation rate ($1/m$), with $m = 1000$. This parameter (m) determines the onset of appearance of cancer cells (defined as cells with any hallmark acquired). The rest of parameters were set to their standard values. Given the high probability of hallmarks acquisition, the cells that acquired the hallmark *evade apoptosis* (EA) present an advantage in this scenario where many cells have acquired several hallmarks, as such cells are not subject to the apoptotic process. Thus, the predominant hallmark is EA, as shown in the left part of Fig. 35.2, and these cells can acquire more hallmarks in subsequent divisions.

The right part of Fig. 35.2 shows snapshots of sections of the multicellular system evolution corresponding to different time iterations. The snapshots correspond to a plane that crosses the central part

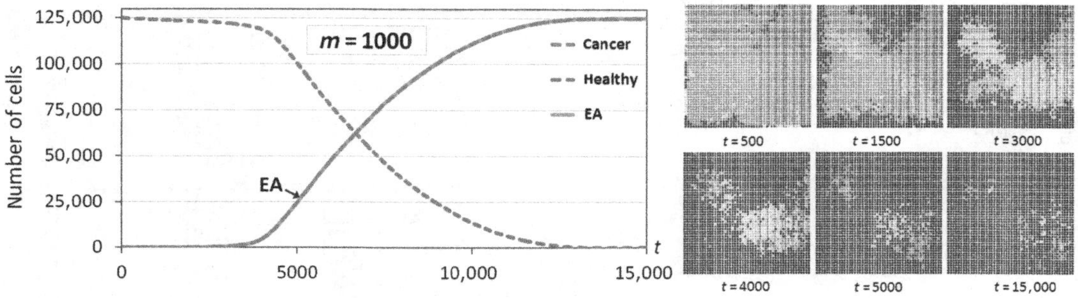

FIGURE 35.2

Evolution through time iterations of the number of healthy cells, cancer cells, and the most predominant hallmark (EA) with $m = 1000$ while the rest of the parameters were set to their standard values (grid initially full of healthy cells). The right part shows snapshots of a central section at different time iterations.

of the grid. This 2-D representation gives more information than a 3-D representation, because it shows the internal distribution of cells with different hallmarks (each combination is represented with a different color/gray level). The snapshots show that the tumor growth behavior begins in the outer part, because cells with the hallmark *self-growth* (SG) acquired can rapidly grow in this area without growth factor, acquiring more hallmarks in next divisions (the blue/dark gray cells have acquired all the hallmarks).

Fig. 35.3 shows another example when using shorter telomere lengths ($tl = 30$) in all cells with respect to the default value ($tl = 50$). In this scenario, even with the low hallmark mutation rate ($m = 100{,}000$), if very few cells acquire the hallmark *effective immortality* (EI), they have a clear advantage over the other cells without that hallmark, so they propagate rapidly when the healthy cells begin to decrease because these cells have performed the maximum number of mitoses. Thus, the hallmark EI is the most predominant in the tumor progression, as it can also be seen in the snapshots of the right part of Fig. 35.3, where the green/light gray cells correspond to such cells with EI acquired. This example began

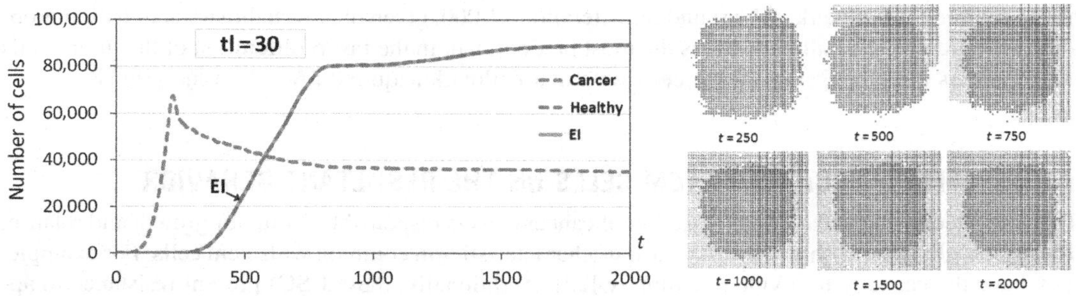

FIGURE 35.3

Evolution through time iterations of the number of healthy cells, cancer cells, and the most predominant hallmark (EI) with $tl = 30$ while the rest of the parameters were set to their standard values. The simulation begins with only one healthy cell at the center of the grid. The right part shows snapshots of a central section at different time iterations.

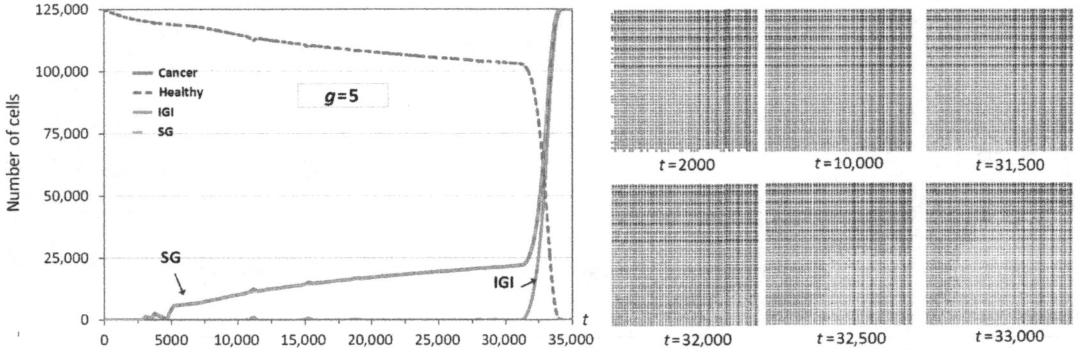

FIGURE 35.4

Evolution through time iterations of the number of healthy cells, cancer cells, and the most predominant hallmarks (SG in the beginning and IGI for the fast increase of cancer cells) with $g = 5$ while the rest of the parameters were set to their standard values (grid initially full of healthy cells). The right part shows snapshots of a central section at different time iterations.

with only one healthy cell at the center of the grid, so the healthy cells perform in few iterations the maximum number of mitoses. Starting with the grid full of healthy cells, the behavior would be the same but requiring many more iterations to reach the same situation where the healthy cells performed their maximum number of divisions, as most of the time they are surrounded by other cells.

The third example corresponds to a scenario where cells that acquired the hallmark *ignore growth inhibit* (IGI) have a high invasion potential in the surrounding tissue, because we used a low value in parameter g (5) while the rest of parameters are maintained in the default values. Thus, cells with IGI acquired have a high probability ($1/g$) to propagate in the immediate neighborhood sites, ignoring the contact by inhibition mechanism. In Fig. 35.4 tumor growth behavior begins, again, in the outer part, because cells with the hallmark *self-growth* (SG) acquired have an advantage in the outer area of the grid without growth factor. Nevertheless, the sudden fast increase of cancer cells is when a few cells have acquired the hallmark IGI, around time iteration 31,000, given the low hallmark acquisition probability. Therefore, the hallmark IGI is the most predominant in the fast proliferation of the tumor cells which allows the propagation of the cells with that hallmark acquired toward all the grid sites.

35.3.2 EFFECT OF CANCER STEM CELLS ON THE RESULTANT BEHAVIOR

The CSC theory states that a small fraction of cancer cells is responsible for tumor growth and relapse. These CSCs have been shown to have various characteristics in common with stem cells. For example, they have the capacity to divide indefinitely [22]. Additionally, these CSCs present resistance to apoptosis and they present heterogeneity, that is, potential for multidirectional differentiation [20]. In our model it is easy to incorporate these properties, as they imply that CSCs have acquired the hallmarks *effective immortality* (EI) and *evade apoptosis* (EA). The importance of the presence of these cells is because, if current treatments of cancer do not properly destroy enough CSCs, the tumor will probably reappear [21]. In fact, CSCs are relatively resistant to standard cytotoxic and irradiation therapies because, for example, cytotoxic therapies affect rapidly proliferating cells, whereas evidence suggests that only a small fraction of CSCs actively proliferate.

We followed the CSC simulation used by Enderling and Hahnfeldt [21] regarding their differentiation. Thus, CSCs will divide symmetrically, with a low probability ($p_s = 0.01$ in [21]) or asymmetrically (with probability $1 - p_s$) to produce a CSC and a nonstem cancer cell (differentiated cancer cell (DCC)). In our simulation, in the asymmetric division, the differentiated nonstem cancer cell acquires (randomly) one of the five hallmarks considered in our modeling as well as the initial telomere length that defines its finite replicative potential (unless it acquires the hallmark EI). In the simulations, beginning with the grid full of healthy cells, a low number of CSCs will be incorporated in the inner area with growth factor to check their effect on the behavior of the multicellular system evolution.

Fig. 35.5 includes an example of an scenario previously used for considering a high invasion potential ($g = 5$ and default values in the rest of parameters). The left part of Fig. 35.5 shows the evolution through time iterations of nonstem cancer cells (DCCs), when a number of CSCs corresponding to a 1% of the grid size (125,000) was introduced at the beginning. This small percentage is sufficient to show CSC implications. In several cancer types, that proportion of identified CSCs varies, being, for example, about 2.5% in colon cancer population [23] and 1–5% of primary tumors in human mammary carcinomas [24].

As there is not practically any free site, most CSCs remain quiescent until they have free space to perform mitoses. Given the low probabilities of symmetric division and random cell death, the number of CSCs remains stable during the 9000 iterations shown in Fig. 35.5, so CSC evolution is not shown. However, the nonstem cancer cells begin to grow due to the asymmetric division of CSCs and thanks to the acquisition of the hallmark *ignore growth inhibit* (IGI) in few of such DCCs, which can rapidly proliferate because of their advantage in this situation with practically no free sites (the daughters acquire the same hallmark). Thus, in comparison with Fig. 35.4 (no CSCs), the increase of DCCs logically

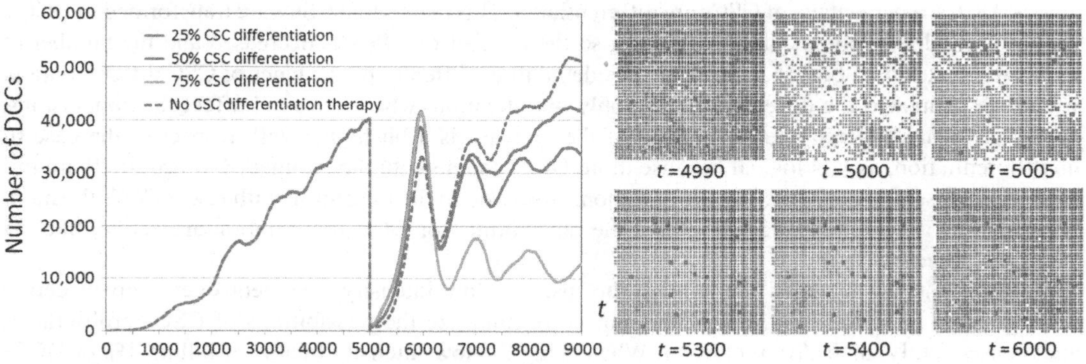

FIGURE 35.5

Left: Evolution through time iterations of the number of DCCs with $g = 5$ while the rest of the parameters were set to their standard values (grid initially full of healthy cells). At $t = 5000$ a standard treatment is applied, killing 100% of DCCs. After that, a CSC differentiation treatment is applied, with three different percentages of CSCs differentiated. Right: Snapshots of a central section at different time iterations corresponding to the case without CSC differentiation therapy. Colors: Healthy cells in gray/light gray, DCCs in different colors/gray levels depending on the hallmarks acquired, CSCs in red/dark gray with enlarged size.

begins in earlier iterations. The fluctuations in the expansion of these hallmarks and cancer cells are a consequence of the contact inhibition mechanism simulation: the cells with IGI acquired proliferate faster when they are surrounded by healthy cells. However, when the clusters of cells with IGI acquired reach a certain size, then the apoptotic process can decrease their size for a small time, until reaching another lower size where the proliferation continues again.

At time iteration 5000 100% of nonstem cancer cells is killed, simulating a (perfect) cancer therapy, causing the drastic drop of the nonstem cancer cells. Nevertheless, because CSCs are more resistant to therapeutic interventions such as chemotherapy or irradiation compared with their differentiated counterparts [25], the CSCs remain in the simulation.

The right part of Fig. 35.5 shows cross sections at different time iterations. The snapshot at $t = 5000$ shows how these DCCs are eliminated by the effect of a treatment. The next snapshots show how the healthy cells that have not performed the maximum number of divisions rapidly fill the free space, but DCCs recover quickly because the CSCs not killed again produce nonstem cancer cells (see for example the cross section at $t = 5300$). These DCCs produce a similar evolution pattern like the one at the beginning of the simulation, as shown in the cross sections and in the left graph of Fig. 35.5.

Nevertheless, there is an important and clear difference with respect to the first growth pattern of DCCs: this second proliferation on nonstem cancer cells is faster. This counterintuitive effect is because, after the elimination of DCCs, CSCs have more opportunities to proliferate and differentiate in the small amount of time until the grid is completely filled with mostly healthy cells. So, the few DCCs, after the CSC differentiation, can produce the faster tumor regrowth.

Vainstein et al. [26] considered the stimulation of CSC differentiation. A "differentiation therapy" (like retinoic acids) force CSCs to differentiate terminally and lose their self-renewal property [27]. Therefore, Vainstein et al. [26] proposed that, in clinical trials, CSC differentiation therapy should only be examined in combination with chemotherapy to substantially reduce the population sizes and densities of all types of cancer cells. We considered also this possibility, so, after the standard treatment against DCCs, a percentage of CSCs are differentiated. This means that CSCs are transformed to DCCs, acquiring randomly one of the 5 hallmarks, so the number of CSCs is decreased and the number of DCCs is increased. In Fig. 35.5 we have considered three different percentages of CSC differentiation, where we simulated the differentiation in only one iteration, which does not affect the conclusions. When CSCs are differentiated, the slope of the increase is a bit higher with respect to the case of no differentiation, as it is logical because more DCCs (some with the hallmark IGI acquired) are immediately present to begin the fast proliferation. However, in the long term, with fewer CSCs the number of DCCs is best controlled (note that the other limits for DCC proliferation are active, like the apoptotic process).

In Fig. 35.6 we repeated the strategy but using a low intensity treatment over a given period (between $t = 5000$ and $t = 6000$). The aim is to minimize the possibilities of CSCs proliferation and, consequently, their differentiation. When using the low-intensity treatment killing 1% of DCCs in each time iteration, the healthy cells almost immediately fill the few free spaces, so CSCs do not have as many opportunities to proliferate and differentiate as in the previous case using a high intensity treatment, resulting in a slower increase of DCCs in next iterations. This can be seen in the snapshots of Fig. 35.6. For example, the snapshot at $t = 5100$ shows how CSCs have no free spaces to proliferate and differentiate, so the increase of DCCs is not favored as in the previous case.

We also included the cases in which very low intensity CSC differentiation treatments are applied in the same interval ($t = 5000$ to $t = 6000$). With a treatment that differentiates 0.01% of CSCs in each

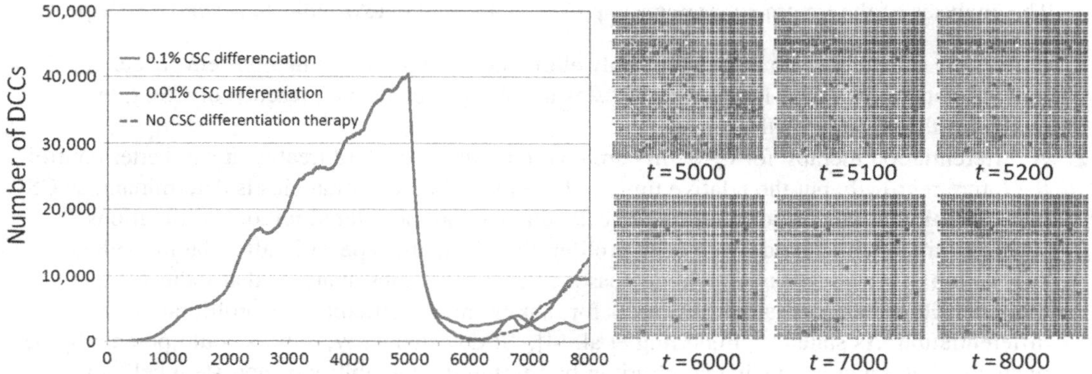

FIGURE 35.6

Left: Evolution through time iterations of the number of DCCs with $g = 5$ while the rest of the parameters were set to their standard values (grid initially full of healthy cells). Between $t = 5000$ and $t = 6000$ a standard treatment is applied, killing 1% of DCCs in each iteration. The graph also includes the cases when, in the same interval, a CSC differentiation treatment is applied, differentiating 0.01% and 0.1% of CSCs in each iteration. Right: Snapshots of a central section at different time iterations corresponding to the first case (no differentiation therapy). Colors: Healthy cells in gray/light gray, DCCs in different colors/gray levels depending on the hallmarks acquired, CSCs in red/dark gray with enlarged size.

time iteration, practically there is not any difference with respect to not using a differentiation therapy as the key aspect is to block CSC proliferation. Meanwhile, using a treatment that differentiates 0.1% of CSCs in each time iteration, no CSCs remain at $t = 6000$, which could contribute to the continuous increase of DCCs.

35.4 CONCLUSIONS

We used computational models based on cellular automata and the abstract model of cancer hallmarks to analyze the emergent behavior of tumor growth at a cellular level. The advantage of the "in silico" models is that we can run experiments that would be too expensive and time-consuming to carry out in the lab [28]. As indicated by Savage [28] regarding the complexity of cancer, "Researchers have tended to focus on genes and proteins, but to understand and fight the disease, it must be viewed as a system, rather than merely as a set of cellular activities." Thus, "the recent focus on genetics and pathways in individual cells has caused many researchers to neglect the systemic view" [28]. The simulations based on CA are within this idea emphasized by Savage [28], as the model permits an analysis and view of the system working with different levels of abstraction or with the focus on particular simulation aspects. Moreover, the abstract model of cancer hallmarks is the ideal one for the study of the multicellular system in terms of behavioral characterization, which is our objective, rather than particularizing in a cancer type and without the need of characterization of the pathways involved in the acquisition of the hallmarks.

The analyses of the treatment strategies applied in a CSC context indicate several key aspects:

1. Using only standard treatments, which only eliminate rapid proliferating nonstem cancer cells, not only do not stop possible future regrowths as a consequence of the presence of CSCs, but facilitates that the regrowth is faster.
2. A differentiation therapy for CSCs in combination with a standard treatment can better control the future regrowth, but the relative timing of the two treatment strategies is determinant, as CSC differentiation produces nonstem cancer cells that can promote rapid tumor proliferations.
3. The ideal treatment should make CSC proliferation difficult, especially after the immediate application of a standard treatment, as reasoned in the previous analyses that indicates that a low-intensity standard treatment is better for making more difficult CSC proliferation and differentiation. As stated by Enderling et al. [4], "If detected early, tumors could potentially be maintained at a non-advancing equilibrium by reinforcing the ability of non-stem cells to competitively suppress CSC proliferation." So, as indicated by Han et al. [27], targeting CSC niche and the quiescent state of CSCs is a therapeutic possibility as "Maintaining the cells in a quiescent state by blocking specific receptors and signaling pathways within the CSC niche can inhibit CSC functions of tumor initiation and metastasis." Our analyses show that this is one of the most important factors to control, which was not intensively considered.

ACKNOWLEDGMENTS

This work was funded by the Ministry of Economy and Competitiveness of Spain (project TIN2013-40981-R).

REFERENCES

[1] Hanahan D, Weinberg R. The hallmarks of cancer. Cell 2000;100:57–70.
[2] Hanahan D, Weinberg R. Hallmarks of cancer: the next generation. Cell 2011;144(5):646–74.
[3] Patel M, Nagl S. The role of model integration in complex systems. An example from cancer biology. Berlin: Springer-Verlag; 2010.
[4] Enderling H, Chaplain M, Hahnfeldt P. Quantitative modeling of tumor dynamics and radiotherapy. Acta Biotheor 2010;58:341–53.
[5] Adami C. Introduction to artificial life. Santa Clara: Telos-Springer Verlag; 1998.
[6] Ilachinski A. Cellular automata. A discrete universe. Singapore: World Scientific; 2001.
[7] Langton C. Life at the edge of chaos. In: Langton CG, Taylor C, Farmer JD, Rasmussen S, editors. Artificial life II. Redwood City, CA: Addison-Wesley; 1992. p. 41–9.
[8] Ribba B, Alarcon T, Marron K, Maini P, Agur Z. The use of hybrid cellular automaton models for improving cancer therapy. In: Proceedings of 6th international conference on cellular automata for research and industry, ACRI 2004, LNCS, vol. 3305; 2004. p. 444–53.
[9] Gerlee P, Anderson A. An evolutionary hybrid cellular automaton model of solid tumour growth. J Theor Biol 2007;246(4):583–603.
[10] Gevertz J, Gillies G, Torquato S. Simulating tumor growth in confined heterogeneous environments. Phys Biol 2008;5(3):1–10.
[11] Rejniak K, Anderson A. Hybrid models of tumor growth. WIREs Syst Biol Med 2010;3:115–25.

[12] Bankhead A, Heckendorn R. Using evolvable genetic cellular automata to model breast cancer. Genet Program Evolvable Mach 2007;8:381–93.
[13] Abbott R, Forrest S, Pienta K. Simulating the hallmarks of cancer. Artif Life 2006;12(4):617–34.
[14] Spencer S, Gerety R, Pienta K, Forrest S. Modeling somatic evolution in tumorigenesis. PLoS Comput Biol 2006;2(8):939–47.
[15] Basanta D, Ribba B, Watkin E, You B, Deutsch A. Computational analysis of the influence of the microenvironment on carcinogenesis. Math Biosci 2011;229:22–9.
[16] Santos J, Monteagudo A. Study of cancer hallmarks relevance using a cellular automaton tumor growth model. In: Proceedings PPSN 2012 — Parallel problem solving from nature. Lecture notes in computer science, vol. 7491; 2012. p. 489–99.
[17] Santos J, Monteagudo A. Analysis of behaviour transitions in tumour growth using a cellular automaton simulation. IET Syst Biol 2014;9(3):75.
[18] Monteagudo A, Santos J. Cancer stem cell modeling using a cellular automaton. Lect Notes Comput Sci 2013;7931:21–31.
[19] Monteagudo A, Santos J. Studying the capability of different cancer hallmarks to initiate tumor growth using a cellular automaton simulation. Application in a cancer stem cell context. BioSystems 2014;1(115):46–58.
[20] Gil J, Stembalska A, Pesz K, Sasiadek M. Cancer stem cells: the theory and perspectives in cancer therapy. J App Genet 2008;49(2):193–9.
[21] Enderling H, Hahnfeldt P. Cancer stem cells in solid tumors: is 'evading apoptosis' a hallmark of cancer? Prog Biophys Mol Bio 2011;106:391–9.
[22] Wodarz D, Komarova N. Can loss of apoptosis protect against cancer? Trends Genet 2012;23(5):32–41.
[23] Ricci-Vitiani L, Lombardi D, Pilozzi E, Biffoni M, Todaro M, Peschle C, et al. Identification and expansion of human colon-cancer-initiating cells. Nature 2007;445(7123):111–5.
[24] Korkaya H, Paulson A, Iovino F, Wicha M. HER2 regulates the mammary stem/progenitor cell population driving tumorigenesis and invasion. Oncogene 2008;27(47):6120–30.
[25] Sottoriva A, Verhoeff J, Borovski T, McWeeney S, Naumov L, Medema J, et al. Cancer stem cell tumor model reveals invasive morphology and increased phenotypical heterogeneity. Cancer Res 2010;70 (1):46–56.
[26] Vainstein V, Kirnasovsky O, Kogan Y, Agur Z. Strategies for cancer stem cell elimination: insights from mathematical modeling. J Theor Biol 2012;298:32–41.
[27] Han L, Shi S, Gong T, Zhang Z, Sun X. Cancer stem cells: therapeutic implications and perspectives in cancer therapy. Acta Pharmacol Sin 2013;3(2):65–75.
[28] Savage N. Modelling: computing cancer. Nature 2012;491:S62–3.

Index

Note: Page numbers followed by *f* indicate figures, *t* indicate tables, and *b* indicate boxes.

D

Q

R

S

T

U

V

W

Printed in the United States
By Bookmasters